MORALITY
AND THE LAW

MORALITY
AND THE LAW

SAMUEL ENOCH STUMPF

VANDERBILT UNIVERSITY PRESS 1966

TO MY PARENTS

REVEREND LOUIS STUMPF
ELIZABETH JERGENS STUMPF

*though this is not to suggest that one
was the law and the other morality*

ACKNOWLEDGMENTS

I HAVE incurred many obligations in the preparation of this book—probably many more than I can acknowledge here. But I do want to mention the constant encouragement I have had from A. Ray Forrester, Dean of the School of Law at Cornell University, the generosity of the Rockefeller Foundation for making possible the writing of this book, and the stimulation I derived from H. L. A. Hart's lectures at Oxford University.

For permission to quote materials of other authors I am grateful to the publishers of the following works: Triska and Slusser, "Treaties and Other Sources of Order in International Relations: The Soviet View," *American Journal of International Law* (1958); Gray, *Nature and Sources of the Law*, Beacon Press (1921); Pound, *Contemporary Juristic*

Theory, Claremont Colleges (1940); Dewey, "Logical Method and Law," *Cornell Law Quarterly* (1924); Gsovski, "Soviet Concept of Law," *Fordham Law Review* (1938); Winfield, "Ethics in English Case Law," *Harvard Law Review* (1931); Babb, *Soviet Legal Philosophy*, Harvard University Press (1951); Radbruch, "Anglo-American Jurisprudence through Continental Eyes," *Law Quarterly Review* (1936); Vishinsky, *The Law of the Soviet State*, The Macmillan Company (1948); Whitehead, *Adventures of Ideas*, The Macmillan Company and Cambridge University Press (1933); Wright, *Contemporary International Law*, Random House, Inc. (1955); Bin Cheng, *General Principals of Law as Applied by International Courts and Tribunals*, Stevens & Sons, Ltd. (1953); Lauterpacht, *Development of International Law by the International Court*, Stevens & Sons, Ltd. (1958); also, chapters one and three appeared in the *Vanderbilt Law Review* in Volumes Six (1952) and Fourteen (1960) respectively.

SAMUEL ENOCH STUMPF

Vanderbilt University
November 1965

CONTENTS

INTRODUCTION

THIS book on law and morality grows out of the contemporary concern of men everywhere to understand
the phenomenon of law—that law by which governments direct and order the behavior and destinies of human
beings. The concept of law has become ambiguous, and men
have become suspicious of the regime of law, for in the name
of law men have been compelled to commit horrendous acts
and through law large numbers of people have suffered severe restrictions on the development of their normal human
expectations. At the same time, the law has been the fundamental agency in preserving social order and stability; what
is more, among certain peoples of the world the rule of law
has meant the progressive realization and preservation of a
new and higher human dignity. The "law" has therefore

presented itself to modern man with a double face, being under some circumstances the agency of tyranny and under others the instrument of humanitarian passion.

Men wonder whether the word "law" properly applies to those orders and directives of governments which violate their moral sensibilities or whether the word "law" should be reserved for those rules fashioned by governments which are clearly consonant with morality. The fundamental question is whether the concept of law must include the element of morality if we are to describe adequately and correctly the phenomenon of law, or whether the concept of law is sufficiently defined as the regime of official power or coercive force. What, in short, is the relation between law and morality?

Modern legal philosophy has led us to believe that law is morally neutral or, as a leading jurist has said, that "law has no moral connotations whatsoever." Whether this is the case is the central question of this book.

There is a disarmingly simple way of viewing the relation between law and morality—a way so simple that it could bring an abrupt end to the discussion at this point. For the law could be likened to a knife, an instrument with many potential capacities. With a knife one can stab and kill another person; also, with a knife one can cut bread. Whether the knife is used to kill or to cut bread does not change the intrinsic character of the knife as a knife. Why should we not think of the law in this manner? The law can kill and it can sustain; the law can be the tool of a dictator and the beneficial instrument of a democracy. The implication here is that the law, like the knife, is morally neutral, that it is an instrument that can fall into malignant or benevolent hands. This would mean that our concern about the law is misplaced, for about the law there is no ambiguity; it is simply a question of how men will use the law.

If the analogy between law and a knife could be successfully pursued, most of the theoretical difficulties concerning the relation between law and morals would disappear. But to pursue this analogy is to assume that we can discover law, or the essence of law, in some pure form, the way we can isolate a neutral knife. One can imagine a knife lying inertly on a table and for the time being unused—it can be admired as a work of art or used in the course of a meal or grasped as a weapon. But what is a law, or where is a law, *before* it is used for good or ill? Is there any clear way of thinking about law as an independent entity, independent of moral characteristics? Is it possible to analyze the phenomenon of law and thereby distinguish between the *fact* of law and the *use* of law the way we can consider the fact that a knife exists without any reference to its uses? Or is it the case that laws are necessarily related to morality?

The plan of this book is to explore the relation of law and morality in five different ways, each way representing a major theory of law. The first three chapters deal successively with the theories which say first that law is what the courts do in fact, second that law is the will of the economically dominant class, and third that law is the command of the sovereign. Each of these theories was originally designed to show that there is a separation between law and morality, but I have tried to show that not even in terms of these theories themselves can such a separation be demonstrated or sustained. The fourth chapter looks at international law as a striking example of a new kind of law coming into existence in our time, giving us a testing ground for the theories presented in the first three chapters. Here we ask whether in the development of international law it is the case that law is uniquely bound up with a court, is the product of an economically dominant class, or is simply the command of a sovereign. Moreover, what is the role of morality in the development of international law? The fifth chapter deals with the theory of natural law and is concerned chiefly with the question whether a legal order rests upon the moral order. To indicate the necessary connection between law and morality, I employ here an illustration from Thomas Hobbes, holding that he not only developed a clear theory of natural law but that he also argued that the legal order rests upon the moral order. In the final chapter I indicate ways in which law and morality are to be differentiated, but I also point out their similarities, concluding that these similarities account to a great extent for the intimate relation between morality and the law.

Morality and the Law

1

WHAT THE COURTS DO IN FACT

The Moral Element in
Supreme Court Decisions

THERE is an attractive simplicity in the definition of law which says that "law is what the courts do in fact." Much mist and mystification were cleared away from the study of law when Justice Holmes uttered these words.

This Holmesian concept of law seemed to lead jurist and layman alike in a surefooted way to the very threshold of the meaning of law. Instead of thinking of law as a system of logically connected principles, the law was now to be seen as the outcome of a very human process which reflected, not logic, but rather the felt needs of the community as these needs were understood and expressed by the court. Instead of an inflexible and mechanical set of ideas, law was now to be viewed as a supple process for achieving social goals. In a memorable passage, Justice Holmes perceptively wrote that the life of the law has not been logic; it has been experience. The felt necessities of the times, the prevalent moral and political theories, institutions of public policy, avowed or unconscious, even the prejudices which judges share with their fellowmen, have had a good deal more to do than the syllogism in determining the rules by which men should be governed.[1]

It is remarkable that this Holmesian preoccupation with what the courts do in fact has brought into prominence precisely that feature of law which it was intended to tone down —the moral element. The earlier classical theory of law, particularly the doctrine of natural law, had tried to indicate an intimate relation between law and morals, suggesting that law is a system of rules of conduct the content of which can be deduced from certain major moral premises. If this were true, then the student of law would have to study these basic moral and legal principles and try to understand how they are related and how conclusions could be drawn from them in deciding specific cases.

Legal realism, to which Holmes had given the decisive impetus, took the view that to look for law in such a set of principles, moral or legal, was to look in the wrong place. Here the jurist would confuse the realms of law and morals; the judicial mind must be deflected from moral conceptions and notions of human purpose and look rather to the factual arena where the law is actually at work. This was not to deny that moral notions lurked everywhere in the law but to suggest that this moral element was not the essential element in the law. It was assumed that all one had to do was to describe the work of the court and this analysis would yield a clear picture of what is meant by *law*.

1. Oliver Wendell Holmes, *The Common Law* (Boston: Little, Brown, 1881), p. 1.

On the basis of such an analysis, moreover, the lawyer could predict how the court would work in the next case. To be concerned with what the courts do in fact, and to predict on this basis what the court *will* do, clearly set the stage for a way of thinking about the law which only indirectly raised the question of the moral element in law. It appeared that through this realism the minds of jurists were unhinged from broad moral and legal principles and attached instead to the day-by-day work of the courts, the activities of which were now taken to be the very definition of law itself.

But the curious outcome of this emphasis on the court's activities was twofold: first, it gave the practicing lawyer a sense of emancipation from the abstract, mechanistic, and logical conception of the law and led him right to where the law really could be found and handled; the other result, however, was to bring to light for the legal theorist or philosopher an extraordinary corroboration of the intimate relation between law and morals.

If law is what the court does, then we need to ask, "What does the court do?" If one is concerned only with the immediate practical consequences of the court's action, then the answer can be given simply in terms of the final decision. But when one asks what lies behind this decision there opens up a far more significant conception of what the law is. What, for example, is involved when a judge renders a decision? Clearly this process is not a precise and automatic movement from premise to conclusion. What does, in fact, happen has been described by Professor Max Rheinstein in this manner:

> For the new case a decision is in existence, hidden and unconscious, perhaps, but indicated by those faiths, ideals and aspirations which guide, inspire, and determine the community, but not upon the basis of his own, individual predilections and personal ideals, but in con-

formity with the value judgments of that society of which he is a functionary. These value judgments of the community are, of course, those of the individuals of which it is composed, and, especially, of those who are its recognized guides and leaders. Of these individuals, the judge is one himself and in that sense his individual value judgments help to shape those of the community. But, as judge, he is not to give way to them unless they have become those of the community. As judge, he has to search for that solution which is the "right" one in the eyes of his society. In this sense he has to "find" the law. But he has also to "make" it, since he has to articulate the norm which has only been vaguely felt before. That process of articulation is delicate and difficult, it requires skill, tact, training, craftsmanship, and above all, sensitivity. It is of a truly creative character, like that of the artist, poet, or musician, who feels the sentiments living in his people and gives expression to them, so that each individual can now recognize them as his own and make them into a new source of strength and inspiration. . . . The judge, the watchman of society, holds power in his hands, which he can use and abuse. No institution can ultimately safeguard the proper use of that power. . . . Nothing but moral virtues restrain the watchman.[2]

If we consider the work of the United States Supreme Court, for example, and ask what that Court does, we discover some major elements in the anatomy of law. In particular, we discover just how and why there exists a moral element in the law. There is, of course, a persistent belief that law finds its deepest validation in its conformity to moral and ethical values and principles. As the highest organ of law in our society, the Supreme Court cannot avoid confronting from time to time this moral dimension of law. Wherever the destinies of men are involved, a decent respect for their reason and conscience demands rationally articulated decisions in controversies.

That the Supreme Court occupies such a strategic role in our society is beyond question. More than a century ago

2. "Who Watches the Watchman?" in *Interpretations of Modern Legal Philosophies*, ed. Paul Sayre (New York: Oxford University Press, 1947), pp. 602–603.

Chief Justice Marshall said that "The Judicial Department comes home in its effects to every man's fireside; it passes on his property, his reputation, his life, his all."[3] Aware of this unique status, the court has frequently broken the restrictive bounds of technicality, feeling, as Justice Frankfurter once wrote, that "there comes a time when even the process of empiric adjudication calls for a more rational disposition than that the immediate case is not different from preceding cases."[4] Whenever this happens, the moral and ethical convictions of the judges, or of society as understood by the judges, begin to move into the reasoning of the Court.

What do we mean by the *moral element* in judicial opinions? The moral element of a decision is that portion of the argument or line of reasoning which rests primarily upon such moral and ethical conceptions as "right" and "wrong," "good" or "bad," "desirable" or "undesirable," or "preferable" or "not preferable." The moral element in an opinion has the effect of contrasting an action, a given conduct, or a particular law as it "is" with what it "ought to be" in terms of moral as compared with legal standards.

Whether the moral element is a legitimate or necessary element in judicial opinions is the subject of considerable controversy in many quarters, including the Court itself. For example, in a dissenting opinion, Justice Frankfurter took issue with the majority decision in the *Mercoid* case on the nontechnical grounds that "litigants and lower courts ought not to be embarrassed by gratuitous innuendoes against a principle of the law which, within its proper bounds, is

3. Chief Justice John Marshall, in the course of the debates of the Virginia State Convention of 1829–1830, cited by Justice Sutherland in O'Donoghue v. United States, 289 U.S. 516, 532.
4. New York v. United States, 326 U.S. 572, 575.

accredited by legal history as well as ethics."[5] This dissent
moved Justice Black to write a separate opinion, specifically
to protest Frankfurter's reference to ethics, in which he said:
"It seems to me that the judicial error (in this case) of discussing abstract questions is slight compared to the error of
interpreting legislative enactments on the basis of the court's
preconceived views on 'morals' and 'ethics.' "[6]

This disagreement over the propriety of judicial reference to morals and ethics is symptomatic of the ambivalent
character of the Court's work, for the Court is conscious of
its restricted sphere in our system of government, yet it cannot avoid moving into the realm of value judgments. In
order to understand the status of the moral element in judicial decisions, three aspects of the problem need to be considered: the general question of the relation between law
and morals, the objectivity of the judge, and the decisions of
the Court.

Law and Morals

Since it is the *law* that the Supreme Court administers,
any ambiguities lurking in men's conception of that law will
plague the work of the Court. This is true not only when it
is a question of interpreting the meaning of a particular
statute, which long ago prompted Justice Brown to remark
that "the province of (statutory) construction lies wholly
within the domain of ambiguity . . ."[7] or when the vague
phrases of the Constitution are involved; it is more clearly
true when, in light of our present concern, there is a suspen-
sion of agreement about the relation between law and morals.

5. Mercoid Corp. v. Mid-Continent Investment Co., 320 U.S. 661, 678.
6. 320 U.S. at 672.
7. Hamilton v. Rathbone, 175 U.S. 414, 421.

The Court could hardly be expected to fill its decisions with vignettes on ethical and moral responsibility if the dominant theory holds that law and morals represent two mutually exclusive modes of social control. On the other hand, it would be unrealistic to expect the Court to refrain from considering the moral and ethical implications of controversies if it were held generally that the nature of law is such that it needs more than proper enactment to be valid, that it must be in harmony with the ethical and moral insights of men. The uncertainty on the part of the Supreme Court in the area of value judgments is traceable to this fundamental disagreement about the nature of law.

The Interdependence of Law and Morals

The present problem should be viewed against the fact that in all periods law has been shaped to fit the contours of moral conviction. Dean Pound has said that "the attempt to make law and morals identical by covering the whole field of morals with legal precepts, and by conforming existing precepts to the requirements of a reasoned system of morals, made the modern law."[8] In a similar generalization, Justice Cardozo held that "The scope of legal duty has expanded in obedience to the urge of morals."[9]

The law has never been able to dissociate itself fully from the notion that there is a difference between an arbitrary command and a law. For Plato, every law had to have two parts: the substantive part and the preamble, where the preamble was to provide the rational and moral justification of

8. Roscoe Pound, *Law and Morals* (2d. ed.; Chapel Hill: University of North Carolina Press; London: Oxford University Press, 1926), p. 31.
9. Benjamin Nathan Cardozo, *The Paradoxes of Legal Science* (New York: Columbia University Press, 1928), p. 46.

the substance.[10] It was this moral defensibility of the law which differentiated it from an arbitrary command.[11]

Added to this classical view of law was the theological formulation of natural law which had its fullest expression in the Middle Ages. We are concerned here, not only with the fact that the creation of law by the legitimate lawmaker had to follow the dictates of a higher law, but, more significantly, with the fact that the judges were to treat any law which was contrary to the higher law of nature as null and void.[12] Whereas in the Middle Ages judges were thus under formal obligation to pass on laws in terms of natural moral law, in our day judges have responded, as Justice Cardozo has said, merely to a "moral urge." But the phenomenon is the same.

A point of view which Kant stated further imbedded into legal thought this conception of the judge's dependence upon moral norms in adjudication. For although he distinguished sharply between a moral and legal duty[13] and firmly denied to the people the right to rebel against unjust laws,[14] he did

10. See Plato's *Laws* 722D–723B (Jowett ed., 1892) and George Miller Calhoun, *Introduction to Greek Legal Science*, ed. Francis de Zulueta (Oxford: The Clarendon Press, 1944), pp. 82–83.

11. See Kessler, "Natural Law, Justice and Democracy—Some Reflections on Three Types of Thinking about Law and Justice," 19 Tulane Law Review 32, 35 (1944).

12. See Otto Friedrich von Gierke, *Political Theories of the Middle Age*, translated with an introduction by Frederic William Maitland (Cambridge University Press, 1938), p. 84:

The properly Medieval and never completely obsolete theory declared that every act of the Sovereign which broke the bounds drawn by Natural Law was formally null and void. As null and void therefore every judge and every other magistrate who had to apply the law was to treat, not only every unlawful executive act, but every unlawful statute, even though it were published by Pope or emperor.

13. Immanuel Kant, *Lectures on Ethics*, trans. by Louis Infield, introd. by J. Macmurray (London: Methuen & Co., Ltd., 1930), 33, 34–36, 48, 69–70, 71.

14. Kant, *The Philosophy of Law*, trans. by W. Hastie (Edinburgh: T. & T. Clark, 1887), 176–177.

hold that: "The Science of Right . . . designates the philosophical and systematic knowledge of the principles of Natural Right. And it is from this science that the immutable
principles of positive legislation must be derived by practical
jurists and lawgivers."[15] It is questionable whether such a
systematic body of natural rights with a moral and ethical
foundation is available to the judge today, but that the judge
does from time to time adjudicate cases on the basis of some
moral and ethical values seems beyond question.

Again, Justice Cardozo revealed the moral element in the
judicial process when he wrote that

> the judge stretches a point here in response to a moral urge, or makes a
> new application of a precedent there. Before long a new tradition has
> arisen. Duties that had been conceived of as moral only, without other
> human sanction than the opinion of society, are found to be such that
> they may effectively and wisely be subjected to another form of sanc-
> tion, the power of society. The moral norm and the jural have been
> brought together, and are one.[16]

What Cardozo has here expressed, very likely after a close
analysis of the working of his own mind on the bench, has
been underscored by other students of the judicial process.

15. *Id.* at 43–44.
16. Cardozo, p. 43. An elaboration of this same point is made by William E.
Hocking:
> It may clear up some of the difficulty if we remark that the bearing of
> ethical right on legal right is due not more to the specific nature of law
> than to human nature and the nature of ethics. It is due to the fact that
> the same behavior which is the subject matter of law comes under or may
> come under the cognizance of ethics; and that the man who is behaving
> cannot divide himself into two personalities, a legal and a moral person-
> ality, for the purpose of an identical action. If he has to raise a moral
> question in regard to the act, the law is not the abstract action, but the
> man behaving; hence everything that enters necessarily into the man's
> consideration of a given deed enters by consequence into the law's con-
> sideration of the same deed.
Hocking, "Ways of Thinking about Rights: A New Theory of the Relation
Between Law and Morals" in *Law: A Century of Progress, 1835–1935* (New
York: New York University Press, 1937), II, 4.

The continental jurist Ehrlich has argued that no scientifically trained jurist could doubt that a great part of the law is even now not created by the state. Indeed, "there never was a time when the law promulgated by the state in statutory form was the only law, even for the courts. . . ."[17] The ambiguities of statute law leave considerable room for the independent reasoning of the judge. His reasoning frequently proceeds under the influence of the concept of justice, and "on the basis of this concept, the judge finds the norms for his decision. . . ."[18]

Even where the law already embodies a particular concept of justice, the judge, moved by a deeper concept, strives to bring the prevailing concept into closer accord with the demands of moral and ethical values. Justice Cardozo could not have made this more explicit than when he wrote: "What we are seeking is not merely the justice that one receives when his rights and duties are determined by the law as it is; what we are seeking is the justice to which law in its making should conform."[19] It is thus clear that judges have at all times considered the realm of moral ideas an intrinsic part of law.

The Tendency Toward Separation of Law and Morals

However formidable may have been these ideas of Cardozo, Kant, the natural law advocates, and those who, like Plato, would rest the concept of justice on the contrast between what law *is* and what it *ought to be*, they are by no

17. Eugen Ehrlich, *Fundamental Principles of the Sociology of Law*, trans. by Walter L. Moll; introd. by Roscoe Pound (Cambridge: Harvard University Press, 1936), p. 15.
18. *Id.* at 214.
19. Cardozo, *The Growth of the Law* (New Haven: Yale University Press, 1924), p. 87.

means the controlling ideas in contemporary juristic thought. The notion has developed gradually that the law has no real concern for moral and ethical values. John Chipman Gray considered this development away from a moral concern the great gain in jurisprudence during the last century, for he argued that law "is not that which is in accordance with religion, or nature or morality; it is not that which ought to be, but that which is."[20]

A major reason the judges of our Supreme Court do not indulge more frequently in overt value judgments is the restrictive effect of the separation of powers. Even in England as early as the eighteenth century this effect on judges was produced by the growing doctrine of the separation of powers; for the division of the legislative powers from the judiciary led to the conception of judges as passive agents limited to "finding" the law. "Even the vigor of Lord Mansfield's injection of moral concepts into the law led to rebellion when his personality was removed from the scene."[21] The medieval echo in Lord Coke's decision in Dr. Bonham's case where an act of Parliament was declared null and void because it was contrary to common right and reason never did become the dominant note in the English judiciary.[22]

The division of powers between the legislative and judicial branches had such a decisive effect upon the judges in the land of the common law that in our generation Percy Winfield could say that

20. John Chipman Gray, *Nature and Sources of the Law* (2d. ed. from the author's notes by Roland Gray; New York: Macmillan, 1921), p. 94. Cf. Brecht, "The Myth of Is and Ought," 54 Harvard Law Review 811 (1941).

21. Landis, "Statutes and the Sources of Law," in *Harvard Legal Essays*, ed. Roscoe Pound (Cambridge: Harvard University Press, 1934), pp. 213, 217.

22. See Plucknett, "Bonham's Case and Judicial Review," 40 Harvard Law Review 30 (1926).

there is not the faintest trace in current English case law of any attempt on the part of the judges to make the law conform to any ideal ethical standard. Where there is any scope for the application of morals to the law, what they do apply is the practical morality which is prevalent for the time being in the community. They have no general formula, whether utilitarian or otherwise, as to what morality *ought* to be. It is enough for them if they can keep abreast of what *is* now.[23]

To a great extent, this separation of law and morals in the judicial process is a procedural matter. This means theoretically that if moral and ethical values are to be injected into the law, the injecting must be done not by the judges but by the legislature. Moreover, to keep a watchful eye peeled for procedural irregularities is held by many to be more important than for the court to pronounce on the moral aspects of the case at hand. That is why the Supreme Court can dispose of so many cases which appear to involve grave moral questions without showing in the slightest degree any moral concern in their decisions. There is great merit in this procedural exactitude, for in most cases where a scrupulous obedience to procedure has been followed the outcome has also measured up to moral demands. Indeed, Justice Frank-

23. Winfield, "Ethics in English Case Law," 45 Harvard Law Review 112, 132 (1931). See Douglas, J., dissenting in McLeod v. J. E. Dilworth Co., 332 U.S. 327, 335. "I would make the result under the Commerce Clause turn on practical considerations and business realities rather than on dialectics." But see Justice Black's dissent in S.E.C. v. Chenery Corp., 318 U.S. 80, 97–98, 63 Sup. Ct. 454, 87 L. Ed. 626 (1943):
Entrusted as the Commission is with the responsibility of lifting the standard of transactions in the market place in order that managers of financial ventures may not impose upon the general investing public, it seems wholly appropriate that the Commission should have recognized the influence of admonitory language like the following it approvingly quoted from Meinhard v. Salmon, 249 N.Y. 458, 164 N.E. 545: "A trustee is held to something stricter than the morals of the market place. Not honesty alone, but the punctilio of an honor the most sensitive, is then the standard of behavior. As to this there has developed a tradition that is unbending and inveterate. . . . Only thus has the level of conduct for fiduciaries been kept at a level higher than that trodden by the crowd."

furter has said that "the history of American freedom is, in no small measure, the history of procedure."[24]

But this well-known limitation upon the Court does not entirely account for its reticence to indulge in moral judgments. There is another powerful pressure upon the judicial mind in this regard; it is the fact that judges partake of the general contemporary uncertainty regarding the actual content of moral truth. Holmes's philosophical skepticism is familiar enough, although it is worth repeating that his judicial self-control was not so much a matter of procedural propriety[25] as it was uncertainty. "I enforce," he said, "whatever constitutional laws Congress or anybody sees fit to pass—and do it in good faith to the best of my ability. . . . I am so skeptical as to our knowledge of the goodness or badness of laws that I have no practical criticism except what the crowd wants."[26]

Such an attitude, if consistently held, could have but one effect, for as Holmes's great friend Sir Frederick Pollock wrote in reply to this comment: "If you deny that any principles of

24. Malinski v. New York, 324 U.S. 401, 414. Cf. Paul H. Douglas:
Most young men tend to be impatient with what the lawyers term procedural matters and to be far more interested instead in substantive issues. Only the latter seem to the young to have vitality. But as time passes and a man grows older, it dawns upon him that a great part of our progress has been made through transforming substantive issues of conflict into accepted matters of procedure. For it is in this way that the society peacefully disposes of issues which, if not so handled, would tear it apart. May there not be a moral guide for action in this fact?
Douglas, "A Possible Method of Dealing with the Closed Shop Issue," 14 University of Chicago Law Review 386, 398 (1947).
25. Although Holmes emphasized propriety too, e.g., "I cannot believe that the [Fourteenth] Amendment was intended to give us *carte blanche* to embody our economic and moral beliefs in its prohibitions." Baldwin v. Missouri, 281 U.S. 586, 595.
26. *Holmes-Pollock Letters* (Cambridge: Harvard University Press, 1941), I, 163. For further light on Holmes' philosophy see the recent debate between Professor Howe and Hart on "The Positivism of Mr. Justice Holmes," 64 Harvard Law Review 529, 929, 937 (1951).

conduct at all are common to and admitted by all men who try to behave reasonably—well, I don't see how you can have any ethics or any ethical background for law."[27] Nor is it surprising that Holmes conceived of the nature of law as a regime of force,[28] for whenever the moral dimension is eliminated from law what is frequently left is nothing more than coercion.

To be sure, skepticism is not a uniformly undesirable attitude. Important values have been preserved in our society precisely through the reluctance of judges to speak in terms of absolutes. Justice Learned Hand remarked in a significant decision that freedom of speech "rests upon a skepticism as to all political orthodoxy, upon a belief that there are no impregnable political absolutes, and that a flux of tentative doctrines is preferable to any authoritative creed."[29] But when this case moved up from the Court of Appeals to the United States Supreme Court, Chief Justice Vinson went considerably further in expressing the theme of intellectual uncertainty than Justice Hand's remark on "political orthodoxy" and "political absolutes" had intended. "Nothing is more certain in modern society," said the Chief Justice, "than the principle that there are no absolutes . . . that all concepts are relative."[30]

Inevitably this means that, whereas the Court has the final word in adjudicating cases, it should not have the last word "in those basic conflicts of 'right and wrong—between

27. *Holmes-Pollock Letters,* I, 275.
28. 2 *id.* at 36. Cf. *Hegel's Philosophy of Right,* translated with notes by T. M. Knox (Oxford: The Clarendon Press, 1942), p. 16. "That force and tyranny may be an element in law is accidental to law and has nothing to do with its nature."
29. United States v. Dennis, 183 F 2d 201, 207 (2d Cir. 1950).
30. Dennis v. United States, 341 U.S. 494, 508.

whose endless jar justice resides.' "[31] Even Justice Cardozo who, as we have indicated above, argued that the judge responds to a "moral urge" in rendering a decision, was aware of the fact that however consciously the judge wanted to implement morals in his juristic reasoning he faced a bewildering complex of conflicting moral standards, not only between different communities, but within the same community. There is still uncertainty, for a choice still must be made between one group standard and another before the moral norm can be converted into the jural one.[32] It is no wonder that, faced with such a dilemma, the judges prefer to take a narrow view of their work and limit their concern as strictly as possible to procedural standards and statutory law.

The philosophers have done their share to bring about this result in the judicial process. To the extent that judges depend upon a general knowledge of nature and its laws to inform them about the nature of law as applied to human conduct, the denial of any absolute laws in nature cannot avoid producing an unsettling effect upon the judges' conception of the nature of the laws with which they are concerned. Chief Justice Vinson's dictum that "all concepts are relative" is qualitatively no different from Alfred North Whitehead's statement that

since all laws of nature depend on the individual character of the things constituting nature, as the things change, then correspondingly the laws will change. . . . Thus the conception of the universe as evolving subject to fixed eternal laws regulating all behavior should be abandoned.[33]

31. Hand, "The Contribution of an Independent Judiciary to Civilization," in *The Supreme Judicial Court of Massachusetts 1692–1942*, (Boston: Massachusetts Bar Association, 1942), pp. 59, 66.
32. Cardozo, *Paradoxes of Legal Science*, p. 37.
33. Alfred North Whitehead, *Adventures of Ideas* (New York: Macmillan, 1933), p. 143.

John Dewey has stated in forceful terms that the very
health of the law depends upon ridding legal reasoning of all
universal principles:

> The sanctification of ready-made antecedent universal principles as
> methods of thinking is the chief obstacle to the kind of thinking which
> is the indispensible prerequisite of steady, secure and intelligent social
> reforms in general and social advance by means of law in particular. If
> this be so infiltration into law of a more experimental and flexible logic
> is a social as well as an intellectual need.[34]

The effect of such philosophical notions has been to concentrate the attention of the judges upon the particular statute and to deflect it from principles of morals and ethics. The
concept of right and wrong gives way to the notion of lawful
or unlawful. And in extreme cases, though with increasing
frequency, the right and lawful are considered identical, the
"right" being made so by the law rather than the law being
considered "just" because of its conformity to "right." This
is the residual influence of Hobbes who argued that "laws are
the rules of just, and unjust; nothing being reputed unjust,
that is not contrary to some law."[35]

One of the severest blows leveled at those who would
argue that there are antecedent moral principles and natural
rights to which the law must conform came from the powerful
pen of the English legal reformer Jeremy Bentham:

> All this talk about nature, natural rights, natural justice and injus-
> tice proves two things only, the heat of passion, and the darkness of
> understanding. . . .
> Property the creature of law?—Oh, no—Why not?—because if it were

34. Dewey, "Logical Method and Law," 10 Cornell Law Quarterly 17, 27
(1924).
35. Thomas Hobbes, *Leviathan*, ("Everyman Library" [New York: E. P.
Dutton, 1950]), chap. 26.

the law that gave everything, the law might take away everything: if everything were given by law, so might everything be taken away.

The case is that in a society in any degree civilized, all the rights a man can have, all the expectations he can entertain of enjoying anything that is said to be his is derived solely from the law. . . . Till law existed, property could scarcely be said to exist. Property and law were born and die together.[36]

And, long before Holmes said that "the common law is not a brooding omnipresence in the sky but the articulate voice of a sovereign that could be identified," Bentham said that "customary law is a fiction. . . . Try to produce any such rule: if it appears in any shape it must clothe itself in the similitude of some particular provision of the nature of statute law. . . ."[37] It is not too much to say that the philosophical uncertainty about the content of moral truth has led to this preoccupation with statutes both in the theoretical and in the practical spheres of legal endeavour.

One of the most extensive contemporary treatments of the nature of law identifies law with the sum of the positive statutes of the state and in the opening section states that "the concept of law has no moral connotation whatsoever."[38] Kelsen means by this statement that the validity of laws rests not on their conformity to moral principles but upon proper enactment. And again, limiting the area of legitimate law to properly legislated statutes rests on the assumption that laws cannot depend for their validity upon moral correctness, since there are no pre-existing moral norms: "There are no *mala in se*, there are only *mala prohibita*, for a behavior is a

36. Bentham, *The Limits of Jurisprudence Defined*, introd. by Charles Warren Everett (New York: Columbia University Press, 1945), p. 84.

37. *Id.* at 282.

38. Hans Kelsen, *General Theory of Law and State*; trans. by Anders Wedberg (Cambridge: Harvard University Press, 1946), p. 5.

malum only if it is *prohibitum*."[39] The division of powers and philosophical uncertainty have thus led to an attempted separation of law and morals and to a greater preoccupation with statute law.

Impossibility of Separating Law and Morals

With this attempted separation of law and morals the strict adherence to precedents becomes a way of achieving certainty, stability, and continuity. Consequently, the process of *stare decisis* takes on greater importance. For if the Court does not attempt to achieve justice by satisfying the demands of morals and ethics, it is felt that the Court can achieve a kind of justice by at least treating alike all people in similar circumstances. This is the importance of Justice Brandeis's famous comment that "in most matters it is more important that the applicable rule of law be settled than that it be settled right,"[40] though it is instructive that Brandeis specifically exempted constitutional questions from this rule. Frankfurter has also said that it is important for judges to bear in mind that "continuity with the past is not only a necessity but even a duty."[41]

But more than fifty years ago Mr. Justice Field stated in an opinion that "it is more important that the court should be right upon later and more elaborate consideration of the cases than to be consistent with previous declarations."[42] Justice Cardozo warned against the danger of depriving the judicial process of its "suppleness of adaptation to varying

39. *Id.* at 52.
40. Burnet v. Coronado Oil & Gas Co., 285 U.S. 393, 406 (dissenting opinion).
41. Frankfurter, "Some Reflections on the Reading of Statutes," 47 Columbia Law Review 527, 535 (1947).
42. Barden v. Northern Pacific R. R., 154 U.S. 288, 322.

conditions."[43] And Justice Douglas recently elaborated extensively on this theme, providing an impressive chart showing the Court's frequent overruling of major precedents and arguing that in constitutional law "*stare decisis* must give way before the dynamic component of history."[44] This conflict of opinion concerning *stare decisis* indicates the impossibility of resting the judicial process solely upon a systematic use of precedents. The compelling urge to achieve the morally right, instead of simply the technically correct, solution in controversies has led the judges to find ways of implementing moral convictions into their decisions.

Consequently, it cannot be said that the law moves in well-fixed grooves where precise statutes shore up the flow of judicial reasoning, preventing it from spilling over into the broad expanse of value judgments. In spite of the separation of powers, the restrictions of federalism, and the force of moral skepticism, it cannot be said that a decisive breach has been achieved between law and morals, even though overt expressions of moral and ethical judgments in Supreme Court opinions are notoriously elusive, being found frequently only in "the accent and atmosphere of speech through which [the Court] conveys a particular decision."[45]

Morals and the Judge

It is one thing to say that law contains a moral element; it is quite another thing to say that judges are bound to consider the moral element of law in the reasoning process which leads to their decisions. The recurring theme in the opinions

43. Landis v. North American Co., 299 U.S. 248, 256.
44. Douglas, Stare Decisis, 49 Columbia Law Review 735, 737 (1949).
45. Frankfurter and Hart, "The Business of the Supreme Court at the October Term, *1934*," 49 Harvard Law Review 68 (1935).

of the Supreme Court is that the law admittedly embodies moral conceptions but that the validity of a law cannot depend upon the judges' appraisal of that moral element. This amounts to saying that the law which the court handles is freighted with moral and ethical content, but that the manner in which the judges handle this law renders it morally neutral. Essentially, this involves a contrast between the creation of law, which is the province of the legislature, and the judicial process, which operates under the aegis of the Constitution and the proliferation of its intent. The untenability of this distinction between the creation and interpretation of the law has been frequently urged, and much has been made of Bishop Hoadley's remark that "Whoever hath an *absolute authority to interpret* any written or spoken laws, it is he who is truly the lawgiver to all intents and purposes, and not the person who first wrote or spoke them."[46] And the objectivity of the judges has often been seriously questioned, though rarely with the cynicism of William Graham Sumner who said about the Taney Court that "The effect of political appointments to the bench is easily traceable, after two or three years, in the reports, which come to read like a collection of old stump speeches."[47] Whatever may be the *de facto* lapses in judicial objectivity, the judges theoretically consider their role as being determined objectively by the law of the land and not by moral and ethical principles.

The objectivity of the court is heightened by the fact that today most controversies have gradually come under some specific statute. Until these controversies were brought under the rule of statutes, they were left to a great extent to what

46. Gray, pp. 102, 125, 172.
47. Frankfurter, "Taney and the Commerce Clause," 49 Harvard Law Review 1286, 1287 (1936).

Frankfurter has called "judicial lawmaking." But once a state had passed a statute bearing on a particular problem, it ceased to be the court's business to engage any further in such "lawmaking," nor was it "for us to assess the wisdom of the policy underlying the law of [a state or Congress]. Our duty is at an end when we find that the Fourteenth Amendment does not deny her the power to enact [a] policy into law."[48] In the early days of the Court, practically all questions were open ones, giving wide range to the creative and imaginative power of the judges.[49] Even as late as 1875 more than 40 percent of the controversies coming before the Supreme Court were common law litigation. By 1925, such litigation was reduced to 5 percent, and by 1947 it had almost reached the vanishing point. This means that practically every case that comes before the Court has a statute at its core,[50] and this in turn reduces the scope for judicial application of moral and ethical principles.

The Concern for Judicial Objectivity

The judges of the Supreme Court have never tired of reiterating the fact that their function is not to consider the goodness or the badness of laws or of conduct, nor the wisdom nor unwisdom of statutes. Constitutional and statutory interpretation has developed a frame of mind among them which, by and large, has weaned them away from the broader philosophical implications of their work. Justice Brandeis once said: "I have no general philosophy. All my life I have

48. Carpenters & Joiners Union of America, Local No. 213 v. Ritter's Cafe, 315 U.S. 722, 728.

49. See Attorney General Jackson's speech to the Supreme Court on the occasion of the Court's 150th Anniversary. 309 U.S. v–vii (1939).

50. Frankfurter, "Some Reflections on the Reading of Statutes," 47 Columbia Law Review 527 (1947).

thought only in connection with the facts that came before me. . . . We need, not so much reason, as to see and understand facts and conditions."[51] That is why for him the function of the court was not to be "an exercise of the powers of a super-legislature. . . ."[52] Even when conditions in industry reached the point where those who were involved in the clash of interests could continue to engage in their struggle only by endangering the community, Brandeis held that it was not the function of the court to say that things had gone too far and then to set out the legitimate bounds for industrial warfare; such a task he felt was reserved for the legislatures.[53]

If Brandeis added any liberal views to the law through his opinions, he achieved this without compromising his objectivity as a judge. This was true also of Cardozo, although in his case judicial objectivity was the more remarkable in the light of his explicit and broad philosophical concerns. For Cardozo, the standard of judgment was not subjective, except in a very limited area. The judge "may not," he said, "substitute his own reading [of the social mind] for one established by the legislature, acting within constitutional limitations, through the pronouncements of a statute."[54] Only when there were no such pronouncements and when objective tests failed could the judge "look within himself."[55]

Justice Frankfurter's opinions abound in reminders that the role of the judge is severely circumscribed, particularly when the judge would inject his own value judgments overtly

51. 317 U.S. ix, xxxix (1942).
52. Dissenting in Jay Burns Baking Co. v. Bryan, 264 U.S. 504, 534.
53. Dissenting in Duplex Printing Press Co. v. Deering, 254 U.S. 443, 488. "This is the function of the legislature which, while limiting individual and group rights of aggression and defense, may substitute processes of justice for the more primitive method of trial by combat."
54. Cardozo, *Growth of the Law*, p. 94.
55. Cardozo, *Paradoxes of Legal Science*, p. 56.

into his decision. "It can never be emphasized too much," he wrote, "that one's own opinion about the wisdom or evil of a law should be excluded altogether when one is doing one's duty on the bench."[56] Even if it could be demonstrated convincingly that a law is socially undesirable it is still not the business of the Court to say so. Judicial objectivity for Frankfurter is a primary requisite if there is to be a democratic order and if the Court is to escape the charge of being oligarchic. And "The Court is not saved from being oligarchic because it professes to act in the service of humane ends."[57] Nor must the failure of Congress to speak on a matter be construed by the Court as having any concrete meaning, for "The search for significance in the silence of Congress is too often the pursuit of a mirage. We must be wary against interpolating our notions of policy in the interstices of legislative provisions."[58]

To stay thus within the bounds of proper judicial power calls for "the severest intellectual detachment and the most alert self-restraint," qualities which Frankfurter considers the unique marks of the greatest judges of the Court.[59] In another explicit disavowal of judicial competence in making value judgments, Frankfurter held:

Matters of policy . . . are by definition matters which demand the resolution of conflicts of value, and the elements of conflicting values are largely imponderable. Assessment of their competing worth involves differences of feeling; it is also an exercise in prophecy. Obviously the proper forum for mediating a clash of feelings and rendering a prophetic judgment is the body chosen for those purposes by the people. Its func-

56. West Virginia Board of Education v. Barnette, 319 U.S. 624, 647, (dissenting opinion).
57. A.F. of L. v. American Sash & Door Co., 335 U.S. 538, 555 (concurring opinion).
58. Scripps-Howard Radio, Inc. v. F.C.C., 316 U.S. 4, 11.
59. United States v. Lovett, 328 U.S. 303, 319 (concurring opinion).

tions can be assumed by this Court only in disregard of the historic limits of the Constitution.[60]

Is Complete Judicial Objectivity Possible?

But the judicial process contains a recalcitrant element which prevents its achieving the rarefied objectivity which Frankfurter has here sought to portray. And, strangely enough, no one seems to be more aware of this condition than Frankfurter himself. The Achilles heel in the objectivity of the judicial process reveals itself at many points. Whereas Brandeis liked to think that the great need was the marshalling of facts, Frankfurter makes the telling point that "facts do not assess themselves" and that "the decisive element is the attitude appropriate for judgment of the facts. . . ."[61] In a dissenting opinion he pointed out that facts do not automatically produce a satisfactory result; on the contrary, he felt that in this case "the Court's opinion seems to me to snarl a straight thread of facts into a confusing skein of legal principles."[62]

Moreover, objectivity is somewhat modified when in light of the purpose of judicial review it is necessary to ascertain whether lower courts have offended or observed the standards of justice, for the problem here is that "These standards of justice are not authoritatively formulated anywhere as though they were prescriptions in a pharmacopoeia."[63]

That the subjective element is present is further revealed by Frankfurter's disagreement with Holmes's famous phrase that "general propositions do not decide concrete

60. A.F. of L. v. American Sash & Door Co., 335 U.S. 538, 557.
61. Baumgartner v. United States, 322 U.S. 665, 666–667.
62. Maggio v. Zeitz, 333 U.S. 56, 81.
63. Malinski v. New York, 324 U.S. 401, 417.

cases";[64] to this Frankfurter has replied that "Whether they do or do not often depends on the strength of the conviction with which such 'general propositions' are held."[65] And after scrutinizing the hundreds of cases in which Holmes, Cardozo, and Brandeis construed statutes, Frankfurter concluded that "the area of free judicial movement is considerable."[66]

There is a last infirmity in the judicial process, for judges are human, the rational process is treacherous, "the ramparts of reason are fragile," and judgment can be influenced and confused by arousing passion.[67]

Strict objectivity is therefore an impossibility on the bench, both because of the human limitations of judges and the ambiguity of the law itself. In spite of all the canons erected to insure the objective operation of the judicial process, subjective elements intrude, sometimes overtly, more frequently covertly; sometimes in the form of personal predilections, at other times through interpretations of natural law and justice. Moreover, disagreements develop between various members of the Court, and the Court at one time will rule in favor of one set of interests and at another time shift to a different set of interests.

The fact that the Court will at one time exalt the right of property over personal rights and at a later date give civil liberties a preferred position as against property rights is indicative of many things about the law, not the least of which is that law is dynamic and adjustable to changing circumstances and also that the judges are provided with no absolutely binding and objective set of ideas that will in all cases

64. Lochner v. New York, 198 U.S. 45, 76.
65. Harris v. United States, 331 U.S. 145, 157.
66. Frankfurter, "Some Reflections on the Reading of Statutes," at 527, 533.
67. Frankfurter, J., in Pennekamp v. Florida, 328 U.S. 331, 350 (concurring opinion).

and at all times insure a uniform result. After all, the Court can and has reacted against its previous point of view. Indeed, the crisis of the Roosevelt Court which issued in a new line of decisions represented so marked a change in point of view that Justice Jackson took occasion to warn his brethren: "If the reaction of this Court against what many of us have regarded as an excessive judicial interference with legislative action is to yield wholesome results, we must be cautious lest we merely rush to other extremes."[68]

We are concerned here with the simple fact that the Court consciously changes its mind on important matters and consciously seeks to implement its judgments of value into the judicial process. Even if the values which the judge injects into the law are not his own in the sense that his reason demands that they become recognized by the law; even, that is, if the judge merely feels that society is seeking a change in the values which law will protect, it is nevertheless he who must decide to adjust his judgment to the new values in one way or another and in that sense his subjective action and reaction become a part of the law. Looking back over his juristic career, Cardozo admitted that phenomenon when he said that "it has been an interesting time to live in, an interesting time in which to do my little share in translating into law the social and economic forces that throb and clamor for expressions."[69]

Whether the Supreme Court's shift of emphasis from one set of values to another represented a change in the substantive beliefs among the judges has been a much debated subject. The case can be argued two ways, though one cannot

68. Concurring in Duckworth v. Arkansas, 314 U.S. 390, 401.
69. Hughes, Mr. Justice Cardozo, 305 U.S. xiv, xxvii (1938).

get the same explicit evidence to prove the case both ways. One argument is that as the New Deal developed the Court did not change its economic philosophy or its moral judgments; it simply took a new attitude toward the right of state legislatures and the Congress to experiment in the social and economic fields. Or, as Frankfurter said in a dissenting opinion,

> when the tide turned, it was not merely because circumstances had changed and there had arisen a new order with new claims to divine origin. The opinion of Mr. Justice Brandeis in Senn v. Tile Layers Union, 301 U.S. 468, shows the current running strongly in the new direction—*the direction not of social dogma but of increased deference to the legislative judgment.*[70]

This amounts to saying that, if anything, the Court became even more objective, since it deferred more completely to the will of the legislative branch. The other way of arguing this shift in the decisions is to say that the Court itself became imbued with dominant beliefs which superseded the old ideas. The evidence to support such a point of view is available only in scattered areas in the opinions, for it is not necessary for the judge to say he believes in the substance of the new legislation; to sustain a new law, it is enough for him simply to rule that the law does not violate the Constitution. Even where some of the boldest social innovations were involved in cases at hand, the Court reduced these cases to their legal nexus, as in the first *T.V.A.* case where the decision turned, not upon the acceptibility of the social philosophy underlying the T.V.A. project, but upon the validity of a contract.[71] Nevertheless, it does not stagger the imagination,

70. A. F. of L. v. American Sash & Door Co., 335 U. S. 538, 544 (dissenting opinion). Emphasis added.
71. Ashwander v. T.V.A. 297 U.S. 288.

nor does it stretch the limits of credulity, to say that one of the reasons that the Court deferred more readily to the new legislation is that it accepted the new and emerging system of values.

We need not stop here to analyze any further the reasons for the shift in the Court's attitude of judgment, for our concern is with the factual question of whether there has been such a change and to what extent there are evidences in the written opinions which indicate that the decisions turned on any overtly expressed value judgments in the form of moral or ethical principles.

So far we have discussed rather abstractly the question of the nature of law and the problem of the objectivity of the judge. For whether Supreme Court decisions turn on ethical or moral principles is determined to a great extent by whether law and morals are in any way related and whether the judges are free to indulge in value judgments in the normal course of their judging. We have said that the law the judges deal with contains implicit and frequently explicit references to moral and ethical principles, not only as side references, but as their very justification. Similarly, we have argued that in spite of the several canons of objectivity, the judges still find ample room for their own value judgments. The question to which we now turn is to what extent these value judgments actually enter the reasoning of the written opinions and in general what values govern various decisions.

The Court and Morals: Some Cases

It helps in understanding the Supreme Court's attitude toward morals to remember that the function of the Court is to try cases. And no case can ever reach the Court if it involves merely a moral problem, for then by definition it is not a case.

If, for example, a person is drowning and someone happens to be sitting on the shore watching the desperate struggle of the victim without lifting a finger to help rescue him, he cannot be held liable, for as Ames once said: "he took away nothing from the person in jeopardy, he simply failed to confer a benefit upon a stranger. . . . The law does not compel active benevolence between man and man. It is left to one's conscience whether he shall be the good Samaritan or not."[72] This is the primary datum in this problem, for the heart of a case can never be, for the Court at least, a moral issue. Only insofar as a particular law embodies a moral concept can a case be tried on moral grounds, because then in reality it is being tried on legal grounds; and in such a case the moral issue is taken for granted or is made by the Court to be either peripheral or absent altogether.

Yet, as the following cases will show, the question of morals lurks everywhere, even though the cases are decided on the basis of pure law. Just how the moral element enters into the Court's reasoning and what is achieved by its inclusion varies from case to case. But the fact that discussions on moral themes *are* found in the opinions leads to the presumption that moral value judgments are operative in the reasoning of the Court.

How Does the Moral Element Enter Judicial Opinions?

There are, among others, six ways in which the moral element is referred to in the opinions of the Court. The following cases do not exhaust all the possibilities, but they do

72. Ames, "Law and Morals," 22 Harvard Law Review 97, 112 (1908).

indicate some characteristic ways in which the subject of morals arises and is treated in cases coming to the Supreme Court.

A given action may lie well within the limits of the law but may be so questionable morally that a judge will consider the case from the moral standpoint. When the Bethlehem Steel Corporation case[73] reached the Supreme Court, the judges were confronted with the fact that the steel company had made huge profits out of producing ships for the government during the First World War and the government was now refusing to pay what it considered abnormal profits. The technical basis on which the case really rested, and in terms of which the steel company won the case, was the fact that the government had entered into a contract with the company and had to live up to its bargain. In the majority opinion, Justice Black took cognizance of the 22 percent profits but was not particularly impressed; for in light of the much higher profits made by others whom he cited, this 22 percent was relatively small. Besides, all the argument about these profits seemed to him to be beside the point: there was no concrete way in which the size of the profit could influence the reasoning toward a decision. To the government's argument that unconscionable profits ought not to be tolerated, Black replied: "If the Executive is in need of additional laws by which to protect the nation against war profiteering, the Constitution has given to Congress, not to this Court, the power to make them."[74] Inevitably, the discussion on the bench centered around the moral dimension of the case. In a concurring opinion, Justice Murphy felt moved to make

73. United States v. Bethlehem Steel Corp., 315 U.S. 289.
74. 315 U.S. at 309.

clear the distinction between law and morals as it applied to this case in the following words:

The question before the Court . . . is not whether an arrangement like the one presented for review accords with our conceptions of business morality or with correct administration of the public business. Having made a bargain, the Government should be held to it unless there are valid and appropriate reasons known to the law for relieving it from its obligations. It is the duty and responsibility of the courts, not to re-write contracts according to their own views of what is practical and fair, but to enforce them in accordance with the evidence and recognized principles of law.[75]

But Justice Frankfurter refused to let the moral factor get such summary treatment. To him it made a serious difference that the steel company had assumed no risks of loss in connection with the rising costs of labor, materials, and transportation, nor did Bethlehem have to make any capital expenditures, since the government agreed to advance all the funds that were required for the performance of the contracts.

So clear was the moral obligation of the company to Frankfurter in this case that not even the objectivity of the judicial process which Black invoked here and which Frankfurter himself had so frequently expounded could prevent him from a vigorous dissent:

However circumscribed the judicial area may be we had best remain within it. But the function of the judiciary is not so limited that it must sanction the use of the federal courts as instruments of injustice in disregard of moral and equitable principles which have been part of the law for centuries.[76]

Obviously there was a moral problem in this case, but only

75. *Id.* at 310 (concurring opinion).
76. 315 U.S. at 312 (dissenting opinion).

Frankfurter's dissenting opinion would decide the issue on the moral element.

There are times when, although there is agreement on the moral element in a case, the judges find themselves unable to translate this moral duty into legal rights. The plight of the American Indian involves such a problem and was vividly revealed in the case of the *Shoshone Indians.* In a concurring opinion Justice Jackson said:

> We would not be second to any in recognizing that—judgment or not judgment—a moral obligation of a high order rests upon this country to provide for decent shelter, clothing, education, and industrial advancement of the Indian. Nothing is gained by dwelling upon the unhappy conflicts that have prevailed between the Shoshones and the whites—conflicts which sometimes leave one in doubt which side could make the better claim to be civilized. The generation of Indians who suffered the privations, indignities, and brutalities of the westward march of the whites have gone to the Happy Hunting Ground, and nothing that we can do can square the account with them. Whatever survives is a moral obligation resting on the descendants of the whites to do for the descendants of the Indians what in the conditions of the twentieth century is the decent thing.
>
> It is most unfortunate to try to measure this moral duty in terms of legal obligations and ask the Court to spell out Indian legal rights from written instruments made and probably broken long ago and to put our moral duty in figures as legal damages. The Indian problem is essentially a sociological problem, not a legal one.[77]

Here the moral element of the case was clearly admitted, but since there was no way for the Court to translate it into a legal remedy, the Indians left empty-handed, and once again it was made clear that the Supreme Court cannot right every wrong.

The moral element enters most frequently in cases where there is a conflict of competing values. Justice Cardozo ad-

77. Shoshone Indians v. United States, 324 U.S. 335, 355.

mitted that he had worked out a system of priorities in cases which presented a conflict of values. He said: "There is no common denominator to which it is possible to reduce [opposing values]. . . . In general we may say that where conflict exists, moral values are to be preferred to economic, and economic to aesthetic."[78] In recent decades, the Court has resolved several conflicts among competing values by raising moral values above economic values.

In the conflict between civil liberties and property rights the Court has more and more emphasized the priority of civil rights. The written opinions seem to affirm this priority primarily on constitutional rather than moral grounds. This is, of course, based upon the judgment that the Constitutional rights laid out in the First Amendment lie at the heart of our form of government. In *Marsh v. Alabama*,[79] Justice Black said,

When we balance the Constitutional rights of owners of property against those of the people to enjoy freedom of press and religion, as we must here, we remain mindful of the fact that the latter occupy a preferred position. As we have stated before, the right to exercise the liberties safeguarded by the First Amendment "lies at the foundation of free government by free men" and we must in all cases "weigh the circumstances and . . . appraise the . . . reasons . . . in support of the regulation . . . of the rights."[80]

The phrase "preferred position" does not, of course, appear in the Constitution but is itself the result of "appraisal" and interpretation. As Justice Frankfurter has pointed out, the philosophy underlying the phrase was developed in the opinions of Justice Holmes "for [whom] . . . the right to

78. Cardozo, *Paradoxes of Legal Science*, p. 57.
79. 326 U.S. 501.
80. 326 U.S. at 509.

search for truth was of a different order than some transient economic dogma," and so Holmes "was far more ready to find legislative invasion [of the Constitution] where free inquiry was involved than in the debatable area of economics."[81] Furthermore, "indispensible conditions of an open as against a closed society come to this Court with a momentum for respect lacking when appeal is made to liberties which derive merely from shifting economic arrangements."[82]

Brandeis held many years earlier that "Where only property rights are involved, mere postponement of the judicial enquiry is not a denial of due process, if the opportunity given for ultimate judicial determination of the liability is adequate."[83] Justice Rutledge implied that such a priority of values is the underlying philosophy of our law when in a concurring opinion he wrote:

Since in these cases the rights involved are rights of property, not of personal liberty or life as in criminal proceedings, the consequences, though serious, are not of the same moment under our system, as appears from the fact that they are not secured by the same procedural protections in trial. It is in this respect perhaps that our basic law, following the common law, most clearly places the rights to life and to liberty above those of property.[84]

Justice Jackson made the same point when he said, again in a concurring opinion, that "Property can have no more dangerous, even if unwitting, enemy than one who would make its possession a pretext for unequal or exclusive civil rights."[85]

These opinions provide us no sustained analysis of the reasons, apart from mere affirmation, for the priority of civil

81. Kovacs v. Cooper, 336 U.S. 77, 95 (concurring opinion).
82. *Ibid.*
83. Phillips v. Comm'r, 283 U.S. 589, 596.
84. Bowles v. Willingham, 321 U.S. 503, 525.
85. Edwards v. California, 314 U.S. 160, 185.

liberties, but there is little doubt that such preferential treatment of civil rights grows out of a judicial value judgment,
since the Constitution does not indicate the position of various rights in the hierarchy of values. Faced with conflicting
values, the judge has to decide on the "preferred position."
It is at this point that moral judgments can enter the reasoning of the Court, even though this may not be apparent in
the written opinion.

Considering this same problem in other areas, it can
hardly be doubted that in the minimum wage cases, the conflict between such values as freedom of contract, private property and the guarantee of a wage adequate for a decent standard of living was resolved in favor of the latter value through
the moral urge of the Court.[86] Similarly, the line of cases
leading to the right of collective bargaining reveals a gradual
modification of the doctrine of freedom of contract, due
largely to the moral concern of the Court.[87] The conflict between the individual's rights and the general welfare has likewise been resolved in terms of moral preference.[88]

Whether the preferences employed here by the Court
are good ones is not our chief concern at the moment. The
point we wish to make is that in those cases which present a
conflict of values, the Court inevitably indulges in value
judgments of its own.

*In other cases, a moral end is achieved on technical legal
grounds with no moral arguments appearing in the majority*

86. West Coast Hotel Co. v. Parrish, 300 U.S. 379; Morehead v. New York
ex rel. Tipaldo, 298 U.S. 587; Adkins v. Children's Hospital, 261 U.S. 525.
87. Lincoln Federal Labor Union v. Northwestern Iron & Metal Co. 335
U.S. 525; Coppage v. Kansas, 236 U.S. 1; Adair v. United States, 208
U.S. 161.
88. Helvering v. Davis, 301 U.S. 619; Steward Machine Co. v. Davis, 301
U.S. 548; Nebbia v. New York, 291 U.S. 502.

opinion. Frequently, cases are decided on technical legal grounds where the net result is to uphold a moral value judgment although the opinions contain no reference at all to such a value judgment. In such a case it is not unusual to find one of the judges writing a separate opinion to point out that the real principle governing the case is not simply legal but something quite deeper. In this way the moral element is at least recognized.

The issue in the *Bob-Lo Excursion Co.* case[89] was the validity of a Michigan statute which forbade racial discrimination on boats taking people to an amusement park and at the park. The reasoning of the Court was deflected from the civil rights issue by the circumstance that in this case the park was an island near Detroit but actually in Canada, so that the point for decision turned out to be whether Michigan could legislate in a situation where "foreign commerce" was involved.

Justice Rutledge held in favor of the colored girl who had suffered discrimination on one of the boats going to this island, but his opinion was restricted to the technical question of ·Michigan's power to pass the statute here involved. Since the moral value of ending discrimination in this area was achieved by the Court's decision, albeit without any direct reference to the problem of values implicit in the case, the matter could have rested there.

But Justice Douglas wished to make explicit the value judgment which controlled the case for him, and in a concurring opinion he wrote:

The case is, I think, controlled by a principle which cuts deeper than that announced by the Court and which is so important that it deserves to be stated separately . . . the question here is . . . whether a State can

89. Bob-Lo Excursion Co. v. Michigan, 333 U.S. 28.

prevent a carrier in foreign commerce from denying passage to a person because of his race or color. For this is a case of a discrimination against a Negro by a carrier's complete denial of passage to her because of her race. It is unthinkable to me that we would strike down a state law which required all carriers—local and interstate—to transport persons regardless of their race or color.[90]

This is a good example of a judge's concern to make the moral grounds of the Court's decision explicit, even though the reasoning of the opinion based on technical law reached the same conclusion. But it is more often the case that a moral end will be achieved without any recognition in the opinions of the moral grounds of the decision. Nowhere, for example, is there any treatment of the moral evil of child labor in the opinions which finally abolished that practice.[91]

Statutory interpretation provides another occasion for the inclusion of moral judgments in Supreme Court opinions. The *Mercoid* case[92] involved a patent infringement, and the argument was concerned chiefly with the matter of "contributory infringement." Justice Douglas's treatment of the doctrine of contributory infringement in the majority opinion led Justice Frankfurter to dissent on explicit moral grounds.[93] It was Frankfurter's dissent with its reference to the ethical basis of the legal doctrine of contributory infringement that prompted Justice Black to write a concurring opinion for the sole purpose of protesting against Frankfurter's attempt to rest a case on a moral interpretation of a statute, in which he said:

If there is such a wrong as contributory infringement, it must have been created by the federal patent statutes. Since they make no direct

90. *Id.* at 40–41.
91. United States v. Barby, 312 U.S. 100; Carter v. Carter Coal Co., 298 U.S. 238; Hammer v. Dagenhart, 247 U.S. 251.
92. Mercoid Corp. v. Mid-Continent Investment Co., 320 U.S. 661.
93. *Id.* at 676 (dissenting opinion).

mention of such a wrong, its existence could only be rested on inferences as to Congressional intent. In searching for Congressional intent we ordinarily look to such sources as statutory language and legislative history. The dissent in question mentions neither of these guides; in fact, it mentions no statute at all. Instead, the chief reliance appears to be upon the law of torts, a quotation from a decision of a lower federal court which held that no infringement was shown, and the writer's personal views on "morals" and "ethics." Not one of these references, unless it be the latter, throws enough light on the patent statutes to justify its use in construing these statutes as creating, in addition to a right of recovery for infringement, a more expansive right judicially characterized as a "formula" of "contributory infringement". *And for judges to rest their interpretation of statutes on nothing but their own conceptions of "morals" and "ethics" is, to say the least, dangerous business.*

If the present case compelled consideration of the morals and ethics of contributory infringement, I should be most reluctant to conclude that the scales of moral value are weighed against the right of producers to sell their unpatented goods in a free market. At least since Adam Smith wrote, unhampered competition has not generally been considered immoral. While there have been objections to the Sherman Anti-Trust Act, few if any of the objectors have questioned its morality.

It has long been recognized that a socially undesirable practice may seek acceptance under the guise of conventional moral symbols. And repeated judicial assertion that a bad practice is hallowed by morals may, if unchallenged, help it to receive the acceptance it seeks. With this in mind, I wish to make explicit my protest against talking about the judicial doctrine of "contributory infringement" as though it were entitled to the same respect as a universally recognized moral truth.[94]

This case is particularly interesting because it involves a doctrine created, not by a statute, but by the courts. It could have grown out of an earlier court's moral urge but, as this opinion indicates, it did not have binding influence on members of a later court. That the doctrine of contributory infringement rested on a moral conviction did not give it more authority. Instead this made it a somewhat more precarious doctrine precisely because it grew out of a statutory interpre-

94. *Id.* at 673–674. Emphasis added.

tation based on conceptions of morals and ethics which, as Justice Black argued, is "dangerous business."

Lastly, the doctrine of natural moral law continues to figure in the opinions of the Court, though not without vigorous intramural opposition. The *Adamson* case is interesting because a natural law doctrine was employed by the majority of the Court to deny a defendant a right which the non-natural law reasoning of Justice Black would uphold.[95] The technical question here was whether the Fifth Amendment guaranty that no person "shall be compelled in any criminal case to be a witness against himself" is made effective against state action by the Fourteenth Amendment.

It is Black's contention that the Fourteenth Amendment incorporates the Bill of Rights, and the importance of this lies in the fact that it supposedly spells out in detail the content of due process, thus eliminating the need for a subjective determination of fundamental rights. The majority argued that pure objectivity would not be achieved simply by saying that the Bill of Rights is applicable to state action, for it would still be necessary for the Court to select from among the first eight Amendments which were thus to be incorporated, since clearly no one could argue that all the provisions embodied in those Amendments were carried over into the Fourteenth. Justice Frankfurter in a concurring opinion held that

in the history of thought "natural law" has a much longer and much better founded meaning and justification than subjective selection of the first eight Amendments for incorporation into the Fourteenth. If all that is meant is that due process contains within itself certain minimal standards which are "of the very essence of a scheme of ordered liberty" *Palko* v. *Connecticut*, 302 U.S. 319, 325, putting upon this Court the

95. Adamson v. California, 332 U.S. 46.

duty of applying these standards from time to time, then we have merely arrived at the insight which our predecessors long ago expressed.[96]

But Justice Black held that the law ought to be declared void. Black's purpose, of course, was to limit the subjectivity of the Court, for in his opinion the natural law formula announced in this case and its precedents could "license this Court, in considering regulatory legislation, to roam at large in the broad expanses of policy and morals. . . ."[97]

But the Court cannot avoid considering the moral implications of cases, and not even a deliberate attempt to follow closely the Constitution can eliminate the occasion for turning to the vague phrases of natural law, and this for the simple reason that the laws or conduct can be considered unjust for reasons not indicated in the Constitution. Even Justice Black argued from what appears to be a moral concern when dissenting in *Muschany* v. *United States*:[98] "We are squarely confronted with the issues of fraud, unconscionable dealing, and unjust enrichment. I think we should remand the case to the Circuit Court so that it can pass upon *those* questions."[99] Justice Holmes referred to the fact that the common law required a judgment not to be contrary to "natural justice" and cautioned against letting constitutional fiction deny "fair play."[100]

96. *Id.* at 65.
97. *Id.* at 90 Black sought to prove that the Bill of Rights was incorporated in the Fourteenth Amendment by showing that such an incorporation was intended by the framers of the amendment. After an extensive analysis of the history of the passage of the amendment, Professor Fairman concludes: "In his [Black's] contention that Section I was intended and understood to impose Amendments I to VIII upon the states, the record of history is overwhelmingly against him." Cf. Fairman, "Does the 14th Amendment Incorporate the Bill of Rights?" 2 Stanford Law Review 5, 139 (1949).
98. 324 U.S. 49.
99. *Id.* at 78.
100. McDonald v. Mabee, 243 U.S. 90, 91.

In yet another case Justice Black disagreed with the reasoning of the Court on grounds other than legal. This was a case where the young parents of three children were killed on a train and the guardians were unable to receive compensation because that father was a railroad employee riding on a pass. In his dissent, Justice Black said that "the subjection of railroad employees while passengers to the hazards of uncompensated injuries is at war with the basic philosophy which has found expression in other industrial and social legislation for many years."[101] This "basic philosophy" is not much different from the "natural justice" Black resents so much, since neither of these phrases is elucidated in any specific statute applicable to the instant case but is more akin to what Cardozo has called a "moral urge."

The conclusion is unmistakable—that a moral element permeates the judicial process. The moral element enters law in the first instance through the legislative process where the moral and ethical value judgments of the people are translated into statutes. Since the moral element already resides in the law, the judge can remain silent about it in a particular case. That the judge's opinion does not contain an elaborate dilation on the moral point does not mean that there is no conscious concern on his part for the moral element. This can mean only that for the time being the Court is in accord with the value judgments implicit in the law, and in the particular case it simply *applies* the law. This accounts for the fact that there are so comparatively few discussions of moral issues in the opinions.

Yet, even the few cases referred to in this discussion reveal the frequency with which the Court finds itself arguing

101. Francis v. Southern Pacific Co., 333 U.S. 445, 468.

over the relevance of moral value judgments. The obvious reason for this is that the Constitution has to be interpreted, and constitutional interpretation opens rather wide areas in which the Court's moral urge can come into play. The more significant point is, however, that not only the Constitution but statutes too have to be interpreted. The reduction of most cases to a particular statute has therefore not eliminated the possibility of viewing a case from a moral point of view. The remarkable thing is, as Professor Freund has already pointed out, that "the process of statutory construction has likewise become an aspect of political philosophy."[102]

102. Paul Freund, *On Understanding the Supreme Court* (Boston: Little, Brown, 1949) p. 36.

2

THE SOVIET CONCEPT OF LAW

Natural Law with
a Marxist Slant

SOVIET law may be one thing in theory and something else in practice. Even so, from the earliest days of the revolution, the Communists took the scattered ideas about law in the writings of Marx and sought to employ them literally, which meant that since the revolution was to abolish the state, and since the state and law were so closely identified, this would mark the end of the existence of law. The Russian Revolution thus produced one of the most significant episodes in recent history so far as the study of law is concerned, for it produced a society which deliberately abolished the regime of law: "from November 1917 to 1922," writes Stuchka, "law was formally lacking."[1]

1. Rudolph Schlesinger, *Soviet Legal Theory* (New York: Oxford University Press, 1945), p. 79.

In place of law in the formal sense, there was government by decree, and these decrees were enforced by the newly instituted People's Courts which were specifically ordered to refrain from any dependence upon the conceptions of law identified with the overthrown governments; or, as the statute put it, "No reference can be made in the decisions to the laws of the overthrown governments."[2] In this manner, an abrupt and complete break of continuity with all previous governments and their laws was achieved.

The radical revolt against law proceeded on both the theoretical and the practical level, and while Soviet thought about the nature of law has undergone many adjustments since 1917, the fundamental attitude toward law has not been changed. In the early days, the Soviet jurist Gintsburg wrote that "Marxism declares a merciless war against the bourgeois legal concepts. . . ."[3]

In the 1927 edition of "The General Theory of Law and Marxism," Pashukanis argues this point with great thoroughness and fidelity to Marxian premises, showing that from these Marxist principles nothing less than the total elimination of law would ensue:

The dying out of the categories . . . of bourgeois law by no means signifies that they are replaced by categories of proletarian law. The dying out of the categories of bourgeois law will in these conditions signify the dying out of law in general; that is to say, the gradual disappearance of the juridic element in human relations.[4]

Lenin stated that the Soviet system is in theory a dicta-

2. Vladimir Gsovski, "The Soviet Concept of Law," 7 Fordham Law Review 20, n. 76 (1938).
3. *Id.* at 4, n. 12.
4. E. B. Pashukanis, "The General Theory of Law and Marxism," in *Soviet Legal Philosophy*, trans. by Hugh W. Babb, introd. by John N. Hazard (Cambridge: Harvard University Press, 1951), p. 122.

torship of the proletariat which is a "power unrestrained by any law and based upon force and not law."[5] Vishinsky more recently expressed this point when he wrote that "The dictatorship of the proletariat is authority unlimited by any statute."[6] That is to say that the radical revolt against law was precisely against that which in the West is termed the "rule of law," and it is for this reason that Rudolph Schlesinger writes that "even today it is more difficult in the USSR than elsewhere to establish a clear-cut distinction between administrative and legislative acts."[7]

While it would not be correct to say that today there is no Soviet law, the gradual rebuilding of this law, from a condition of no law, has proceeded upon the same theoretical bases which had earlier led to its abolition. This dramatic episode of the abolition of law and the gradual attempt to reconstruct the concept and regime of law provides us with a vivid case study of what is involved in the complex phenomenon of law.

The Soviet Conception of the Cause of Law

The most conspicuous feature of Soviet philosophy of law is its rigorous analysis of the manner in which law is supposed to emerge in human society. Most legal theories devote substantial attention to what is called the "source" of law, and in this respect Soviet theory is far more detailed than any contemporary theory, with the exception of the theories of natural law with which Soviet reflections have much in common. Most noticeable in Soviet legal theory is the at-

---

5. Gsovski, p. 18.
6. Andrei Vishinsky (ed.), *The Law of the Soviet State* trans. by Hugh W. Babb, introd. by John N. Hazard (New York: Macmillan, 1948), p. 48.
7. Schlesinger, p. 60.

tempt to push the doctrine of the source of law beyond those theories which hold that law is "what the courts do in fact," or that law is the "aggregate of commands of the sovereign." The activity of the courts and the commands of the sovereign are taken by the Soviet theorists as simply "proximate" rather than "ultimate" sources of law, for the activities of both judges and primary sovereigns are, for them, simply symptomatic of some deeper phenomenon. Judicial decisions and legislative acts reflect some prior reality.

In order to understand the meaning of law, it becomes necessary to put the acts of judges and sovereigns into a fuller perspective, for if these activities are only symptoms of something else, that something else must be located and defined. Moreover, if the acts of judges and sovereigns are considered symptoms of something prior, the concept of the source of law takes on new meaning; for in this sense the source of law is more like the "cause" of law rather than a body of principles to which jurists consciously go for information.

Marx was concerned most with determining how law is "caused." The decisive point in his analysis was the status of the human mind; for whatever else can be said about the phenomenon of law it must be agreed that law is in some way fashioned by the human consciousness. Only a conscious being is able to grasp law; when one says that law is what judges or legislators do, this necessarily means what they do as conscious or "rational" beings. Austin had defined law as "a rule laid down for the guidance of an *intelligent* being by an *intelligent* being. . . ."[8]

8. John Austin, *The Province of Jurisprudence Determined*, introd. by H. L. A. Hart ("Library of Ideas" [London: Weidenfeld and Nicolson, 1954]), p. 10.

In Soviet law, it is held that "Without the consciousness of law there is—and can be—no law."[9] But where does the mind stand in relation to the law? If the mind fashions the rules for human behavior, can it be said that the mind *originates* the rules; does the mind have the capacity to penetrate to a realm of eternally true principles from which to draw the content of the rule? This was, of course, the position of those who, with Hegel, said that reality was Idea—that the material order of human experience was the embodiment or reflection of ideas. From this point of view the mind originates rules and transforms human behavior and relations to fit these ideas.

Marx felt that this was a grotesquely incorrect analysis of the status of the mind and a thoroughly incorrect account of the relation of ideas to reality. For Marx, ideas are derivative; that is, they are caused by the material reality which is the only thing that is real. This is, of course, the heart of Marxist materialism, for Marx wrote that with him the idea is nothing but the material transformed and translated in the mind of man. If law is a matter of consciousness, if it has to do with men's ideas, then law is really the transformation or reflection of the material order by the mind of men.

The mind, then, does not stand in any kind of independent relation to the material order; the mind is not free to "create" rules of human behavior; it is able only to "transform" the material forces which impinge upon it into conscious formulations of rules. Consciousness is the effect of prior material conditions in human experience. Law is therefore *caused* by the material order, since the mind of man

9. S. A. Golunskii and M. S. Strogovich, "The Theory of the State and Law," in *Soviet Legal Philosophy*, p. 383.

simply reflects this order. The human mind occupies a middle position: at one end is the material order which is producing or causing effects upon the consciousness; at the other end is the rule. But the rule emerges from the mind in the particular form that it does only because of the particular impact of the prior material order upon it.

Were this interpretation of how the mind works taken literally, one would have to conclude that the human mind at all times reflects the prior material order perfectly. Thought and consciousness would always bear a one-to-one relation to the material reality, and consequently thought would always be "correct" or "true," for the mind would mirror "reality." Moreover, thinking would proceed along strict lines or channels and would be shored up against any spilling over into "error" or "unreality." So strict would be the mechanism of thought that it would not even be possible to ask oneself whether his ideas were true, for if in fact ideas proceed from the material reality, then there would be no other position that the mind could take in relation to that material order. For the mind to "reflect" upon its own operations supposes that the mind has some independent status and possesses certain powers.

This is the kind of difficulty Hume found himself in when he reduced all ideas to impressions or sensations but continued to speak of the mind as being able to "handle" these impressions in such a way as to "transpose" or "augment" ideas. The capacity for "imagination" indicates an ability of the mind to operate, at least in some sense, independently from the external impress the material order may have on the mind. Marx was aware of this difficulty, for it arose at one of the crucial points in his argument about law, namely, when he designated law as "ideology."

To say that law is "ideology" has two different meanings in Marxist theory. First of all, in the strict sense, law is ideology in that law is the cluster of ideas which the actual material order creates in men's consciousness, so that ideas "confirm" the order of society. The second meaning of the term "ideology" is a critical one, for it means a set of ideas which represent a distorted view of the real material order. It is this second meaning of ideology which is found throughout the writings of Soviet legal thinkers, for they all hold that law is ideology, that is, a set of ideas, transformed into rules of behavior but based upon a distorted view of reality. This notion of ideology is best understood when we consider the economic basis of law.

The Economic Basis of Law

The material order or matrix from which law springs is the economic order; the way in which men are actually related to each other in producing goods and wealth causes them to think about the rules of social behavior—about law. Although these rules of behavior are, as we have said before, formulated by the mind, they do not originate there but are only reflections of the material order. These rules have their overt expressions in the pronouncements or commands of the state.

For the Marxist, the relation of the law to the state does not represent as serious a question as it does for most democratic philosophers, for this relationship is simplified by arguing, as Lenin did, that "Law and the state are not two distinct phenomena—one preceding the other—but are two sides of the same phenomenon: class dominance."[10] Whereas Locke

10. *Id.* at 366.

argued that men have certain natural rights even before there is a state, the Marxist would argue that the very idea of "rights" is simply a reflection, not of some natural law or natural right, but of the simple fact that a person is in a position, especially economically, to assert his "right."

This concept of right has its origin in the actual economic order, becomes an "idea" or "law," and is then enforced by the state. Without the state, there would be no law, for as Lenin wrote, "without an apparatus capable of compelling the observance of legal rules the law is nothing."[11]

Thus the law and the state emerge from the same matrix —the economic fact, or the way in which men are related to each other in the processes of production. As Marx put it, "Legal relations as well as forms of the state could neither be understood by themselves, nor explained by the so-called general process of the human mind, but they are rooted in the material conditions of life."[12]

In one of his most famous statements, Marx indicated his concept of law when he wrote that "Society is not based upon law; that is a juridical fiction. Just the reverse is the truth. Law rests upon society, it must be the expression of the general interests that spring from the material production of a given society."[13]

We have come to the point where Marxist theory seems to be offering a new approach to the understanding of law by distinguishing its own "scientific" approach from the "idealistic" or "ideological" approach of most bourgeois theorists. We shall see later whether there is as much difference be-

11. *Ibid.*
12. Gsovski, p. 5.
13. *Ibid.*

tween the Soviet and Western theories as the two sides think there is. At any rate, the Marxist rests his claim for scientific precision upon the fact that he looks for the phenomenon of law where alone it is possible for law to exist, namely, in the orders of society.

All law, according to this view, is the law of the ruling economic class. The Western jurist is accused by the Marxist of looking in the wrong place for the essence of law when he seeks it in rational principles fashioned by the mind and originating there. "The jurist imagines," wrote Engels, that "he is operating from *a priori* principles, whereas they are really only economic reflexes."[14] This is why Marx could say, speaking to the bourgeoisie, that "your law is the will of your class given the authority of a statute."[15] It may be that the framers of this statute think that they are expressing the requirements of "justice," but their concept of justice is affected by their status in the economic order; their legal consciousness reflects the actual material reality.

What is this reality? In the simplest terms, the "makers" of the law are the economically superior or dominant class in society. But if this dominant class is in fact dominant, and if its law reflects this dominance, then the law is a clear reflection of the material order, and in that sense the law must be "correct." And yet, the Marxists' argument against law is that it is "ideology," by which they mean that law is a distortion of reality.

Nowhere does the weakness of the Marxist argument show itself more clearly than when it designates law as

14. Hans Kelsen, *The Communist Theory of Law* (New York: Frederick A. Praeger, Inc., 1955), p. 13.
15. "Manifesto of the Communist Party" in Karl Marx and Friedrich Engels, *Selected Works* (Moscow: Foreign Languages Publishing House, 1958), I, 49.

"ideology," and this in spite of the fact that the notion of ideology is a profound insight into human nature. The weakness of the argument stems from the assumption that the scientific analysis of the source of legal consciousness can provide the data for designating what ideology is. If by ideology is meant a distortion of reality, and if reality is the actual historical economic situation—and if the actual situation is that one class dominates another, and if the laws reflect this domination, then where is the distortion of reality?

To be sure, the Marxist argues that the distortion comes about when jurists forget that they are simply expressing the will of the dominant class and wrongly think that they are dealing with eternal principles of justice. This would mean that ideology is essentially "illusion," but illusion about what? The illusion would pertain, not to the law, for about the "fact" of law there can be no mistake. The law, in fact, can be assumed for purposes of argument to reflect the actual social reality. The illusion would have to pertain to what men think *about* the law.

The fact of the law is thus one thing, whereas men's interpretation of the law is another. But how is it possible, in terms of Marx's scientific method, to account for the possibility of ideology? What makes it possible to go so wrong with respect to the law? That men do indulge in the illusion that their laws (however notoriously prejudiced in favor of their self-interest) are "just" and represent universal and eternal verities is unquestioned. But the theoretical problem here is to inquire how, in terms of Marxian principles of analysis, this can be accounted for.

To speak of ideology the way Marx does assumes a far different concept of the human mind and of reality than Marxism admits. While the doctrine of ideology as Marx has developed it is one of the most fruitful of his insights, it cannot rest securely upon its premise. For even though this doctrine of ideology assumes that the mind knows truth only insofar as the mind reflects actual reality, Marx continues over and over again to interpret and appraise actual reality from the vantage point of what is not yet real.

Thus he can speak of the English Factory Acts as laws which were just as necessary to modern industry as cotton, yarns, and electric telegraph; these factory laws are therefore a true reflection of the situation in the economic order. The ideological aspect of these laws lies in thinking that they embody the norm or the picture in terms of which human beings will or must be related to each other permanently. How can Marx know that these laws do not possess eternal forms of human association?

The most cogent scientific evidence which would support his view is the fact of change, both in the laws and in the actual relations of persons in the economic order. But Marxism does not rest its case on the simple fact of change. Its critical power stems from its vision of the *direction* historical change is taking. Thus, the perspective from which Marxism is alone able to provide the meaning for the concept of ideology is the perspective of the ultimate end, which is not yet a fact. It is not simply that there is change and that for this reason it is illusory to think that any particular laws can at any one time grasp the full possibilities in human relations; Marxism criticizes laws as ideological, rather, because they represent only approximations of some future social reality whose configurations can even now, before they exist, be described, namely, the classless society.

Thus, whereas some observers analyzing the factual social order arrive at one interpretation, for example that there are inequalities, and from this conclude that there always will be inequalities, others can take the same facts and come to a different conclusion, as, for example, the Marxist who "interprets" these facts in such a way as to predict that the future, contained in the present, will necessarily eliminate all inequalities.

The question here is whether it is ever possible for any observer to achieve a truly objective view of reality, particularly if it is assumed, as in the case of Marxian analysis, that all views are affected by one's status in society. Marxism assumes that the ultimate end of history can be known even now before it "exists," and only in terms of this end can it say about the present that it is misunderstood when it is considered eternally just or right. Nowhere does Marxism resemble natural law theory more than at this point, where it assumes that the law is hidden in nature from which it must and can be derived.

Soviet jurists never tire of accusing Western legal philosophy of misconceiving the true nature of Western legal theory. There is some truth in their attack, for no one will deny that laws represent class interest in many instances. But when it is a question of analyzing the true nature of the phenomenon of law and not of its borderline cases and its exceptional manifestations, the question is whether this attack is accurate.

It is true, for example, that Western law considers law to exist abstractly "independently of human actions and relationships, and independently of the social relationships which it regulates."[16] It must be admitted that, indeed, altogether too much Western legal theory gives the impression

16. Golunskii and Strogovich, p. 371.

that law has nothing at all to do with human beings. Austin can speak at length about law as a command and Kelsen, too, restricts the concerns of legal theory to the legal norm. When one studies these dominant Western theories there seems to be some plausibility in the Soviet criticism that these theories have their

inception in the fact that bourgeois legal science ascribes to law an independent existence unrelated to the reality of human life in society, and contemplates it rather as expressing eternal principles than as possessing the reality of a social phenomenon which exists in definite social conditions.[17]

But what we have been trying to indicate here is that the very conception of ideology in the center of Marxist analysis assumes an ideal standard by which to judge the present and predict the future; this Soviet picture of the future resembles very much the ideal element in the natural law philosophy.

The Material Order, the Ideal Order, and Law

Against the so-called idealism of Western legal theory, Marxism focuses upon the concrete sources of the law which it finds in the forces of production and the relations of production. Marx had argued that the mode of production in the material life determines the general character of the social, political, and spiritual process of life. This is to emphasize once again that the material, not the spiritual, order is primary. For again Marx held that "it is not the consciousness of men that determines their being, but, on the contrary, their social being determines their consciousness."[18] Law,

17. *Ibid.*
18. Preface to "The Critique of Political Economy," in Marx and Engels, *Selected Works*, I, 363.

religion, and morals are all in the same category as being produced by the social or material order, and to that extent they are all ideological.

This conclusion is reached through a distinction between the substructure and the superstructure, where economic relations are the substructure or foundation, and law, religion, and morals are the superstructure. "Law emerges out of definite economic relationships."[19] The "scientific" aspect of this analysis comes from the emphasis upon the concrete relations which can be identified. Vishinsky, who at one time was the director of the Soviet research program whose purpose it was to draft and develop a theoretical basis for law, wrote that the "essence" of law is "rooted" in the material conditions of life, and that law is merely "the will of the dominant class, elevated into a statute."[20] This scientific definition, he continued, "starts from the proposition that political, legal, philosophical, religious, and literary development is defined by—and is a superstructure over—economics."[21] How is this major theme in Marxism to be understood?

According to a one-time Soviet jurist, Pashukanis, this general theory is made more specific by saying that "every sort of juridic relationship is a relationship between subjects. A subject is the atom of juridic theory: the simplest element, incapable of being resolved further."[22] But this subject of legal theory is viewed solely from the economic point of view, chiefly because the Marxist believes that it is a person's economic status that determines his attitudes and relationships to other persons.

19. Golunskii and Strogovich, p. 373.
20. Vishinsky, p. 13.
21. *Ibid.*
22. Pashukanis, p. 160.

But the decisive fact determining the economic status of an individual is his relationship to property. When a person owns property, he develops a cluster of "interests" around that property and this is what forms in him his attitudes towards others. Between man and man, and between groups and other groups, there is interposed the fact of property—ownership—and it is out of this fact that there flows the consciousness of "mine," which is fashioned in turn into the "rule": "thou shalt not steal." It is at this point too that all those who own property join forces, literally, to protect what they have against those who do not have but look longingly at the "property" of others.

The institution of private property is what gives rise to those relations between people which call forth the phenomenon of law. For it is the institution of property which causes, more than anything else, the clash of "interests" which it is the function of law to settle. This, then, is what is meant in Marxist legal theory when it is said that "law does not have a history of its own." It means that there is no law apart from production relationships, apart from the clusters and conflicts of interests which are generated by the ownership of property. This is why Pashukanis concluded that "the pivot—the content—of each historical system of law is the relationship between the owners of the means of production and the immediate producers. This relationship is responsive to the fundamental class interest of the dominant class and is maintained by the organized force of that class. . . ."[23] The clash of class interests, whose roots are in private ownership is the "cause of the development of the juridic superstructure,"[24] that is, the "cause" of law.

23. *Id.* at 261–262.
24. *Id.* at 137.

Marx pursues this analysis of the economic cause of law with even more precision. In his *Capital*, he points out that material things can enter into relationship to each other only if their owners place themselves in relationship to each other. Each person's will, he says, resides in his property, and therefore no one can take this away from him unless he agrees to part with it. And all commodity exchanges are therefore achieved by mutual consent in accordance with the rules men have formulated.

These rules are laws, but these laws have come into being only because owners of commodities recognize in each other private proprietors. The relations between men about which law is concerned have their inception, therefore, in two wills: the will of an individual or group as proprietor against the will of another individual or group interested in the property in question. This legal relation is expressed in the form of contract and is simply the reflex of the real economical relation between the two.

The consequences of this theory of the source of law are most significant, for it means in the first place that law is now viewed not as the embodiment of principles of justice and of right but the reflection of class interests based upon economic position and considerations. This argument is impressive when viewed in the perspective of history, for it is a fact that the legal orders of most major societies have changed as their economic structures have been altered.

What is not clear about the argument, however, is whether all these changes in the laws are the effect of changes in the economic order, or whether men's changing view of what is "right" causes the economic order to be transformed to fit these conceptions of right. Moreover, even the Soviet jurists at one point criticized the rigour of the Marxist view of law, for they recognized the quality of "law" in those laws of capitalist countries which protected the "oppressed classes," for example, in the form of labor legislation or laws which pertain to neutral spheres such as public health.

Some writers have seen in the Marxist theory of law, not the reduction of all law to economics, but rather simply an emphasis that along with other noneconomic factors determining the content of law there are economic origins to the human conceptions which influence the law. This emphasis, according to these views, leads Marxism to deny any ultimate validity to these human conceptions of law.[25] But the literature reveals no such qualification, for the economic order is continually singled out as the decisive matrix of law.

Against this claim of the primacy of the economic order in shaping the law is the other historic fact that economic changes have not always caused a radical reconception of the law but have simply created new demands, new interests, and new desires. The law has at points been radically changed to fit these new demands, but even more important is the fact that basic principles of justice have been adjusted to meet the new conditions. More than that, what is impressive in this connection is the evidence in legal history of the way in which a taught tradition in law, in the hands of judges drawn from any class, has stood out against class interest.[26]

The radical attitude of the Soviets toward law is best understood when the line of reasoning we have been follow-

25. See Schlesinger, p. 22.
26. See Roscoe Pound, "Fifty Years of Jurisprudence", 51 Harvard Law Review 779 (1938); see also Paul Freund, *On Understanding the Supreme Court* (Boston: Little, Brown, 1949), Chap. 2, "Portrait of a Liberal Judge: Mr. Justice Brandeis." In another place, Roscoe Pound describes how judges arrived at their judicial decisions in these words:
We are exhorted to be scientific. Let us employ scientific method and instead of dogmatizing *a priori* on how judges must decide, let us see how

ing here is taken to its logical conclusion. For when law is viewed as simply the reflex of economic relations, it follows that law cannot be viewed as embodying anything perma-

---

common law judges did decide a typical case of conflicting class interest as to which, on the face of things, the economic interpretation might well show us the decisive determinant. The case I am to relate established an every day and universally admitted proposition in the Anglo-American law of wrongs which is enforced against property owners in every part of the English-speaking world. How does it compare with the realist theory of judicial decision? If there was any class which was socially and economically dominant, whose desires the English bench might have been expected to reflect in its decisions in the first third of the nineteenth century before the reform of parliament, it was the landed gentry. If there was anything in which this class was deeply interested it was preserving game and hunting. If there was anyone against whom this class would have sought to employ the most effective weapons at its command, it was the poacher and trespasser. To the landowner a right to set traps and spring guns to catch or injure trespassers and so deter them and others in like cases was an obvious corollary of his rights as owner. The question came up in a well-known case in 1828. A landowner who had a garden of valuable tulips and had had plants and bulbs to the value of 20 pounds stolen, set a spring gun to protect his garden. A trespasser climbed over the wall into the garden and was injured by setting off the gun. He sued for damages and the court rendered judgment in his favor. The property owner claimed a right to take measures for the protection of his property during his unavoidable absence and that a wrongdoer should not be allowed to recover for an injury occasioned by his own wrong. The court's answer was that there had been an intentional aggression in setting a trap for trespassers and such aggression to the extent of wounding would not be justified by a privilege of defending property. Since the 15th century, certainly a time when the bench was not hostile to the interests of landowners, it has been part of the taught tradition of the common law that one might justify woundings to defend his person but not to defend his property other than his dwelling. Of the four judges who sat in this case and agreed in deciding it, the chief justice was the son of a squire and his mother was the daughter of a knight. He had inherited property before he came to the bar. One of his colleagues was the son of a landed proprietor. All four were Tories. If the landed aristocracy had set out to choose judges to formulate their desires and interests as the law of the land, it would not have been easy for them to make a better choice. But whatever might have been the individual views of these judges as to poachers and trespassers, the traditional principle of liability for intentional aggression governed their judicial action. One might recount such cases in every part of the law.

Roscoe Pound, *Contemporary Juristic Theory*, (Claremont, Calif.: Pomona College, Scripps College, Claremont Colleges, 1940), pp. 48–50.

nent. Law is the tail which follows the animal, and wherever the animal goes the law is sure to follow.

Here Marx's general theory of history with all its determinism and relentlessness comes into play, for Marx sees in history an inner logic compelling events to move in accordance with economic necessity. So far as law is concerned, the importance of this theory of history lies in the fact that it provides Marxism with the theory of how the substructure constantly changes, thereby inevitably "causing" changes in the superstructure. Since law has no permanent status of its own but is only derived from the economic substructure, and since there is constant movement and change in the substructure, there will inevitably be change in human consciousness and therefore in the law.

Vishinsky stressed the relation of this economic theory to the Soviet definition of law, for he points out that "law and statute draw their content from the definite economic or production conditions dominant in society . . . production and exchange define the entire character of social relationships. Law is the regulator of these relationships."[27] We need to be reminded that Soviet writers do not intend to restrict this conception of the source and nature of law to Soviet law but consider it a general theory which is supposed to unveil the nature of law wherever there is law. Stuchka writes:

I consider this formula [the economic source of law] perfectly applicable even now, since it comprises the chief *indicia* incorporated in the concept of law of every sort in general [and not of Soviet law alone]. Its most fundamental merit is that for the first time it puts upon firm scientific ground the problem of law in general: it renounces the purely

27. Vishinsky, "The Fundamental Tasks of the Science of Soviet Socialist Law," in *Soviet Legal Philosophy*, p. 337.

formal view of law and sees in law a changing social phenomenon rather than an eternal category.[28]

The particularly radical feature of this view of law is found in its notion that there are no stabilities in the law. To be sure, no legal theory would presume to know the absolute formulations for the rules of human behavior nor desire to fix it with absolute rigidity. One of the well-known difficulties of Western legal theory is that of finding a way to deal simultaneously with the needs of stability and the needs for change.

Soviet jurists feel that they have broken through the confining strictures of this dilemma by refusing to talk about stabilities within the law. Having put their whole emphasis upon the economic order as the matrix of law, they have formulated a "clean" and uncomplicated explanation of what law is. But it appears that they have achieved this theoretical simplicity by abandoning the very notion of law.

The clear logic of this position was best seen by Pashukanis, who looked upon Western legal theories after this manner:

After high-flown phrases concerning the "eternal idea of law" or "the absolute significance of personality," the reader who is searching for a materialistic explanation of social phenomena turns with particular satisfaction to theories which treat law as resulting from a struggle of interests as something manifesting state constraint.[29]

But having turned to the materialistic matrix of law, what conclusions can be drawn from it for the legal order?

With clear precision, Pashukanis drew the fateful conclusion from this analysis that if the substructure is con-

28. P. I. Stuchka, "The Revolutionary Part Played by Law and the State—A General Doctrine of Law" in *Soviet Legal Philosophy*, p. 20.
29. Pashukanis, pp. 115–116.

stantly changing there is a constantly changing system of law. More than that, inasmuch as the drift of history is not aimless, that it is gradually working itself out in such a way that the disharmonies and the contradictions between classes will ultimately be reconciled, it follows that when there are no classes there will be no private interests. When private interests no longer exist, there will be no need for law, for law has been defined throughout as the will of the economically dominant class.

There can, therefore, be no sense in fashioning a permanent philosophy of law. "How can you wish to build a final legal system when you start from social relationships which already involve the necessity that law of every sort wither away?" asked Pashukanis. His point was, of course, that "when this dominant (socialist) sector shall have absorbed everything, the disappearance of law will begin forthwith."[30]

To be sure, this radical interpretation of Soviet legal theory was later condemned as a "wrecker" theory, but the logic of it follows clearly from Marxian premises. Moreover, the argument against Pashukanis which resulted in his own withering away was not so much against the theoretical accuracy of his conclusion as the effect his teaching had upon the Soviet society, namely, that of subverting the sense of legality and the sense of obligation to the law. It is quite obvious that if it is held that the law contains nothing permanent, then it loses its hold as a norm of obligation. Alternatively, to make out of law simply the expression of the will of the economically dominant class clearly reduces law to the naked force of that class.

30. See Harold J. Berman, *Justice in Russia*, (Cambridge: Harvard University Press, 1950), p. 34.

While this is indeed how the Soviet writers have always looked at law, and do so even now, they at the same time could not rid themselves of the desire and need for a sense of legality. But Pashukanis had reduced law to a political force which is actively involved in recreating the economic order. Whereas bourgeois states can develop a superstructure of law which exhibits aspects of permanence, this is not possible in the dynamic conditions of the perpetual revolution, or, as Pashukanis put it: "It is different for us: we need the utmost elasticity of our legislation. We cannot tie ourselves up with any system because we are everyday breaking up the economic system. Politics is law; we have a system of politics, but we do not have a system of proletarian law."[31]

These words were uttered in the same mood as were those of Goichbarg, who early had said that "We refuse to see in law an idea useful for the working class. . . ."[32] But these earlier and more specifically revolutionary expressions have been considerably toned down, even though there has been no fundamental shift in the theoretical approach to law. In the intervening years the idea has been accepted that law must continue as an important factor in Soviet society. Having, however, so cogently argued away its foundation, the Soviet theorist faced the difficult task of reconceiving the status of law in the conditions of socialism.

The Logic of Lawlessness and the Desire for Law

The justification of the use of law in the socialist phase is not entirely consistent with the earlier premises of the Marxist argument, for there the basis of law was found in

31. Gsovsky, p. 31.
32. *Id.* at 12.

private ownership. The clear implication was that when the condition of private property was left behind, there should be no further use for law. But Marx had seen the possibility that not even the abolition of private property would mean the total elimination of law, for there would still be "property." And since some form of property would remain, law, too, would continue. There can be no society, he says, where there is no property in some form. Since the property was not private, neither would the superstructure of law which it brought forth be private, but there would be law. And even where the classes are no longer in existence or recognized, the Soviet system has not been able fully to dispense with law.

Lenin had made it clear that "in the first phase of Communist society (generally called socialism), 'bourgeois law' is not abolished in its entirety, but only in part, only in proportion to the economic transformation so far attained, that is, only in respect of the means of production." Bourgeois law recognizes the means of production as the private property of separate individuals. Socialism converts them into common property. To that extent does bourgeois law disappear.

This seems to say that law is not abolished all at once but will be eliminated in the long run. The constant reference to bourgeois law also implies that only portions of bourgeois law will remain; that is, to the extent that law remains in the Soviet systems it is bourgeois law, for law is an anachronism in pure communism.

Yet the rigor of this logic is so radical in its consequences that not even the Communists are willing to take it to its obvious conclusion. On the contrary, there has been a tremendous effort to build a more creative philosophy of law. Indeed, as Professor Berman has said, "the 'Struggle for Law' during the past fifteen years remains one of the most important internal developments in Soviet Russia since 1917."[33]

But what can be the basis for a Soviet jurisprudence? To have a jurisprudence it is more or less necessary to assume the continuity of the order of law in society, and this is apparently what the present Soviet writers assume; they are not prepared as were the earlier exponents of radical Marxism to write off the category of law. But again, so decisive are the presuppositions of Marxism that the creative task of building a fresh legal theory is almost impossible.

Pashukanis had said that "if the proletariat is forced to use (bourgeois law) it does not mean that there is a possibility of a further development of this law by way of filling it with a socialist content." Still, in the transitory period, "the proletariat must use in its own class interest these forms inherited from bourgeois society and by this exhaust them. . . ."[34]

The extent to which Pashukanis has been superceded is indicated by the quite different approach taken by Vishinsky to the possibility of fashioning a Soviet form of law. Vishinsky saw no contradiction in saying that "the will of the workers merges with the will of the entire people," and this led him to speak of "Soviet socialist law as an expression of the will of the whole people."[35]

---

33. Berman, p. 195.
34. Gsovsky, p. 12.
35. Vishinsky, "The Fundamental Tasks of the Science of Soviet Socialist Law," p. 339.

One does not wish to focus upon these logical inconsistencies, however glaring they may be, for our concern is not to prove that if you are going to define law as the will of the economically dominant class in society, then there can be no meaning to the phrase that Soviet law expresses the will of the whole people; against whom is this will expressed? We are concerned with understanding the nature of law and look to the Soviet experience as a fascinating source of information and a unique exposure of the anatomy of law.

That the Soviet jurists should no longer see in law a simply bourgeois remnant is quite instructive, although equally interesting is the fact that the theoretical basis for the new concept of socialist law has not yet been found. Vishinsky seems mostly to have posed rather that solved the problem, although his "Fundamental Tasks of Soviet Law" indicates a clear intent to fuse into a more creative legal theory the Marxist premises which formerly led to the renunciation of law. He has raised

the question of the very form of Soviet law, of the special characteristics and specific features possessed by the Soviet legal form as a socialist form. In this domain, new paths must be opened and new forms of law must be worked out, as well as new forms of the statute—all these forms and paths reflecting the socialist content of the new social relationships created by the proletarian revolution. . . .[36]

In the meantime, law continues to exist in Soviet society, and the ostensible justification for it is that there are "enemies" obstructing the transition to the Communist order. The law then becomes a weapon to use in the continuing revolution. The question at this point is whether Soviet law is made to fit any system of morals.

36. *Id.* at 339.

Common Critique of Law and Morals

Soviet jurists do not distinguish law and morals as sharply as do most contemporary Western writers in legal theory, for the Soviet jurists see in morals a phenomenon almost identical with law. In one sense at least, both law and morals are the same, namely, in that they are both part of the superstructure, they are both ideology. More than that, ethical principles provide the content of law, according to these jurists, and to that extent they suffer the same criticism as the form of law.

Law and morals are said to emerge from the same matrix, from the economic relations in society. The category of moral thought is as artificial as the category of law, so that, just as the whole category of law must ultimately be eliminated from social consciousness, so also must the ethical category be eliminated. From the Marxist point of view, ethical forms are criticized, not because they manifest some defect here or there, but because as a category of consciousness they represent a distorted view of social reality. The deep fault in the moral consciousness of man cannot be overcome by the correction of any particular fault of capitalism: nothing less than the transition to a planned social economy, and particularly the abolition of private property, can correct the fault, for this would mean "the destruction of (ethical form) in general."[37]

Again, the destruction of the ethical form of consciousness occurs simultaneously with the destruction of law; "ethical fetishes can be completely overcome in reality only if the fetishisms of good and of law are vanquished at the same time."[38] What is argued here is that even to think in

37. Pashukanis, p. 199.
38. *Ibid.*

terms of moral concepts is to mistake the true nature of life by confusing it with some idealized version of things. Aristotle may have thought that slavery was the natural state for some men and therefore justified this institution in his ethical system, not realizing that what, in fact, was going on was an economic order of dependence, wherein the dominant class used other classes in the processes of economic production.

To look at institutions in this way leads the Marxist to give up all ethical criticism; even now the Marxist does not say that slavery was unjust, for that would involve him in the use of ethical language. Rather, he says that these institutions are all products of the economic order and to that extent are necessary. One cannot use ethical terms in relation to events which do not transpire in the context of freedom; one cannot condemn a man who acts under duress. According to Marxism, even the capitalist must do things simply because the system forces him to do them. In Marx's *Capital* there is almost a complete absence of "explicit moral argument" or "appeals to conscience or to principle,"[39] for he is concerned with providing a "scientific" and not a moral analysis of society.

We have already intimated that this scientific analysis does not eliminate the use of ethical categories, for the very notion of ideology has specific moral characteristics. To say that morals and law are ideology is to say that they distort reality; but, again, this distortion is such chiefly when compared with the state of affairs which will not only one day come into existence but which "ought" to come into existence. Surely, the tremendous activity of the revolution

39. Isaiah Berlin, *Karl Marx*, ("Home University Library" [London: Oxford University Press, 1948]), p. 9.

and its aftermath is more than a quiet prediction of the general drift of history; it is a rallying cry to the masses for action. And however much this is explained as simply the means by which to shorten and lessen the birthpangs of history, it carries with it all the intensity and conviction of not only ethical but religious belief.

Law and morality are put into the same category by the fact that both of these are forms in which human behavior is prescribed. The prescription of behavior inevitably is unscientific, for it is idle to suppose that by means of prescriptive rules it is possible to alter the fundamental wellsprings of human actions. These actions are determined by the economic reality, particularly by the existence of private property; therefore the most ethical ideals can do is to confirm the facts about behavior, as in the case of Aristotle's ethics of slavery.

To say, for example, that it is immoral to steal is simply to say that there are those who own private property and do not want anyone to disturb it, but the stealing does not, in this theory, represent any universal or timeless delict or wrong, it is simply the reflex of the present economic order. Stealing is a necessary consequence of the existence of private property, and it is idle to assume that is can be dealt with effectively through moral injunctions. The only way to eliminate stealing is to eliminate the conditions which are producing it, and this can be done only by abolishing private property.[40]

40. The melancholy naivete of this analysis of the moral dimension in human existence is graphically revealed in Konstantinovsky's account of theft in Soviet society in *Soviet Law in Action*, ed. Harold J. Berman (Cambridge: Harvard University Press, 1953).

The criticism of morality, not only bourgeois morality but the very category of morality, is that it is inseparably connected with law and is indeed the chief channel by which law becomes infected with ideology, with the dominant class view of reality. So closely tied into law is the category of morality that it would be difficult to separate the two, except for the fact that law is held to be that part of morality which is fashioned into a statute and has behind it the power of the state.

This puts law and morality in the category with religion, the chief form of ideology. Marx's attack upon religion is based upon his conviction that religion attempts to provide a general theory of the world and man's place in it. He regards religion as a perverted consciousness of the world, the "opium of the masses," and an "illusion." Religion, for him, is the creation of the dominant class whose purpose it is to keep the structure of society at any given time in a static state and thereby to preserve the interests of the owners of private property. Religion sees only one aspect of man's condition in society but does not understand the true reality. When religion observes the inequality among men, it seeks to justify this inequality by ascribing it to the will of God or by saying that paradoxically the poor achieve a higher degree of morality and happiness than the rich because the poor are not distracted from spiritual pursuits by their wealth.

Even worse, according to the Marxist, religion deflects man's attention from the true economic forces at work by directing his thought to his future existence in the spiritual world. For the Marxist, this religious consciousness is the most debilitating form of ideology of all; more than any other form, religion stands in the way of an aggressive and self-conscious assault upon the natural order. This is why, particularly in the early days, the Communists had to fight the ideology of religion.

But they fought law just as much, if not more. Goichbarg had written that "at the present time [1922] we have to combat juridical ideology even more than the religious."[41] These two ideologies are not very different from each other, for again religious faith is one of the most powerful sources of morality, and morality is the first version of law. Consequently, the relation of religion, morality, and law is extremely intimate, and this is something that the Soviet jurists recognized from the beginning. All three of these forms have in common that they provide the norms for behavior, and it is this control over human behavior which law, religion, and morals have that Marxism wants to break.

One aspect of the whole concept of ideology which keeps recurring in Marxist literature needs to be more carefully analyzed: why should Marxists be so concerned with ideology? If the material order is the only reality, then what danger can there be in ideology?

Again, we have already questioned the adequacy of the Marxist theory of knowledge, since to hold that all ideas are reflections of the material reality, all ideas would reflect reality, and to that extent these ideas would be correct or true. But if ideas are truly reflections of some prior reality, then these ideas must have some existence of their own, otherwise they could be neither reflections nor could they ever be wrong. That ideas exist in some way prior to and independent of the economic context is clearly assumed by the Marxist, for the Marxist is very seriously concerned about

41. Gsovski, p. 12.

the effect a person's or group's ideas can have upon other minds.

Ideas are, therefore, not only effects of prior causes but are themselves causes of the social consciousness. This is to say that while law is the reflex of economic conditions, the law can, in turn, be the cause of a particular consciousness in those to whom the laws are addressed. It cannot be said, therefore, that all our ideas are the consequence of the economic conditions, unless this means that all ideas can ultimately be traced to these economic relations.

Engels admitted this casual efficacy in ideas when he wrote that although the economic situation is the basis, still, the various elements of the superstructure (political, legal, philosophical theories, religious ideas) also have their influence upon the course of the historical struggles. This means that it is necessary to distinguish between the source of ideas and their use. Insofar as ideas reflect only the contemporary situation in the social order, they are scientific. If ideas derived from a particular point in time or stage of history become inflexible, if, that is, a set of ideas remains static while change takes place in the economic order, these ideas are reactionary, since they pertain to an era which is past.

Forms of thought which tend to remain static possess a double fault; first of all, they represent the class interest of a group based on economic position, and secondly they represent that group's interest as it once existed in the past. To retain such ideas is to be hopelessly out of touch with reality.

Now it is law in particular which embodies this double fault more than any other form of ideology, for by its very nature law tends to be conservative, and in trying to conserve the interests of its framers, the economically dominant class, the law inevitably lags behind the momentum of history.

Moreover, the law tends to perpetuate the ideological consciousness of society by inculcating into the minds of men the ideas which are its content.

From the critical point of view, then, Marxism is committed to the elimination of the several elements in the "superstructure," including religion, morals, political ideals, and, above all, law, for it is the law which turns out to be the bearer of all the ideological freight of this superstructure.

The Necessary Connection between Law and Morals

But just as it was not possible to eliminate law from Soviet society, so also it is not possible to reinstate law without at the same time providing it with moral content. From the point of view of understanding the nature of law, this fact is of immense importance, for we see in Soviet law the impossibility of separating law and morals. In the creative task of rebuilding law, however, the Soviet jurists have tried always to be consistent with their critical views about law. Law for the Soviet jurist thus is still the will of the economically dominant class—in this case, the will of the proletariat. Whereas Marx defined bourgeois law by calling it, in a derogatory sense, the will of the dominant class raised to the level of a statute, contemporary jurists use almost precisely these words as their creative definition of law when they say that "socialist law is the will of the Soviet people elevated into legislation."[42]

Moreover, just as the early jurists leveled their criticism against law by charging that it was the bearer of ideology, so now this character of law is reaffirmed, only there is now an attempt to furnish the law with "a socialist consciousness."

42. Golunskii and Strogovich, p. 366.

This means that wherever and whenever there is law, there must also be a moral consciousness.

There is no attempt in Soviet legal theory to obscure the fact that legal and moral consciousness is class consciousness. On the contrary, it is precisely this class or socialist consciousness which the law is calculated to reflect and also to inculcate throughout society:

Socialist legal consciousness is a powerful *factor in the formation of law* —in the creation of law, the emergence of new legal norms: on the other hand, the socialist law in force is a most powerful means of strengthening and developing the consciousness of citizens.[43]

This is why in Soviet legal theory it is now held that "the bond between law . . . and morality is very close."[44] And this bond is viewed from two ends: at the point where law is created, where morality provides the direction for the law, and at the point where the law is employed, where the law in turn forms the sense of moral obligation.

Legal theory in the West, insofar as it wishes to reflect the scientific point of view, has emphasized the radical distinction between law and morals. Kelsen expressed this point of view most sharply when he wrote that "the concept of law has no moral connotations whatsoever."[45] One can appreciate this view if it means that since there are different moral systems built into various systems of law no definition of law can incorporate all these different moralities. Kelsen may also admit that in the earliest stages of the formation of law a society's moral convictions may work their way into the

43. *Id.* at 384.
44. *Id.* at 375.
45. Hans Kelsen, *The General Theory of Law and State*, (Cambridge: Harvard University Press, 1945), p. 5.

content of the law. But having made these concessions, he argues that the phenomenon of law in no way connotes anything moral.

It must be said in this regard that the Soviet jurists have a more accurate analysis of what law is. The most important aspect of the Soviet experience with the law is to demonstrate that wherever you have law you have some moral convictions. It is not at this point necessary to argue the merits of socialist morality; it is sufficient to point out that the destruction of law in Soviet society required the destruction of the ideology of religion and morality. The rebuilding of law has required that a new moral consciousness be fashioned.

However incorrect this moral system may be, it does represent the indispensible element in the law. Western jurists are fond of pointing to the element of force in law as the decisive element, reducing the concept of law to the *commands* of the state, as did Hobbes, Bentham, Austin, and Kelsen, each in his own way.

The fact of power no doubt plays a substantial role in the phenomenon of law, but it can hardly be the "essence" of law. On the other hand, in spite of the relativity of moral ideals, their relationship is more than an accidental feature of law. It seems to be more accurate to say that "legal consciousness is so closely interwoven with morality that no exact boundary between them can be drawn, since legal and moral views and convictions constitute a part of the general conception of life prevailing in society."[46] Or again, "by their very content many legal norms comprise moral norms."[47]

The separation of law and morals has been most frequently urged by those who consider the domain of morals to

46. Golunskii and Strogovich, p. 384.
47. *Id.* at 375.

be almost exclusively internal to human nature, whereas the law's domain is taken to be the external life of man in society. Moral action is supposed to spring from internal motives, while behavior in the legal sphere is supposed to be directed by external compulsion. Moral behavior is thought to be the effect of altruism or love, whereas legal behavior is thought to be engendered by the fear of physical pain or constraint.

No doubt these distinctions can be made; who can compel one to be "pure in heart" by any threat of imprisonment? But surely the injunction to be pure in heart does not exhaust the full spectrum of moral behavior, so that although it is not possible to command purity of heart it is possible to enjoin consideration of the welfare of others.

Kant argued that a person cannot be moral if his actions are in response to a will that is not his own; it is not enough for conduct to be "in accordance with the moral law"; to be moral, conduct must proceed "out of respect for" the law and must be the product of the individual's free will: he must *choose* to behave in a given way. But it is quite difficult to sustain this distinction between "autonomy" and "heteronomy," between internal and external motivation, for there are many ways in which the so-called "autonomous" will is influenced by an external will.

Theologically, it is plain to see that even for Kant the ultimate basis of the law is God as the legislator, so that the will of the moral man merges with the will of God: an individual wills to treat his fellow man as an end in himself, not only because he wants to be treated that way himself, but also because the ultimate lawgiver, God, stands behind this particular universal law. And even if the only consideration of the moral will were the concern to retain one's rationality, then the concern for rationality would represent the external or heteronomous element in the moral act.

Similarly, it must be admitted that the external agency of law is not wholly devoid of the internal element of morality. We have seen that it is not possible even to think the concept law without at the same time recognizing the fact of legal consciousness, which includes moral consciousness. Only the most abstract conception of law which sees in law only some huge impersonal club or weapon could maintain that law is devoid of consciousness. And even if law were a club, there would still have to be a consciousness which would have to know when and why to use it, thus bringing us back to internal consciousness.

It would, of course, be possible for a madman to wield a club without any coherent conception of what he is doing, but in normal discourse we are assuming that lawgivers and rulers have at least as much consciousness as we do. To that extent the law as a means of regulating behavior rests upon the internal experience of men, and this is not entirely different from what occurs in any moral act.

The reason, therefore, for the coalescence of law and morals is that they both partake, not only of a similar *type* of internal experience, but frequently of the very same internal motives. The stimulus which affects one's moral sensibilities as he confronts his fellow man in society is the same stimulus which may lead him to deal with that occasion through the medium of the law. And the very question of the relationship of the individual to the law raises a very important question, for if there are no moral connotations to the law, then it must be held that the law must be obeyed only because it is "official," which is to say, as Austin argued, only because if one does not obey he will suffer pain.

This view of law seems to put man in the status of an animal who is taught to react to certain commands, knowing that if he does not obey he will be hit or in some other way punished. But this altogether misconceives that which is, in fact, going on in the phenomenon of law, for the law is the product of consciousness and is directed by one consciousness to another, that is, to quote Austin again, "by one intelligent being to another intelligent being." This being the case, it is inevitable that law as a phenomenon possesses the same internal characteristics as morality. This is, of course, not to say that all law is morality and that all morality is law; but where there is law there is morality.

Again, we may disagree with the moral content of Soviet law, but the question is whether in theory it is possible to separate the realms of law and of morals as decisively as our own jurists do. We are asking whether a theory that does not indicate that conscious formulations of moral values are an intrinsic part of what is meant by law is an adequate theory at all.

The Soviet jurists pursue this relation of law and morals to the extent that law becomes for them the agency for creating moral consciousness. For them, the law has moral ends, and the obedience to the law becomes in itself a moral act. Thus, whereas the earlier conception of Soviet law emphasized law as the weapon of the dominant class—the ideology of the superior economic group, backed by the power of the state—the emphasis has now shifted to the moral element in law. What was once labeled ideology in the derogatory sense is now admitted to be the will of the proletarian class, but not in the derogatory sense.

Ideology has now become not only respectable but has assumed the ethical characteristic of "ought." The law is not only the bearer of social consciousness but the law ought to be respected precisely because of this moral element in it. Whereas the law was at one time viewed solely as a power mechanism, it is now viewed as a moral vehicle which should be respected because of its intrinsic moral content. Whereas it was formerly defined as the command of the sovereign who had the right to order the conduct of subjects chiefly because it had the power, law is now to be obeyed because of the fundamentally moral ends it is seeking to achieve.

The Soviet law is therefore conceived today, not only as a means of affecting mass behavior by coercing men externally and physically, but as touching their internal consciousness as well. All this, of course, transpires under the ideology of socialism: "Law . . . seeks to influence man's internal stimuli; our socialist law thus strives that people voluntarily fulfill its requirements because they are convinced that these are reasonable and expedient, and because of conscious socialist discipline."[48]

This means that the objectives of the Soviet law are roughly the same as that which may be called Soviet morality. Soviet morality is the sense of obligation with respect to certain kinds of behavior, and these can be specified so far as the social realm is concerned for

the tasks of socialist law—to destroy exploitation, to eliminate the survivals of capitalism in human consciousness, and to co-operate in the building of classless communist society—are at the same time moral tasks, in the sense that they are requirements of socialist morality.[49]

Even more specific is the provision of article 2 of the U.S.S.R. Constitution which establishes the rule that "labor in the U.S.S.R. is an obligation and a matter of honour, of

48. *Id.* at 377.
49. *Id.* at 379.

every citizen capable thereof, in accordance with the principle: he who does not work does not eat." This is a legal norm—a constitutional measure—but by its content it is also a norm of socialist morality.[50]

It becomes quite plain that the revival of law in Soviet Russia rests upon the recognition of the moral dimension of human existence, a dimension which Marxists have consistently labeled as ideology in the derogatory sense. At every turn now, the moral consciousness is viewed, not as the hopelessly distorted reflection of the material reality, but as the fundamental basis of the moral obligation, of the imperative "ought". The law, again, is now the instrumentality for the inculcation of this "ought" in the consciousness of the people. Also,

the fulfillment of norms of socialist law—of socialist laws—is the moral duty of the Soviet citizen, irrespective of the threat of constraint in case a law is broken, while on the other hand, socialist law is a powerful factor in the development and confirmation of moral views and ideas among the popular masses.[51]

It may seem strange that the function of law today is to develop an affirmative attitude among the citizens about those things which in the Marxist analysis were the very items, for the most part, which were objects of ridicule, especially when it is remembered that the state and the regime of law were in particular the worst aspects of the superstructure. Now the courts are charged with the task of "the fundamental remaking of the conscience of people"[52] which includes

educating the U.S.S.R. citizens in . . . a spirit of unswerving precision in carrying out the Soviet laws, of care for socialist property, of labor

50. *Ibid.*
51. *Id.* at 380.
52. I. T. Golyakov: *The Role of the Soviet Court*, trans. by Richard Kramer, (Washington: Public Affairs Press, 1948), p. 16.

discipline, of an honorable attitude towards state and social duty and of respect for the rules of socialist life together.[53]

Rarely has the law been called upon to carry so great a burden, to operate in such a wide area of human activity, to penetrate so deeply into the internal life of man. With its all-embracing theory of reality, with its claim to scientific accuracy and truth, Marxism has at first radically revolted against the very category of law but has subsequently tried to reconstruct the theory of law. Since it assumes that the truth is hidden in the existing reality and that it is possible to deduce from this reality or nature the norm for the right or just, it is no wonder that it has been said that Soviet jurists have given the old theory of natural law a "Marxist tonsure."[54]

Soviet Law and the Rule of Law

Although the relation between Soviet law and Soviet morality is clearly demonstrated, there is still the question whether Soviet law as a legal system is itself under any sense of moral constraint. It is one thing to define the ends of a political regime and make these the ends of the legal order which that regime controls. It is quite another thing to say that in the formation of these ends, and in the procedures employed in their application, moral norms are recognized and adhered to.

There are serious questions about the Soviet legal order in this regard, for it is just here that the Soviet system cannot be said to represent the "rule of law" in the fundamental sense of that phrase. In its simplest form, the notion of the rule of law implies that the whole legal order is viewed as

53. Golunskii and Strogovich, p. 380.
54. Pashukanis, "The Soviet State and the Revolution in Law" in *Soviet Legal Philosophy*, p. 253.

being under the rule of justice and right. This implies limitations upon the lawmaking power of the sovereign, for the very reason for acknowledging a sovereign is to insure a reliable and predictable regime for the protection of persons and rights. The affirmation of the existence of human rights even before the existence of government, for the protection of which governments are instituted in the first place—this is the minimum meaning of the rule of law.

The rule of law thus carries the clear implication that the rulers themselves operate under rules and are not the sole makers of rules. Yet it is precisely at this point that the rulers of the proletariat dictatorship do not feel bound by any higher laws. This is the residual influence of Marx himself who, although he sounded like a thundering Old Testament prophet condemning the injustices against the poor, was mainly concerned with the scientific description of the drift of history. For him, "the conceptions of natural rights, and of conscience, as belonging to every man irrespective of his position in the class struggle, are rejected as liberal illusions."[55]

Even in a rather sympathetic analysis of Soviet law there is the halting conclusion that the "so-called private rights in Soviet Law are *not actual rights of private persons,* but *rights established by the State in favor of private persons,* in order to secure the public interest in the latter's welfare."[56] It is part of the official theory that the state cannot be bound by any superior norm: "law is not above the state but emanates from it, and socialist legality, likewise, is always the modus operandi of the socialist state and cannot become an impediment to its realization of its historical tasks."[57]

55. Berlin, p. 9.
56. Schlesinger, p. 95.
57. Golunskii and Strogovich, p. 393.

The procedures of law are made to fit the needs of the continuing revolution, and everything, including individual rights, is subordinated to this end. Earlier, the curriculum of the Soviet law schools reflected this approach, in that

> law concerning the rights of individuals was relegated to a few hours at the end of the course in economic-administrative law and given apologetically, as an unwelcome necessity for a few years due to the fact that capitalist relationships and bourgeois psychology had not yet been wholly eliminated.[58]

Lenin had rejected any division between administrative procedure and the powers of legislation on the ground that such a distinction would threaten "the homogeneity and efficiency of the revolutionary regime, and this principle has been followed."[59] Law is then viewed as the "binding rules of conduct . . . by the entire force of its apparatus of constraint: the state."[60]

The use of force and constraint are typical elements in all systems of law, and to this extent there is nothing unusual in the Soviet notion that "legal norms are those rules of human conduct established or affirmed by the state, whose coercive force guarantees their being put into operation."[61] And this fact, that state authority is the source of its force and binding character "distinguishes a legal norm from a moral norm"[62] is theoretically an acceptable distinction.

Yet, as one follows the analysis of the use of force and power, it becomes more and more apparent that the power of law, although it is employed for the purpose of implementing Soviet morality, nevertheless proceeds in a manner

58. John Hazard in Berman, *Justice in Russia*, pp. 36, 296.
59. Schlesinger, p. 60.
60. Golunski and Strogovich, p. 365.
61. *Id.* at 368.
62. *Ibid.*

that destroys the notion of the rule of law. This seems to be cynically expressed by Krylenko, who described the Soviet court as a class institution and an organ of government power which is "completely under the control of the vanguard of the working class."[63] He also makes it clear that the judge self-consciously operates under the aegis of the Marxist philosophy of social revolution, recalling the words of Gintsburg who had written that "the Communist party decisions are the direct and the Marx-Lenin doctrine the indirect sources of Soviet law to be used by the courts."[64]

Professor Berman asks the pertinent question, why is it necessary, under these circumstances, to erect such an elaborate structure of rights and procedures and courts? He finds the answer in the words of Krylenko, who said that "a club is a primitive weapon, a rifle is a more efficient one, the most efficient one is the court."[65] In this connection, Rudolph Schlesinger makes the point that in Soviet law there are no formal rules, for example, as regards admissable evidence: "any evidence is admitted which, according to the circumstances of the case, may prove helpful in clearing it up. . . ."[66]

But, again, the most serious challenge to the concept of the rule of law is found in the definition of law which Vishinsky had formulated, which is that law is

a system of norms established by legislation by the State of the Toilers and expressing the will of the whole Soviet people, led by the working classes headed by the Communist party, in order to protect, to strengthen and to develop socialist relations and the building of a Communist society.[67]

63. Berman, p. 28.
64. Gsovski, p. 32.
65. Berman, p. 28.
66. Schlesinger, pp. 64–65.
67. Schlesinger, p. 244.

Particularly important in this definition, so far as our present question is concerned, is its placing of the Communist party in a rather strategic position regarding the principle of the validity of law. It appears that, quite apart from the proper legislative enactment of the law, the validity of these enactments would be conditional upon the consent of the Communist party.[68]

It is here in particular that the "rule of law" breaks down, especially as we recall that the dictatorship of the proletariat is a "power unrestrained by law and based upon force and not law."[69] This is why Gsovsky was able to write that "Law is still viewed primarily as an instrument of rulership, and not the guardian of rights. The very soul of law is thereby negatived. . . ."[70]

68. *Id.* at 245.
69. Gsovski, pp. 17–18.
70. *Id.* at 42.

3

LAW AS COMMAND

*Austin's Theory of the
Separation of Law and Morals*

THE lingering influence of the natural law theory in England brought forth a powerful new philosophy of law. The chief features of this new theory were developed by Hobbes and Bentham and found their most compelling formulation in the works of the "analytical" jurist John Austin. These men were concerned most with ways to deal with the existence of morally bad laws.

Sir William Blackstone had said in his *Commentaries* that the laws of God are superior in obligation to all other laws, that no human laws should be allowed to contradict them, that human laws are of no validity if they contradict God's laws, and that all valid laws derive their force from the Divine original.[1] When Austin confronted these ideas, he

---

1. Blackstone, *Commentaries*, (4th ed.; London, 1770), Vol. I, Sec. II, p. 42.

immediately focused upon the central issue in legal theory, for he remarked that if these ideas of Blackstone's have any meaning at all it must be this, "that no human law which conflicts with the Divine law is obligatory or binding; in other words, that no human law which conflicts with the Divine law *is a law.* . . ."[2] The problem, as Austin saw it, was to determine how the authority of a legal order is achieved. From whence, in other words, do laws derive their character as law?

What impressed Austin was the fact that there are many rules for human behavior which are morally desirable but which are not laws. Similarly, there are many laws which violate moral standards but are nevertheless laws. Unlike the natural law school, for which he had only contempt, Austin distinguished two aspects of the inquiry into the nature of law:

The existence of law is one thing; its merit or demerit is another. Whether it be or be not is one inquiry; whether it be or be not conformable to an assumed standard, is a different inquiry. A law, which actually exists, is a law, though we happen to dislike it, or though it vary from the text, by which we regulate our approbation and disapprobation.[3]

To separate the inquiry about what laws exist from the inquiry about what laws are good or bad was Austin's great achievement. But by this separation he also brought about the theoretical separation of law and morals.

Whereas Blackstone argued that a rule derived its character as law from its conformity to God's law, Austin developed the point that a rule's conformity to morals is irrelevant

2. Austin, *The Province of Jurisprudence Determined*, introd. by H.L.A. Hart ("Library of Ideas" [New York: Noonday Press, 1954]), p. 185 (hereinafter *Province*).
3. *Province*, p. 179.

in determining whether that rule is law. The "bad" law is as much a law as the "good" law, wherefore goodness or badness is not the decisive element in the authority of a law or of the legal order.

Austin thought that by this distinction between what law is and what it ought to be he could clarify the meaning of law which had been obscured by the advocates of natural law who, like Blackstone, had injected the notion of morality as a necessary element in the definition of law. This distinction between law and morals has since Austin's time had a powerful influence throughout the juristic world, and John Chipman Gray has described Austin's great contribution by writing that:

> The great gain in its fundamental conceptions which Jurisprudence made during the last century was the recognition of the truth that the Law of a State . . . is not an ideal, but something which actually exists. It is not that which is in accordance with religion, or nature, or morality; it is not that which ought to be, but that which is. To fix this definitely in the Jurisprudence of the Common Law, is the feat that Austin accomplished.[4]

But equally since Austin's time men have been uneasy about this separation of law and morals. There is no doubt that certain legal rules have no moral connotation, as, for example, the rule that automobiles should be driven on the right or the left. There are rules, too, that are not at all moral in the sense of being intrinsically moral. That a will should have two or three witnesses can hardly be considered the requirements of God, nature, or morality.

Similarly, there are rules of law which raise for man a hypothetical question instead of placing him under the pres-

---

4. Gray, *The Nature and Sources of the Law* (2nd. ed., from the author's notes by Roland Gray; New York: Macmillan, 1921), p. 94.

sure of a categorical imperative. Thus, the law of contracts holds that *if* you want a binding contract, you must fulfill certain requirements, or *if* you want to give someone the legal power to act on your behalf, as for example when a broker buys and sells securities for you, these legal arrangements have specific requirements and the law makes specific imperatives; but these imperatives are hypothetical, for a person may very well choose not to enter a contract or may decide not to engage a broker.

In this significant sense it is clear that the law governs a man's behavior only if he chooses to enter these particular spheres of behavior. There is nothing about these modes of behavior which any system or morals would include among those things which all men, in order to be men, must adhere to. It is analogous to the case of baseball; *if* one decides to play this game, then he immediately submits himself to the rules of the game, but there is nothing in the moral code of mankind that requires that all people should play baseball. Because the law contains so many rules, such as traffic laws, which regulate a person's conduct at points where morality is unconcerned, and because other laws raise only hypothetical obligations, pending a person's choice to come under the law's control, positivists have held that law is quite different from the rules of morality.

But not all the rules of law are of this hypothetical nature. The most characteristic thing about laws is that they positively command certain kinds of behavior, and in these cases the content of the law is frequently identical with a moral rule. The prohibition against the use of child labor is surely an expression of a moral sentiment. Even if the reasons which are used by the moralist for prohibiting child labor are different from the reasons men use for passing a law against that practice, in both cases the reasoning is based upon moral convictions. If, that is, the abuse of children is denounced by the moralist because it represents a tragic exploitation of a defenseless minor and a ruthless denial of the rights of the child to a normal childhood, on the one hand, while the law is justified by the legislator, on the other hand, on the pragmatic grounds that the prohibition will produce healthier adults and a stronger society, these are, nevertheless, *both* moral arguments. The fact that the law in its very inception becomes freighted with moral elements is what causes skepticism in many quarters about the positivistic doctrine of the separation of morals from the law.

Austin did not deny that moral influences were at work in the creation of law, but he allowed nowhere in his theory any place for this moral element when defining the nature of law. In order to maintain the sharp distinction between law and morality, he defined law in its most abstract and severe terms as a command of the sovereign. It was Austin's reduction of law to a command which has ever since his time aggravated the debate over the nature of law.

This is a difficult debate, because whichever way we choose to think of the relation between law and morals we come upon undesirable conclusions. If we identify law with morality, then whatever is commanded by the state would be obeyed, not only because it is commanded, but also because the command prescribes morally desirable conduct. If we make such a close identification between law and morals, however, we run into the danger of losing the basis for a moral criticism of laws, since there would be a confusion between one's moral and legal obligations. An iniquitous law could not on principle be criticized because it would already be identified with morality.

The alternative approach is to say that law and morals represent two separate kinds of rules for behavior and that they have no necessary relation to each other. This is a convincing view, particularly when it is used by those who argue that only by making this distinction can we preserve the possibility of the moral criticism of law.

But this view leaves unsolved the problem of the obligatoriness in law; the positivist view implies that the only element at work in determining our duty to the law is the fact of the state's command and the power the state is able to mobilize to support its command. It really argues for a complete separation of law and morals and the reduction of law to the force of the state. According to this view, the concept of law is formulated without any reference to the law's moral aspects.

The bald identification of law and force in the positivist theory calls for a careful analysis of the argument by which this identification is reached. Conversely, if positivism argues for the separation of law and morals, it is necessary to examine the argument by which this separation is urged. The reconception of the meaning of law to which the positivist view leads is so radical that it is necessary, not only to try to come to terms with this point of view, but even before that to determine whether it is in fact possible for the positivists themselves to achieve what they announce they intend to do. Has Austin really developed a consistent argument in which he demonstrates the separation of law and morals, and is Austin guilty of all that his critics say about his treatment of law and morals? The full anatomy of Austin's thought can be most conveniently unraveled by considering how he treated the problems of the "source," the "validity" and the "ends" of law.

Positivism and the Source of Law

The problem of the source of law dominates the positivist theory because its definition of law is essentially a doctrine of the source of law. When Austin defines law as the command of the sovereign, he is saying that only those rules are laws which emanate from the sovereign. The notion of law is thus identified with the notion of command. In order to differentiate various possible kinds of commands, Austin specifies that only those commands are law which have their source in the will of the sovereign. Moreover, law is defined as those commands of the sovereign which are based upon a sanction, where the sanction is defined as the threat of evil which the sovereign can mete out upon those who disobey the command. Practically the whole of the Austinian legal theory is found in these three concepts of *sovereign, command,* and *sanction,* and these terms are defined in terms of each other; they are variations of each other.

The picture one gets from this abstract and severe description of law is one that no positivist really intends to convey but which Austin's theory certainly suggests. It appears that the sovereign is a morally indifferent entity, barking out commands after the manner of an animal trainer, directing these commands at persons who are trained to respond the way an animal responds to his master's voice, and who respond only because, like the animals, they know that certain kinds of behavior bring about painful consequences. This is the interpretation of legal positivism which horrifies the casual observer, for it seems to provide the foundation for the most arbitrary kind of ruler.

As it stands, the conception of law based upon sovereign, command, and sanction has indeed achieved the desired theoretical result, namely, the separation of law and morals: there is the sovereign, who is the undisputed ruler; there is his command which orders man's conduct; and there is the threat of punishment or some form of pain if a person does not obey. Now only if this severe statement is left unembellished is there any successful separation of law and morals. When Austin does elaborate his notion of the source of law, the relation of law and morals turns out to be a rather close one.

There are various ways in which the notion of the source of law can be considered, but Austin takes the view that there is only one source of law: the command of the sovereign. No rule has the quality of law except the rule commanded by the sovereign. No law can emanate from any source other than the sovereign, for by definition only the sovereign's commands are law, and the rules he commands are laws because he commands them and for no other reason.

Here again, the breach between law and morals appears to be absolute, for positivism allows no other consideration to enter the definition of law than the fact of command. While Austin can differentiate, as we shall see, between what others confuse as sources of law other than the sovereign, he maintains that law does not exist in any fashion as law prior to the sovereign's command; if there is law anywhere, it is the product of that command.

If all that positivism wanted to achieve in this account of the source of law were to specify how the word law is to be used there would be no cause for concern. In that case, we would simply agree that we would reserve the word law to apply to the commands of the sovereign. There would be no difficulty in assigning the source of law, for obviously law would emanate only from the sovereign if we have already agreed that only such commands are law.

But men raise the question about the source of law precisely because this arbitrary restriction of the use of the term "law" is not at all satisfactory when we are dealing with human beings. For the law, understood even as simply a command of the state, also implies that the contents of these commands are binding upon those to whom they are addressed. Laws prescribe how men shall act. The notion of law is incomprehensible when law is viewed solely as a command; it is always a command directing human behavior. A theory of law which does not suggest that legal rules concern the behavior of men is certainly an irrelevant and useless, if not dangerous, theory.

It is precisely because the commands of the law involve the life of man in its most sensitive and intensely human aspect that men continue to raise the question about the source of law. Even though positivism obviously admits that the sovereign's commands are directed to human beings and that these commands direct human conduct, it leaves the phenomenon of command bare, for it requires of the sovereign nothing else than to be sovereign, to be in the habit of being obeyed, in short, of being the supreme power in society. By making the sovereign's command the sole source of law, positivism is led to its distinctive conclusion, which is that whatever the sovereign commands is law, and, more important, that the sovereign is bound by no moral considerations in the process of commanding. Moreover, a subject is bound to obey the sovereign's command for no other reason than that he is commanded.

But the fact that men's lives are ordered by the law has led them to look for the source of the law in places other than in the commands of the state. Even though men are willing to admit that the word "law" should be limited to what the sovereign commands, they are not willing to admit out of hand that the sovereign can command whatever he wants.

The British Parliament is said to be absolutely sovereign, that it can do anything "except change a man into a woman." But this is certainly an oversimplification of the nature of sovereignty in England as well as other places. Men have been willing to reserve the word law for the commands of the state, but they have never agreed that the commands of the state can be arbitrary. That is, men have never agreed that there should be a separation of law and morals. They have agreed to call bad laws "law" only because they know that in the process of lawmaking bad laws as well as good laws will be made—that there will be mistakes. Though men have agreed to obey the laws the sovereign issues, they have invariably set down rules by which the sovereign will fashion or make his commands, his laws.

Thus, in the very process of making laws, the sovereign is already bound by the conditions by which he became the sovereign. Men do not agree to form a society for their own destruction but for their preservation, and if we brought in no consideration other than survival, for the time being, we would be compelled to hold that the moral value of preservation of life is already a basic precondition of sovereign power —that in the beginning of lawmaking the relation of law and morals is present.

To prove the close relation between law and morals, it is not necessary to prove that every single law is a moral law or is in conformity with morality. The law's concern over human behavior relates the phenomenon of law to morality. In the process of creating or fashioning a legal rule, the lawmaker must constantly ask himself what kind of behavior is appropriate for man in society; that is, he asks how men ought to behave, and the legal rule is frequently made in the light of this "ought."

For the sake of conceptual purity, we may divide the full phenomenon of law into two parts; one part has to do with the gestation of the contents of the rule—this process includes the vital moral, religious, and general value-convictions a society or legislator wants to express through the medium of law; the second part is the mechanical process of formal promulgation by which these ideas are invested with the form of a statute. If one is to describe the full phenomenon of law, he must include both processes. Austin, however, attempted to formulate the concept of law solely in terms of the second aspect of the lawmaking process. That a meaningful concept of law cannot be achieved this way, that is, by separating technical promulgation from the concerns over the moral direction of human behavior, was later evident even to Austin. The very concept of law is meaningless until the nature of man is brought into consideration.

The Concept of Law and the Common Nature of Man

The most important link between law and morals in Austin's system is found in his conception of man's nature. While Austin spoke of natural law as the "veriest foolishness," he nevertheless reiterated one of the most important tenets of that school—that the conceptt of law rests upon what is "necessary" and what is "bottomed in the common nature of man."[5] With this concern over the nature of man, Austin identifies his system with the tradition of natural law in which the very starting point is the nature and condition of man.

5. *Province*, p. 373.

Austin wishes to derive from his conception of man the obvious point that one can make no sense out of the conception of law until he focuses upon certain features of human nature. Hobbes painted a gloomy picture of the anarchy of the state of nature and saw in man's selfishness and predatory bent the need for law. Theologians had accounted for the law in the fact of human sin. For Hobbes, as well as for the theologians, the breakdown of order through the willfulness of men and the capacity for man to understand anarchy as less desirable than some form of order are the pre-conditions for the emergence of law. Austin says that the very idea of law is incomprehensible until it is seen in connection with the problem of human evil and is viewed as the correction of evil. He writes:

> But the notion or idea of evil or imperfection is involved in the connected notions of law, duty, and sanction. For, seeing that every law imposes a restraint every law is an evil of itself: and, *unless it be the work of malignity, or proceed from consummate folly, it also supposes an evil which it is designed to prevent or remedy*. Law, like medicine, is a preventive or remedy of *evil*: and, if the world were free from evil, the notion and name would be unknown.[6]

It becomes clear at once that Austin is far from considering law in the arbitrary terms which his technical formulation would suggest. While his theory of command sounds as though law is something arbitrary, he said this would be the case only if it were "the work of malignity" or proceeded "from consummate folly." Law is at the very first seen as a corrective of evil and as such proceeds upon some conception of what is the opposite of evil, namely, good. And this "good" is to be seen as "bottomed in the common nature of man." Without this conception of good and evil the notion of law

6. *Province*, p. 85. Emphasis added.

would be "unknown." There can be no more forceful identification of the ideas of law and morality than this, although
Austin does provide even more illuminating illustrations of
this connection.

Jeremy Bentham, to whom Austin is most deeply in-
debted for his positivistic views of law, had the same contempt
for natural law as did Austin.[7] But in a revealing passage Bentham too made a very close identification between the concerns of law and morals when he said that the function of law
"is to increase the efficacy of private ethics, by giving strength
and direction to the influence of moral sanction."[8]

This passage comes from that part of Bentham's analysis
of law where his specific concern was "to ascertain what sort
of thing *a* law is . . . what it must contain in order to be
complete."[9] While Bentham too would identify law as a command, he would not consider this the complete idea of law,
for lurking in the back of his mind was a constant concern
over the moral content of the law, where good is determined
by the good of the community.

To be sure, Bentham said that a law is whatever the community decides to punish as an offense, but he immediately
adds that "The good of the community cannot require . . .
[the punishment of] any act . . . which is not . . . in some way
or other detrimental . . . [and] an act cannot be detrimental
to a *state*, but by being detrimental to some one or more of
the *individuals* that compose it."[10] Thus, unless an act is detri-

---

7. Jeremy Bentham, *Limits of Jurisprudence Defined*, introd. by Charles
Warren Everett (New York: Columbia University Press, 1946), p. 84.

8. *Works of Jeremy Bentham*, published under the superintendence of his
executor, John Bowring (Edinburgh: W. Taft; London: Simpkin, Marshall &
Co., 1843) p. 146.

9. *Id.* at 142.

10. *Id.* at 97.

mental there should be no law against it, "for in the case of such an act, all punishment is groundless."[11] It appears then that the notion of law is, not only that law originates in the command of the sovereign, but that such commands must threaten punishment and should therefore be commands only in those cases in which there are grounds, that is, moral grounds, for such a command. From this analysis it develops that, although there seems to be a sharp distinction between what the law "is" and what it "ought to be," between the laws sovereigns actually make and laws they ought to make, Bentham urges that the very completeness of the idea of law requires the recognition that the commands of law emerge in the context of the moral concern of the legislator and society.

In this same vein, Austin identified the areas of law and morals through a very careful analysis of the kind of acts the law should consider as offenses. He said, "every act . . . that ought to be an object of positive law, ought to be an object of the positive morality. . . ."[12] Even more interesting is Austin's notion that every act that ought to be an object of morality "is an object of the law of God."[13] The object of the positive law is therefore the same as the object of the law of God, the only difference being that the law of God is concerned with a wider area of offenses than is the positive law. Austin speaks at this point not so much of the intersection of law and morals as that which is even more intimate—their concentric relation:

[T]he circle embraced by the law of God . . . is larger than the circle which can be embraced to advantage by positive law. Inasmuch as the two circles have one and the same centre, the whole of the region comprised by the latter is also comprised by the former. But the whole of the region comprised by the former is not comprised by the latter.[14]

11. *Ibid.*
12. *Province*, n. 163.
13. *Ibid.*
14. *Ibid.*

When Austin speaks of law as a command, he is assuming that in its formation the sovereign has in mind the moral nature of man, so that the very "is" of law contains some feature of moral "ought" the moment the law is born. It is not entirely correct to say that the concern over the "ought" is the concern only of the legislator and not the legal scientist. Austin explicitly says that "it was not a deviation from my subject to introduce the principle of utility."[15]

This supreme principle of ethics, both in Bentham and in Austin, has an intrinsic relation to the very notion of what law is, for as Austin points out, "I . . . should often be unable to explain distinctly and precisely the scope and purport of a law, without having brought the principle of utility directly before you."[16] The idea of command, apart from some conception of how someone ought to behave, is so abstract that it can hardly have any meaning by itself. Only as the act of articulating directions to action does command take on meaning, and such directions carry moral implications. For the moment it makes little difference whether the particular moral content of the law is acceptable, because it needs only be said here that both Bentham and Austin see an intimate relation between the ideas of morals and of law because they see the intimate relation between the moral nature of man and the moral concern of law.

The notion of a command cannot be understood apart from one other way in which law is "bottomed in the nature of man." For Austin emphasizes that law "in its literal meaning" is a rule laid down "for the guidance of an intelligent being by an intelligent being having power over him."[17] It

15. *Province*, p. 59.
16. *Ibid.*
17. *Id.* at 10.

must be observed that the political superior from whom a positive law flows is one who not only possesses power but who has intelligence, and the person whose conduct is to be ordered is not simply an entity capable of receiving signals in the way animals do but has the capacity for intelligence. By intelligence, Austin means the faculty of reason. The idea of law is thus intimately connected with the faculty of reason, both in its creation and in the object to which it is directed. Law can exist only where there are intelligences, for as Austin says, "where *intelligence* is not, or where it is too bounded to take the name of *reason*, and, therefore, is too bounded to conceive the purpose of a law, there is not the *will* which law can work on, or which duty can incite or restrain."[18]

This suggests that one of the "necessary" aspects of law is its rational character and its inevitable connection with purposes, especially human purposes. It cannot be assumed that when men deal with laws their reasoning is different from their reasoning about moral duties. Nor do we need to think that when their lives are ordered about by the laws men cease to reflect on the moral defensibility of the law. The law does not in every case have to be identical or in conformity to the rules of morality in order to show the relation between the two. Austin showed that the law flows, in an important sense, from human reason which is also the source of morality. It is not simply that law and morality have the same source that is important here but, again, that they flow from the same kind of reasoning, frequently about the identical kinds of behavior.

Thus, while Austin wishes always to say that a law is a law whether it is good or bad, he certainly did not contemplate

18. *Id.* at 12.

that law had no moral characteristics. And what we have tried to show is not simply that here and there one can find a moral element in the law but that the law is "bottomed" in the nature of man and is the extension of his moral nature, therefore reflecting both man's strengths and weaknesses.

The Moral Basis of Sovereignty

When we analyze Austin's notion of sovereignty, we again find a far more intimate relation between law and morals than positivists usually admit. The stark theory that there are no legal limitations to the power of the sovereign was stated in its sharpest modern form by Hobbes. His notion that "there could be no unjust law" was the logical outcome of his account of the source of law. When he wrote that "laws are the rules of just, and unjust; nothing being reputed unjust, that is not contrary to some law,"[19] he insisted that it was impossible for any statute to be unjust. The theoretical basis of this notion is that for Hobbes there are no moral principles which precede the law; the creation of law and of morality occur simultaneously. There is no perspective from which to criticize law, for there is no law of nature behind the positive law, only the law of preservation.

There is, in Hobbes's theory, moreover, a pessimistic view of man which is far less creative than the theological doctrine of sin, for it considers man so irretrievably selfish and predatory that he must be restrained by the absolute authority of the state. Hobbes's account of the lawlessness of the state of nature is the decisive element of his account of the source of law, for by lawlessness in this state he means,

19. Hobbes, *Leviathan*, ed. with introd. by Michael Oakeshott (Oxford: B. Blackwell, 1946), p. 173.

not only the absence of positive law, but seems to imply the absence of man's awareness of an order of right. Thus, as Hobbes traces back the source of law to its origin, he arbitrarily stops with the fiction of the social contract as the starting point of all law.

Although Austin has written one of the most brilliant refutations of the social contract theory,[20] he nevertheless follows Hobbes by reiterating in his own argument that "the power of a sovereign is incapable of legal limitation."[21] He comes to this conclusion because of the way he has defined both positive law and the nature of the sovereign. Having said that the sovereign is the individual or group of individuals who are political superiors habitually obeyed by political inferiors, and having said that laws emanate only from a sovereign, he thought it followed that the sovereign cannot bind himself by his own laws.

Because Austin thought chiefly in terms of English monarchy and aristocracy, he made the mistake of thinking that in all governments the sovereigns are not bound by the laws they make. In America the rulers are bound by the laws they make, and even more significant is the fact that the lawmakers are also bound by the fundamental law of the Constitution.

Austin emphasized that there is no *legal* limitation to the sovereign's power. This is simply a play on words, because it means that there are no laws when the sovereign *begins* being a sovereign. First there is a sovereign, then his commands become the law, so it may be theoretically correct that there are no legal limitations to the sovereign. But again, in constitutional government, the constitution is the basic law and it

20. *Province*, p. 306.
21. *Id.* at 245.

limits the powers of the sovereign, so that in this case not even the verbal symmetry in Austin's argument will hold.

Austin's theory of the sovereign is not as bald as his original statement leads one to suppose. We get the picture of the sovereign without any *legal* limitation issuing commands and threatening evil pains and punishments. In the best criticism of Austin's theory, Sir Henry Maine writes that Austin's "theory of Sovereignty neglects the mode in which the result has been arrived at. . . . And thus it is that, so far as the restrictions contained in . . . [his] definition of Sovereignty . . . [are] concerned, the Queen and Parliament of our own country might direct all weakly children to be put to death. . . ."[22] Surely this is the first impression one gets from the short version of Austin's theory. But upon a closer look at his theory we find that the acts of the sovereign, though capable of no *legal* limitation,[23] are certainly hemmed in by *moral* limitations.[24] The way in which these moral limitations affect the sovereign comes out in Austin's careful analysis of the meaning of the phrase "the source of law."

There is a "loose" way and a "strict" way of defining the word "source," and Austin's view of the sovereign's legal status depends upon this distinction. For the loose meaning of the source of law is that whatever influences the shaping of a law is a source of law. But in the strict sense there is only one source, namely the command of the sovereign. Again, in the loose sense, one can refer to the *remote* causes of the law, whereas in the strict sense we must look only to the *proximate* source of law.

22. Henry James Sumner Maine, *Lectures on the Early History of Institutions* (New York: Henry Holt & Co., 1875), p. 360.
23. *Province*, pp. 230–231, 245, 255–256.
24. *Id.* at 258–259.

Behind the distinction between the loose and strict interpretation of the source of law lies the even more important distinction between the "cause" and the "source" of law. Austin's contention is that there has been a confusion between
those influences which have "caused" a law to be formed and
the actual "source" from which the law, as law, springs. This
confusion, he feels, is what complicates or distorts all discussions about the nature of the sovereign. For if law has its
source in nature, or God, or custom, then it could rightly be
said that the sovereign is under legal limitations, since there
are laws "prior to" or "above" the sovereign. These rules
which emanate from nature or custom are, for Austin, not
laws in the strict sense of the term; they are only positive rules
of morality. Austin writes:

God or nature is not a source of law in the strict sense. . . . God or nature
is ranked among the sources of law, through the same confusion of the
source of law with its remoter causes. . . . But . . . [law] is law, strictly so
called, by the establishment it receives from the human sovereign. . . .
God or nature is the remote cause of the law, but its source and proximate cause is the earthly sovereign, by whom it is *positum* or established.[25]

To say that the proximate source of law is the sovereign
does not in any sense mean that on that account there is a
separation of law and morals. It only means that the process by

25. Austin, *Lectures on Jurisprudence*, revised and edited by Robert Campbell (5th. ed.; London: J. Murray, 1885), II, 548 (hereinafter *Lectures*):
Taking the term "source" in a loose signification, customs may be styled
sources of laws. For the existence of a custom, with the general opinion
in favour of it, is the cause or occasion, or is one of the causes or occasions,
of that legal rule which is moulded or fashioned upon it. But taking the
term "source" in the same loose signification, the causes of the custom from
which the law emerges are also a source or fountain of the law itself: and,
generally, any cause of any law must be ranked with its sources or foun-
tains. . . . Hence certain writers have ranked experience and reason, together with external circumstances wherein mankind are placed, amongst
the sources of the laws whereby mankind are governed.

which moral convictions become transformed into law has been clearly exposed and analyzed. But for the present Austin's most important point is that the very way in which the sovereign is constituted already means that the sovereign works under moral limitations, or, as Austin says in a significant passage:

> The law of England, for example, cannot be understood without a knowledge of the constitution of Parliament, and of the various rules by which that sovereign body conducts the business of legislation: although it is manifest that much of the law which determines the constitution of Parliament, and many of the rules which Parliament follows in legislating, are either mere law imposed by the opinion of the community, or merely ethical maxims which the body spontaneously observes.[26]

While it is true therefore that the sovereign cannot be limited by "strictly legal" boundaries, his authority is nevertheless constituted upon a moral foundation. To say that the sovereign has no legal limitations is therefore a misleading notion, insinuating that the sovereign could do anything it wished.

But even Austin saw the absurdity of that conclusion and felt it quite necessary to indicate in detail how the Parliament works. He was concerned with the workings of the sovereign, chiefly because it was in this activity that he centered all his theory about the law. The most decisive feature about the sovereign, for Austin himself, was not the fact that it was curbed by no legal limitations but that it was, in fact, curbed by "moral" laws.

This led Austin to say that without understanding these moral limitations upon the sovereign one could not really understand what positive law is. The moral limitations upon the sovereign had the effect, too, of joining the moral and legal

26. *Id.* at 746.

elements in the positive law, which means that instead of achieving a separation of law and morals, which positivism is reputed to do, Austin's analysis reveals just the opposite— the conjunction of law and morals. Referring to these moral laws in the structure of constitutional lawmaking, he regrets that he has found them there because they upset the logical rigor of his system, but with admirable candor he writes,

> though, in logical rigour, much of the so-called law which relates to the Sovereign, ought to be banished from the *Corpus Juris,* it ought to be inserted in the *Corpus Juris* for reasons of convenience which are paramount to logical symmetry. For though, in strictness, it belongs to positive morality or to ethics, *a knowledge of it is absolutely necessary in order to have a knowledge of the positive law* with which the Corpus Juris is properly concerned.[27]

Austin next indicates the indissoluable relation between law and morals when he says that "the case which I am now considering is one of the numerous cases wherein law and morality are so intimately and indissolubly allied, that, though they are of distinct natures and ought to be carefully distinguished it is necessary nevertheless to consider them in conjunction."[28] He thus reiterates here in detail what he had expressed earlier when he spoke of "the compound of positive morality and positive law, which determines the character of the person, or . . . persons, in whom, for the time being, the sovereignty shall reside. . . ."[29] The sovereign must not be looked upon, even in theory, as independent of the moral law, for the sovereign's activities transpire under the constant influence of the moral law, wherefore there is a constant relation between law and morals.

27. *Id.* at 745–746.
28. *Ibid.*
29. *Province,* p. 259.

There may be serious questions over whether anything can be gained by demonstrating that there is such an intimate connection between law and morals. Bentham wondered just what Blackstone had achieved by arguing that the natural law places limits upon what the positive law can control.[30] Bentham's objection was that if it is held that there is a close connection between law and morals, the effect will be for people to identify their moral obligation with their legal duties.[31] And to say that the law already contains its moral justification is to stifle any serious criticism of the law.

But everything depends upon which end of the argument we are considering. When law is considered at the point of its creation, the very idea of law requires that it bear some relation to moral standards. But after the law has been made, it is still necessary to consider whether it is morally justifiable. The pressure of moral criticism of law exists at both points. To argue for the relation of law and morals does not mean that morality must be or will be reduced to the commands of the law. But even such an effect is not totally undesirable, for it is one of the functions of law to urge those moral actions which men in their selfishness will not voluntarily undertake, or, as Bentham put it, "to increase the efficacy of private ethics." What is gained by this analysis is a demonstration that the sovereign cannot separate the act of making law from a consideration of the requirements of morality.

The Problem of the Validity of Law

The positivist has a simple formula for legal validity, for he argues that whatever the sovereign commands is valid law.

---

30. Blackstone, I, 38.
31. Bentham, *The Principles of Morals and Legislation,* II (Oxford: B. Blackwell, 1948).

We have already seen in our analysis of Austin's theory of sovereignty that this simple formula is far more sophisticated than it first appears. This is true also in the positivism of Hans Kelsen, for what first appears to be a self-sufficient account of legal validity turns out to be a natural lawlike grounding of the legal order.

The key to Kelsen's system is the word "normativism."[32] To this word he gives a novel meaning which is not to be confused with moral norms. A norm is "an impersonal and anonymous 'command.' "[33] All laws are norms. If that which we call a law is not a norm, then it is not a law.

Whence does this norm come? Every norm derives from another norm. Kelsen is not concerned with the problem of the source of law which leads other jurists to discuss the role of custom, morality, nature, and God as sources of law. For him there can be no entity different from or existing independently of the law as the source of law. "[T]he 'source' of law," he says, "is always itself law."[34] All laws are related to one another.

Here Kelsen is reiterating Austin's theory, for he too is saying that there is only one true source of law in the juristic sense—the sovereign, or a superior norm. The legal system is a hierarchy of norms whose regress can be traced finally to the "basic norm," beyond which there is no other norm or law. The "basic norm" is ultimately the source of all laws; it is the starting point of the norm-creating process. The basic norm is a hypothetical assumption lying behind the first legislator—

32. See Kelsen, "The Pure Theory of Law," 50 Law Quarterly Review 474 (1934).

33. Hans Kelsen, *General Theory of Law and State*, trans. Anders Wedberg, ("20th Century Legal Philosophy Series" [Cambridge: Harvard University Press, 1946] hereinafter *General Theory*).

34. *Id.* at 132.

the assumption that he is legislating validly; the basic norm is the norm which authorizes the historically first legislator. The function of the basic norm is to confer law-creating power upon the first legislator and on all the other acts (of legislation) based upon the first act. In Kelsen's theory, everything depends upon this last statement; for every norm, that is, every law, is valid only insofar as it is based upon the basic norm, or, subsequently, upon some other norm which issued from the basic norm.

Kelsen likens the basic norm to the transcendental logical principles of cognition which are not empirical laws but merely the conditions of all experience. So, too, the basic norm is itself no positive rule because it has been made but is simply presupposed as the condition of all positive legal norms. The final presupposition is not, for example, the first constitution, but the validity of that constitution. The final postulate is that at a given time in history there existed a condition which validated the first constitution—that condition, not itself an act or statute, is the basic norm.

Thus from the basic norm there emerge types of law, for example, the civil and criminal law. The criminal law in turn produces a specific statute, and from that statute specific decisions are arrived at by the court affecting individuals. The sequence here is from norm to norm, from law to law. For the constitution, criminal law, statute and decision are each norms and constitute the hierarchy of norms. These positive laws become valid only on one assumption: that there is a basic norm which establishes the supreme law-creating authority.

But this does not mean that the basic norm itself can in any way be proved to be valid. "The validity of this basic norm is unproved and must remain so within the sphere of positive law itself.''[35] Moreover, this does not mean that the system of laws is a closed logical system,[36] for the laws in this hierarchy are not deduced logically but conform to the higher norms. Kelsen simply makes the point that, just as one cannot know the empirical world from the transcendental logical principles but merely by means of them, so positive law cannot be derived in its content from the basic norm but can merely be understood by it. This means fundamentally that norms do not in any way correspond to reality but derive their ultimate validity simply from proper enactment. Kelsen puts this central point in these words:

> The norms of positive law are valid, that is, they ought to be obeyed, not because they are, like the laws of natural law, derived from nature, God, or reason, from a principle of the absolutely good, right or just, from an absolutely supreme value or fundamental norm which itself is clothed with the claim of absolute validity, but merely because they have been created in a certain way or made by a certain person. This implies no categorical statement as to the value of the method of the law-making or of the person functioning as the positive legal authority; this value is a hypothetical assumption.[37]

Also, this basic norm "is presupposed to be valid because without this presupposition no human act could be interpreted as a legal, especially as a norm-creating, act.''[38]

This intricate argument for a "science of law" which attempts to separate law and morals turns out in the end to be neither science nor successful in separating law and morals. If anything, Kelsen's system greatly clarifies the relation between law and morals, for he makes it unmistakably clear just

---

35. *Id.* at 395.
36. See Julius Stone, *The Province and Function of Law* (Sydney: Associated General Publications, Ltd., 1946), p. 141.
37. *General Theory*, p. 394.
38. *Id.* at 116.

where the moral element enters the system of law. The two avenues through which morals pass into the law are through the basic norm and at the occasion on which each new norm is created. It is quite true, as Kelsen argues, that law proliferates within the structural framework of civil government, that laws proceed from laws. But he has made it clear that norms do not in fact, nor do they need to, proceed logically from one norm to the other.

This means that the hierarchy of norms provides at most the mechanism or procedure by which the laws are created. But at each point in the hierarchy the laws become imbued with morality as they are fashioned into statutes. "It is possible for the legal order," says Kelsen, "by obliging the law-creating organs to respect or apply certain moral norms or political principles or opinions of experts, to transform these norms, principles, or opinions, into legal norms and thus into true sources of law."[39]

The validity of a law rests only upon its proper enactment; in this view, positivism seems to say nothing about the law's content. But it is precisely because the basic norm does have the effect of directing the sovereign in its act of law-making to consider the requirements of morality that in the end the positivistic system takes on some of the characteristics of natural law theory.

Austin modified his theory when he elaborated the context within which the sovereign formulated his command, a context which included particularly the dimension of moral imperatives. Similarly, Kelsen's system takes on a different mood when he distinguishes between the validity of an ordinary legal norm and the validity of the basic norm. The va-

39. *Id.* at 132.

lidity of an ordinary norm rests solely on proper enactment and not upon the validity of the content of the norm. But with the basic norm the situation is just the opposite, for when he speaks of the validity of the basic norm he says it

is not valid because it has been created in a certain way, but its validity is assumed by virtue of its content. *It is valid, then, like a norm of natural law, apart from its merely hypothetical validity. The idea of a pure positive law, like that of natural law, has its limitation.*[40]

Neither Austin nor Kelsen succeed in producing a coherent account of the separation of law and morals, for they both inject a moral element just where their system would have led us to believe that validity is totally independent of morality. One cannot, therefore, take Kelsen literally when he writes that "law has no moral connotations whatsoever."[41]

Morality and the Judicial Process

The impossibility of separating law and morals is frequently argued by referring to the judicial process.[42] The argument here is that the judges frequently make the law, and when they do this they invariably inject their own or the society's moral standards into their decisions and thereby bring about a union between law and morals.

We need to consider how the positivist meets this argument. Austin was aware that much law comes from the activity of the courts.[43] Not only was he aware of the practice of judicial legislation, he even urged judges to engage in it.[44] But what Austin and Kelsen do reject in this argument is

40. *Id.* at 401. Emphasis added.
41. *Id.* at 5.
42. See, e.g., Paul Vinogradoff, *Common Sense in Law*, revised by H. G. Hanbury (2d ed.; London, New York: Oxford University Press, 1956), p. 150.
43. *Lectures*, p. 612.
44. *Province*, p. 191.

that judicial activity represents a novel or unique source of law. For them, the fact that the courts engage in moral reasoning in arriving at their decision and therefore in their act of creating law does not mean that these courts are an entity independent of the sovereign. "Sovereignty," says Austin, "includes the judicial as well as the legislative power."[45] When the courts make law, this is the sovereign making law, for the courts are part of the sovereign, and unless the supreme sovereign revokes the act of the subordinate sovereign, there is the "tacit" assumption that it is the sovereign itself which is legislating when the court makes a decision.[46]

Judicial lawmaking is for Austin one of the recognized ways in which law gets made. But what needs to be understood here is that this demonstrates not only the logical symmetry of his argument where the supremacy of the sovereign as the only source of law is preserved; it also illustrates that it is in the constant attempt to implement the moral norms of a society that judges make the law, or at least that moral rules are constantly being transformed into legal rules. Austin is very explicit on this when he writes:

> Now a merely *moral,* or merely customary rule, may take the quality of a *legal* rule in two ways:—it may be adopted by a sovereign or subordinate legislature, and turned into a law in the direct mode; or it may be taken as the ground of a judicial decision, which afterwards obtains as a precedent; and in this case it is converted into a law after the judicial fashion. In whichever of these ways it becomes a legal rule, the law into which it is turned emanates from the sovereign or . . . judge, who transmutes the moral or imperfect rule into a legal or perfect one.[47]

But Austin adds immediately, with respect to these moral rules, that "Those who maintain that it existed as a law before

45. *Lectures,* p. 520.
46. *Id.* at 512.
47. *Id.* at 536.

it was enforced by legal sanction, or that it was established as law *consensu utentium* confound law with positive morality."[48] And while he will admit that "courts of justice are a source of law, insofar as law consists of judicial decisions," he nevertheless places the courts into the direct line from the sovereign as "legislating in subordination to the sovereign" and that therefore the courts are only "reservoirs . . . fed from the source of all law, the supreme legislator, and again emitting the borrowed waters which they receive from that Fountain."[49] But surely behind this metaphorical diction there resides more than a conception of an arrangement of superior and subordinate sovereigns; for the quality of rule, whose content is fashioned for the direction of human conduct, comes out of the moral sentiment of the lawmaker and not the abstract recesses of the sovereign.

Moreover, if the law does not represent a self-contained or closed logical system, then it must follow that the judges are not tied to the specific implication of a prior statute or even of a precedent. Courts are always "distinguishing" new cases for the purpose of taking them out of the restrictive bounds of previous cases and precedents. When judges distinguish cases in this manner they are expressing their urge to achieve "justice," which might not be achieved by a mechanical application of a previous decision.

The central philosophical question raised by this activity of the judge is whether in distinguishing cases and interpreting statutes he is creating new law based on moral considerations, independent of the supreme sovereign.

Professor Hart has made the distinction between the *core* of a law and its *penumbra*, suggesting that it is indeed

48. *Id.* at 537.
49. *Id.* at 510–511.

necessary for judges to interpret the meaning of statutes in those rare cases where an unexpected example comes before them.[50] A statute regulating the interstate traffic of "vehicles" may thus become obscure when the case involves an airplane. Did the legislators have in mind only automobiles, trucks, trailers, and motorcycles? Or did they have in mind the maintenance of the safety of people against the danger of improperly operated vehicles? In the latter case the emphasis shifts from the limited list of vehicles to the more basic question of the danger to people from mechanically operated vehicles, whatever their nature. But to put the problem in that form suggests that it is only in the penumbral situation that questions occur and only on these occasions that there is an extension of an otherwise clear core of law.

To speak of a core of a law implies that once a law is made there is only the problem of applying it, that the core has a permanent life, and that all decisions based upon it must in some way be tightly tied to it by logic. If we were to look at decisions in this manner we would have to hold that every interpretation of a law is already contained in the law as it is.

The most this would do is preserve the fiction that law is a command of the sovereign and this would be stretched to include the judicial interpretations of statutes. It would also mean that judges are concerned only with the law as it *is* and not as it *ought to be*. When judges have to deal with a penumbral situation, they are, it is held, dealing only with an exceptional situation. But do laws have such a core? Does the Fourteenth Amendment have a specific core? Is the problem

---

50. Herbert Lionel Adolphus Hart, "Positivism and the Separation of Law and Morals," 71 Harvard Law Review 607 (1958); See Holmes's dissent in Schlesinger v. Wisconsin, 270 U.S. 230, 241 (1925): "[T]he law allows a penumbra to be embraced that goes beyond the outline of its object in order that the object may be secured."

of racial segregation part of the core or penumbra? Is the ruling of the Supreme Court that it is unlawful to segregate the races in schools part of the core or the penumbra? Is the interpretation of the Fourteenth Amendment to be tied rigorously to the intent of the framers of that amendment? Should the judges' opinion rest on an historical study of whether the framers had in mind the segregation of schools? Or, is it possible that the Fourteenth Amendment is the expression of the sovereign, in this case the people, that the law "ought to be" such as to conform to the moral dimension which that amendment expresses?

There can hardly be any question that in the process of making a decision judges must refer, not only to the premises of the "core" of the law, but to the circumstances of the particular case and to the general question of the justice of the decision. It is clear that the "slot machine" concept of the law is far too great an oversimplification of what law is. But are we, then, justified in saying that the activity by which judges seek to arrive at a decision and their consideration of what ought to be the purposes and aims of the law in terms of social policy are part of the law? To this question the positivists have always replied in the negative, for they have based their science of law on the description of the "is" and not the "ought to be."

But, again, in terms of the argument of positivism itself, the judicial concern over what a law is or ought to be and the concern over the justice of the decision is part of the phenomenon of the law. Moreover, since the positivist holds that the court is the sovereign, then what the court says and does is the law. The meaning of the term "law" therefore includes what the judges do in formulating their "command," that is, their decision. It is not accidental that the judges constantly strive to achieve justice (what the law ought to be). The judge's engagement in weighing the requirements of justice and thereby going beyond the mechanical approach of the machine is an intrinsic part of what the law is.

The fact that the judge engages in these activities is far more intimately related to what law is than that he writes his opinions with a pen or with a pencil or that he walks to the court or drives in a car. All these activities are involved in the process of rendering a decision, but only the activity in which he is concerned with the right decision is, among these examples, truly part of the law.

Again, this would have to follow from the view of sovereignty offered by Austin, for the law is the command of the sovereign directing the conduct of those in the habit of obeying. And just as we say that Austin's primary legislator was not free to make laws in any arbitrary manner, that he was under moral limitations, so also the judge, still under the influence of that original moral constraint, is engaged in the activity of realizing the whole intent of the law—justice.

This process is very subtle and is attended with many dangers. But the dangers suggested in this procedure indicate something about the nature of law which would otherwise be overlooked in the interests of having a neat theory. The danger is, of course, that this interpretation of the judicial function might open up the courts to the subjective whims of individual judges. But this danger has to be put over against the danger that the law will become irrelevant and that fictions will constantly have to be invented in order to give the semblance of continuity and certainty in the law. Certainty in law must collide with the quest for justice, and this collision ought to indicate that the nature of law is misconceived if it is treated as a static structure; for such a static form cannot reflect the subtle variations in which human beings confront each other, nor does it recognize that human life is dynamic and cannot be contained in any partially conceived framework of behavior.

The judicial process is an intrinsic part of the law because it is the means by which the stabilities of the rules are applied to the dynamic behavior of men, and this process operates under the aegis of the quest for justice. In this sense, what a philosopher thinks the law ought to be might not be part of the law in the strict positivistic sense of the word, but what the judge thinks it ought to be is part of the law. And since the judge is part of the sovereign, the judicial process must be contained in the definition of law. In this sense, too, what the law "ought to be" is already an aspect of or is contained in what the law "is."

Force, Reason, and the Law

Positivism identifies law with force; it could be no other way if law is to be defined in the narrow sense as the command of the sovereign. Justice Holmes frequently spoke of the *ultima ratio* of law as force. When it comes to the development of a *corpus juris*, he said, the fundamental question is, "What do the dominant forces of the community want and do they want it hard enough to disregard whatever inhibitions stand in the way?"[51]

He argued that the most fundamental of the supposed pre-existing rights, the right to life, is sacrificed whenever the interest of society, "that is, of the predominant power in the

---

51. Max Lerner, *The Mind and Faith of Justice Holmes* (Boston: Little, Brown, 1943), p. 432, (letter to J. C. H. Wu); See *Holmes-Pollock Letters*, I, 163; Roscoe Pound, *Social Control Through Law* (Published for Indiana University; New Haven: Yale University Press, 1942), p. 107.

community is thought to demand it."[52] The fact that the state forces the conscript with bayonets to die for a cause in which he does not believe gave Holmes no scruples, not because the safety of the state required such sacrifice, but because he did not feel that there was any defensible concept of justice or morality which could overcome the supremacy of force which he therefore raised to the highest principle of law. "Our morality," he said, "seems to me only a check on the ultimate domination of force, just as our politeness is a check on the impulses of every pig to put his feet in the trough."[53]

This rhetorical connection between force and the skepticism about morality is not fortuitous but is the technical doctrine of positivism. Force becomes the ultimate principle of law simply because there is no other alternative once the notion of justice is removed as the ground of law.[54]

We have already seen that Austin's theory of sovereignty is rigorously limited to the fact of command, and in this regard he is restating the conclusions of Hobbes and Bentham. It would be difficult to sustain the notion that these men singled out force as the central characteristic of law because they did not admit the possibility of any moral truth. Indeed, a careful reading of their works reveals that they all utilize the language of natural law.[55] But it can be said of them that they did not believe that there was any universal validity to moral systems, nor did they believe that moral ends could be "proved" by natural reason. The scope of reason is for them limited to the empirical world, and they all wished to employ

52. Holmes, "Natural Law," 32 Harvard Law Review 42 (1918).
53. Lerner, p. 431.
54. *General Theory*, pp. 18–21.
55. Pollock, "The History of the Law of Nature: A Preliminary Statement," 1 Columbia Law Review 30–31 (1901).

the methods of empirical science in developing their theory of law.

Because they saw such a severe limitation to the scope of rational competence, they refused to conceive of law in such nonempirical terms as "justice." The most fundamental characteristic of law which the method of science was able to reveal was the element of coercion, or force. The whole concept of law therefore revolved for them around the notion of sanction, or threat of evil or pain. The "essence" of law therefore becomes force, for not only does "the idea of coercion . . . become inseparably connected with that of a law," but even more specifically "it is upon punishment that everything turns."[56]

It does not help us in this problem to remind ourselves of the truly deep moral sensitivity of such men as Holmes, Bentham, and Austin, for it is with the consistency and accuracy of the theory that we are concerned. To point to their moral insights, particularly in the judicial capacity, as we frequently do in Holmes's case, is to point to that very quality in the jurist for which we all instinctively look, which is the opposite of arbitrariness.

The fact of force is without doubt a substantial element in law, but to define law in terms of force is to define, not law, but force. When we come to the defense of such men as Holmes by saying that he would be incapable of using the power of his position without regard to moral considerations, we are in effect saying that a judge, or the sovereign, "ought not" to disengage the fact of his power from the requirements of justice. If this were not the case, there would really never be any debate about the nature of law, for, if indeed the

56. Bentham, *Limits of Jurisprudence Defined*, n. 227.

essence of law is its coercive element, if the sovereign is defined solely in terms of power, then man would not be so exercised over the question whether might is right.

Is it not rather the case that by the idea of law is meant the domestication of force by morality? Does not constitutional law indicate that what is binding upon the subject by the threat of ultimate physical coercion is binding on the sovereign by a moral sanction?[57]

Yet Austin stripped all other considerations from his definition of law except force, or, as Maine has said,

Sovereignty, for the purposes of Austin's system, has no attribute but force, and consequently the view here taken of "law," "obligation" and "right" is a view of them regarded exclusively as products of coercive force. The "sanction" [force] thus becomes the primary and most important member of the series of notions and gives its color to all the others.[58]

This exclusive preoccupation with force is what renders Austin's theory of law inaccurate, for it puts the center of gravity in the wrong place in the phenomenon of law. Radbruch says:

A certain behavior is not lawful because it is commanded or enforced, but it is commanded or enforced because it is law, because it is just and socially necessary in the opinion of the law giver. . . . To see the essence of law in command and sanction is therefore a falsification of the reality of law.[59]

The separation of law and morals in positivism is the understandable result of the attempt to differentiate between a legal order, a system of morality, and a set of religious be-

57. Vinogradoff, p. 29.
58. Maine, p. 363.
59. Radbruch, "Anglo-American Jurisprudence Through Continental Eyes," 52 Law Quarterly Review 530, 534 (1936).

liefs. But it does not follow from any kind of logic that the legal order does not contain elements of moral and religious beliefs. Indeed, our argument has been that it is because positivism has tried to urge that law has "no moral connotations whatsoever" that it has obscured the meaning of law.

To be sure, the object behind the formulation of, say, Kelsen's "pure" theory of law is to rid the definition of law of all political and subjective ideological ingredients. That ideology moves into the content of law cannot be questioned. For example, Professor Panunzio declared in his inaugural lecture that "we must 'fascicize' the instruction of law. . . . *Instruction in the theory of the law is like instruction in religion.*"[60] Even the Marxists, whose chief criticism of bourgeois law is that it is simply the instrument of ideology, have begun to reconstruct law along ideological lines: "The Soviet Courts," writes Gintsburg, "were designed to render specific 'class justice.' . . . [They] are called upon to carry out the policy of the Soviet government and Communist party as well as the Marx-Lenin doctrine."[61]

Recognizing that a system of law can embody ideology in its most pathological form, does it follow that legal theory must isolate the phenomenon of law from moral and religious elements? Is it even theoretically possible to define law accurately without taking into consideration its moral aspects? It is important, to be sure, for scientific reasons, to be able to distinguish law from other modes by which human conduct is controlled; still, the jurist's chief concern should not be the preservation of certain "scientific" presuppositions if this makes it impossible to render a faithful analysis of the total

60. Steiner, "Fascist Concept of Law," 36 Columbia Law Review 271 (1936).
61. Gsovski, "The Soviet Concept of Law," 7 Fordham Law Review 4 (1938).

phenomenon of law. If it is a presupposition of the science of law that only what can be physically observed[62] will have a rightful place in the construction of a theory of law, then obviously there will be no place in legal theory for the concept of justice.

But this does not prove that justice is not an essential element of law; it proves only that legal science has no way of handling the question of justice—that the science of law is incapable of dealing with the total phenomenon of law. By virtue of its methodological premises the science of law is forced to distort the meaning of law because it does not ask, "What is the full nature of law?" but asks instead, "With what aspects of the phenomenon of law can scientific method deal?"

In this case, the scientific method is like a net which catches only some fish, while the rest escape. That the ideological content of law may be "subjective" or "relative," and on that account not acceptable to everyone, does not alter the fact that there can be no law at all without the presence of "value content." An adequate theory of law must be broad enough to deal with all the facts in the phenomenon of law, including the fact of value.

To say that the essence of law is force is to say that law is essentially a technique of social control. And to call law a "technique" is to disengage it from any particular ends, from its moral purposes. Kelsen argues that to analyze the law as it is, is to free the law from "the metaphysical mist" with which it gets covered by speculations about justice.[63] But the error Kelsen seems to make is to think that if he "declines to give a

---

62. *General Theory*, p. 79.
63. Kelsen, "Function of the Pure Theory of Law," in *Law: A Century of Progress* (New York: New York University Press, 1937), II, 237.

moral judgment on the positive law,"[64] he has thereby eliminated from the phenomenon of law the value content that is already there.

It is not the scientific jurist's moral judgment about the law that is decisive here; it is the moral concern of the legislator which produces the law's moral element. Even as a "scientific" observer, the theorist should see that law is not just abstract force; it is always force in conjunction with "ends." Yet Kelsen argues that the only way to distinguish the legal order is to see it as a technique of force:

> What distinguishes the legal order from all other social orders is the fact that it regulates human behaviour by means of a specific technique. If we ignore this specific element of the law, if we do not conceive of the law as a specific social technique, if we define law simply as order or organization, and not as coercive order (or organization), then we lose the possibility of differentiating law from other social phenomena.[65]

Nowhere do we see the radical reconception of the meaning of law so vividly as in this attempt to "reduce" law to force. For along with this identification of law with force comes a new meaning to the word "ought" or to the whole notion of obligation. The command theory of law would say that men should obey the law simply because they are commanded to do so. They "ought" to obey the law, not for any moral reasons, but solely because there is a threat of force. This is what the separation of law and morals entails. From this positivistic view the law does not prescribe ways in which men "ought" to behave; it simply prescribes norms for behavior, and if men do not comply with these rules, then the officials of the government "ought" to bring down the sanction upon such nonconforming persons.

64. *Ibid.*
65. *General Theory*, p. 26; cf. pp. 21, 22, 438.

The concept of "ought" is therefore quite radically reconceived. As Kelsen says, "That somebody is legally obligated to certain conduct means that an organ [of the state] 'ought' to apply a sanction to him in case of contrary conduct."[66] This is truly the negation of whatever men have heretofore thought to be the meaning of law, for while at all times jurists have seen the importance of the sanction behind a legal rule, there has rarely been such a decisive separation of morals or justice from the structure of law. This has the effect, again, of making force the principle of law.[67] But as Radbruch writes, "The legal principle cannot . . . have the character of a command, but must be a judgment of values. Its primary form is not: Do this! or: Forbear from doing that! but: This is necessary for the sake of justice and the general good."[68]

What is behind this persistent identification of law with force and the apparent horror of finding the value element in law? One answer seems to be that ever since Hobbes sought to establish legal theory on a scientific basis, force has displaced justice as the essence of law. The problem has to do with the theory of knowledge. Kelsen phrases the problem in very sharp terms by saying:

Positivism and (epistemological) relativism belong together just as much as do the natural law doctrine and (metaphysical) absolutism. Any attempt to push beyond the relative-hypothetical foundation of

66. *Id.* at 60.
The concept of legal duty also implies an "ought." That somebody is legally obligated to certain conduct means that an organ "ought" to apply a sanction to him in case of contrary conduct. But the concept of legal duty differs from that of moral duty by the fact that the legal duty is not the behavior which the norm "demands," which "ought" to be observed. The legal duty, instead, is the behavior by the observance of which the delict is avoided, thus the opposite of the behavior which forms a condition for the sanction. Only the sanction "ought" to be executed.
67. *Id.* at 58–59.
68. Radbruch, p. 52.

positive law . . . means the abandonment of the distinction between positive and natural law.[69]

As one pursues Kelsen's positivistic separation of law and morals, it becomes clear that he is concerned, not merely with separating these two modes of ordering behavior nor even with distinguishing them. His argument is rather that the difference between law and morals is that while we can "know" something about law, we cannot have any "cognition" of value or moral terms. The impact of his scientific method is therefore not simply to say that the contents of legal science are different from legal philosophy but that we can get reliable knowledge about law only through empirical description.

Over against the classical view about law as announced, for example, by Plato, who said that "no law or ordinance whatever has the right to sovereignty over true knowledge,"[70] Kelsen radically rephrases legal theory by saying that "cognition can grasp only a positive order evidenced by objectively determinable acts. This order is the positive law and is known only by positivism, which is a radically realistic and empirical theory. It declines to evaluate positive law."[71]

The separation of law and morals is therefore an attempt to conceive of law independently of morals precisely because moral discourse is "subjective" and incapable of objective proof. But it does not follow logically that, just because we cannot furnish the same kind of proof for the concept of justice which the law contains as we can about the mechanism of force involved in law, this value element is not there as a most significant part of law.

69. *General Theory*, p. 396
70. Plato, *Laws* IX, 875.
71. *General Theory*, p. 13.

It would follow logically to admit the presence of value elements and then reserve the problem of dealing with the "measure" of values as a significant part of the study of jurisprudence. The law is always employed at the point at which men confront real alternatives in their behavior, and the law is used for signifying which direction they must take in the face of several other possible ways of action. To be involved in fashioning such decisions for the direction of behavior is precisely the concern of morality, and at this point the function of law and morals becomes the same. The law could have no other meaning, could not indeed be "thought," if it were not seen as the agency by which men were confronted by an imperative to choose an "ought."

The fact that the "ought" and the "is" are two different realms makes law possible in the first place. It is true, as Bentham says, that "every legal command imposes a duty,"[72] but is this duty simply the consequence of the "fact" that it was commanded? Can legal duty be based simply upon the command without any reference to its moral defensibility? No more difficult question can be raised in legal theory, because here again we come face to face with the problem of the "bad" law. But we need to ask whether it would be more accurate to say that the law's command is the mode and means by which men are reminded or recalled to a duty that exists prior to the law in a moral form.

Austin said the latter when he pointed to men's evil tendencies as the very cause for law; wherefore it must follow that law is engaged in the consequences of men's evil and its correction, and there must always lurk in the law some concep-

72. Bentham, *Limits of Jurisprudence Defined*, p. 142.

tion of what the law is trying to achieve. It would make no sense to say that the law attempts to overcome the evil of human nature by perpetrating its own fresh evils. Whether the law succeeds in this attempt to rectify human evil is one question, and the fact that this attempt to rectify evil characterizes the regime of law is another.

The more we consider the characteristics of law, the more it becomes evident that the law is a matter of "thought" or of "consciousness." It represents the capacity men have of transcending, that is, stepping back from and looking at their own and other's behavior, "evaluating" or "judging" that behavior as desirable or undesirable, then "thinking" of alternative ways of behavior which would be "better" and would more adequately lead to the "greater good" or "happiness" of the "greatest" number.

This is what in fact lies behind all law, and to hold that men do not have the capacity to achieve a perfect knowledge of the absolutely and eternally good does not change this characteristic of law. Nor are men relieved of the necessity for grappling with what the law "ought" to be just because such discussions have to transpire under the cloud of subjectivism. In spite of the difficulties of epistemological relativism, the persistence of the question of moral ends suggests that such ends cannot be separated from our understanding of what law is. And nobody was more aware of this than those who sought to fashion the positivistic separation of law and morality, namely, Bentham and Austin.

The Ends of Law

Positivism raises doubts about the possibility of finding trustworthy guides in human nature for the ends of law. Nevertheless, Austin had focused upon the significant fact that all legal systems embody certain fundamental notions which are "necessary" and "bottomed in the common nature of man." Austin's thought nowhere resembles the natural law mode of reasoning more than at the point at which he looks to man's nature for the ends of law and indeed for the understanding of the fuller meaning of law. His severe and cryptic conception of law as a command is greatly modified when the meaning of law is connected with those fundamental notions which are "bottomed in the common nature of man."[73]

So significant did Austin consider these notions which go into the making of laws that he said that "it is impossible to consider jurisprudence quite apart from legislation," and that "if the causes of laws . . . be not assigned, the laws themselves are unintelligible."[74] The rather large section devoted to ethics in his *Province of Jurisprudence Determined*, about which he said that "it was not a deviation from my subject to introduce the principle of utility," certainly shows how close Austin considered the relation of law and morals. Thus, the principles of legislation turn out to be fundamental also to understanding the prior question of the nature of law.

Not one of the early positivist jurists ever successfully disengaged the idea of law from the notion of the ends of law. They all begin by announcing that law and morals are two distinct subjects, that law is simply a command. But within the same treatise they deal with the problem of ends in such a way as to indicate that without such a connection between "ends" and command there can be no full understanding of what is meant by law. Hobbes had raised order or security as the minimum end, and Bentham had pushed far beyond this minimum to the much wider end of "happiness," or the

73. See the lecture, "Uses of Jurisprudence," in *Province*, pp. 365, 367, 369.
74. *Lectures*, p. 1113.

greatest good for the greatest number; and Bentham took his cue from "the natural constitution of the human frame."[75]

Whereas present-day positivists recoil from discussions of morals and on that account wish to disengage the law from moral concerns, the founders of this school discovered that they could not sustain this separation. Even though Bentham and Austin were particularly concerned to rest their theories on scientific and empirically verifiable information, they soon found themselves, and with no apology, dealing with morals just the same.

Their initial impetus to work out a new system of jurisprudence had come from their dissatisfaction over Blackstone's theological conception of man and his attempt to relate law to these characteristics of human nature. A good idea of the paradoxical attitude the utilitarians showed on this matter is found in Gibbon's note on Blackstone's *Commentaries*. When he came to that part which deals with "The Nature of Laws in General," Gibbon wrote:

> I have entirely omitted a metaphysical enquiry upon the nature of Laws in General . . . and a number of sublime terms, which I admire as much as I can without understanding them. Instead of following this high a priori road, would it not be better humbly to investigate the desires, fears, passions and opinions of the human being, and to discover from thence what means an able legislator can employ to connect the private happiness of each individual with the observance of those laws which secure the well being of the whole.[76]

In one stroke Gibbon rejected one system of morals underlying the law and offered another system—utilitarianism. Bentham, too, had raised the principle of utility to the center of attention in defining the ends of law. Although Bentham

75. Bentham, *The Principles of Morals and Legislation*, p. 4.
76. Holdsworth, "Gibbon, Blackstone, and Bentham," 52 Law Quarterly Review 46, 50 (1936).

wanted to rest jurisprudence upon science, he nevertheless made the art of legislation part of that science, thus indicating that jurisprudence is also concerned with what the law "ought to be."

John Stuart Mill said about Bentham that he "expelled mysticism from the philosophy of law, and set the example of viewing laws in a practical light, as means to certain definite and precise ends."[77] But "ends" have to do with values, and these are not capable of the kind of proof the scientist looks for, not even when based upon the principle of "utility." Bentham was aware of this for he wrote:

> Is it [the principle of utility] susceptible of any proof? it should seem not: for that which is used to prove everything else, cannot itself be proved: a chain of proofs must have their commencement somewhere. To give such proof is as impossible as it is needless.[78]

Yet he clearly specified the principle of utility, the idea of the greatest good of the greatest number, as the measure for the ends of law: "The common end of all laws as prescribed by the principle of utility is the promotion of the public good."[79] This could be looked at from the reverse side too, that is, looking not only at the common good, but also listing the offenses which subvert the common good: "By classing offenses . . . according to their mischief, laws have already been classed according to their ends: so that in giving an analysis of offenses, we have given, as far as it has gone, an analysis of legal ends."[80]

Bentham has, then, pursued the matter of ends far more extensively than those positivists who suggest that we can

77. *Id.* at 51.
78. Bentham, *The Principles of Morals and Legislation*, p. 4; cf. Bentham, *Limits of Jurisprudence Defined*, 115–116.
79. Bentham, *Limits of Jurisprudence Defined*, p. 115.
80. *Ibid.*

agree only upon a few minimum notions about the requirements of society,[81] for Bentham goes far beyond the mere
notion of order for physical security, provision for keeping
promises and contracts, and the security of possessions. For
Bentham, the principle of utility was a radical, creative, and
"dangerous" principle, dangerous precisely because it would
call for vast reform, not only in the laws, but in the actual
behavior of the society.[82]

Thus, Bentham brought into the law the moral principle of behavior, the moral "ought." Since law and morality
were for him concerned with the same conduct, they had to be
based upon the same principle. Since the law was concerned
with the behavior morality labeled as "ought" to be done,
this same principle thereby also determined what the law
ought to be. When jurisprudence studies a system of laws,
according to Bentham's analysis, it is also studying in "that
branch of jurisprudence which contains the art . . . of legislation" what the laws ought to be.[83] Thus what starts in Bentham
as an attempt to separate law and morals ends with a most
intimate, natural law-like identification of law and morals.

This was also the case with Bentham's illustrious prede-
cessor, Hobbes, who when he considered the ends of law,
went far beyond the original empirical analysis of man's nature when he said:

[T]he duty of a sovereign consisteth in the good government of the
people; and although the acts of sovereign power be no injuries to the
subjects who have consented to the same by their implicit wills, yet when
they tend to the hurt of the people in general, they be breaches of the

81. Hart, "Positivism and the Separation of Law and Morals," 71 Harvard
Law Review 621 (1958).
82. Bentham, *The Principles of Morals and Legislation*, xi-xiii.
83. *Works of Jeremy Bentham*, I, 148.

law of nature, and of the divine law; and consequently the contrary acts are duties of sovereigns, and required at their hands to the utmost of their endeavor, by God Almighty, under the pain of eternal death.[84]

Bentham's conception of ends is far more profound than just any ends men might agree upon. He wrote that, "[B]y *end* is here meant not the eventual end, which is a matter of chance, but the intended end, which is a matter of design."[85] This was why Bentham felt that "the limits of the law seem . . . to be capable of being extended a good deal farther than they seem ever to have been extended hitherto."[86] Bentham had in mind here the very kind of case Ames had talked about, namely —the law could compel one to be "the good Samaritan."[87] Whereas Ames concluded that "the law does not compel active benevolence between man and man," Bentham came to quite a different view of the matter, asking, "why should it not be made the duty of every man to save another from mischief?"[88] Then he goes on to indicate the kind of situation the law, following the lead of morality, should incorporate into its "ends":

A woman's head-dress catches fire: water is at hand: a man, instead of assisting to quench the fire, looks on, and laughs at it. A drunken man, falling with his face downward into a puddle, is in danger of suffocation. Lifting his head a little on one side would save him: another man sees this, and lets him lie. A quantity of gunpowder lies scattered about the room: a man is going into it with a lighted candle: another, knowing this, lets him go in without warning. *Who is there that in any of these cases would think punishment misapplied?*[89]

84. Hobbes, *Elements of Law, Natural and Politic*, ed. with preface and critical notes by Ferdinand Tönnies (Cambridge, Eng.: The University Press, 1928) p. 142; cf. pp. 22, 71, 72–73.
85. Bentham, *Limits of Jurisprudence Defined*, p. 113.
86. *Works of Jeremy Bentham*, I, 148.
87. Ames, "Law and Morals," 22 Harvard Law Review 97, 112 (1908).
88. *Works of Jeremy Bentham*, I, 148.
89. *Ibid.* Emphasis added.

Thus, whereas Kelsen, limiting himself strictly to a description of the ends of law, can only say that the end of law is to bring about certain reciprocal behavior of human beings, "to make them refrain from certain acts which, *for some reason*, are deemed detrimental to society, and to make them perform others which, *for some reason*, are considered useful to society,"[90] the natural law theory always implies that this phrase, "for some reason," can be drawn from the nature of man, and in this respect Bentham followed the pattern of natural law.

Similarly, Austin was bound to consider the ends of law, for although he defined law as an aggregate of commands he was also aware of the fact that "commands . . . proceed not from abstractions, but from living and rational beings."[91] As such, those who set the commands were bound to consider the proper ends which human beings should pursue in their behavior.

Austin emphasized at this point, the close relation between the law of God and the positive law. While he never confused the two, he did argue that the positive law must be fashioned in accordance with the law of God. The law of God, he said, could be known in one of two ways: by direct revelation or through the "index" of utility. Since God intends the well-being of all his creatures, it is possible to determine the goodness or the rightness of a law by simply applying the test of utility: does the law increase the happiness or the good of the society?

The ends of the law are therefore to be derived from the nature of man as understood in a theological sense. Comment-

90. *General Theory*, p. 15. Emphasis added.
91. *Province*, p. 43.

ing on the careful analysis he had made of the principle of utility in the previous three chapters, he goes on to say:

I made this explanation at a length which may seem disproportionate, but which I deemed necessary because these laws [of God], and the index by which they are known, are the standard or measure to which all other laws should conform, and the standard measure or test by which they should be tried.[92]

To be sure, although the sovereign "ought" to shape his commands with these laws of God in mind, it is nevertheless the sovereign who issues the command, and his command is not identical with the law of God but is at most a "copy . . . of the [divine] model."[93]

But the importance of this passage is that Austin conceived of law as springing from something essential in the nature of all men and all societies, as if to say that the basis of law, and therefore ultimately the basis of obedience, is not simply the fact of command but rather the universal perception by men of the utility of government. But by this he also meant that there are certain ends which the law must seek—ends which the very notion of law entails.[94]

92. *Id.* at 131.
93. *Id.* at 163.
94. *Id.* at 301.

4

INTERNATIONAL LAW

The Testing Ground of Theory

W E have considered in the preceding chapters the theories which focus in turn upon the court, economic relations, and the sovereign as the essential element in the phenomenon of law. There, it was our conclusion that these three elements could not give us an adequate conception of law, for in no case did they account for the "rule of law," or for the basis of obligation to law. It appeared that to be concerned chiefly with the court, economic relations, or the sovereign was in a sense to suffer from an optical illusion, for the essence of law is to be found in none of these, even though each plays a significant role in the law. When these elements are employed in the theories of international law, their inability to account for the nature of law is even more dramatic. If these theories say respectively that law is what the courts do, or what is willed by the economically dominant class, or what the sovereign commands, then we are driven to the conclusion that there can be no international law. For the World Court has no automatic jurisdiction and nations are not bound to submit their cases to it, and even if they do they are not bound by its decisions. If, on the other hand, law is defined as the will of the economically dominant class, there can be no international law, for there is no economic class which has the same characteristics in all nations; on this definition, for example, the will of the capitalist class must be at variance with the will of the proletariat, in which case there can be no international law since there is no homogeneous economic class in the international community. Also, if law is defined as the command of the sovereign, then the conclusion must again be that there can be no international law for there is no international sovereign legislator, only independent sovereign nations.

It appears impossible to achieve a coherent conception of law in terms of these three dominant explanations of law. We need to examine these theories afresh to determine whether they are adequate to deal with the relation of law and morality and with the urgent problems of achieving the rule of law in the world of nations.

International Law and the Judicial Process

The theory which holds that the law is "what the courts do" is seriously misleading when we consider it in the light of the status and work of the international court. What strikes one first is that such a theory could only have been developed, as it was by Holmes and Gray and earlier by Bishop Hoadley, in a highly developed society with a settled judiciary. The theory pays little or no attention to the manner in which the court itself receives its powers and jurisdiction.

A brief glance at the status of the World Court, however, quickly indicates that the court itself must be brought into existence by international law and must look to specifically designated "sources" for the "law" which it will apply. Thus, before the court utters a word, the channels within which its reasoning will move have been, to a large extent, set for it. This comes about by the fact that the statute which has brought the present court into being specifies how the judges will be selected, what classification of cases will be heard, and how many judges will sit in each class of cases.

Representation on this court is limited to those nations which are members of the United Nations and are duly elected by particular nations, forming a list of nominees from which the Security Council and the General Assembly each separately choose fifteen judges; any person on this list who is chosen by a majority of both bodies is elected. There are additional detailed provisions for this procedure of election and tenure, but the significant point is that every attempt is made to create an independent judicial body and to reduce as much as possible the political, compared with the judicial or legal, complexion of the court.

Although it is not possible to eliminate all such political elements from the creation and operation of the court, by and large the court has been designed to reflect and make its decisions in terms of international law. But the existence of this court has not resulted in the court's being the center of the operation of international law. The court appears to be powerless unless the parties to a dispute are willing to submit their controversies to it and are further willing to be bound by its decisions.

Quincy Wright has made the telling point that

the new international law implies an acceptance by all states of the duty to submit to judicial procedure for the interpretation of their legal obligations and the opportunity to invoke adequate procedures for assuring obedience to the judgment. Such a development is envisaged by the court statute, the charter provisions, and the resolutions of the General Assembly, but insofar as states have not accepted the court's jurisdiction, the charter leaves the matter to diplomacy unless peace is threatened, in which case the Security Council or the General Assembly may make recommendations.[1]

This precarious status of the court, its indecisive position in the community of nations is taken by many to prove that there is today no international law. Our only concern here is to argue that the theory which holds that the law is what the courts do does not give us a fruitful insight into the meaning of law. Such a theory become plausible only after a judiciary has been firmly established, but even so it only *appears* that the law is what the courts say.

The most significant thing about the present status of the international court is that it reveals how a court comes into being and how it becomes related to the law. What we are observing today in the development of the international court is that the court can have no power or jurisdiction until the nations of the world are fully satisfied that it will not be the case that the law is "what the court does."

It is precisely the suspicion in many quarters that the court may decide cases either in political terms or according to the subjective opinions of the judges that has hindered the development of international law. The deep conviction which lies behind this suspicion is that the function of a court must be to administer the law—the court must not be the creator

1. Quincy Wright, *Contemporary International Law: A Balance Sheet* (Garden City, N.Y.: Doubleday, 1955), pp. 50–51.

of the law and thereby usurp the role of the legislature, an argument heard frequently today, even concerning national courts.[2] This is to say that the nations of the world rightly refuse to accept the notion that law is simply what the courts do, "and nothing more pretentious."

Although the community of nations has no clearly defined concept of international law, it is agreed that there is more to law than simply what the court says. To be sure, the refusal of most states to submit their controversies to the court is not always or only based upon this quest for the true law; it is often rather their stubborn refusal to give up certain interests or advantages.

It is not enough simply to have a court, even one which has a very determinate structure, in order to have law. The United States Supreme Court is effective, not only because of the rules of its organization, but particularly because it has

2. According to Hersh Lauterpacht:
Judicial caution is an attitude of mind resulting . . . from the fact that courts have to *apply* the law and that they have to apply the *law in force*. They have to apply—and no more than that—the law. It is not within their province to speculate on the law or to explore the possibilities of its development. . . . It is not their function deliberately to change the law so as to make it conform with their own views of justice and expediency. This does not mean that they do not in fact shape or even alter the law. But they do it without admitting it. . . . The same considerations apply to the administration of international justice. Moreover, there exist in this sphere additional reasons for the exercise of restraint. These include, in the first instance, the importance of the subject-matter on which the courts have to decide. They cannot experiment or innovate as easily in matters in which States have an interest. . . . [Also there is] the fact of the voluntary nature of the jurisdiction of international tribunals. An international court which yields conspicuously to the urge to modify the existing law—even if such action can be brought within the four corners of a major legal principle—may bring about a drastic curtailment of its activity. Government may refuse to submit disputes to it or to renew obligations of compulsory judicial settlement already in existence.
The Development of International Law by the International Court, rev. ed. of *International Law by the Permanent Court of International Justice* (1934) (London: Stevens, 1958), 75–78.

available in addition a fairly definite guide to the legal terrain, a creative articulation of the fundamental law of the land, the Constitution. There is as yet nothing comparable to the Constitution in international law.

Moreover, the formulation of an effective constitution or basic instrument of law must be more than the pronouncement of an effective sovereign. The weakness of international law is not due solely to the absence of a superior coercive force, for the emergence of law is neither the activity of the courts nor the will of powerful entities. We are again faced with the problem of discovering how the nations of the world can agree to be bound responsibly to certain rules of behavior. The court must not expect to have its jurisdiction established simply through the development of some superior force to administer sanctions and thereby enforce the law. The problem is one which is not related solely to power.

Indeed, the whole concept of power as the basis of law in the international field becomes even more untenable when one considers what such a force would have to be concretely to deal effectively with our largest and most powerful nations; the use of force here would result in nothing less than war, which would be precisely the condition the law is trying to alleviate. But besides this consequence, the concept of power is incapable of solving the problem of the grounds of obligation. Thus the reason that the court is ineffective is not that it does not have the backing of sanctioning power but that there is no sufficient agreement among the nations upon the rules to which they should be bound.

The problem of obligation in international law is fundamentally a moral one, because it is impossible to separate the question of obligation in law from the question of obligation in general. De Visscher has argued that "the distinction of the ethical and juridicial categories . . . ought not to be pushed to the point that the law is isolated from the primary notions of morality to which are connected, as to their common stem, all the normative disciplines."[3]

Between nations, argues De Visscher, as in the case of a single nation, the law derives from morality to the extent that the idea of the "just," which forms the specific content of the law, is inseparable from the idea of the "good," which is a moral idea. What, he asks, does it take in the international milieu, with its order of facts, interests and ideas and sentiments—to furnish the moral substratum of obligation? "No society can have a juridical foundation without the belief among its members in its necessity. The final explanation for a society as for law is found beyond society: it is found in individual consciences."[4]

This former judge of the World Court thus takes the position that to look for the law in the work of the court is to look in the wrong place; the matrix of law, whether in the municipal or in the international sphere, he argues, is the moral capacity of man, not the mechanical structure of the state or the court. The court becomes a vital institution only after the moral sentiment of men has been sufficiently crystallized to articulate general principles by which men are willing to be bound in their conduct and which they propose as the rules of others' conduct as well. The court cannot come into being without this broad conviction in the international community that there are certain principles of right by which controversies are to be considered and judged.

---

3. See Charles de Visscher, *Theories et Realities en Droit International Public* (Éditions A. Pedone; Paris: Libraire de la Cour d'Appel et de l'Ordre des Avocats, 1953), pp. 126–127.

4. *Ibid.*

And even where a court is established, as is the case with the World Court, by common agreement, it does not possess the power to proceed without some specification of the rules it will enforce and which will govern its judicial reasoning. Thus, although the court renders a final decision, this decision is not the "source" of the law. The sources to which the court must turn are expressly listed in the Statute of the Court, and even though the court, in its process of adjudicating and reasoning finds it necessary to expand, embellish and interpret these sources, they are nevertheless the true sources of the law in the field of international law. And a careful examination of the four sources designated by Paragraph 38 of the Statute indicates that to a very great extent these sources are moral in nature—the positive morality Austin spoke of.

Sources of Law

Article 38 of the Statute of the International Court of Justice lays out the following law-creating processes of which the court may avail itself; this statute therefore determines authoritatively the sources of law which the court is required to consult, namely:

(1) International conventions, whether general or particular, establishing rules expressly recognized by the contesting states;
(2) International custom, as evidence of a general practice accepted as law;
(3) The general principles of law recognized by civilized nations;
(4) Subject to the provisions of Article 59 (which provides that "the decision of the Court has no binding force except between the parties and in respect of that particular case") judicial decisions and the teachings of the most highly qualified publicists of the various nations, as subsidiary means for the determination of rules of law.[5]

5. These are set forth in *Statute of the International Court of Justice*, art. 38.

Treaties as a Source of Law

To understand the manner in which treaties produce law, it is important to recall Salmond's comment on conventional agreements when he wrote that "agreement is a law for those who make it, which supersedes, supplements, or derogates from the ordinary law of the land. *Modus et conventio vincunt legem.*"[6] In the sphere of international law, this general rule means that there is almost complete freedom of contract. A treaty is an agreement between two or more nations in which they stipulate which rules they will be bound by and which rules they will not be subject to. Such an agreement is in most cases entered into for the purposes of achieving a specific objective. For this reason treaties represent the formulation of a principle of general law. Moreover, there is some question whether treaties actually create new law, for in most cases the point of the agreement is to create an obligation which would not have existed by the general law or to make ineffective some existing rule which would not have otherwise applied.[7]

There is, however, a class of treaties which can be considered a major source of law, and these are the treaties which are entered into by a substantial number of nations and whose purpose it is to declare what their understanding of the law on a particular problem is or ought to be. Their purpose may also be to lay down a general rule for future conduct or the creation of some new institution. These treaties turn out to be the closest approximations of international legislation and are frequently referred to as "lawmaking" treaties.

6. J. W. Salmond, *Jurisprudence* (10th ed.; London: Sweet and Maxwell, 1947) p. 89.
7. James Leslie Brierly, *The Law of Nations: An Introduction to the International Law of Peace* (5th ed.; Oxford: Clarendon Press, 1955), p. 59.

It must be borne in mind, however, that these lawmaking treaties are limited to those nations which participate in their creation and are not binding upon those who are not parties to them.[8] This means, again, that such treaties are not the source of a general law. Nevertheless, because they are the closest substitute there is to legislation, they do represent an important source of law. That this results in conventional law is also true, for it is the product of an agreement. But to call it conventional law does not necessarily mean that it is not law, as Austin's use of the phrase implied. Nor does the conventional character of treaty law mean that nations can agree to do just about anything they want, as though the word "conventional" is construed to mean that agreements between nations are not subject to moral rules. A first requisite of a treaty is that it must contemplate a purpose which is "legal," that is, a purpose which is defensible in the councils of the international community.

This source of law leaves the least amount of room for the court's independent reasoning in a case involving a treaty, for the treaty, not the court's decision, is the source of the law.

Custom as a Source of Law

It is not entirely clear how, why, or when a custom becomes law. The transition from custom to law is a difficult process to describe, for, as Fischer Williams has said, "The Rubicon which divides custom from law is crossed silently, unconsciously, and without proclamation."[9]

8. Note that the United Nations Charter binds nations which are not parties to it, "so far as may be necessary for the maintenance of international peace and security." U. N. Charter, art. 2, para. 6.
9. John Fischer Williams, *Aspects of Modern International Law*, (Oxford, Eng.: Oxford University Press, 1939), p. 44.

There are two considerations which the court weighs heavily in looking for customary law: that the rule has been actually used by nations to govern their conduct and that in using these rules the nations have consented to their legal character. That is, a customary law is a rule which is recognized as binding and which results in some form of sanction if it is violated.

In this way, a customary *rule* of behavior is to be differentiated from a *habit* of behavior. It is extremely difficult for the Court to find adequate evidence of a customary law, particularly if it must determine whether a nation has *consented* to the legal nature of the rule. The strict positivist holds that a customary rule is not a law unless there is explicit consent to its obligatory force. But in a famous case the court held that

international law is for the most part uncertain and lacks sanctions. It rests on a general consensus of opinion, on the acceptance by civilized states, members of the great community of nations, of rules, customs and existing conditions, which they are bound to respect in their mutual relations although neither committed to writing nor confirmed by conventions. This body of rules is called international law.[10]

That custom should be a source of law which the court must consider can be explained only on the assumption that the rules of conduct which custom creates are more in accord with the moral sentiments of mankind than rules which are simply the edict of a sovereign. If the element which differentiates custom from habit is the conscious recognition that the custom has obligatory force, then a custom is transformed into a law by the rational process which ascribes to certain rules of behavior the attribute of "right" or "just." Hence,

10. Case of the Steamship "Lotus," Permanent Court of International Justice, series A, No. 10 (1927) (dissenting opinion).

only those patterns of behavior which possess this moral stamp have the character of law.

There are, of course, customs which are morally reprehensible and whose effect is to destroy human freedom, integrity, and self-respect. It could not, therefore, be argued, without serious qualification, that a custom becomes law because of its moral content. Nevertheless, when a mode of behavior represents more than just a habitual way of action—when, that is, people consent to be bound by a rule and give it the force of law—then such a custom springs from the moral consensus of the community.

A customary rule which becomes law is not an eternal or perfect rule, but it frequently exhausts the powers of rational discernment of right for the time being. Until some higher perspective is reached, this rule may very well be the fullest expression of right and justice available. The court has thus available a source of law which lies as close as is possible to those who will be bound by it. When this customary law is ambiguous, a larger scope for judicial discretion and interpretation opens up, where the judges take the fragmentary tissues of the custom and weave them into a whole concept. Judge Altamire pointed out this aspect of the judicial process when he wrote in the *Lotus* case that often in this process

there are moments in time in which the rule implicitly discernible has not as yet taken shape in the eyes of the world, but which is so forcibly suggested by precedent that it would be rendering good service to the cause of justice and law to assist its appearance in the form in which it will have all the force rightly belonging to rules of positive law.[11]

In this process, the court participates with the community in the law-creating process, being led by the consensus of the

11. *Ibid.*

community. The court is surely engaging in a creative process here, but the true source of the law is found, not in the court, but in the moral sentiments of the community.[12]

General Principles of Law

Nowhere is the creative function of the court made more possible than in the authorization to employ the general principles of law in arriving at its decisions. The only qualification made by Article 38 is that the court must use only those principles of law which are "recognized by civilized nations." Since it is chiefly civilized nations that have achieved the stage of articulated principles of law, there is nothing particularly restrictive about this provision of the Statute.[13] It does, however, raise difficulties in the modern world, which has seen the inclusion of nations of various levels of development into the community of nations.

It is sometimes the case that the principles of law prevailing among the majority of civilized nations is invoked, even though one of the parties to a dispute may not have heard of it. Although it was not in the strict sense the decision of an international arbitrator, Lord Asquith highlighted this issue in his award in the Arbitration between *Petroleum Development . . . Ltd.* and the *Sheikh of Abu Dhabi* (1951). In

12. According to Fischer Williams:
A court of international law is not entitled to lay down as new law what it conceives to be morally right or what might in its view properly or conveniently be made law. Such a court is, however, bound not merely to apply existing treaties, and respect such obligations as states have in terms or by custom accepted, but also—and this function is of great importance in international matters—to intercept what may be called the general sense of civilized humanity, and to declare that to be law which after an objective consideration of all the necessary evidence it esteems that the legal conscience of the contemporary world . . . has already, tacitly or expressly, accepted as law, binding states and men."
Williams, pp. 61–62.
13. 1 International and Comparative Law Quarterly, 250–251 (1952).

determining the proper law of a concession contract, the arbitrator ruled out the law of Abu Dhabi on the following ground:

This is a contract made in Abu Dhabi and wholly to be performed in that country. If any municipal system of law were applicable, it would *prima facie* be that of Abu Dhabi. But no such law can reasonably be said to exist. The Sheikh administers a purely discretionary justice with the assistance of the Koran; and it would be fanciful to suggest that in this very primitive region there is any settled body of legal principles applicable to the construction of modern commercial instruments.

The Arbitrator, relying on the terms of the contract, also ruled out any other system of municipal law as proper law and found that the contract prescribed the "application of principles rooted in good sense and common practice of the generality of civilized nations—a sort of 'law of nature.' "[14]

But it is not clear just how this provision of the Article 38, that the court should apply "general principles of law," is to be understood. Some jurists suppose that these general principles are to be drawn from some ideal view of obligation, while others hold that it is the actual principles in use in living systems of law to which reference is here made, such as that promises should be kept, or *res judicata*. Whether Article 38 refers to some form of natural law or to the principles of actual systems of law makes little difference, for the full force of this provision is to reject the positivistic notion that only statute law is law. At the same time, this does not mean that the judge is hereby set free to develop *his* principles of law; these principles are drawn from the fund of juristic wisdom which represents the fusion of long practical experience and intellectual reflection.

Early writers on international law were in the habit of

14. *Ibid.*

drawing on the Roman law, and this process continues and is justified on the grounds that principles which are found to be generally accepted by civilized legal systems can well be assumed to be so reasonable that they can be relied upon to maintain justice in any system.[15] And it is inevitable that the court should find it necessary to turn to such principles in the course of its work; otherwise, it would have to say, in those controversies where there is no specific statute or "law" that the issue "is not clear," that there is no way of resolving the case. In a decision rendered by a tribunal which was set up by an agreement between the United States and Great Britain, the status of general principles was referred to in this manner:

> Even assuming that there was . . . no specific rule of international law formulated as the expression of a universally recognized rule governing the case . . . , it cannot be said that there is no principle of international law applicable. International law, as well as domestic law, may not contain, and generally does not contain, express rules decisive of particular cases; but the function of jurisprudence is to resolve the conflict of opposing rights and interests in applying, in default of any specific provision of law, the corollaries of general principles, and so to find . . . the solution of the problem. This is the method of jurisprudence; it is the method by which the law has been gradually evolved in every country resulting in the definition and settlement of legal relations as well between states as between private individuals.[16]

When we look back upon the activities of the court, then, we find that only in a very narrow sense can it be said that

---

15. Admitting that the judge must at times have recourse to general principle, Lauterpacht adds, "This is far from signifying that wherever the Court has had recourse to general principles of law its action amounted to judicial legislation. On the contrary, normally it has constituted no more than an interpretation of existing conventional law by reference to common sense and the canons of good faith." Lauterpacht, p. 166.

16. Eastern Extension, Australasia and China Telegraph Co. (Great Britain v. United States), American and British Claims Arbitration, Nielsen's Report 73, 75, quoted in Brierly, *The Law of Nations*, 67–68.

international law is "what the court does." If any single and distinctive contribution of the Court emerges from an analysis, besides applying the settled law, it is that the Court is the channel and the instrument by which morals (not the judges' but the community's) enter the law. As Judge Lauterpacht has pointed out,

> courts as distinguished from formal legislation—have been mainly responsible for the infusion of morals into law. While in the international sphere judicial empiricism must . . . proceed with great caution, this aspect of the contribution of the Court provides one of the not least significant features of its activity.[17]

Soviet Conceptions of International Law

From the earliest days of the Soviet state, the question of international law loomed as an urgent yet difficult problem. How should the Soviet state relate itself to the other nations of the world? Were there any rules which it could recognize as binding upon its conduct in the international sphere, and did such rules have the character of law? To these questions, the Soviet jurists brought their standard Marxist doctrines in an attempt to formulate a theory of international law. The story of this attempt by the Soviet jurists to develop a theory of international law on the basis of Marxist concept of law is a highly illuminating account not only of the failure of this attempt; even more important is the light which this failure throws upon the question of the true nature of law. The way in which the Soviet experience helps to clarify the nature of law can be indicated by an analysis of the three most important stages in the Soviet conception of international law.

17. Lauterpacht, p. 172.

The Theoretical Marxist Stage

The first attempt of the Soviet jurists to formulate a theory of international law was a failure because the Marxist principles from which they started did not fit the facts of international relations. Marxist theory had said that law is the will of the economically dominant class, that it was a weapon of domination, that it was the product of a state, and that it was the ideological superstructure of a particular arrangement of the factors of economic production. But not one of these elements was present in the international scene.

At the very beginning, at least, the revolution was supposed to have destroyed the state—without a state there could be no law, and without a superstate over all the nations, there could surely be no international law. Moreover, the nations of the world were not related in the same way as classes are within a state. Without classes or a dominant class, there could be neither the occasion nor the basis of law, for there would be no "will of the economically dominant class." Hence the conclusion again had to be drawn that there was no international law.

Also, there was no uniform mode of production and distribution, that is, no uniform economic structure throughout the world. There were instead many different modes of production, and at least the Soviet nation with its type of socialism was sharply different from the capitalistic economies with which it had to deal. But without such a uniform economic structure of which the law is supposed to be a reflection there could not be any single system of law. There would have to be as many legal systems as there are economic orders which produce them. Again, therefore, the conclusion had to be that there is no international law deriving from and binding upon all nations.

Even more destructive of the Marxist theory was the

fact that insofar as international law was effective in the world, its function was just the opposite of what Marxist theory said it was. This theory holds that the function of law is to dominate—law is a weapon for domination. But the facts indicated that international law was a system of rules by which sovereign and equal nations were attempting to remain sovereign and equal. The law sought to protect rather than dominate, and to the extent that Soviet Russia was willing to be bound by international law, she did so as a sovereign through which doctrine she sought the protection of her rights, sovereignty and independence.

With these facts it was impossible to make the Marxist theory of domination by law stand. And when the further fact was added that there was no international organization of force whose very expression is the essence of law, the Marxist theory ended in total bankruptcy, for as Pashukanis wrote, "if we take the proposition of Lenin, 'Law is nothing without a mechanism capable of compelling the observance of legal norms,' international law must then be regarded as nothing. . . ."[18]

If this breakdown in the Soviet theory of international law seems to be only a *logical* difficulty, it must be remembered that the Soviet jurists as well as the leaders of the nation had tried to fashion from the beginning the closest bond between Marxist theory and Soviet practice. It was not the critics of the Soviet jurists but the jurists themselves who pointed up the problems of logical contradiction, for the logical extension of Marxian principles was held to be the surest way of making the revolution succeed. Pashukanis had argued that "bolshevism requires unswerving logic in politi-

18. E. B. Pashukanis, "The Soviet State and the Revolution in Law," in *Soviet Legal Philosophy*, trans. by Hugh W. Babb, introd. by John N. Hazard (Cambridge: Harvard University Press, 1951), p. 244.

cal ideas," and that "everything that works to the detriment of logic causes detriment thereby to the cause of the proletarian revolution and must be pitilessly anatomized and swept away."[19] And it was Mirkine-Guetzevitch who pointed out that "a state involved itself in contradiction if it claimed to be recognized as a state, but interpreted itself as a class organization engaged in a life-and-death struggle with the class organizations constituted by the other states."[20]

The only way out of this contradiction is either to change the theory or to take it literally and follow its logic wherever it leads, and in the first phase the Soviet jurists drew the obvious conclusion that "from the point of view of Marxian definition of the law, so-called international law is no law at all."[21]

Behind this strictly logical difficulty there is, however, a far deeper problem, for Soviet thought represents a fundamental break in the continuity of the kind of European thought which produced the broad principles upon which the classical theories of international law had been built. Although these classical theories have been discredited for the most part by the Western powers themselves, the latter nevertheless possess a common fund of ideas and ideals from which militant Marxism represents a sharp and abrupt deviation.

This means that by its own design Soviet thought declares itself alien to this common fund of Western ideas which gives rise to, and even now to a great extent sustains, the

19. *Id.* at 242.
20. Quoted in Rudolf Schlesinger, "Recent Developments in Soviet Legal Theory," 6 The Modern Law Review 21, at 34 n. 49 (1942).
21. Hans Kelsen, *The Communist Theory of Law* (New York: Frederick A. Praeger, Inc., 1955), p. 150. See also Stoyanovich, "The Reality of International Law," Journal du Droit International 39 (1959).

structure of international order. It is for this deeper ideological, and not only logical, reason, that Soviet jurists in this first state denied the existence of international law. They wished to say that they did not recognize as in any way binding upon them those rules of behavior for states which were simply the expression of bourgeois social ideas.

The inevitable involvement of the Soviet Union in the affairs of nations, stemming most immediately from the need for economic relations with capitalist states, forced a more realistic attitude toward international law to be developed. The attempt to apply the Marxist view of law in this sphere had failed. That it had failed surely indicated that the attempt to define the nature of law in terms of economic class conflict had also failed. Instead of holding to "unswerving logic," the Soviet jurists began to reconstruct their theory of law.

The Realist Stage: the Doctrine of Sovereignty and the Use of Treaties

The new and realistic attitude is best expressed in the candid works of Korovin who made the obvious point that "it is impossible to reject international law simply by denying its existence and to dispatch the entire set of international legal norms of the present time (1924) as a bourgeois remainder by a stroke of the pen."[22] Korovin helped shift Soviet theory from its earlier preoccupation with Marxist principles to the classical doctrine of state sovereignty as a basis of international law.

This was a big step, for it moved Soviet theory from the

22. Yevgeni A. Korovin, "Mezhdunarodnoe Pravo Perekhodnogo Vremeni" (International Law of the Transitional Period) 2 (1924), quoted in Kelsen, p. 156.

position of denying the existence of international law to the position wherein such law was recognized. But Korovin did not admit that there was an international law "above" all the nations and especially not above the legal systems of each nation. The most his new theory would concede was that there could be rules governing the conduct of nations toward one another but that these rules were the product of the sovereign nations concerned.

Korovin had actually injected into Soviet theory the notion of sovereignty as developed by such writers as Jellinek, who held that a state binds itself to international law because, as he said, a state had the power to determine exclusively by its own will the legal relations under which it will live. In this manner, a state is not submitting to some objective law which hovers "over" the nation; it simply extends its internal legal system to include those rules by which it has agreed to be bound in relation to other nations.

The effect of this shift in theory was to say that law is the product of agreement between sovereigns as expressed in international treaties. This is a long way from the older concept of the economic matrix of law. Of course, this reconception of law in terms of the doctrine of sovereignty and treaty agreements may have been chiefly a "practical" concession to the requirements of coexistence with capitalistic nations. Much has been made of the fact that "the absolute dependence of Soviet theory on the practice of the Soviet State is a well-known fact."[23] It is held, too, that the Soviet jurists fastened upon the doctrine of sovereignty only when

---

23. Jan F. Triska and Robert M. Slusser, "Treaties and other Sources of Order in International Relations: The Soviet View," 52 The American Journal of International Law, 721 (1958).

they realized that this doctrine could, more than any other, be used in their own and best interests. This point is quite clear, for the doctrine of sovereignty is well suited to making a nation independent and inaccessible to foreign ideas and laws.

But the Soviet jurists attempted at this stage, too, to retain the earlier distinction between the "material" and the "formal" sources of law. If it was no longer possible to argue the Marxist theory literally, it could nevertheless be held that the "real foundations" of law among nations must be found in the facts of "struggle, coexistence and competition."[24] The formal rules of international law merely reflect struggle, coexistence and competition. To explain law in this fashion is to express much more than the former notion that law is the reflex of economic relations, for this new explanation focuses upon the conflict between peoples as the source of law. The attempt to resolve these conflicts leads to the formation of legal rules. International law thus becomes the mechanism by which peoples seek to establish order and harmony rather than an instrument of domination. The treaty is the means by which sovereigns express these rules by which they agree to be bound, and by building upon the doctrine of sovereignty and the practice of treaty agreements the Soviet jurists were able to reconstruct a defensible theory of law. Shurshalov wrote in 1957 that "the international treaty is the fundamental source of international law . . ." and that "contemporary international law is basically treaty law."[25]

At this stage there was still the severe Marxist mistrust, if not outright rejection, of "moral laws and the laws of hu-

24. *Id.* at 724–725.
25. *Id.* at 717–718.

man conscience"[26] as the source of law or of international obligation. Moral laws, said Troianovski, were too subtle and lacked precision and could therefore not be taken seriously as a basis for international order. What was needed was "something more positive, more concrete and more definitive," and this could be found in "very precise international theories duly signed" and based on "exact formulas and determined obligations."[27]

This is, of course, a repetition of legal positivism which limits legal obligation to specific positive enactments. It says that there is law only when sovereigns say there is and that law is what they say it is. Thus, the spirit of realism had led the Soviet jurists to acknowledge the need for coexistence and therefore the need for a workable theory of international law. They accepted the classical theory of sovereignty and in general adopted the positivistic concept of law which ruled out the notion of moral obligation as the basis of law and limited the source of law to the formal technique of treaty agreements.

The Soviet jurists, however, put two serious qualifications upon the doctrine of sovereignty and the use of treaties. They maintained first of all that not every nation should enjoy unlimited sovereignty but that this should be limited to "peace-loving" nations. Secondly, the Soviet jurists would not admit that any and every treaty was a "valid" one. Sovereign power and treaties, they held, could be and have been used as the instruments of imperialism. Both sovereignty and treaties must therefore be used in such a way as not to "conflict with the basic principles of international law."

26. Address of Aleksandr A. Troianovski, 1934 Proceedings, American Society of International Law 195, at 196 (1934).
27. Korovin, pp. 25–26; quoted in Triska and Slusser, p. 702.

"Basic principles" play no significant role in the positiv-istic theory of law which envisages only positive enactments or agreements. But this reference to "basic principles" by the Soviet jurists, whatever their reasons may have been, has had the effect of injecting a new conception of law into their theory. To require that treaties be in accord with "princi-ples" must mean that law in the international sphere is more than just an agreement between nations; it suggests that such agreements must concern morally defensible ends.

We are led, then, to the third stage in Soviet theory of international law which might be called the "idealist" stage.

The Idealist Stage

It would be incorrect to suggest that there is a clear pro-gression from the theoretical Marxist, to the realistic, then to the idealistic stages of Soviet legal theory. All three of these elements are actually present in the Soviet juristic thought of today. Our only concern is to indicate that the first two stages revealed severe limitations to these jurists as they at-tempted to build a theory of international law. It is signifi-cant that in spite of the clear rejection of any universal moral norms the Soviet jurists do engage in the moral criticism of the acts of sovereign nations and of treaties.

Korovin had expressed this rejection of morality as a source of law in clear and forceful terms when he argued that *"the theory of natural law* merits rejection not only for reasons associated with its origins but chiefly because from the Marxist standpoint it is inconceivable to speak of any ideal law common to all mankind which stands above classes." In the same vein, he said that "we must equally reject the arguments of *the idealistic school.* Neither the moral nature of man as an individual (an ethical variant) nor his intuitive experiences (the psychological variant) can be considered as sources of any law whatsoever and much less a source of international law." He concluded that *"the historical school is the most instrumental where the problem of the source of law is adequately formed; it reasons not with reference to a 'national spirit' of types and nations but uses materials of collective (mass) psychology."*[28]

Despite this forceful rejection of natural law and the idealistic view of law, the Soviet jurists do engage in the moral criticism of treaties and sovereign acts and raise considerations that are clearly moral in deciding by what rules they will be bound. About this curious ambivalence De Visscher writes that

having pushed relativism to the point of at least theoretically denying any moral absolutes, they are visibly embarrassed when they have to define the criteria by which Soviet international law separates norms which, despite their bourgeois origin, it can regard as sufficiently progressive for adoption, from those to which it attributes an imperialist character and which it therefore holds inacceptable.[29]

It may be that the Soviet jurists are not at all "embarrassed" but turn to moral principles when it becomes helpful. They have even been willing to see in custom a helpful source of law: "Regardless of the uncertainty, instability and relativity of international custom," wrote Koshevnikov, "it would be incorrect to underestimate, let alone to ignore, this significance as a source of law for international relations." Again, this could have been argued chiefly because of the advantage acquired from such a view, or as Pashukanis asked, "Why should the Soviet government be deprived of those rights which re-

28. Triska and Slusser, p. 702.
29. De Visscher, p. 162.

quire no treaty formulation and derive from the very fact that normal diplomatic relations exist?"[30]

We are not concerned with emphasizing the political aspect of this problem, although it admittedly permeates Soviet juristic thought. Important here is that it became necessary, once Soviet thought recognized the existence of international law, to provide an adequate basis for the validity and the binding force of international law. This basis could not be supplied effectively, either by Marxist principles or by the positivistic concept of sovereignty. In spite of its moral relativism, Soviet thought turned to the sphere of morals for the "deeper" sources of law.

In addition to treaties, custom was thus recognized as a source, and even more emphasis was placed upon certain "general principles." These principles were the criteria for testing the "justice" of acts and treaties. Shurshalov defined these principles as follows: universal peace and the security of nations; respect for the sovereignty and territorial integrity of nations which are members of the international community; noninterference in the internal affairs of states; equality and mutual benefit as between nations; and the rigorous fulfillment of obligations assumed under treaties— *pacta sunt servanda*. Any treaty which proves to be incompatible with these principles, Shurshalov argues, is not valid.[31]

This means that although treaties are still regarded as the fundamental source of precise obligations, the making of the treaty, and therefore the making of a law, transpires under the influence of the above mentioned principles. To the extent that these principles seek ostensibly to channel the

30. Triska and Slusser, pp. 720–721.
31. *Id.* at 717–718.

conduct of nations along lines which are moral in character it could be said that Soviet theory on international law has moved to a moral instead of a severely positivistic basis. Even if we were to allow for the political motives which lie behind much of the Soviet legal theory the point remains that insofar as a theory of law needs to be developed, such a theory cannot be developed without explicit recognition of the moral basis of obligation. Only a theory which is not followed logically nor employed in actual practice can separate the concerns of law and morals.

The Idea of Sovereignty and International Law

The most formidable impediment to the realization of the rule of international law today is the doctrine of national sovereignty. In its simplest form, this doctrine means that a nation reserves for itself the right to decide what rules shall govern its own behavior. Nations are understandably jealous of the prerogative to govern themselves and it is obvious that if a nation is to govern itself it cannot be subject either to another nation or to a supernation.

The conscious identity of races and peoples and nations is a very powerful fact in social and political life. The sovereign nation is, above all, the institution which today provides men with the strongest sense of belonging to a definite group and geographical location in the world. Modern man's life is profoundly linked to his state in a far more decisive way than to any other institution. Because of the deep historical roots of nations, and because of their influence upon the social, economic, and even psychological security of individuals, nations have developed an extraordinary sense of individualism and independence.

This individualism expresses itself in a peculiarly force-ful way through the notion of sovereignty, for it is in the name of sovereignty that nations resist the application of rules traditionally called international law. Why should the doc-trine of sovereignty have such a destructive effect upon the rule of law among nations? There can be no simple answer to such a difficult question, but to a considerable extent this outcome is the consequence of the conceptual apparatus which supports the doctrine of sovereignty.[32]

The modern theory of sovereignty is largely the product of the imaginative philosophy of Hobbes. Whenever one asks why states are sovereign, some of Hobbes's mythology is in-variably given in the answer. When Hobbes was criticized for resting his argument on a "fiction" of the social contract which had no historical basis to which he could point, he turned triumphantly to the condition in the international community of nations, observed the anarchy, and announced that here was the condition of the state of nature writ large for all to see.

This anarchy between nations is what must have been the condition as between particular individuals before the social contract. Just as individuals lived in a state of "war of

32. Lauterpacht says that there is international law only as there is a decrease of sovereignty, and in particular

the results of the activity of the Court may appear to be to a large extent coextensive with—or expressive of—limitations upon the sovereignty of the states . . . What [this] amounts to is that insofar as the Court declares the the law and insofar as that law implies restraint upon freedom of action, its decisions are liable to be interpreted as being in the nature of a re-straint upon sovereignty. This is perhaps no more than a transposition into the international sphere of what is a general phenomenon in the administration of law—for law, although its ultimate end and effect in a society are the realization of freedom, normally operates in the first in-stance by way of restricting the freedom of action of one of the parties. Lauterpacht, p. 166.

all against all," so nations are in a "perpetual posture of war." And just as each individual possessed the right to determine for himself what line of conduct would secure his survival, so each nation decides what it must do to survive. As each individual possessed a right to any and everything in order to survive, so each nation has such a right to whatever it can get to assure its survival. And just as there is no law, apart from that of survival, binding upon individuals, so there is no law binding upon all nations until they consent to it. If there is such a thing as the "law of nations," this can be no other, says Hobbes, than that law of nature by which each individual and each nation has the right to determine what course of action will lead to its survival. All this Hobbes has said in that classic passage in the *Leviathan* where he writes:

> Kings and Persons of Sovereigne authority, because of their Independency, are in continual jealousies, and in the state and posture of Gladiators: having their weapons pointing and their eyes fixed on one another; that is, their forts, Garrisons, and Guns, upon the Frontiers of their Kingdoms; and continually Spyes upon their neighbours; which is a posture of War. But because they uphold thereby the Industry of their subjects, there does not follow from it, that misery, which accompanies that Liberty of Particular Men. . . . The Law of Nature and the Law of Nations, is the same thing. And every Sovereign hath the same Right, in procuring the Safety of his People, that any particular man can have, in procuring the safety of his own body. . . . [xiv] The natural law may be divided into that of *men* which alone hath obtained the title of the law of *nature*; and that of *cities*, which may be called that of *nations*. The precepts of both are alike. But because cities once instituted do put on the personal proprieties of men, that *law* which speaking of the duty of single men we call natural, being applied to whole cities and nations is called the *right of nations*. And the same elements of *natural law and right* which have hitherto been spoken of, being transferred to whole cities or nations, may be taken for the elements of the *laws and rights of nations*.[33]

33. Hobbes, *Leviathan*, ed. with introd. by Michael Oakeshott (Oxford: B. Blackwell, 1946), chapt. 13.

During the nineteenth century, and to a great extent even today, this picture drawn by Hobbes has been the prevailing view of the sovereign state. If we look behind the doctrine of sovereignty we find nothing more profound than this fundamentally egotistical view of man and nations. The self-interest of individuals and of nations is raised to the rank of the law of nature.

With respect to its own citizens in its own territories, writes Quincy Wright, "sovereignty was omnipotent. . . . The state could treat its nationals unjustly or even barbarously; it could deny them fair trials or execute them without a trial; it could permit discrimination, starvation, or massacre *and violate no rule of international law*."[34] What made it possible up to our day for such acts as these to be immune from the rule of law was the preponderant view that it was not sufficient that an act be morally iniquitous in order to make it contrary to law. In a state of nature in the international scene, it was assumed that each nation could do whatever it wished to its own citizens and the assumption was that even a moral criticism would not invoke a principle of conduct superior to the will of the sovereign.

But such a limitation of sovereignty would destroy the essence of sovereignty. Even during the Nuremberg trials one line of defense taken by some of the Nazi officials was that the "crimes" for which they were being tried were not crimes at all because there had been no specific law designating their acts as crimes; in addition, these officials said they acted on behalf of and in the name of their sovereign state and were therefore accountable to no one else.[35]

34. Quincy Wright, p. 20.
35. What made it possible up to our day for such acts as these to be immune from the rule of law is the preponderant view that it is not sufficient that an act be morally iniquitous in order to make it contrary to law. Even more disas-

The artificial character of the doctrine of sovereignty is particularly glaring when we observe nations committing injustices against their own citizens. But the manner of thought engendered by this doctrine over the centuries makes it difficult for peoples to give up their sovereign rights. While one nation would like to limit the sovereignty of another nation to prevent what it considers an unjust behavior, this first state frequently would not itself be willing to submit to a limitation of its own sovereignty. Still, the claim to absolute sovereignty has become less and less plausible in the modern world, and the artificial conceptual structure developed by Hobbes is showing a disintegration at many points. In the field of international law the conception of law is apparently being shaped not so much by the considerations of sovereignty as by the growing moral consensus of mankind.

Consent and the Moral Basis of Law

We have seen that to take the doctrine of sovereignty either literally or strictly is to destroy the possibility of an international law. But there have been attempts to derive a basis for international law without rejecting the doctrine of sovereignty, and this approach is to be found particularly in the theory of *consent*. The premise of this theory is that there is nothing necessarily contradictory between the existence of sovereign states and international law, since the latter is the product of the consent of nations. This means that there is no reason that a sovereign nation cannot limit itself through an agreement with another nation.[36]

---

trous was Hobbes's view that where there is no law there is no morality, for law and morality are born together. Sheldon Glueck, "The Nurenberg Trial and the Aggressive War." 59 Harvard Law Review, 436 (1946).

36. Cf. treatment of Georg Jellinek's theory in Wolfgang Friedmann, *Legal Theory* (3rd ed.; London: Stevens, 1953), p. 417.

The most ingenious version of this theory of consent was formulated by the Hegelian jurist Jellinek in his doctrine of the self-limitation of the state. According to Jellinek, the essence of the sovereign state is that it possesses the power of self-determination. One aspect of such self-determination is self-limitation, as when a state binds itself to its own law within its own territory. By this same faculty a nation can enter into agreements with other nations, can recognize them as legal entities, and can choose to bind itself to agreements or contracts between them and itself. In this way a state acts somewhat like Hobbes's man in the state of nature, whereby through his consent to be bound he transmutes himself from an absolutely free agent into a legally responsible entity.

Through this consensual theory, Jellinek sought to avoid the logical impasse created by the notion of sovereignty where the imposition of a law upon a nation by another nation, or even by a super-national legislative body, would be incompatible with the sovereignty of each state. But in the consensual theory it is the consent or the willingness of each sovereign state to be bound by an international law which provides the basis of that law. On this view one aspect of sovereignty is the faculty of the state to limit itself.

There are at least two serious objections to this theory. In the first place, the facts do not seem to accord with it. States do not expressly consent to all the rules by which they find themselves bound when they become states. When a new state is formed it becomes bound to many rules which it did not create and even about which it may not have been expressly familiar. It is, of course, possible to argue via a legal fiction that each state "tacitly" consents to the prevailing rules of conduct to which membership in an international community binds it, but this notion of a tacit consent is clearly only an attempt to repair a defect in the consensual theory.

A far more important objection to the consensual theory of limitation is that it does not provide an adequate basis for international law because it does not explain how or why a state should be bound by a rule of international law. If law means at least that the wills of those to whom it is addressed must be limited, how can the principle of limitation be derived from an unlimited, that is sovereign, will? Can a self-imposed limitation be a true limitation? For example, if a nation agrees to be bound by its promise, can it really be bound if the only reason for its obligation is its consent to be bound? If the basis of the obligation rests upon its consent only, cannot a sovereign will "take back" its consent? The ground of this objection is that in the consensual theory the obligation is created by the consent of the nation; it did not exist in any form before that consent. Having created it, the nation can annul it. The theory of consent does not account adequately for the binding nature of agreements; behind any particular promise is the fundamental rule that promises ought to be kept, and this rule is not the product of anybody's consent.

Although it would appear that individuals limit themselves in their behavior when they observe the moral law, it is of paramount importance here that individuals do not create the moral law. The moral law has an unconditional and imperative quality and is addressed to an individual who senses an obligation to it; he believes in the objective existence of the rule and wills to conform to a rule he did not create. A promise is binding because there already exists the prior rule that promises ought to be kept. This is substantially the argument used at the Nuremberg trials when Justice Jackson held that even if there were no specific positive consent on the part of nations to be bound by certain rules of behavior, to indulge in such acts as genocide and torture is clearly a violation of rules to which nations are obligated to conform.[37] The basis of obligation to the law cannot be found in the will of the party who is to be bound.

And again, the act of consent cannot create international law, for at most this act of consent would have the effect of extending the sphere of a state's own law to the international scene. When a state agrees to be bound and retains its sovereignty, it is, in effect, incorporating the rules to which it is now bound to its body of internal law. This has not created an international law but a certain form of international relations or "a certain coexistence between states whose foundations must rest upon their sovereign wills and which they can terminate when they wish."[38]

Hence, this consensual theory does not solve the logical dilemma created by the doctrine of sovereignty because each of these theories amounts to the same thing. And to these there are two additional objections. First, doctrines of sovereignty and consent turn to a fictionalized entity for an explanation of obligation, namely, the state. Of course, the law frequently deals with fictions in order to deal effectively with unique forms of institutions, as in the case of the corporation. The state or nation does not possess the attributes of personality, and insofar as this is the case it is almost impos-

---

37. *Ibid.*
38. Stoyanovich. "The Reality of International Law," 1959 Journal du Droit International 41–42.

sible to derive from the doctrine of the state the foundations of the rule of law. For law in its clearest sense is a matter of reason and is addressed to rational and conscious beings.

To speak of a state as exercising its "will" must be to speak only figuratively. Yet the literature on international law deals almost exclusively with these abstract fictions, of which the state and its sovereignty is the most notorious. This means for the enterprise of law that no satisfactory theory of law can be derived from them precisely because they are not the true foundations nor the fundamental elements of law. All that can be derived from the concept of sovereignty is a conceptual mechanism by which a people can retain the possibility of doing what they wish.

A second objection, closely related to the former, is that the doctrines of consent and sovereignty obscure the basis of obligation by separating the spheres of law and morals. The breakdown of international law is indeed the consequence of this refusal to see in moral obligation the basis of "legal" obligation in the system of international law. If one were to take the terminology of sovereignty seriously and accept such phrases as the "will" of the state, then one should stress the analogy between the individual and the state at many other points.

We take it as axiomatic, particularly in democratic countries, that the individual is of the highest value and that the function of law is the protection of inalienable human rights. In a real sense, individuals are sovereign entities, but the very notion of the importance of human values means that the positive existence or preservation of these personal values imposes limitations upon all individuals. Any positive faith in the value of the individual necessarily carries with it the corollary conviction that each individual is obliged to respect the value of the other. Each individual shares in the objective value from which he derives his own value; the reason one seeks respect for his own person is fundamentally the same reason other persons desire equal respect. The condition on which any one is respected is that everybody must be respected.

The doctrine of state sovereignty might imply this, but it is never stated this way; it is always formulated in a unilateral sense and thereby becomes nonsense. State sovereignty always implies that a state's rights must be respected but that the first state is under no obligation to respect others. The basic immorality of the doctrine of sovereignty is its unblushing egotism. This type of egotism is precisely the cause of the breakdown of any community of any size but is particularly destructive in the community of nations. As between individuals, we refuse to accept the notion of absolute sovereignty chiefly because the status of each as a person is dependent upon the protection of all as persons; individual freedom is qualified both by the reciprocal basis of the dignity of each as well as the interdependence of all.

The interdependence of nations has until recently been obscured by the facts of geography and slow communications. But even with the shrinkage of the world which has made close neighbors of practically all peoples, nations in their collective behavior act in ways that would destroy their internal communities if the same type of behavior were pursued there. At any rate, a fundamental objection to the theory of consent and sovereignty is that it argues for an amoral relation between states, and to destroy the moral basis of obligation is to leave only the element of force as the ground of compulsion between states.[39]

---

39. See Bin Cheng, *General Principles of Law as Applied By International Courts and Tribunals*, (London: Stevens, 1953), p. 122:
The theory of abuse of rights (abus de droit), recognized in principle . . .

Persistent use of the analogy between the individual and the nation suggests that the grounds of international law can be understood more creatively when these attributes of personality are introduced, for it is in relation to persons that the concept of law finally makes sense. Moreover, it is only by introducing these considerations of persons that the element of obligation in international law is discovered, for it is in the sense of moral obligation, which only persons are able to possess, that the ground of obligation is found in the international community.

If the personal qualities of will and obligation are ascribed to the state only metaphorically, no great advance is necessarily achieved. But even this metaphorical use of the language of personality is evidence that the doctrine of sovereignty is too abstract to stand by itself; it needs the support which the concept of law requires, namely, the character of personality.

Ever since the rise of the sovereign state, however, the personality of the state was raised above that of its members and given a life of its own. For international law this meant that the subjects of international law were not human beings but states. If, for example, an individual was injured by another state his government was the subject of the controversy. He could not have access to any tribunal for restitution nor even receive damages if they were paid:

---

by the Permanent Court of International Justice . . . is merely an application of this principle [the principle of good faith which governs international relations] to the exercise of rights. . . . The exercise of a right—or supposed right, since the right no longer exists—for the sole purpose of causing injury to another is thus prohibited. Every right is the legal protection of a legitimate interest. An alleged exercise of that right not in furtherance of such interest, but with the malicious purpose of injuring others can no longer claim the protection of the law.

If he sometimes gained compensations for injuries which he received in foreign lands after the local courts had denied him justice, it was not in his own right, but as a consequence of the rights of his state to protect him and, if it wished, to give him reparation which it had in its own right received for the injury to its national.[40]

It is one thing to consider the state as a personality with rights of its own for its own sake, which is the view that prevailed in the last century and possesses some adherents even today. It is another thing to see in the state the agency for the protection of actual persons. The profound movement toward this view in the last decades is a recognition of the fictional character of the state as a person and the conviction that concrete persons are in a true sense the subjects of international law.

Persons become the subjects of international law chiefly because it is from human values and relations that the law takes its shape. The shift from the notion that a state exists for itself to the newer view that it is the agent for human beings was affected by a series of events that in our day is most dramatically expressed in the Universal Declaration of Human Rights. Preceding this document were a series of earlier attempts to place human beings instead of merely states into the role of subjects of the law. There were several treaties which set forth the rights of aborigines, of minorities, of workers, of women, of children, and of other classes of persons who were in danger of oppression.[41]

The United Nations Charter represents a major move to put individuals in the forefront as subjects of the law, and this means not only a recognition of human rights but also its

40. Wright, p. 20.
41. *Id.* at 21.

corollary—personal responsibilities. The charter calls for "international co-operation . . . in promoting and encouraging respect for human rights and for fundamental freedoms for all without distinction as to race, sex, language, or religion."[42] The modern developments in international law are thus considerably altering the rigid positivism which saw in the state a legal entity only. Today,

the new international law recognizes the individual, whatever his nationality or lack of nationality, as a subject of international law with certain rights which are in principle under the protection of the society of nations, anything in the law of his nationality or residence to the contrary notwithstanding.[43]

This trend toward separating the fictional state from the concrete person also affected the disposition of the leaders of the aggressive nations after the Second World War, this being the appropriate conclusion that if individuals have rights, then it is individuals too who are accountable for the violation of those rights. We are concerned to show here, of course, that the development of international law has required the gradual abandonment of the theory of sovereignty, and this for the reason that such a doctrine does not fit the facts of the nature of law. The law emerges from the consciousness of living persons and is addressed to concrete persons, for its function and purpose is to order the conduct of rational beings.

To say that law emanates from the will of a state is to misconceive the nature and the true source of law. Both historically and analytically it appears to be incorrect to account for the emergence of law in terms of the command of a sov-

42. Article 1.
43. Wright, p. 22.

ereign. Maine has said that "it is certain that in the infancy of mankind, no sort of legislature, nor even a distinct author of law, is contemplated or conceived."[44] And in our day some leading jurists are attempting to clarify a new basis for international law which is to be found, not in the command of the state, but in the moral consensus of the community of nations. The dominant positivistic theory of today would rest the structure of the positive international law upon the hypothesis that only sovereign states can create law.

But the facts of recent history point to a rather different element at work in the development of international law. This is the rational and ethical postulate of a community of interests and functions and values. A far more creative principle in the formation and development of international law is the postulate of moral obligation; this obligation is grounded, not in the physical force of sovereigns, but in the common concerns of the human beings who make up the international community. Thus the "first cause" in international law is not so much the will of individual states as it is the rational and moral rules which the emerging international community is finding increasingly new opportunities to express.[45]

Lauterpacht argues that "undoubtedly the effectiveness of the law depends to a large extent upon the prevalent practice and general level of morality, by the very fact that the reign of law is, and tends to become, part of common practice and morality."[46] A former judge of the international court,

44. Henry James Sumner Maine, *Ancient Law* (London: J. Murray, 1919), p. 7.
45. See Lauterpacht, *The Function of Law in the International Community* (Oxford: Clarendon Press, 1933), pp. 429–423.
46. *Id.* at 437.

in a significant and penetrating book, makes substantially the same point when he writes that

in the international order, as in the internal order, the human values are the final reason for the rule of law. Founded upon the moral conceptions which are the essence of civilization, they impose themselves upon the State whose mission is to assure their protection and their free development.[47]

But to ground the international law upon the moral consensus of the world community is a slow and ambiguous process. The law must take concrete and precise form and must be reducible, if not to a code, then at least to a working set of principles. For the law must provide the instrument of adjudication, the court, with the guides for decisions. Ultimately, the rule of law must mean the settlement of controversies on the basis of clear rules by the competent judicial organ.

This is, of course, the very point at which legal theorists confront their most difficult task, for they seek a precise source of law; this is the reason they look to the sovereign which is such a definite entity and turn away from the more ambiguous realm of "moral consensus" which is almost incapable of exact identification or delineation. This is the reason, too, for identifying law with what the courts do, for in the last analysis the decision of the court represents the *law* in the realistic sense of the term.

47. *Id.* at 420–423.

5

NATURAL LAW

*The Moral Basis
of the Legal Order*

O F the many issues raised by the theory of natural law, only one is pertinent to the concerns of this book— whether there is a necessary, rather than only an accidental or intermittent, relation between law and morality. The question is whether we find moral values embodied only occasionally in particular laws or whether the whole legal order rests upon a moral foundation.

It is, of course, the central premise of all natural law theories that the positive legal order is not autonomous, that the regime of law is founded upon morality. This audacious premise has been affirmed and maintained by advocates of natural law notwithstanding the virtually insoluable problems it has provoked. To argue that the legal order rests upon

morality assumes that there is some clear standard and content to morality upon which all men can agree. There is the
assumption also that any law which lacks moral defensibility
lacks the character of law, raising the question whether such
a law should be obeyed.

One may also ask whether it is helpful to use the word
"law" in speaking of natural law and whether the doctrine
of natural law clarifies our understanding of the very concept
of law. In spite of those nagging questions, and in spite of the
rather high degree of analytic imprecision in most natural
law discourse, there is the persistent claim in natural law
theory that law bears at once an intimate, legimate, and even
necessary connection with morality.

It has been said that in both the Roman and English legal systems there was such an intimate relation between law
and morality, between the positive law and the natural law.
Thus, in Roman Law, the *ius civile* or positive law, and the
ius gentium, a form of natural law, were not distinguished
as two fundamentally different kinds of law but were at
points considered theoretically the same. Jolowicz has said
that the Romans "did not in fact succeed in distinguishing
morals from law in theory."[1] Although the Romans attempted
to set certain boundaries between law and morals, they never
tried to separate law from morals but rather specified certain
areas within the domain of morality as the chief concern of
the law.[2] Similarly, regarding the common law, Goodhart
has said that "there is in England . . . a close bond between law
and morals and it is impossible to understand the nature of

1. Herbert Felix Jolowicz, *Historical Introduction to the Study of Roman
Law* (Cambridge, Eng.: The University Press, 1932), p. 104.
2. Michel Villey, *Leçons d'Histoire de la Philosophie du Droit* (Nouvelle
edition; Paris: Dalloz, 1962), pp. 156–157.

English law unless we also recognize the various moral ideas which it represents."[3]

It would be misleading to suggest that there is no difference between natural law and positive law. The point is, rather, that the idea of natural law is always developed in relation to some specific system of positive law. The reason that positive and natural law bear such a close relationship is that, at one point at least, they represent the same kind of activity—an activity of the intellect directed toward fashioning rules for human behavior.

When the legislator fashions a law, roughly the same considerations go through his mind as those usually ascribed to one who is concerned with natural law. The chief difference is that the legislator is constantly affected by and aware of the conflicting interests of the people for whom he must legislate. Although he may have in mind certain ideal solutions to these conflicting interests, he is forced to scale down this ideal solution to the level of compromise in order to get on with the job of legislation.

Because of this compromise, there is always a spread between the actual and the ideal, or between the "natural" and positive law. But even though there is this gap between natural law and positive law, the natural law does influence the process of legislation and the judicial process. It is not as though natural law is a subject which one group of people thinks about while others think about positive law. There is only one kind of "law" in the strict sense of the term—the positive law, and it is in connection with the creation of this law that natural law thought emerges. All the categories of

3. A. L. Goodhart, *English Law and the Moral Law* (1953), (London: Stevens, 1953), p. 8.

positive law, such as "sovereign," "command," and "sanction," are precisely what concern the natural law thinker.
But he interprets these categories of positive law in such a
way as to link them with morality.

Even in his exaggrated or "maximum" theory of natural
law Thomas Aquinas was particularly concerned with describing and interpreting the elements of the positive legal
order. Aquinas thus makes it clear that only those rules of
behavior which emanate from the proper legislator can be
properly called human law for "it is he alone [who] . . . has
the right to make the laws."[4] Aquinas moreover agrees that
it is the sovereign's *command* that conveys the law, but, he
says, "a command denotes an application of a law."[5] Law is
not synonymous with a command; rather, "law is a dictate
of reason commanding something."[6] He thus argues that "a
private person has no authority to compel right living,"[7]
that private persons may only "advise" and that if their advice is not accepted, they "have no power of compulsion" for
such power "belongs either to the community as a whole or
to its official representatives."[8] Aquinas accepts even more
strongly the elements of sanction as part of the law when he
says that "law, to be effective . . . must have compelling
force."[9]

All this indicates the element of positivism in natural
law theory. But unlike legal positivism, natural law theory
does not identify the essence of law with its positive elements,

4. *Summa Theologica*, Question 90, Article 3, Reply 2.
5. *Id.*, Question 90, Article 2, Reply 1.
6. *Id.*, Question 90, Article 1.
7. *Id.*, Question 90, Article 3, Reply 2.
8. *Id.*, Question 90, Article 3.
9. *Id.*, Question 90, Article 3, Reply 2.

for it finds the essence of even positive law in the realm of rational activity. Aquinas thus accepts the notion that law is the will or command of the sovereign but adds that it is not any and every expression of the sovereign's will which is law. He holds, rather, that "if it is to have the authority of law [the will] must be regulated by reason when it commands."[10]

Still, even when the sovereign commands a tyrannical law, such a command has some vestige of law; for, although "tyrannical law, not being according to reason, is not law at all in the true and strict sense but is a perversion of law," Aquinas argues that it does, nevertheless, assume the nature of law "to the extent that it provides for the well-being of the citizen."[11] This last point is, of course, very imprecise because it suggests two quite different criteria for law, one being a rule "according to reason" and the other a rule which provides for the "well-being of the citizen."

It may be that these two criteria are in the last analysis the same insofar as any rule which provides for the well-being of the citizen is at the same time in accord with reason. Aquinas does want to reject, however, the bare notion that any and every command of the sovereign is equally a law. He is here reaffirming the ancient natural law theme which one finds in Plato's remark that "no law or ordinance has the right to sovereignty over true knowledge,"[12] and in Augustine's even more explicit conclusion that "that which is not just seems to be no law at all."[13]

---

10. *Id.*, Question 90, Article 1, Reply 3.
11. *Id.*, Question 92, Article 1, Reply 4.
12. *Laws*, IX, 875.
13. *De Libero Arbitrio*, I, 5.

These extreme views imply that the very idea of law requires the inclusion of morality. There are, as we have seen, areas of agreement between legal positivism and natural law, for positivists recognize that moral ideals have influenced the development of law, and advocates of natural law recognize the roles of the sovereign, command, and sanction. They disagree, however, on the question of what constitutes the essence or nature of law.

A contemporary version of the strong views just mentioned of Plato and Augustine is found in Gustav Radbruch who says that "the idea of law can be none other than justice."[14] His argument is that the very meaning of the idea of law is that it is the "reality the meaning of which is to serve justice."[15] Kelsen had made the point (See Chapter Three, p. 112) that law is a norm which derives from another norm, which is to say that laws come from other laws, to which Radbruch responds that "law cannot originate in law alone,"[16] for the matrix of law is the moral judgment of man. The validity of law is therefore not to be found merely in the formal components of the law. "In morals alone," writes Radbruch, "may the obligatory force of the law be grounded"[17] and not in the official character of its enactment.

Radbruch was reacting to a system of law which had satisfied every criterion of validity that positivism had set forth. But he was convinced that the Hitler regime represented the destruction of the idea of law, and he lamented that "legal positivism that ruled unchallenged among legal scholars for decades and taught that 'law is law'—this view was

14. "Legal Philosophy," in *Legal Philosophies of Lask, Radbruch, and Dabin* trans. by K. Wilk (Cambridge: Harvard University Press, 1950), p. 73.
15. *Id.* at 75.
16. *Id.* at 125.
17. *Id.* at 84.

helpless when confronted with lawlessness in a statutory form."[18]

Earlier in his career, Radbruch might not have had these theoretical scruples. He had recognized that any system of law had to contend with irreducible conflicts, with "antinomies." It is not possible, he said, to reconcile the conflict of values created by the divergent claims arising respectively from the individual, the nation, and culture.[19] Besides discovering these conflicts[20] he thought that there was no way of overcoming a basic relativism in the realm of values, for "the ultimate statements concerning the 'ought' are incapable of proof, axiomatic. They may not be discerned but only professed."[21]

Moreover, Radbruch had believed that this relativity of value judgments was inevitable if one retained a scientific approach to the study of law. But with the breakdown of the idea of justice and law in Germany, Radbruch tried to meet the problem posed by totalitarian government in three different ways: first, he urged relativists to oppose any attempt of government to force value judgments upon those who did not share them; second, he sought to find "in the nature of things" some limitations for governmental decrees; and finally, he emphasized the "idea of justice" as requiring, not only that equals be treated equally, but also the recognition that all men are equal and that they all possess inalienable rights.[22]

18. Quoted by Lon L. Fuller, "American Philosophy at Mid-Century," 6 Journal of Legal Education 483–484 (1954).
19. "Legal Philosophy," p. 73.
20. *Id.* at 48.
21. *Id.* at 55.
22. See Arnold Brecht, in *Natural Law Forum*, III, 1, 196.

It is clear that in these three attempts, particularly in the last two, Radbruch had gone beyond the limits of science as he had earlier conceived it. If the validity of law is based upon the command of the sovereign and nothing else, then Radbruch could have no complaint regarding the validity of this totalitarian regime and its decrees. Yet Radbruch's argument is destroyed if the moral element which constitutes its end is denied.[23] Radbruch thus expresses the classical natural law doctrine that the very notion of law is incomprehensible apart from morals, saying that "the validity of law, the nature of legal duty cannot be conceived without the aid of ethic."[24]

The rhetorical force of these statements by Radbruch and the classical natural law advocates has seemed impressive to many, although others have failed to find in them a clear argument for natural law. What complicates the discourse of natural law theory is that its advocates have seldom indicated with clarity what they mean by "nature" and, more importantly, exactly how nature becomes related to law. To be sure, Aquinas described a neat architectonic relationship between "eternal law," "natural law" and "human" positive law, but this theory rested, in the end, upon a theological base. His theory of nature required the perspective of supernature. In the end, law must, for Aquinas, accord with God's reason.

Similarly, the grand theories found in Plato, Aristotle, Augustine, and others assert the desirability of resting law upon morality. But in most of these cases, the theory of natural law becomes so wrapped up with special concepts of

23. "Legal Philosophy," p. 85.
24. Radbruch, "Anglo-American Jurisprudence through Continental Eyes," 208 Law Quarterly Review 535–536 (Oct., 1936).

purpose and belief that they appear presumptuous to readers whose thinking is pursued in a pluralistic setting.

This is not to say that such natural law theories are necessarily wrong; it does mean, however, that they do not strike one as an argument for natural law. If one insists that Thomism, for example, does provide an argument in the logical sense, this would certainly have to be granted, since there is the consistent movement from premises to conclusions.

The real difficulty with natural law theories is, however, that in presenting their "arguments," the more "maximal" their premises and assumptions are, the more "minimal" their acceptability seems to be. There is reason to believe that from a more minimal set of premises it would be possible to formulate an argument for natural law which would be more maximally acceptable. One who has formulated such a minimum argument for natural law is, surprisingly enough, Thomas Hobbes.[25]

HOBBES'S MINIMUM ARGUMENT FOR
NATURAL LAW

The striking feature of Hobbes's theory of natural law is his insistence that law and morality have the same content and that the obligatory force of law is to be found in morality. He starts with the basic assumption that as a minimal purpose men endeavor to survive. He derives from this drive toward survival a consistent argument for the necessary connection between law and morality. As a basis for his argument, Hobbes makes certain observations about human nature.

25. For an articulate contemporary version of this argument, see Herbert Lionel Adolphus Hart, *The Concept of Law* ("Clarendon Law Series" [Oxford: Clarendon Press, 1961]), pp. 189–194.

Some Characteristics of Human Nature

Ever-Present Possibility of Injury

No one, says Hobbes, is self-sufficient. It is not possible for a man to make himself completely invulnerable. All men, by nature, have "fear," by which Hobbes means "a certain foresight of future evil."[26] One's survival is always in jeopardy, so that "they who go to sleep, shut their doors; they who travel carry their swords. . . ."[27]

This ever-present possibility of injury provides the most obvious basis for both law and morality, because bodily harm is a direct threat to survival. If by nature men could be perfectly secure, the primary reason for law and morality would not exist. Whether men protect themselves by locked doors, swords, morality, or law amounts really to the same thing: without some protection, without some mode of restraint, men are subject to attack or injury. The first fact about human nature is, therefore, that life is precarious and that injury and death at the hands of one's fellowman is always a possibility. This fact is the first link between human nature, morality, and law, for both law and morality are fashioned to overcome the fixed fact of individual vincibility.

The "Natural Equality of Men"

Men are, of course, unequal in many ways: in wealth, in physical strength, in imaginative power, and in the use of their rational capacities. If the rich, strong, and brilliant could employ their advantageous inequalities to control others permanently, there would be no occasion for law and morality.

26. *De Cive*, ed. S. P. Lamprecht (New York: Appleton-Century-Crofts, 1949), p. 24.
27. *Ibid.*

An equilibrium between men would be achieved, whereby the strong would control the weak. But Hobbes asks us to "consider how brittle the frame of our human body is," concluding from this fact that "there is no reason why any man trusting to his own strength should conceive himself made *by nature* above others."

What makes all men equal in spite of their other inequalities is that it is easy "even for the weakest man to kill the strongest." Men are equal when they can do equal things against each other; and "they who can do the greatest things, (namely, kill) can do equal things."

By nature, then, all men are among themselves equal. Such equality renders everyone vulnerable. Natural equality and vulnerability become the reasons for morality and law, for morality and law seek to overcome men's "mutual will of hurting" by providing rules of behavior and a system of restraints. Given the nature of human equality, says Hobbes, "we can neither expect from others, nor promise to ourselves the least security"; to achieve security, morality and law are necessary.[28]

The Scarcity of Things

It is not a part of man's nature that there is a scarcity of things. Some men live in fertile regions with relative abundance while others suffer severe privations. It is an aspect of human nature, however, that man's continued existence depends upon a steady stream of nourishment which he must derive from sources outside his own organism. Within himself he is constantly forced to overcome a form of scarcity—the scarcity of sufficient nutrition, as his body regularly uses up

28. *Id.* at 25.

what he eats. This fact of human nature, namely, the absence of a self-sufficient organism, forces men to rely upon resources around them to support and sustain their existence. By nature, men are dependent upon a regular and reliable source of sustenance.

Although by nature men are dependent upon external resources, their needs are not by nature automatically fulfilled. Men must either discover or produce food. Here men face their most serious threat from each other, insofar as there is no natural or mechanical mode of distribution of things; instead, everyone sets out to get what he can. "The most frequent reason why men desire to hurt each other, ariseth hence," says Hobbes, "that many men at the same time have an appetite to the same thing; which yet very often they can neither enjoy in common, nor yet divide it. . . ."[29] To internal scarcity is thus added external scarcity; but it is the natural fact of internal scarcity constantly threatening man's survival that requires that his relations to the outside sources of his sustenance be made reliable. Morality and law fulfill this task as they seek to protect the mechanism of survival from disruption by invasion from others. The mechanism of survival will vary from time to time but can include such elements as the possession of land, equipment, and the practice of exchange and promise. Whether the mechanism be simple or intricate, the fact of survival requires protection, forebearance and dependability. Moral rules and the legal regime come into being to stabilize the mechanism of survival which the fact of scarcity makes necessary. Otherwise, given limited resources, "it follows that the strongest must have it. . . ."[30] But the "strongest" will eventually encounter their

29. *Id*. at 26.
30. *Ibid*.

"equals," since everyone is vulnerable, so that if scarcity does not lead directly to morality and law, it leads to these through natural equality.

Man by Nature Is Able to Make Moral Distinctions

Human nature is complex. Like a watch, it has many parts. But like a watch, says Hobbes, where the "motion of the wheels cannot well be known, except it be taken in sunder, and viewed in parts," so also "what the quality of human nature is" requires that we consider it "as if [it] were dissolved."[31] that is, we must consider human nature's constituent parts in order to understand the nature of the human act. When we do this, we find a mixture of capacities and motives.

We have already mentioned the element of fear, the expression of egotism growing out of the drive to survive, for fear is chiefly the "foresight of evil." To those who would want to describe human nature, not as a fearful self, but as loving and altruistic, Hobbes issued the reminder that even in well-governed states with settled laws men travel with swords and do not go to sleep without locking their doors and even in their houses lock their trunks. Because of the natural equality of all men, fear plays a significant role, and so Hobbes argues that "the original of all great and lasting societies consisted, not in the mutual good will men had toward each other, but in the mutual fear they had of each other."[32]

Fear is only one element in the complex nature of man. There is also the subtle combination of lust and reason. Men have "natural lusts . . . for every man is desirous of what is good for him, and shuns what is evil." Lusts revolve around the matter of survival, for men desire what in their opinion

31. *Id.* at 11.
32. *Id.* at 24.

will secure their existence. Likewise, they shun what is evil
or what threatens their existence, for "the chiefest of natural
evils . . . is death." Against this threat of death man has "a
certain impulsion of nature, no less than that whereby a
stone moves downward."[33]

But unlike a stone, man moves whichever way his reason
leads him; man makes choices and decisions. He can anticipate and evaluate dangers and can devise means for protecting himself. This is the precise context in which the word
"right" emerges, for it means acting, that is, choosing or
deciding or using one's reason in such a way as to survive.
Hence, "the first foundation of natural right is this, that every
man as much as in him lies endeavor to protect his life and
his members."

In this context, Hobbes gives limited meaning to "reason," especially to "right reason." For by "right reason" in
natural man he does not mean "as many do, an infallible
faculty" which grasps eternal truths, "but the *act* of reasoning by which man uses all means to insure his survival." Reasoning is "the peculiar and true ratiocination of every man
concerning [his] actions. . . ."[34] It follows, therefore, that the
relation between lust and reason is not a simple one, where
reason merely devises the mans for securing any and all the
objects of lust. The decisive natural fact is the drive to survive, and it is the function of right reason to sort out those
objects of lust which secure survival from those which would
endanger survival.

Even in the so-called "state of nature" man has, in addition to the elements of fear, lust or desire, and reason, the
capacity to make moral distinctions. Hobbes does say that

33. *Id.* at 26.
34. *Id.* at 32.

"nature hath given to everyone a right to all," that is, "to do what he would, and against whom he thought fit, and to possess, use, and enjoy all what he would, or could get." Moreover, whether the means he is about to use and the action he is performing is necessary for his survival "he himself, by the right of nature, must be judge."[35]

But the "war of all against all" that results from each person's seeking his own survival is not an amoral phenomenon. Although each person has the natural right to adopt ways and means for his survival and has the sole right to judge which means he will choose, it does not follow that all his actions are necessary means for his survival! Even in the state of nature, says Hobbes, it is possible to distinguish between acts which are and those which are not necessary for survival.

"Right reason," then, is not simply ratiocination whereby a man devises means to achieve whatever ends he may choose, but "true ratiocination [concerns] actions of his which may either redound to the damage or benefit of his neighbors."[36] From the primary natural right to survive is derived a fundamental standard of human behavior, providing a clear standard of morality. For even though every act in self-defense is in a sense "right," Hobbes explicitly says that *even in the state of nature* "if any man *pretend* somewhat to tend necessarily to his preservation, which yet he himself doth not confidently believe so, he may offend against the laws of nature. . . ."[37] The capacity to make moral distinctions is natural; natural man knows the difference between a bona fide act of self-defense and an outright act of plunder.

These, then, are some of the characteristics of human

35. *Id.* at 27–28.
36. *Id.* at 32.
37. *Id.* at 28.

nature which provide the causes or the reasons for morality and law. For morality and law are derived from the natural facts of man's susceptibility to injury by his fellowman, from the natural equality of men, from the scarcity of things, and from man's natural capacity to make moral distinctions. These human characteristics have in common that they all bear in one way or another upon the human drive for survival. It turns out, therefore, that morality and law have the same content since the "good" which morality prescribes and the "right" which the law enjoins both involve survival. In their original form, morality and law are "natural" in the sense that "every man by natural necessity desires that which is good for him" and possesses the "right reason" which enables him to understand what he must do to survive.[38]

Natural Laws Derived from Human Nature

Although Hobbes gives a rather conventional definition of natural law when he speaks of it as the "dictate of right reason," he is particularly concerned to show that natural law is "a part of human nature." And this he does by deriving all natural laws from the natural functioning of reason. Everyone agrees, he says, that those actions are good or right which are "not done against reason" and those are wrong "which are repugnant to right reason."[39] Right reason means the act of reasoning from some true principle without contradiction. That all human actions should facilitate man's endeavor to survive is such a true principle.

Although a man is capable of acting in a wide variety of ways, and although Hobbes says that in the state of nature "everyone has a right to all," right reason requires that from

38. *Id.* at 29.
39. *Id.* at 32.

all the possible ways he can act, a man should, following right reason, act consistently with the requirements of survival. In general, then, natural law is not merely some abstract "dictate of reason" but is rather "a dictate of right reason, *conversant about those things which are either to be done or omitted for the constant preservation of life and members. . . ."* From this general concept of law, Hobbes derived, among others, the following specific "natural laws."[40]

The first and fundamental law of nature, derived by reason from the condition of human nature, is that "peace is to be sought after." It is part of man's elementary rational knowledge that survival can best be guaranteed under conditions of peace.[41]

Another law of nature, derived from the first, is "to perform contracts." Nature "commands every man, as a thing necessary, to obtain peace, to convey certain rights from each to other . . . and this is called a contract."[42] Good faith and the keeping of promises are indispensible if there is to be a peaceful and stable community. Such acts are required by right reason as the conditions of peace and survival. But not all contracts are in accord with right reason or natural law, and therefore not every promise is right or obligatory. For example, "no man is obliged by any contracts whatsoever not to resist him who shall offer to kill, wound or any other way hurt his body."[43] To obey contracts is a command of reason, but reason also prescribes the scope of contracts so that "no man is tied to impossibilities,"[44] "no man is tied by any compact whatsoever to accuse himself," and, in general, "if what [men]

40. *Ibid.*
41. *Ibid.*
42. *Id.* at 43.
43. *Id.* at 39.
44. *Id.* at 40.

vow be contrary to the law of nature, they are not tied by their vow, for no man is tied to perform an unlawful act."[45]

Although reason requires that for the sake of peace and survival a man should willingly convey certain of his rights to others, reason also dictates that he should retain some others, including "the right of bodily protection, of free enjoyment of air, water and all necessaries for life."[46] These rights which men retain and must not convey through any compact they must also be willing for every other man to retain.

A corollary to the natural law requiring that contracts and promises be kept is the enjoyment "without molestation" of what has been conveyed, "as for example, if any man shall sell or give away a farm, he utterly deprives himself . . . from all right to this farm. . . ."[47] What earlier all men were free to use acquires, through contract, a new status. Various forms of property have their foundation therefore in the natural law.

There are many other natural laws, and altogether "the laws of nature are the sum of moral philosophy."[48] We have seen, then, that even in the state of nature, natural law, or right reason, requires that men should seek peace or refrain from injuring others, that promises be kept, and that what has rightly become a person's property be respected. Actually, Hobbes's list of natural laws is a long one, including such rules as that "both parties disputing concerning the matter of right submit themselves unto the opinion and judgment of some third" and that "no man must be judge or arbiter in his own cause."[49] All natural laws, again, are derived from the

45. *Id.* at 37.
46. *Id.* at 51.
47. *Id.* at 34.
48. *Id.* at 59.
49. *Id.* at 53.

initial premise that the indisputable purpose of human nature is to survive.

Can it be assumed that these natural laws will be known by all men? If they are not known, can they be binding upon all men? Hobbes realized that some "will say that the deduction of these laws is so hard, that it is not to be expected they will be vulgarly known, and therefore neither will they prove obliging."[50] It is true, he said, that fear, anger, ambition, "and other perturbations of mind" do hinder a man's knowledge of natural laws. Indeed, he thought that natural law requires that a man refrain from actions which would weaken or disturb the mind and thereby destroy the faculty by which the natural laws are known, "which most manifestly happens to drunkards and gluttons."[51] Actually, says Hobbes, "there is no man who is not sometimes in a quiet mind," and in such a condition nothing is easier for him to know than the rules of natural law. All anyone needs to do is to test his proposed action by the principle of reciprocity, to "conceive himself to be in the other's stead," and he will know what is right. All men know the ancient rule, "do not to others, you would not have done to yourself."[52]

Because the "end" or purpose of human nature will always be at least survival, all the laws which reason deduces from this condition of human nature are "immutable and eternal." What the laws of nature forbid can never be lawful, and what they command "cannot be abrogated by any custom or law whatsoever."[53] Even in the state of nature all the laws of nature are binding upon all men. Hobbes distinguishes

50. *Id.* at 55.
51. *Ibid.*
52. *Ibid.*
53. *Id.* at 57.

between the internal court of conscience and the external court of the community, saying that "the law of nature doth always and everywhere oblige in the internal court, or that of conscience, but not always in the external court, but then only when it may be done with safety."[54]

From Natural Law to Positive Law

We come now to the central question: whether the positive legal order is morally neutral or whether there is an intimate and necessary connection between the regime of positive law and morality. The argument so far has been that because of certain inherent human characteristics, some rules must be formulated to guide human behavior, and that from the nature of man certain rules can by all men be deduced and these rules have the quality of natural laws. Finally, all men have the obligation to obey these rules of natural law. This argument assumes that there is yet no civil society.

To return to Hobbes's analogy: if we want to understand how a watch works we have to take it apart and discover all the causes of the motions. Similarly, the positive legal order of a civil society is best understood when its constituent parts are analyzed. When we take a civil society apart, we find at least these elements: individuals, rules of law, a sovereign, and obligation. Whether these four elements emerge in history in exactly this chronological order or whether this sequence signifies an order of logical priority does not make too much difference for the sake of the argument. In either case, the task of understanding the positive legal order requires that we make some assumptions about each of these four elements.

54. *Id.* at 56.

The manner in which these elements are put together will determine whether we can argue that the legal order is grounded in morality.

The Individual

Any system of positive law must assume a particular quality in human nature, namely, the quality of understanding, of rationality. If we assume that there was a time when there was no positive legal order, when men lived in a state of nature, we must also assume that men possessed at that time the same natural capacities they exhibit in civil society. Unless we make that assumption, the alternative is to say that prior to civil society men possessed no understanding or rational capacity. If this was the case, by what act could human nature have been transformed from a nonrational to a rational condition? Some accounts of the origin of civil society attempt the logically impossible feat of deriving a rational system of laws from what can only be interpreted as brutes. Only rational beings are capable of understanding a rule of behavior; and only such individuals can understand the desirability of creating a legal order in the first place. The presupposition, then, of a legal order, is intelligent human beings.

Rules of Law

Rules of law do not exist for the first time only after civil society is instituted. Admittedly, it is the case that positive law comes into being only after a sovereign is established. But the issue is not simply to designate the proximate origin of positive law; the question is, rather, to account for the origin of the rules of law. If human nature is given, if all its characteristics are relatively permanent, if, that is, men have by nature the rational capacity to deduce from human nature certain rules for human behavior, then these rules are the laws of nature and are the primary forms of the rules of law. There is no basic difference between the laws which natural reason deduces in the state of nature and the positive laws which the sovereign commands. This follows from the fact that individual human nature is the same in the state of nature as in civil society.

Hence Hobbes says that "the Law of Nature, and the Civil Law, contain each other, and are of equal extent;"[55] he also says that "Civil and Natural Law are not different kinds, but different parts of Law; whereof one part being written, is called Civil, the other unwritten, Natural."[56] The force of this argument derives from the fact that natural law and morality are the same; this would mean, therefore, that civil law, being a version of natural law, emerges from morality.

The positive law does not create the category of morality, although it frequently provides its official definition: for example, "theft, murder, adultery, and all injuries are forbid by the laws of nature; but what is to be called theft, what murder, what adultery, what injury in a citizen, this is not to be determined by the natural, but by the civil law."[57]

The core of positive law is always, says Hobbes, derived from the natural law; the details for implementing natural law appear in the positive law. That promises should be kept is prescribed by the natural law, but that there should be two or three witnesses to a contract is a positive mechanism for enforcing the keeping of promises. That men should not injure each other is a rule of natural law, but that automobiles

55. *Leviathan* ("Everyman Library" [New York: E. P. Dutton 1950]), p. 227.
56. *Id.* at 228.
57. *De Cive*, p. 81.

NATURAL LAW · 203

should travel at specific speeds per hour in various zones is a positive means for preventing injury. Although nature nowhere prescribes that there must be two witnesses to contracts, it does enjoin the keeping of promises, and although nature nowhere contains a rule requiring speeds at 32 miles per hour, it does enjoin care for others' safety. When Hobbes says that "Law was brought into the world for nothing else, but to limit the natural liberty of particular men, in such manner, as they might not hurt, but assist one another. . . ,"[58] he was referring to the rules of Natural Law from which specific rules of Positive Law are to be deduced.

The positive law is not always a perfect expression of the requirements of natural law. Nor is the natural law always understood accurately or fully. That there can be such variability in both the positive and natural laws might suggest a degree of relativism which is inconsistent with the idea of natural law. There is the assumption in many natural law theories that the content of natural law is invariable and that human reason is capable of discovering absolute norms of behavior. Such theories also assume that natural law provides the positive law with a perfect pattern for legislation.

The fact is, however, that laws are constantly being challenged and changed. Laws require one mode of behavior at one time and a different mode at a later time. It would appear from this fact that there are no permanent norms of natural law to guide the making of positive laws. If the positive laws are in a constant process of revision, and if what was called "natural" at one time (for example, slavery) but contrary to nature at a later time, why not abandon the whole idea of natural law and look upon the positive law simply as a set of

58. *Leviathan*, p. 228.

rules fashioned by each generation to fit its own conception of desirable human behavior?

There is great theoretical simplicity in describing law as merely the command of the sovereign. Conversely, there is considerable theoretical imprecision if it is argued that positive law should rest upon natural law while saying at the same time that natural law has no static or permanent content. Everything, it would seem, turns upon whether the theory of natural law requires one to say that the content of natural law is absolutely and fully known at any given time.

It is not necessary, in order to have a viable theory of natural law, to say that there is a presently known set of absolute rules of human behavior. Nor is the relevance or value of natural law theory diminished because of the historical fact that men constantly revise the content of natural law. There are certain permanent facts about human nature from which Hobbes, as we have seen above, derived certain natural laws. But whether these are the only laws which can be derived from human nature is open to question. Nor is it necessary to assume that the interpretation of the laws of nature is always accurate or adequate.

Although Hobbes had, for clear reasons, assigned to the sovereign the authority to interpret the law of nature, and although he once said that "there can be no unjust laws," he did not deny that sovereigns and judges could give erroneous interpretations of the natural law. Although he defined law as a command of the sovereign, Hobbes did not intend by that definition to separate law and morality. The peculiar authority of the sovereign and his judges is that they alone have the right and power to command and render interpretations and decisions. But these acts of authority are not equivalent to morality. Sovereigns and judges can err, says Hobbes, and their decisions can and must be evaluated by the moral standards that precede their acts.

For example, the function of the judge, "the act of judicature," is, says Hobbes, to consider "whether the demand of the party be consonant to natural reason, and Equity; and the sentence he giveth is therefore the interpretation of the Law of Nature."[59] His sentence is authoritative, not because it accords perfectly with the requirements of natural law but because he was authorized to give the sentence, the interpretation, by the sovereign. The moral authority of his decision is separable from his functional authority to render it. Hence, says Hobbes, because there is no judge and no sovereign "but may err in judgment of Equity," it follows that "if afterward in another like case he find it more consonant to Equity to give a contrary sentence, he is obliged to do it." Indeed,

"all the sentences of precedent judges that have ever been, cannot all together make a law contrary to natural Equity: Nor any examples of former judges, can warrant an unreasonable sentence, or discharge the present judge of the trouble of studying what is Equity . . . from the principles of his own natural reason."[60]

Hobbes apparently would not accord to positive law a morally neutral status. From his conception of human nature, he derived natural laws, and he never divorced his conception of civil law from these natural laws. The very concept of law, as he saw the matter, is derived from morality or natural law. That he placed such emphasis upon the role of the sovereign in the phenomenon of law must not obscure his constant reminder that positive law must satisfy, as much as possible, the requirements of morality.

Nor did Hobbes wish to limit the function of civil law to

59. *Id.* at 236.
60. *Id.* at 237.

merely preserving order. The general obligation of the sovereign to procure the safety of the people was more than a duty to insure their survival. By safety, said Hobbes, "is not meant a bare preservation, but also all other contentments of life, which every man by lawful industry, without danger or hurt to the common-wealth, shall acquire to himself."[61] The rules of civil law contain therefore more than the minimum natural requirements for survival. Just what else they should contain will vary as human horizons are extended, for says Hobbes, "Time, and industry, produce everyday new knowledge."[62]

We have compared "rules of law" with "civil laws," saying that natural reason understands the requirements of the rules of law even before there is a sovereign and that civil laws are the positive enactments of the sovereign. It is perfectly consistent to argue, as Hobbes does, that the rules of law, the natural laws, are not "properly" laws, but that "when a commonwealth is once settled, then are they actually laws, and not before. . . ." The issue is not how the word "law" is to be *used*, but rather what the word law *means*. To say, rightly, that laws properly so-called are the commands of the sovereign does not mean that law consists simply in the fact of such commands. Hence, although Hobbes says that "the civil laws are nothing else but the commands of him who hath the chief authority in the city, for the future actions of his citizens,"[63] he is simply designating the "official" rules in a particular legal system; by this definition of law he did not intend that law has no reliance upon morality.

On the contrary, his whole argument has been to show

61. *Id.* at 288.
62. *Id.* at 290.
63. *De Cive*, pp. 74–75.

that the rules which natural reason can deduce from human nature—these rules become the content of the positive civil law. Civil society and its legal order are built upon the conditions of human nature and its requirements. That is why Hobbes asserts that "the law of nature, and the civil law, contain each other." Similarly, when Hobbes says that "there can be no unjust law," or that "before there was any government, just and unjust had no being," he is again stipulating the use of the word justice in the technically legal sense.[64] In this context, justice means "in accordance with the positive law" or the official decision of a court. He certainly did not mean to say that justice in the moral sense had no being in the state of nature. "The Laws of Nature," says Hobbes, ". . . consist in Equity, Justice, gratitude and other moral virtues on these depending, in the condition of mere nature. . . ."[65] Although the sovereign has the sole authority to command and to define justice, he is not exempt from the requirements of natural law and natural justice.

The principle difference between law in the state of nature and in civil society is that in the former laws are unwritten and everyone is free to interpret the requirements of justice, whereas in the latter there is an official sovereign who promulgates laws and renders interpretations and decisions. Positive law, therefore, does not begin simply with the fact of sovereignty as though sovereignty does not have its prior conditions and causes. The preconditions of sovereignty are intelligent human beings, knowledge of natural laws and justice, and some form of consent empowering a sovereign to make positive laws.

64. *Id.* at 129.
65. *Leviathan*, p. 227.

The Sovereign

Although Hobbes expressed a personal preference for monarchy, his concept of sovereignty is not tied to any particular form of it. And although the very concept of sovereignty implies powers and rights, Hobbes made it clear that the sovereign also has duties. The most significant aspect of Hobbes's theory is that he describes the origin of sovereign power in moral terms.

At one technical point Hobbes sees no difference between the sovereign who is "instituted" and one who becomes sovereign by conquest. In both cases the moral rule of survival is the cause of sovereign authority. In the first case, men fear each other and to avoid death or injury choose a sovereign, "a Man, or Assembly." In the case of a victor, the people "subject themselves to him they are afraid of. In both cases," says Hobbes, "they do it for fear. . . . But the rights, and consequences of sovereignty, are the same in both."[66] In the case of conquest, "it is not . . . the victory that giveth the right of dominion over the vanquished, but his own covenant."[67] Hobbes does not deny the possibility of despotism, but his theory of sovereignty is neither a blueprint for nor a justification of the totalitarian despot.

Again, certain conditions prevail before there is a sovereign; the existence of intelligent human beings, their knowledge of the natural laws, and their obligation to obey these rules, unless there is a genuine threat to their security. The reason for instituting a sovereign is to create the conditions of security that would enable men to obey the requirements of

66. *Id.* at 167–168.
67. *Id.* at 171.

natural law. The war of all against all is caused, not by the absence of rules of conduct, but rather by their violation, forcing everyone to be his own defender. Men know by nature that they should seek peace, refrain from injuring others, keep their promises, and refrain from stealing.

The function of sovereignty is not, therefore, to create morality or law as though these did not exist before the sovereign. The sovereign, when instituted, comes into being through the moral law which enjoins men to seek peace, to enter into agreements, to yield certain freedoms for the sake of peace, and to keep promises when agreements or contracts are made. The social contract cannot be the origin of morality; the obligation to keep promises precedes the social contract, and this prior moral commitment secures the contract from which the sovereign authority is derived.

The fiction of a social contract is not the decisive point here; what is important about the contract theory, however, is its insistence that, either chronologically or logically, there is, prior to the sovereign, a moral order and that the function of the sovereign is to implement it.

In this view, the origin of sovereignty lies in morality— in the natural moral law which logically leads men, in the interests of peace, survival and the enjoyment of human contentments, to create a civil society. From its inception then, the sovereign has a moral cause and a moral end. That his origin and his duties are defined by morality does not mean, however, that whatever the sovereign does is moral. In this regard, the sovereign is no different from an individual who is also subject to the natural laws of morality but does not always act in conformity to these laws. The sovereign can make bad laws and, what is more, he is capable of violating the very natural law he was instituted to enforce. All the duties of the sovereign, says Hobbes, "are contained in one sentence, the safety of the people is the supreme law."[68]

The sovereign is under moral obligation. He is not autonomous. His reason for existing is not found merely within himself. The decisive point is that "the city was not instituted for its own, but for its subjects' sake. . . ."[69] Nor is mere survival all that the safety of the people requires, for "by safety must be understood, not the sole preservation of life in what condition soever, but in order to its happiness. For to this end did men freely assemble themselves, and institute a government, that they might, as much as their human condition would afford, live delightfully."[70]

A sovereign "would sin against the law of nature," says Hobbes, if he did "not study as much as by good laws" he could provide his subjects "abundantly, not only with the good things belonging to life, but also with those which advance to delectation."[71] Hence, says Hobbes, "to the sovereign, belongeth the making of good laws. But what is a good law? . . . A good law is that which is *needful* and *perspicuous*."[72] It is not proper for the sovereign to "bind the people from all voluntary actions." Rather, it is the sovereign's function "to direct and keep them in such a motion, as not to hurt themselves by their own impetuous desires, rashness, or indiscretion; as hedges are set, not to stop travellers, but to keep them in the way."[73] Hence laws that are not needed for these constructive purposes are not "good."

Nor are those sovereign acts in accordance with the safety

---

68. *De Cive*, p. 142.
69. *Ibid.*
70. *Id.* at 143.
71. *Ibid.*
72. *Leviathan*, p. 299.
73. *Ibid.*

of the people which favor the rich against the poor. Justice must be administered equally "to all degrees of people . . . as well rich, and mighty, as poor and obscure persons." For, says Hobbes, "in this consisteth Equity; to which, as being a precept of the law of nature, a sovereign is as much subject, as any of the meanest of his people."[74]

To say that law is a command of the sovereign does not necessarily imply a separation of law and morals. The very ground of the sovereign's authority lies in morality, and the sovereign's responsibility is morally circumscribed. His duties, in addition to those mentioned above, include the obligation "to cause justice to be taught," that is, to cause men to refrain from depriving their neighbors by fraud or violence of their possessions, their own life and limbs, "those that concern conjugal affection," and also their "riches and means of living." The sovereign's pedagogical function is not limited to these negative prohibitions but extends to engendering a high motive for behavior, the motive that gathers up the whole intent of the Second Table of the Commandments: *Thou shalt love thy neighbor as thyself.*[75]

If the sovereign's authority is thus grounded in morality, and if his actions are clearly required to enhance the safety of the people in the broadest sense of that phrase, what duties rest upon the citizen to obey the sovereign when in the judgment of the citizen the sovereign has departed from the requirements of morality?

Obligation to Obey the Law

It should not be surprising that Hobbes rejected the position that the citizen has an absolute duty to obey the law. To be sure, much of his argument reads like a grammar of strict

74. *Id.* at 296–297.
75. *Id.* at 294–295.

obedience. At the same time he recognized that for certain reasons, a citizen could, "without injustice," refuse to obey the law. Hobbes's argument regarding obedience is therefore a double one, giving reasons for obedience and describing the conditions under which obedience could not be required.

As we have seen already, Hobbes argued that the citizen's obligation to obey the law is a moral one. The logic of his argument for sovereign authority is clear, consisting of the following: only by instituting a single authoritative voice can men overcome anarchy; by conferring authority upon the sovereign, men thereby convey to the sovereign the right they each originally had for determining right actions. For this reason, the sovereign's acts are in a special sense those of each citizen—as though each citizen expressly said in the social contract that *I authorize all his actions*; if after the social contract each citizen were to reserve the freedom to decide whether the sovereign's commands are just and therefore whether they should be obeyed, anarchy would once again result; therefore, to avoid anarchy, the citizens must obey the civil laws, that is, the sovereign's interpretation of the natural law.

But in addition to this argument for obedience, Hobbes recognized that there can be some things "which, though commanded by the sovereign, [the citizen] may nevertheless, without injustice, refuse to do."[76] The reason Hobbes gives two answers to the question whether men have an obligation to obey the law is that his argument for sovereign authority contains two perspectives: for one thing, sovereign authority is necessary for overcoming the confusion of opposing opinions that leads to anarchy; secondly, men consent to be governed only because they assume that their quest for survival and the

76. *Id.* at 183.

fullest enjoyment of their natural aspirations—in short, the fulfillment of natural law—can better be achieved in civil society. Hobbes is thus concerned, not only with order, but also with justice; not only that laws should be definite and clear, but that they be clearly right.

For "the two arms of a Commonwealth," says Hobbes, "are *force*, and *justice* . . . as if a commonwealth could consist, where the *force* were in any hand, which *justice* had not the authority to command and govern."[77] We have already recognized that for Hobbes one use of the words "just" and "right" is merely tautological, since they mean whatever the law prescribes. But the extensive analysis Hobbes makes of the state of nature, of man's rational capacity, of man's ability to discern the natural laws, of man's clear obligation to the laws of nature even prior to civil society, and his explicit statement that "the city was not instituted for its own, but for the subjects' sake"—all this indicates that there are moral rules and the concept of justice even before the legal system is instituted.

Hence, even though the express words of the social contract might be "I authorize all his actions," Hobbes argues that "no man is bound by [these] words themselves," to obey every command of the sovereign. The significant fact about the contract is not its precise wording, says Hobbes, but rather its intent. Hence, if the express words are interpreted so as to frustrate the intention of the contract, then they do not have to be obeyed. If, for example, the sovereign "commands a man to kill, wound or maim himself; or not resist those that assault him . . . yet hath that man the liberty to disobey."[78]

The intention of the contract is twofold; namely, to create a condition of ordered security in society, and to enable

77. *Id.* at 230.
78. *Id.* at 184.

men to fulfill their natural capacities for endeavors consistent with the natural law. As the contract has a twofold intent, it is possible to frustrate this intent in two ways: first, the citizens can frustrate order, security and predictability by civil disobedience; secondly, the sovereign can frustrate the purpose of sovereignty by disregarding or damaging the welfare or safety of the people.

It is not necessary to retain the language or terminology of the social contract to discuss the grounds of obligation to the law. Hobbes seems to have limited this contract to the citizens and excluded the sovereign from it. In this view, the citizens have contracted with each other to obey the sovereign; but there is no contract between the citizens and the sovereign. The sovereign cannot break a contract, therefore, because he was never a party to one.

Although the sovereign has no contractual obligations to the citizens, he does, nevertheless, have duties toward them which are prescribed by the natural laws, by God. But the sovereign's violation of a natural law does not justify a citizen's disobedience; the sovereign is answerable to God and not to the citizens. Still, it is not necessary to use this language of contract, since the chief point being made is that the very concept of sovereignty, the very presupposition of civil society is that somewhere there has to be a locus of authority. Such authority ceases to be authority if it is constantly subject to every individual citizen's interpretation and possible disobedience. Whether there was or was not a contract, there is the implied assumption and requirement of obedience to authority if anarchy is to be avoided. Indeed, Hobbes says that "the obligation to perform grows not immediately from that contract, by which we have conveyed all our right on the city, but from hence, that, without obedience, the city's right would be frustrate, and by consequence there would be no city constituted."

If it is the case that the citizen has a moral obligation to obey the law and also a right to disobey it, what is the formula for deciding when to obey and when to disobey? Hobbes did not provide an exact formula for answering this question. It may be that there is no such precise formula. The criterion he proposed is the general one: whether disobedience will cause the breakdown of society, that is, frustrate the intention all men have, even in their disobedience, to live in civil society. Hobbes thus says that "there is so much obedience joined to [the] absolute right of the chief ruler, as is necessarily required for the government of the city. . . ."[79]

It is not enough for a citizen to say that he is disobeying the civil law in the name of the natural law. For even though the law of nature is easy to discern for those who think impartially, still, "there be very few, perhaps none, that in some cases are not blinded by self love, or some other passion" making thereby the law of nature "of all laws the most obscure."[80] Most important of all in this connection is the fact that one who disobeys the sovereign now puts himself in the position he has just denied to the sovereign—that of giving the authoritative interpretation of the natural law. Moreover, such a person is in effect asking for obedience from the rest of society to his own version of morality and law.

Even more complicated is the case wherein one disobeys the civil law in the name of the law of God. The vexing question is how it can be determined what God's law is. Hobbes's central point here is not that there is no law of God; indeed, he believed that the laws of nature are the commands of God.

79. *De Cive*, p. 78.
80. *Leviathan*, p. 235.

Rather, his point was that well-meaning individuals could disagree over what constituted God's law. One has to be prepared, he said, to allow, not only this or that particular citizen to claim exemption from the civil law, but anyone who felt that God's law required him to disobey the sovereign. Yet, "if men were at liberty, to take for God's commandments, their own dreams, and fancies, or the dreams and fancies of private men; scarce two men would agree upon what is God's commandments; and yet in respect of them, every man would despise the commandments of the commonwealth" and once again anarchy would prevail.[81] It is helpful to remember that the logic of disobedience implies retaining the concept of absolute authority. As Hobbes says, those persons "who dispute against absolute authority, do not so much care to destroy it, as to convey it on others."[82]

The right Hobbes would give to the citizen to disobey the sovereign is, in the end, restricted to those cases wherein the elementary purpose of civil society, the preservation of life, is threatened. Conversely, the chief authority the sovereign has over the citizen lies in those cases wherein the actions of the citizen can threaten the foundation of civil society. This means in actual fact that civil disobedience is an exceptional occurrence. But it does not follow from this that there can be no moral criticism of the sovereign.

Such criticism, however, does not always require civil disobedience. The very structure of civil society can provide the apparatus for protest and the mechanism for orderly change, especially in a democratic legislature and judicial system. But the legislature and the courts are part of the sovereign authority, and not even in a democracy does a private citizen have the right to disobey these.

81. *Id.* at 246.
82. *De Cive*, p. 78.

Legislatures and courts can fail to satisfy a citizen's legitimate expectations. Even Hobbes argued that the responsibility of the sovereign to insure the "safety of the people" implied more than simply physical preservation; it should include, he said, "all other contentments of life," not preservation of life "in what condition soever, but in order to its happiness." The sovereign, it would appear, will be constantly under pressure from the citizens as they press beyond the conditions of mere survival toward the attainment of the "other contentments of life."

The line between civil society and anarchy is a thin one, and the desire to achieve an orderly and a just society is a deep one. Whether the thin line will be crossed from civil society to anarchy will depend upon how men set out to achieve the just society. It would be the greatest irony if the very foundation of society, the rule of law, were destroyed in the process of seeking justice. The natural law keeps man's situation in a perpetual tension, for it enjoins him at once to obey the laws as the condition of an ordered society and at the same time impels him toward justice.

What is clear from Hobbes's theory of natural law is that he never divorced law from morality. He saw the legal order as founded upon morality—a morality derived from human nature and for that reason natural. His theory is a minimum theory of natural law because it asks one to make the least number of assumptions about man and his purposes. But he saw as the purpose of human life more than its mere preservation. Still, the intent of our analysis has been to show that even from a positivistic version of natural law Hobbes viewed law as a moral phenomenon, insisting that the legal order cannot be separated from the moral order.

6

THE MORAL ORDER AND THE LEGAL ORDER

Some Points of Intersection
Between Law and Morals

T H E most formidable difficulty encountered in understanding the nature of law is, as we have seen, the difficulty of accounting for the moral element in law. Law moves in a strange and imprecise way between the domains of power and morality. While the existing law is capable of accommodating these diverse domains in their fluctuating proportions, recognizing the function of power at one moment and the demands of morality at another, the process of conceptual definition is less successful in grasping this dual nature of the law. The process of definition is, after all, a process of inclusion and exclusion. A definition of law is therefore both a statement of what law is and of what it is not.

The use of simple definitions for explaining law has very little success or value in dealing with the nature of law.

The chief limitation of the technique of definition in this case is that a definition is most successful when dealing with a *thing*. But the word "law" does not refer to a simple thing in the same manner that the word "table," for example, does. There is a marvelous correspondence between the definition of "table" and actual tables. The jurist would like to achieve this same precision and accuracy when he uses the concept of law. But a simple definition of "law" is incapable of suggesting, by itself, the rich freight borne by the concept of law. For this reason, whenever jurists seek to define "law" with the precision achieved in defining "table" there is bound to be some major distortion of the concept of law. Most definitions of law have lifted out of the full phenomenon of law that element which lends itself most easily to a direct identification, as in the case of John Austin's definition of law as "the command of the sovereign" and Justice Holmes's remark that law is "what the courts do in fact." Since the moral element is the most difficult element either to identify or to manage in any definition, it is this element which gives the most difficulty when we attempt to formalize the concept of law.

The separation of law and morality is not solely a result of the stringent process of definition. This separation is mandatory if we are to preserve both the clarity of the concept of law, on the one hand, and the purity of moral obligations on the other. There is the constant danger that if the association of law with morality is too close, then the law will become the substitute for our moral standards; and if the law is our moral standard, we have lost the possibility of a moral criticism of the law. Moreover, the requirements of moral obligations are such that the law cannot encompass or enforce them. Hence the separation of law and morality reflects a recognition of the differences between them.

The similarities between law and morality, however, are as significant as the differences. Moreover, the discovery of these similarities has an important bearing upon how we shall understand what is meant by the concept of law, for if we discover a close relationship between law and morality, then we can quite legitimately say that law is a moral phenomenon and that the legal order rests upon the moral order.

The word "law" will be used in the following analysis to refer to the laws of governments. The word "morality" will encompass the conceptions men form of the rules for prescribing human behavior. Whether these rules of morality are based upon a particular conception of human nature, are derived from a theological interpretation of man, or are simply the outcome of the considered consensus of the community does not, at this point, make much difference. Our sole concern here will be to consider whether we can argue successfully that law is a moral phenomenon and that in order to understand the full nature of law we need to recognize the intersection of law and morality.

Command and Choice

The difference which strikes us first is the fact that law *commands* us to act, whereas in morality we *choose* to act. To be sure, there is the commandment to love our neighbor. Still, the moral command or imperative is distinguished from the legal command by the fundamentally different type of force which lies behind each. Behind morality lies the force of conscience or even of persuasion. Men react to this force with a mixture of deliberation, internal struggle, and a conscious decision to obey or disobey. Apart from the pressure of the community about us, our final decision in the moral realm is rooted in our personal choice of whether to conform to the moral rule.

The command of the law, however, is never independent of the apparatus of society's organized force. Our immediate reaction to such a command is to consider the physical or punitive consequences of our failure to comply. We obey because we have to. Although we choose to obey the law, for after all we could also disobey it, we did not choose to be subject to the law. The moral law is something from which one chooses to draw the rules of behavior, provided that these moral precepts are sufficiently clear and intellectually coercive. Men move with a subtle freedom through the domain of moral discourse, taking and leaving what suits their interests and tendencies, and they do this with no immediate adverse result.

On the other hand, while men do from time to time deliberate over whether they will obey the law, neither the substance of the law nor its obligatoriness is in doubt. The legal command at once signifies what should be done and what will happen if it isn't done. In this sense, then, the law commands, whereas in morality we are persuaded. This certainly represents a fundamental difference between law and morality—the difference between external compulsion and internal affirmation of an obligation.

But are we willing to say that this difference, which is made dramatic by the threat of force lurking behind the command of law, entails a separation of law and morals? Do we obey the law only because it is commanded? Does the quality of obligatoriness attach to the law only because it is guaranteed by physical power? I think not. It is surely more accurate to say that, granted the law is obeyed in most cases because of its threat of pain, nevertheless the law does not obligate us solely because of this threat. We are willing to be bound by the command of the sovereign because, in addition to the power available for enforcing the command, the content of the command "makes sense," is "reasonable," or is "just." We resent and resist commands which are "arbitrary." We tend to evaluate lawmaking by moral criteria; that is, we expect the substance of the legal rule to be morally defensible. The legal "ought" partakes of the moral "ought," and for this reason there can be no thorough separation of compulsion and choice.

Abstract and Concrete

A second difference is that the law is *general* and *abstract*, whereas morality is *concrete* and *personal*. The law must necessarily be phrased in an impersonal way because it is addressed to hypothetical persons who may or may not fit the category of behavior for which the law is framed. Furthermore, the law treats all persons in the same way when they come under its operation. Although under certain circumstances differences among people are taken into account, the general character of law has the effect of treating all persons alike. This makes the law necessarily impersonal and abstract; and officers of the law must likewise think in terms of rules, not people, giving at times the impression that the preservation of a rule has a higher value than preservation of human dignity. Morality, on the other hand, stresses obligations, not to rules, but to persons. A rule for the moralist has no meaning apart from the concrete persons who live by it, whereas the abstract nature of law frequently demands certain types of behavior, solely in the name of the law.

Moral rules can and do come under the same criticism as legal rules, for, like the latter, moral rules can also be abstract. The injunction "love thy neighbor" still leaves unclear what exactly is meant by love and just who is one's neighbor. Furthermore, a person can very well follow the moral rule out of concern for the rule rather than for his neighbor. Moreover, a moral rule will often be accepted out of respect for the source from which it issues. This shows that moral rules also possess a general and abstract character and at times take precedence over persons. To this extent moral rules resemble legal rules.

The difference, however, is that the moral rule possesses the possibility of wide flexibility in a way that the legal rule does not. The requirements of morality render the moral rule more supple and adjustable to concrete circumstances than the legal rule, which requires enforcement even when in a particular case this clearly seems harsh.

Too much can be made of the abstract and general character of law in distinguishing it from morality. Although a legal rule is, in fact, general, it nevertheless refers to concrete human beings whose behavior it is designed to regulate. Whoever formulates a legal rule certainly has in mind the possibilities, tendencies, and dispositions of human beings, and he proceeds on the assumption that these conditions of behavior are common to most men.

It is hardly correct, therefore, to say that the law is abstract if this means that the law does not take into account the capacities of concrete persons. In this respect, the moral rule is founded upon the same premise as the legal rule, for the moral rule also assumes that there are basic similarities in all human beings. Even a highly flexible and dynamic morality which puts great emphasis upon the peculiar requirements imposed by the special circumstances of the moment must proceed on the conviction that, not only this person or these persons should act in this way, but that any person under these circumstances should act precisely in this way because this is the human thing to do. Morality has its own way of being general, of abstracting certain stable structures from human nature and assuming that these qualities will be present wherever human beings are present. The very notion of "person" already implies certain determinate characteristics which at once identify a moral agent and at the same time prescribe his obligation. Moral obligation assumes the stability and the primacy of certain human characteristics, and it is possible to speak of these in general terms, (for example, "worth," "dignity," "equality," "freedom," and "rights") without speaking of any person in particular.

Both legal rules and moral rules thus envision a human nature, both are general in their formulation, and both are abstract in that they rise above particular persons. The legal rule, just as the moral rule, is chiefly concerned with the behavior of human beings, and for this reason the category of law is not fundamentally different from the moral category. Indeed, the moral element as here described is built into the legal rule. Many of the criticisms one can level at the law can be directed at moral rules as well. It becomes quite clear that there is not simply a separation of law and morality but rather that there are some differences between the two. The conclusion, therefore, is not that the law is incapable of taking into account the lives of concrete persons in the way that morality does; it is rather that the law contains reasons for its enforcement which go beyond the special concerns over the persons immediately involved. The importance of the quality of "generality" in law is not that it deflects law from personal concerns but rather that it seeks to be relevant to many persons and many times. In order to retain the relevance of a law for a continuous period of time it is necessary to preserve its general character, not identifying the law with any particular event.

The law against murder does not stipulate anything about the instruments used or the times at which the act may be committed, for it must be able to control all the great variety of ways in which the act is committed. But even here the law shows considerable flexibility, for the specific result of killing a person has a wide variety of legal consequences. The law takes into consideration such factors as self-defense, duress, accident, and mistake. Still, it is true that the law will at many points lead to a different action than a solution suggested by morality.

Universal and Particular

Laws are binding in a particular place, whereas moral rules are without boundaries. A system of laws is effective and applicable in a limited geographical or cultural area. Only under special circumstances does a person in one state or nation have any legal liabilities under the laws of another state or nation. Laws apply for the most part only to the regular members of a community or to those outsiders who actually enter the community either physically or through such channels as trade and commerce. A moral rule, on the other hand, does not have such boundaries. If a person is under the moral obligation to love his fellow man, this obligation is not limited to a special or restricted group of people. A catastrophic earthquake in Chile creates no legal obligation upon Americans to come to the aid of stricken and homeless victims, but it does lay a moral obligation on them. Legal obligations thus have a limited scope of applicability; they apply to a specific group of people who have a certain formal relation to the lawgiver.

There is, of course, a limited relevance to certain systems of morality and certain moral rules, for not every moral rule is recognized as universally acceptable or binding. We are all familiar with the relativities of moral standards, both in time and in place. This fact of moral relativism has the effect of creating limitations upon the applicability of moral rules similar to the limitations characteristic of legal rules. But moral discourse and moral philosophy, by intention at least, deal with human nature and not with local mores, customs, or habits. The moral philosopher may in fact be influenced by his cultural setting in his quest for the standards of human behavior. But it is *human* behavior that concerns him, and not solely French, English, American, or African behavior.

The premise of moral obligation therefore is that wherever human beings confront each other certain moral obligations will always be present, as, for example, to be honest, to refrain from taking what belongs to another, and to refrain from injuring another person. Exceptions to these obligations are, of course, easily conceivable, but there is a virtually universal expectation that these rules will be respected between men. There is no similar universality attaching to any municipal law, for the area of its applicability is set off by specific boundaries. Only when a law is mutually recognized, as between two nations, does it travel beyond its original boundaries.

It is very much to the point here to recall that the jurist Austin would not accord to international law the quality or character of "law." For him these rules governing matters between nations were called "positive morality" and not law. This suggests that law differs from morality, not only by virtue of a different sphere of applicability, but also by virtue of the fact that a legal rule is a command of a sovereign, which alone can invest a rule with the quality of law. In any case, we have seen here an important difference between law and morals. This difference, however, does not yet indicate that law and morality are separate; at most it uncovers the limits within which the law moves.

External Control and Internal Motivation

Another way of contrasting law and morality is to say that law is concerned with *external conduct*, whereas morality deals with *internal motive*. There must be a standard of behavior by which the law can measure an act—a standard on which reasonable men will agree. But to get such agreement from reasonable men, they must be offered some evidence of external behavior which they can confidently analyze. The law is capable of making important distinctions between various types of behavior, and it makes these distinctions chiefly on the basis of external facts.

The same act can transpire under different circumstances with correspondingly different legal consequences. For example, a man repairing a chimney throws or drops a brick down from the roof, thereby hitting another man and killing him. Consider three possible sets of circumstances in which this might have taken place: a passerby climbed over a fence, was walking along the side of the house where there was no path and where no one was accustomed to walk, and was struck on the head when the bricklayer discarded a defective brick over the side; the bricklayer had carelessly piled some bricks on the roof and one of them slid over the other side, striking a mailman who was approaching the side door where he always delivered the mail; the bricklayer recognized an old enemy and hurled the brick at his head. The differences between these three variations are obvious to a reasonable man analyzing the specific details of the external act; there is no need to know any more about these acts for reasonable men to understand the different degrees of responsibility and culpability involved.

The marks of morality, however, are not so external; hence they are harder to enforce and therefore are not the immediate concern of the law. There is not only humor in the headmaster's injunction, "Boys, be pure in heart or I'll flog you," but also a dramatic reminder of what the law can and cannot do. The law cannot reach into the subtle wellsprings of benevolence; it cannot animate by force what by its very nature must be spontaneous and free. Nor can the law pursue people through all their waking moments, guiding and controlling them as they touch each others' lives in an indeterminate number of ways and in varying degrees of intimacy. The gentle suppleness of human existence with its constantly novel experiences, enlarging horizons, and delightful and tragic new turns and surprises cannot at any one moment be adequately anticipated nor fully captured in the form of a legal principle.

The law must wait for a particular act, a single event lifted from an endless chain of human behavior before its mechanism of control can operate. But the event which triggers the mechanism of law enforcement is an external event, some mode of external behavior. Morality, on the other hand, is so definitively a matter of internal sentiment and motive that it can rarely be discovered by the apparatus of law. Such subtle attitudes as respect, considerateness, patience, forgiveness, sympathy, and love are deeply submerged in the center of the self, far removed from the touch of law. While the law can command the payment of taxes, it cannot require the additional element of cheerfulness, and while some aspects of marriage can be controlled by law, there is no way for law to guarantee true tenderness. The efficacy of law seems to end at the threshold of man's internal self, and at this point morality becomes the arbiter of the human act.

Upon closer inspection, however, this distinction between external and internal behavior is not so sharp or clear as it first seems. External behavior is never unrelated to an internal act or to internal motivations. The same external act can, however, be produced by a variety of internal motivations. While the law is concerned chiefly with the external act and, indeed, will come into play only where there is such an act, the law nevertheless takes into account the factor of motivation, usually speaking of this element as "intent." It thus makes a difference in law whether there was intent to murder, and the law goes to great pains to discover this intent. To be sure, intent can be discovered only if there is some accompanying public act which is objective evidence of intent. The law is nevertheless profoundly concerned at appropriate times with the inner life of the actor as the decisive element in determining the fact and degree of guilt or responsibility.

The law reflects the internal working of the moral self in still another way. Even though the legal rule applies ostensibly and in most instances to an external act, it is of utmost importance to bear in mind that the emergence or creation of the legal rule in the first place is an internal act. At its very inception the law is an internal sensitivity to a configuration of external fact.

The initial impulse which suggests that "there ought to be a law against it" is frequently a simple moral judgment of an act whose repetition the law is then fashioned to prevent or discourage. That workers should be compensated for injuries suffered in the factory becomes a matter of legal obligation only after the internal judgment that this is "right" or "desirable" has been made. The moral sense of obligation between man and his fellow man is frequently the energizing factor in the creation of law. Once this moral judgment is fashioned into a legal rule, the legal rule has a life of its own and gives the impression of having a purely legal and not a moral complexion. An employer who violates a workmen's compensation law is not interrogated about his love for his fellow man but is only asked whether he has met the specific external requirements of the law.

Still, a full view of the law which looks, not only at its mechanical application, but also at the reason and manner for its creation indicates that the law is the embodiment of internal moral sentiments. The law emerges from the comprehensive consciousness of the community and seeks to control the external behavior of men. But, again, the law can do this chiefly because it is addressed and communicated to the internal consciousness of the governed. Whether laws are good or bad, out-dated or too far advanced for local public opinion is one thing; but that law, as a rule of conduct, is a reflection of the internal life of judgment seems clear. Hence, even though the law cannot enforce the injunction to "bear one another's burdens," in the sense that the law should require every factory manager not only to compensate for injuries but also to express the attitude of compassion and benevolence, the law does in effect enforce the moral injunction in its external aspect.

Differences in Scope

The above contrast between external and internal behavior suggests that the law is concerned with *minimum moral standards,* whereas morality envisions the truly good or *ideal life.* The scope of law is certainly far more limited than the scope of morality. In most societies the law limits itself to those requirements considered basic to the social order.

This is particularly true in a society which exalts the value of human freedom. The scope of freedom is in inverse proportion to the scope of law, for as the coercive power of law is extended over man's life, to that extent man's freedom is diminished. In a free and open society, therefore, the law is restrained and restricted to guaranteeing the minimal conditions for an orderly and peaceful community. The law provides the structure within which men can live with reasonable assurance that promises will be kept, property will be safe, and that people will not suffer intentional physical harm.

Once these minimal guarantees are secured, the law can refrain from prescribing man's conduct in more specific detail. The law has frequently been considered as playing the role of an umpire: it watches the race only to insure that nobody is pushed off the track or tripped. It is not the function of the law to make sure that everybody wins the race, but only that the lanes are kept clear. In this view, the law is limited to providing a race course within which various kinds of races can be run, depending upon what the people find interesting and compelling. This is to say that the law as such is not the agency for bringing to fruition the full possibilities latent in human nature or its destiny.

There may also be a deep skepticism in this view over whether there is any particular destiny or discernible structure in human nature, the possibilities of which should be coaxed into reality by the agency of law. And even if human nature did require special modes of behavior, this view asks, is it by law that this behavior should be ordered? The law simply liberates man from daily concern over survival so that within this secure context he can turn his attention and energies to those more intricate and personal relations which his moral nature urges upon him.

In this context men assemble to marry, do business, debate, study, and worship. They express ideas about goodness, justice, truth, and about ultimate reality. They communicate through speech, the printed word, and various forms of art. They form associations for the production of goods, education of children and adults, and for the worship of God. Out of all these activities are distilled the rules of morality and the system of obligations between man and man. Here the concern is with the proper conduct through which the full life is to be achieved, hence a concern over the methods and opportunities for successful survival, the maximum fulfillment of intellectual and aesthetic capacities and the commitment to what is considered ultimate in the nature of things.

The way men act in this broad sphere cannot be fully prescribed by law because life in this sphere is too protean. Large areas of life must be left untrammeled and uncoerced in order to preserve the possibility of free and creative discovery of new human values. That this involves risk to older and settled values goes without question. In the economic order at least, the element of risk is clearly accepted, for here the prospect of loss is overshadowed by the possibility of great gain. In art and literature there is also the need for freedom. Otherwise we see the dreary repetition of standard forms and lose the unique contribution of the artist, which is freshness of perception and expression. Education and religion, too, must be pursued under conditions of widest freedom if the deepest values inherent in the pursuit of truth are to be realized.

The law is brought into these areas under great peril, for the law, before it can be the guide for the community, must itself be informed by the highest insights of the community. Can the law, however, decisively control those areas of behavior which by their very nature are still in the process of discovery? Can the law define what is truth or how God is to be worshipped? Only on the assumption that ultimate answers are already available to these questions can the law move into these areas with any degree of confidence. But, again, even if reasonably reliable truth is available to a community, is it within the scope of the law to regulate the broad area we have here been describing, or is this to be reserved for the more subtle control of morals?

Does the concept of law necessarily imply a concern with only the minimum standards of behavior, leaving to morality the role of making men moral? Historically this question has been answered for the most part in the negative, although the breadth of the law's concern is in no wise suggested by what the nature of law is. Whether the law will be used narrowly or widely is not a matter of the meaning or nature of law but a consequence of a society's decision about its use.

Aristotle saw in law the instrument for habituating men to the morally good life; Soviet jurists see in law the agency for the remaking of human nature; and in the United States the law has gradually absorbed many areas of behavior which were previously considered the proper province of morality. Law and morality are not successfully separated or distinguished by holding that the scope of law is narrow while the scope of morals is wide. The scope of law changes from one era to the next, and in our era the law has spread its control over a very wide span of human behavior. It may be that the intimate relation between law and morals, and not their separation, is what is indicated by this variation in their relative scope, for if men do not perform voluntarily their moral obligations these obligations must be enforced by the law. The law never self-consciously or deliberately enforces an immoral mode of behavior; those who fashion the law, for the most part, believe that the substance of the law is either required by moral considerations or at least by the general welfare of the community.

The scope of law seems to increase as a society becomes more sensitive to how men "ought" to be living or how the social life of men can be improved. At each step in the march of the law there is resistance to its invasion into previously "free" domains of human behavior; at the same time there is constant pressure for the law to move into these previously uncontrolled areas. What at one time were considered the minimal concerns of the law have over the years been so elaborately reconceived as to proliferate the law's influence with astonishing thoroughness. The simple guarantee that promises will be kept has expanded into a broader control over what kinds of promises or contracts will be permissible in the first place (e.g. contracts in restraint of trade or contracts requiring or prohibiting union membership) ; the guarantee of the safety of property has also been accompanied by a radical reconception of what private property means and what rights collective society has in this property (e.g. minimum wage and social security laws); the protection from injury has also been broadly reinterpreted so that today injury is no longer limited for the purposes of law to physical harm but now includes such forms as injury to reputation caused by slander and injury to personality caused by segregation. The legal rules and decisions regulating these sensitive areas are, nonetheless, laws for having moved into areas once held more exclusively by morality.

Making and Discovering Rules

The law is *made*, whereas a rule is *discovered*. Early jurists were fond of saying the opposite—that laws are not made, they are found. But by this they meant simply that the obligatoriness of a law was to be found in its moral defensibility. Surely laws are made in the sense that they emerge from a formal process of enactment. Certain modes of behavior are neither just nor unjust, neither good nor bad, until a formal rule is made to regulate them.

Traffic laws transform otherwise neutral behavior into delicts or misdemeanors as soon as they become official. It is an offense to travel at certain speeds or park in certain locations only after rules declaring these as offenses are made or promulgated. Without such an applicable rule these acts are legally indifferent. The positing or making of the rule is the only way law comes into being for these acts. But the positive law prescribes our behavior not only in these areas which are morally indifferent before the law is made, for we have already seen that the law as often enforces behavior which is suggested or required by moral obligations. Even here, however, the law is made and has a positive character only because of an act of the official lawgiver. Whether the substance of the law is morally neutral or morally freighted, the quality of law attaches to a rule only when it becomes part of an official system of rules through an act of the sovereign, either through the legislative or the judicial process.

Moral rules, on the other hand, are not made but found. There is no way to repeal a moral obligation. A law, however, can be made and then repealed; a judicial decision can be made and overruled or reversed. The peculiar quality of a genuine moral obligation is that it is categorical, that it is required by the very nature of man. A person must respect another person, not because somebody made a rule or law to this effect, but because human beings intrinisically ought to treat each other in this way.

Although there are exceptional occasions when moral responsibilities seem to be waived, such as killing in time of war, there is no way of being released from the demands of morality. Whatever type of moral system we may confront, the assumption on which the moral rule is based is that human nature, being what it is, already contains or prescribes in some way the nature of our obligation to our fellow man. The moral rule is discovered or found in the sense that certain ways of behaving appear fundamentally appropriate, whereas other ways appear inappropriate and in varying degrees damaging to personality. Human beings are capable of an almost indeterminate variety of conduct which does not conflict with the quality of appropriateness; nevertheless, at critical points the requirements of human nature clearly call for a certain type of behavior for no other reason than that we are men.

How does this distinction, between the law as made and the moral rule as found, help to clarify the concept of law?

For one thing, it helps us to isolate from all the many kinds of rules those which are peculiarly legal. Moreover, of the many ways in which the word "law" can be used, we can now limit this concept to those rules which are the official norms of behavior for a society and which are made official in some positive way by the sovereign authority. To say that law is a rule of behavior commanded by the sovereign means no more than that until a rule has this element of positive enactment or recognition it may be a customary rule, a moral rule, a religious precept, but not a law. When people say "there ought to be a law against it" they are saying that what at the moment may be only a moral obligation ought to be made a legal obligation. The moral obligation may have broken down and it may then be desirable to supplement the moral obligation with a legal obligation supported by the apparatus of official force. The moral rule and the legal rule may very well have the same substance, but what transforms the moral rule into a legal rule is its official recognition or promulgation by the sovereign. The moral rule by itself is not a law. But the moral rule can be or become relevant to the process of law. Likewise, laws do not in every instance have a moral basis. This means that, in the narrow view, the quality of law is conferred on a rule by the act of positive recognition or promulgation.

To say that law is made should not confuse the relation between law and morality. It is not necessary to accept the severe conclusion that a person has rights only if the law makes them or confers them upon him. It is one thing to say that to make a legal rule is to create a right and that until the legal rule is made a person has no right at all. It is quite another thing to say that when the legal rule is made the conditions for dealing with human rights in a legal way have been established. Rights have their initial form in morality; the legal rule is only the official recognition and the technical means of enforcement of rights. That is the meaning behind the phrase, "to secure these rights, governments are instituted." The law does not invest a human being with the qualities of worth and dignity and the other values which flow from these: these values are intrinsic to human nature when viewed from the standpoint of morality. The identification of rights is never complete, either in the fullness of their description or in their number, for specific rights come to light only as conditions focus upon them.

The moral priority of rights, however, does not alter the fact that a right becomes legal only after a law has been made, either by legislation or a judicial decision. There are times when a moral right has not yet been legislated but becomes relevant for the first time in the course of a controversy in the judicial process. The judicial process involves both finding and making, for where there is no specific statute or precedent governing a controversy, a moral norm is sought, and when it is discovered, or when the process of judgment has matured under the influence of a moral norm, this moral norm is transformed into a legal norm by judicial recognition, interpretation, and application. The making of law is, therefore, not in every instance the beginning of a right, but in critical areas of human behavior it is the extension and transformation of the moral right into law.

It is certainly not the case that every law is the extension of morality. Law in the making often reflects the weakness, selfishness, and predatoriness of which men are capable. There is no guarantee that the law will be made in accordance with man's moral insights or the requirements of his moral nature. But even where a law has been made in violation of a moral right the law is subject to criticism only because there is this discrepancy between the law as it is in fact and what the moral right indicates that it ought to be.

Levels of Obligation

Legal obligation is not nearly so ultimate as is moral obligation. In spite of the intimate relation between law and morality, the law is not the standard of morality. Law and morality are bound together because the function of law as an agency for controlling human behavior cannot proceed without reference to moral imperatives. To a large extent, the direction in which the law will lead human behavior is suggested by the moral tendencies of a community. But a community's moral vision is dynamic, and it is affected and influenced by a struggle of competing interests. The moral quality of law will constantly reflect the outcome of contests of power between representatives of different interests, and not all interests have the same moral quality.

A law which seeks to enforce fair trials for all people clearly has a different moral quality from a law which prohibits members of a minority race to own property. Every legal system is made up, on the one hand, of laws which reflect clear moral imperatives and on the other hand of laws which clearly cannot be justified morally. If the law were to represent our only standard of right, we would lose the independent perspective which moral insight provides from which to evaluate the law. We constantly speak of good laws and bad laws, and we do this from whatever moral position we have taken. When our moral judgment condemns a law as bad, we are faced with the dilemma of obligations contradictory to the legal rule and to the moral rule.

In a democratic system of law there is a double basis for

legal obligation. The law is obeyed, for one thing, because of its moral quality. Secondly, it is obeyed because it is a proper and official part of the structure of law. It may be that not a single law can ever arouse complete or unanimous consent about its moral defensibility. Yet it is obeyed by virtually the whole community. There is a kind of morality which compels one to obey the law for the sake of the community, even when one does not accept the moral substance of the law.

The members of a democratic community will to varying degrees always have some criticism to make of the laws. Most of these moral criticisms have the effect of reducing or eliminating for such a person the moral obligation to obey the law; he may decide that the law simply violate elementary justice, as in the case of an unjustly discriminatory tax. But the fact that a law is morally deficient does not immediately lead to disobedience of the law, for there is still the second basis of obligatoriness—that the system of law, which encompasses the remaining rules and procedures, must be upheld. This is particularly important when it is considered that an individual's criticism of the law may not be shared by other members of the community who also presume to be expressing their moral judgments. Again, even the bad law is obeyed under certain circumstances, because in this way the structure of the legal order is preserved.

In democratic society there are specific remedies available for dealing with a bad law without threatening anarchy or chaos. Chief among these are the legislative and the judicial processes. It is possible, therefore, to renounce one's obligation to the questionable morality of the law and at the same time to obey the law for the sake of the legal order upon which other important values continue to depend.

In such a case one affirms his higher obligation to the moral rule in whose light the law now becomes morally deficient. The degree of "badness" in the law will vary from law to law, wherefore the intensity of one's reaction to it will also vary. The bad law can either be superseded by a new law or challenged through the judicial process. If neither of these procedures is available because either the mode of power or the predominat opinion is contrary to a person's moral sensitivity, he then must decide whether to continue to obey the law out of a desire to preserve the legal order or whether his moral obligation overrides even this second basis of the law's obligatoriness.

The life of the law involves a continuous process of protest. No formulation of laws can ever be taken as absolute or eternal. The basis of continuity in the law is provided by those accurate and fundamental insights into human nature and rights which history continues to affirm. Legislation and court decisions prevail only as they continue to fit the moral and pragmatic expectations of society. Where these laws have lost their contact, either with the practical necessities or the moral sensitivities of the time, they either fall into desuetude or are altered or eliminated altogether.

There are times also when the whole structure of law, and not simply a particular law, is looked upon as of secondary importance by some in the solution of grave social problems. The overwhelming sense of moral obligation concerning human relations overrides the more deliberate processes of law. The feeling that the solutions to these problems are immediately mandatory and cannot wait for the inherently sluggish pace of the law nor take the risk of a technical diversion or obstruction has often led men to bypass the procedures of law by disobeying the law.

The law has learned to anticipate this problem and has made provisions for predictable protest. The objections voiced by those who could not conscientiously bear arms in any kind of war have led to an alternative to conscription laws, so that one who "must obey God rather than man" does not face the dilemma which the conscription law once posed for him. Still, although there is some postponement of disobedience to law through the double basis of law's obligatoriness and through the availability of regular procedures for challenging and altering the law, the time may very well come when a person feels that his obligation to law is not ultimate, that his moral obligation is of a higher order.

From this analysis of the relation between law and morality we can derive at least three major characteristics of law: that law is a body of rules fashioned for the purpose of regulating human behavior and in the making of these rules there is dependence upon the conceptions of morality; law is also enforced by the coercive power of the state, but this power is not the "essence" of law, for it is brought to bear upon persons only in conjunction with a rule; and law is directed toward ends which the society is trying to achieve.

The two main ingredients of law are therefore power and morality; but law cannot be reduced to either. The intersection of law and morality is what renders law a moral phenomenon. Finally, law is here seen as a flexible tool for regulating human conduct, and its flexibility is the outcome of man's ever new insights into what is morally right. The law is the mechanism of stability and predictability, and until the law is altered to fit our fuller moral insights the law is the bearer of our social morality.

INDEX

Almonte's
Brothers
of the Wind

R. TAIT McKENZIE
and JAMES NAISMITH

by
Frank Cosentino

Published by

 GENERAL STORE
PUBLISHING HOUSE

1 Main Street Burnstown, Ontario, Canada K0J 1G0
Telephone 1-800-465-6072 Fax (613) 432-7184

ISBN 1-896182-54-2
Printed and bound in Canada

Layout and Design by Derek McEwen

Copyright © 1996

The General Store Publishing House
Burnstown, Ontario, Canada

Canadian Cataloguing in Publication Data

Cosentino, Frank, 1937 –
    Almonte's brothers of the wind : R. Tait McKenzie and James Naismith

Includes bibliographical references
ISBN 1-896182-54-2

    1. McKenzie, R. Tait (Robert Tait) 1867-1938.
    2. Naismith, James, 1861-1939.
    3. Physical education and training–Biography.
    4. Physical education and training–History.
    5. Sculptors–Canada–Biography.
    6. Basketball–Biography.
    7. Almonte (Ont.)–Biography.   I. Title.

GV331.C67 1996   796'.092'2   C96-990073-2

First Printing October 1996

Dedication

For my parents, Vincenzo and Maria,
my brothers and sister and their spouses:
Dom and Isobel, Lena and Louie, Ang and Maureen,
and Teresa, the sister I never knew,
with all of my love and thanks.

—❖—

My appreciation goes to John Stevens for his
efforts in the preparation of
this manuscript.

Preface

BROTHERS OF THE WIND is the story of Robert Tait McKenzie and James Naismith. It could be the story of many Canadians. Their parents left the land of their birth, Scotland, and arrived in an underdeveloped yet promising new country. As is the case with any immigrant group, one has to ask why. The answer, typically, is the same: They sought to give their children the opportunities for growth they couldn't have at home. Both Naismith and McKenzie were born in the new land, Canada, before the birth of the nation. The families settled in a Scottish settlement in Ramsay Township of Lanark County in the Ottawa Valley. The area provided the backdrop to their growing up. There was work to do, fields to plough, forests to explore, rivers to navigate, school and play to absorb their time. As with all immigrant groups, heritage was important; it was lived out in many ways, through their dress, the Highland Games, the Celtic language, the Kirk, the community. At the same time the new land, its diversity and its people, shaped an emerging identity.

It was an experiential existence. There was always something to do. Imagination was just as important as those tasks which were ordered to a specific end. Life was to be lived, sometimes with great hardship and difficulty, more noted by the parents than the children. In the living were countless reminders to be filed away for the right time, to be drawn upon when needed. Their rural education in Almonte stood them in good stead. Both attended McGill University. The extrovert Naismith chose the ministry; McKenzie, the nature lover, decided on medicine. Their university careers were vehicles which carried them into other fields. McKenzie chose medicine because he felt that it was the best way to prepare himself for the emerging discipline of physical education. Naismith took a detour from the traditional ministry. He chose to develop the whole person through sport, Muscular Christianity it was called. He enrolled, at age twenty-nine, in the YMCA Training School at Springfield, Massachusetts. Fourteen years later, in 1904, McKenzie moved to the University of Pennsylvania to head its physical education department.

On the surface, it might appear that these were simply two early examples of Canadians who became validated in their native country's eyes only after achieving success in the United States. And they were successful: Naismith, just one year after arriving at Springfield, called upon his Ottawa Valley background to invent basketball; McKenzie, his youthful curiosity piqued by nature, explored new avenues of expression. The wide acceptance of his experimental first works, his masks, encouraged the budding artist to continue to portray the human body much as the classical Greeks had. Each was acclaimed in the United States and overseas for their work. Even so, McKenzie remained a Canadian citizen for all of his life; Naismith until he became an American in his 65th year.

They were discovered belatedly by Canadians because of the huge impact they have had on the wider world. These two "brothers of the wind" reached out to the world from Almonte, deep in the Ottawa Valley, to share their efforts with generations past and to come. This book is a tribute to all those who have left their native land to find new life and growth in Canada. It is a small way of saluting the lives and contributions of Naismith and McKenzie in the hope of dispelling some of the cultural amnesia Canadians have about our rich heritage.

Frank Cosentino
Eganville, Ontario
May 22, 1996

Table of Contents

CHAPTER 1

Early Days in Almonte and Ramsay Township

ROBERT TAIT MCKENZIE and James Naismith, two of Almonte's most distinguished citizens, were as alike as two peas in a pod. Both of fierce Scotch background, they were boyhood friends. More than that, they were spiritual brothers imbued with a love of sport who even today continue to make an impact in the far regions of the world.

Their paths crossed at an early age. McKenzie, "Rob" as he was known in his youth, was the younger of the two. He was born May 26, 1867, at Ramsay Township in Lanark County only thirty miles away from the new capital, Ottawa, of the new country, Canada, that was to come into being thirty days later on July 1, 1867. Naismith was almost six years older at the time. The two would meet some three years later. McKenzie's father, William, was a minister in the Free Church of Scotland as was his father Patrick before him. When William came to Canada in 1857, he was thirty-two, a graduate of Edinburgh's New College and a bachelor. Locating in Montreal, Canada East, he was an assistant to Dr. Simon Fraser and delivered the odd lecture at the New Presbyterian College.[1]

William was also an itinerant preacher whose travels took him wherever Scottish communities had settled. After hearing this young and dynamic preacher, the congregation of the Free Church at Ramsay Township must have felt that God had answered their prayers. They sent William a call to become pastor of their congregation. The young transplanted Scot was captivated by the area. It was a beautiful spot, much like the home he left behind. Cherry trees lined the road leading up to a stone wall surrounding the church and the manse; a row of

1

poplars stood like tall sentinels. There was a garden with primroses, a box hedge and an eye-catching orchard. The people were similar, Scots of his religious bent as well as many Irish who had left their home because of the potato famine. All were in hope of a better life. The new minister "drove up with the ruling elder, Andrew Toshak, in 1858, greeted the assembled people gathered in their buggies and farm wagons from the wide country-side and, from the high pulpit, raised his hand and said, 'Let us worship God.'" [2]

There was one slight problem. William was a bachelor. The parish preferred a married man. Back to Scotland went William, one year after becoming pastor, there to wed his bride Catherine Shiells. He first met her at the Sunday school classes where Catherine and Nellie Shiells [3] also taught on Sunday afternoons. William, a divinity student at the time, walked them home "over the mound, down through Princes Street Gardens, to their home in New Town. The acquaintance thus begun soon ripened into something warmer, and he and Catherine were betrothed before he left for his Canadian adventure." [4] It must have been a dramatic change for his young spouse. McKenzie wrote later that she was full of terror at the thought of leaving the "security of her home and an old civilization and culture for the unknown terrors of the Canadian backwoods." [5] She was a timid and shy lass; the duties of a minister's wife loomed large. There was a certain amount of pride evident as he wrote that "the learning of the new ways of which she was profoundly ignorant was faced with courage and determination. Her generous fun-making ability due to an inner joyousness brought to her many friends." [6] She left Edinburgh with its refined life for a rugged existence in Ramsay Township and its outpost mentality. It was a strength-sapping life for the young woman but she soon found herself "strengthened by" (the congregation's) "natural love and affection. She speedily became the leader of this little community of which she found herself the centre." [7] A family followed: three children in quick succession. William junior was born first; next came Agnes and then Robert Tait, named for his maternal grandmother.

A year after Rob's birth, 1868, the family moved the short distance to the more developed Almonte. The town itself was full of surprises. Was there any other town in the Valley with a Spanish name? Already, it was a manufacturing centre, the Manchester of Canada it was called, specializing in woollens. The reason it was named after Juan Nepomuceno Almonte is lost. He had been a soldier and diplomat, fought at the Alamo, survived numerous military coups d'état, civil wars and always seemed to land on his feet. He died in exile in Paris, March 20, 1869.[8] His struggles apparently so captured the imagination of the residents of Ramsay and Waterford, two small settlements on the Canadian Mississippi River, that they named their community after him. It is certainly the only town in Canada to bear the name of a Mexican general.

The move was a shared decision. For three years, the two parishes, Ramsay and St. John's Presbyterian, in Almonte, proved to be too much for the minister and his young family. Both William and Catherine were often sick, run down from the continual work involved. Visitations to the two churches became more and more difficult. The congregations decided to merge. The Ramsay church was closed; St. John's Almonte would serve the combined group. The congregation would do the travelling.

The change brought a revival of spirit and health. Almonte was a beautiful and bountiful town with the picturesque Mississippi River flowing gently through it, providing the source of power that attracted woollen and grist mills. Almonte manufactured tweeds of such high quality that they were exported to the mother country. The Parish provided a white brick manse opposite the church in south western Almonte.

> In its Free Kirk Manse, he (Rob) was nurtured on
> porridge and the Shorter Catechism. For to this
> pioneer settlement came his father Reverend William
> McKenzie, "Meenister" to the hardy gaels who, on
> Sabbath mornings, loaded the family into wagons to
> take them to the Kirk where the presenter sounded
> the Covenanting note of Old Hundred.[9]

It was a close-knit Scottish community bound by heritage, religion and in many cases the common struggle against the bush and the land. When Rob was three, the demanding pioneer life caught up with Catherine McKenzie. She was taken ill. The doctor's advice was that she could not be treated locally; she must return to Scotland, to Edinburgh. The congregation banded around the "Meenister" and his wife. William and Catherine returned to Scotland for her treatment. Parishioners Robert and Anne Young took in the McKenzie children in the interim. The surrogate grandparents took great interest and delight in their young charges. They were there constantly, showering affection and attention on the youngsters, introducing them to a whole new dimension in family life.

They and their surroundings made a great impact on Rob. The setting was idyllic. There were huge shade trees, an old stone house with a "verandah on three sides, the fragrant lilies in the garden, its hedges and beehives were places of delight. The patient collie on its treadmill worked the churn. Its spacious barn housed the products of the well tilled fields and the stable pump and horse trough supplied the horses and cattle." [10]

It was quite comfortable for Rob to call the Youngs Grandfather and Grandmother. His family had made many visits to their farm. It was a fun place to be. There were also three children there, Annie, James and Rob Naismith, the Young's true grandchildren who had recently come to live with them. The three were orphans, their parents John and Margaret having recently died. John Naismith had come to Ramsay in 1842 as a nine-year-old. He lived with his uncle Peter Naismith on a farm along Clayton Road. On January 18, 1858, he married Margaret Young who lived close by. John was a teamster and a building contractor; he found work in the Outaouais at Fort Coulonge. They moved there in 1869 when he bought a sawmill to manufacture his own lumber and cut his costs. Disaster struck the next year at the sawmill on Grand Calumet Island. The Naismith's world, so secure at first, began falling apart. First, Grandfather Young died. Then fire consumed the mill in the summer of 1870. All their hopes had been pinned there. It seemed as if all the stability was being taken from the Naismith children's world. Then, without warning, John Naismith contracted typhoid fever and died on October 19, 1870.

Gravestone of Naismith's parents   *Naismith Foundation*

As soon as Margaret's brother

heard the news that John was ill, he loaded up his wagon for the long journey to Grand Calumet. Typhoid was so feared, so contagious, that the Naismiths would be quarantined. On his arrival at their makeshift home, he called from the outside for Margaret. He knew that she would not leave her husband. She packed some clothes for the children and sent them out to their uncle. The last image James Naismith had of his mother was her waving from the doorway; his father was too weak to rise from the bed. In a few short days he was dead. Margaret contracted typhoid as well and died less than three weeks after her husband on November 6, 1870, James Naismith's ninth birthday.

James Naismith's world had come crashing down around him. Within the space of six months, three of the most cherished people in his life had left it: His grandfather in July and now his father followed by his mother. All three had naturally been important to him, but his grandfather had been a special influence. He had delighted in the quiet moments when he "helped" Grandfather Young. The older man accepted him as he was, never scolding or admonishing, continually encouraging. Jim could still hear his grandfather's voice saying: "Don't think you can't master it! Do it and make a man of yourself!"[11] Occasionally, Jim would find himself looking longingly out his window across a gully to the house he had been born in and lived in before the family moved on to Fort Coulonge. Life was so much happier and secure then. Memories flooded back to him, happier times when all of his loved ones were together.

Grandmother Anne did her best to make sure that all the Naismith children and her McKenzie visitors were brought up with staunch Presbyterian values. There were prayers in the morning and evening; readings from the Good Book and Pilgrim's Progress; good work habits. Services, prayers and a quiet Sabbath were all part of the normal routine. But on February 3, 1873, Grandmother Young died. Again, the Naismiths and McKenzies were in mourning. Jim became a ward of his uncle, Peter; fourteen-year-old Anne became the woman of the house, not only tending to the domestic chores for her bachelor uncle Peter, but trying to be a mother to her younger brothers.

Now a twelve-year-old, James Naismith was expected to help out on the large farm. There were chores early in the morning before school, a long walk to school, a day spent fidgeting in the classroom, the walk home to more duties, a meal cooked by Annie and perhaps some free time to spend with friends. Uncle Peter was a no-nonsense type of man. Industry, thrift, self-reliance and devotion to duty were all stressed. He made it quite clear to Jim that he wasn't going to be coddled, he would have to pull his own weight and earn his keep. The more he could do for himself without distracting his uncle from his work, the better. And Jim Naismith took the lesson to heart. There were plenty of rivers and lakes around Almonte. The Mississippi, Misiwaka and Indian Rivers were all playgrounds, summer and winter.

On one late fall evening after a prolonged early cold spell which had frozen the Indian River, Jim strolled over to watch his pals who were out for the season's first skate. There was a fire burning on shore to ward off the chill. Naismith's friends were obviously enjoying the frozen delight, their voices rising in excitement as if they were newly found after having been stilled during the harvesting. Standing by the fire, Jim looked on longingly. He wanted so much to join in; he took so much joy from playing and being part of the game, whatever it happened to be — tag, prisoners' base, lacrosse on ice, speedskating or crack the whip. There was the sheer relief from the sunrise-to-sunset work to school regime. But he had no skates; and he refused to ask his guardian, not after all the speeches he had heard about self-reliance. He was just too proud, and perhaps a little intimidated, to ask Uncle Peter to buy him some. After a few minutes of watching, Jim turned abruptly and made the three mile hike back to the farm. He headed straight into his uncle's workshop. Already he was developing a talent for confronting his problems and tackling them head on.

The gas light burned far into the night and early morning. The noise of sawing and grinding was muted while the youngster fashioned a solution to his problem.

> The next evening when the group gathered at the
> river, this young fellow was among them and over his
> shoulders hung a pair of skates. These skates were not
> like those of the other boys but were made from a
> pair of old files set firmly into strips of hickory wood.
> Years later, when necessity arose, this same inventive
> lad gave the world not a pair of home made skates but
> the game of basketball. [12]

While his uncle stressed self-reliance and initiative as good, solid Scotch family virtues, there was another influence on Naismith's inventiveness. The Young homestead was almost halfway between

Almonte and Bennies Corners. The latter was a small settlement and a meeting place for the youth of the area, farm boys all, once their chores were finished. It gave them a chance to play together, trade stories and roam freely, something they couldn't do during the day. At the Corners there were a few houses, a blacksmith shop, the local school, a store and trees, lots of trees in a stand which provided the delicious syrup in early spring and the chance to test oneself and one's fellows in feats of strength, balance and agility. Who could climb the fastest? Who could swing from a limb the longest? Who could chin himself the most? Who could walk along a limb the farthest before having to jump because it was about to break? They lived in a physical world. At their farms, morning and night, and sometimes all day, they tried to outdo each other with stories of how much work they did, how heavy a load they had lifted, how quickly they loaded and unloaded the hay wagon.

The blacksmith shop provided many opportunities for demonstrations of strength and skill. The boys stood in awe of the smith who bent and shaped huge weights of steel and iron. They vied with each other to lift the heavy anvil, sometimes impressing one another "by

Bennies Corners School   *Naismith Foundation*

grasping the tapering end which is called the horn."[13] The long heavy rope which was part of the smith's gear and "used to hobble refractory horses when they were to be shod" was well used by the boys. Sides were chosen, a command given, and a tug-of-war would ensue. There was grunting, straining and herculean efforts by each side until the winner prevailed and the losing side fell to the ground, completely exhausted. The rope might also double as a high bar as they competed to see who could jump the highest. Invariably, there would be the type of testing common to all groups, the establishment of some sort of pecking order. Wrestling eventually surfaced as a natural way of finding out who could put everything together in the activity most basic to human development and probably the oldest of all sports. More often than not, it was James Naismith; the others, especially young Rob McKenzie, could only look at him with astonishment and respect.

No one was left out. In the evenings, especially in the lengthening summer days, one of the favourite games was duck on a rock. The rules were fairly simple.[15] Behind the blacksmith shop sat a large rock imbedded in the ground. It stood about a foot high and was as round as a washtub. Each player searched for a "duck," a stone about fist size. One was chosen to be "it," to be a guard and place his duck on the rock. The rest of the group stood behind a line some twenty feet away. They took turns trying to knock the duck off the rock. With a miss, the thrower had to retrieve his thrown rock within a prescribed area, without being tagged by the guard. If a tag was made, places were exchanged, the thrower becoming the new guard. If the duck was knocked from the rock, the guard had to retrieve it, place it back on its perch and then scramble to tag the others who were busy picking up their stones and heading back to safety. The guard could only tag someone after retrieving his duck and placing it back on the rock. It was a simple game, a children's game, yet one which would stay with Naismith for years and form the core of his contribution to sport history.

There was some strategy involved. When a player threw his rock as hard as possible on a flat plane, it travelled a long way and he had to go a long distance to retrieve it. At the same time, it meant that the guard had more time to tag him. Eventually, they determined that if the rock were lobbed in an arc, it didn't travel far if it missed. If it hit the duck and knocked it off, invariably the duck fell behind the rock, and the one thrown landed to the side or front. In such a case, the guard was less likely to tag someone because he had to travel farther to get the duck. Finesse and accuracy were just as important as strength. The game and its strategy were filed deep in the recesses of James Naismith's mind, to resurface some twenty years later.

On those hot, dusty, summer days, a ritual of sorts developed. At the end of the Duck On a Rock game and before it turned completely dark, it was time for a swim. Naismith recalled years later how "the boys filed down the dusty road, crossed the old rail fence into Anderson's pasture and made their way to the old swimming hole in the Indian River. It was typical boys' play in the water; they ducked one another and used the mud bank for a slippery slide."[16] Feeling refreshed and clean, each made his way to his own house under the darkening late summer sky. It was time to catch some sleep before rising with the sun in the morning for another day of chores and school before meeting once again at Bennies Corners.

The change of seasons brought a change in play. With the bright blaze of autumn reds, yellows and golds of the woods serving as a backdrop, hunting and fishing occupied the young boys' time. A boy might catch a great northern pike, its huge size and sharp teeth sure to be a topic of conversation whenever and wherever they gathered to swap stories. As in all rural communities, hunting season in Lanark County was a special time of year. While the men went out searching for deer or lynx, the youngsters' excursions were a rite of passage, as they went out hoping to bag a partridge or rabbit.

With the onset of winter, skating at the "old swimming hole" on the Indian River became a focal point. There was no hockey, since the game was not yet invented, but there were races, tag, and attempts at "fancy skating." And there was always a blazing log fire on shore for welcomed warmth. Rather than allowing the winter of snow and cold to confine them indoors, the youngsters treated the landscape as a huge playground to explore and engage. When someone arrived with horses and sled, a "bob-sled" as it was called:

> boys and girls would pile into a sled filled with
> straw and singing and yelling, they would go
> from house to house, rousing out some of their
> friends who had failed to start with the group.
> Often the whole crowd would enter some
> kitchen to laugh and chatter as they ate
> doughnuts and drank cider. [17]

There were also sports introduced by the native people during the winter time. Tramps on snowshoes through the fields were popular, as was tobogganing. Where there were no hills, snow was moved to create a long ramp serving as a slide, and the toboggan with its crew of screaming boys and girls gathered speed from the push at the top and the build-up of momentum.

As far as Rob McKenzie was concerned, Jim Naismith was a marvel. Partly a natural result of the age difference of six years, Naismith's heroic physical feats inspired the younger Rob to idolize him. He was all that the youngster wanted to be. McKenzie was a gentle kind of youth: slight of body, shy and reserved.

Even at an early age, he had developed an appreciation for beauty and form while trying to fit in with the rugged play of his environment. School, especially, was distasteful. His first master, a former blacksmith named McCarter, terrified young Robbie. His use of the strap reminded the children of the way the blacksmith swung his hammer when trying to bend an object into the required shape. The students had a special name for the brawny disciplinarian: Juno. He, in turn, had a pet name for young Rob whose body was present in the classroom but whose mind wandered far off in some more idyllic setting. There were so many delights outdoors; the fresh air, the sunshine, the animals and birds in their abundance all made the school seem like a prison. The school house with its dusty floors and musty smell, the long hours of sitting erect, struggling to give meaning to the words and blackboard marks of the giant McCarter were too much for Rob. His mind was his vehicle of freedom.

> Later, he recalled being a rather delicate child, sensitive at being called pale faced, a roamer of the woods and fields with a mind filled with the romance that Sir Walter Scott and Fenimore Cooper alone could instill, going unwillingly to school, distracted by thoughts of the deerslayer, making clothyard shafts from the strait cedar rails looted from the fences of unwilling farmers, feathered with care to be sped by bows of rock elm against squirrels, chipmunk or groundhog, the wild pigeon then still with us, the partridge sitting low on its branch and failing all this, even the domestic hen.[18]

There were those Sundays when after services Rob would exit the church, the hymn How Great Thou Art echoing in his head, giving him a new feeling for the wondrous works of the world of nature. His mind wandered constantly in school, his reverie frequently shattered by Juno who, observing McKenzie drifting off, eyes glazed, sent a question in the young lad's direction. Rob's "stupid-like" response was greeted typically by McCarter's "Eh, Rabbie, ye're a meeserable tool!"[19] In the one-room school house, the comment brought forth giggles and chuckles from the other students; not that they enjoyed seeing McKenzie so singled out, but they were so surprised at how often it happened. He just never seemed to learn.

One can only speculate how young Rob McKenzie would have turned out had he had to endure McCarter for all of his eight elementary years. But good fortune was with him. In 1875 a new school was built on Martin Street to accommodate both elementary and secondary grades. McCarter was to stay behind at the old country school. It was a Godsend for McKenzie. He was able to join his sister Agnes and brother William, both of whom were in high school. The trek to classes became enjoyable once again. Passing the river on the way might call for a quick cooling-off swim or a wade in the shallows of the river known by all as Rock Bottom. More often than not, however, Rob was peeking into the cleverly disguised oriole nests hanging like ornaments from the many elms. Each was a miracle in itself, never ceasing to fascinate the young man. He could only marvel at the weaving of the hanging object of fibres, bark and string suspended from the tip of a branch. And to think that a bird, a "dumb animal," was able to make it!

But the happiest aspect of the move was that Robbie had a new teacher, Miss Nelson. He began enjoying school again. She understood him, encouraged him, praised him for his artistic talent and insights. She even went so far as to suggest to his parents that they should send him for art lessons. And the perfect opportunity presented itself. An artist was coming to Almonte, was available for instruction and his lessons were reasonably priced. The parents agreed. Rob was enrolled and gained a solid foundation in seeing with the eye of an artist. The sketching skills he learned were to come into play again and again throughout his life.[20]

It was only the first of many awakenings and influences for young Rob. The next year, in early 1876, his father, the Reverend William McKenzie, died. Robert Tait McKenzie wrote later that it was as a result of "a night drive home in the cruel winter cold from Clayton after conducting services in a hot and overcrowded hall as a substitute for another who could not go."[21] He was only fifty-two, but having been ill for a long time and having insisted on continuing to minister to his flock, he deteriorated rapidly and died. That was sad enough but there were additional burdens. Rob's mother, Catherine, was pregnant with her fourth child. Never healthy, she found it was an additional preoccupation. Regardless, the manse would have to be turned over to the new minister and his family.

Again, the community came to the young family's assistance. They cooked meals, did chores, and most helpful of all, raised money for a new house. Catherine understood that she could only accept such help for so long. After all, her friends could not support her indefinitely, and in any event, she was too proud to accept charity beyond a certain point. The family had to look after itself. The children would have to do chores, run errands and look for odd jobs to help support the growing family. Just a short time later, in June, the baby, a boy, was born.

He was named Bertram for Catherine's brother-in-law, John Bertram, a successful lumberman living in Peterborough. He and his wife, Helen Shiells, had offered much support, financial and otherwise, to Catherine to see her through the difficult adjustment of the death and birth.

Whether it was the sketching Rob was doing or the removal of the subtle pressures of being a preacher's son or no longer being the baby of the family, he grew more mature and observant. To be sure, he was very sad at the loss of his father; his visits to the Young farm became more frequent. He became more aware of Jim Naismith, remembered how he had coped with the death of his father. He had only admiration for the independence, the strength and self-assurance of Naismith, now a strapping fifteen-year-old. He became even more of a role model for the nine-year-old.

Indeed, Jim Naismith was coming much into his own. He had recovered well from the death of his parents, which now seemed so long ago. He had not been a burden on his uncle, Peter Young. In fact, he strived to ensure that he would live his life without being a drain on anyone. He was in his second year at high school and somewhat restless. School was confining. It was as if his energy was welling up, straining to be released. He just couldn't sit still for so long when there was a whole physical world out there to explore and discover. He dropped out. Uncle

Peter was not pleased but he agreed to it if Jim could learn to support himself and contribute to the upkeep of the farm. He gave Jim responsibility, provided a team of horses to work full time around the farm. Jim's father had been a teamster as well and he was determined to show that he was capable of handling a team and wagon.

It wasn't easy. One time he was crossing the Misiwaka River to pick up a load of hay. It was winter time; there was a coat of ice on the water. The normal fording spot was down river where the water was shallow. It was also a longer way from his destination. He decided to cross closer to the hay pick-up where the water was deeper. It was winter, the water had frozen; surely it would be safe. The crossing with the empty sleigh was uneventful; he was pleased with his time-saving shortcut. He quickly loaded up the wagon.

He crossed back at the same spot. All was going smoothly, he was relaxing, congratulating himself on his time-saving decision. He was almost at the shore when there was a sharp crack and the horses crashed into the water. There was no time to call for help, and in any event, it was too far away to be of any help. And there was no way he would call for Uncle Peter to bail him out, not after all his talk about self-reliance and looking after yourself! Jim felt his throat tighten as he watched the horses thrashing in the icy water.

For a moment, he was immobilized. Then, he swung into action. The sleigh with its load of hay had not gone into the water. He clambered down from his seat and rushed to loosen the doubletrees to free the horses. Still they floundered and kicked at the water, trying to secure a foothold on the ice. Jim grabbed a rein and threw it around the head of the horse that was kicking at the side of the hole. He moved to the other side and started pulling. Momentarily, he was reminded of all those tug of war games at the blacksmith's shop at Bennie's Corners. With a huge effort, he pulled once again; the horse's front hooves held the ice. Jim led him to safer ground. He returned to repeat the feat with the other horse.

At once exhausted and exhilarated by having averted a catastrophe, for a moment he was aware of nothing but his heavy panting. He sat down on the bank to catch his breath. The horses were behind him and Jim turned to make sure that they were okay. As he turned, he caught a glimpse of his Uncle Peter watching from behind the trees. He had seen it all but preferred to stay in the background, allowing Jim to work his own way out of the mess he had got himself into.

This was the type of experience that fueled Jim Naismith's boundless self-confidence. He seemed to excel in any activity related to his country environment. There might have been an absence of organized sport in his life but there was no lack of competition. And he thrived on it. Teams of horses vied with each other to pull huge loads; logs and stones were lifted in contests of strength; young unbroken horses were mounted to see who could stay on the longest. There were the straightest furrows to plough, contests to see who was the most accurate shot, canoeing skills to be tested, trees to be felled in predetermined paths. It was a wonderful, testing life; so many ways to bring joy to the effort and labour of rural life.

And there were many occasions for competition. During harvest time, for example, neighbours would gather at each farm to help, moving from one location to another. These were the days of little or no machinery. A strong back was a necessity; the term "farmhands" for labourers could be taken quite literally. Wheat sheaves had to be tied up in individual bundles before they were loaded on the wagon. It was just a matter of time before workers would compete to see who could process the most sheaves of wheat and it was just a matter of time before Jim Naismith was the acknowledged champion.

Years later an older McKenzie reminisced to recapture this scene of his youth, still seemingly in awe of his friend:

> a powerful youth bestrides an unbound sheaf of wheat,
> while in one hand he holds a sheaf he has just bound.
> He throws it up in the air and binds the other one
> before the first one comes back to earth and challenges
> anyone on the harvest field to do the same thing. [22]

Jim Naismith was at home in the country. Every aspect of it seemed to agree with him. He had remarkable quickness. Spearfishing in the early evening by jacklight was a test of his reactions. He relished it; invariably, he won out over the fish. There were occasions when Rob McKenzie accompanied Jim and was wide-eyed at his strength, skill and quick decisive actions. It was as if Jim was trying to introduce Rob to the outdoor life, trying to build up the frail young boy using the activities of the robust life he loved.

And it seemed to be working. He learned to ride a horse bareback, hanging on for dear life to whatever tufts of hair were in reach, which was even more difficult when "the trot of the thirsty horse to the water trough made the problem of balance acute."[23] He learned to harness a horse, milk a cow and plough a furrow.

Part of the transformation of young Rob from a passive to an active participant in his environment occurred in the pivotal summer of 1876. His father died; his brother was born. Both had an impact but as well, the circus came to town, and to a nine-year-old boy, it was a wonder to behold. In addition to the rides, the exotic animals he had only read about and the barkers with their enticing spiels, the New Golden Menagerie Circus exposed the wide-eyed young lad to a different sort of athleticism.

He had always associated athletic ability with the feats he had seen Jim Naismith perform at school and at the Young farm. Among the Scots, the great Donald Dinnie and his inspiring performances, which were becoming legendary at the Highland Games, were a constant subject of conversation. Young Rob's idea of an athlete might have been "Roy Moe MacLennan, Glengarry County's pride, who could leap over three horses, the centre one being sixteen hands high, and throw a ten pound blacksmith's hammer further than a man could fling a finger stone of his own choosing."[24]

Like all small towns, Almonte was occasionally visited by wandering "pedestrians," individuals who would appear at a tavern or inn, barber shop or livery stables and challenge all comers to a race. These characters were not always on the level. They would demonstrate their skill to a select few and get them all worked up about a sure thing. A match would be arranged with side bets and what seemed to be a certainty dissolved into misfortune and a quick exit from town by the "tourist." There were legendary figures who made an impact on a young boy: Larry Frost, "the king of the lumber-jacks who could plant the print of his spiked heel in the ceiling beam of a Bryson bar room and land on his feet, 'leaving his calling card', he called it; in the villages and towns the visiting firemen already ran their course, laid their hundred feet of hose, coupled it to the hand engine, and with labouring backs, pumped a stream of water through it against time."[25] It was obvious who were the heroes of the day. It was they who "could make their team of horses pull a load where another had failed, who took pride in lifting the heavy end of the log, who could tame a wild colt, run a straight furrow with his plough, handle a canoe, shoot straight, or make a tree fall where he wanted it to lie."[26]

Now, however, nine-year-old Rob watched open-mouthed as

slight, muscular people, their timing perfect, balanced on the high wire, swung from one trapeze to another, tumbled and twisted and turned high in the air, seemingly about to plunge to the ground, only to be snatched by hands or a bar swinging by at the right time. It was something of a turning point. These were trim, lithe individuals performing these skills; they looked no bigger than he was. Robert Tait McKenzie was determined to raise the level of the physical side of his being.

> There were plenty of opportunities but it wasn't an automatic transition. His primary model, of course, continued to be Jim Naismith. One night Rob accompanied Jim, rifle in hand, to determine who or what was killing sheep on the farm. As McKenzie later recalled, it was an unforgettable pitch black night, we pitched the punt quietly on the low bank of the meadow, a lighted lantern concealed in an empty firkin, carefully covered, Jim with his gun across his knees and I holding the nose of the punt against the bank, waiting in silent anticipation for what was to happen. Presently, we heard the rush of frightened feet coming toward us; the flock of sheep came stampeding by. I raised the lantern high and there was a sudden startled pause as I saw reflected in the phosphorescent light, startled eyes. The gun cracked and a neighbour's dog, long under suspicion for sheep killing dropped in his tracks.[27]

In Rob's case, the use of the rifle did not come without trial and error and some good luck. On one occasion, while driving the wagon over a rock-strewn, bumpy road, he ignored the advice that had always been given to him and held the rifle by the barrel while resting the butt on the floor of the buckboard. The jarring and jostling of the wagon caused the rifle to fire; his hat was sent flying. The brim was partly blown away. His ears were ringing. His heart was thumping. He broke out into a cold sweat when he realized what had happened. Rob counted himself lucky to be alive. He had learned his lesson with only a fright rather than any permanent or serious damage.

With time, McKenzie widened his appreciation of nature and in some ways sought to tame it. His eager attempts to duplicate Jim Naismith's feats drove him to learn how to milk a cow, handle a plough, ride a horse bareback and eventually to remain comfortably in the saddle whatever the horse's gait. But it was the water, winter and summer, that helped to inspire confidence and poise in the youngster. He learned to swim the hard way; his older brother, William, threw him "into the pond off the boom at the sawmill and made (him) swim back to the log in dog-fashion."[28] It was so commonplace and so natural. Just as the oar and the paddle on the waterways opened up Canada, so too did they expand McKenzie's horizons. The rivers and lakes became a constant playground, no matter the season. In the winter, he joined his friends in screwing his skates to his heels and strapping the fronts over his toes. Many of the games played on dry land were the games of winter. They were fun. In addition, they allowed the young budding artist to test his powers of observation, taking in the scene of his friends striving to catch up or stay ahead in a speed skating race or elude or catch someone in a game of prisoners' base. Occasionally, all eyes would shift to someone who was skating with the latest Acme strapless skates; they were a marvel. They all watched intently, so aware that the straps on their skates were bound so tightly that they restricted the blood circulation and hastened the onslaught of frozen toes. They knew that the inevitable painful tingling was to come as they thawed out.

With the coming of spring, it was a common sight to see the youngsters gathered by the great log slide. Over the winter the timber had been accumulating; at the thaw it would be slid down the ramp into the Mississippi to float down to the Ottawa. The lumbermen were the stars of the day; wherever they could, people watched in awe as they probed and picked, poked, pushed and pulled, stepped over and around, balanced and jumped from log to log, breaking up jams and ensuring the free flow down the chutes and into the swollen waters, their voices rising above the roar of the crashing water and timber. They were a sight to behold — and to emulate:

> We stepped lightly from stick to stick as they sank under our weight, till we could come to rest on a big one. Sometimes we would come suddenly to a space of clear water too late to stop and then we had to throw ourselves belly down across one and warily regain our place on top. Good exercise it was and practical for it had an element of risk without which the sporting spirit is lacking.

> The sinister power of the water was brought to us by
> the drownings that were recounted to us as warnings
> as we learned the risks men run in their contest with
> nature.[29]

It was this contest with nature that appealed to McKenzie. He didn't particularly want to compete with his friends; he might alienate them or make them feel badly. He was interested in testing himself and nature was the perfect foil. He wanted to duplicate it, to challenge it, to co-operate with it, to flow with it and be part of it. By the time he was fourteen, he had become the proud owner of a birch-bark canoe, able to propel it with or against the current or wind with a single paddle without changing sides. He was ready to explore the lands downstream. There were rapids to shoot, portages to take, camps to make. He would stay away for weeks at a time, moving past the mouth of the Mississippi and into Marshall's Bay on the Ottawa. There he would camp, fish, hunt and gather berries for his day-to-day needs much the way people of the first nations had done for years before. He had become a self-sufficient young man, brimming with confidence. He felt equally at home in Almonte or in the rural areas where he might have to hitch horses to a wagon, fell a tree, pitch a tent, make a campfire, cook a meal or work the fields.

Life was a voyage of discovery. He was introduced to lacrosse. He had seen the Indians play it, but now the rules had been codified and distributed so he and his friends could play it as best they could on the village common which doubled as a cow pasture. Players had to be nimble indeed as they moved to avoid the many cow pies which dotted the field. Then too, there were the many animals who didn't appreciate the disturbance in their grazing area. A high fence rail was often the last resort for a youngster who had run out of manoeuvring room trying to avoid a menacing bull, developing the leg strength necessary for competitive high jumping.

The fence rail also served to introduce the group to another concept. During the winter, the same field was covered with high banks of snow, particularly around the fence. Tumbling just like circus performers became possible; the soft snow would break their fall and cushion them. The boys climbed the fence, jumped off it, tucking in their heads and rolling and landing on their feet. It was a springboard which would serve both McKenzie and Naismith well in the future.

Meanwhile, Jim Naismith was moving towards his future date

McKenzie and Naismith as teens   *U of Penn. Archives*

with destiny. When he was fifteen and half way through his grade ten, like many country boys at that time, he figured he had enough education and wanted to quit school and get on with his life. With his Uncle Peter's permission, he took his team of horses and joined the lumbering trade. A strong, strapping lad, he made an impression and carried it through wherever he went. He was accepted in all the lumber camps. He soon demonstrated that he could saw, ride and load logs as well as anyone and better than most.

There was nothing halfway about Jim Naismith. He learned to swear and drink with the best of them. On one occasion, while in a tavern, he was keeping up a steady banter, his words sprinkled with obscenities. His tongue had been well loosened by liberal shots of whisky. He was feeling good, almost cocky; he belonged, he was accepted. He ordered another whisky. The man next to him, a stranger, asked if he were Margaret Young's boy. Not knowing what to expect but obviously well pleased that he was recognized and known, with a big smile on his face, he replied that indeed he was. He wasn't prepared for the next comment:

> "She'd turn over in her grave to see ye." Jim Naismith set the glass of whisky down before it reached his lips. He got up and walked out of the saloon, never to return. That night he went back to the grain bin. He made a solemn vow to his mother that she would never again need to be ashamed of him. He would drink no more, nor would he ever let himself be provoked into profanity. [30]

He made another decision. After five years of drifting, he returned to school. There are two versions of what happened. One [31] is that when Jim approached his uncle Peter to inform him of the decision, he met with resistance. After all, there was work to be done on the farm, work that Jim had been doing, and he couldn't afford to hire someone else to do it. Naismith understood. He promised to do the chores before and after school and he'd still be available for the summers too. He was now almost twenty years old. The principal, Peter Campbell McGregor, agreed to take him on as a student. That was all Naismith needed. He became a dedicated pupil; he learned Latin and Greek and finished the rest of his high school diploma in two years, earning grades suitable for entrance to university. When he informed his uncle that he wished to enrol at McGill, once again there was resistance. With Jim being out of town, there would be no one to do the daily chores. Naismith promised to come home every summer to work on the farm. Peter Young wanted one further concession. If Jim Naismith agreed to study for the ministry, he would give his consent. Jim agreed. The compromise was reached and the soon-to-be twenty-two-year-old left for McGill in September of 1883.

Naismith himself had a slightly different version. He wrote:

> It was with a firm determination and a great sense of confidence that I was to enter the study for the Ministry. For several years, I had been wondering what I wanted to accomplish; finally, I decided that the only real satisfaction that I would ever derive from life was to help my fellow beings. At that time, the Ministry was the way one attempted to help his fellows. I knew that there would be seven years before I could go out into the world and begin my life work but I felt that the time spent would be worthwhile. [32]

It would be three years before his young friend, Rob McKenzie, would join him at McGill. It was not something that he had contemplated but, as with so many facets of his life, James Naismith was showing the way. It wasn't easy. The young sixteen-year-old McKenzie was still finding it difficult to concentrate on his school work. Math was especially hard. And there was always the overpowering presence of McGregor. He treated everybody alike, made no allowances for individual differences; he just didn't seem to understand Rob's temperament. He was such an intimidating presence. He taught Latin and Greek, demanding full attention while he paraded across the front of the room in his long black academic gown. He was the principal, led by example, worked long hours, drilled his students incessantly and paid attention only to what was on the printed page without detouring into historical or lyrical insights. Students worked hard, McKenzie included. Much of his work was done in his seat beside the window in the diminishing light of the short winter day. Being next to the windows made it irresistible for McKenzie's mind to wander through the woods and meadows of the enticing outdoors. More than once, McGregor's booming voice shattered his reverie with "McKenzie, your head is full of rats and straw."

In 1883, the year that Naismith left for McGill, McKenzie went to Ottawa to attend Lisgar Collegiate Institute to take his preparatory work to enter McGill. In 1885, at eighteen years of age, he enrolled at McGill as a pre-med student, reunited once again with his soul brother and inspiration, James Naismith.

1. Jean McGill, The Joy of Effort, (Bewdley:Clay Publishing Company Ltd., 1980), p. 1.
2. R. Tait McKenzie, "The Bench of the Minister And His Wife" address, University of Pennsylvania Archives, p. 3.
3. Some sources have Shields but it most certainly is Shiells as reported in Who's Who in America, 1936-37. *Journal of Health, Physical Education and Recreation*, February, 1944, p. 96.
4. R. Tait McKenzie, "The Bench of The Minister and His Wife" dedication address, University of Pennsylvania Archives.
5. ibid.
6. ibid.
7. ibid.
8. *Appletons' Cyclopedia of American Biography*. New York: D. Appleton and Co., 1887, Volume 1. p. 57.
9. A.S Lamb, "Tait McKenzie in Canada," JOHPER -1944, Vol. 15, #2, p.69.
10. Jean McGill, op. cit., p. 2.
11. Bernice Larson Webb, The Little Basketball Man. (Lafayette: Spider Press, 1991) p. 4.
12. James Naismith, Basketball: Its Origins and Development, New York: Associated Press, 1941, p.16.
13. ibid., p. 14.
14. ibid..
15. See appendix for the published rules in their entirety.
16. ibid., p. 15.
17. ibid., p. 16.
18. Jean McGill, op. cit., p. 3.
19. ibid., p. 13..
20. ibid., p. 4.
21. R. Tait McKenzie, "The Bench of the Minister and His Wife", op. cit., p. 6.
22. R. Tait McKenzie, "Reminiscences of a Good Friend". Almonte *Gazette*, A Celebration of Basketball, November, 1991, p. 5.
23. R. Tait McKenzie Notes, University of Pennsylvania Achives, p. 6.
24. ibid. p.1.
25. ibid., p. 2.
26. ibid., p. 7.
27. Jean McGill, op. cit., p. 9.
28. McKenzie notes, op. cit., p. 3.
29. Jean McGill, op. cit., p. 6.
30. Bernice Larson Webb, op. cit., p.9.
31. ibid..
32. Naismith, op. cit., p.19-20.

CHAPTER 2

Montreal and New Horizons

ONTREAL in the 1880s was a huge city by Canadian standards. Among its population of some 150,000 were a number of contrasts. There were, of course, the two solitudes, the French and English, who co-existed but seldom interacted, unable to speak a word of each other's language. As well, poverty existed side by side with tremendous wealth, old with new: "frame houses, some of them scarcely better than an Irishman's hovel on his native bog and squalor and dirt; (and nearby) are great streets of great houses, all of fine cut stone." [1]

The city was divided by language and religion: East of St. Lawrence Main was French speaking, west of it English. Within the English group were the prominent Scots, who by virtue of their numbers and their wealth were most influential. There was "perhaps no wealthier city area in the world" as the section between "Beaver Hall Hill and the foot of Mount Royal and between the parallel lines of Dorchester and Sherbrooke in the west." [2] In the southwestern portion was Griffintown, an Irish enclave, a little world in itself, separated by choice and design.

Ever since 1807, when a group of Scots created the Montreal Curling Club, sport had played an important role in the social life of the city. Indeed, the Anglo community used it as an instrument for contact among its various members; it was after all an island of English-speaking people in a sea of French. They built a flourishing sport culture and worked to ensure its spread much as did the graduates of the British public schools in England. Indeed many of our sports were first codified in Montreal and made their way to the rest of Canada and to the United States and England.

Perhaps the centre of Anglo prominence and culture was McGill University. Ever since its founding by James McGill, the university was a beacon for the English, an important rite of passage for those wishing to do well. It had a flourishing medical faculty, a respected arts program and a theological college. It was the clear and logical choice for James Naismith.

When he made the decision to work towards his BA at McGill, Jim Naismith did so with the idea that he would graduate in the ministry, some seven years down the road. There were to be no detours. His years away from high school and his eventual return gave him a renewed focus. It was almost as if he had tunnel vision about the matter. Nothing would interfere with it. Then, too, at twenty-two, older than the average freshman, he didn't think he had much in common with them. He was there with no friends, a young man from

McGill Rugby team: Naismith is second row, left   *Naismith Foundation*

the country in this huge metroplitan city; he had been warned by almost everyone in Almonte to gird himself against the excesses that were part of big city living. And so he did. He kept to himself, worked hard in his classes, did his assignments dutifully, and much out of character, became a loner. His whole approach to life, challenges, obstacles and athletics was consciously submerged.

It might have been that he was guided by the principle "when I was a child, I did the things of a child; when I became a man, I did the things of a man." He had spent years looking for fulfilment, as he put it: "wondering what I wanted to accomplish; Finally, I decided that the only real satisfaction that I would ever derive from life was to help my fellow beings."[3] That being Naismith's overriding goal, the ministry fit neatly into the framework. That and the fact that Naismith had missed almost five years of schooling meant that there was no time to waste:

> I was determined to study as hard as I could. I
> spent long hours over my books and everything
> else was forgotten in my desire to finish my
> education and get into the field as soon as
> possible.[4]

Yet there was something about the big strapping farm lad that other students began to notice. There was a magnetism about him; when he entered a room conversation would momentarily stop as everyone's gaze turned in his direction. He seemed made for movement, for strength, quickness and leadership, not the kind to stay in his room at residence, venturing out only for meals and classes.

One evening, a few weeks into his first term, Naismith was in his room. Dinner was over; he was already positioned at his desk, dutifully poring over the day's notes. A knock on the door startled him. He blurted out a hesitant "come in," his eyes moving to see whom it might be. Students Jim McFarland and Donald Dewar entered. Naismith was surprised to see them. He knew who they were, but true to his newly introverted perspective, didn't think that they knew he even existed. They were third year students, closer in age to him. There were a few stiff moments of awkward conversation, small talk about the residence, meals, teachers and the like.

Naismith began taking in his visitors: McFarlane was a well-built, strong-looking type, a member of a number of McGill athletic teams.

He had an ease of movement that Naismith recognized; he moved like an athlete, he was confident. There was an economy of motion; he felt comfortable with himself. Jim was inwardly pleased that such a well-known campus figure had sought him out. On the other hand, Dewar seemed to be an unlikely chum for the other. He was slight of build, almost scrawny; he certainly didn't look like an athlete. He looked like a bookworm. His thoughts flashed to a picture of how he and Rob McKenzie must have appeared together in the eyes of others back in Almonte.

In time, McFarlane steered the conversation to the point of the visit. "Naismith, we've been watching you for some time and we see that you never take part in any of the activities. You spend too much time on your books."[5] Naismith didn't know whether to laugh or cry. Too much time on books? Wasn't that why he was at McGill? What were these people talking about? When the initial effect of the blunt statement wore off, he began to appreciate what was behind it. Certainly McFarlane was an excellent example of harmony, of a sound mind in a sound body. His eyes turned towards Dewar. A slight smile curled his lips. Here was no athlete. How could he be part of the advice

Presbyterian College Newspaper staff; Naismith is second from right
Naismith Foundation

McFarland was giving? Almost as if he could read Naismith's thoughts, Dewar spoke: "Believe me, Naismith, what McFarlane says is true. I wouldn't listen to the fellows either and you see the results."[6]

The conversation continued for some time, the visitors attempting to draw the reluctant Naismith into a greater sphere of university life; the fledgling minister-to-be, his Presbyterian upbringing in full gear now, just as adamant that he had no time. He had to apply himself as fully and as diligently as possible.

When they left, Naismith returned to the studies he had set out for himself for that evening. He had difficulty concentrating. He retired to bed but sleep came with some difficulty. He lay on his back, his arms under his head, and gazed into the blackness, replaying the earlier scene with his two visitors. Why had they, juniors both, come to see him, a freshman? They didn't seem to have any ulterior motives; they weren't trying to get him to join any specific team. They just wanted to see him get involved in some physical activity. They were evidently suggesting it for his health. He stifled a laugh: Jim Naismith having to be encouraged to take physical exercise! In the back of his mind he could hear Thomas Carlyle admonishing:

> Produce! Produce! Were it but the pityfullest
> infinitesimal fraction of a product, produce it in
> God's name. . . . Up! Up! Whatsoever thy hand
> findest to do, do it with thy whole might. Work
> while it is called To-day for the Night cometh.[7]

On the other hand, certainly, at home, Naismith felt much better, more alive and vigorous, when he was active and moving, whether it was in the hayfield, on the skating pond, swimming or canoeing. He continued to toss and turn. Should he keep his hand to the plough and continue on the way he had begun?

Finally, sleep came. Morning arrived; too soon! A tired Jim Naismith made the decision to visit the gymnasium McFarlane and Dewar had spoken of so enthusiastically. Anything that could keep him from having a peaceful sleep, he reasoned, should be confronted.

A gymnasium was something new to Naismith. He had never seen the likes of one in Almonte. Indeed, there were few in the whole country. But they existed in Montreal. In 1861, the year of Naismith's birth, only one gymnasium existed in Montreal, at the Jesuits' College.[8] Perhaps not so coincidently, that same year a start was made on the next one. It was to be built by McGill College in conjunction with the Montreal Gymnastics Club under the supervision of Frederick Barnjum. It was a co-operative venture with the Montreal High School which was an affiliate of McGill. Barnjum, an expatriate Englishman, had definite ideas about exercise and physical education programs. When he arrived in Canada in 1859 he exhibited some skill as an artist, horseman and gymnast. Soon after his arrival, he formed the gymnastics club. It was an instant success and outgrew its facilities. Members were attracted to this new approach featuring movements and routines. He sought to have each person achieve his fullest physical potential with a series of exercises on apparatus and with free movements modelled on Archibald McLaren's English system. It was a movement in sync with the times. Many were leaving the active life of the farm for the burgeoning urban centres and their sedentary way of life.

McLaren was a Scot, a doctor who had studied in Paris. He was also an athlete, enjoying fencing, boxing and forms of gymnastics. He had opened a gymnasium in London, England in 1858, the object being to study physical education scientifically. He took a holistic approach of health over strength. He recognized that activities which were taken for granted in the rural areas – walking, riding, and swimming along with physical work – were seldom possible in the city's schools and factories. His gymnastics program sought to be a replacement and therein lay its value. He even went so far as to formulate an "overload theory" of training as an antidote to the physical underdevelopment that he found among his students. While he had all the respect in the world for the games favoured in the British public schools, he felt that games were inadequate in promoting body development and health. They were too one-sided and encouraged practitioners to continue doing only what they did well. Certain bodily areas were being exercised; others were excluded. As well, not all schools were endowed with wide expanses of fields for sport. He became an expert in the field of anthropometry, thinking of the human body in terms of ideals, of what it could become within the limits of each individual. He "synthesized the British passion for sports with the Scandinavian stress on formal gymnastics."[9]

Barnjum was won over by this approach and soon introduced it to Montreal where he was rapidly gaining a reputation among its English-speaking elite. Like his English public school graduates, he believed in the evolving concept of "Muscular Christianity;" there were social and moral virtues promoted with physical education. He was critical of the notion of an education without attention being paid to the physical, leaving it to "'the benevolent care of chance' and to individual inclination."[10] To a group of Anglos living in the midst of a larger number of French and wanting to preserve their dominant role in society, his message of cultivating both the mental and physical, in order to produce "noble specimens of our race"[11] was eagerly grasped.

After he made the arrangements with McGill to affiliate the gymnasium, he toured many cities in North America to see what apparatus was available. In the best amateur tradition of the day, he refused to take any salary even though he was appointed Drilling and Gymnastics Master. He was becoming a well-known, if somewhat eccentric, member of Montreal society.

Outside the gymnasium at 19 University Street, Jim Naismith hesitated only briefly. Students of all ages, from university to high school, were coming and going. He entered with them. He moved down a narrow corridor past the open dressing rooms with its stove and benches. On the walls were fixed wooden lockers; there was a noticeable locker room smell of sweat. To one side of the room in the corner was a single shower cubicle – with only cold water, Naismith discovered later. Opposite the locker room was the office of Frederick Barnjum. Moving into the open gymnasium, Naismith spotted the "Major," as Barnjum was known. He was shorter than he had imagined, legends always seem to be, he mused, and yet for his age was well developed. He wore dark brown, a jacket and knickerbockers with dark stockings and flat black shoes. His moustache and long side burns ended in a hint of whiskers which combined to give him the look of a master of foxhounds.

Naismith's eyes were riveted on the compact leader as he strode across the floor to the centre of the gym. On his command, the students began to hang and move on the numerous bridge ladders along the walls. They initiated a number of exercises designed to warm up and strengthen the upper part of the body, each side equally. That done, another command and the group split into smaller squads, each one with a leader. Here too, there was a predetermined program revolving first around vaulting and barbells and finishing with a spirited display of Indian club routines. There were other groups, more advanced, they seemed to be, tumbling and building pyramids. It was all so active and yet so symmetrical and fluid.

Jim Naismith was hooked. He was especially impressed by the

crest of the Guards, the advanced group. He decided to join the club. He was particularly taken with the competitive atmosphere introduced by Barnjum. After all, he thought, if there were just exercise with nothing to look forward to as far as measuring with something else, it could be boring. That seemed to reach deeply into Naismith's psyche. The Major took great pains to reward his students. On the ladder routine, he watched them move forward and back, using only their arms for locomotion. As if for effect, Barnjum moved over towards those who performed the best. He took them by the arm and directed them close to the front of the line. It was immediate feedback and Naismith liked that. The top ten would start in that position the next class. Similarly with all of the other exercises; the barbell drills, the vaulting box, the parallel bars and the Indian Clubs. When there was a formal competition, there was another opportunity to move higher in the ranking. Now there were three judges to evaluate the movements; the resulting scores serving to order the students in terms of merit.

Naismith's introduction to sport at McGill was somewhat different than at the gymnasium. The term gymnastics at that time was simply another word for exercise. It was more like the fitness clubs of today offering different levels of activity according to the needs of the participants. Outside of the gym, on the playing fields of McGill and Montreal, there was a whole host of sports waiting for Jim Naismith to discover them.

In the fall of 1883 he was returning to the campus from a trip downtown with a friend. They noticed the football team practising and stopped to watch. McGill was renowned for its rugby football. While other centres were playing the soccer variety of the game, McGill had been introduced to the style in vogue at Rugby School in England. There, in 1823, legend had it that William Webb Ellis, a student, picked up the ball in a soccer game and ran with it. It was against the rules but students enjoyed the subsequent chase and tossing of the ball back and forth to teammates in order to elude the opposition that they developed their own version of the game and named it rugby after their school. Wherever graduates went throughout the wide expanse of the British Empire, either as immigrants or as members of the civil service or military, they took the game with them.

As early as 1865 in Montreal, citizens, the garrison and the university were engaging in games of rugby football or a variation of it since all the rules could not be recalled exactly. A hybrid form developed at McGill and in 1874 the university team made an historic visit to Massachusetts, as would Naismith later on. In games with Harvard University, McGill introduced their game to the American school, which had been playing a soccer version. The Americans enjoyed the new approach so much that they adopted it and next year introduced it to the other schools in the north-eastern United States, Princeton, Rutgers, and Yale, forming the basis of the Ivy League. Changes continued to occur in the game, its evolution being somewhat faster and different in the United States than in Canada. By 1884, however, it had changed from the closed scrum of English rugby to an open formation with the ball being heeled back by a centre. The defence was not allowed to move until the ball was put into play by the centre tapping it back to the quarterback with his heel.

At this particular practice in Autumn, 1883,[12] Naismith was enjoying the experience. It was his favourite time of year. The trees were in the midst of changing their colours from dark greens to yellows, golds and reds. There was a crispness in the air, not yet cold but without the hot sun and humidity of a summer in Montreal. The sun was still up in the west but it was sinking earlier each day; the noise of the starlings in the trees provided its own background to the scene. On the field was the confusing movement of thirty players. At times, it seemed as if everyone was on his own; there seemed to be no pattern; there was a wonderful spontaneity to it all. On closer examination Naismith could see that players were where their teammates expected them to be. He began to enjoy the rhythm of the game. The sounds and the voices of the players added to a wonderful scene for the Lanark lad.

Suddenly, it all stopped. There was a cluster of players around one of their own who had been injured. While some team mates carried the injured player off the field, a couple of others were walking from the practice field towards Naismith and his friend. One of them, the captain, called out: "Won't one of you fellows come in and help out?"[13]

There were others watching the practice. Naismith's head turned about as if on a swivel, looking to see who would respond. When no one did, he took off his coat, handed it to his friend, and volunteered his services. It was a new game for him but it was soon obvious that he was strong, quick, competitive and a fast learner. When practice was over, Naismith was elated when the captain of the squad asked him to play in the upcoming Saturday game against Queen's University. He scarcely hesitated, even though he had to buy his own uniform and equipment since the school provided none. That Saturday he played at centre in his first college football game.

He loved football. There were so many aspects to it. To some it simply looked like a trial of brute strength. He was learning otherwise. There was the constant necessity to perform a highly coordinated and precise task under the pressure of being pursued by an opponent. Such grace, dexterity, quickness and speed left him enraptured by the game. He played for seven seasons at McGill and a further two at Springfield College in Massachusetts. Indeed, James Naismith was flourishing. He was the prototypical student athlete. He worked hard in school and came alive on the playing field.

When he returned to Almonte for the summer, as he had promised, he worked on his uncle's farm. But, while the days were filled with the work he had been used to and it felt good to be back into the rural lifestyle, the gatherings at Bennies Corners took on a new direction. Jim's circle of friends had grown older. No longer were they playmates; the Prisoner's Base, Duck on a Rock and tag type of pals. They were young men who worked hard in the field, who still had their enthusiasm for life but were now faced with the realities of being grown-ups. Their strength was developed through their work and way of life. They had fully expected that Jim Naismith would return from the big city anaemic and weak. Books would be the heaviest objects he had lifted for months. McKenzie, especially, was even more in awe. Ironically, Barnjum's exercises were modelled on McLaren's who consciously formulated his program for city people who had moved there from the active farm life. And just to show his friends that all of that book learning hadn't hurt him, he reached for the beam in the old blacksmith shop and chinned himself with one arm, something he used to delight in doing after a hard day's work in the field. Naismith was the picture of health. The new and exciting movements he demonstrated were a wonder, especially to Rob McKenzie. Always in awe of Naismith's boldness and strength, he silently made up his mind to complete high school and follow Jim to McGill.

On his return to university, Naismith continued to explore his new-found world. He played lacrosse, later to join the world champion Montreal Shamrocks in the National Lacrosse Association. In 1884, he was selected the best all-round sophomore gymnast at McGill; the next year he won a silver medal in the prestigious Wicksteed Medal competition offered by the university for the outstanding gymnast. In 1886, he won first prize in a one-mile walk and earned the highest standing in all-round physical attainment. In 1887, his awards included a gold in the Wicksteed, his selection as McGill's best senior athlete, a prize in music (he was a soloist with the Literary Society chorus) and he graduated with his honours BA. All the while, in addition to his sports and studies, he was active in student government and the debating club. He remained faithful to his heritage. From 1883 - 1890, he joined and drilled with the Royal Scots Regiment where he attained the rank of captain. He seemed to be the perfect example of a "sound mind in a sound body."

However, all was not without sorrow. When he returned to Almonte for Christmas of 1884, what should have been a joyous occasion and reunion turned out to be a tragedy. His younger brother Rob was working with a lumbering crew for his Uncle Peter. The eighteen-year-old took sick, stricken with severe stomach pains. He went to bed early New Year's Eve knowing that the work day started at 5 a.m. The cramps were still there the next day. Robbie Naismith was doubled over in pain. Jim felt helpless. There was nothing he could do.

> During a moment when Uncle Peter and Annie
> were out of the room and Jim was left with his
> brother alone, Robbie spoke words which would
> haunt Jim, he admitted years later, for the rest of
> his life. "You wouldn't see a rabbit suffer like this
> and not kill it," he cried clutching Jim's hand,
> "Why don't you kill me?" [14]

Jim turned away as Annie returned. She had nursed the family through sickness before. Perhaps she could do it again. She had used salts and they had worked. Not this time. Within an hour Robbie Naismith was dead, his appendix ruptured. It was all that Jim Naismith could do to return to McGill in January of 1885, his only brother dead. He immediately immersed himself in his school and activities, trying desperately to fill the void within him.

When Rob McKenzie enrolled at McGill in September of 1885, Naismith greeted the eighteen-year-old like a long-lost brother. They roomed together; both were in the faculty of arts. Each was good for the other. They had known each other from their earliest days and while McKenzie had always held Jim in great admiration for his abilities and outgoing nature, the older Naismith was very protective of Rob. He wasted no time in introducing him to the gymnasium and the athletic scene. McKenzie looked frail, in need of some hardening up. He had been in Ottawa for the year, away from his Almonte life and home. Naismith knew that Barnjum's exercise program would do wonders for him.

McKenzie was impressed. The whole panorama of movement, tumbling, vaulting, lifting, clubs and bodies swinging made an immediate impact. He didn't know where to look first. He signed up for evening classes. It was more than he could have imagined. He wanted to try everything, but perhaps harkening back to his first introduction to the circus, acrobatics became a passion. At the residence, he took his mattress off the bed, put it on the floor and used it as a landing pad when doing handsprings or flips. Any new movement he saw he attempted. Before long, the uniform development of his scrawny physique was noticeable. He couldn't get enough of it. With his friends, he sought out the burlesque theatres and vaudeville shows at the Theatre Royal. Here were the practical applications and innovative movements he was learning, and more so for McKenzie than Naismith, trying to emulate.

The two practised the seemingly impossible moves. With persistence they mastered them. They formed a "brother act." The stunts they performed so captivated Barnjum's fancy that he allowed them a separate spot at the annual gymnastics exhibition. They even took the act on the road. That Christmas, they returned to Almonte for the high school's concert at the Town Hall. It was an unforgettable night, McKenzie later recalled:

> Our act ended in a Catherine Wheel in which each held his partner's ankles and by a series of dives rolled across the stage like a revolving wheel. We were accustomed to make six revolutions but unfortunately, the stage was small and we found ourselves across before we realized it and too late to stop. So we burst through the dressing door in the wings and collapsed in the midst of a chorus of girls who were changing their dresses.[15]

Never one to enjoy school at any age, McKenzie was ever more interested in exploring and observing the world around him. He had been bitten; he wanted to try every activity. He played football, sprinted, ran the hurdles, jumped high and long, swam and boxed. He experimented, tried as many sports as he could, making mental notes on the techniques. Some he kept up; others he dropped. He found that while he had quickness and speed, he did not have much endurance. After a half-mile run which he completed in 2:30, he was exhausted. He gave up that sport but filed the memory of the feeling he had. In the tug-of-war he found that by entwining himself with the rope around his waist, knees, arms and hands, that he could outpull bigger and stronger opponents. It was a technique used at the Highland Games he had seen and it came up in conversation wherever Scots gathered. After all, it was a group of Scots from Zorra Township, outside Woodstock, Ontario, who had recently captured the World Tug-of-War Championship.

His Scottish heritage was never far from him. Both McKenzie and Naismith took delight in walking around the McGill campus wearing their red jackets and kilts when attending sessions of their regiment, the Fifth Royal Scots, later to become the Thirteenth Royal Canadian Highlanders. They eagerly anticipated the weekly march-outs; almost nothing could keep the two from the gatherings. Once Rob McKenzie decided to go in spite of a badly strained ankle. Normal care would have demanded rest, ice and elevation of the leg but none of that for the fledgling doctor. He took part in the evening's drill. He ignored the increasing pain and the throbbing which accompanied each step he took. The ankle swelled under the tight laces of his boot. It was too much; he fainted. An embarrassed McKenzie was taken home in a carriage by his room-mate Naismith.

McKenzie was game for almost anything. He even tried boxing, impressed by the way his instructor was able elude his opponent's guard and cuff the nose just enough to make it

McGill University pyramid team. McKenzie, second from left, standing   *Mill of Kintail*

bleed. He would even tell him in advance what he was going to do but could still feint, flick his wrist, and slap the nose just enough to start the flow.

It is an amazing testimony to the abilities of both that they were able to keep up their grades in spite of the their many activities. No specialists were they. Perhaps because of their hyper-involvement they knew there was only so much time for classes and study. Yet even there, they found it difficult to sit still poring over text books in their room or in the library. There was just too much energy to keep pent up for very long. Often when it became too much, the east wing of the residence invaded the west. Usually the raid was led by Naismith: "when study became too oppressive. . . many times (Naismith) had to appear before the 'powers' for explanation." [16]

But these times became fewer and fewer for Naismith as he moved closer to the completion of his BA and entrance to the theological seminary. It was time for him to begin serious preparation for the ministry. In the summer of 1886, with the blessing of his Uncle Peter, he went to the young province of Manitoba to do mission work. Perhaps not so curiously, Rob McKenzie went there too, but for a different reason.

When British Columbia entered Confederation, it did so on the condition that a railway connect it to the rest of Canada. Prime Minister Macdonald had stated that he hoped to look down and see the two oceans tied together by a band of steel. Opposition leader Alexander McKenzie, quick to score points at the prime minister's expense, replied: "You might be looking up." The massive undertaking that was the Canadian Pacific Railway was completed in 1885 when Donald Smith, a transplanted Scot known better in Canadian history as Lord Strathcona, "took the maul in hand to drive the last spike, and after missing it a few times he drove it home amid cheers from all present" [17] at Craigellachie, B.C. The province of Manitoba at the time was only a small area around Winnipeg and the Red River settlement. Canada's motto, From Sea To Sea, was somewhat optimistic. The vast amount of land to the north and west to British Columbia was purchased from the Hudson's Bay Company in 1869. It was a necessary move, since American settlers were moving west and north and in the wild west, it seemed that possession was nine tenths of the law. In return for the 3.9 million square kilometres, Canada paid 300,000 pounds, about $1.5 million, gave the Hudson's Bay Company land around their trading posts and a further five percent of the fertile land in the north-west. [18]

It was a huge expanse of country, including the present provinces of Alberta and Saskatchewan, northern Manitoba, the Yukon and Northwest Territories. It meant that the west had been opened up, but just barely; roads had to be built along with the railway. Surveying jobs were available to map out a future Trans-Canada Highway.

McKenzie was in his element, back in the outdoors he loved so well, exulting in the new landscape and images he was seeing. During that first summer, in 1886, he helped survey the Indian trails which had served the first nations for years; they would become the foundation of the road system in the west. They were widened to sixty-six feet, guaranteeing that enough width would be available as settlers moved into the area and claimed land. He travelled throughout Manitoba from Portage La Prairie to Lake Manitoba along the Assiniboine and Souris Rivers. His crew consisted of three French-Canadians, one of whom was Ibrahim DuFresne, an engineering student from McGill. Only the cook spoke English. McKenzie saw it as an opportunity to improve his French. In only a short time, he was conversing easily. Evenings were spent around the campfire; though it was summer, they were at fifty-three degrees north latitude. The nights were wondrous. The stars seemed so close McKenzie felt at times that he could reach out and touch them, these sparkling jewels on a black velvet background. McKenzie reminisced about his family. It was the first time he had been so far from home. He carried with him a small trunk which his father had brought with him from Scotland. In it was a picture of his mother. He was very close to her, especially since the death of his father. He marvelled at the way she was able to continue on in what must have been obvious pain and loneliness. She was just so "good and intelligent." [19]

It was a great life for a nineteen-year-old boy who loved the outdoors. Food was plentiful; there was bacon, molasses, dried fruits, potato chips in good supply and plenty of opportunity to fish, and hunt birds and small game. This was a good thing, too, because the cook was a novice. Many times his attempts ended up poured down one of the many prairie dog holes. There were plenty of liquids to wash the food down, ranging from spring waters to a case of Hennessy brandy and a ten-gallon keg of Jamaican rum! It was a busy summer. There was much to do and it was October before Rob could return to his classes at McGill.

The next summer, he was in Alberta. He had taken a train to Calgary. It was a real frontier town, the living "wild west." He saw the extremes of the first nations people. In his crew was the chief surveyor, a full-blooded Iroquois by the name of Tom Greene, who had graduated from McGill. There was also his brother, described by Rob as "a real Indian." They made their base by the Bow and Elbow Rivers. It was another growing experience for McKenzie. Not only did he learn to rely on himself in his numerous sorties from camp but he was able to witness first-hand the new country emerging from the old. In his spare time, he drew; his sketching pad was always busy. He outlined numerous scenes which he later painted in water colours. His eyes took in everything.

He saw his first boxing match in a newly-constructed building used for everything from dancing to roller skating. This was in Lethbridge, where the ever-blowing winds and distinctive coulees had already made an impression. The local bartender, a burly Irishman named of Gorman, renowned for his toughness, was to fight "Denver Ed" Smith. Even then, a contest involving a Canadian and an American had its appeal. The audience was a melange of those forging a new life in the rugged land that was the west. Surrounding the ring were the Mounties in their red coats and black riding pants with their distinctive yellow stripes. They were interspersed at strategic spots among workers from the coal mines, "ranchers, railway men and loafers with a sprinkling of women who haunt all frontier towns."[20] To the back of the hall were interested Indians: Sarcees, Blackfoots and Bloods, some blanketed, silent and seemingly indifferent as they watched the white man's novel spectacle. The fight went forty-six rounds before Gorman, who seemed to be the superior boxer, was too exhausted to continue. Rob couldn't help wondering as he watched the ebb and flow of the battle just how his instructor at McGill would have done in a match with these two.

The young man's work was not without danger. It called for grace under pressure. On one occasion, he had been sent out alone with his pick and shovel. In the midst of his digging, he was confronted by six Blackfoot braves. They were well armed, on horseback and obviously angry. They gestured to McKenzie to leave. He continued digging. They threatened; he refused to stop. The six moved their horses back some distance, wheeled around and charged McKenzie, whooping and brandishing their rifles. All McKenzie had was his spade. He jumped up from the pit and stood his ground ready to swing the shovel at the closest rider. At the last moment, the party split and swerved to either side of him and rode off, their faces revealing their disappointment and their realization that they were losing the battle against the encroachment of the white man. From that point on, the crew decided to work in pairs.

There were advantages and disadvantages to the new arrangement. Certainly, it was safer with two. But having Ross, the Queen's student, with him meant that McKenzie could no longer work at the leisurely pace that he had established for himself. Previously, he had stopped for a tea after digging seven mounds. It would be about 11 a.m., the sun high in the sky. McKenzie would relax under the shade of his cart and escape into the world of Victor Hugo's Les Miserables or Fielding's Joseph Andrews. After an hour, sometimes longer, he would re-emerge into the real world, far from these literary scenes. There were compensations though; Mckenzie had an audience. He could perform his acrobatics. When Ross mounted his cart, hitched to the horse they called Bill, Rob began to turn handsprings towards them. Bill did not know what was happening when the blurring, whirring, turning arms, legs and head flipped menacingly towards him. McKenzie got the exact effect that he wanted. The horse, fearing the unknown, bolted across the landscape with Ross hanging on to the reins for dear life and yelling "Whoa! Whoa!" McKenzie coiled on the ground in laughter.

Ross, too, had his chance to demonstrate his abilities. The survey party happened to be working by the Blackfoot reserve on Treaty Day, when payments of blankets and money were to be made to the Nation. There were celebrations: races, gambling and feasting. Ross was a good sprinter, faster than anyone there; he proposed his idea to McKenzie. Why not race a horse over fifty yards with a turn? Ross had done it before and had won. The heavier horse's momentum didn't allow him to turn as quickly as a human. It would go beyond the twenty-five yard point and nullify its greater straightaway speed. It was a sure thing! McKenzie remembered his youthful days in Almonte when hustlers used to come into town and make some sort of bet which on the surface seemed ridiculous but on reflection was a sure thing. The two of them put up all of their money. It was covered eagerly by the Blackfeet. The city slickers hadn't counted on the "Indian ponies accustomed to the chase (which could) stop in their own length and wheel like a flash, so we made the mistake of our lives when we backed Ross."[21]

Rob couldn't wait to get back to Montreal to tell Jim about his summer and show him his sketches; each one triggered a torrent of memories of the wondrous wild west of Canada.

Meanwhile, Jim Naismith's pursuit of his degree in divinity was proceeding into the next phase, theological studies. If the truth were known, his theology faculty classmates were hoping that the athletic side of him would diminish, if not disappear altogether. They wanted all of Jim's energies directed towards theology and the ministry and none of it dissipated in these frivolous and unimportant activities. His work in attaining his BA degree in philosophy and Hebrew had certainly given every indication of the former high school dropout's great promise. But all that time spent on the sports field! And in the gymnasium! They were constant worries to the faculty and his classmates. They were rivals for Jim's attention; aimless amusements which took away from the work of the Lord. And certainly, they were a bad influence on Naismith, these preoccupations with the body rather than the mind. They pointed out the hard tackling and blocking of football, along with the unsavoury language that one occasionally heard from other players. How could a divinity student participate in such an environment? That was bad enough. Even worse was Naismith's decision to play lacrosse with the Montreal Shamrocks, a group of Irishmen! And mostly Catholics! An unsavoury lot who certainly couldn't be called a gentlemanly side. In fact most referred to them as outright professionals and there were few worse words which could be used to describe an athlete or a team at that time. Not only that, the game of Lacrosse itself was thought to be a form of legalized mayhem and certainly no place for a young man committed to carrying out the work of the Lord. His classmates and professors prayed for his soul. They gathered in groups and asked God to release James Naismith from these tools of the devil.

All of this of course was going on without Naismith's knowledge, but still he did have that heightened feeling that his peers and professors were disapproving, that there were doubts on their part of his commitment to the life of the ministry. He was aware of their whispers: if he really wanted to dedicate his life to the service of God, why was he wasting so much of his time on sport? Couldn't it be better spent in pursuit of all that there was to learn about his true calling? When they chided him openly, it was done in a joking fashion. He continued to play and occasionally showed up in class with an assortment of bumps and bruises, strains and sprains. After one especially hard fought football game, in which, being a centre, Naismith always seemed to be in the middle of the fray, he returned to McGill having received a crack on the nose. It was his turn to preach that Sunday as part of his practical training. He ascended to the pulpit. There was an audible gasp; he had two blackened eyes! Now the advice came fast and furious. Classmates, professors, even the Reverend Principal advised him that it was time to put these foolish, time-consuming, evil diversions aside. Prayers were again volunteered for his soul.

It was a conundrum for Naismith. He loved sport; he saw it differently from his fellow theologs. He loved the thought of being a minister but he also enjoyed using all of his talents and his abilities. He wanted to give his God glory with all of his body as well as his soul and mind.

And then there were the other university officials. If he was receiving a lot of negative feedback from the theology wing, he was receiving large amounts of praise from the university. Following his graduation with his BA and beginning with his studies in theology, he was offered a position as instructor in what was becoming McGill's physical education program. It was a great opportunity for him to learn more about Barnjum's approach and planning. Much to the consternation of the theology staff, he took it. His balancing act continued: his athletic involvement, new teaching duties and seminary life all competed for his time. The prayers for Jim Naismith's soul continued at Presbyterian College of McGill University.

The dismay among theology officials increased in 1888. Two events of major import occurred at McGill. Firstly, Frederick Barnjum died. McGill was left without a director for its burgeoning physical education program. It looked no further than the multi-talented Naismith for a replacement. After all, Jim Naismith epitomized all that the university was trying to do with its students. He was a young man who had grown and developed in so many ways, who was the personification, particularly on the athletic field and in the gymnasium, of a healthy and informed way of life.

And there was more. During the year that he had worked as Barnjum's assistant, it became obvious that he had the respect of his charges and that he was conscientious and an effective teacher. There was subtle pressure from the theology principal, Reverend Donald

Harvey MacVicar, to turn down the offer. At the same time, McGill officials were persistent. The board of governors' representative Sir William Dawson was persuasive. Then too, there was the matter of extra money, meaning he would no longer be a burden on his Uncle Peter. There was much thought, much prayer by many. In the end, Jim Naismith accepted the position. He would continue his theological studies and his athletic involvement but now he would also become the first native-born Director of physical education at McGill.

In some ways, the time of year, autumn, with its changing hues, its transition from one season to another, its movement from the sultry, humid, hazy days of summer to crisp, sharp, fresh temperatures always signalled a period of change for Naismith. Perhaps it was the many years of farm life, each culminating in the harvest amid the muffled sounds of the fall; it was a time for reflection, for looking back over the past and looking ahead to the future. He was in such a state of mind when another momentous event took place.

McGill had invited a young American, Amos Alonzo Stagg, to come and address its students. Stagg had made quite a name for himself at Yale University where news of him and his exploits on the football field, his selection as an All-American and his reputation for sportsmanship had made him a well-known figure in Canada as well as his own country. Naismith went to hear him speak. Stagg's message was not what he expected. There was none of the puffery and bravado that some athletes engaged in, none of the self-serving stories, crafted to entertain, that most invited athletes delivered. Stagg had a clear, distinct and haunting message. Naismith had been a student of the classical age of Greece and Rome. He was aware of the term that had originated and evolved in the early church, "Athletes of Christ." These were ascetics

Amos Alonzo Stagg
Naismith Foundation

who took the approach of athletes training their bodies and applied it to the cultivation of the spirit. Indeed the term describing these people, ascetics, was derived from the Greek askesis which literally means "an athlete in training." Just as an athlete had a goal and worked hard to reach it, eliminating those practices which diverted him from it and concentrating on those which brought it closer, so too was the ascetic training himself. Naismith was enthralled by Stagg who spoke of the athletic experience in terms so familiar to him. There was no conflict between sport and the Christian life, said Stagg. They were eminently compatible. The same characteristics needed on the sporting field were the ones needed to live a fulfilling Christian life. One needed a vision, a clear-cut goal, to pursue with determination, enthusiasm, sincere and unstinting effort.

Jim Naismith was re-affirmed. No longer was he in doubt or confusion about the mixed messages the world was sending him. He was confident now that he was on the right path and had been so all along.

Uplifted by Stagg's insights and presentation, Naismith was all the more sure that he wanted to continue playing sport, that, if anything, it would enhance his spiritual being. Up until that time, he had felt that he was living two separate existences which were apparently incompatible, especially when he listened to his fellow theologs and seminary professors. Now he could see a connection between the two; one could be the expression of the other, the theory of life and its practice, a recipe for life. There was no dichotomy at all; that was the central epiphany. It hit home and was reinforced, of all places, on the football field.

Naismith had never been the preachy type. When he played football for McGill he put all his effort into completing his assignments. At no time did he flaunt the fact that he was a divinity student heading towards ordination. Nor did he at any time attempt to proselytize his team-mates or try to convert them to his way of thinking. He was simply one of the guys. They, in turn, had no preconceived notions about him. Or so he thought.

In the autumn of his last year, prior to graduation, an incident occurred which caused Naismith to reflect more deeply upon his life's direction. During a football game, the left guard missed an assignment. The mistake resulted in a loss for McGill. The player was upset with himself and spewed out a torrent of profanity directed more at himself than anyone else. In the midst of this stream of cursing and swearing, it suddenly struck the player that Jim Naismith was next to him, certainly within hearing. He quieted down as soon as he recognized this. Sheepishly, the chastened athlete leaned toward his team-mate and whispered: "I beg your pardon, Jim. I forgot you were there."[22]

The apology took Jim by surprise. Not once had he reproached his team-mates about profanity; he could not understand why the apology was made. The incident stayed with him as he tried to interpret its meaning. He could only think that he knew, and apparently others did too, that he could put his all into the game and still keep himself in control and true to his being.

Clearly, Jim Naismith was at a crossroads. Somehow he had preached his Christian message without the aid of a pulpit. He decided to visit the Young Men's Christian Association (YMCA) and speak with its director, D.A. Budge. The YMCA originated in England and established its first North American operation in Montreal in 1851. It had made quite a reputation for itself in the city, with its emphasis on the Christian life lived through the body, mind and spirit. He recounted the football incident to Budge and mentioned that perhaps there "were other effective ways of doing good beside preaching."[23]

Once Budge heard the story and the musings of his young visitor, he told him of a school in Springfield, Massachusetts, that was "developing men for this field."[24] Naismith's head snapped up. He wanted more details; he was hooked. He wanted to rush out, drop the ministry program he was so close to completing and jump into this new approach which was so much more in keeping with his athletic life.

A few years earlier, he might have done that, made a rash decision based on a gut reaction. He was a little older now and on reflection, decided to speak with one more person before he made his decision. He sought out his favourite teacher, Professor Campbell. He received sound advice: "I can't tell you what you should do. While this new field appears good, I would finish the course in Theology; then if you do not like this new work, you can return to your original field."[25]

While all of this was happening in the life of James Naismith, his Almonte "brother" and room-mate was also moving along his career path. His Uncle Bertram had written to Rob with an offer to work at his Collins Inlet lumber company on Georgian Bay. It was just the type of new experience that he was yearning for. It was outdoors with lots of fresh air and physical enough to continue building up the twenty-one-year-old's still slight build.

It was in true pioneer country. There was no access by train; only wagon trails, little more than paths, wound their way over gentle sloping mounds. Water provided the main access just as it had in the time of the early explorers who opened up the land. McKenzie was left to wonder how the voyageurs did it with their heavy canoes and loads of supplies. He arrived in a lumber tug, a sturdy snub-nosed boat which was knocked about in the rough waters of the bay. When he wasn't wondering whether the tug was going to plough through the turbulence, he was fascinated by the wildlife and the rocks smoothed by centuries of pounding surf.

The captain of the tug noticed his young slightly-built passenger's eyes taking all in. After the roller coaster ride, with the dock in sight, he casually asked Rob if he would like to pull the steam whistle. He pointed to the cord hanging down from above; it was knotted tightly at the end. McKenzie nodded and grasped it. It took all of his strength to sound the three blasts signalling the boat's arrival. The captain had a huge grin on his face, shook Rob's hand and told him that he was a fine sailor. McKenzie could only imagine that a summer of lessons was just beginning.

On landing, there was a tour of the mill by the manager. His uncle, John Bertram, was an MP for Peterborough; Parliament was still in session. McKenzie would have to rely on himself and fellow workers to familiarize himself with the lie of the land. The mill was the heart of a company town. Amid the rocks and forests and wild blueberry bushes were tidy little homes, most with an abundance of blooming flowers and porches inviting one and all to come and pass the time of day. Arriving at the boarding house which was to be his home for the summer, he was shown to his room. After his McGill residence, this was spacious. It had an ornate, white iron bed and a patchwork, multi-coloured Indian quilt. To one side was the ever-present wash stand supporting a jug and basin. There was the smell of baking bread in the air. Rob followed it to the kitchen where he introduced himself to the cooks. Moving outside, he spotted the ice house, which on the surface seemed to be a storage site for sawdust; a lot of digging and scraping would uncover huge blocks of ice stored since the winter freeze. Occasionally, the cook would ask him to bring in some ice with the tongs or turn the crank for the ice cream maker. He was only too happy to oblige; invariably his reward would be a generous portion of the latter or fresh blueberry pie. Mealtimes were feasts. Hungry men reached for generous amounts of food; conversation was at a minimum as their strength was being replenished. After dinner, most retired to the porch where they lit their pipes or pulled out a plug of chewing tobacco. Inevitably, there would be a competition to see who could hit the spittoon with the greatest accuracy.

McKenzie took all of this in. He watched the mill operation. The logs were floated down river to a pond just outside the village. From there they were directed to an upper dam and through to a lower one, coming to rest in the mill pond where they waited to be selected for cutting. A worker, peavy in hand, clamped a log and sent it to the sawyer where it was cut. It was an outdoor operation, a roof protecting workers from sun and rain. On the top of the mill stood a whirligig – a little mechanical man who moved his arms as the wind blew and stood at ease when it was calm. It seemed to be working just as hard as the men.

There was just the hint of home to the whole surroundings. Here, too, McKenzie was fascinated by the tall Scot who was the blacksmith. He had a physique that McKenzie envied. Muscles rippled and glistened with sweat; more than that, he was artistic. Works of copper and brass stood beside the horse shoes and functional iron mill parts. McKenzie was constantly amazed that beauty might be found in the most unlikely of places.

Across from the boarding house was the company store, a wagon path in between. There was also an open space. Rob was excited to see a make-shift running track, long jump and high jump pits complete with sawdust. Audiences gathered on the porch to witness the goings-on; bets were taken on the track events or a slugfest to settle the arguments which seemed to be a natural result of the close quarters and some mens' need for excitement. He stopped gorging himself at supper, aware that the college boy would be challenged by the tough school-of-hard-knocks-trained workers.

The manager's office contained a rolltop desk, a first-aid box and a pair of forceps which could be used to extract an aching tooth. Under the desk cover was a picture of a can-can girl adjusting her garter, looking back over her shoulder at someone entering the room. McKenzie smiled when he remembered the manager giving him a quick peek as part of the tour.

His job was to load up the flat cars which ran on rails but were pulled by horses to the ship loading dock. He guided the lumber to the cars, measured and counted the number of board feet, experimented with different configurations to find out if more could be carried. It was strength-building work. His arms, back and legs were constantly stressed. He felt pumped up and stronger after each day of lifting and moving. He could also feel himself becoming more comfortable; his shyness leaving. He enjoyed hearing the ship's crew telling their stories, spinning their yarns; the mouth organ playing was fascinating. The hard work, the huge meals, the walks in the woods, the "ragging" with fellow workers and sailors, the competitions on the field, his observations of the quiet strength of the smith all made for a magic summer.

When he returned to school in the fall for his final year in arts, he had already decided that he would pursue a career in medicine – quite a leap for a young man who had been told by his Almonte principal that his head was full of rats and straw. His Almonte ways were far behind him. He was twenty-one, gaining confidence and self-assurance with each passing year. His mother had decided to move to London to be with Agnes who was teaching kindergarten. His brother William had moved to Manitoba, to Fort McLeod where he was a lay missionary in the Presbyterian Church. Bertram, at twelve years old, had just finished elementary school. He would eventually attend another fine Presbyterian institution, Queen's University, for an engineering program.

In the summer of 1888 when Frederick Barnjum died suddenly after contracting meningitis from an infection in his ear, the university asked Jim Naismith to assume the position of Director of Gymnastics and Physical Training. Just as Barnjum had invited Naismith to be his assistant, Jim in turn sought out his Almonte "brother" to assist him. The two of them talked it over in their room. McKenzie was hesitant: He had never led a class before; he had only one year of limited experience under Barnjum. The excuses poured out: McKenzie raised them; Naismith resolved his fears. Finally, they arrived at an arrangement: Naismith would be responsible for the classes; Mckenzie would assist in other areas, thus lightening the load for Jim who continued to maintain his active academic and athletic life. Indeed, McKenzie was more and more encouraged as the year continued. After a football game, Naismith would show up at the gym for his classes, physically and emotionally drained. He was never one to do anything halfway. Every play of the football game was given his total involvement. McKenzie could see that. He could also see that he was in no condition to expend any more physical effort on his class. He offered to take them. In the process, he was building up his confidence and his expertise which by now was gaining recognition throughout the university. In the spring of 1889, he won the Wicksteed gold medal. He had succeeded Jim Naismith as the acknowledged gymnastics champion.

Robert Tait McKenzie was far from the shy introverted young man he once was. There was no doubt that his involvement with sport and his association with Jim Naismith was having its effect. In the pyramids constructed by the gymnastics class, he was the central figure. Others relied upon him for their support. His physique was becoming so well-developed and proportioned, he was a living testimonial for the exercises. He wrote an article entitled "The Growth of Gymnastics in Montreal" for the May, 1891, issue of the *Dominion Illustrated Monthly*. He "personally posed for the Barnjum Bar-Bell exercises, some twenty-five in number and had them printed."[26] This drill, which originated in England, featured McKenzie with a four-foot bar weighted by wooden balls at either end. It received wide distribution and was published in the magazine *Mind and Body*.

He was also becoming a keen performer on the playing fields. He entered long and high jump competitions, his ability in the latter leading to his representing McGill in the fledgling intercollegiate competitions with the University of Toronto and Queen's. He was a classic proponent of theory and practice. He wrote an article "Helps in Teaching the High Jump" for *Triangle*, November 1890, and won five consecutive championships in the sport from 1887 to 1891. His 5'9" jump, a record for five years, was really a testimony to his will-power and leg strength. Only straight-on jumping was allowed at the time; the world's record was less than nine inches higher.

Like Naismith, he went out for the McGill football team. He was such a student of the game, his powers of observation so keen, that he wrote articles in 1890 and 1891[27] comparing Canadian and American football in one and giving the characteristics of Canadian football in the other. Football was a revelation to him, not for the sport itself, but for the public intensity and scrutiny it received compared to the more reserved and controlled gymnastics and track and field. It was the big fall sport; the whole university and the city seemed to get involved. Conversation everywhere focused on the upcoming match. The opposition took on "wolf-like ferocity;" the game appeared to be bigger than life itself. There was a noticeable tension in the dressing room on game days, a culmination of the no-nonsense practices that occurred during the week. It seemed that the reward, a medal or a cup when it was all over, did not reflect the huge build-up, the impression that an important battle of epic proportions was taking place.

That summer of 1889, McKenzie chose to stay in Montreal. He took a job on the waterfront with Hansa Steamship Lines; their boats plied the Atlantic from Canada to England and return. Very much still a rural country, Canada shipped cattle among other agricultural products to the mother country which in turn sent its manufactured goods. He oversaw twenty to eighty dock workers, depending on the ships being loaded or unloaded. He noted the hours they worked and arranged for their midnight supper at a nearby boarding house. The company depended on McKenzie's accurate count of the cattle being shipped; the tally at the other side of the ocean had to match. It was pressure work since the boats were loaded in the evening and steamed out in the morning. Occasionally an animal was counted, backed up and was counted again. If the tally and the manifest disagreed, McKenzie had to go downstairs to the holding area. There, in the stale oppressive air, he made his way through and over the cattle to see if any were lying down, counting all the while. He often wondered what he would have done if he hadn't his farm upbringing, if he hadn't been at home with the cattle. It certainly wasn't a boring job. A different emergency seemed to come up every night. The lifting, crawling, pulling, pushing and straining made for a strenuous yet rewarding summer. It also provided McKenzie with another perspective on how muscles, different from those used in sport, could stand out and strain during the various tasks. When he returned to school in the fall of 1889, he was in great shape. When McGill was invited to the University of Toronto for an autumn track meet, he won the two events he entered, the hurdles and the high jump.

Of course, like all athletes, McKenzie had his share of troubles. He practised his high jumping with a string rather than a pole between two upright bars and a mat underneath. On one occasion, he landed on the edge of the mat, tumbled and broke his leg. He was not a good patient. He walked out of the hospital on his discharge and promptly fell on the sidewalk, breaking the leg once again. He also had his problems with boxing even though he had a lot of confidence in his ability. When an opponent in a friendly match told him in advance about his right uppercut, McKenzie was sure that he could handle it. He suggested his opponent use when he least expected it. He was sure that he could parry it. When the uppercut came, McKenzie was knocked out.

With Jim Naismith's graduation in 1890, it was only natural that McGill turned to Robert Tait McKenzie. He followed in Naismith's footsteps and was appointed Director of Gymnastics at a salary of $200 per year. He continued to work on his degree in medicine and prepared himself for the new position. He also decided to spend the summer in Massachusetts, James Naismith's new location.

1. E.A. Collard, *Call Back Yesterdays*. Toronto: Longmans, 1965, p. 176.
2. ibid. p. 180.
3. James Naismith, *Basketball: Its Origins and Development*. New York: Associated Press, 1941. p. 19.
4. ibid. p. 20.
5. ibid. p. 21.
6. ibid. p. 21.
7. Arnold Edinborough, *Arnold Edinborough, An Autobiography*. Toronto: Stoddart, 1991. p.198.
8. Montreal *Gazette*, May 1, 1861.
9. Wise, S.F and D.Fisher, *Canada's Sporting Heroes*. Don Mills: General Publishing Co., 1974, p.21.
10. ibid. p.21.
11. ibid.
12. While some sources such as Bernice Webb, *The Little Basketball Man*, Lafayette: Spicer Press, 1991, p.12, give 1884 as the year that Naismith started playing football at McGill, that would have meant that he could have played only six years at McGill. Naismith himself, however, *Basketball, Its Origins and Development*, New York: Associated Press, 1941, p. 26, stated that he played seven years at McGill which would have made his first year 1883..
13. Naismith, <u>Origins</u>, p. 22.
14. Webb, <u>op.cit.</u> p. 13.
15. R. Tait McKenzie, "Reminiscences of a Good Friend", in *A Celebration of Basketball*, op. cit., p. 5.
16. Almonte *Gazette*, op. cit., p. 5.
17. Toronto *Globe*, November 8, 1885.
18. A. Evans, I. Martinello, *Canada's Century*, 2nd ed. Toronto: McGraw Hill Ryerson Ltd., 1988, p. 12.
19. McGill, op. cit., p. 15.
20. McGill, op. cit., p. 15.
21. McGill, op. cit., p. 18.
22. Naismith, *Origins*, op. cit. p. 23.
23. ibid.
24. ibid.
25. ibid., p. 24.
26. W.G. Anderson, "A Tribute to Robert Tait McKenzie", *JOHPER*, February 15, 1944, p. 53.
27. "Rugby Football In Canada", *Dominion Illustrated Monthly*, February, 1892 and "Foot Ball: A Report of the Yale-Harvard Game", Springfield, Mass., 1892.

CHAPTER 3

Massachusetts (New Careers)

IT should come as no surprise that both McKenzie and Naismith decided to travel to nearby Massachusetts in order to prepare themselves for their new careers in physical education. The New England area had always been attractive to Quebeckers and eastern Canadians; Boston had always been the hub of the latest developments in physical education, a field which was becoming more accepted and growing in importance. In fact, in 1889, the so-called Boston Conference was held to see if Americans could agree on one scientific approach to physical education. Representatives from every competing system were there: drill, and the discipline it was thought to inspire; German apparatus gymnastics imported with the immigrants who were adherents of Freidrich Jahn and the Turner movement; followers of the manual labour approach because of its social usefulness and calisthenics, the beauty-through-strength approach mostly aimed at women and based on the Swedish Ling system of non-apparatus gymnastics or exercise popular in Scandinavia.

Massachusetts had long been a pioneering state in the area of physical education. In 1862, the first professor of hygiene and physical education was named at Amherst College.[1] Edward Hitchcock was a medical doctor and his aim was to develop a sound body with a sound mind by instituting an enjoyable program with none of the tedium of drill. He stressed moral aspects as well: the body was the "temple of the Holy Spirit"[2] and all that flowed from that. On a visit to England he encountered the work of Archibald McLaren, who had been such an influence on Barnjum in Montreal. He became an advocate of the use of anthropometric measurements as a guide for each person's goal. He

53

influenced many and when the American Association for the Advancement of Physical Education was formed in 1885, he was selected president after first being honoured for his pivotal role in physical education in the American colleges.

At the Boston Conference, the Americans agreed to disagree. The melting pot might be okay for the country but not for physical education. There was to be no one system which all schools could agree to promote. The American approach was to be eclectic, a mosaic; it would thrive on diversity. The various schools would compete with each other in order to bring out the best in each other. Each system seemed to have its own inspirational leader and two of them were to have a direct influence on McKenzie and Naismith.

McKenzie's choice as a role model was Dudley Allan Sargent. He was born in Belfast, Maine and had worked as an acrobat. While pursuing an undergraduate degree at Bowdoin College, he was the director of gymnastics, earning five dollars per week. He enjoyed his work so much that he entered Yale's medical faculty in order to prepare himself for the field. Remarkably like McKenzie, he paid his way through Yale by becoming the director of the gymnasium and an assistant professor of physical training. After ten years at Yale, he moved to Harvard and its Hemenway Gymnasium, a prototype of the facility he considered necessary for his work. He did not care for the heavy apparatus of the German system nor were wands and bar bells enough, he thought, to develop strength. He individualized programs. He developed a whole series of machines using weights, pulleys and hydraulics aimed at developing specific muscle groups. He developed the Sargent Jump, still in use today to determine leg power. He gathered, tabulated and compiled results to form charts and establish norms for comparative purposes. It was all wonderfully "scientific."

He opened Sanatory Gymnasium for women which eventually became Radcliffe College. He formed a normal school, a teaching institution, to promote his approach in which he attempted a synthesis of

> the strength giving qualities of the German
> gymnasium, the active and energetic properties
> of English sports, the grace and suppleness
> acquired from French calisthenics, and the
> beautiful poise and precision of the Swedish
> movements, all regulated, all systematized and
> adapted to our particular needs and institutions. [3]

When Sargent offered a summer course at Harvard in 1890, one of his students was the new director of gymnastics at McGill University, Robert Tait McKenzie. It was a double bonus for McKenzie. He wanted to join Naismith but, as well, the young Canadian wanted to be on the leading edge in his field. He felt it was important to know as much about it as he could, to develop objectives, to be aware of what was happening elsewhere at similar levels. He was fascinated by Sargent's use of anthropometry, the proportions of the human body and the strength available from harmonious development. Sargent was a treasure trove of information. He had taken photos of athletes in a variety of sports. They were well known figures, familiar on both sides of the border and well known to the sports-loving McKenzie. He was amazed at the abundance of statistics and accumulation of data Sargent had gathered from the date he became director of Hemenway Gymnasium in 1879. He had charts showing the direct influence of proportion on strength and skill in athletics.

McKenzie was completely taken with the empirical approach advocated by Sargent. Students' information was taken: How did they perform on certain standardized tests? What was their height? Weight? Waist size? Chest? Legs? Calves? Did they have a healthy or florid complexion? Were the muscles loose or flabby? No question seemed too insignificant. All relevant information was placed on a graph, a chart used to indicate the physical condition of each student. It would then be up to the examiner to prescribe a regime of exercises to improve the student's condition. According to Sargent, the key was to have each student compete with himself rather than with others. In that way the student would take an interest in his body, to strive to be the person he wanted to become. By continually remeasuring, he could plot his development toward the new person he was becoming. The nature of the exercises were such that improvements were noticeable very early adding to the incentive to continue on the path to the ideal. After six months, another examination was taken, results recorded and a new prescription of exercises assigned, if needed. Sargent was so convincing in his presentation that McKenzie could understand why Harvard had made the program compulsory for all incoming students. He took notes and filed everything for future use.

The summer course was intense. It was interesting and involved but it was summer and Sargent was aware of that. Students were allowed to go to the beaches on Saturday afternoons. They were an extrovert's delight. Most of the class were agile products of gymnastic programs themselves. It was an ideal setting for them, wide expanses of sand, water to cool off in, and a chance to demonstrate their skill in tumbling, handstands and acrobatic skills. It was a revelation to the uninitiated. Crowds gathered to watch the well-developed exhibitionists, young men moving effortlessly, with total bodily control, seemingly defying gravity, to a chorus of oohs and aahs. They walked on their hands as easily as most people moved on their feet! Flips, forward and back, were executed so fluidly. And not just one! The speed they built up with continuous movement of hands and feet on the ground was astounding. The look of amazement on everybody's faces said it all; their exclamations an involuntary expression of what they were witnessing.

McKenzie enjoyed it thoroughly. His summer was a distinct success. He had also made an impression. Luther Gulick invited McKenzie to join his YMCA staff at Springfield. It was tempting. After all, it would allow him to continue his close association with Jim. He wavered but when he found out that his duties included the conducting of religious services, he declined.[4] He had decided, long ago, perhaps with the death of his father, that the life of a minister was not his calling. He would miss his friend Naismith with whom he spent some time during the summer but he couldn't wait to get back to Montreal to try out these new ideas he had been exposed to which reinforced in his own mind the importance of the physical education field.

Meanwhile, at Springfield, Massachusetts, a different approach to physical education was in the forefront. The Young Men's Christian Association, the YMCA, had opened up a training school to develop new teachers in its version of "Muscular Christianity," a belief that character and moral values could be developed and transferred through sport. The YMCA was originally an English organization formed in 1844 by Sir George Williams as a response to the industrial revolution which had attracted many young men, the wage earners of the day, from the countryside to the cities. Williams was a clerk in a dry goods store employing about eighty young men. Countless other businesses had similar situations. Williams was instrumental in forming the YMCA to conduct prayer services and Bible-reading sessions. The name had been suggested by his room-mate, Christopher Smith, and its objectives were laid out: the spiritual and mental improvement of men employed in the drapery trade; membership open to young men who lived out their Christian beliefs; management to be provided by a directorate chosen from the membership. As it expanded, premises followed and programs were added; by 1848, there was a library, reading room, restaurant, social parlour and lecture halls. Young men who did not profess their faith were invited to become associates.

The lecture hall was a way of communicating with the public. There was a missionary zeal about the membership; they were encouraged to evangelize "to win young men to lead a religious life."[5] It was a time in England when there were many public school graduates who were attracted to the fledgling organization. These were the future leaders of England, members of the military, the professions and the civil service. Many of them were imbued with the values of Muscular Christianity in the schools which taught sport as a central part of their curriculum. The playing field was where the student learned not only strength, discipline and courage but also developed his character, practised sportsmanship, fair play, respect not only for the rules but for authority and his fellow human being. And of course, all of this was wrapped up in the concept of doing your best against all odds and exhibiting persistence and leadership at all times. These precepts eventually made their way into the core beliefs of the YMCA since they were, in effect, a reflection of Christian virtues.

By 1851, the association had twenty-four branches throughout the United Kingdom as well as some 2,700 members. Like English colonists, culture and ideas, it too spread throughout the world, including across the Atlantic where it opened its first North American branch in Montreal on November 25. A month later, on December 29, 1851, it opened its Boston agency, which served mainly as a social centre. Voting membership was restricted to those who were members of an evangelical church. It was an immediate success; over a thousand members flocked to it. Some 10,000 copies of its constitution were spread around the eastern United States. By 1854 there were twenty-six other YMCAs established; a convention was held in Buffalo that same year. There it was decided to formulate an international policy to implement its goals in Canada as well as the United States. In the next year, 1855, another convention was held; the affiliates from Europe were included this time. It was held in Paris, France and approved its statement of belief called the Paris Basis:

> The Young Men's Christian Associations seek to
> unite those young men who, regarding Jesus
> Christ as their God and Saviour, according to
> the holy scriptures, desire to be His disciples in
> their doctrine and in their life, and to associate
> their effort for the extension of his kingdom
> among young men. [6]

It was a defining moment for the YMCA. After its creed, the Paris Basis, received unanimous endorsement, the assemblage knelt spontaneously "to acknowledge the Mercy of God and to entreat his benediction on the decision at which they arrived." [7]

While it might be thought that games and sport were always an integral part of the YMCA, this was not the case. At the convention in 1867 in Montreal, it was moved, seconded and passed

> that this convention regards the introduction of
> games into the rooms of the Young Men's
> Christian Association, for the entertainment or
> amusement of young men, as fraught with evil,
> dangerous to the best interests of Associations,
> compromising to Christian integrity, and
> dishonouring to the blessed Master and Teacher,
> the Lord Jesus Christ. [8]

While in Canada games and sport were not encouraged until the 1880s, it was not the case in the United States. The New York branch opened the first gymnasium as part of the YMCA in 1869. A building suitable for all of its activities was erected at 23rd Street and 4th Avenue at a cost of $487,000. It was a prototype for future Ys. It had a lobby which included the general office of the secretary, as the administrator was known. Everyone entering passed through this area on the way to the reading room, gymnasium, library, classrooms and the secretary's private office. The movement also spread through the universities in the form of student associations and among railroad workers as North America expanded its frontiers westward. As it did so, it acquired property and began to train full-time secretaries to carry on the work of developing young men physically, socially, intellectually and spiritually. By 1885, the Association Training School was formed at Springfield, Mass. to train secretaries. The following year, the physical component of the Y had assumed so much importance that "a physical department was added for the training of Physical Directors."[9]

Initially, it was a two-year program, later extended to three. Students took a variety of religious courses as well as psychology, sociology, physiology, anatomy, anthropometry, physical diagnosis, physiology of exercise, gymnastics, athletics, aquatics and a history of the YMCA.[10] The physical department's aims were straightforward. Not only did it strive to give young men physical training and rugged vigorous bodily development, but also to develop character.[11] Indeed, in Canada at the Toronto branch of the YMCA in 1890, the physical aspect of the program was said to attract "more young men than any other Department of our Association."[12]

At Springfield, Luther Gulick was charged with instituting the physical component. He was appointed instructor of physical training in 1886. Gulick came from a missionary background and later, in 1889, graduated in medicine from New York University. Until then, the YMCA had used sport, exercise and games as a drawing card, knowing that they appealed to young men. Once they were attracted, the Y worked on their spiritual and moral guidance. In other words, the athletic component was simply an instrument to be used for higher purposes. Gulick had other ideas. He wanted to promote physical education as a value in itself. He believed:

> Each nature, (physical and spiritual) is an
> essential part of the man himself. Thus we
> believe that Physical Education is important not
> merely because it is necessary to order the
> perfect intellectual and spiritual manhood but
> because the physical is in itself part of the
> essential ego.[13]

Gulick was responsible for the now familiar logo of the YMCA, the triangle. It represented his approach and the philosophy upon which the Y was to rest - the supremacy of the spirit when supported by the body and the mind.[14] He advocated his version of the British approach of Muscular Christianity. Christian virtues were to be displayed on the sporting fields. Sportsmanship was to be practised at all times. He instituted a "Clean Sport Roll," a nine-point code to encourage a spirit of fair play and honesty of approach and effort. Inter-YMCA competitions were promoted in order to demonstrate and display the approach for all to see. Gulick was young himself, not quite twenty-five, when Naismith met him, but a remarkable man and just the type of person the Almonte native needed to meet at that time.

When he graduated from McGill and was licensed as a minister on April 18, 1890, and was now able to accept a call from a congregation, Jim Naismith's decision to forego the ministry for a new direction in his life — physical education — did not come easily; nor was it readily accepted by all. His Uncle Peter and sister Anne were deeply disappointed. He was accused of putting his hand to the plough and turning back, a reference to a passage in Luke 9:62 wherein followers of Christ were exhorted to persevere, to stay the course in that direction rather than give up and try something else. Naismith knew the quotation very well. He had agonized for long hours about whether he was in fact turning away from his chosen path. He had concluded that he was not. He was simply taking a different approach to achieve the same end. He reasoned logically: If athletics was an instrument of the devil as some had said, and the devil wanted to lead him to do evil, he could only do that because sport was so attractive. And if it were attractive, why couldn't it be used for good rather than evil? As far as his Presbyterian College seminary professors were concerned, James Naismith was rationalizing; he had chosen a path away from God and was on the road to perdition. Faculty and classmates resolved to pray for his soul.

Naismith spent the summer of 1890 visiting various YMCAs in the United States. He was quite familiar with the one in Montreal. He wanted to see first-hand whether the practical applications reflected the impressive philosophy he had heard so much about: "A sound mind in a sound body" was so sensible to him. While he was attending summer school sessions at the School for Christian Workers in Springfield, Massachusetts, the forerunner of the YMCA training school, he met Luther Gulick.

Naismith had arrived unannounced. He asked to see the dean. Told that Dr. Gulick was in class, he sat down to wait. Naismith wasn't sure just what to expect. Still, he was mildly surprised when a young man, his junior by four years he later found out, fresh-faced, red-headed, tall and athletic in movement with piercing blue eyes and a winning smile, entered the waiting room. He checked his desk and moved towards Naismith with his hand extended in greeting and welcome.

The warmth and sincerity was obvious. Jim Naismith couldn't help but make comparisons with his McGill superiors who were such serious, stolid types. He found himself engaged in an absorbing conversation, speaking freely and naturally. They discussed their experiences, ideas and beliefs openly. The more they spoke, the more the Y seemed to be the place for him and the more he seemed so right for the Y. Gulick was between classes. Would Naismith be interested in sitting in on the next one? He would, gladly. Naismith was enthralled with the dynamism and the sincerity of the rapport between student and professor. The two met again that evening. They spent more hours discussing and dissecting each other's ideas. Gulick sought his visitor's input on a pentathlon competition he was planning for the YMCA. Jim was pleased at the gesture. It was as if two equals were sitting down rather than a prospective teacher and student. The more the two spoke, the more Naismith was convinced by Gulick's whole being of the importance of the work of the physical director [15] and this combination of missionary zeal and medical knowledge. He couldn't wait to tell Rob about him.

His interview over, his commitment and acceptance to the YMCA school agreed upon, it was a Jim Naismith with mixed emotions who returned to Almonte. It wasn't so much that he had to convince himself that he was making the right decision; it was more that he had to soothe his sister Anne's and Uncle Peter's doubts about this sudden apparent shift in his life's direction. It meant that he was leaving the valley, Ramsay Township, Lanark County and Almonte behind, perhaps forever. He knew how others might be affected by that. There had been great hope that he would settle in the area, like his ancestors, and be a minister to his own. Now that seemed out of the question. If he went on to graduate from the training school, he could locate anywhere in North America, perhaps even overseas, but almost certainly not in Almonte. But he was twenty-nine, head-strong, fiercely independent and adapting to a new path, intent on living it as it was unfolding before him. There were many discussions, much of them forced when he spoke with Annie and Peter; hopeful and free when he spoke with Rob.

The two of them, these brothers of the wind, were at complete ease with each other. They had been together almost a lifetime, shared the same interests, outlooks, sports, room, university. Curiously enough, where Robbie had always looked to Jim as a role model, someone to emulate, it seemed now that Rob was better positioned for the career they both wanted. He was a director of physical training well on his way to acquiring a medical degree, a necessity for a career in the new field. Between the two of them, they would have the perfect qualifications, Rob with his medicine, Jim with the charisma. The two of them resolved to keep in touch. Since Rob was following in Jim's footsteps at McGill, he would be sure to contact him for advice. In any event McKenzie was looking forward to visiting Jim at Springfield as well as keeping himself current with new developments in their emerging field.

Summer ended. Rob McKenzie left Almonte to return to McGill. Jim Naismith met up with T.D. Patton in Ottawa and Dave Corbett in Montreal. The three of them bought their tickets on the Vermont Central Railroad and headed for Springfield, Massachusetts. Another Canadian, Lyman Archibald from the Maritimes, joined them, the four of them making up a strong Canadian contingent at the YMCA school. Soon after his arrival, Jim went to Gulick's office. The director was speaking with a short, stocky man. Naismith recognized him immediately. It was Amos Alonzo Stagg, the speaker who had so impressed him at McGill. Gulick motioned to Naismith to come and join them.

Curiously enough, the two had never met in Montreal. Jim was in the audience of course when Stagg addressed the class but for whatever reason, he didn't go up after the address to meet the man whose message of the compatibility between sport and religion had influenced him so much. Yet there were so many common interests. They had been theology students, had a great interest in sport, were prominent football players with their respective universities, were both in their late twenties and here they were both students at the YMCA Training School. Each had been filled in about the other by Gulick, who showed his joy at having these two prizes at his school. Indeed, Stagg had been offered $5,000 a year to play professional baseball.[16] His decision to attend Springfield was news throughout the land.

The two students took to each other immediately, forming a lifelong friendship. Their first meeting in Gulick's office resulted in a little good natured competitive one-up-manship: Each demonstrated the firmness of his handshake, Stagg's having been formed pitching at Yale; Naismith's by the wrestling and gymnastics he had done at McGill. It was a delightful meeting. The two hit it off sensationally. Already, James Naismith was losing any doubts he might have had about his decision to join the Y.

Naismith and Stagg in football exchange, 1891   *Naismith Foundation*

As for Luther Gulick, his eyes were gleaming. These were two exceptional young catches, perhaps the best the universities of two countries could produce. Naismith at 5'10" was the picture of glowing health. He had a luxuriant moustache, a perpetual grin on his face and an attitude which declared that he was ready to try anything; a remarkable *joie de vivre*. Stagg was probably the best known athlete in the north-east if not the whole United States. As well as having been a star pitcher at Yale he excelled at right end as a member of the famed "Eli" juggernaut football team of 1888. Most importantly, both were committed to using their immense athletic talents in the service of the Lord and for that, Luther Gulick was thankful indeed. After all, that's what the YMCA was all about!

Gulick was so caught up with the moment that he made a decision. The training school would have a football team. Ever since the game had been introduced into the northeastern United States by McGill in 1874, it had taken off. The Ivy League Schools, well known for their academic programs, were almost as famous for their football teams. Harvard, Princeton, Yale, Rutgers and Amherst all turned out the leaders of tomorrow. A schedule of football games against them would put the YMCA in the public's eye and perhaps attract some of those schools' graduates to its programme. Just as important, however, the YMCA could provide a model for how the game should be played. There were those who said that it was too demanding physically, too intimidating and rough, some said dirty, and had no place in an educational institution. This was a chance for the YMCA to demonstrate some leadership.

Naismith and Stagg were enthusiastic about the decision. Football had played a major role in their life. They hated to give it up. They loved the game. Stagg was appointed coach, captain and fullback; Naismith was put at centre, a position he played at McGill for seven years. Experience wasn't the only thing he brought from his school; he had his whole football uniform complete with short pants, red and white stockings and short sleeved shirt. He wasn't trying to be conspicuous; Stagg had asked each of the thirteen players he had chosen to provide his own uniform. The others, all products of American schools, were outfitted in long pants and long sleeved canvas jackets. There were chuckles all around as they compared the Canadian's traditional lighter garb to the heavier "warrior" look of the Americans. Ever the team man, Naismith knew that he had to change to the American style garb. He recalled later:

> It was only a few days later that I sheepishly bought one of the long sleeved jackets like the others. The only remnant of my McGill uniform that I retained was the red and white striped stockings. [17]

There were other changes. Unlike the Canadian game with its heeling out, the Americans used the snapback system. It meant that Naismith had to learn a new approach. He had to execute his assignments from a bent over position rather than his tradtional stand up one. It was an easy transition. In the Canadian system he could end up being in position for a lateral pass and running with the ball. The result was that he could never put all of his energy into his play. Not so in the American game. He was to be a blocker after his primary task of snapping the ball was over and he could put all of his energy into that and come up with all sorts of variations and approaches. Oh, it felt good to be playing football again. He had thought that his playing days were finished, but now he returned to it with renewed vigour. He enjoyed the rough and tumble of it. He was creative in his approach to his assignments, staying always within the rules. He had to be, for he elevated the game in his mind and heart to the level of an offering. Before the first game and at each one thereafter, the players, led by Stagg, would pray. It was a familiar ritual. Stagg would issue the final reminders about the game plan and then turning to the assembled team, said:

"Let us pray for God's blessing on our game."

He did not pray for victory but he prayed that each man should do his best and show the true Christian spirit. For two years, it was his custom to ask different members of the team to lead; during those two years, I never heard anything but the same spirit breathed by the men.[18]

They came to be known in the press as "Stagg's Stubby Christians." They played an indoor game against Yale in Madison Square Garden; newspaper accounts were enthusiastic about the team which displayed innovative tactics. It had a novel wedge attack which featured interlocking legs and arms; the mass combined to push back the opponents. It was probably a variation of the McGill University football scrum which Naismith had introduced to Stagg. In the game with Yale, they pushed the mighty and bigger Eli back some twenty-five yards, which amazed and surprised spectators and media alike. Naismith was also given credit for inventing the football helmet. He wore a home-made bonnet, the forerunner of the leather helmet, strapped under his chin in order to protect his "cauliflower ears." But it was his football play which was the talk of the team. He was described as "160 odd pounds of concentrated TNT."[19] When Naismith asked Amos Alonzo Stagg why he kept playing him at centre rather than giving him the chance to carry the ball sometimes, his reply was a direct: "Jim, I play you at Centre because you can do the meanest things in the most gentlemanly manner."[20]

It was the best of times for Naismith. He was enjoying his environments. His class- and team-mates were all enthusiastic about sport and the approach of the Y. Not only that, he was able to room at the YMCA and take his meals close by at the Sherman home where Maude, one of the two girls in the eleven-children family, had caught his eye.

At the end of the first year of the two-year program, Luther Gulick offered his two star pupils, Naismith and Stagg, the opportunity to join the teaching faculty while completing their studies. Both jumped at the chance. Naismith was responsible for instruction in boxing, wrestling, swimming and canoeing while continuing with his football and his studies. He enjoyed it. He loved to keep busy physically and mentally; he enjoyed knowing that his pupils would be going out and influencing countless others because of his instruction.

In many ways, the physical education classes at the YMCA in 1891 reflected the problems with the field throughout the United States. All of the competing systems which had surfaced were exercise- and fitness-oriented. The Boston Conference had not been able to identify any approach as being *the* one to follow; all continued to be taught. It was left up to the delegates to decide by their preference what was to be featured. Each area would continue to emphasize the approach preferred by the leader in charge of the institution.

The YMCA was particularly aware of the problem. Its students, mature individuals and graduates of universities from throughout North America, had a common complaint: Members of gymnasium classes were losing interest in the program being offered at the Y. It had been developed and refined by a former circus performer, R.J. Roberts. He had removed all of the daring acrobatic skills and emphasized only those repetitive movements designed to exercise the body. There was nothing to divert one's attention from the tedious repetition. Its intent was to build up one's "physique, health and vigour with little thought for the interest of the participant."[21] It was "dull," "boring," "spiritless," "without challenge." The students were turned off by it.

At the same time, games and track and field were more prominent and attracted a larger following at the universities. Sport had become part of the graduates' lifestyles and they flocked to join different organizations, the Y included, where they could continue to live active lives. The summer posed no problem but in the winter there were no indoor sports offered; gymnastics or exercise classes were the alternatives and, to many, not attractive ones. They did not provide the highs one could get from making a good play on the sports field or executing a tricky manoeuvre on a piece of apparatus. It was almost impossible to lose oneself in the heat of the competition. It appeared that the new generation wanted "pleasure and thrill rather than physical benefits."[22] Not only that, there was a whole new group of administrators who were now part of the YMCA, people who had an appreciation for sport but wanted less intensity and more diversion.

Technically, James Naismith was still a student when he joined the teaching faculty. His role was much like that of a graduate teaching assistant in a university today. He brought many strengths with him. His wide background in sport helped him to instruct in a variety of different activities, all from a practical, experienced point of view that the students appreciated. There was no question about his religious commitment; he was in tune with the values that the school was advancing. This was an important consideration since the YMCA wanted its faculty to be living witnesses to their philosophy. Jim Naismith would do as he taught others to do.

There was another major reason he was added to the faculty: He seemed to be a perfect counterweight to Luther Gulick. The director of the Y was impetuous at times, much in keeping with the stereotypical redhead. He was an idea man who appeared to need a supporting cast to actualize, to carry out the details. He knew that the secretaries and the physical directors of the Ys needed a new winter game. He also knew that they disliked the program as it was now being taught at the college. He was rapidly losing faith in the notion that a good teacher, using creative approaches, could solve the problem. He saw that something new had to be introduced, but as Naismith remarked: "He could only see the mountaintops forgetting the valleys that lay between." 23

On the other hand, Naismith was more analytical. He could stand back and see the number of obstacles that had to be overcome, not dwell on them, but simply be aware that they had to be dealt with. It irritated Gulick because whenever he expounded on some vision he had, Naismith would inject a dose of reality. Naismith preferred to lay down a firm foundation, building gradually to the point where the activity would generate its own momentum.

Occasionally, Gulick, in a fit of frustration, would label Naismith as an obstructionist. The Canadian didn't see himself that way; he preferred to think of himself as a pathfinder, a problem solver. This was probably as a result of his sport background. There was always a goal to reach but at the same time there was an opponent to stop you from attaining it. The challenge of the game was to develop a strategy and evolve tactics created to succeed.

In the summer of 1891, the challenge to find a solution to the winter activity problem was a priority of the whole school. Members of the faculty were asked to join in the effort. Gulick himself investigated various systems in use in Europe. Naismith was assigned to go to Martha's Vineyard. There, the Swedish system, possibly the most popular in all of Europe, was being taught in a summer school session by the famous Baron Nils Posse. It was made for class instruction. It was free standing with little or no apparatus and had applications to health education, harmonious development, even military preparation.

It was a refreshing change for Naismith. He could see the alertness, the poise and posture developing in the students. It took him back to his days at McGill. On his return to Springfield, he reported that while some of the Swedish system could be incorporated into facets of the YMCA curriculum, it was not the answer to the problem. Gulick also reported that the solution wasn't to be found in Europe's systems. The heavy apparatus of the German program and the posture and carriage emphasis of the French way were not the way for the Y.

Classes began once again in September of 1891. The problem was still there. There were only four months to come up with a "made in the Y" answer. Gulick decided to offer a new course to his second year students, including Stagg and Naismith. It was a seminar in psychology. Issues and problems were discussed. One of them was "the need for some game that would be interesting, easy to learn, and easy to play in the winter and by artificial light."[24]

1. Cosentino, Dinning, Jones and Malszecki, *A History of Physical Education*. Toronto: Captus Press, 1987, p.217.
2. ibid.
3. ibid., p. 219.
4. McKenzie autobiographical notes, chapter 2, p.10. University of Pennsylvania Archives.
5. *Encyclopedia Americana*, "Young Men's Christian Association". New York: USA Book-Stratford Press, 1953, volume 29, p. 654.
6. ibid., p. 654.
7. ibid.
8. Murray G. Ross, *The YMCA In Canada*. Toronto: Ryerson Press, 1951, p. 35.
9. *Encyclopedia Americana*, ibid. p. 658.
10. ibid., 658.
11. ibid..
12. Ross, Op. cit., p. 88.
13. Ellen Gerber, *Innovators and Institutions in Physical Education*. Philadelphia: Lea and Feabiger, 1971, p. 350.
14. ibid. p. 350.
15. Naismith, *Origins*, op. cit., p. 25.
16. McKenzie notes, op. cit., chapter 2, p. 10.
17. Naismith, *Origins*, p. 27.
18. ibid.
19. Webb, op. cit., p. 20.
20. Naismith, *Origins*, p. 28.
21. Naismith, *Origins*, p. 29.
22. Naismith, *Origins*, p. 30.
23. Naismith, *Origins*, p. 31.
24. Naismith, *Origins*, p. 33

CHAPTER 4

Naismithball?

THE summer of '91 was over. Jim Naismith returned to his studies and to his second year of teaching. Aside from his classroom work, his fall promised to be busy. He still had his instructional assignments in boxing, wrestling, swimming and canoeing; the football season was here again and there were added responsibilities there. He was now the captain and in addition to playing centre would occasionally carry the ball from the fullback position. All of that was something to anticipate, but he wasn't looking forward to the early faculty meetings. It was Jim Naismith's season. He wanted to be outdoors, moving about, not stuck indoors talking about all sorts of details that didn't really concern him. Well, at least that's what he wanted to believe. He would have to give a report to the faculty about his summer findings. He would have to inform them that the Swedish system of Nils Posse was not the panacea the school was looking for. Some other resolution to the "secretaries problem" would have to be found. [1]

In a way, the situation was a microcosm of the need which led to the Boston Conference of 1889. Here too, there was no one system which would satisfy the need. Springfield College would have to develop its own approach. Surely there were enough high powered thinkers around that a solution could be found, thought Jim. He was quite content to be on the periphery, to let the others analyze and invent. He had more pressing matters, a heavy schedule of classes to teach, a football season to play and a fall to enjoy. He was coming up to his thirtieth birthday. There weren't too many years left where he would be able to throw himself with abandon into the physical play he so enjoyed. He was bound and determined to balance off his intellectual development as much as he could with the joyful physical sport that he loved so much.

Nonetheless, James Naismith found himself back in the classroom those early weeks in September. The new course in psychology brought all the five graduate students, including Naismith and Stagg, together with some faculty. While the course was ostensibly designed to relate to physical education in general, the real intent of it soon became obvious. It was really a think tank. The object was increasingly clear: How could a game be developed which would be interesting, easy to learn, was not rough and could be played indoors in the winter under artificial light at a time when the days were shortest and darkness fell early? Hardest of all, the game had to be stimulating and interesting enough to hold the attention of a group of men who had a love of sport but at the same time, were administrators and not athletes per se.

At times while he was in class, Jim's mind was a thousand miles away. It wandered back to those youthful days when the gang congregated at Almonte and Bennies Corners. Memories of that play-filled era flooded back to him. Then, as only the mind can, the focus switched to Springfield's football season and the big games with Yale or Amherst or Dartmouth before him. Just as quickly, there was an abrupt awakening. He became conscious of Luther Gulick's voice: "There is nothing new under the sun. All new things are simply combinations of the factors of things that are now in existence."[2]

It sounded so biblical. Jim was alert now. His attention had been captured; he was back in the present, entirely in the classroom. He was intrigued by Gulick's statement. He listened to an illustration of how new chemical substances were simply repackaged in different combinations, old forms dressed in new clothes. Naismith sat up now. He was involved in the class. He recalled that he spoke up: "If that were the case, the answer to the problem facing everyone is to be found in what games are presently available. It was necessary to cast only a wide net, experiment and by trial and error, eliminate and refine until the right combination was found." Naismith had long ago given up the fear of sounding like a know-it-all. He had learned to speak his mind.

The impetuous redhead Gulick reacted immediately. The class was given an assignment. Take Naismith's concept, try it out and return next week for the class, each with a suggestion. When the six people left the seminar, they were convinced that the forthcoming week would see the solution to the problem. Springfield and the YMCA would have its new winter game.

It was not to be. When the session resumed, there were no suggestions, let alone solutions. Each was so heavily into his teaching term, with class preparations and various activities, that there had been little time left to spend analyzing. The situation was urgent and yet with the busy fall season, all activities played outdoors, the need seemed muted. The secretaries were as actively involved as everyone else. They might be administrators but they were still drawn to the Y college because of their love of sport. In some cases, they were more than able to hold their own with the physical directors in training. Four of them were among the Springfield eleven football team: a guard, a tackle, an end and a halfback. The rest of the team were directors in training; one couldn't tell who was who from their play.

The problem wasn't that they didn't like sport. They loved it. The rougher the better. They loved the outdoors; there was lots to do. Indoors was stultifying, boring. That's when all the problems occurred, when they had to move into the gym. They simply did not want to play the less challenging kids' games like three deep or prisoner's base and longball.

But the end of the autumn came; classes did have to move indoors. Once again, the topic surfaced in the seminar class and in faculty meetings. The difference in attitude between the two trainee groups was once again obvious. The physical directors were eager. They lapped up the instruction in all areas. They had a vested interest. They would have to pass this knowledge on when they were in charge of their own Ys. The secretaries reverted to form. They were frustrated. There was no real need for them other than to occupy their time and try to whet their interest. They were bored with the indoor program and with the boredom came the usual grumbling, slackness and stepping out of line — anything to create a diversion and some interest.

Again, they became a focal point of faculty discussion. That one hour per day class seemed to be occupying an inordinate amount of their time. Yet they all seemed to recognize the urgency because of the long range programme effects it would have on the YMCA all across the country. Most of Canada and the United States had winters where games could not be played outdoors, where instruction had to be moved inside. If the training college could not make the indoor activities interesting for those who had a genuine love for activity, how would they be able to retain their public membership clientele?

Gulick assigned the class to an expert in marching and calisthenics, Dr. A.T. Halstead. It was a move which might have been appreciated by the physical directors. Halstead's reputation with drill and calisthenics and his facility with commands was much publicized and in demand. They would surely use it in their positions. Not only that, the larger ratio of exercisers to instructors was what they would typically run into. But the secretaries? Not interested! Marching and moving their arms and legs to shouted commands wasn't their style. This wasn't the military! Were they intentionally taking turns being out of step? Or a count behind? Or just out of sync? The snickering and laughing was somewhat stifled but it was still too much for Halstead. At the next faculty meeting, he asked to be reassigned.

Gulick could only agree and move down the list. The secretaries' group was moved to Dr. R.A. Clarke. He was a medical doctor, an extremely intelligent man who was perhaps the best athlete and gymnast in the country. He was a man accustomed to success. Everything that he had done, he had excelled at. His students were among the best prepared, they attended classes with enthusiasm, moaned aloud when they finished and looked forward to the next one. He was a very confident teacher. He wasn't prepared for the reaction he received. He had dropped all marching and drill from the program. That made his charges happy. He wanted to make maximum use of the sixty-five by forty-five foot space. He decided to introduce apparatus work. Surely, they would find that challenging. As a change of pace, he interspersed track and field events which could be accommodated in the area. Again, enthusiasm waned; the antagonism of the class was increasing. Of what use was any of this going to be in their jobs, they questioned. After all, were they not there for job training? Clark was losing his confidence. Gulick was fretting even more. Two of his most senior and best qualified staff were unable to turn things around.

At the next faculty meeting, Clark asked to be removed. What he was doing was not working. He wondered aloud whether anyone could do anything with that group. He seemed a thoroughly chastened man. It had been a new experience for him. By now, the end of the football season had come. It meant that Jim Naismith had some time to reflect on the situation. He became a more active participant in the discussions. Perhaps it was only natural that he proceeded slowly. After all, he was a junior member of the faculty; there was still that nagging thought that some people might think he was a know-it-all if he started to spout off his theories. At the same time, however, he was a member of faculty; he did know something about the secretaries in speaking with his football cohorts and he did have a pretty good feel for what people enjoyed and the difference between sport and play; he knew there could be joy in effort.

He spoke up: "The trouble is not with the men but with the system we are using. The kind of work for this particular class should be of a recreative nature, something that would appeal to their play instincts."[3]

It seemed as if everyone in the classroom turned to look at him. Jim felt all of their eyes. How would they react to this junior member's observation? He breathed an inaudible sigh of relief when he saw nods all around; they were all seemingly in deep thought. Or was it just that they all had the fear that whoever spoke up would be assigned the malcontent group? Certainly, Jim Naismith didn't feel that way. This situation clearly needed senior faculty, not a novice in the field. A momentary twinge of fear shot through his body as his eyes turned to Gulick, who was speaking in reaction. He recognized that twinkle in his eye, that slight smile on his lips. "Naismith," he said, "I want you to take that class and see what you can do with it."[4]

The other members of the group raised their heads and sat up, aware that they had been spared for another week at least. Naismith reacted defensively: What about his classes in boxing, wrestling, swimming and canoeing? How could he still do those and find the time for this new assignment with the "incorrigibles?" Accommodations would be made, he was told. He had more questions, objections really, trying to find a way out. All queries were dismissed off-handedly by Gulick. Naismith couldn't help thinking: Was the Springfield head simply uniting two problems the class and Naismith? The Canadian knew about the obstructionist label, some might have said know-it-all but he was sure that it was out of frustration on Gulick's part, not only because of his great experiential knowledge in sport but also because he seemed able to pronounce on every topic that came up. He was almost the antithesis of Gulick. Naismith chose to reason things out; Gulick was for the quick reaction and implementation. His ideas flowed from the top of his head. The two would always make a good team. Gulick had the vision, the idea; Naismith was the one to slow him down, to ask questions, volunteer observation, to suggest that a remote point was the place to start to build a solid base of support before the idea could be effected.

Naismith left the class, and walked slowly down the hall. His mind was lost in the maze of what was probably his biggest challenge since arriving at Springfield. He was unaware that Gulick was walking alongside him until he felt his arm around his shoulder and heard his voice. "Naismith, now would be a good time for you to work on that new game that you said could be invented."[5] It sounded like a dare and all through his life, Naismith had responded to challenges that were thrown his way. He hadn't changed. He could feel his fist tighten. He stared at Gulick. Was that a smirk or a nervous questioning grin on his face? He eased up. There was nothing for him to do but accept the test, and try to put his theories into practice.

Naismith spent a week developing an approach. He looked over the class list. There were seven Canadians on it but he couldn't count on them for support if they weren't interested in what he had to teach. There were four members of the football team. They knew him and

YMCA Training School gymnasium, site of first game of basketball
Naismith Foundation

respected him because they had seen him put his all into each play of every game. Indeed, the team, five and three after the first season, finished with a 3-3 record the second year in spite of the fact that there were only two holdovers. Naismith had played a dominant role too, carrying the ball as a fullback when necessary in addition to being captain of the team.[6]

Of the forty-two men enrolled in the school, eighteen of them were in the secretary class. From the list, two names jumped out at him: Frank Mahon and T.D. Patton. Each was a football player. More than that though, they were the informal but acknowledged leaders of the group. If they were convinced that the activity was interesting and worthwhile, the others would follow.

His first move was to do away with any formal apparatus and drill exercises to commands. Of that he was sure. He wanted to concentrate on a games approach, something which would be recreational and so stimulating that the class would be literally carried off, unaware that they were engaged in a physical activity. He would concentrate on the play aspect. The fitness would take care of itself. He searched through a mental list of games. There were those low organizational types, the ones people played spontaneously between classes. He would try those first. Three Deep and Sailor's Tag lightened things up but held the grown men's interest only for a short time. Similarly with any gymnastic games introduced. He tried the games developed by Sargent of Harvard and by Gulick. Spheres were used, ranging in size from a cricket ball to a medicine ball. Each new game was greeted with some enthusiasm (he wondered if it was only because of many in the class wanting to see him succeed) but soon it waned. He decided to try modifying some existing sports.

Football was first. There was a solid core in the class who played it and enjoyed the game. But how to convert it to the indoors? He had to remove the roughness. He went back to its roots, to English rugby. The difference in the two games was in the tackling. In football, the tackle was usually made low, a shoulder driven into the player to immobilize him and bring him down, stopping the play. In rugby, the tackle was made from the top down. It was more necessary to restrict the ball carrier's ability to pass the ball back to another player. To tackle low would mean that the tackler was effectively removed from continuing play. What would happen, he wondered, if the rugby type tackle was incorporated into football? Would it be less rough? Was that the answer? He was anxious to try it, to see the results. They weren't what he was hoping for. The class wasn't having any of it. They had played "real" football, had been taught the "proper" way to tackle. This namby-pamby approach to a game which was already becoming the American fall pastime wasn't for them. They let Jim Naismith know it too! Indoor football was scratched.

Next was soccer. Naismith thought that the soft indoor running shoes, so different from the hard leather cleats worn outdoors, would be enough to restrain the members from kicking the ball too hard. He forgot about the heat of competition. With each opportunity to score or make a quick pass to an open man up the floor, they kicked the ball with the usual effort. The inexperienced kicked the ball with their toes, much to their painful chagrin. Naismith remembered ruefully: "instead of an indoor soccer game, we had a practical lesson in first aid."[7]

Those who were experienced fared better. They kicked the ball with their instep. Their feet were safe but that was more than could be said for other objects. Windows, unprotected by mesh or bars, were smashed by misguided balls; Naismith winced. He didn't know which he hated most about it, facing Mr. Stebbins, the building custodian, or Luther Gulick when another window had to be replaced. Oh well, he thought, the windows would be protected with the screening purchased to cover them. He could still remember Stebbins' glance as he climbed the ladder to install it. Still, the onslaught continued; clubs, barbells and apparatus were knocked from their wall perches. A great cheer was likely to go up when this happened. He began to wonder if the players had the goals mixed up. It almost seemed as if they were trying to do it. What with damaged toes, broken windows and apparatus strewn about like bowling pins, indoor soccer was soon abandoned. Jim Naismith was running out of ideas.

His confidence began to flag. It was already December and still he was no closer. All he had done was eliminate some possibilities. He began to doubt himself. Had he made the right decision in refusing the call of the parish in Almonte? Was the YMCA where the Lord wanted him to be? It had all seemed so right at the time. Was he being tested? He moved back in time. What had he enjoyed? He was aware of two games which had been "invented" in Canada, right in Montreal. He had heard about the first hockey game played at the Victoria Rink on March 3, 1875. It was before his time at McGill but it was already part of the lore of the McGill football team. He wondered if McKenzie had tried to introduce hockey to his students. Coincidentaly, there were two nine-man sides then, the same number he had in his class. The teams were a combination of members of the skating club and football players. He chuckled as he recalled that the game was called before it was over. A regular brawl had broken out: "Shins and heads were smashed and the lady spectators fled in confusion,"[8] he recalled the Kingston paper had printed. One of the McGill players during Naismith's time had the actual write-up. The football players had really taken to the game, seeing it as a way to stay in condition during the winter months. Again, his mind turned to McKenzie. He wondered what kind of a hockey player he was or whether he had even the time to play it. No, hockey was out of the question, even if there were a rink available.

Lacrosse! He would try the Canadian game of lacrosse. Now there was a game. Ever since the Montreal dentist, George Beers, had codified the native game of *baggataway* in 1867 and formed the National Lacrosse Association, it had grown by leaps and bounds. It was a game he had played as a youth, carried on and enjoyed recreationally at McGill, but it was the year that he spent with the Montreal Shamrocks, world champions they were, that was among the most enjoyable in his sporting life. It too was a field game. He had to turn it into an indoor game, in effect anticipate the formation of box lacrosse. If only there was more time, he thought, he would cut the crosse and make a shorter version of the stick, one which could be handled with one hand. But there wasn't. He had to go with what he had, the full sized one.

He introduced the game, explained the rules and tactics. The Americans had bewildered looks on their faces; the Canadians, knowing confident grins. All seven of them were beaming as their countryman explained and demonstrated the technique. They marvelled at his ease with the stick, the accuracy of his passes and the facility he displayed in catching the hard passes. He was obviously someone who had played the game. They had heard rumours of his playing ability but this was the first chance they had to see him in action. Now was their chance to demonstrate their skill. Every little nuance and trick that they had learned they were able to try now; the Americans were simply too bewildered to respond at anything but an elementary level of play. When the novices did have the ball, sticks and arms and elbows rained upon them. Yet those who knew the game seemed to be inhibited. It was when two opponents who knew the game were vying for the ball that the real action took place. Naismith reminisced:

> football and soccer appeared tame in comparison. No bones were broken in the game but faces were scarred and hands were hacked. Those who had played the game before were unfortunate for it was to these men to whom the flying crosses did the most damage. The beginners were injured and the experts were disgusted; another game went into the discard. [9]

It was getting closer to the time when Jim would have to make his report to the faculty and Luther Gulick on his progress or lack thereof towards a solution. He felt as if he was drifting. His last class seemed uneventful, anarchic. He visualized the order and precision of his classes at McGill, sure that they were still like that under Tait McKenzie. His mind seemed to be far off, preoccupied for the whole hour. He wasn't used to failure. He disliked losing, whether it was a game or a debate. He simply wanted to marshall all of his God-given talents into a maximum effort. It was no guarantee of victory, but usually it was good enough. But this was discouraging. How could he go back to everyone and admit defeat, admit that all of his fancy theories wouldn't work? With the class finished and the students headed off to the locker room, he trudged upstairs to his office. He felt much older than his thirty years. He sank into his chair, slumping in body and spirit. He could hear the class downstairs in the change room. Their voices were excited now; a constant level of joyful, noisy bantering and laughing. He could hear the snap of the towel, visualize someone turning and yelling a loud sharp "ow!" Lockers were banged. It was a scene so familiar to him. It was exactly the spirit and camaraderie he was trying to see in the gym. Sadly, he knew that it hadn't happened there. He was determined to find out why.

His mind started to work. He reviewed his efforts. No wonder, he thought, the play he introduced failed to generate any interest among the class. They were children's games; they couldn't appeal to men! There was nothing in them to sustain interest. They might last with children because of their short attention span but not with these grown adults. He thought back to the three sports he introduced. Why had they failed? There had been some interest, particularly among those who were proficient in them but it was obvious that they liked the sport the way they knew it. They didn't care for the modified game. It was almost as if the traditional game had been a rite of passage and not to be fooled with. If that was the case, thought Naismith, any attempt to change an established game would result in failure. He had been right all along. Something new had to be the answer.

Now he was alert. He had snapped out of his momentary self-pity. His analysis continued. What was there about games that were so popular that they could hold so many people's attention? He remembered Montreal, the cradle of so many great games. Each one seemed to attract a following. Clubs were formed around almost every one. They were opportunities for people to socialize or compete at as high a level as they wanted. Everybody seemed to be so absorbed in some form of sport. Again, he asked, why? If he could find the answer to that question, he was sure that he would have the solution to his problem.

He began again thinking about the games that he played: football, rugby, lacrosse, hockey, golf, cricket, baseball, tennis, squash. They all had one thing in common, a ball. His new game must include a ball. But what kind? There were large ones and small ones. Why? Again, he continued to analyze. The smaller the ball, the more necessary it became to have some kind of implement to strike it: a bat, a club, a racquet. Not only that, it appeared that one had to be introduced to such a game at an early age. He noticed that in the lacrosse session that he tried, the Canadians handled the stick as if by second nature; the Americans, unused to it, were awkward with it. But the Americans were far more comfortable with a baseball bat in their hands; the Canadians seemed to have the difficulty there. He concluded that an implement was out of the question. Good thing, too. He was afraid that a club or bat in some of these people's hands would be murderous. He was reminded of the lacrosse stick experience. Besides, there wasn't enough time. And, he concluded logically, a small ball was out of the question. One more thing eliminated. It was a start.

He had decided on a ball, a large one. But what kind? The sport with the greatest following in the world was football. North America had its version of the game; in the rest of the world, it was the association or soccer variety. He remembered his attempt to introduce all of them in an indoor environment. No question about it, the men enjoyed the North American football the most. What spoiled it was the tackling. Again, he began to reason. Tackling was necessary because the players advanced the ball by running with it. They could only be stopped by tackling. Hence the rough play.

A light went on. Suppose the running was removed! He blurted out loud: "If he can't run with the ball, we don't have to tackle; and if we don't have to tackle, the roughness will be eliminated."[10] He was overjoyed at this simple solution. Why hadn't he thought of it before? He literally jumped up from his chair, snapped his fingers and whooped: "I've got it!" He calmed himself down. He had something but he had to put more flesh on its bare bones. All that he had was the rudimentary outline of a game which used a large ball and allowed no running. There was much more to do but for the first time since he had taken over the class, he was beginning to feel his old confidence returning. He continued his musings.

If the players couldn't run, what could be done? And where were they going anyway? He hadn't even addressed the notion of the purpose of the game. That would come later. He disciplined himself. The ball had to be thrown or batted to another player, a team mate. He returned to the roughness aspect. What would happen if the player in batting the ball, closed his fist and hit an opponent? Accidentally, of course? He grinned at the thought of some members of his class politely saying "oops" after decking someone while batting the ball. He decided to minimize this effect. If the ball were batted, it had to be with an open hand. Now to the running aspect, he thought. If the player receiving the ball were running, he would have to stop as quickly as possible, or pass the ball immediately to another. He was formulating the rules in his mind as if he was ready to explain them to a group. Players could run but not with the ball. Teams would advance up and down the floor by passing the ball.

It was in this last aspect of his new developing game that Naismith was far ahead of his time. The sports of the day had an "onside rule." In other words, the person receiving the pass had to be behind the initiator. Football, rugby, lacrosse, soccer and the recently invented Canadian game of hockey all called for the onside pass. He ignored that. He would allow passing in any direction, forward, backwards, sideways. It was a novel idea but this was to be a novel game. He would try it.

He paused for reflection. A fear came over him. Was this just another version of "keep away?" He had vivid and painful memories of how the class had reacted to that type of game. He had to come up with a purpose, an objective, a goal. Lover of sport that he was, Naismith recognized that every sport had a goal, some literal, some figurative, demarcated area or a net. Usually, it was placed at field level at each end. What would happen, he speculated, if a net, similar in size to the 8' by 6' lacrosse goal, were placed at either end of the gym. He visualized it. Players would throw hard in attempting to overpower the goal keeper. It could lead to flaring tempers and that old problem of roughness. Players would resent any limitations on the swing of the arm or the speed of the throw in an attempt to slow down the ball. That, then, was out of the question.

Naismith seemed to have plateaued in his thinking. He sat for over an hour wrestling with this next phase. His mind began to wander. He wondered how Rob McKenzie was doing at McGill. He missed his boyhood friend. He would have been a good person to talk all of this over with. Most of all though, he missed his friendship. Indeed, he longed for all of his friends and the gang around Bennies Corners. It was such a large part of his growing up. Those days when everybody gathered at the smithy shop would be with him forever. There was something about the play that they enjoyed. Even such a simple game as Duck on a Rock brought such delight. Jim had slumped down in his chair as his mind wandered deeper and deeper into his youthful days.

Suddenly, he bolted upright. The same problem that he was having had existed in Duck on a Rock. When the guard put his stone, the duck, on that wash-tub-sized rock for the others to try to knock off with their stones, a strategy developed. When the throw was made parallel to the ground from the twenty foot distance, the harder the throw, the farther behind the target it would travel if it missed the duck. That meant that the guard had more time to replace the duck when it was knocked off and tag one of those attempting to retrieve their missile. A new technique developed. The rock was lobbed in an arc towards the duck. That way it would fall closer to the restraining line when the duck was knocked off; the guard had a more difficult time tagging the throwers because of the time he needed to retrieve and replace the duck. That simple throwing strategy made for a more entertaining game.

There seemed to be an answer there, the missing ingredient. Somehow, the goal must be elevated above the players' heads. That way, they couldn't throw in a straight line and overpower or hurt anyone. Finesse would be the operative means of scoring. Force would be of no use; if there was no force there would not likely be any roughness. Now his mind was working quickly. If the goal area was elevated, what could he use? A box! He would find two boxes, big enough to receive a football or soccer ball, small enough to demand a touch, some practiced skill, and place one at either end.

He turned his attention to the start of the game. Winning it would take care of itself. Whichever team scored more goals would win but how to begin it? Quickly, his mind raced through the various sports. There was water polo, where the ball was placed in the middle of the pool by the referee. Both teams made a mad dash towards it. He liked the fairness of it but he winced at the thought, chuckling out loud at the picture of nine secretaries at each end of the gym some thirty feet from the ball, given a signal and racing towards the centre. It would be a disaster, a regular melee; fair but too rough.

Rugby was next. He remembered that when a ball went out of bounds, there was a throw-in from the sidelines. It was tossed between two lines of opposing players. He winced at the memory of one game against those good presbyterian lads from Queen's. When he leaped upwards to snare the ball, he received a well-placed elbow in the ribs on the way down. He felt the sharp pain all over again. Still, he liked the concept of a throw-in. His mind moved to the bully or face off in hockey and lacrosse. Only one player was involved. He liked that. Again, his thinking was vertical. He would have one member from each team at the centre of the court. They would compete with each other for the ball that the umpire would throw up in the airspace between the two of them.

That night, Jim Naismith slept fitfully. He couldn't get the game out of his mind. In his waking moments, he kept going through the developments that he had conceived. When he slept, he alternated between exhaustion and exhilaration and doubt. His feet churned and would come to a sudden stop. His arms flailed as if passing or receiving a ball. The ball! He hadn't decided on the sort of ball he was going to use!

When he rose, early, he hardly tasted his breakfast. He made his way quickly to his office. There were two balls there side by side, a football and a soccer ball. Seeing the two physically beside one another cinched it. He would use the soccer ball; it was obvious that the football was made for carrying. You could tell by the contour. He remembered cradling it in the crook of his elbow as he carried it down the field. It had to be the soccer ball.

Moving out of his office, he spotted Stebbins, just the man he wanted to see. His inquiry about the availability of two boxes about eighteen inches square was met with a scratch of the head and a definite "Nope!" A slight pause and he continued. There were no boxes but he had a couple of peach baskets he was using for storage. Would they do? In any event, he needed them back, he said. They would do. Naismith took the peach baskets and a hammer and moved to the opposite end of the gym. A running track on a balcony ringed the perimeter above the gym. It was about ten feet high. Jim took the peach baskets, larger at the top than the bottom, and nailed them to the base of the balcony.

Everything was in place now. He returned to his office. He wanted to be fully prepared for this class. He knew exactly what he wanted to write down in the way of rules. Within an hour, he had refined everything to thirteen regulations:

The ball was to be an ordinary Association football.

1. The ball may be thrown in any direction with one or both hands.

2. The ball may be batted in any direction with one or both hands (never with the fist).

3. A player cannot run with the ball. The player must throw it from the spot on which he catches it; allowances to be made for a man who catches it when running at a good speed.

4. The ball must be held in or between the hands; the arms or the body must not be used for holding it.

5. No shouldering, holding, pushing, tripping or striking in any way the person of an opponent shall be allowed; the first infringement of this rule by any person shall count as a foul, the second shall disqualify him until the next goal is made, or, if there is evident intent to injure the person for the whole of the game, no substitute allowed.

6. A foul is striking at the ball with the fist, violation of rules 3, 4, and such as described in rule 5.

7. If either side makes three consecutive fouls, it shall count as a goal for the opponents. (Consecutive means without the opponents in the meantime making a foul.)

8. A goal shall be made when the ball is thrown or batted from the grounds into the basket and stays there, providing those defending the goal do not touch or disturb the goal. If the ball rests on the edge and the opponent moves the basket, it shall count as a goal.

9. When the ball goes out of bounds, it shall be thrown into the field and played by the person first touching it. In case of a dispute, the umpire shall throw it straight into the field. The thrower-in is allowed five seconds. If he holds it longer it shall go to the opponents. If any side persists in delaying the game, the umpire shall call a foul on them.

10. The umpire shall be the judge of men and shall note the fouls and notify the referee when three consecutive fouls have been made. He shall have the power to disqualify men according to rule 5.

11. The referee shall be the judge of the ball and shall decide when the ball is in play, in bounds, to which side it belongs, and shall keep the time. He shall decide when a goal has been made, and keep account of the goals, with any other duties that are usually performed by a referee.

12. The time shall be two fifteen minute halves, with five minutes rest between.

13. The side making the most goals in that time shall be declared the winners. In case of a draw, the game may, by agreement of the captains, be continued until another goal is made.

He took the list down to the stenographer, Miss Lyons. He wanted a copy to be posted so that the players would have a chance to look them over before the game began. It was almost class time. Rules in hand, he made his way to the gym. He attached them to the bulletin board. Those entering the gym knew that any important announcements would be posted there; they would be sure to check it before class. The first class member to arrive was Frank Mahon. The unofficial leader of the group, he was an imposing fellow, a tackle on the football team. He loved the rough and tumble. He spotted his team-mate, now teacher, Naismith, standing by the board, soccer ball under his arm. His eyes moved to either end of the gym where he expected to see a couple of standard goals. Instead, there were the two peach baskets suspended from the balcony, about ten feet from the ground. He looked at Naismith, then at the bulletin board, and up to the baskets. A snort emerged. To Naismith, it "sounded like a death knell as he said: 'Huh! Another new game!'."[11]

Smiling weakly but undeterred, Jim Naismith called the class together. All eighteen surrounded him. He was introducing a new game. Eyes rolled. Smirks were stifled. He was such a universally liked man that they would humour him and give him a chance. They perked up when he told them that if it didn't work, he would try no others. He read the rules, explaining where necessary. He chose captains and allowed them to pick the remainder of their teams. The squad members were positioned strategically into the fore court, mid court and back court, three in each section, two wings and a centreman. He called the two centremen from the mid zone together, explaining what he was going to do. They got themselves into what they considered to be the best position to react to the tossing of the ball into the air between them. He later reminisced: "It was the start of the first basketball game and the finish of the trouble with that class."[12]

To be sure, there were kinks to work out. Fouls were numerous at first until the players got the feel of the game. The floor was small enough that some tried to score from far away. Tactics began to evolve, away from an individual approach to a team one. The idea was to move the ball up to the forward line who were closer and therefore had a better chance of scoring. Those in the back court became defenders; they guarded the goal and if successful in stopping a shot or catching the rebound, moved the ball quickly to the centres and forwards. A jump ball took place after a basket was scored. Play was slowed down because every time a goal was scored, Stebbins had to haul out the step ladder and climb up it to retrieve the ball from the peach basket.

It was taking too much time; the players on the losing side especially were anxious to speed things up to try to gain back the score. Naismith called over Stebbins. Would he please cut the bottom out of the peach basket? Good custodian that he was, Stebbins declared that the peach baskets would be of no use for carrying things if he did that. He suggested a compromise. He would make a small hole in the bottom, just large enough for a broom handle to be poked through. After each goal, he would poke the ball out from the bottom with the broomstick! It was an ideal solution; the game would speed up, the baskets would still be serviceable.

Once the game and the class were over, Jim Naismith went back to his office. He could hear the noise from the locker room. Unlike other days, it seemed almost a continuation of the excitement from the gym floor. For the first time, he felt that the secretaries had actually enjoyed the class, that they looked forward to returning the next day. And they did; they genuinely enjoyed the new experience. Here they were, these grown men, moustaches and beards glistening with sweat, moving the ball around the court until one paused, raised the ball over his head to loft it towards the peach basket only to have someone, an opponent, come up from behind and steal the ball right from his hands. There were loud guffaws, excited noises, bewildered expressions, good natured ribbing. Every minute of play seemed to provide a lesson on how and how not to play. Directions were shouted; warnings from team-mates, calls for passes, directions, voices yelling "shoot! shoot!" Naismith thought it was wonderful in spite of the many times he had to call a foul, something he was sure would stop once the rules became more familiar to all.

If he needed any more confirmation that the game was a success, he was to receive it with each passing day the class met. The very next morning, when he went down to the gym, he noticed that the rules were missing from the bulletin board. He was a bit miffed but in his characteristic way, he took it as a sign that somebody thought enough of the game that he wanted to study them or even spread them around. When class began, he noticed a few visitors in the gallery. The noise from the gym attracted them. They wanted to see what was going on that could cause such mirth and excitement. After the class was over, another joyful experience, he discovered that the people in the gallery were teachers from the nearby Buckingham elementary school. As classroom teachers responsible for supervising gym classes for the youngsters, they often wandered over to the college to see what was new in the way of activities or teaching techniques. Did he think, they asked, that there was any reason why girls couldn't play this game? As far as Naismith was concerned, there were none. The excited teachers went back to their school and formed the first girls' team.

It was Frank Mahon who gave the final confirmation of the success of the game. He approached Naismith to inform him that it was he who took the rules from the bulletin board. He was convinced that the game would be a success, he enjoyed it so much himself. He wanted a souvenir of it and as well, since the Christmas break was due shortly, he wanted to take it back to his YMCA in North Carolina to introduce it there. He knew, though, that Naismith would also want them. Out he went to his locker, opened it up, and returned with the two typewritten sheets.

Mahons idea was one shared by many. They would be going home for the break. It would be great to take the rules of this new game with them. Mahon, on his return to Springfield, approached Naismith once again. There was a curious bond between the two. Both shared the same philosophy which brought them to the Y; both were leaders. Each played football on the line where some said the real lovers of the game played. They jokingly teased that the backs should pay their way into the game since most of the time they seemed to be removed from the action and watched what was going on. Occasionally, when Naismith moved back to the full back position, he could see the look that Mahon was giving him in the huddle. A knowing grin was on each of their faces. Naismith recalled from his days at McGill that occasionally the middle wing, the tackle in American football, would be brought back into the backfield to carry the ball on a key short yardage situation. He asked Mahon if he would like to try it. After a couple of carries, Mahon was ecstatic. The big North Carolinan guffawed that there was nothing to the backfield position as long as the men in the trenches were opening up the holes for you. If it was possible, he became even more outgoing and a lifelong booster of James Naismith.

Now, back from Christmas holidays, he told Naismith how much the people at his Y enjoyed the game. Almost in the same breath, he asked if Jim had a name for it. He dismissed the Canadian's assertion that he was only interested in getting it started; he hadn't even thought of one. He persisted: It had to have a name. "Let's call it Naismithball". This evoked a hearty laugh from Naismith who volunteered that such a name would kill it quickly. Mahon persisted. The game had to have a name. He blurted: "Basket Ball!"

Characteristically analytical, Jim Naismith thought out loud: There was a basket. There was a ball. Sure. Basket Ball it would be.

1. Much of the material in this section is dependent upon Naismith's work *Basketball: Its Origins and Development*. New York: Associated Press, 1941.
2. ibid., p. 33.
3. ibid., p. 33.
4. ibid.
5. ibid., p. 57.
6. John Dewar, *The Contributions of James Naismith to Sport in Canada*. Ed.D dissertation, Florida State University, 1965.
7. Naismith, op. cit., p. 40.
8. J.W. Fitsell, *Hockey's Captains, Colonels & Kings*. Erin: Boston Mills Press, 1987, p. 36.
9. Naismith, op. cit., p. 41.
10. ibid., p. 46.
11. ibid., p. 53.
12. ibid.

CHAPTER 5

The Road Less Travelled

S OMETIMES, looking back over the path one has taken in life, one wonders at how one arrived at the present position. Yet, upon reflection, it becomes obvious that there was no other way. This was the case with both Tait McKenzie and Naismith.

The year 1892 was a busy one. McKenzie had heard about Naismith's project and success even before his Almonte brother had told him about it. The Montreal Y had introduced a demonstration game during the Christmas break of 1891 and proudly announced that it was a product of the mind of James Naismith, the former McGill man. McKenzie was happy for him. Meanwhile, Tait had graduated from McGill with his degree in medicine and "resolved to write at least one paper a year of scientific interest."[1] He interned at Montreal's General Hospital and continued to teach in the gymnasium where he was quite anxious to try out the innovations he had learned at the Harvard summer school sessions. As well, he was still heavily involved in sport, particularly football, at McGill. He was the school's team doctor. His interests in orthopaedics and the game he had come to love combined to keep sport as a focus in his life. There were many times when McKenzie finished his rounds at the hospital and rushed to class or a game, his black medicine bag in hand. He administered iodine for scrapes, stitched up a cut with his curved needle and thread, wafted ammonia under the nostrils of a woozy player and occasionally brought one back with him to the hospital where he could monitor a concussion through the night.

His diagnostic abilities were not lost on others. When the Canadian Rugby Union, formed in 1882 to convene championship games between the Ontario and Quebec Unions, found itself unable to do so because of the disparity of rules between the two bodies, it decided to reorganize itself in 1892. It was looking for a new set of rules that would be acceptable to all. It asked McKenzie to travel to the Yale-Harvard game and report if the American game had anything to offer. It was an ironic arrangement. Football had been introduced into the United States in 1874 when McGill played Harvard. The Massachusetts school so liked the game that it convinced the other northeastern colleges, including Yale, to adopt the Canadian style of football. Those schools weren't as bound to the British traditions and so the game evolved to be more of a possession-type game. They introduced the snapback system. It meant less spontaneity and chance and relied more on order and management – "scientific" was the term used.

The visit was an opportunity to see old friends but at the same time it was an eye opener. He spent some time speaking with Naismith about the American game, its style and approach. He was glad to do so since he saw Jim so little these days, but he wasn't prepared for the real thing. Perhaps it was just that it was Harvard and Yale. These were two traditional rivals both in the classroom and on the athletic fields. McKenzie couldn't understand the sheer intensity on the field. It looked as if the players hated each other. They battered one other with reckless abandon; their followers in the stands seemed to live or die with each play. Indeed they looked as if they might join in the fray at any time. And a fray it was! Players were being carried off the field on a regular basis. He looked at the benches; there were a number of medical men and they all seemed to be engaged. He couldn't help contrast the American approach with the almost genteel style of the McGill games.

On his return to Montreal, he could not recommend that any American features be adopted. Yet it was as if he had seen the future. He didn't like it but he could see it coming. The game would change, as would the equipment and the preparation. He wrote a report on the Yale-Harvard game as a contrast to an earlier description of the Canadian game for the *Dominion Illustrated Monthly* in February, 1892. In the end, the CRU received his report and decided to adopt the rules of the Ontario Union, seeking to convince the other unions to play by them.

McKenzie's busy schedule of interning, instructing in the

gymnasium, demonstrating in the anatomy labs and being available for McGill's sporting competitions was beginning to take its toll. He contracted the dreaded typhoid fever in the spring of 1893. A rest from his hectic life was in order. But he couldn't sit still. The SS *Lake Superior*, a ship crossing the Atlantic regularly between Montreal and Liverpool, was looking for a surgeon. It seemed to be the perfect solution. McKenzie would have a restful voyage attending only holidayers and any crew who were ill. He had time available to rest, read and, most of all, to think. He began to formulate ideas about the need for exercise and its ability to assist the body to be on guard against disease and sickness. He had only to look at himself as an example of its value. He was convinced that had he not been in good physical condition, the typhoid which had struck him would have gained more of a foothold in his system and overcome him.

Above all, he felt that he had something to contribute to society. He wanted to be as well-prepared and knowledgeable as possible. Once the ship landed in Liverpool, he had a week layover while the boat prepared for the return trip home, loading cargo and supplies. McKenzie used the time to visit hospitals to learn the latest techniques; to visit gymnasia, again to see what was current. It was a time in England when the sports and games approach of the pubic schools was not part of the curriculum of the common schools. Recruits to the armed forces, particularly the navy, were being rejected in record numbers. To a nation which prided itself as being Queen of the Seas, it was a dangerous situation. The Common Schools did not have the elaborate fields and gymnasium space of the Public. England turned to the style in vogue in Sweden, the Ling System, a method whereby large numbers could be led by a single instructor. Competing with it for the nation's favour was the system of Archibald McLaren, who sought to develop programs tailored to the individual.

McKenzie's respite from his duties gave him renewed vigour and an even more forceful vision. On his return to his McGill duties in the autumn of 1893, he decided to approach the board of governors with a plan to upgrade the physical education requirements. His ability to overcome typhoid played a role in his decision. Being a medical doctor was, of course, an advantage since he was aware of the symptoms and medical treatment to combat the all too often fatal illness. However, just as important in McKenzie's mind was the fact that he was in superb physical condition and that had a preventive effect against the ravages of the often fatal disease. He recalled, too, how he had been relatively sickly as a youth; it was only when he developed an active lifestyle that he became full of vigour. He couldn't remember the last time he had been ill before the typhoid struck. He was convinced that being exposed to the bacteria from patients and the overloaded schedule of an intern were the reasons that he succumbed. His physical reserves built up from his years in gymnastics and sport were the reasons why he overcame this mighty obstacle.

Having thought all of this out and combined it with the summer school sessions he had attended at Harvard, as well as the information gleaned from his overseas expeditions, he acted. He approached the board of governors with a plan to increase the amount of attention given to the physical, not a small chore in an institution dedicated to the development of the mind. In a way, he was aligning himself with James Naismith and the Y movement. They believed in strengthening the spirit while paying attention to the strong foundation of body and mind. McKenzie wanted to strengthen the body in order to promote not only its health but the strength of the mind. He wanted a sound mind in a sound body. He was also fully aware that to begin at university age might be too late; such a program should begin much earlier. He was aware that so many strong country folk, used to working in the fields all day, began to deteriorate physically when they enrolled in school and sat at their desks all day.

But he was at McGill; he could only address the problem there and hope to influence others. He knew that various students arrived at the university in different phases or levels of fitness. Yet they were all treated the same and given like programs. For some it was too strenuous; for others not strenuous enough. He recommended that each entering student be given a medical examination followed by a specific and personalized program based on the inadequacies found. His aim was to improve academic performance by improving physical condition.

He quoted statistics which he knew well. He was forceful. While there was a tendency on the part of some university people to downplay sport since it was non-academic, there was some solid evidence close by to help dispute that contention. The student newspaper, the *Gazette*, published a survey in 1890 of the grades of 105 McGill University football players from 1880-1886.[2] The results were enlightening, especially to those who considered that intercollegiate sport took time away from important studies. Twenty percent of the players had graduated with first-class honours; twenty-one of them had won university medals. Another fifteen percent, – sixteen student athletes – graduated with second-class honours. Included in the results were twenty-three who graduated as doctors, eleven in law and forty with a science degree.[3]

He provided further ammunition. He reviewed the winners of the Wicksteed Medal competition. Over a ten-year period, starting in 1883, sixteen of the twenty had been at second-class honours or above. He ensured that the board was aware of the time spent by these student athletes on their activities; he recounted in detail the amount of practice and preparation a member of a school team had to go through. Contrary to what some academics felt about such activities taking time away from more important studies, it was clear that just the opposite was a better reflection of reality: Regular and systematic exercise contributed to the persistence and dedication needed for good academic work.

He had one more piece of evidence to support his conviction. When Harvard University (McKenzie knew that the mention of a prestigious institution such as Harvard would cause them to perk up their ears) opened its new gymnasium in 1880 all incoming students were tested in the area of general strength. By 1893, there were 245 students who tested higher than the strongest person from 1880. Harvard was a magic name; it had an enviable reputation. He used the figures to point out where McGill could improve its approach, to continue to call itself the Harvard of the North with even more validity. That base knowledge of each student's strengths and weaknesses would provide instructors with an idea of where improvement was needed. He also proposed that the university not schedule classes and bring in guest lecturers during the common gymnasium hour.

Just as important to McKenzie was the need for a new facility. The gym was old and outdated, with a number of inadequacies. He catalogued them: Showers were cold and in a dark corner; the old lockers were an invitation to thieves. There was an ever-present smell of gas when the lanterns were lit and not enough heat from the old coal stove during the winter months. Not only that, the ventilation was poor and it was a standing joke among the classes that exercise in the gym was bad for their health; they could be hit by falling chunks of plaster from the ceiling! Rain brought large pools of water through the leaking roof "where besides the inconveniences when many were on the floor, (were) dangerous to the health from dampness and wet feet."[4]

His presentation had its effect. The new gymnasium was approved in principle, although it was delayed until funds became available. McKenzie was given a new title, medical director of physical training, the first in Canada. He was to supervise the physical examinations of incoming students, again a first in Canada. Perhaps it was just as well that the expanded physical education program he visualized wasn't adopted right away. He was busy. He was also demonstrating in anatomy, a job taking four hours a day, five days a week; in the evenings, he conducted gymnastics classes, one of his special duties, to train future directors for the YMCA which would open a new facility in 1895. Perhaps he recalled Jim Naismith's stories about his experience with the secretaries but the new duties revealed another side to McKenzie yet one familiar to all starting a new endeavor:

> As I sit waiting tonight (Nov 6/94) I have the feeling of impending danger an urgent vague sensation that I always have in beginning of any enterprize. I feel that this is going to be a failure, that tonight nothing will be done and that the club will never come to anything. A feeling comes over me that the would-be-members will treat it as a joke, – will not take it seriously and that would hurt me more than a row over it. I hardly know what my future plans with regard to it will be if this first attempt to organize fails. I don't know whether I would ever have the confidence to start it again. The fear of failure has always prevented me from undertaking projects in the past until I was certain that they could not fail but this time I feel that I have gone into it without having taken all precautions against this possibility although it seemed fairly sure in talking it over at home. What it really wants is men who will always want to come instead of having to be dragged out. I begin to fear for the hour. Perhaps Ten is too late. I will be tired myself and may not be in condition to enthuse tired men. If so it will terminate in yawning and disgust for all concerned.[5]

Indeed the YMCA connection was never very far from McKenzie. He continued to correspond with Jim Naismith and was aware of the new game that he had invented. It had made its way into Canada through the Canadian graduates of Springfield. One of Naismith's class members who played in the original game, T.D. Patton, became the director of physical education at the Montreal Y in September of 1892 and introduced the game during that year.[6] By 1894, McGill had a league running within the university which competed for a trophy donated by the Graduates Society.[7]

As if McKenzie's schedule wasn't hectic enough, he was asked to provide swimming lessons for the son of the Governor General, Lord Aberdeen. It was the beginning of a friendship between the two. Aberdeen was so pleased with the approach taken by McKenzie – there was no "mollycoddling." McKenzie offered a fine program of responsibility with guidance; he asked him to accompany his oldest boy, Lord Haddo, to England in 1895 and later, on a cycling trip to France, where it was hoped that the young sixteen-year-old's proficiency in French would improve as well as his fitness. McKenzie struck him as the perfect tutor, but more than that he would act *in loco parentis*, like a wise and judicious parent. Aberdeen had a further request. He asked McKenzie to join his staff as a personal physician. It was a major decision for Tait. Not only would he have to take a leave of absence from McGill and the job and his connection with sport that he enjoyed, as well as from his own practice, he would also have to learn a whole new protocol for living in a stratum of society he had never been part of. It was a long way from his growing up days in Almonte.

Ever one to face challenges and to expand his horizons, he decided to do it. Dr. J.J. Ross was put in charge of the physical training program. McKenzie was paid $1500 for the year. It was a considerable raise over what he had been earning from his previous duties: $476 from his medical practice and $400 from McGill. It turned out to be an intensive fifteen-month immersion into the world of high society. It also provided him with contacts he would never have otherwise been able to make. Once the term was over, Aberdeen left for his U.K. home and McKenzie returned to McGill as a demonstrator in anatomy and instructor in physical education.

He continued to practice medicine. Yet he realized that the only reason he had entered the field was to prepare himself for a career in physical education. He was torn between his two callings much like Jim Naismith. Orthopaedics were important, as was physical education which seemed to be evolving so rapidly. Hovering in the background was his whole artistic side. He had been interested in sketching from his youthful days, since he had taken those first rudimentary lessons. He continued to carry a sketch pad with him, pulling it out and recording quickly, planning to fill out the details later when he had the time, which it seemed to him was seldom. He began to make drawings based on his anatomy observations and delivered a lecture in artistic anatomy to the Montreal Art Association. It was 1897 and in the same year, he attended a preliminary meeting of the Society of College Gymnasium Directors, an American-based group. They were still searching for a unique American system, yet each one wanted to defend the approach taken in his institution. Nevertheless, it was an interesting experience for McKenzie. He returned to Montreal full of renewed enthusiasm for his profession and its vitality.

It was as if something very deep in McKenzie's being was bursting to surface. On the one hand, he was observing real, live human beings filled with energy, experiencing movement which was innovative, creative, exploring the bounds of humanity. Yet his drawings were two-dimensional, static. Not that he was dissatisfied with his ability; it was the medium. His presentations to the Montreal Art Association were somewhat like his anatomy: lifeless forms dissected; drawings of sinew, tendons, bones and inanimate objects were losing their appeal. He had chosen medicine because of his preoccupation with a healthy life. He needed to find another mode of expression, one which would challenge his powers of observation and his ability to portray life.

He remained close to a variety of sports. He always had been, it seemed, as an athlete, a teacher or an attendant. He began to muse occasionally as he watched the tremendous effort and strain which appeared on an athlete's face. He recalled his own career as a high jumper. People told him of the intense look on his face, the concentration he portrayed as he ran down the approach, focusing on the bar. If eyes were the mirrors of the soul, his face reflected the whole range of emotions he felt. Was it the same as the strain which appeared as a result of mental anguish, he wondered? He began to pay closer attention. They appeared to be different, these athletic tensions and emotional ones. Slowly, he collected data. He built up a storehouse of knowledge about which muscles were effected. He sought a way to give expression to his findings. Sketching and painting couldn't do it. He decided to try his hand at sculpting.

He used clay. It was malleable, something he could shape easily with his fingers. His first work was a life-size mask, realistic rather than impressionistic. He had come across a photograph of "B.J. Wefers, a famous sprinter of the day, which showed his tense expression as he put everything into the finish of a race."[8] In addition, McKenzie enlisted the help of his students to scour numerous sources for photographs of faces of athletes straining to perform. He titled his finished work: *Violent Effort*. He was so pleased with it that he attempted three more: *Breathlessness*, *Fatigue* and *Exhaustion*.

His works met with overwhelming success. Photos of them and an accompanying article were published in the *Journal of Anatomy and Physiology* in London, England. These were chiefly scientific studies, yet they had enough artistic merit that they were also shown at art salons in the United States as well as Paris, France.

He was scheduled to attend the Society of College Gymnasium Directors annual meeting at Yale. It was at this American meeting that McKenzie's career took yet another turn. At the same time, during the Christmas break, and also on the Yale Campus was a gathering of the American Society of Anatomists. The contrast between the two groups was immediate and striking. The anatomy group was reserved, staid, dry and, to McKenzie, very much like the subject matter it studied and dissected. On the other hand, the gym group was as vibrant as it was different. McKenzie had come to know most of them from his frequent visits to Harvard's summer school. He never felt in awe of them but nonetheless, he enjoyed Sargent, striking with his mass of figures, statistics and apparatus for measuring strength and power. So many of the men who had pioneered methods that McKenzie came to rely on were there: Hitchcock, a specialist in anthropometry and a pioneer in testing for students' strength at the beginning and end of each year. One could see the improvement; he published the results for all to see. Naturally, other schools took up the challenge to see if they could better the results. At the other end of the spectrum was George Goldie, a superb and renowned Scot who had McKenzie's attention the first time he met him because of his great practical experience and knowledge of almost every sport of the day. He was a legend among the Hibernians with their Caledonian Games and McKenzie had heard of him long before meeting him.

Violent Effort   *Mill of Kintail*   **Breathlessness**   *Mill of Kintail*

Fatigue   *Mill of Kintail*   **Exhaustion**   *Mill of Kintail*

It was a turning point. McKenzie's paper, and his original way of illustrating the data, so captured his audience of anatomists that he was offered a job at the University of Pennsylvania. He was flattered but he declined. His mind was made up and it was the gymnasium directors who had done it for him. Their camaraderie, innovations, commitment and vibrancy convinced him to concentrate on physical education.

It was not unlike James Naismith's decision. Each had trained for what he thought he wanted more than anything, Naismith as a minister and McKenzie as a doctor. In the end, each of them chose to move into an area which seemed at first to be only an interest but was to grow into a lifelong love, physical education as perceived and defined by each one. McKenzie had a deftness of hand, honed by his being a surgeon. His success with the clay masks, later cast in bronze, prompted him to attempt other forms of modelling. He tried bas-relief, took some lessons to ease the transition. His eye needed an object to refer to. He thought back to the ancient Greek sculptures he remembered. They were harmonious, idealized to represent the god which dwelled in the athlete and was responsible for his victory. They couldn't be taken as a realistic representation. He could see that from the athletes he was viewing. Sprinters such as Wefer and Duffy were either tall and lanky or short and thick-set.[9] Reality was far different from the ideal.

Again his inspiration came from the gymnasium directors. He presented his paper and masks to them. They were so enthusiastic and encouraging. He sat back and listened to the next presentation by Paul Phillips of Amherst College. He was a disciple of Hitchcock and had gathered measurements from a large group of American sprinters. It was exactly what McKenzie wanted. With Phillips' approval, he took the measurements and combined them with those gathered by his class at McGill. Then he sought out four prominent McGill athletes, Percival Molson, John D. Morrow, L.O. Howard and Frederick J. Tees. They would strike various poses in order for him to study and re-create the musculature as it was defined. He decided that since it was to be a free standing statue, it would be quarter size. The result was *The Sprinter*, McKenzie's first figure in the round. It was a nude in the Greek classical sense. The pose was that of a sprinter in a crouch start, just recently approved for track and field. Previously, even in the ancient games, the start had always been a standing one; the viewer's attention was attracted and held immediately.

The Sprinter   *Mill of Kintail*

The finished product looked so graceful, so lifelike, so full of youthful confidence. The feedback was all enthusiastic. McKenzie's confreres asked him to make another figure, that of an idealized all-round athlete. Again measurements played a role. Four hundred general measurements plus an additional fifty superior athletes were taken into account. McKenzie produced what some have called his finest work, *The Athlete*. "It represented a beautifully developed young man in the bloom of youth bending slightly to the side to place in his right hand a spring dynamometer with which to test the strength of his grip."[10]

It seemed as if McKenzie was spending more and more time with his New England confreres. Probably in the beginning it was because of Naismith that he did so. The connections became deeper. Not only was he using the anthropometric data provided by the University of Pennsylvania, he was also taking advantage of sculptor friends he had made in Massachusetts. Indeed, while touching up his bronze *Athlete* in the studio of Henry Kitson, he attracted a reporter looking for an article for the Boston *Globe*. The paper praised his work, *The Sprinter*, remarking that even the President, Theodore Roosevelt, had purchased a copy for the White House.[11] The article enthused about McKenzie's new work, *The Athlete*, commenting on its likeness to the Greek classical statues. A bright future was predicted for the Canadian who was said to have "the genius and capacity as have few . . . rare scientific training . . . will stand him in good stead . . . a student . . . maintains the attitude of a student which is what all successful artists and sculptors have ever done."[12] Critical acclaim followed from England, France and the United States. McKenzie's horizons were expanding. Perhaps it was time to give them a freer rein.

Meanwhile, James Naismith was undergoing his own metamorphosis. He was falling in love with his landlady's daughter. He had moved to the Sherman boarding house in Springfield and was more and more attracted to Maude. It was a mutual admiration society.

During the Christmas vacation of 1891, a short time after the invention of basketball, they had their first date. She made him feel as if he was the centre of everything. She even took up the game of basketball and played in what might have been the first game for women in March 1892. It made Jim feel very special. Maude wasn't particularly fond of sports but because he had invented the game, she began to play and enjoy it. He saw it as an appreciation of his work and support for the time he was putting into its spread.

And spreading it was, through a variety of means. It made its way through Canada and the United States first by students who were part of the original class. In addition, the *Triangle*, a publication of the Y, first printed the rules in January 1892. The issue was mailed to Ys throughout North America. It added to his workload. Letters poured in from everywhere requesting clarification and details. At the same time, there were problems. Some YMCAs were vehemently opposed to the new game. They couldn't accept the fact that the gym floor would be tied up by ten persons while so many others would be left without the use of the facility. Indeed, one Y in Philadelphia, the north branch, "refused to allow basketball on the gym floor."[13] Part of the problem was that many of the gym directors had little or no experience in team games or competitive sports. As a result, when they saw the intense competition, fights and arguments breaking out, they were unable to control the situation; the Y consequently was getting a reputation it did not want.

Naismith was even getting letters from overseas. Two of his students in the class of 1893 were from France and Japan. Each of them took the game home, helping to spread it there as well. All of this was enough for Naismith to continue his hectic pace: Basketball, his teaching duties and the courting of the beautiful and charming Maude Sherman.

They were married on June 20, 1894 in Hope Congregational Church in Springfield; best man was his brother of the wind Robbie Tait McKenzie. It was a joyous occasion. The two valley boys were together once again to share yet another aspect of life and share each other's joys and accomplishments. McKenzie had beaten his typhoid and was still on leave from McGill as house physician to the Governor General. Naismith had given the world a new game, was feeling very fulfilled, surrounded by the ones he loved. There was one nagging irritation. Annie, his sister, had come down for the wedding. She was still decidedly cool towards her brother, unable to rid herself of the judgement that she had previously expressed to him: "you put your hand to the plough and turned back." She was still unable to forgive him for leaving the ministry. Jim was hurt but too busy to dwell on it. He had made his decision and wasn't about to start looking back and questioning it now. It was good to see Rob; he seemed so excited about his work. Medicine seemed to be such a natural extension of physical education.

On July 1, 1895, the Naismiths had their first child, a daughter, Margaret Mason. Perhaps it was only fitting that she be born on Dominion Day, Canada's birthday. Jim Naismith considered himself very much a Canadian but, as well, it was very close to the American Independence Day of July 4, Maude's national day. It all made the birth seem like an international event.

Otherwise, Naismith was becoming somewhat restless. Basketball seemed to be evolving. Five players were now the accepted number on each team. Outfits and shoes were being especially designed for the game and were available through the Spalding catalogue. The soccer ball had been abandoned and the first ball specifically for basketball was produced in 1894 by the Overman Wheel Company, a manufacturer of bicycles from Chicopee, Mass. One year earlier, in 1893, the peach containers were replaced with a basket similar to one used today, with an iron rim and a cord to release the ball. The Narrangansett Machine Company developed the iron hoop with a braided cord netting; the ball was released by pulling the cord. It sold for $15 a pair in 1893. In 1895, the backboard was brought into the game. It was a protection from overzealous fans who reached out to deflect the ball towards or away from the basket according to their loyalties. The dribble, an integral part of the game today, made its way into it in a roundabout way. It began as a defensive measure. When a player was unable to pass the ball, the ball could be released and attempt was made to capture it again before the oposition. Players began experimenting and by 1896 a specific style, the dribble game, was being played in some sections of the northeast, particularly around Yale. [14]

All of these variations were for Naismith to pronounce upon. Did he agree? Was it allowed? How would he rule? Naismith's guidelines were five in number, five general principles which would govern and maintain the integrity of the game.

1. There must be a ball; it should be large, light and handled with the hands.

2. There must be no running with the ball.

3. No man on either team shall be restricted from getting the ball at any time that it is in play.

4. Both teams are to occupy the same area, yet there is to be no personal contact.

5. The goal shall be horizontal and elevated. [15]

It was certainly a busy time and in some ways a flattering time. He was the centre of attention on so many occasions. Yet he also realized that he needed more education in his adopted field. It seemed obvious that in order to become an accepted authority in the field, it was necessary to become a doctor. McKenzie had recognized that and Gulick was one as well. He made up his mind. He, too, would pursue medicine, not so much to practice it but rather to prepare himself better as a physical educator. But where? And how could he do it with his added responsibilities, a wife and child?

The answer came in the summer of 1895. The central branch of the YMCA in Denver, Colorado, offered him the position of physical director. There were certain cons which struck him immediately. It would mean leaving Springfield where he was in the centre of developments both in basketball and in physical education; he would be even further from Almonte and his family and from Montreal where McKenzie was practicing. It would be especially difficult for Maude who would be alone with the baby far from her family, left on her own to cope with the trials of motherhood. On the other hand, Denver was also the home of the Gross Medical School, an institution with a good reputation for turning out quality doctors. The pros won out. They made their decision and moved to Denver where, in September of 1895, thirty-four-year-old James Naismith began his career in medicine.

It was a busy three years. He combined his intense medical studies with his duties at the Y in addition to being a model father and husband. Maude was happy too. However, she became pregnant in 1897, and there were complications. She contracted typhoid. Jim was worried. He had lost his parents to the illness; he didn't want to lose a wife and child too. Her condition worsened; pneumonia set in. He hired a nurse to be with her at all times. He broke away from his studies and his job as often as he could to sit with Maude. She was in decline. He could see it. Memories came flooding back. He was a small boy once again, sitting on the wagon with his Uncle Peter, waving to his mother who was staying to look after his father, sick with typhoid. He fought back tears as those sad days were relived and drifted in and out of his thoughts. His bride was dying.

Occasionally she would awaken, apparently lucid, and her eyes would meet his. A faint smile would come to her lips. She would drift back into a semi-conscious state. Jim's mind was in torment. Had she given up? Had she accepted that this was the end? He sat back and dabbed her forehead, occasionally speaking to her in a reassuring way. Outwardly, he maintained an air of confidence; inwardly, he was praying as hard as he could for a miracle. It was almost too much for him when, on one occasion, he returned from a particularly trying day at the Y and school. He again sat in the bedroom where Maude was lying, still feverish, in the four-poster bed. She seemed peaceful but he was disquieted. He held her hand. Almost immediately, she opened her eyes, looked at him and beyond to the posts of the bed. She seemed lucid now and "chanted softly: One to watch and one to pray and two to bear my soul away." [16]

A tearful Naismith realized that Maude was speaking of angels. Had she seen them sitting on the bed posts? Was she hallucinating? Speaking in allegory? Was she giving up? He didn't know what to say and so said nothing, giving her hand a gentle squeeze. Later, he instructed the nurse to pay special attention that evening. It was a good thing. As he dozed, the nurse had noticed that Maude was very still. She reached over and searched for a pulse. There was none. Frantic, she awakened Naismith. Now alert, he moved to Maude. He could find no pulse either. He called her name. There was no response. He slapped her face. Why, he didn't really know. It seemed such an impulsive thing to do. Some instinct seemed to be telling him that she needed to be awakened from her deep sleep.

Maude stirred. Took a breath. Another. It seemed as if Jim was trying to breathe for her. He felt for her pulse. It had reappeared. And was getting stronger! No one could convince Jim Naismith and the nurse that this wasn't a miracle. Maude had returned from the dead! Her doctor later gave her a clean bill of health. The only reminder of the ordeal would be loss of hearing but it was a small price to pay for her return. Not only that, the baby was saved. Helen Carolyn was born on December 21, 1897, the first day of winter, and as if to signify that, Maude's hair was beginning to turn prematurely white, another consequence from her bout with typhoid. There was another part of family lore associated with the child. As a baby, she cried often; perhaps from colic. Jim took his turn carrying her through the night, pacing the floor. He marvelled at her lungs. At times, they seemed too large for such a little baby. He joked that instead of Helen Naismith, she should have been called Hell 'n blazes. When her parents told her this story she decided that she would spell her name "Hellen" as a reminder, something she did for the rest of her life. 17

James Naismith graduated with a degree in medicine on April 8, 1898. It had been a hard three-year struggle. It was beginning to seem to him that he had spent the better part of his life in school, preparing himself for the future. He had been trained for the clergy, yet had decided against entering that service. Now, he was a doctor. But he didn't want to practice medicine. It was simply the best way he knew of to prepare himself for the field which appealed to him, physical education. It was time for another turn in the road.

During a tumbling class at the Y, Jim was supervising students while they were performing various floor routines. A student was performing a somersault. His timing was off; he landed on his neck, breaking it. The student died. Naismith was shattered. Through sleepless nights he questioned himself. Could he have "spotted" the youth better? Could he have prevented the death? Was this punishment from God for his moving away from the ministry, ignoring His call? When he slept, it was fitful. Awake, he was constantly distracted. Spiritually, he was in disarray. What had he done to deserve this? All of his Presbyterian upbringing came to the fore. Why had it happened? Was he in God's disfavour? The remorse and doubt was so all-pervasive, his bewilderment so absorbing that he could no longer bear it. He went to the spot in the gym where the student died. He knelt and spoke with his God. If he had offended him, he was sorry but he needed relief. He asked for it. There was nothing more he could do on his own. He abandoned himself to his Lord and asked Him to take over. Jim Naismith would become His instrument. He would be open to whatever came his way, wherever he was led.

On September 1, 1898, the Naismith family moved to Lawrence, Kansas, where he accepted a post at the University of Kansas. It was a curious set of circumstances that took Jim Naismith there. Once again,

Amos Alonzo Stagg intervened into his life. The university was looking for a director of chapel and religious services who could also head up the fledgling department of physical education as well as coach. The Kansas president had contacted his counterpart at the University of Chicago where Stagg was performing the same function. Stagg wired the Kansas president and recommended Naismith, the "inventor of basket-ball, medical doctor, Presbyterian minister, tee-totaller, all around athlete, non-smoker and owner of vocabulary without cuss words." [18]

That might have been the background to the move but as far as Jim Naismith was concerned, it was Divine Providence working. God had answered his prayer. On many occasions after that, whenever he returned to Denver, Jim Naismith visited that site in the gym, knelt at the exact spot and gave thanks for yet another sign of God's working in his life.

At Kansas, he settled into his new duties. He promoted basketball to the university and the community. In addition to being director of athletics, he coached the Jayhawks, compiling a 54-44 won-lost record. In the classroom, he was a one-man department, teaching the required first-year courses in hygiene and gymnastics. His main job was that of chapel director. Students attended chapel daily where there was singing, prayer and a talk. As time went by, the daily devotionals gave way to alternating days, later weekly; compulsory attendance gave way to voluntary. His duties at the chapel were soon virtually eliminated, replaced with others. He introduced courses in kinesiology, analysis of motion in sport, became the university's physician until one was hired specifically for that task. Meanwhile, his family continued to grow. John Edwin, "Jack" was born November 3, 1900, Maude Annie on October 28, 1904.

Jim Naismith, as often as not now known as "Doc," entered fully into the life of his new community. And as often as he could, he communicated with Tait McKenzie, seeking his opinions and ideas. Being so far west and away from developments in the east where ideas about physical education and sport seemed to always be in ferment, he wanted to keep up as best he could. He introduced new sports into the athletic program: fencing, rowing, football, track. There was a new and free health service for students as well as novel approaches to developmental and remedial physical education. He became a practitioner of the anthropomorphic approach, filing statistics on every aspect of student activity and using them for comparative and personal purposes. Because he was known throughout the state, the university sent him to deliver speeches and lectures to groups of all sorts. He spoke on a variety of subjects but became something of an expert in the physical development of children. He advocated that children be treated individually, that physical differences and later maturation be given more importance. He delighted in making new apparatus to achieve a desired effect.

He became thoroughly involved in the community. He taught Sunday school and the youngsters looked forward to his classes, sprinkled as they were with analogies from the world of sport and presented in concepts easily understood by the youngsters. His adult denominational and non-denominational sessions were over-subscribed. He continued to promote the YMCA in Lawrence and opened a branch on campus. In recognition, the Springfield YMCA Training School granted him an honorary masters degree in physical education on February 12, 1911. During a severe flood of the Kaw River, it was the experienced paddler, Jim Naismith, who risked his life to take people to safety. This man with the funny Canadian accent was endearing himself to the people of his adopted home. The Naismiths' fifth child, James Jr., was born on May 7, 1913. Naismith was now fifty-two; Maude almost forty-five, still deaf and almost completely white haired, constant reminders to them both of her brush with typhoid and the miracle of life. She enthused at Jimmy's birth that she had stolen him from the angels.[19]

More and more, Naismith was gravitating towards actively practicing his religious beliefs. Ideals were important to him in an era when results and pragmatism held sway. It was only in 1916 that he was finally ordained as a minister. The United States had not yet entered the First World War but was having its own border skirmish with the Mexican Pancho Villa. Naismith was still a Canadian and could have gone to Canada to join up but he wanted to be closer to home. As well, he was making his living in the States, had been there for some twenty-five years now; he wanted to be with the American forces. He had been appointed chaplain in the Kansas National Guard and underwent active training. On April 12, 1916, he was ordained by the presbyter at Clay Centre, Kansas. He was now Reverend Dr. James Naismith.

With the call-up of the National Guard, Naismith, a captain, was sent as a chaplain to the Mexican border war. Part of his duties involved promoting sport as a means of taking soldiers' minds off war and keeping them out of trouble away from the senoritas of the streets when there was time on their hands. In a way, it was the same sort of problem which he had had at Springfield. He had to come up with innovative ways of occupying young men's time or lose them. His duties lasted until October 30, 1916, when he was discharged, having served out his term. Less than a year later, the United States declared war on Germany. Naismith took a leave of absence from the university and volunteered for duty with the YMCA National War Work Council. He sailed for France in September 1917, too late to see his boyhood friend McKenzie who, he knew, had volunteered to serve with the British command.

And McKenzie? It was a busy dozen years for him too. There had been many changes, twists and turns which had made him a well-known figure on two continents. In 1904, the same year as Naismith's marriage, he decided to accept a position with the University of Pennsylvania as professor and director of the department of physical education. He had given it much thought and in the end, saw it as the only way. At McGill, he really had little academic standing within the university, although he had recently been named lecturer in anatomy. It seemed to be a constant uphill battle. His salary for his physical education work was paid by the athletic association and he answered to that committee rather than to the university directly. Also, there was little progress that he could see towards a new gym. There were plans; it was said to be on the list of buildings to be constructed; it had official priority but it seemed as if everything else was continually moved ahead of it on the list. Pennsylvania offered him everything he wanted. His salary would be paid by the school. He was to be a full-fledged professor in the faculty of medicine with full academic status, director of the physical education department. A new gymnasium, Weightman Hall, was being built, its construction still at the point where he could have a say in the design of it. Perhaps the final sweetener was that McKenzie would have an office and a studio in Weightman Hall overlooking Franklin Field, the university's up-to-date stadium. Not only that, he would be allowed to continue his medical practice if he wished.

If anything made McKenzie's decision easier, it was Pennsylvania's approach to physical education. It was all that he could ask for. It was an academic department within the university rather than a student service as at McGill. Incoming students underwent a compulsory medical examination and were required to take two periods of physical education per week during a four-year degree. Academic credit would be given for the course on a par with any other one taken.

He began to make his presence felt almost immediately. Within the university community, he began receiving accolades for his approach of improving the general health of the whole student body against the trend of spending time and resources on the few who represented the university on its teams. He was instrumental in forming the Playground Association of Philadelphia, a group which assured that children would have space for imaginative recreation. He was a pioneer in advocating better physical education programs for elementary school children; he invited the children to have a sports day at Franklin Field and in the process, endeared the department and the university to the wider Philadelphia community. His studio was put to good use. Amid a variety of medallions and bas reliefs, he completed a death mask of boxing legend John L. Sullivan; sculpted the *Competitor* and the *Supple Juggler*. It was a hectic time but he loved it in spite of the feeling that there never seemed to be enough hours in the day.

His work was attracting international attention, and in 1907 he

The Boxer   *Mill of Kintail*   **The Competitor**   *Mill of Kintail*

The Relay   *Mill of Kintail*

was invited to address conferences in London and Paris. He decided to accept; the ocean crossing would give him a much-needed rest and help him recharge his batteries to return revitalized and re-energized for the next term. It was a momentous decision. Aboard the ship, McKenzie was struck immediately by the beauty of a passenger, Ethel O'Neil. He inquired about her. She was a Canadian, from Hamilton, the daughter of the owner of the Hamilton *Spectator*. She was a concert pianist who also taught music, on her way to Berlin to study during the summer break. She was twenty-seven, McKenzie, forty; he was smitten. They were drawn to each other immediately; they seemed to have so much in common considering they had not known each other before. The voyage ended all too quickly. On their arrival in London, they parted but not before McKenzie brashly told her that he intended to marry her. They continued to correspond. On August 18, 1907, they were married at the Chapel Royal of Dublin Castle, McKenzie's friends, the Aberdeens, having played a prominent role in the arrangements.

When they returned to Philadelphia, they soon found the quarters at 26 South 21st Street too cramped. They moved to 2014 Pine Street where the three floors plus an attic provided the needed space for each other's pursuits. Athletes came to pose for McKenzie in his studio on the second floor while strains of classical melodies wafted down from Ethel's third floor piano room. McKenzie's work blossomed. In addition to the continuing bas reliefs and medallions, he sculpted *The Relay* in 1909 and *The Onslaught* in 1911. He had reached back into his own athletic past, his love of track and field and football seemingly wanting to burst through and be expressed concretely. At the same time, he was aware of the role that both sports played in the life of the community. Pennsylvania's Franklin Field was the site of the famous

Penn Relays and McKenzie's work was guaranteed a ready audience. The work portrayed a member of the team, the third runner, eagerly following the course of the race as the baton was carried towards him. There is a look of intense concentration on his face; one can almost see the race being run through the concentration of his gaze. *The Onslaught* was a football piece. McKenzie was becoming a devotee of the American game with its fewer men and more scientific play because of the snapback system. He chose, however, to create an image of the ball carrier breaking through the line, giving the whole work the appearance of a wave cresting, about to break upon the shore. As if all of this wasn't enough, McKenzie even found time to write a book; *Education In Exercise and Medicine.* Like his sculptures, it was a classic, described as a Bible for those in the field, a blend of theory and practice in the developing discipline.

Perhaps his best known work, the one which is synonymous with his name, was created in 1912. *The Joy of Effort* was commissioned by the American Olympic Committee. Again, it was McKenzie the hurdler giving expression to his talent. He remembered the preparations, the steps between the hurdles, the constant practice needed to get them down, the control under full-speed conditions and the need to bestride the hurdle without slowing down or striking it, all the while aiming for victory. Three hurdlers are represented clearing a bar. There is an intense yet relaxed look about them, a close sense of competition and their sheer joy in it. The bronze, a forty-six inch diameter circle, was set in the stadium wall at Stockholm, site of the 1912 Olympic Games. Everyone was thrilled with the work but none more so than King Gustav of Sweden. He presented McKenzie with a silver medal in honour of the work. It wasn't the only joy in his life. In that same year, 1912, he produced a bas-relief of Ethel. It had a Gaelic inscription: "To Ethel, the thousand times beloved daughter of Neil, the royal hearted, the dark haired, the precious, joy

The Onslaught, now the CIAU Winston Churchill Trophy   *Mill of Kintail*

Joy of Effort, **encased in the Stockholm stadium for the 1912 Olympics**   *Mill of Kintail*

of my youth, pride of my life, darling of my heart, with my soul's devotion."[20] One of the first bas-reliefs he had made was of his mother, the first love in his life. It seemed only fitting to do one of Ethel.

McKenzie's largest piece of work to that time was unveiled in 1914. The university had asked him to create a statue of Benjamin Franklin. He was only too pleased, not only because Franklin was an acknowledged hero in Pennsylvania, but also because he had pronounced on the importance of educating youth in body as well as mind. The eight-foot representation was of a young Benjamin leaving home, ready to carve his niche in the world. It was unveiled in June, its site close to Franklin Field, in front of Weightman Hall. It stands today at the entrance of the physical education building.

These were days of immense satisfaction to Tait and Ethel. Summers were spent at Noank, Connecticut, where they rented a cottage on the seashore. Athletes came to pose and pass the time playing sports. From his window McKenzie could see the lithe and supple athletes. They moved with such grace. They were so fluid, so natural, so effortless. Yet he knew how their appearance belied the tremendous effort which had gone into what seemed so natural. Visitors from teams competing at the relays were brought to the cottage to relax, including the competitors from Oxford and Cambridge along with olympic champion Lord Burghley. There was time for family. His mother, who had lived with Tait for some years before he married, and his brothers and sister along with their family, all came to spend time with Rob and Ethel. And still the sculpting continued. There was *The Plunger*, a figure about to dive into the water, the athletes at the sea side offering inspiration. There was an interpretation of a discus thrower. Every sport sculptor seemed to want to create his version of the ancient olympic event which was captured classically by Myron in his *Discobolos*. He continued to sketch for future

Boy Scout, 1914; original copyright was presented to Lord Baden-Powell

Mill of Kintail

works, keeping up a steady stream of subjects. There was a *Man Watching The Pole Vault*, another *Discus Thrower* from a different angle, *Shot Putter Resting, Shot Putter Ready, High Jumper Cleaning His Shoe, Relay No. 1, Relay No. 2*. His bas-reliefs were continually improving. His medallions were many; he was in constant demand while his teaching and physical education duties increased. In 1907, he had been given the additional rank of professor of physical therapy. Even the Boy Scouts commissioned McKenzie to create a one-quarter size statue. It was a piece of art that Lord Baden-Powell was very pleased to have as his own.

The harmony and tranquility of McKenzie's life came to an abrupt end in 1914. His mother died in October. The funeral took him back to Almonte. His father's old congregation rallied again and came from far and wide to gather for her funeral. They "reopened the closed doors of the old church to conduct the funeral service in the building haunted by her memory."[21] It turned into a nostalgic visit. The only thing missing was his friend Jim as he took Ethel to all the old haunts he had as a youth. They walked through the woods and by the river, and generally soaked in all the memories he had as a youth. At the same time, the talk everywhere was of the war which had broken out in Europe and which Canada, by virtue of its semi-colonial status, was a part of. He had been somewhat sheltered from the immediacy of it in Philadelphia since the United States was still at peace. Everywhere McKenzie went in Almonte, there was talk of war, of mobilization. Would conscription be necessary? There were recruiting drives to attract volunteers for the effort. He resolved to be part of it.

On his return to Philadelphia, he requested and received a leave of

The Fountain of the Laughing Children, **Philadelphia** *Mill of Kintail*

absence. Eighteen months was the most allowed. It was granted, to begin immediately after the winter term. In May 1915, the McKenzies sailed for England and there applied to join the Canadian Medical Service. There was red tape and misunderstandings. Such applications could only be made through the government in Ottawa. McKenzie had been told otherwise. He turned to the Royal Army and its Medical Corps. They were overjoyed and immediately assigned him a lieutenant's commission and sent him to Connaught Hospital at Aldershot where surgeons were needed. There, he was assigned to partake of a physical training program for the newly arrived. Ethel, meanwhile, settled to a rented house in nearby St. John. While McKenzie physically went through the training procedures each recruit went through before heading for the front, it was discovered that he was the author of the text, *Exercise in Education and Medicine*, which was being used in the course. The commander, chagrined and at the same time elated, pulled him from the classes and sent him on a special inspection assignment to the camps along the south coast to ensure that they were being properly run.

It was not unlike the problems that McKenzie had seen at McGill and Pennsylvania. There were basically two groups of men: those who were physically unfit for service and had to be made fit, and those who were convalescing. In both cases, remedial work was needed. He outlined his plan to the director of military services, Sir Alfred Keough. The British were enthusiastic. McKenzie was promoted to major. Remedial equipment was brought in; training courses were designed for instructors and masseurs. A chain of command was set up for each section or camp depot. New equipment was invented specific to the remedial needs of the patients. Swedish non-apparatus gymnastics, or exercises, were used to handle the large numbers of soldiers, up to 5,000 in the camp. All exercise was made progressive to increase strength. Light work that could be handled easily gave way gradually to more intense movement until the soldier was fit for active duty once again.

It was a huge success. It was as if all of the ideas that McKenzie had developed at McGill and the University of Pennsylvania had been tailored to his work in England. Within four months, 1,200 men were returned to class A condition. Indeed, the whole approach was so successful that an additional sixteen other command depots were established.[22] Once the organization of the camps was complete and the bugs of the move from peace-time to war ironed out, McKenzie spent the remaining six months of his leave attached to the orthopaedic centres. Ethel moved to Manchester where she, too, was actively involved with the Red Cross. She joined women from all walks of life making bandages, splints and such items as needed for the front and the hospitals.

McKenzie's work in the orthopaedic hospitals was an example of his modelling with human clay.[23] He took individuals who were disabled from the war and designed apparatus specific to their needs. His "extra-ordinary blend of anatomical knowledge and athletic stimuli made him a healer of great power."[24] McKenzie later documented these advanced ideas in remedial work in a book, *Reclaiming the Maimed: A Handbook of Physical Therapy* in 1918.

His overseas work finished by 1917. He was disappointed that he had not seen Naismith whom he knew to be in France. He returned to Philadelphia and the University of Pennsylvania in keeping with the term of his leave of absence. He was in demand in the United States and Canada because of the reputation he had gained overseas with his inventive approach. He became a consultant to the Walter Reed Hospital and designed equipment for it. The Canadian government asked him to advise its hospitals on a similar basis. McKenzie oversaw the Canadian effort until November 11, 1919, when the war ended. In addition to designing equipment, he turned his sculpting talent to other uses, working with plastic surgeons in the reconstruction of faces disfigured during the war.

While McKenzie continued to reclaim the maimed and broken bodies, Naismith had set his sights solidly on the spirit. The United States declared war on Germany on April 6, 1917. The YMCA was asked to play a role in preparing soldiers for the front as well as keeping their spirits up. In turn, the Y asked Jim Naismith to be part of the team dedicated to bringing moral and physical preparation to the soldiers. He was in his element introducing games and recreational activities and satisfying his new ministerial status by preaching the good life of purity in mind, body and spirit. His lectures on the pitfalls of loose sex were a combination of biology and moral guidance. Indeed his approach was so filled with common sense and so well received that he was asked to join the troops overseas in France in September of 1917.

Naismith was fifty-six. While his reputation as the inventor of basketball always preceded him, it was "Doc" Naismith, the counsellor who was being sent. It was a rugged existence. Only because he had kept himself in good condition throughout his life was he able to cope. Paris was bombed regularly. Sirens wailed throughout the night. There was as much mental anguish as physical for those in the city. It was damp; there was mud everywhere. Naismith had to trek through it when he made his way out of the city and into the hinterlands closer to the front. He was resourceful, he had to be. In some ways it was as if he was a youth again back in Almonte during the cold Ottawa valley winter. He smothered his boots with goose grease to make them more water resistant; wore insoles and extra socks, always had extra long underwear, whatever would keep the chill and the dampness at bay. There never seemed to be enough covers at night. He solved the problem by spreading open newspaper pages between his blankets in order to insulate himself from the cold.

The Y and Jim Naismith were responsible for addressing the American troops as they arrived at the French ports. He gave speeches on the need to resist the temptations of Paris, the necessity of maintaining good, clean, moral habits. Afterwards, small knots of men gathered around him to ask questions, to discuss and elaborate. News had begun to circulate that the Doc had invented basketball. Soon the men who showed up for the lecture on the pitfalls of Paris were easing into questions about the game. Naismith found the subject hard to stay away from. Students were students, he thought. His own classes at Kansas did the same thing in order to get him off the topic of the day. Whatever. The important thing is that he had their attention and he would get his point across.

There was always a fear that men, sitting around with time on their hands before their marching orders came in, would gravitate towards trouble. It was the challenge of the Y not only to lecture them on living good clean lives but also to fill their free time with good wholesome activity. It would keep them out of trouble and maintain their level of fitness for the front. In a way, it was much like the work that McKenzie had done in England. Sport was used to improve the quality of the men's condition as a by-product of the enjoyment they took from the competition. The Y also tried to help the men by setting up local headquarters, like a little bit of home, a meeting place where the men could be sure of feeling as if they were in a part of America. On November 16, 1917, Naismith was put in charge of the Y's bureau of hygiene, designed to deal with the problems of alcohol, sexual promiscuity, communicable disease, standards of morality and relations with the French. A staff of eight assisted Naismith in the work.

The bureau seemed to take its cue from the old song "How are you going to keep them down on the farm after they've seen the lights of gay Paree?" Naismith arranged for counter-attractions whenever leave was given to the soldiers. He set up boxing matches or wrestling competitions, races, games of all sort in order to keep the men in camp and, relatively speaking, out of trouble. Where possible, he visited as many soldiers as he could, paying special attention to the Kansas personnel. He brought letters from home, newspapers, bits of conversation he had picked up. His visits were eagerly anticipated as he was continually upbeat and cheery. His motto was written across the inside of his well-used, tattered New Testament, which he always had with him: Strong in Body, Clean in Mind, Lofty in Ideals. [25]

If McKenzie was sculpting with human clay, it was sculpting done on the outside. Naismith was working on the inside and war was the perfect circumstance to guarantee an audience. He had seen the faces of young men caught in the shelling, witnesses of the carnage of war. He had seen the devastation they felt throughout their whole being as a buddy was brought back dead. Their faces reminded him of the many cornered squirrels and rabbits he had seen at home in the woods, looking desperately for a tree to climb or a hole to escape to. It was so true: There were no atheists in foxholes. These were broken men; they needed rebuilding. Naismith took care to reconstruct from the inside out; his goal was to revitalize the human spirit.

1. Robert Tait McKenzie, biographical notes, chapter 2, p. 18, University of Pennsylvania archives.
2. John Dewar, *The Contributions of James Naismith to Sport in Canada*. Ed.D dissertation, Florida State University, 1965.
3. ibid., p. 29.
4. *JOHPER*, February, 1944, p. 82.
5. McKenzie notes, University of Pennsylvania archives.
6. Barry Mitchelson, "The Evolution of Men's Basketball in Canada", unpublished paper presented to the First Canadian Symposium on the History of Sport and Physical Education, University of Alberta, May 13-16, 1970, p. 2.
7. ibid., p. 32.
8. F. Tees, "Tait McKenzie", McGill *News*, Autumn, 1941, p. 28.
9. ibid., p. 28.
10. ibid., p. 29.
11. Jean McGill, *The Joy of Effort*. Bewdley: Clay Publishing Co. 1980. p. 42.
12. ibid.
13. James Naismith, *Basketball, Its Origins And Development*. New York: Associated Press, 1941, p. 113.
14. ibid., p. 62.
15. Webb, op. cit., p. 41.
16. ibidWebb, op. cit., p. 41.
17. ibid. p. 43.
18. ibid., p. 61.
19. *JOHPER*, 1944, p. 74.
20. R. Tait McKenzie, "The Bench of the Minister and His Wife", op. cit., p. 7.
21. *JOHPER*, p. 88.
22. *JOHPER*, p. 81.
23. Hussey, Christopher, *Tait McKenzie: Sculptor of Youth*, London: Country Life, 1929.
24. Webb, op. cit., p. 85

CHAPTER **6**

Post-War Memorials

S OME called the conflict of 1914-1918 "the war to end all wars." In the beginning there was a certain amount of enthusiasm associated with it. It was Good versus Evil and certainly Good would prevail. Young and old citizens eagerly rallied under the British flag to join the new crusade. No one, it seemed, paused to reflect on the consequences, the loss of the flower of a nation's youth. Certainly, those far from the front only became aware of the immensity of the conflict when news came of a fallen neighbour or member of the family. Only then did they question the folly of the conflict. Yet just as often the intense patriotism they were encouraged to feel helped to blunt the pain of their loss.

Not so at the front, not close to where the dead and broken bodies were constantly on view. And not so for Robert Tait McKenzie and James Naismith. They witnessed enough of the so-called Great War to cause them both immense anguish. As much as McKenzie had sought to prepare his charges for the conflict, he was at a loss to explain how such a horrific event could happen. He had seen trainloads of soldiers leave every six hours by steam engine for the front. For days on end, the human cargo was moved out, led like lambs to the slaughter. Not many would return. Everybody knew that. McKenzie knew it and cringed at the thought, the cheap disregard for human life. He began to see his art as a means of keeping those memories of the sacrifice alive, hoping to induce in his viewing public some of the emotions that had been felt by his subject as well as evoking a response. The better he carried it out, the more lasting would be the memory of those lambs.

The war also signalled the end of the Victorian era. True, the

Queen died much earlier but her traditions had lingered, traditions with which Naismith and McKenzie felt comfortable. In the world of sport, amateurism was one concept that was losing its grip, being replaced by a commercial professionalism. All the conditions were right for it. Communications had improved; travel was much easier. The new medium of radio was gaining popularity and would soon be used to broadcast descriptions of sporting competitions to an eager and expectant audience. The economy was growing as industry used the assembly line techniques which had served the war effort so effectively. Consumers were eager to enjoy the new prosperity that seemed to be just around the corner. Spectators were willing to pay money, more and more of it, to see the best athletes perform. Players were being attracted to teams by promises of jobs or money. After all, wasn't the war fought for freedom, they rationalized. And shouldn't the athlete be free to negotiate the best deal for himself?

These were trying times for both Naismith and McKenzie. They had been schooled in the old virtues, believing that the ideals behind the sport took precedence over the skill, that the occasion for competition was much more important than the outcome. To them, sport was not an end in itself, it was a means, an instrument for developing character, morality, fitness, health, leadership. In many ways, they were still attached to the traditional British and Victorian public school notion of sport. It became obvious that they were in the minority; they were being left behind. Competition between schools, specialized training, appeal to alumni, the stress on athlete-students as opposed to student-athletes, was all coming to the fore.

Naismith encountered it at Kansas when he was relieved of his basketball duties. The traditional Victorian view of coaching was that it was illegal, like a bystander at a card game seeing the cards in each player's hand and telling one which card to play. Not that he thought he was cheating when he coached basketball at the University of Kansas. His idea was that the players should be given the ball and make their own decisions based on what was happening around them, just the way it was in life. He was replaced as coach in 1909 by Forrest C. "Phog" Allen, a new breed of professional coach, interested in turning out highly skilled performers on the court and letting life take care of itself. Ten years later, in 1919, Allen was named director of athletics; Naismith was later replaced as track and field coach in 1920 and as chairman of the department of physical education in 1924.

It was disconcerting to say the least. Naismith had originally been hired by the University of Kansas as director of chapel, physician, head of athletics and physical education as well as basketball coach. Now in the early post-war period, he had been replaced in each area. He might have simply been behind the newly-emerging times, out of step with new developments in a changing world. But there is some indication that the First World War had done great damage to Jim Naismith. He might have had what today would be described as post traumatic stress disorder.

In those immediate post-war months, Naismith stayed in Europe still trying to counsel and recreate, literally, the broken spirits, minds and bodies of the soldiers. Inter-Allied competitions were begun and held in a variety of sports, including basketball, for the soldiers involved in the mopping-up stage of the combat. Naismith was unable to stay for the championship of the game he invented. He returned to Kansas, a shell of the person who had entered the service. He had lost weight; he was down to 150 lbs. from his normal 190. He moped about, had no interest in anything. The image of war was with him always. He couldn't get it out of his mind. He was aware that some 300 allied soldiers had been shot for "cowardice." He also knew that they hadn't suffered from fear; it was what was termed "shell shock." Only those who had lived through the horrific blasts from big guns and bombs from out of nowhere could understand. He was one of many who wanted only to shut out the world. In some ways, he had lost his will to make sense of what had happened, to continue to live in this world where man could be so inhumane to man. He had regular flashbacks, images from the war forever etched in his mind.

When he returned to campus life there were so many returning servicemen, decked out and looking so resplendent in their military garb. But what a difference between those who had served overseas and those who had remained Stateside! Veterans of combat seemed to carry invisible scars on the inside. It was their dark night of the soul and Naismith knew exactly what they were going through. He was feeling it too. He was a forlorn figure moping about the house. When he did go out, much to the relief of those at home who simply didn't know how to bring back the Jim Naismith they knew, he was liable to be off, hitching up the horses and taking the wagon out to the countryside around Lawrence. It reminded him of his younger days, of his dad driving the wagon, his own youth on Uncle Peter's farm in Almonte.

He was distraught at the attitude of the non-combat veterans who whispered about the "whackos" who were "crazy" and should be put into the "loony bin." It was a desperate time for those who had "preserved the freedom of the civilized world." All they wanted was peace in their minds. They opted out of life, disinterested, apathetic. Jim Naismith simply withdrew from all that had once been so important to him, waiting for the nightmare to play itself out and leave his being. He did a lot of praying. He desperately needed something to displace the memories.

Perhaps there was something stirring in the deep recesses of his mind which took him back to his youth. Maybe that was why he enjoyed hitching up the horse and wagon; there was that connection with a life back in Almonte, that seemed so simple, so joyful, where it was easy for him to be carefree and in control of his life. He turned to another activity from his past. There had been many skilled wood carvers in the Ottawa valley; his own Grandpa Young had been one. Jim, along with all of his boyhood chums, always carried a carving knife. It was part of growing up. There was always wood around. He remembered the good feeling of creating something out of a formless block of wood. Competitor that he was, he wanted to carve better than any of his friends; he wanted to be the best.

He was inspired to buy some tools. The decision, any decision at that time, seemed a sign of hope, that Jim Naismith was re-entering the world of others. He organized a workshop, gathered wood. Once again, it would be his link with the Ottawa valley which would renew his being.

Meanwhile, in Philadelphia, Robert Tait McKenzie was undergoing some of the same problems on his return to the United States and the University of Pennsylvania. There, too, a schism had appeared in the program. The academic group wanted resources put into the programs for the student body. But funds were in short supply; athletics was a way to bring revenue into the school. A decision to make athletics subservient to physical education was sidetracked when it was referred to a committee. It "died of anemia . . . after a sojourn in a pigeon hole."[1] It was obvious that athletics was winning the day. In 1922, Franklin Field was enlarged to a seating capacity of 50,000, three years later to more than 60,000. McKenzie was embittered. He wrote: "Obviously nothing must interfere with the extraction of the last ounce of gold from this mine . . . The struggle between the ethics of an

Amusement Enterprise and an Educational Institution which was abroad in the college world, became more and more acute."[2]

It was a frustrating period for McKenzie. He, too, needed to return to an outlet and sculpting would provide it. Almost as much, however, there were signs that McKenzie's contact with his homeland had re-ignited his attachment to that country. He had remained a Canadian and would be so for the rest of his life. But he was virtually unknown in Canada outside of the Montreal and Ottawa areas. Even there, however,

The Flying Sphere   *Mill of Kintail*

he was mostly noted for his work in physical education. Almost all of his sculpting had been done while he was at the University of Pennsylvania where he gained his reputation as a skilled artist. Perhaps it was one more indication that a prophet is least honoured in his own country.

All of that began to change at the end of the war. When former Prime Minister Wilfrid Laurier died in 1919, it was suggested by a Montreal MP that McKenzie be commissioned to sculpt a statue of him. He was flattered but declined and in doing so made some allies because of his sensitivity. He recommended that it should be done by a Canadian of French descent. The request was a sign of things to come. Perhaps the devastation of war was so felt by all, including McKenzie, that there was a need to memorialize the heroic deeds of those who had played a role in it, particularly those who had fought and fallen. "Lest We Forget" seemed to be the guiding principle that propelled McKenzie into the next phase of his work.

In rapid succession, he was sought out to effect a memorial to Captain Guy Drummond, a Canadian who died in a poison gas attack in 1915. Another memorial was requested by Prime Minister Mackenzie King in honour of a mutual acquaintance, poet Wilfred Campbell. Still another work, this one a remembrance of the only member of Parliament to have been killed during the war, Lt. Col.

G.H. Baker, was commissioned. The flurry of work from Canada seemed to be the tonic needed by McKenzie. It dawned on him that recognition from his native land was important to him. When McGill University conferred an honourary degree on him in 1921, it was one more indication that he was becoming less of a stranger in his own homeland and for that he was pleased.

At the same time, his focus was international. His sculptures had always been appreciated in centres of art in London and Paris. He decided to travel to England to have a showing of his completed sculpture in London. It was 1920. The war was over but only too recently for many. England had made huge sacrifices, there had been many casualties. Every day on the streets there were vivid reminders of the huge impact of the war. People flocked to his exhibition. They seemed relieved to see such perfectly harmonious bodies, whole and unbroken, full of energy and bursting with sensitivity and life.

Representatives from Cambridge University attended the

The Homecoming, **Cambridge Memorial**   *Mill of Kintail*

showing. They were impressed. McKenzie was approached. Would he be interested in doing a memorial dedicated to the soldiers of Cambridgeshire who had served in the war? He accepted immediately and as he was doing so his memory began to sort through the hundreds and thousands of faces he had seen in search of a typical English man. He had seen many in the camps but sought more. He went out to the university, surveying the student body as they moved about. He decided to sculpt the head in England, and the body in Philadelphia.

The result was *The Homecoming*. Unveiled by the future King George VI, it was a triumph but came close to disaster. There was not enough time to meet the deadline and complete the bronze casting process in London. McKenzie decided to bronze the plaster statue for the unveiling and cast it later on. As it turned out, it was a typical rainy London day when the unveiling took place. Some of the bronze began to disappear during the heavy deluge. But it was a blessing in disguise. When Mckenzie saw the statue on its public pedestal from his new perspective his sharp eye noticed some modifications that he wanted to make in order to improve it. McKenzie recalled the impression he wanted to portray:

> The statue shows a private soldier in full kit on
> his triumphal return after the War. With
> discipline relaxed, he is striding along
> bareheaded, helmet in hand, a German helmet as
> a trophy slung on his back and partly concealed
> by a laurel leaf, carelessly flung over the rifle
> barrel. In his hand he holds a rose. Another rose
> thrown to him has fallen to the ground. His head
> is turned to the side, his expression is alert,
> happy and slightly quizzical, and his lips are
> slightly parted as if he has recognized an old
> friend in the welcoming crowd and is about to
> call to him. In this face I have tried to express
> the type on whom the future of England must
> depend. [3]

There was an inspiring quality to the work. One observer remarked that she stood "unmindful of the pouring rain and the hurrying footsteps about me, enthralled as I was, with the lilting beauty of that triumphant figure." [4]

McKenzie had always believed that the best way to get something done was to get started on it immediately. He lived by that credo and it was a good thing. Commissions were now being offered to him on a regular basis; he was beginning to be known as the Sculptor of Youth and his reputation was spreading. Much of the impetus for it came from his London exhibition. People had come from both sides of the ocean. They were impressed with the statues which were so life-sustaining and in sharp contrast to the mangled and crippled bodies of so many veterans returned from the war. And of course, there were so many who didn't come back. Aside from the understanding of the folly of war, there was the overwhelming conviction that a debt was owed by those who survived to those who had fallen during the conflict.

Still, there was some evidence that McKenzie's talent and reputation as a sculptor was largely unknown in his own hometown. Two representatives from Almonte appeared at the London exhibition. They were in search of a sculptor who could undertake a memorial to their fallen soldiers. It is not known whether they went specifically to check out the quality of McKenzie's work for themselves or whether they had simply come to London as a major centre with many artists to choose from. In any event, they were suitably impressed with their native son's work and asked him to undertake the task.

The result was McKenzie's memorial *The Volunteer*. It stands today beside the Town Hall in Almonte. Eight feet high, the Rosamond War Memorial named for Alec R. Rosamond of the woolen mills family, a volunteer who had lost his life in the Great War represents one of the more mature subjects in Tait's works. Indeed, it looks very much like a self-representation. There is a forward look to the statue indicating perhaps the unknown and also the resolve to push ahead and face the challenge of it. A list of names accompany the statue, individuals from Almonte who had

The Volunteer at **town hall**
Author's collection

The Volunteer **at its dedication**

Mill of Kintail

lost their lives. Another major dedication was made in 1923. The Baker Memorial in the House of Commons was unveiled before an appreciative throng in Ottawa.

Another country, another site and another memorial followed. The citizens of Woodbury, New Jersey struck a committee to commission McKenzie to sculpt their homage to their war dead. The result was the *The Victor*. It was almost a thematic copy of *The Homecoming*, the returning soldier marching home victorious, symbolized by his carrying of the laurel, and recognizing someone as he passed by. Yet his youthful face had a certain tenseness about it; lines appeared on it as if the reality of war had been a greater shock for the American "doughboy" than for his English and Canadian counterparts.

The Baker Memorial **in the Parliament Buildings**

Mill of Kintail

The Victor, **memorial to the people of Woodbury, New Jersey**

Mill of Kintail

A fourth country beckoned and the result was perhaps the most famous of his memorials. Certainly, it was the most ambitiously designed and sculpted of his tributes to the war effort. The Scottish-American War Memorial was unveiled on September 7, 1927, at the Princes Street Gardens in Edinburgh, Scotland.

It had been a labour of love for the Scottish-Canadian. Throughout Canada and the United States, St. Andrew's Societies had been formed to maintain the Scottish connection through Highland or Caledonian Games (his own community of Almonte was later to be noted for them), the Gaelic language, dances and lectures. McKenzie was president of the Philadelphia branch when it decided to honour fallen Scots from the first war. He was commissioned to come up with, and effect, a suitable design.

It was more than a labour of love for McKenzie. He had always

Scottish American War Memorial, **Princes Street Gardens**

Mill of Kintail

McKenzie addressing the assemblage at the dedication of the Scottish American War Memorial   *Mill of Kintail*

been intensely proud of his heritage, probably considered himself more of a Scot than a British Subject or Canadian. He was aware, having lived in Montreal, of how the Scots had contributed to the opening of the country, how they had made such a cultural impact on life throughout the land. He seemed to prefer the wearing of the kilt, whether as part of some ceremony or not. He took great delight when people teased him about his traditional thrift and ascribed all the general Scottish stereotypes to him. He always cherished his visits to the Aberdeens as much because of the countryside and geography as their company.

McKenzie travelled to Edinburgh with a group from Philadelphia to explain the idea to the proper authorities. It was well received by the civic officials; they offered a site, part of the Scottish National Memorial. It was politely declined. The St. Andrew's Society was afraid that its effort would be overshadowed and lost in such surroundings. McKenzie, who by now had full confidence in his sense of perspective, suggested an alternate, along Princes Street facing Castle Hill where the national monument would be. He immediately recognized that pedestrians would be certain to pass by it and would notice it for itself. Permission was secured. McKenzie made sketches of the area, taking in all of its features. He returned to his studio in Philadelphia where he began to construct a model from the drawings and his impressions. His mind pored over all of the many thousands of Scots with whom he had come into contact. Sketches of them were made as well and filed. He had already decided how to place the work; it would face the Scottish Memorial on Castle Hill to symbolically join the Scots of the new world with their ancestral homeland as they answered the call for assistance in the Great War of 1914-18.

He continued his research. Regimental dress, coats of arms, plaids and any detail related to the Scots were meticulously detailed. He knew that as a North American Scot his work would have to be above reproach in every way. He searched the Philadelphia campus and settled on a model for his main figure. Granville Carrel was his answer. The student was a member of the university's football team. He was from out west, Colorado, and as a result there were few occasions when he could travel home. McKenzie, as athletic director, knew him both as an athlete and a student. For his part, Carrel was "thunderstruck by the fee which Dr. McKenzie offered him 'just to sit'."[5] Perhaps it was because of their natural empathy or possibly because the McKenzies had no children of their own, but Carrel became a frequent guest of theirs, usually on weekends or holidays. He stayed for dinner often and was made to feel quite at home. Years later he was to remark that he counted "McKenzie as one of his greatest friends . . . one of the finest men he has met . . . Mrs. McKenzie could not have been nicer to him."[6] Carrel's face was the model for that of the soldier; his body was the model for the various Scots shown on the frieze of the monument.

He posed over four years for the monument. He listened as McKenzie explained his approach. He saw the smaller version which Tait constructed; marvelled at the use of his body as the faces of others were linked with the form of his body. He saw his own face on the main figure. He witnessed it all until it was ready for shipment, wondering for years how it would look on its pedestal in Edinburgh. He had to wait until the middle of the second war to see it in its location. As Major Granville Carrel of the United States Army, he was stationed in Scotland and saw *The Call* in all of its solemn splendor at the Princes Street Gardens.

What Carrel saw was inspiring, not only to him but to countless others, particularly the Scots who encountered it as a daily reminder of the considerable contribution made by their expatriate countrymen.

There was the seated, kilted youth, rifle on his knees, giving the impression that he is ready to move forward, rising from a bench covered by his military coat which he has thrown off. His gaze is fixed on the castle. He has a determined and resolute look about him. He will not hesitate to answer the call to arms to defend his proud heritage. He is the universal Scot. There are no identifiable regimental badges or insignia. He is the quintessential citizen as identified by the Lion of Scotland on his sporran — the pouch in front of the kilt. Below the statue is a frieze of the many Scots from different walks of life along with "the Recruiting Party." They answered the call, these people from all walks of life, each one ready to "jeopardy his life unto the death." The cost of the memorial was raised by St. Andrew's Societies throughout North America. It was unveiled on September 7, 1927.

The inscription was there for all to read: From Men and Women of Scottish Blood and Sympathies in the United States of America To Scotland A People That Jeopardized Their Lives Unto The Death in The High Places of The Field. The frieze behind the figure was a fourteen-foot wall, twenty-five feet in length. The first section has pipers and drums; the second a recruiting party of military personnel; the third the recruits, representatives from all walks of Scottish life. There were farmers, miners, fishermen, shepherds, clerks and gamekeepers. The eye naturally moves from the eager and untrained to the disciplined and the ordered military effect. The American ambassador, Alanson B. Houghton, unveiled it. Lord Atholl was to say later that although no one could say how many Scottish Americans gave their lives, "the monument told in some subtle way why they came, why they were ready to make the sacrifice and why the memories would be cherished, so far as possible, for all time to come."[7]

Perhaps the most stirring moment of the unveiling was when someone began to sing a Scottish traditional hymn of the 121st psalm, "I to the hills will lift mine eyes From whence does come my aid." It was a well known song, one that McKenzie recalled from his boyhood days at St. John's Presbyterian Church in Almonte. It brought back to him the memory of his father leading the congregation which included his family, young Robert and James Naismith and all of his boyhood friends, all joining in. Here, too, years later in the land of his ancestors, the thousands gathered for the dedication joined in and became one with the young soldier gazing toward and beyond Edinburgh Castle, the "Heart of Scotland."

McKenzie putting finishing touches on *Wolfe Memorial*

Mill of Kintail

McKenzie received yet another memorial commission. Again, the site was the United Kingdom, at Greenwich Royal Park in London. In celebration of Canada's sixtieth birthday as a united country, a statue of General Wolfe, the victor at the Plains of Abraham, was to be erected. After much deliberation, McKenzie chose as his theme a planning Wolfe, telescope in hand, having observed that the French forces had moved away from the Plains of Abraham.

The statue, completed in 1928, was erected June 5, 1930, by the current Marquis De Montcalm, a fact not lost on the press of the day. The reporter of the London *Times*[8] opined that the British and French blood of the fallen that day in 1759, including that of Wolfe and Montcalm, gave rise to united Canada's gift of the monument to Britain. Both leaders who shed their blood were united in the memory of all. They were worthy opponents, continued the report. Each was aware that this might be his last battle. Wolfe was said to have declared that "the paths of glory lead but to the grave." Montcalm was filled with foreboding. The new Marquis continued:

> Both faced death with the same disregard for life
> . . . their last words were for their soldiers. . .
> Both leaders were mourned and respected at
> their tombs and citizens of two great peoples,
> adversaries yesterday, friends to-day, pay
> homage. Allow me to thank you for your gesture
> and acknowledge your great kindness, not only
> in the name of the descendants of the French
> who fought for Canada but also in the name of
> those who wish with pious faith to keep in their
> heart the ties which bind them to the vanished
> past.[9]

If there were only memorials and university duties, McKenzie would have been a more than busy man. However, there were other pieces of work. He continued with his athletic sculptures, some of which recalled his youthful days. Perhaps aware of his own background and because of the numerous track and field events he was able to follow from his studio overlooking Franklin Field, he turned some of his talent to that area. The shot putter fascinated him. He had always marvelled at the explosive power needed to propel the stone. There was the concentration, the movement of the body into the appropriate path and the summation of the forces in the timely release. He made a small bronze of the *Shot Putter Resting* in 1919; later one of *The Hop* and *The Ready*, the latter of the putter beginning his event. Perhaps because of the classical Myron's *Discobolos*, a piece which he saw as an inaccurate representation, he was interested in the throwing events. *Discobolos* had always been considered a classic piece of scupture. Classicists debated over the style and form. McKenzie was more convinced that it was not representative. He knew that the head always led in the ultimate direction of the throw, contrary to Myron's presentation. It might have been beautiful art but it wasn't grounded in fact. In 1920, he fashioned the beautiful *Flying Sphere*. It was an eighteen-inch representation of an athlete after having launched his missile in the air.

He was also preoccupied with the pole vault. It was a modern phenomenon, one that the Greeks had no equal to. As a result, there were no guidelines as to how to represent it. He was uncertain how to sculpt it. He was afraid it would be top-heavy were he to fashion it with only the pole in contact with the base. His first work was *Watching The Pole Vault* in 1919. The athlete gazed either at the bar itself or another vaulter. In 1923 he produced his *Pole Vaulter*. It was a combination bas-relief and sculpture. To authenticate the musculature involved in the push off leading to the jump, he had his model, pole vaulter Neville Sherrill, walk on his hands, his feet in the air similar to his position when he crossed the bar. His arms and shoulders were taut as if pushing up from the pole. It was a recognition of the lofty heights man had reached. The inscription stated: "Nelson B Sherrill of the University of Pennsylvania vaulted over a bar 13 feet in height May 1923. The world may yet produce an athlete who will go higher by another foot." This was obviously in the era of bamboo rather than fiberglass poles.

A combination of factors turned McKenzie to winter sport themes after the war. They had always been part of his days in Almonte. As

Brothers of the Wind   *Mill of Kintail*

well, the Antwerp Olympic Games of 1920 featured a program of winter sports for the first time. He and Mrs. McKenzie joined the Philadelphia Skating Club in 1920 as well; it reminded him of those days on the frozen Indian and Mississippi Rivers. He was enthralled with the skaters as they prepared for competitions, amazed at the way they could transfer their horizontal momentum into the vertical. What leg strength and muscle control it must have taken! He knew that from his own attempts on the Mississippi. This was new sculpting territory for him; his inspiration, the Greeks, had never done any studies of the

body in winter settings. They had no opportunity to do so. It would have to be his own approach and he relished the challenge. He completed *Ice Bird* in 1925. It was a young male skater in a graceful glide after landing a jump. There was "a long line formed by the skater's outstretched right arm . . . in a sensuous arc through to his extended left foot. The slightly bent right knee is in the perfect position to catch the full weight of the body and the skating manoeuvre."[10]

In the same year, 1925, McKenzie finished his relief entitled *Brothers Of The Wind*. It showed eight speed skaters in various modes of competition. Perhaps McKenzie saw himself and his Almonte friends in it. In the days of his youth, speed skating

The Plunger   *Mill of Kintail*   was a popular pastime on winter's frozen rivers. A huge open area was cleared of snow; the ice was thick and crystal clear, smooth as glass. Hockey was virtually unknown; lacrosse on ice could have been a possibility but it was the sheer joy of skating, the wind blowing freshly across the ice, which was a favourite. Invariably there was the athletic Jim Naismith in the lead, so relaxed. Others would follow, like Billy Drummond, later a renowned poet; MacIntosh Bell, the famed geologist; Andy McPhail, later to be knighted; John Carter, the friend next door; the comical Rob Knowles who became a minister in Toronto; Eddie Peacock, also knighted in England where he became a director of the Bank of England and comptroller of the Duchy of Cornwall, and of course, himself. They all competed, all shared in the joy of skating against and with the stiff breezes. They were all brothers of the wind. McKenzie was perhaps the least athletic of them all in his youth. Was that he, the last of the skaters, struggling to keep up, eventually to be lapped and having to drop out and watch? Or was he in the middle of the group, his rhythm broken, trying hard to spurt back into contention, head down and so determined? Surely that was Naismith showing such beautiful and relaxed form, effortlessly in the lead. An original cast bronze of the work, "305 cms in length is in the collection of the University of Calgary, permanently installed at the entrance of the Olympic Oval" [11] constructed for the 1988 Winter Games. Those who saw the film *Cool Runnings*, the story of the Jamaican bob-sled team at the 1988 Games, might remember seeing the frieze there.

McKenzie turned 60 in 1927. He was tiring of the constant bickering between the approach he believed in for physical education at the University of Pennsylvania and those who wanted athletics to operate independently and receive greater emphasis. He contemplated resigning but was talked out of it. It was suggested that he take time away from the university, devote himself to his sculpting. He received a leave of absence in 1929. Clearly, Robert Tait McKenzie was trying to make a decision about his future.

Jim Naismith, too, had decisions to make during the twenties. At times he felt like a fifth wheel. He began the decade as a 150-pound shell of himself, some forty pounds below his normal weight. His university had relieved him of many of his duties. Some felt that the times had passed him by. He was no longer responsible for the direction of physical education or the athletic program. Everything was out of sync for him. He struggled to find a way back to his normal, upbeat self. The prayers and woodworking seemed to be helping. They made him feel as if he had returned at least somewhat to his roots. He was also able to put his hand to the plough again. Now an ordained Minister, he turned more and more to preaching, teaching Sunday school and substituting for ministers on weekends or when needed. His steady workload of pastoral duties, preaching, baptizing, performing wedding ceremonies and funerals worked wonders for him, and gave him a renewed sense of purpose. Soon he was back to his normal 190 pounds, moving with his characteristic quick athletic grace and renewed joy in his efforts.

In keeping with his character, he bore no malice towards Phog Allen who had replaced him as basketball coach and director of athletics. He knew that it was a university decision to give athletics more emphasis, to keep its name before the public in the hopes of attracting more alumni support. He didn't agree with it but he knew that Allen hadn't made the decision. Still, it didn't make matters any better or easier for Naismith when Allen also replaced him as chairman of the physical education department in 1924. Well, he rationalized, he was now sixty-three and the university wanted younger men. Allen wasn't even forty; it was just his turn, the man who some called the father of basketball coaching replacing the father of basketball and shaping the programs. Allen was one of the new breed who believed that marketing and promotion of athletics was important. People had to be given reasons to come to the stadia and gyms. It was no longer enough to simply put on the game. And he was fundamentally different from Naismith; he believed in coaching. Naismith was a throwback to the old ways: Any coaching or teaching should be done during the week, at practice. During the games the players should be left on their own to use their ingenuity and develop their reliance on their own wits. It wasn't that Naismith's model of what a coach should be called for any less knowledge than Allen's. He knew as much about Xs and Os as anyone. The fundamental difference was that he was interested in developing people, more focussed on the psychology involved and the best coach-player relationship to effect a performance. When coaches like Allen began to develop and use zone defences in order to slow down the opposition and in effect to help them win the game, Naismith abhorred the trend. It slowed down the game, "decreased the value of athleticism,"[12] denied the athlete the chance to respond to a higher tempo challenge. It is interesting to note that the National Basketball

Association (NBA) has outlawed the use of zone defences because it mutes the spectacle and reduces the athleticism of the game and its players. But for Phog Allen, it was the victory that was important; tactics and strategy for winning the contest were vital; zone defences and coaching from the sidelines were all key ingredients in the mix.

Like others, Allen seemed to have a genuine affection for Doc Naismith. When he discovered that the rule book for basketball had no reference to or picture of the inventor of the game, he lobbied effectively to change it. It is likely that he played a role in the NCAA decision in 1923 to grant Naismith honourary life membership, and the rules committee's move to make him honourary chairman for life. In one way this reconfirmed Naismith's feeling that he was in his declining years. After all, these were the sorts of kudos given to someone when he was on the way out and his time had been served. But they were nice gestures and appreciated. When the *Jayhawker*, the university's yearbook, dedicated its 1925 issue to him, it eased the pain somewhat of having his duties lifted from him one by one. It was public praise which lifted his spirits at a time lifting was needed: "Twenty-six years at the University as Director of Physical Education, father of basketball, exponent of clean sportsmanship, believer in the Kansas spirit and true friend of all KU students."[13]

One of the reasons Naismith bypassed the ministry when he graduated from McGill's theology school was that he felt that he could do his preaching with his actions rather than from a pulpit. The dedication helped him to see that he had continued to succeed at this. It was still important that his Uncle Peter and sister Annie knew that too. After all, they had supported him financially through McGill. It seemed as if his whole life, since he had left McGill for Springfield thirty-six years ago, had been spent trying to prove that he had not really taken his hand from the plough and turned back. He had simply chosen another method of cultivating. He sent them a copy of the book and inscribed it: "To Pete and Annie who made it possible for me to be of some use in the world. Jim"[14]

He had other news for them too. On May 4, 1925, he became an American citizen. He had decided to do so as the war was ending. He was in the United States Army, had made his living there, indeed lived there longer than he had in Canada. Other than occasional contact by letter with Rob McKenzie or mail from Almonte, the closest he came to reminders of his past was when he saw Mississippi Street close to the university or when people teased him about his Canadian accent. He didn't think that he had an accent but those occasions served to trigger a flow of memories to a world of long ago. His mind drifted back to the river by the same name which flowed picturesquely through Almonte, the town where he had so much joy in his youth. And more and more, there were only those memories left. Annie died in March of 1929, followed three years later by Peter. There was a depression on in the world; Naismith was doing his best to not let it engulf his life.

1. R. Tait McKenzie, "Physical Education at the University of Pennsylvania – from 1904 to 1931 – and the Gates Plan". *The Research Quarterly*, May, 1932.
2. ibid.
3. Hussey, op. cit.
4. Mabel Lee, *JOHPER*, op. cit., p. 88.
5. *JOHPER*, op. cit., p. 69.
6. ibid.
7. *JOHPER*, op. cit., 1944, p. 68.
8. London *Times*, June 6, 1930.
9. ibid..
10. Richard Graburn, *Robert Tait McKenzie, 1867-1938*. Calgary: The Nichols Arts Museum, 1977. p. 46.
11. ibid. p. 48.
12. Toronto *Globe and Mail*, October 7, 1995.
13. Webb, op. cit, p. 96.
14. ibid.

CHAPTER 7

Thirties

As if in rhythm with the pulse of the world, the careers of Jim Naismith and Tait McKenzie mirrored and moved along with the current of time. When the stock market crash of 1929 signalled the beginning of the Depression it was as if their lives reflected the times. Jim Naismith not only lost his sister Annie in 1929 and his Uncle Peter a short time later, but he and Maude lost their house as well. He was unable to keep up the payments on the mortgage. The bank foreclosed. Unlike Rob McKenzie, he had never been one to keep a close tab on his finances. Not only that, but as a coach and counsellor to students he had continually been there for loans when they were short of cash. In time it caught up with him. The Naismiths gave up the house. The children now married and on their own, Maude and Jim moved into a smaller, more modest home.

It was a dark period in the Naismiths' life. Yet through it all, there was the continuing glimmer of light, flickering ever so dimly at times but enough to sustain Naismith, who by nature was an optimistic and confident individual. He had written a book in 1919, *The Basis of Clean Living*. It was a title which characterized his life and as the decade unfolded, it was that way of living which allowed him to emerge with his head above water once again. He had never considered himself a coach in the sense of concentrating on the skills of the game. He saw himself as, and made his reputation by "building character in the hearts of young men." [1]

Two individuals who had played major roles in his life became part of it once again. On April 1, 1931, Naismith, along with Amos Alonzo Stagg and Robert Tait Mckenzie, were inducted as fellows of

Annie Naismith, James' sister

the American Association of Health, Physical Education and Recreation. The creator of basketball was said to have had "a wisdom, far ahead of his time, of the social values of recreation and competitive athletics."[2] Towards the end of that year, in December, the YMCA honoured him with its Springfield Emblem. He represented "an ideal in education, in leadership and in inventive ability."[3] When Naismith was presented with the first Edward Norris Tarbell Medal, he was doubly pleased. It was a replica of McKenzie's *Joy of Effort*. In January of 1932, he delivered a paper to the Society of Physical Education. The next year, the thirty-fifth year of basketball at Kansas, saw him honoured in a ceremony where seven of his original players came from all across the United States to pay homage to Doc Naismith. It was a wonderfully uplifting event. Naismith was far from being a rich man in terms of money but it was obvious that he had touched many during his career and they were anxious to let him know of their appreciation.

The 1936 Olympic Games served to bring Naismith once more to the greater public's attention, this time internationally. Held in Berlin, they gained later notoriety when they became known as the Nazi Olympics, where Hitler was such a pervasive figure and where Jesse Owens, the great American sprinter, demolished before the whole world the myth of Aryan supremacy. It was also at the Berlin games where basketball made its debut as an Olympic sport. It had previously appeared as a demonstration sport at St. Louis in 1904, a team from the Buffalo German YMCA winning the medal, and in the 1924 and 1928 games, but this was the first time that it would be accorded full olympic status. Plans were made to ensure that the Father of Basketball would be there to see the game on display. The American National Association of Basketball Coaches made plans to honour Naismith during the Olympics. All that remained was to get the cash-strapped Jim Naismith to Berlin.

A scheme was hatched; a National Naismith Fund was set up. The week of February 7-15 was designated as Naismith Week. Every basketball game played in the United States was asked to appropriate one penny from each ticket sold.[4] The whole exercise served to draw attention once again, to Naismith. His university duties were minimal now; still some teaching, membership on the athletic board, speeches to the community at large. The publicity prompted requests from throughout the mid-west for Naismith to officiate at opening ceremonies and appear at dinners. The pace was hectic, one which

A proud and mature Naismith holding a basketball

Naismith Foundation

would have done in someone younger than his seventy-five years. The Denver YMCA presented a gold medal to their former director at a ceremony attended by returned members of the Y team which Naismith had taught from 1895-98. The Denver tournament was where the American Olympic team would be selected. It was officially opened by a smiling James Naismith who was "more pleased and excited than a farm boy at a first circus."[5]

Plans were moving smoothly along to send the Naismiths, Jim and Maude, to the Olympics. It was a grandiose scheme. A tour following the games to wherever basketball was played was proposed; a cairn would be erected in Lawrence or perhaps Springfield; a life annuity would provide security for the couple. It was all on too grand a scale. It soon became obvious that one cent from each ticket would not provide the necessary funds. The Olympic trip became the priority. Then Maude was stricken with a heart attack. She was not well enough to go, but it was not so severe that she couldn't be cared for by daughter Hellen in Dallas.

On July 10, 1936, Jim Naismith and Phog Allen left New York for the Berlin competitions, due to begin on August 1. They were intended to showcase German recovery and might. Basketball had only been added after much discussion and persuasion, having been approved only in mid-March, virtually on a trial basis. Two tennis courts were set aside in the outdoors. All games were to be played there in spite of the fact that there were eight indoor gyms close by. They would be used only if made necessary by heavy rains.[6]

Eighteen countries were split into two divisions. Each team played all other members, the first place nation from each section to meet each other for the gold and silver medals. Canada was represented by the Windsor Fords, national champions. The team included Irving Meretsky, Gordon Aitcheson, Ian Allison, Jimmy Stewart, Tom Pendlebury, Norm Dawson, Don Gray, Ernie Williams, Malcolm Wiseman and Stanley Nantais from the Fords, plus Norm and Charlie Chapman and Doug Peden from the west.[7]

There were hitches. It was discovered that the German Olympic Committee had neglected to have any official ceremonies or program put into place to honour Naismith as the inventor of the game. A makeshift one was arranged. On August 8, in the Hall of German Sports, all eighteen competing teams marched and gathered in a mini opening ceremony before a presiding Jim Naismith. There was a small crowd, approximately 200, but to him it was an honour he had never ever expected and would never forget. After short welcoming speeches to the clubs and their representatives by officials, Naismith was asked to say a few words. Ever gracious, he congratulated the players for having made their country's team; he thanked them for the great honour being bestowed by them, the parade of the athletes and the dipping of their flags along with the ceremonial olive wreath. "When I walked out on a Springfield, Massachusetts playground with a ball in my hand a game in my head I never thought I'd live to see the day when it would be played in the Olympics,"[8] he said. Naismith then left the dais; it was his turn to walk around. He visited each country's team, pausing to speak with the representatives and taking in the exuberant "cheers of each nation."[9] He had a special few moments for the teams from Canada and the United States.

As it turned out, the game to determine the gold and silver medals was played by those two nations. Each team had gone through its division undefeated. Canada had won games over Brazil, 24-17, Uruguay, 43-21, Poland, 42-15, Latvia, 34-23 and Switzerland, 28-9. On the afternoon of August 14, 1936, in a "rain drenched" setting outdoors, the United States prevailed, winning the first basketball gold medal at the Olympic Games, defeating Canada, the silver medal winner, by a 19-8 score.[10]

It was a proud time for Naismith, made even more so by his being able to see the fabled Edmonton Grads team in action. He had seen no reason why women couldn't play basketball and he became aware of a team of young ladies from Edmonton who were the perennial North American champions. Coached by Percy Page, they won 502 games in a twenty-five year stretch, losing only twenty-two. They had appeared at four Olympics while basketball was a demonstration sport. In addition to setting the stage for the acceptance of the game for a full-fledged medal competition, they had won every game that they had played over the four Olympics. At the 1936 festival they played and won all thirteen games. They played basketball exactly the way that James Naismith envisioned it should be. He was thrilled to see them and just as excited that they were from his native land. He wrote:

> . . . on this your twenty-fifth birthday. . . your
> record is without parallel in the history of
> basketball. My admiration is not only for your
> record of clean play, versatility in meeting teams

at their own style, and more especially for your
unbroken record of good sportsmanship. My
admiration and respect go to you because you
have remained unspoiled by your successes, and
have retained the womanly graces,
notwithstanding your participation in a
strenuous game. You are not only an inspiration
to basketball players throughout the world, but a
model of all girls' teams. Your attitude and
success have been a source of gratification to me
in illustrating the possibilities of the game in the
development of the highest type of
womanhood. [11]

Naismith concluded his Olympic trip with a visit to fourteen
countries, including Switzerland where he was selected President of the
International Federation of Basketball Leagues. He returned to his
Kansas home by way of Almonte and Bennies Corners for a nostalgic
look at where it all began, hoping that his brother of the wind, Tait
McKenzie might still be there. He had missed him in Berlin, one of the
few Olympics that McKenzie did not attend. It was also said that when
he returned to Kansas, he still had some money left from the fund and
turned it back to the committee. [12]

McKenzie wasn't in Almonte. He was back in Philadelphia for the
winter. He would have liked to have gone to Berlin for the games —
the Olympics were always a special time for him — but doctors had
recommended against it. He, too, was having heart problems.

It had been a busy time for the sculptor who seemed to thrive on
being overworked but perhaps it was all catching up with him now. In
1930, a year off to think over his resignation was over; he decided to
carry through with it. He left his post as director of the department of
physical education. It was no longer an enjoyable part of his life. He
had too many more compelling things to do than sit in interminable
committee meetings which seemed to go around in circles. He was still
held in very high esteem in the physical education field. That was no
problem. When the American Academy of Physical Education was
formed in 1930, it was McKenzie who was invited to address the select
group of twenty-nine members and to become its first president. The
field was still exciting to him. There was much to do but the
administration, the minute details which seemed to prolong meetings,

the growing number of petty disputes among the faculty and the continual bickering between physical education and athletic factions took him away from more important activities. Physical education was a growing field in the world and McKenzie wanted the academy to do its part in attracting top students into the field and to continue to recognize those making a contribution to it.

He was also making an impression elsewhere. In Almonte, the town was celebrating its fiftieth anniversary of incorporation in 1931. His reputation in the area had been enhanced by *The Volunteer* which was constantly in public view. The Mayor invited him back and offered him the "Freedom of Almonte." McKenzie was pleased. He had been back irregularly, in 1914 for the burial of his mother and in 1925 for the dedication of *The Volunteer*. There were a lot of memories in the area for him. Jim wouldn't be there; nor would Annie and Peter Young. He would probably go to the old high school, even though P.C. McGregor would be gone. He chuckled at the thought of old Williams the janitor who let the students know who was boss. He had kicked Eddie Peacock, later to become Sir Edward, down the stairs because he was being obstinate. He was sure much had changed; hadn't everything? He knew that there was a new train station. Patty McGarry was surely gone, as were the old hangouts: Wattie Lawson's livery stable and George's barber shop. Whatever happened, he mused, to those wonderful and enchanting Thrall girls? All sorts of images played in his mind. The Youngs, the Campbells, the McFarlands, Sneddens, Bill Thoburn, the mayor, all were part of his early life and all came flooding back into his memory. He didn't realize how much he missed the place, how much he defined himself as an Almonte native.

McKenzie returned and was accorded the Freedom of Almonte. He was taken to the high school where he reminisced with the students about his own youth in the area. While he was there, he decided to revisit some of his old haunts. He came across Baird's Mill. It was abandoned now, but it had been important when grinding grain into flour for Bennies Corners and the surrounding area. The mayor of Almonte encouraged Tait to consider buying the abandoned building and grounds. McKenzie's studio lease in Maine was running out. It was a good time and he was quite sure that Almonte would welcome their native son gladly; the mill would make an ideal retirement home and studio.

Mill of Kintail, prior to restoration, circa 1931   *Mill of Kintail*

Artist that he was, McKenzie saw beyond the "heaps of stones" that the building now was. He visualized what it could be: "an amazing place . . . accessible but isolated . . . like the retreats . . . of the highland robbers."[13] McKenzie was a thrifty man. He had no cash problems. He paid $10,000 cash for the mill and the fifty acres surrounding it. There was a lot of work to do. Fences had fallen; the barn was in a state of near-collapse. There was only a pile of stones nearby where the carriage house and the workshop used to be. As for the mill itself, the walls of Nepean sandstone were firm even if the floors and roof were rotted out. The mill wheel which used to turn so majestically was gone, as was the dam. It all looked like a shambles but McKenzie could see the final result, as with his works of sculpture when he started out. He liked what he saw and set about the restoration. He was eager to tell Naismith of his discovery. He had seen him in April when they were both made fellows of the American Association of Physical Education. Wouldn't it be wonderful if he could find a similar spot and move back?

Tait McKenzie and Naismith at the Mill of Kintail, circa 1937   *Mill of Kintail*

Like everything else, however, it had to be fit into his busy schedule. He was gradually easing himself out of his physical education duties. He had resigned his position at the University of Pennsylvania but the president, Thomas Gates, had asked him to remain as an advisor to him. He picked McKenzie's brain for a new approach to physical education and athletics. A lengthy report was prepared. Known as the Gates Plan, it became a model for physical education programs throughout North America. A dean of physical education reporting to the president was to be responsible for three divisions, each with a director reporting to the dean. There was one for health services, one for physical education and one for athletics. One departmental budget was to be in place, minimizing the need for athletics to function outside the academic milieu as a business enterprise. To further integrate athletics into the academic function, coaches were sought out with academic qualifications as well as knowledge in their sport and given faculty appointments.

The plan was an immediate success. Gates was greatly impressed with McKenzie; he asked him to change his mind about retirement. This was flattering but McKenzie had too many other things he wanted to do with his time. The renovations of the mill were underway. He still had many unfinished projects at his summer studio in Maine. His studio in Philadelphia was filled with work in progress. He and Ethel enjoyed the few free hours they had together socializing and visiting with friends. He declined Gates' invitation. The president was persistent. As a final attempt at having McKenzie maintain his contact with the University of Pennsylvania, he asked McKenzie to accept a research professorship in physical education. McKenzie was pleased to accept the honour. It would allow him the freedom to sculpt, give him some financial support, keep him in touch with the academic community without the meetings and detail of administration and of course he was pleased with the recognition both of himself and the field. Only a few years earlier, in 1928, the University of Pennsylvania had presented him with an honourary degree.

With the publication and spread of the Gates Plan, widely known to be based on his ideas, McKenzie received many acknowledgements from around the United States, one from Jim Naismith. He stated that he thought the proposal was exactly what was needed, that it would

Naismith and McKenzie reminiscing in 1937 at the Mill

Naismith Foundation

become a model for universities across the land. He was proud of his boyhood friend and asked for a picture to replace the one he had of McKenzie in his track outfit at McGill. Naismith wanted his physical education students at Kansas to be able to put a current face to the names of prominent physical educators they knew by reputation, in this case by virtue of McKenzie's book which was used as a text.

Triumph of Wings; the later *Falcon* was adapted from this

Mill of Kintail

Sculpting became McKenzie's major preoccupation now. It was probably his eye for detail that contributed to the great recognition he earned in this field. In 1931, he finished a tribute to aviation, *The Falcon*. He wanted to fashion the wings of a bird on the body of a human. In preparation, he took a pupil, Joe Brown, to the zoo, sketch pad in hand. They were ushered into a special room, there to observe the bird while it perched, flew, ate and moved about. For three hours, the two counted feathers as it spread its wings, took copious notes about its habits, felt the muscles of the bird as it was held by its keeper. They studied the falcon from a variety of perspectives. Its head, beak and gaze of its eyes were all recorded. When the two returned to the studio, Brown assumed that McKenzie would immediately work on the wings of his sculpture while it was all fresh in his mind. He didn't. Instead, he devoted all of his time to the human figure. Brown was curious. He asked why he didn't correct the head and the wings according to the new information that they had gained, while it was still fresh in his mind. McKenzie replied that he would like to let it all simmer and percolate for a few days to see what remained with him. What they had observed that day, he remarked, was superficial; he wanted to do more observation, "to get to know the bird not just meet him." [14] Only after three trips did McKenzie feel ready to incorporate what he had seen.

The Falcon, "with its million feathers," was finished; it was eventually placed outside the McLennan Library at McGill University. It was a memorial tribute to the aviators, the new military breed which had surfaced in the Great War. McKenzie wanted to portray youth victorious in the sky. It was a symbolic tribute, representative of that bird which was the constant companion of the nobles of the medieval period. It soared to great heights, zeroed in on its quarry and dropped purposefully to attack it. The modern aviator was much like it, showing speed, and daring nerves of steel. To McKenzie, it served as a reincarnation of the chivalric spirit so utterly lost in the plodding warfare of trenches and booming guns.

In 1932, the Olympics came to the United States; the winter games in Lake Placid and the summer in Los Angeles. It was one more opportunity for McKenzie to promote his view of sports in his sculpture. The University of California hosted a seminar series on sport and physical education developments throughout the world. It was part of the Olympic build-up. McKenzie delivered a lecture on the athlete in sculpture. It gave him the opportunity to discuss his latest work, the *Sheild of the Athletes*. It was five feet in diameter and the Olympic art winner. Originally entitled the *Olympic Buckler*, [15] the work was richly symbolic. Around the perimeter was a group of runners, the race in progress from start to finish. All strides used in the event were portrayed. In the middle ring, four inserts represented athletes and the qualities drawn from sport:

Shield of Athletes   *Mill of Kintail*

speed, agility, courage and fair play. The middle and outside circles were connected by four octagonal representations, the high jump, lifting a weight, an athlete in repose and tying a shoe. The middle also had a frieze of hurdlers along with a Latin inscription, *Mens Fervida in Corpore Lacertoso* (An eager mind in a lithe body.) At the top of the middle ring was the Olympic motto: Stronger, Higher, Faster. The middle was connected to the centre by a winged figure, much like *The Falcon*, attributing the same noble qualities to the athletes as McKenzie had ascribed to the airmen. The centre core showed a female figure with two youths shaking hands. All was enclosed in a victory wreath of laurel. It seemed to echo the classical statement attributed to Pierre de Coubertin, the founder of the modern Olympic Games, that it was more important to take part than win. The work was later adopted by Tokyo as its official shield for the 1964 games and was used by the Canadian Post office on its first day covers for the stamp commemorating the first Canada Games of 1967.

McKenzie was liable to gain inspiration from anywhere. Classical sport and the values derived from it were a constant source but he was acutely aware of the number of new activities which had no parallel in the ancient games. The revival of the Olympics and their extension into a winter program, the rich experience of McKenzie coupled with the countless examples he saw in the Pennsylvania area, provided him

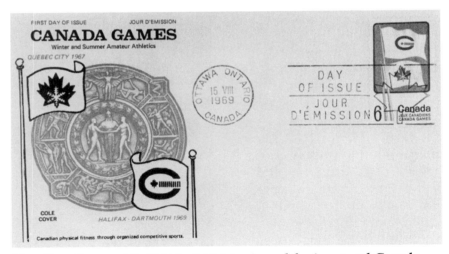

First Day Cover with *Shield of Athletes*, issued for inaugural Canada Games, 1967 (Winter) and 1969 (Summer)   *Author's collection*

McKenzie with *Mercy*, a tribute to the nurses of World War I
Mill of Kintail

Sixtieth Anniversary of Confederation, marble relief at Parliament Building
Mill of Kintail

with all sorts of subjects for his art. Some of his work centred around outstanding Penn athletes like Robert Michelet or William Carr. Some also included non-athletic subjects, special commissions from individuals, companies, friends or colleagues. His lone major female figure, *Mercy* was a tribute to the nursing sisterhood of World War One. It is officially known as the Jane A. Delano Memorial and stands outside the Red Cross headquarters at Garden Court in Washington, D.C. The moving inscription reads: "Thou shalt not be afraid of the terror by night, or the arrow that flieth by day, or of the pestilence that walketh in darkness or the destruction that wasteth at noon day."[16] In 1932, there was yet another expression of McKenzie's gratitude, this time to his native land. A group of Canadians living in the United States wished to celebrate their nationality while giving thanks to their home country with a gift in recognition of Canada's sixtieth year as a country in 1927. They proposed a bronze statue to be housed in the Parliament buildings. Government officials were enthusiastic about the project but they preferred a marble frieze. Even though the cost was some $15,000 more, the group was agreeable; McKenzie was chosen for the work. Delays due to cabinet discussions meant that it could not be unveiled until 1932. It can be seen today adjacent to the commemoration of Confederation of 1867.

There were days when Tait and Ethel sat and watched oarsmen training on the Schuykill river. Often it was in the spring when the ice had broken. The crew had worked indoors all winter long and was anxiously looking forward to resuming its on-water training. It reminded Tait of the days when he took off by himself or with Naismith to explore the Indian or the Mississippi River during the thaw. Winter was in recess and spring had burst forth. The newly emergent rhythms of life seemed to be captured in the crew of eight as they pulled in harmony, gliding over the calm water. He made up his mind that he would do a frieze of them. There was no connection to the classical world, since there was no sporting competition in boat racing even though the Greek city states bordered on the waters of the Aegean and

Eight; oarsmen carrying their shell   *Mill of Kintail*

the rowing of their ships played a huge role in their battles. Because of British influence, rowing had become a major event in the revived Olympic Games. McKenzie searched for the moment he would portray. The pulling of the oars with the arms appealed to him, but how to capture the back and forth, piston-like movement of the arms and the backward lean of the body? He could visualize an elongated frieze over the entrance of a boat house or along a wall of an aquatic facility much the same as his *Brothers of the Wind* graced the walls of Sir Arthur Currie Memorial Gym at McGill. In the end, he was struck by a different co-ordinated movement. He saw the eight athletes lift the boat out of the water and hoist it over their heads to walk it back to the clubhouse. The image stayed with him. In a unique sculpture, McKenzie fashioned a work that showed that the eight were still teammates, still sharing a common goal and, as shown in the pose he caught them in, had submerged their individuality to work together in a common cause.

At the same time as he was working on *The Eight* in 1932-33, McKenzie was completing another work on football. It was a fifty-inch-diameter medallion titled *The Punter*. He had been a student of the game for a long time, had seen it grow from a spontaneous ad lib form of play to a specialized, skilful and practiced activity. The three players are shown kicking the football in three different styles; two are left footed. One has his arms extended, another dropped. Again there seems to be an emphasis on individual style and yet some uniformity is revealed, especially in the high-finishing kicking leg and the flexed supporting one. At this time, McKenzie was beginning to be well- known for his distinctive and stylized signing monogram. It looked like a P and a T printed a space apart, the verticals joined by a V, all of which translated as RTM.

McKenzie felt strongly about the importance of his work, about the need to leave faithful interpretations for future generations. He believed that the image of sport had been shaped for too long by newspapers and their sports columnists and

R. Tait McKenzie in his Scottish tartan   *Mill of Kintail*

photographers. He felt that serious artists had been too content to replay the past "or follow a year or two behind the experiments of the abstractionists, the distortionists and other 'ists' who have been dragging art in the dirt of Europe."[17] McKenzie saw that "the sportsman needs the artist, for if the technique and beauty of our present sports are to be preserved for the future, it must be by him alone."18

By the summer of 1933, Tait and Ethel had most of the renovation work done at the mill. The drawbridge had been refitted with chains, the interior was decorated to reflect the pioneer period. Models of his works were interspersed throughout. A studio was set aside upstairs for his use. Like him, there was little ostentation about the place. An Ottawa report remarked on the "something Spartan in McKenzie's fibre" notwithstanding "his sensitive reaction to the aesthetic." It continued:

> There is nothing decadent or grotesque in all his impressive cavalcade of athletic figures. Like Phidias, he has spent a large part of his time among stripped and striving youth. There he has sought and found the Greek ideal of physical perfection and has given it expression in lines flowing with light, clean rhythm. Whether it be

Robert Tait McKenzie and Ethel, relaxing at the Mill   *Mill of Kintail*

a child's face or an athlete's figure, beauty and
healthy joy of effort is vitally alive in deathless
bronze.[19]

They also found time for company. Guests were often invited to
the mill. The river was dammed in order to create a swimming,
canoeing and paddling area. With no electricity in the mill, and
without even an ice box, necessity became the mother of invention.
McKenzie rigged up an elaborate pulley system which hung into the
water. Guests often expressed surprise when McKenzie, with a great
flourish, announced that the occasion called for a toast. "He ran to the
balcony and leaning over it began to haul on a rope while singing
Heave-ho, Heave-ho. The guests watched curiously. Soon the neck of
a bottle appeared above the rail. Tenderly, McKenzie drew the bottle
into the room."[20] A cork popped; the champagne was poured with a
suitable bow. Ethel was busy as well. She wrote poetry, invited women's
groups from Almonte to tea and always seemed to be able to have
something to do when McKenzie was otherwise involved.

A typical summer day for McKenzie might find him working in his
studio, walking in the woods, swimming, canoeing, going into town,
giving presentations to local groups and where possible, encouraging
others to develop their talents. He was never one to sit still. At times
he seemed driven; his pace was always hectic. He developed heart
problems, was told to slow down. His medication, a form of digitalis,
was a constant companion.

As the Berlin Olympics approached, it soon became obvious that he
would not attend. His doctor had recommended against the trip. He was
approaching seventy years of age and there were signs of rapid
deterioration of his heart. It was a blow to McKenzie. Not only did he wish
to continue his involvement with the games, these were special; he knew
that Jim Naismith would be a guest of honour and his game, basketball,
would be introduced as an Olympic sport and gold medal event.

Still, he refused to slow down. Perhaps he was kept from some of
the travelling he would have liked to have done but his sculpting
continued. One of his works in 1934 was of a boxer, *Invictus*. He was
down on one knee. His eyes were glazed, listening to the referee's
count, waiting for his head to clear before he got up. McKenzie had
always been a fan of the fights. Boxing had always been an event of the
ancient games. As strange as it seems, there was something civilized

McKenzie's parents, from *The Bench of the Minister and His Wife*
Mill of Kintail

about it. Rules had been established to guarantee fairness in the oldest competition in the world, one against one. In the ancient games, the boxers wrapped their hands with *himantes*, stingers. It was more to protect the knuckles than inflict damage on the opponent. The Romans changed the wrapping to the dreaded *caestus*. They were leather thongs with pieces of metal or glass protruding obviously intended to cause the opponent to bleed. Just as the Greek *agon* was replaced by the Roman *ludii*, boxing had moved from healthy competition to an entertainment event, a ludicrous spectacle. McKenzie wanted to illustrate how the modern sport was changed again by the Marquis of Queensbury rules. The modern boxer wore four-ounce gloves called

***The Bench of the Minister and His Wife* by the river and Almonte town hall**
Author's collection

"mufflers when they first appeared in 1747."[21] They effected a change to a scientific approach, "placing a premium on skill."[22] The move to three-minute rounds did likewise. He wanted to convey all of that in his bronze of the boxer waiting to get up at the proper count to continue the match.

More than anything, McKenzie appreciated harmony and grace. He disliked obtrusiveness. In his restoration of the mill, he was careful to use as much of the original material as he could. If a part was not available he searched the countryside for a product which would blend in, perhaps from another building from the same era. Visitors to the mill announced themselves by pulling a chain that rang the "very bell that used to alarm (his) childish ears in the streets of Almonte as the engine went hand-drawn to the fires that periodically devastated that unfortunate village."[23] He bought a birch-bark craft, seeking out "one of the few Indians who still make canoes for old times' sake and paddle it on the safe and shallow water of my own mill pond."[24] Around the grounds he wanted some seating areas to allow people to sit and listen to the sounds of nature from the woods and the fields or to hear the rushing rapids. He used an old millstone as the back of a bench. On it he placed a bronze bas-relief portrait of his mother and father. *The Bench of the Minister and His Wife* rests near the Town Hall, not far from *The Volunteer*, overlooking the Mississippi River. Dedicated to William McKenzie, 1824-1876 and Catherine Shiells, 1836-1914, the inscription below their likenesses reads: Stranger sit, and rest and dream. The noisy millstone turns no more. Before you runs the restless stream that seeks the ocean evermore."

As the depression of the thirties was ending and leading to yet another world war, the era of McKenzie and Naismith was also coming to a close. McKenzie refused to make many concessions to age and to his heart condition. True, he did decide to forego trips to conferences and to the Berlin Olympics and, occasionally, he did decide to be driven someplace that he normally would have walked to but otherwise he maintained his spontaneity of life. About a year before is death, his assistant, Joe Brown, invited some visitors, dancers, to the studio. When the conversation turned to dancing, a space was cleared and they demonstrated some intricate folk steps. McKenzie took an interest. He asked whether they knew the Scottish sword dance. They did not; he demonstrated it for them with much enthusiasm. It was only with great difficulty that his assistant, aware of Tait's heart condition, persuaded him to stop. He did but "afterwards he sulked, 'I had my digitalis right here in my waistcoat'."[25] On another occasion, in 1938, a Canadian folk arts exhibition was held in New York. McKenzie was a member of the board of governors and vice president of the hosting organization. An authority on French Canadian folk songs, Marius Barbeau, was brought in for a lecture accompanied by a "habitant" singer, M. Bedard. He illustrated the lecture with "an unlimited store of folk songs at his tongue's tip . . . speaking only the patois French of his people." When the lecture and demonstration were over, a reception and private viewing continued. So too did the music and singing; this time the folk singer had a partner. In a corner of the room, oblivious to all were McKenzie and Bedard, "each with his arms around the other's shoulders, their heads together, singing *En roulant ma boule roulant* in complete understanding and companionship."[26]

In the spring of 1938 McKenzie took a cruise to Bermuda in the company of two doctor friends. Ethel stayed home but wired him some news while he was aboard ship. He was to receive an honourary degree from the University of St. Andrews in Scotland. In addition, the city of Honolulu commissioned him to do a statue of the great Olympic gold medal swimmer Duke Kahanamoku. Olympic athletes were subjects he always liked to sculpt. He had earlier finished a small bronze of Jesse Owens, the outstanding athlete of the 1936 games. Kahanamoku was already a revered Hawaiian legend.

Honours continued to accumulate. Only a few close friends were aware of his heart condition. The American Academy of Physical Education presented him with an illuminated scroll in recognition of his past work and particularly for designing its seal, *The Column of Youth*. Photographs of students, men and women, considered to be representative of the typical American boy and girl had been collected from physical educators around the States. The original idea of the column was from the old Grecian *herm*, which was used as a boundary marker. Here, too, McKenzie was attempting to link the past with the present. The seal showed a torch being passed from one runner to another in bringing the sacred fire to the altar. It was meant to typify "the Academy and its ideal of increasing knowledge, raising standards and raising the profession to the level of other learned professions."[27] It was unveiled in 1937 when McKenzie was guest of honour at the annual banquet of the American Association for Health, Physical Education and Recreation (AAHPER) in New York City.

Just prior to his death, he was persuaded, once again, to become president of the American Academy of Physical Education. His response was prophetic: "Well, this once more, but this is to be the last time."[28] Six days later, on April 28, 1938, McKenzie collapsed and died. He spent his last hours thinking of others. He worked the morning as usual in his studio on the finishing touches for the Kahanamoku statue, "attended a Board meeting, lunched at his favorite Club, The Franklin Inn, after which he climbed four flights of stairs to the attic studio of a young sculptor who had asked for his criticism."[29] On his return home, he telephoned Ethel who was out supervising arrangements for a charity musical. He offered to come with the car and pick her up. When he crossed the hall to call his driver, he collapsed and died.

His brother of the wind Jim Naismith was not far behind. When he returned from the Berlin Olympics, there were interviews and speaking engagements around the Kansas area. In June of 1937, at the end of the school semester, he retired from full-time teaching. He continued on in a minor, part-time capacity. It was a trying year for him. His wife, Maude, died on March 4, 1937. They had been together almost forty-three years. It was a lonely time for Jim Naismith. It was all he could do to maintain his cheery disposition. His wife was gone, the children had moved out and were on their own, his teaching career was all but over. He did much sitting around and thinking. He even took a car trip to Almonte. It almost proved disastrous. While out in a boat on White Lake, not too far from Almonte, Naismith fell into the water. Luckily, he was able to hold onto the side of the boat until his travelling friend came to his rescue. He returned to Kansas having had some respite from his reminiscing in Lanark County, but in some ways he was a lonely man left with his memories.

One of his remaining duties was as an advisor at the Sigma Phi Epsilon fraternity. There he met Florence Mae Kincaid, the housemother. She too had lost her spouse. They were attracted to each other. They decided to marry, apparently as a way of overcoming their desperate loneliness; each made it clear that they preferred to be buried next to their previously deceased partners when they died.

In the meantime, Naismith had one more recognition to receive. McGill University presented him with an honorary degree, Doctor of Divinity, on April 11, 1939. He had come full circle. When he graduated from Presbyterian College without his accepting ordination there had been many doubts about his decision to enter the YMCA Training School in Springfield. Throughout his life Naismith had often thought back to the pain and grief his decision had caused his sister Annie and Uncle Peter as well as all of those professors and classmates who were so busy praying for his soul. Now, in David Morrice Hall, he heard former classmate Reverend William Reid extol his career at McGill while making his presentation before Reverend Principal F. Scott Mackenzie and the assemblage. After the degree of Doctor of Divinity was conferred on him, Naismith addressed convocation. It was "a never to be forgotten experience to return to one's Alma Mater after half a century and to live again to meet and greet old friends."[30] It was a happy occasion for Naismith. Four of ten of his graduating class of 1890 were still alive and present. If they had parted on bad terms all was certainly forgotten now. With his typical humility, Naismith offered that "one must rejoice to know that they have done great things worthy of this great institution. The College had given the students the will and enthusiasm to accomplish things". He continued: "We did not accomplish all we intended to do or all we wanted to do but we did do a little."[31] He was "guided by the principle to leave the world a little better than when I found it. I thank the Lord for giving me the opportunities."[32] The next day Naismith was given a reception by friends at the Windsor Hotel. He spoke on trends in basketball, critical of the stalling tactics that some teams in the United States were beginning to use in order to protect a lead. Fully aware of whom he was addressing, he was enthusiastic about the game in Canada. Perhaps with the performance of the Canadian men's team and the Edmonton Grads at the 1936 Olympics in mind, he stated categorically: The brand of basketball played in Canada is the kind I envisioned when I invented the pastime."[33]

On June 10, 1939, Jim Naismith wed Florence Mae Kincaid. The two of them travelled to Almonte where once again he could revisit the scenes of his youth with his new wife. The marriage was short-lived. In November, he was hit by two debilitating strokes, the last one on November 28, 1939, when he was reunited in spirit with his boyhood friend and brother of the wind, Robert Tait McKenzie.

1. Affleck, George and Fred Leonard, *A Guide To the History of Physical Education*, Philadelphia: Lea and Fegiger, 1947, p. 476.
2. ibid., p. 475.
3. Webb, op. cit. p. 98.
4. Almonte *Gazette*, November 1, 1991.
5. Webb, op. cit., p. 102.
6. Toronto *Globe*, March 16, 1936.
7. Barry Mitchelson, op. cit., p.108.
8. Toronto *Globe*, August 8, 1936.
9. ibid.
10. ibid.
11. David McDonald and Lauren Drewry, *For the Record:Canada's Greatest Women Athletes.* Rexdale: John Wiley and Sons Canada, Limited, 1981, p. 57.
12. Almonte *Gazette*, November 1991.
13. Andrew Kozar, "R. Tait McKenzie Day, 1976". *CAHPER*, July/August, 1976, p. 24.
14. *JOHPER*, op. cit., 1944, p. 83.
15. R. Tait McKenzie, "The Athlete in Sculpture". *Art and Archaeology*, May/June, 1932.
16. *JOHPER*, 1944, p. 86..
17. R. Tait McKenzie, "Some Studies in the Sculpture of Athletes". A paper presented to AAHPER, Pittsburgh, 1935.
18. ibid.
19. Ottawa *Journal*, May 16, 1933.
20. Ottawa *Citizen*, April 23, 1955.
21. R. Tait McKenzie, "Some Studies in the Sculpture of Athletes. *JOHPER*, September, 1935.
22. ibid..
23. McKenzie notes, op. cit., p. 3.
24. ibid., p. 5.
25. *JOHPER*, 1944, p. 83.
26. ibid., p. 67.
27. ibid., p. 64.
28. ibid., p. 64.
29. ibid., p. 87.
30. Montreal *Gazette*, April 12, 1939.
31. ibid..
32. Dewar, op. cit.
33. Montreal *Gazette*, April 13, 1939.

CHAPTER 8

Mills, Mementos and Museums

PRIOR to his death Robert Tait McKenzie specified that he wished his heart to be surgically removed on his death and an autopsy done to determine if the prognosis was in fact the correct one. It was as much to help his family doctor as anything else. That was the scientist in McKenzie, the person who wanted exactness, the one who wanted to wed fact and theory. There was a second phase to his request. Once the analysis had been done he wanted the heart sent to Edinburgh to be buried with his monument *The Call*, The Scottish American War Memorial in the Princes Gardens. That was McKenzie the dreamer, the idealist, whose heart really was in Scotland, who considered himself a Canadian but also a transplanted Scot, whose ancestors had hailed from that land. He wanted to be united with what he considered his most meaningful work and which was a topic of conversation wherever he went. He wanted to rejoin and be part of the "Heart of Scotland." As for the rest of his body, he requested that it be cremated, the ashes to be interred in the British Officers Plot of Philadelphia's Northwood Cemetery.

His final wishes were not entirely honoured. Officials in Scotland were unable to accede to his request. Church officials at nearby St. Cuthbert's came to the rescue. At a service on September 7, 1938, McKenzie's heart was buried in the southeast corner of St. Cuthbert land; *The Call* was in sight. A simple stone with the monogram RTM marked the grave. His ashes were sent later from Pennsylvania to be buried with the heart. In Philadelphia, the British Officers' Club, in spite of the fact that his ashes had been sent to Scotland, inscribed his name on the Cross of Sacrifice in Northwood Cemetery.[1]

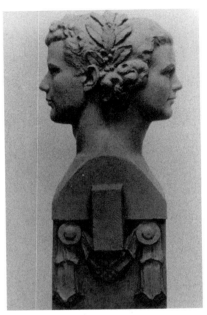

Column of Youth   *Mill of Kintail*

Notes of condolence poured in to Ethel, including one from Prime Minister Mackenzie King. Tributes were many and plans were made to honour his life in a variety of ways. At the University of Pennsylvania, the day of McKenzie's Philadelphia funeral was marked by a unique ceremony. The Penn Relays were scheduled. It was decided to continue them. McKenzie would have preferred that. The flag was flown at half mast at Franklin Field and three minutes of silence were observed. "Then joyously, they continued during the lovely Spring day. The last race was run, the final trophy won."[2]

The American Association of Health, Physical Education and Recreation (AAHPER), looked for ways to honour this Canadian who had made such an impact on their field. His *Column of Youth* was selected as a remembrance. In February of 1944 a special memorial issue of its *Journal of Health and Physical Education* was published. Every story in it was about McKenzie. The following year every issue carried a cover picture of one of his sculptures; the *Column of Youth* appeared on every future issue. The *Joy of Effort* was another popular work much in demand. The Pennsylvania AAHPER branch chose it as its medallion to be presented as its highest award to the membership; in New York State, it became a recognition for service. In Maryland, it illuminated certificates for fitness. The Quebec Physical Education Association and the national group, the Canadian Association for Health Physical Education and Recreation (CAHPER), adopted it as their official crests. The CAHPER *Journal* continues to carry an illustration of the *Joy of Effort* in every issue.

It wasn't the only piece of sculpture to be used by an organization. McKenzie's *Onslaught* was used as a trophy by the Canadian Intercollegiate Athletic Union in 1959. The University of Western Ontario Mustangs were presented with it when they defeated the

University of British Columbia Thunderbirds at Varsity Stadium in what was planned to be the first national university football championship game to be played, a forerunner to the College Bowl and Vanier Cup. At that time it was known as the Sir Winston Churchill Trophy or the Churchill Cup and had been in use in eastern Canada since 1953. It is still used as the trophy for the Western Bowl, the prelude to the Vanier Cup. McKenzie's *Brothers of the Wind* was also used as a token of achievement. It was given to skier Ann Heggtveit in recognition of her winning Canada's first skiing gold medal at the Olympic Games in Squaw Valley in 1960. Consisting of an inscription and a miniature replica, it was presented by CAHPER "for her outstanding courage and sportsmanship."[3]

CAHPER and Canada have continued to honour McKenzie in other ways. Since 1948, each convention has given out the R. Tait McKenzie Honour Awards for "distinguished, meritorious and special service as a mature leader in the field of Physical Education." Two Ontario universities, York and the University of Toronto, present their best physical education students with Tait McKenzie Honour Awards and Book Prizes. At York, the School of Physical Education building is named for Tait McKenzie.

In 1967, it was both the 100th anniversary of the country and McKenzie's birthday. The Canadian government merged the celebrations. There was a festive air of pride throughout the land. The government, always aware of the delicate issue of national unity in the large expanse of land, sought to encourage the new spirit. Expo '67, a world's fair, was held in Montreal to celebrate the national occasion. People were invited to come, to explore their identity and emergence into the world at large. McKenzie's sculptures were put on

University of Toronto *Alumni Shield*, awarded annually for outstanding achievement

Mill of Kintail

Centennial of McKenzie's birth and *Shield of Athletes*   *Mill of Kintail*

display from April to October in the youth pavilion. It served as a rediscovery and reintroduction of McKenzie to Canada. That same year, a film was made of his life; his works were displayed at the Mill of Kintail from June to October; McGill University had an exhibition June 14 - 18; the Ottawa City Hall had its display July 14 - 24.

Commemorative stamps issued by Canada Post for the 1976 Olympics

Author's collection

In New York, the Medallic Art Company commemorated the "birth of one of the most remarkable men in the fields of art, athletics, education and medicine."[4] The obverse had a portrait of McKenzie done by his friend John Sinnock of the United States Mint. The reverse was of the Olympic Shield of Athletic Sports. The medal was struck both in bronze and silver.

On the occasion of another national celebration, the 1976 Olympic Games in Montreal, McKenzie was honoured once again. The Canadian Post Office announced an "extraordinary set of Olympic Commemoratives in Silver and Gold." The 1976 Olympic Precious Metal Stamp Covers were issued in matched pairs. One bore the $1 Tait McKenzie stamp of *The Sprinter* and a .999 pure silver replica; the other was a $2 issue of *The Plunger* as well as a .999 pure silver replica of that stamp. The envelope for the first day cover also carried a replica of the Olympic shield. All of this was advertised as the world's first issue of precious metal stamp covers. Collectors described the stamps themselves as "the most popular issue in Canadian history."[5]

Once again, an effort was being made to re-acquaint the Canadian public with a giant who had fallen from their collective consciousness. His combined knowledge of athletics, anatomy and art was lauded in the post office release as "unequalled since the days of the Artist-Physicians of Ancient Greece". It continued:

> Like these men, Dr. McKenzie believed that athletic sculpture illustrated the link between physical and spiritual virtue. And like his ancient predecessors, he was convinced that the mind and body should be given equal education in order to develop the complete human being. What other modern artist can claim so great an affinity with the men who first conceived and shaped the Olympic Ideal?[6]

McKenzie's studio at the Mill of Kintail Museum   *Mill of Kintail*

Other groups sought to revive and make known McKenzie's works. The Canadian Olympic Association presented plaques bearing replicas of his works to visiting dignitaries. Consistent with the Olympic Games and the cultural events attached to them, art collections with a sport theme were on display. Place Ville Marie in Montreal was the site of such an exhibition, much of it featuring McKenzie's work. It was co-sponsored by the National Centre For Sport and Recreation as well as the Royal Bank of Canada.[7] In Ottawa, a permanent display called *Kaleidoscope* featured a whole range of his works. It was on the mezzanine floor of Esplanade Towers on Laurier St. W.[8]

Without question however, much of the full force of his sculpture was to be found and still is at the Mill of Kintail in Almonte, Ontario. Ethel McKenzie died in December of 1952. She had become an author in her own right. Her poetry had been published in book form and she wrote many verses to accompany Tait McKenzie's sculptures. She was buried in St. Peter's Episcopal Church in Philadelphia. Prior to her death, she sold the mill to Major and Mrs. James Leys. They became so attached to it and the art inside that they began to promote it as an

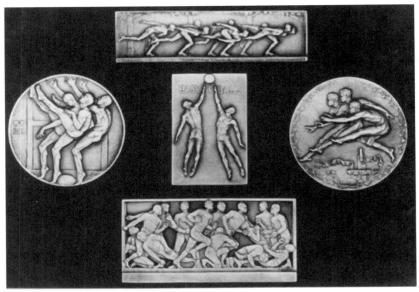

Assortment of reliefs and medallions. Note the only basketball work completed by McKenzie   *Mill of Kintail*

historic site to be preserved. They opened it up for visitors, operating it as a museum. The works of McKenzie were constantly displayed; governments were continually lobbied for support. It was a slow process. Allies were sought. Gradually, it all began to bear some fruit. In 1958, the mill "was declared an historic site by the Archaeological and Historic Sites Board of Ontario."[9]

Both CAHPER and the Canadian Medical Association (CMA) joined with Leys to lobby for the mill to become a national shrine befitting the stature of McKenzie in the world at large. CAHPER passed a resolution at its convention in 1961 to that effect; the CMA a similar one in 1962. CAHPER's stated, in part:

Medal awarded to Buffalo Germans-YMCA at the 1904 St. Louis Olympics   *Author's collection*

> Be it resolved that the National Capital Commission acquire the historic site known as the Mill of Kintail . . . for the purpose of maintaining and administering the said Mill of Kintail as a National Memorial to the great Canadian surgeon, physical educator and sculptor, R. Tait McKenzie and as a shrine devoted to the ideals of mind, body and spirit.[10]

Meanwhile, Leys continued to operate the mill as a museum bearing much of the expense personally. He continued to keep it open for the public. He was enchanted by the works that McKenzie had left behind and sought to bring more in. He and his wife arranged the pieces as best they could "in firm conviction that the Doctor was a figure of international stature . . . one of the greatest sculptors of the male figure since the Greeks."[11] The Ontario government sought to lighten the major's financial load and provided a grant in 1958. It was used for maintenance and repairs. The only additional support was in the "erection of a couple of roadside signs reading Historic Site."[12] Such support was a double edged sword. If more people were attracted it meant additional wear and tear and the old structure could not handle the six thousand visitors a season who were being drawn to the site. Both the building and Leys were growing older; a better solution had to be found.

Leys decided to invoke as much publicity as possible. McKenzie had to become better known and the public had to be aware of the national treasure that was there to be seen by all in the mill. He decided to have an annual Tait McKenzie Day on the weekend closest to his birthday. It was an effective way of spreading the message and acquiring additional works of art by McKenzie from various sources. In 1963, the eleventh Tait McKenzie Day was held on May 25. Some 200 guests gathered at the mill grounds on the banks of the Indian River. There were "distinguished surgeons and physical educators, dedicated artists and craftsmen, athletes and soldiers, each able to give something of themselves in a varied life."[13] The program began with *God Save The Queen*. Girl Guides and Brownies carried various flags. Canon J.W.R. Meakin of St. Paul's Anglican Church, Almonte, opened with a prayer of thanksgiving "for the example set by Tait McKenzie. A Lament, *The Flowers of the Forest*, was played by William Keen, the official Pipe-Major of the Mill of Kintail "in honour of the good doctor."[14]

During the program, Major Leys acknowledged the support of his neighbours, "especially Wilbert and Margaret Monette with their entire family"[15] in helping to establish the Memorial. He continued his efforts before his captive audience. Leys sought to "first safeguard the mill itself with a permanent Authority," before the National Capital Commission or the federal government became involved. He pressed the influential guests to support the concept. Some of those in the audience included Mrs. Vera M. McIntosh Bell who with her husband was instrumental in the McKenzies' purchase of the mill, Professor Winona Wood, chair of physical education, McGill University, who had often brought students to the site to view the sculptures; Professor Iveagh Munro, director of physical education for Women at McGill, who delivered a talk on McKenzie and his work; Gordon Wright, national director of fitness and amateur sport; Dr. G.E. Duff Wilson, chairman of the national fitness committee jointly established by

CAHPER and the CMA; Miss Joan Trott, a student from the University of Toronto and president of the school's Tait McKenzie Honour Society. She was accompanied by fourteen other student members from the U of T. From the Philadelphia St. Andrew's Society, Richard Gregory Sutcliffe came and spoke about the Scottish American War Memorial and the founding by McKenzie of the "British Officers' Club as a means of securing help for all needy veterans in that part of the world who had served in the British Commonwealth and Empire Forces in the First War." 16

The principal speaker was Dr. E.H. Bentley, the associate dean of medicine at McGill. He presented McKenzie's four original masks to the mill. The decision to do so was a testimony to McKenzie's humanity. One of the veterans he assisted through the British Officers Club was Dr. Cyril James. He later became principal of McGill. Before retiring, he wanted to honour his benefactor in this way. He acknowledged that the idea was first suggested to him by Professor Winona Wood.

The steady cultivation of the community at large by Major Leys bore fruit in 1972. In April, the mill was purchased by the Mississippi Valley Conservation Authority. A special fund, the R. Tait McKenzie Memorial Trust, was established by it to receive donations. They would be applied to the development and administration of the museum and conservation area. 17

The R. Tait McKenzie Memorial and the Mill of Kintail Conservation Area were officially opened with ceremonies held on September 8, 1973.

It was a long time coming and a joyful occasion for all. The Cameron Highlanders piped in the guests before playing *God Save The Queen* and *O Canada*. George E. Gomme, chairman of the Mississippi Valley Conservation Authority, welcomed all; Venerable Deacon J.A. Salter, President of the Almonte Ministerial Association, gave the invocation. Greetings were given by C.G. Caswell, chairman of the chairmen's committee of the Ontario Conservation Authorities. There were introductions: A.D. Latornell, director of the Conservation Authorities Branch, G. Hilliard, reeve of Lanark Township and A. Daines, warden, Lanark County. There were politicians present: P. Dick, MP Lanark, Renfrew, Carlton; L. Hopkins, MP Renfrew North, Nipissing East. J.E. Langdon, chairman of the Ontario Heritage Foundation was there and introduced F.A. Wade, chairman of Metro

Toronto and Region Conservation Authority. The guest speaker, J.H. Passmore, past president of CAHPER, was introduced by J. Willard, vice chairman of the Canada Labour Relations Board. The response to the speech was given by George E. Findlay, chairman of the Mill of Kintail Advisory Board. This was followed by a display of physical activities and musical selections by the Cameron Highlanders and refreshments.

It was a festive occasion, the culmination of years of effort. The Mississippi Valley Conservation Area was established in 1968 and in five years had been able to bring the project to a successful conclusion. The ceremony was a "fulfillment of many years of planning and dedicated effort . . . a real joy of effort."[18] The hope was that the memorial would "be a unique Canadian cultural and artistic centre – preserving the classical sculpture, the wonderful ideals and the inspiring philosophy of Tait McKenzie."[19]

In his remarks, Passmore mentioned how impressed he had been as a young man who had been invited to run with his high school at the Penn Relays in 1927. When McKenzie heard that there was an entrant from Canada, and on top of that from Hamilton, the birthplace of his wife, he went out of his way to meet them.[20]

Canada Post commemorative stamp issued for the centenary of basketball, 1991 *Author's collection*

The official name was the R. Tait McKenzie Memorial Museum at the Mill of Kintail Conservation Area. The setting is a sixty-hectare property which includes two hiking trails, the Indian River, a small outdoor theatre, open fields, picnic grounds and forest area. On Wednesdays and Saturday afternoons during the summer months the Ramsay Women's Institute serves tea and cakes on the lawn. A gatehouse at the park's entrance has souvenirs, information and displays. The main attraction is the mill. The first floor has been maintained as it existed in the 1930s when it served as Ethel and Tait's summer residence. The second floor is the studio. It holds many of his works and a table with clay and pottery samples to feel. As well, youngsters are encouraged to use the clay to shape their own works of art. The mill can be reached from Ottawa by taking Highway 17 to Highway 44 to Almonte or Highway 15 from Arnprior.

The Mill of Kintail beckons to all to come and see for themselves the works of this remarkable Canadian.

> There will not come one like him again. He lives, however, in the great tributes all over the world to the young soldier heroes of his time; in the beautiful athletic bronze figures housed at the Mill but above all, in the thousands of buoyant healthy boys and girls thronging in and out of the great gymnasiums into the playing fields."[21]

Dr. James Naismith Basketball Foundation

While the Mill of Kintail has been associated with Almonte and McKenzie, particularly since he bought it and used it for a summer

United States post office commemoratives, 1961 and 1991

Author's collection

studio and residence in the 1930s, the James Naismith Foundation and Museum is a more recent arrival. Honours paid to Naismith had been sporadic. Various nations had issued postage stamps in honour of his creation of basketball. Canada issued its three stamps on October 25, 1991, in denominations of 40, 46 and 80 cents. The catalyst was the 100th anniversary of the game. In the same year, the United States issued a 29-cent stamp in honour of the basketball centennial. It was estimated that at least 100 countries around the world were doing so simultaneously. It was thirty years after the United States had issued one hundred million 4-cent stamps in honour of Naismith. On September 25 of that year, 1961, representatives from Kansas and Massachusetts read a short history of basketball into the Congressional Record.[22] The American stamp was issued on the anniversary of Naismith's birth, November 6, 1961.

Plans were also announced on that date to open a Basketball Hall of Fame in Springfield, Massachusetts. The cornerstone was laid on November 6, 1961, although it was not officially opened until April 16, 1968. A new structure, an outgrowth of the original Naismith Basketball Hall of Fame, opened to the public June 30, 1985. The three-storey building was a further recognition of the growth of the game in the universities and in the National Basketball Association (NBA). Inside, on the third floor, are bronze medallions of the inductees, equipment, uniforms, trophies, videos, indeed all the usual items to be found in such a place. It is also largely interactive. On the first floor, a shootout display encourages fans to test their skill shooting at baskets at various heights from different distances. A scoreboard keeps track of the successful attempts. There is no question that, while the emphasis is on the game, it is portrayed as the "American game." The NBA, college basketball and the Harlem Globetrotters are given prominence. As such, the door had been left open to emphasize a more international approach and a "facility that recognizes how the sport has flourished, not just in the United States, but throughout the world."[23]

Enter the James Naismith Basketball Foundation. In the late 1980s, some Almonte citizens began to prepare for the basketball centenary. They sought a way to give attention to the fact that Naismith was a Canadian, from their community, whose inventiveness in constructing the game was a direct result of his roots. Geoff Mace, a former Carleton University basketball player, and coach of the Naismith Cottontails, an Almonte girls' basketball team, was a pivotal force in establishing the Naismith Foundation. Its purpose was to "spotlight Naismith's accomplishments both inside and outside the game . . . to draw attention to Naismith the man . . . not only a basketball person, he was a well rounded person."[24]

Basketball Canada became interested in the project. They had been considering a hall of fame themselves. Events began to move quickly. Soon the president, Rick Traer and past president, Al Rae, joined the Almonte citizens in sitting on the Naismith Foundation's five-person board of directors. Almonte citizens were also prevalent on the eighteen-person executive group.

Meanwhile, the land along Highway 15 in Ramsay Township, where Naismith went to live with the Youngs after his parents died, was purchased by Greg and Marianne Smith in 1988. The couple became involved with the Naismith project and the home's restoration after Marilyn Snedden, a member of the North Lanark Historical Society and a Naismith Foundation member, showed them a photograph of the original home.[25] The Smiths began to restore the outside to its original appearance. The house was designated as heritage property. Sixty percent of the cost of the exterior refurbishing was picked up by the Ontario Heritage Foundation. As a result, the Smiths signed a heritage easement agreement meaning that "the grounds around the house are also protected as a heritage property."[26]

The Smiths were enthusiastic about the project to honour Naismith. They donated some of their land to the museum and were joined by their neighbour, Daniel Coates, who contributed an adjoining piece.[27] The foundation now had the land, some three acres,[28] for its testimony to Naismith; the site was where he had grown up. It was incorporated

Original rock for duck on a rock game, now situated in front of the temporary location of Heritage Museum *Author's collection*

November 6, 1989, on what would have been his ninety-eighth birthday.[29] A further thirteen acres was purchased in 1995 as plans moved forward with the creation of an architectural model.

Money was needed. Various organizations which had a connection with Naismith began to contribute. Basketball Canada, the YMCA, FIBA, the Pan American Basketball Association along with federal and provincial governments donated funds, the latter over $60,000 for a detailed planning study.[30]

Plans moved quickly. The Baseball Hall of Fame at Cooperstown was studied as a model. Similarly, the Basketball Hall of Fame at Springfield was toured for ideas. Officials saw the new Canadian hall as "promoting something that will be complementary" in allowing the Massachusetts shrine to tell of basketball's American heritage with Almonte to focus on Canada. Almonte celebrated the basketball centennial with enthusiasm. The community's support was everywhere; a more appropriate name might have been Naismithville. During the last week of October 1991, guided tours were held to show where the idea for the game came from; Mill Street shop windows were decorated with basketball and Naismith themes. Visitors to the town were greeted by signs on the outskirts proclaiming Almonte the home town of Dr. James Naismith, inventor of basketball. Naismith Memorial Public School, packed for the occasion, was the site of the unveiling of an historical plaque. A dinner was held to complete the festivities. Jack Donohue, former coach of Canada's national basketball team, and a noted after-dinner speaker, gave the main address. He had done more perhaps than any single person in the country, to elevate Canada's international play in the post-Second World War period. He was named the honorary president of the James Naismith Foundation.

There had been similar bursts of publicity in the past. In 1929, Naismith, himself donated a second trophy to Almonte High School in commemoration of Annie's life. The Naismith Cup was to be awarded to the best female intramural basketball player in the school. As an aside, there was some irony in this. Annie had never quite forgotten nor forgiven Jim for leaving the ministry. He had taken his hand from the plough, she used to say, to pursue a career in the YMCA and invent basketball. One wonders whether she would have agreed to such a memorial. In 1953 the Almonte Lions Club erected a bronze placque, 16x18, to commemorate the sixty-second anniversary of basketball. In 1969, the inaugural James Naismith Trophy donated by the United

Press International for the best American collegiate player was won by Lew Alcindor, later to be better known as Kareem Abdul Jabbar. All of the more recent publicity being generated from the Almonte community seemed to be having its effect throughout the country. James Naismith was being reintroduced not only to his home town but also to the Canadian public. A national children's radio programme, *Treehouse*, sponsored by *Owl* and *Chickadee* magazines, held an essay contest for children. Youngsters across Canada were invited to submit one page on any aspect of Canadian history. Two sisters from Almonte, ten-year-old Laura and seven-year-old Jennie Carlton, entered with their essay on the invention of basketball:

> Did you know that 1991 is the 100th birthday of basketball? This sport was invented by Dr. James Naismith and he was born here in Almonte, Ontario. My sister and I go to Naismith Memorial Public School only two blocks from our house. Our friends the Smith family live in Dr. Naismith's house. Dr. Naismith invented the game when he was a gym teacher at the International YMCA Training School in Springfield, Mass. He was one of Canada's greatest rugby and lacrosse players. He studied to be a Minister but became a physical education teacher instead.
>
> Dr. Naismith wanted to make a team game that could be played indoors in the winter. The janitor couldn't find two boxes for goals, but he found two half bushel baskets. The sport became known as basketball.
>
> The first game was played at the YMCA school on December 28, 1891. It was played with peach baskets and a soccer ball. Only one basket was scored in the game. Each team had nine players. Basketball is now played in 178 countries around the world. Our basketball team is called the Naismith Nighthawks. [31]

The essay was one of four chosen and the "only one read over the air on the national program." [32] Host for the program, Mary Ito, admitted that "she too had learned something new. 'I had no idea that 1991 was the 100th anniversary of basketball.'"[33] The lack of awareness was widespread. The heritage program *Just A Minute* sought to make more Canadians aware with a popular public service announcement. CBC television expanded on the Naismith minute to produce an half-hour analysis hosted by Patrick Watson and Pamela Wallin. The National Basketball Association (NBA) expanded its league into Canada. The Vancouver Grizzlies and the Toronto Raptors began their initial season in 1995. This was done, naturally, for economic reasons but nevertheless the Canadian teams emphasized the roots of the game in their submissions. The Toronto team described one of its team colours and seating areas as "Naismith Silver" as a marketing concept to reinforce the Canadian connection. Vancouver also made a point of inviting to its first free agent camp Almonte native and a member of the Canadian national team, Kory Hallas. The two teams also met in Winnipeg for an exhibition pre-season game. It was promoted as the Naismith Cup, the Raptors winning by a score of 98-77. The Toronto team also had a Naismith as part of its opening ceremonies when it played the New Jersey Nets. Jeffery Naismith Ryder, a great-great-grandson of James Naismith performed the ceremonial tip off. The Raptors won that game by a score of 94-79.

On the international scene, it was probably as a result of the Naismith connection that the world basketball championships were held in Canada in Toronto and Hamilton in 1994. The 6'8" Hallas was a member of the Canadian team and had first been exposed to basketball under the guidance of his coach Fred Forsythe at the Naismith Memorial Public School. The Toronto Raptors seemed to be particularly anxious to develop the Naismith connection, perhaps because Almonte and its proposed museum were in Ontario. When training camp began, October 6, 1995, in Hamilton's Copps Coliseum, part of the official entourage was 80-year-old John McLendon. He was a link with the past, someone who had actually had Naismith as a teacher at the University of Kansas. He described Naismith as "studious, and always seemed quite serious, but he had a little twinkle in his eyes."[34] Naismith's basketball coaching career was long over when McLendon was learning anatomy and the health sciences in the classroom. Regardless, the subject of coaching basketball and the game itself were always close to Naismith's heart. And the students knew it too! McLendon and his classmates were continually trying "to get him off the subject of anatomy. Bring up the subject of basketball, and that was easily accomplished," said the former student.[35] McLendon travelled to Almonte to visit Naismith's hometown and see for himself the roots of this remarkable man.

McLendon, an African-American, had even more special reasons for thinking so highly of him. On one occasion, the young student was part of an instructional swimming class at the university. In those days of segregation, all the white students left the water when he entered. Naismith intervened. He took the class aside, called McLendon to the front along with another student. He took a pin and pricked McLendon's finger. Red blood trickled forth. Naismith took the finger of the white student and did the same with a similar effect. Having demonstrated that each had the same blood flowing in him, he went on to say that each had the same feelings as part of their humanity. Indeed, he continued, the only difference was that very slight thickness of the pigment of the skin.[36] It was a lesson which he was not required to give since segregation was clearly the practice of the day. That he did stayed with McLendon for all of his life. A grateful and adoring McLendon spoke of his prospective visit to Almonte: "I'm so happy about it to be able to go back to his birthplace because Dr. Naismith became my total life."[37]

Almonte had always held a special place in Naismith's heart. When the high school was renovated around 1929, he "donated a

Naismith grave site, Lawrence, Kansas   *Naismith Foundation*

Naismith Memorial, Lawrence, Kansas   *Almonte Gazette*

beautiful silver cup to be competed for annually by basketball teams of the county. The trophy, known as the Dr. Naismith Basketball Cup is one of the most coveted in athletic circles in Almonte."[38]

James Naismith has continued to be honored in his native land and his adopted country. On April 22, 1995, he was inducted into the Canadian Olympic Hall of Fame at Quebec City. His award was accepted by his grandson, Stewart Naismith of Binghamton, New York. Almonte and the Naismith museum were the sites of a premiere showing in mid-September 1995 of a film made about the life of Naismith and the invention of basketball. Parts of it were shot on location in the town. The movie was to be shown over the Baton Broadcasting System which planned to air it "three times in prime time over the next two years."[39] The Naismith Classic is a basketball tournament hosted by the University of Waterloo in Ontario. Indeed, the NBA and its new Canadian teams were thriving. Attendance records were set in the 1995-96 season by the League with an average per game attendance of 17,252 fans, an increase over the 16,727 of the previous season. A total of 20,513,218 spectators attended NBA games, up 10.8% from the previous record in 1994-95. The Vancouver Grizzlies drew more than 700,000 fans for their forty-one games while the Raptors drew nearly 950,000. Basketball was so popular that the Springfield Hall of Fame announced its plans for a new addition and the NBA approved the concept of a women's NBA to begin as a summer league in 1997.

On August 26, 1991, in Lawrence, Kansas, where he is still a legend, the town cemetery was renamed for him. Long time co-worker "Phog" Allen eulogized his life:

> Frederick Froebel gave the world the theory of the Kindergarten – education through play. Dr. Naismith gave to the youth basketball, a game that takes the youngster from the 8th grade to maturity.
>
> I once heard eight nationally known educationists speaking from the same platform declare that basketball had all the qualities necessary to teach the child: poise, rhythm, grace, co-ordination, development of skills, and the development of physical vigour.

The speakers were not competitive coaches nor
were they athletes. The game, the only
international game that is the product of one
man's brains, stamps Dr. Naismith as a great
educationist, a kindly humanitarian and a
practical Christian. He loved youth . . . chose the
profession of physical education over the
ministry because . . . could do more for youth.

The youth of the world will arise and call Dr.
Naismith blessed. [40]

Meanwhile in Canada's Ottawa valley, Lanark County and
Almonte's two brothers of the wind, R. Tait McKenzie and James
Naismith, are once again united in spirit. Each has a museum named
for him, a tribute to their inventive genius. Almonte is proud to host
both of them. Signs on the outskirts proudly proclaim them.
Recognition of the contribution they have made to sport in Canada is
indicated by the site of Canada's national centre for the administration
of sport located outside Ottawa in Gloucester. The governing bodies
are housed in *Place* R. Tait McKenzie Place at 1600 James Naismith
Drive.

In Montreal on September 19, 1996, McGill University,
celebrating its 175 years, inaugurated its Sports Hall of Fame. Two of
the first inductees were Robert Tait McKenzie and James Naismith.
The brothers of the wind were memorialized and united once again at
their *alma mater*.

1. McGill, Jean, *Joy of Effort*, p. 200.
2. *JOHPER*, 1944, p. 87.
3. James Day, "Robert Tait McKenzie, Physical Education's man of the Century". *CAHPER Journal*, April/May, 1967, p. 13.
4. News Release, Medallic Art Company of New York, 1967.
5. Canadian Post Office news release, 1976.
6. ibid., 1976.
7. *CAHPER Journal*, July/August, 1976, p. 27.
8. ibid.
9. Douglas Riley, *McGill Journal of Education*, Spring 1976, p. 73.
10. Day, op. cit., p. 14.
11. Montreal *Star*, November 14, 1964.
12. Almonte *Gazette*, May 30, 1963.
13. ibid..
14. ibid..
15. ibid..
16. Program, Official Opening, September 8, 1973.
17. J. H. Passmore, Opening Ceremonies, September 8, 1973.
18. ibid., p. 2.
19. ibid., p. 3.
20. *JOHPER*, 1944, p. 87.
21. Almonte *Gazette*, November, 1991.
22. ibid.
23. Toronto *Globe and Mail*, October 30, 1991.
24. Almonte *Gazette*, November 1991.
25. ibid.
26. Toronto *Globe and Mail*, October 30, 1991.
27. Almonte *Gazette*, November, 1991.
28. Almonte *Gazette*, November, 1991.
29. Toronto *Globe and Mail*, October 30, 1991.
30. Almonte *Gazette*, November 1991.
31. ibid.
32. ibid.
33. Toronto *Globe and Mail*, October 7, 1995.
34. ibid.
35. Jean Gosset, personal reminiscence from McLendon's visit, Nov.2, 1995.
36. *Globe and Mail*, October 6, 1995.
37. Almonte *Gazette*, November, 1991.
38. Almonte *Gazette*, June 14, 1995.
39. Toronto *Globe and Mail*, April 23, 1996.
40. Toronto *Star*, April 25, 1996.
41. Almonte *Gazette*, November, 1991.

Articles, Books, Etc., By or Relating to Tait McKenzie

1890   Helps in Teaching the Running High Jump; Triangle, November.

1891   "The Growth of Gymnastics in Montreal;" Dominion Illustrated Monthly, May.

1892   "Rugby Foot Ball in Canada;" Dominion Illustrated Monthly, February.
Foot Ball, A Report of the Yale-Harvard Game; Springfield, Mass.

1894   "Therapeutic Uses of Exercise in Education;" Montreal Medical Journal, February.
"Regulation of Athletic Sports in Colleges;" The Week, January 12. Report on Physical Education in McGill University.

1895   "The Typical Speed Skater;" Popular Science Monthly, December.   "Hockey in Eastern Canada;" Dominion Illustrated Monthly.

1896   "Notes on the Examination and Measurement of Athletes;" Montreal Medico-Chirurgical Society, November.

1897   The Speed Skater and His Art; McClure's Syndicate, 1897.   "International Speed Skating;" Outing Magazine, December.
"Natural Selection as shown in the Typical Speed Skater;" Journal of Anatomy, Vol. XXXII.
"The Art of Breathing;" Outing Magazine.
Barnjum Bar Bell Drill; Triangle Publishing Company.
"Frederick Barnjum and his Work;" Physical Education Review, June.
"The Dissection of Two Club Feet;" Journal of Anatomy, Vol. XXXIV

1898   "Accurate Measurement of Spinal Curvature;" British Medical Journal, Dec. 1898; Montreal Medical Journal, Feb. 1898.

1899   "Influence of School Life on Curvature of Spine;" Montreal Medical Journal, March.

1900   Strain, Breathlessness and Fatigue as shown by the Face; International Education Congress, Paris.
"The Place of Physical Training in a School System;" Montreal Medical Journal, January.

1901   "The Treatment of Spinal Deformities by Exercise and Posture;" Montreal Medical Journal, October.
"A Modern Gymnasium;" McGill University Magazine, December.

1904   Address at Opening of the University of Pennsylvania, Pennsylvania Gymnasium; Gymnasium Proceedings, December.
"The Relation of Thoracic Type to Lung Capacity;" Montreal Medical Journal, April.

1905   "Physical Education at Pennsylvania;" Red and Blue, October.
"Building the Physical Side of College Men;" Illustrated Sporting News, August 12.
"An American Sculptor;" The Outlook, March.
"How Far should Physical Training be Educational and How far Recreative in Colleges and Universities?" Journal of Proceedings of the National Educational Association.
"Facial Expression of Violent Effort, Breathlessness and Fatigue;" Journal of Anatomy and Physiology, October.

1906   "Relation of Athletics to Longevity;" Medical Examiner.
"The Legacy of the Samauri;" American Physical Educational Review, December.

1907   "The Development of Physical Efficiency among College Men;" Address at opening exercises of Queen's University Gymnasium, February, Queen's University Journal.
"Systematic Physical Exercises for College Students;" Second International Congress on School Hygiene.
"The Anatomical Basis for the Treatment of Scoliosis by Exercise;" Proceedings of the College of Physicians of Philadelphia.
"The Isolation of Muscular Action;" American Physical Education Review, November.
"R. Tait McKenzie, Sculptor and Anatomist;" International Studio, July.

1908   "The University and Physical Efficiency;" University Magazine, MacMillan & Co. of Canada, Volume VI., No II.
The Regulation of Physical Instruction in Schools and Colleges from the Standpoint of Hygiene (with Drs. Storey, Lee and Hough); American Physiological Society Convention, December.
"Results of the Examination of Students' Eyes" (with Dr. William Campbell Posey); Journal of American Medical Association, March 23.
"Physical Therapeutics;" American Journal of Medical Sciences, October.

1909   "Regulation of Physical Instruction in Schools and Colleges from the Standpoint of Hygiene;" American Physical Education Review, April.

1910   Physical Training of the Seven Ages.
"Sculpture by R. Tait McKenzie;" International Studio, July.
"Annual Address by the President of the Society of Physical Directors of Physical Education in Colleges;" American Physical Education Review, February.
"The City and Fresh Air;" Fresh Air Magazine, March.
"Report on the Department of Physical Education at the University of Pennsylvania;" Old Penn., April 30.
"R. Tait McKenzie, Sculptor;" Old Penn., December.
Book—Exercise in Education and Medicine; Published by W.B. Saunders in Philadelphia and London, 1st edition.

1911 "Chronicle of the Amateur Spirit;" American Physical Education Review, February.
      "The Onslaught;" Century, April.
      "A Visit to the Home of Archibald Maclaren;" read at a meeting of the Directors of Physical Education in Colleges, December.
      "R. Tait McKenzie, Sculptor;" Red and Blue.

1912 "Value of Exercises in Treating certain Cases of Acquired Inguinal Hernia;" International Clinics, Volume III. 22nd Series, January.
      "The Franklin Statue;" Old Penn., February 10.
      "Constructive Patriotism;" American Physical Education Review.
      "Memorial to Dr. Crawford W. Long;" Old Penn., April 6.
      "Dr. McKenzie's recent work in Sculpture;" Old Penn, February 17.
      "The Joy of Effort;" Century. (Picture and Poem by Chas. Wharton Stork.)
      Dedicatory Address at Trees Gymnasium, University of Pittsburgh, July 16.
      "R. Tait McKenzie, Studies from Life;" Life, Town and Country, June.
      The Work of Ten Years in Sculpture; McClees Galleries, March.

1913 "Influence of Exercise on the Heart;" American Journal of Medical Sciences, January.
      "The Royal Central Institute at Stockholm;" American Physical Education Review, March.
      "The Mission of the Artist;" Address to Philadelphia Schools of Design, May 1913.
      "The Quest for Eldorado;" American Physical Education Review, May.
      "The Wisdom of Health;" Old Penn., November 8.

1914 "Non-Military Preparation for National Defense;" The Standard, December.
      The Youthful Franklin; Address at the Unveiling, June.
      "A New View of Benjamin Franklin;" Century, July 1914
      "A Canadian Sculptor;" Toronto Saturday Night, July 4.
      The Moment of Victory, Transcript, Boston.

1915 "The Search for Physical Perfection;" University Lecture and Old Penn., November.
      "Physical Training of the New British Armies;" American Physical Education Review, December.
      "McKenzie, Moulder of Clay and Men;" Waldo Alder, Outing, May.
      "Hate;" The Cornbill Magazine, September 1916 (with Sir Arthur Shipley).

1916 "A National Scheme of Physical Education;" Journal of Royal Sanitary Institute.
      "Treatment of Convalescent Soldier by Physical Means;" Proceedings of the Royal Society of Medicine, Volume XX. p. 31.

1917 "Making and Remaking of a Fighting Man;" American Physical Education Review, March.
      "Treatment of Nerve, Muscle and Joint Injuries in Soldiers by Physical Means;" Canadian Medical
      Association Journal, December, 1917.
      Book–Exercise and Medicine; Published by W.B. Saunders in Philadelphia and London. Second edition.
      Dedication of the Tablet to Weir Mitchell, October.

1917 "A Message from Art in War Time;" Christian Advocate, February 18.

1918   "Mechanical Aids to Reconstruction."
        "Reclaiming the Maimed in War;" Meeting of the College of Physicians,
        Philadelphia, Feb. 7,1918.
        "Functional Re-education of the Wounded;" N.Y. Medical Journal, March.
        "Reconstruction and Rehabilitation of Disabled Soldiers;" Pennsylvania Medical
        Journal, March.
        "Students at War;" Red and Blue.

1919   "Biological Significance of Physical Education"; Current Problems in Social
        Medicine, May.
        "George Whitefield Statue"; Pennsylvania Gazette, June.

1920   "The Newer Mechano-Therapy;" The Pediatrist, July 1920.
        "Un Sculpteur Moderne de l'Athlétisme;" Gazette des Beaux Arts.
        "Physician and Sculptor;" McGill News.

1921   "Physical education in the Universities of the U.S.A.;" Edinburgh Medical
        Journal, December.
        "The Wisdom of Health;" Youth's Companion, May
        "Treatment of Physical Defects;" How to Live, March.

1922   "Physical Education at the University;" Pennsylvania Gazette, May 12.
        "All England stirred by McKenzie Memorial (Homecoming);" Pennsylvania
        Gazette, October.
        "Variations of Athletic Types;" The Outlook, June.

1923   Book–Exercise in Education and Medicine; Published by W.B. Saunders in
        London and Philadelphia. Third edition.
        "A Sculptor of Soldiers and Athletes;" The Century, October.

1924   Report – Physical Education in Europe.
        "The University and the Meaning of Education;" Pennsylvania Gazette,
        October 17.
        "R. Tait McKenzie;" Biographical Notices of Medallists, London 1924.
        "Le Dr. Tait McKenzie, Sculpteur d'Athlètes;" Aesculape, October.

1925   "Le Masque Facial dans L'Effort;" Aesculape, February.
        "Tait McKenzie's Medical Portraits;" International Clinics, Vol. II, Series 35.
        "Dr. R. Tait McKenzie, Sculptor;" Maple Leaf, N.Y., April.

1926   "The Functions and Limits of Sports in Education"; Canadian Medical Journal,
        April.
        Plans for the New Gymnasium, University of Pennsylvania; Society of Physical
        Education Directors.
        "Unveiling of Statue of Former Provost, Edgar F. Smith"; Pennsylvania
        Gazette, July.
        "The Modern Discus Thrower," International Studio, May.

1927   "The Athlete in Sculpture;" The Sportsman, May.
        "The Scottish-American War Memorial;" Country Life, September.
        "Scots and Americans, Edinburgh Unveiling;" The Scotsman, September.
        "Dr. McKenzie designs Scotch War Memorial;" Pennsylvania Gazette, March.

1928   "Le Docteur R. Tait MacKenzie, Médecin, éducateur et sculpteur;" Les
        Nouvelles Médicales de Paris, April.
        "The Place of Physical Education and Athletics in a University;" Address at
        International Congress of Physical Education and Sports, Amsterdam, August.

1929   Christopher Hussey, "Tait McKenzie: A Sculptor of Youth;" Country Life Ltd., London.

1930   "Portrait By G. Gibbs;" Art & Archaeology, March (29:138).
        "Sculpture at the Fine Art Society;" Apollo, August (12:166).
        "Plunger;" Architectural Review, July (68:28a).
        "Plunger;" American Architecture, October (138:61).

1931   "Sculpture From the Medical School;" by B. Abbott, Canadian Magazine, June (75;19+).
        "Art & Athletics;" American Magazine of Art, August (23:153-4).
        "The Eight;" Art & Archaeology, March (31.61).
        "General Wolfe;" Art Digest, October 1 (5:21).
        "Pioneers in Physical Education and the Lessons We May Learn from Them;" Journal Health and Physical Education, November (2:6-7+).
        "Relationships of Physical Education to Art;" (In New York University, School of Education, Symposium on Physical Education and Health, p. 213-16; same in Nash, J. B., editor, Mind-Body Relationships, p183-6).

1932   "Youthful Franklin;" Art Digest, April 15 (6:32).
        "Athlete in Sculpture;" Art & Archaeology, May (33:114-25).
        "Physical Education at the University of Pennsylvania from 1904 to 1931 and the Gates Plan;" American Education Association Research Quarterly, May (3:19-26).
        "American Academy of Physical Education;" Journal of Health and Physical Education, June (3:14 -16+).
        "Sprinter;" American Magazine of Art, September (25:14)

1933   "Reminiscences of James Naismith;" Journal of Health and Physical Education, January (4:21+).
        "Spirit of Nursing;" Architecture (N.Y.), July (68:41).
        "Posture;" Hygeia, November (11:996 - 9+).

1934   "Exhibition, Grand Central Galleries;" Art News, February 10 (32:13).
        "McKenzie's Sculptures of Athletes make a Notable New York Show;" Art Digest, February 15 (8:18).
        "Modern Discus Thrower;" Art News, February 3 (32:2).
        "Shot Putter;" Art News, February 17 (117:24).

1934   "Tait McKenzie, A Sculptor of Youth;" Literary Digest, February 24 (117:24).
        Sprinter; Three Punters; William A. Carr, Running; Sculptures, Survey Graphic, April (23:167).

1935   "Some Studies in the Sculpture of Athletes;" Journal of Health and Physical Education, September (6:9 -13).

1936   "Benjamin Franklin; Illustrious Pioneer in Physical Education;" Journal of Health and Physical Education, February (7:67 - 71+).
        "Falcon;" Art News, March 7 (24:2).

1938   (Obituary) New York Times
        (Obituary) Journal of Health & Physical Education, May (9:298).
        (Obituary) School & Society, May 7 (47:604).
        (Obituary) Time, May 9 (31:65).
        (Obituary) Art Digest, May 15 (21:20).
        "In Memoriam;" R. D. Warden, Journal of Health & Physical Education, June (9:375).

1940   "America's Typical Boy and Girl: R. T. McKenzie's Column of Youth;" Recreation, March (33:678).

1943   "Let Us Honor Dr. R. Tait McKenzie;" Journal of Health and Physical Education, March (14:147+).

1944   R. Tait McKenzie Memorial Issue, Journal of Health and Physical Education, February (15:49 - 94). Thirty biographical and tributory articles.

1959   "R. Tait McKenzie – Educator and Sculptor;" Journal of the Canadian Association for Health, Physical Education, and Recreation, January.

1960   "R. Tait McKenzie;" Journal of the American Association for Health, Physical Education, and Recreation, April.
        "A Physical Fitness Shrine in Canada;" Canadian Medical Association Journal, June 25, Page 1330.

1961   "Physical Fitness;" Canadian Medical Association Journal, April 22.

1962   "Sub - Health;" Canadian Medical Association Journal, February 24.

1963   "Theirs be the Glory;" Journal of the Canadian Association for Health, Physical Education, and Recreation, June-July.

1964   "Olympic Shield of the Athletes;" Journal of the American Association for the Health, Physical Education, and Recreation, September.

1967   "Robert Tait McKenzie: Physical Education's Man of the Century;", James Day, CAHPER Journal, April/May.
        1971Innovators and Institutions in Physical Education, Ellen Gerber, Philadelphia: Lea and Febiger.
        1975Robert Tait McKenzie, 1867-1938, Sculptor of Athletes, Andrew Kozar, University of Tennessee Press.

1976"R. Tait McKenzie Day Observances at The Mill Of Kintail, Official Opening Speech in Remembrance of Robert Tait McKenzie;", CAHPER Journal, July/August.

1980   The Joy of Effort, Jean McGill, Bewdley: Clay Publishing.

1982   "Only Time Will Tell;", Elizabeth Pitt Barron, Mill of Kintail

1988   Robert Tait McKenzie, 1867-1938, Sculptor of Athletes, Richard Graburn Nickle Museum, Calgary.

1991   The Sporting Sculpture of Robert Tait McKenzie, Andrew Kozar, Champaign: Human Kinetic Books.

1992   McGill News, McGill University, Fall.

1995   "A Sporting Life;", Profiles, York University, September.

Appendix II

Works in Sculpture by Tait McKenzie

Before
1902   Tentative works in low relief.
        Speed Skaters, two plaques, about 8 x 12 in.
        The Mother, medallion portrait,12 in., owned by R. Tait McKenzie;
        Four Masks, life size, illustrating violent effort and the progress of fatigue. First
        described before the Society of American Anatomists, 1899, and at the
        International Congress on Physical Education, Paris, 1900; published with
        description in Journal of Anatomy, England, October 1905. Since then greatly
        revised, and described in Exercise in Education and Medicine (W. B. Saunders).
        Sets of the masks are in Museum of Royal College of Surgeons, London;
        Anatomical Department, Cambridge University; and Medical Museum, McGill
        University, Montreal, Canada.

1902   *The Sprinter*, statuette, 1/4 life size, completed after three years' work, modelled
        from the average measurements of one hundred sprinters, showing typical
        sprinter in typical crouching start, then recently introduced. Shown at Society
        of American Artists, 1902; Royal Academy, London, 1903; Salon, Paris, 1904.
        Copies in Fitzwilliam Museum, Cambridge, and many private collections. Used
        as Intercollegiate Trophy in Canada and elsewhere.

1903   *The Athlete*, statuette, 1/4 life size, modelled from the average of four hundred
        Harvard students. The fifty strongest taken over a period of eight years. Shown
        at Salon, 1903; Royal Academy, 1904; Roman Art Exposition, 1911. Copies in
        Ashmolean Museum, Oxford; Museum of Natural History, New York; Toronto
        Art Museum, and in many private collections. First copy owned by Society of
        Directors of Physical Education in Colleges.
        Archibald Lampman, portrait medallion, 12 in., galvano reduction, 2 in. Trinity
        College, Toronto.

1904   *Jeffrey MacPhail*, portrait plaque, 12 x 16 in., owned by Sir Andrew MacPhail;
        galvano reduction, 2 in. high.
        Dorothy B., medallion, 12 in.; Salon, 1904. Owned by Dr. Jonathan T. Meakins,
        Montreal. Galvano reduction 2 in.

1905   *Robert Barr*, novelist, portrait plaque, 8 x 12 in. Owned by R. Tait McKenzie.
        Galvano reduction, 2 in.
        Wistfulness, medallion (6 in.) of Stuart Guilford McKenzie. Owned by William
        P. McKenzie, Cambridge, Mass. Galvano reduction, 1 in.

Discobolus No. 1 and *No. 2*, plaques, 4 x 7 in. Collection of the late Sir William C. Van Horne, Montreal and Franklin Inn Club, and R. Tait McKenzie.
The Boxer, statuette, 1/4 life size; shown at Society of American Artists in 1906, owned by R. Tait McKenzie and in private collections.

1906   *Supple Juggler*, statuette, 1/4 life size; Royal Academy, 1908; Salon, 1909; Roman Art Exposition,1911; acquired by Metropolitan Museum, New York, and private collections.
Competitor, statuette, 1/2 life size; Salon, 1907; Royal Academy, 1907. Acquired by Metropolitan Museum, New York; and National Gallery, Canada; Springfield College, Mass., and private collections.
Wilfred Campbell, poet, medallion, 12 in., galvano reduction 2 in.; Woodland Cemetery, Ottawa, Canada, set in memorial bench of granite.
Maizie and Buzzie, two portrait medallions, 8 in. Owned by Dr. C. H. Frazier, Philadelphia. Galvano reduction, 2 in.
Public School Athletic League Medal, 1 in., New York.

1907   *Dr. William Henry Drummond*, poet, medallion, 12 in.; galvano reduction, 2 in. Original, Western Hospital, Montreal, and Family. Reduction, Surgeon-General's Library, Washington, and Harvard University.
Forbes Robertson, as Caesar, 9 in.; galvano reduction, 2 in. Owned by R. Tait McKenzie.
Gertrude Elliott, as Cleopatra, 9 in.; galvano reduction, 2 in. Owned by R. Tait McKenzie.
Charles Wharton Stork, poet, 9 in.; galvano reduction, 2 in. Owned by Dr. Stork.
Dudley Allen Sargent, 12 in.; medal reduction, 2 in. Owned by the Alumni Association of the Sargent School of Physical Education. Medal struck to commemorate twenty-five years of service.

1908   *Amie Hampton Clark*, medallion, 10 in. Owned by Mrs. C. Howard Clark. Galvano reduction, 2 in.
Clarence Howard Clark 3rd, portrait plaque, 12 x 16 in.
William Cornelius Covenboven Van Horne, portrait medallion, 6 in. Owned by estate of Sir William Van Horne.
James Fletcher, F. R. S. C., medallion, high relief, bronze, 14 in. Set in memorial stele of granite, Experimental Farm, Ottawa, Canada.
George Newball Clarke, 9 in., medallion. Ponfret School Chapel.
Bertram Stuart McKenzie, 9 in. Owned by R. McKenzie.
William Patrick McKenzie, 12 x 18 in. Owned by William P. McKenzie.
Eugene Paul Ullman, painter 12 in. Owned by Eugene Paul Ullman.
Carrie Jacobs Bond, musician, 13 in. Owned by R. Tait McKenzie.
Charles Brockden Brown, first American novelist, plaque 14 x 18 in., galvano, 2 in. Franklin Inn Club.

1909   *The Relay*, 1/2 life size, statuette; Roman Art Exposition, 1911; Montreal Art Gallery; Springfield College, Mass. Viscount Ridley.
Lisl Medallion, 9 in., reduction 2 in. Owned by Dr. Charles Wharton Stork.
Guglielmo Ferrero, historian, medallion, 9 in. Owned by R. Tait McKenzie.
Paul Dougherty, painter, medallion, 9 in. Owned by Paul Dougherty.
Dr. S. Weir Mitchell, 16 x 28 in., portrait plaque. Re-study for Franklin Inn Club, Philadelphia, 1915; re-study made with changed inscription for Library University of Pennsylvania, 1917. Reduction, 4 x 7 in. 100 copies issued by Franklin Inn Club, Surgeon-General's Library, Harvard University,

Pennsylvania Museum and elsewhere.

Dr. W. W. Keen, portrait plaque, 26 x 45 in. Brown University, Providence, Rhode Island. Four reductions 16 x 28 in., for family. Reduction 4 x 7 in., Surgeon-General's Library and Harvard University Pennsylvania Museum and private collections.

Dr. Nathaniel Chapman, Dr. Samuel Jackson, bronze plaques, 38 x 54 in., Medical School, University of Pennsylvania.

Francis Kinlock Huger, 18 in. medallion, Medical School, University of Pennsylvania. Reduction, 3 in., Surgeon-General's Library, Washington, Harvard University and New York Numismatic Society.

College of Physicians' Medal, 2 3/4 in., to commemorate opening of new building, Philadelphia.

Mrs. Bradbury Bedell, portrait plaque, 12 x 26 in. Owned by Margaret Bedell, Catskill, New York.

1910   *Dr. Arthur Adderly Browne*, medallion, 25 in., Medical Library, McGill University, Montreal.

Baron Tweedmouth, Baroness Tweedmouth, two panels, life-size heads, 14 x 18 in., mezzo relief, in fountain Tomich, Ross-shire, Scotland.

Edward Walter Madeira, portrait plaque, 12 x 16 in. Owned by Louis C. Madeira.

1911   *The Onslaught* (1904-1911), football group, 40 in. long, figures 1/4 life size. Royal Academy, 1912. Acquired by Montreal Art Gallery and University of Pennsylvania.

Series of small sketches of athletes in action (at about this time) *Plunger, Man Watching Pole Vault, Discoboli* (forward swing), *Shot Putter Preparing, Shot Putter Resting, Shot Putter Ready, High Jumper Cleaning Shoe, Wounded, The Tackle, Relay No. 1, Relay No. 2*, University of Pennsylvania.

Dr. William Gardner, Portrait plaque, 19 x 24 in., McGill Medical Library.

Dr. Crawford W. Long, 18 in. medallion, Medical School, University of Pennsylvania. Replica with changed lettering, University of Georgia, Athens, Georgia, 1921. Reduction, 3 in., Surgeon-General's Library and Harvard University.

Sign Board, Franklin Inn Club, Philadelphia, 14 x 18 in., bronze.

William Foster Biddle Medallion, medallion 12 in., Episcopal Academy, Philadelphia.

Honourable "Archie" Gordon, plaster bust, life size; Haddo House Chapel, Aberdeenshire, Scotland.

Working Model, Benjamin Franklin, 1/2 life size. Copies, Newark Museum, New Jersey, and Philadelphia Public Library and private collections.

1912   *Mrs. Tait McKenzie*, portrait plaque, 12 x 17 in. Owned by R. Tait McKenzie.

Joy of Effort, medallion, 46 in.; The Stadium, Stockholm, Sweden. Reduction, 20 in. Used as trophy for Philadelphia Public Schools, and reduced to 4 in. used as medal.

Ariston, American Playground Association, 10 in. reduction, medal; award for athletic tests.

They are swifter than eagles, Re-study of P. S. A. L. Medal.

Katherine Clark, medallion, 10 in. Mrs. John W. Clark, Philadelphia.

Honourable Sir George A. Drummond, K. C. M. G., portrait plaque, low relief, 36 x 52 in. St. Margaret's House, Montreal.

General Henry Morris Naglee, memorial, portrait plaque, high relief, 30 x 50 in. St. Jose, California. Set in Memorial Panel, Paul P. Cret, architect.

1913   *Dr. John Herr Musser*, portrait plaque, low relief, 32 x 26 in. University Hospital, Philadelphia.
Wisconsin Plaque, 1 x 2 in., awarded to athletes at University of Wisconsin.
Dr. Horatio R. Storer, portrait plaque, 12 x 17 in. Reduction, 3 in., Surgeon-General's Library, New York Numismatic Society, Harvard and private collections.
Clarence S. Bayne, portrait plaque, 20 x 40 in., set in the wall of the Gymnasium facing Franklin Field, University of Pennsylvania.

1914   *Fencers' Club of Philadelphia*, medal, 4 in.
Dr. John Herr Musser, medallion, 12 in.; Outdoor Department, University of Pennsylvania Hospital, Philadelphia.
Franklin Institute, Medal of Honour, 3 in., awarded for distinguished service to science.
Dr. John Bonsall Porter, portrait plaque, 12 x 16 in. Owned by John Bonsall Porter.
The Youthful Franklin (1910-1914), 8-foot high statue; University of Pennsylvania campus; pedestal by Paul P. Cret.
The Boy Scout, statuette, 1/4 life size; ten copies issued. Owned by Sir Robert Baden-Powell, the late Marshal Foch, and members of the Philadelphia Scout Council, to whom the copyright was presented.

1915   *Honourable Thomas Ryburn Buchanan*, portrait plaque, 18 x 32 in., low relief. Owned by Mrs. Thomas Ryburn Buchanan.
Crawford C. Madeira, portrait plaque 12 x 16 in., low relief. Owned by Louis C. Madeira.

1916   *Intercollegiate Conference Athletic Association Medal*, 3 in., for scholarship and athletic prowess.

1917   *Intercollegiate Conference Athletic Association Medal*, 3 in., for track and field sports.
Lieutenant Hector MacQuarrie, R. C. A., sketch portrait, 12 x 17 in. Owned by R. Tait McKenzie.
Sir Robert Jones, K. B. E., portrait plaque, 12 x 15 in. Reduction, 5 x 7 in. Owned by Sir Robert Jones and R. Tait McKenzie.
Sir Wilfred Grenfell, K. C. M. G., medallion, 8 in. Owned by Sir Wilfred Grenfell.
Philip S. Collins, sketch bust, under life size, for Red Cross. Owned by Philip S. Collins.

1918   *Luther Halsey Gulick*, memorial medallion, 22 in,; Gulick Camp, Sebago, Maine.
Mrs. Nicholas Biddle, portrait bust, life size. Owned by Mrs. J. Bertram Lippincott.
Over the Top, sketch for proposed war memorial.

1919   *The Fountain of the Laughing Children*. Erected in memory of Rosamond Junken Mallery, Athletic Playground, Philadelphia
The Flying Sphere, statuette, 1/4 life size; Art Museum, St. Louis, Mo.
Joseph Pennell, sketch plaque, 12 x 16 in. Owned by Mrs. Joseph Pennell.
John McLure Hamilton, medallion, 12 in. Owned by John McLure Hamilton and R. Tait McKenzie.
Fred G. Mories, sketch, medallion, 10 in. Owned by R. Tait McKenzie.
Walt Whitman, cast medal, 5 in. Issued by Franklin Inn Club.
Boy Scouts Memorial, plaque, 18 x 36 in.; Scout Council, Philadelphia.
Altar of Dedication, 30 x 72 in. Memorial to Captain Howard C. McCall, Church

of the Saviour, 39th St., Philadelphia.

Captain Guy Drummond, statuette, 1/2 life size; Archives, Ottawa, Canada.

Blighty, statuette, 1/4 life size, showing a Seaforth Highlander; H. M. the King's collection, Balmoral Castle, Scotland.

Dr. George Whitefield (1913-1919), eight-foot statue; Dormitory Triangle, University of Pennsylvania Pedestal by John Harbeson.

Grotesques, door knocker, candlesticks. Owned by R. Tait McKenzie.

1920   *Edward Longstreth Medal of Merit*, Franklin Institute, Philadelphia.

Elizabeth Butler Kirkbride, medallion, Kirkbride School, Philadelphia.

Sir Arthur Shipley, G. C. B. E., portrait medallion, 12 in.; Christ's College, Cambridge.

Honourable Christopher G.H. Benson, medallion, 10 in. Owned by Lord Charnwood, London.

The Aviator, statuette, 1/2 life size, of Lieutenant Norton Downes, St. Paul's School, Concord, Vermont.

Intercollegiate Winter Sports Union Plaque.

1921   *Sara Yorke Stevenson*, plaque, 12 x 16 in.; Pennsylvania Museum, Philadelphia.

Lenape Club, medal (cast), 6 in.; Lenape Club.

Philadelphia Sketch Club Medal (cast) 4 in.; Philadelphia Sketch Club.

William James Young, medallion, 12 in. Reduction, 3 in. General Palmer E. Pierce, New York.

John Kendrick Bangs, 8 in., sketch medallion. Owned by Mrs. John Kendrick Bangs.

Pelham Edgar, 8 in.. sketch medallion. Owned by Pelham Edgar.

Frances Pizzi, 8 in. sketch medallion. Owned by R. Tait McKenzie.

Achilles Club Medal, 12 in. Reduced, 1 1/2 in. London.

Lord Seaforth, portrait plaque, 12 x 16 in. Owned by Lady Seaforth, Brahan Castle, Ross-shire.

The Marquis of Aberdeen and Temair, portrait plaque, 12 x 16 in.; Haddo House, Scotland.

Pan, fountain head with spouting mouth; Dr. John L. Todd, Montreal; Dr. Charles Wharton Stork, Philadelphia.

1922   *Dr. J. Wm. White*, medallion, 12 in., set in fountain wall, Rittenhouse Square, Philadelphia.

Grotesque Knife Rests, 2.

Paperknife.

Why not? 1.

Why not? 2.

American Legion Medal, school award for boys, 2 in.

The Home-coming (1920-1922), monument to the men of Cambridge, England. Unveiled by Duke of York, July 3rd, 1922.

Radnor Memorial, "*Over the top,*" bronze panel, 44 x 65 in., in mezzo relief, St. David's Pennsylvania, architect, Adams.

Viscountess Folkestone, medallion, 10 in. Owned by Viscount Folkestone.

1923   *Joseph Trimble Rothrock*, medallion, 12 in., for memorial in State House, Harrisburg, Pennsylvania.

Grant Mitchell, actor, 12 in. J. G. M., R. T. M.

Alexander Wilson, naturalist, 12 in. medallion for Memorial Museum of Natural History, Philadelphia.

William Cooper Procter, plaque, 24 x 40 in.; Procter Hall, Graduate School, Princeton, New Jersey.
Aesculapius, medal, cast 3 in., founded by Dr. Edward Krumbahr for research, University of Pennsylvania.
Luther Halsey Gulick Memorial Medal, 2 1/2 in. Owned by New York Physical Education Society.
Memorial Tablet to Samuel Chew, 18 x 48 in., marble; Old St. Peter's Church, Philadelphia.
Sir William Osler, medallion, 36 in.; Johns Hopkins Hospital; re study for Medical Library, McGill University.
The Javelin Cast, statuette, 1/4 life size. Collection of Lord Broughton.
The Volunteer, statue, 8 ft.; Rosamond War Memorial, Almonte, Ontario, Canada. John Harbeson, architect.
Henry Labarre Jayne, tablet bronze, 24 x 36 in.; American Philosophic Society, Philadelphia.
Lieut.-Col. George Harold Baker Memorial, 7 ft.; Lobby of House of Commons, Parliament Buildings, Ottawa Canada. John Pearson, Architect.
Pole Vaulter, statuette, 18 in. high. Collection of Clifford M. Swan.

1925   *John Cadwalader*, plaque, 12 x 16 in.; Institution for the blind, Overbrook., Pennsylvania.
Relay Carnival Medal, University of Pennsylvania. Three sizes, 18 in., 8 in., and 2 in. Owned by University of Pennsylvania.
American Legion Medal, school award for girls, 2 1/2 in.
Dr. Chevalier Jackson, medallion, 12 in. Owned by C. J. and R. T. M.
Radiance, medallion, 18 in., award for Philadelphia schools; presented by Dr. James Anders.
The Ice Bird, statuette, 1/4 life size. Collection of Lord Broughton.
Wm. Wood Gerhard, 2 in. medal; Philadelphia Pathological Society. Gift of Dr. Arthur Gerhard.
Brothers of the Wind (1921-1925), frieze, eight skaters, 120 x 33 in. Owned by R. Tait McKenzie.
The Chancellor's Medal of Honour, 3 in.; Buffalo University.
The Plunger, statuette, life size; University Club, Boston. Presented by Wm. P. McKenzie.
The Victor, 8 ft. statue, Memorial to the Men of Woodbury, New Jersey; Pedestal by John Harbeson.
Violet Oakley, portrait plaque.

1926   *Sesquicentennial Sports Medal*, 2 in.; Philadelphia.
Dr. Edgar Fabs Smith, 8 ft memorial; Campus of University of Pennsylvania. Horace Trumbahr, architect of pedestal.
The Champion, sketch of Douglas Lowe, 12 in. high.

1927   *Percy D. Haughton Memorial*, portrait plaque, 32 x 20 in. Two panels showing football plays, 28 x 58 in. H. A. Walker, architect. Soldiers's Field, Cambridge, Massachusetts.
Memorial Tablet; County Medical Society, Philadelphia. Carved in wood. By Boris Blai.
The Call, Scottish-American Memorial (1923-1927), figure 8 ft.; *Recruiting Party*, frieze 25 ft.; Princes Street Gardens, Edinburgh, Scotland. Reginald Fairlie, architect.
The Modern Discus Thrower, 1/2 life size statuette. Collection of E. R. Peacock.

1928   *Christine Wetherill Stevenson Memorial*, Art Alliance, Philadelphia. Portrait plaque with two supporting figures in lunette, 8 x 3 ft., cast in coloured cement.
Ellwood Charles Rutschman, medallion, 34 in.; Fraternity House, Spruce Street, Philadelphia.

1928   *Dean Andrew Fleming West* (1925-1928), memorial, 8 ft.; quadrangle of Graduate School, Princeton University. Pedestal by Cram and Ferguson.
General James Wolfe, working model, 40 in., for statue for Greenwich Royal Park, England. A. S. G. Butler, architect.
Shotputter (The Hop), sketch, 12 in. high.
The Upright Discus Thrower, 12 in. high. Collection of Clifford M. Swan.
The Winner, sketch of sprinter, 12 in. high.
Dudley Allen Sargent, plaque and flagpole frieze, 6 in.; for Sargent Camp, Peterboro, New Haven.
Walter Hampden, medallion, 11 in.; the Players' Club, N.Y.
Roy Helton, medallion 11 in. Owned by Mr. Helton.
Lord Burghley, portrait plaque, 32 x 40 in.; the Marquess of Exeter.

1929   *Roy Helton*, medallion, 12 in.

1930   *Swimming*, medal 1 7/16 in.; ICAA.
Tennis, medal 1 7/16 in.; ICAA.
Fencing, medal 1 7/16 in.; ICAA.
Wrestling, medal 1 7/16 in.; ICAA.
Golf, medal 1 7/16 in., ICAA.
Gymnastics, medal 1 7/16 in., ICAA.
Florence Nightingale - - Saunders, medal 2 1/2 in.; American Nurses Association.
Christopher Hussey, man of letters.

1931   *James Sullivan Memorial*, cast medal 5 in., National Junior Forum.
Ellis Paxon Oberholtzer, American historian.

1932   *United Gas Improvement Co.*, medal 1 1/4 and 3 1/2 inch.
Canadian Confederation Memorial, medal, 60 years.

1933   *Franklin Inn Club*, medal 3 1/4 in.
International Nickel Co. Canadian, medal 3 in.; Canadian Institute of Mining and Metallurgy.

1934   *Three Punters*, Springfield College

1935   *Mercersberg Academy*

1936   *Society of Medalists*, 13th issue.

1937   *Skating Club of New York*, medal.
John Sinnock, medal.

1938   *Amherst College Pratt Pool*, medal
American Association of Anatomists, 50 year medal.
University of Pennsylvania Bicentennial, medal.

Duck on a Rock

5 TO 30 OR MORE PLAYERS

PLAYGROUND; GYMNASIUM

Each player is provided with a stone, called a "duck," about the size of a baseball. A large rock or post is chosen as the duck rock, and twenty-five feet from it a throwing line is drawn. On this duck rock one player places his duck and stands by it as guard. This guard is selected at the outset by all of the players throwing their ducks at the duck rock from the throwing line. The one whose duck falls nearest to the rock becomes the first guard. The other players stand behind the throwing line and take turns in throwing at the guard's duck on the rock with their stones, trying to knock it from the rock. After each throw a player must recover his own duck and run back home beyond the throwing line. Should he be tagged by the guard while trying to do this, he must change places with the guard. The guard may tag him at any time when he is within the throwing line, unless he stands with his foot on his own duck where it first fell. He may stand in this way as long as necessary awaiting an opportunity to run home; but the moment he lifts his duck from the ground, or takes his foot from it, he may be tagged by the guard. Having once lifted his duck to run home with it, a player may not again place it on the ground.

The guard may not tag any player unless his own duck be on the rock.

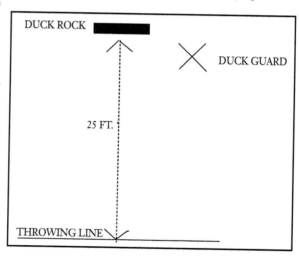

Duck on a Rock

Before he may chase the thrower, he must therefore pick up his own duck and replace it, should it have been knocked off. This replacing gives the thrower an opportunity to recover his own duck and run home; but should the duck not have been displaced from the duck rock, the thrower may have to wait either at a safe distance or with his foot on his own duck if he can get to it, until some other thrower has displaced the duck on the rock, and so engaged the time and attention of the guard. Several players may thus be waiting at once to recover their ducks, some of them near the duck rock with a foot on their ducks others at a distance. Any player tagged by the guard must change places with him, placing his own duck on the rock. The guard must quickly recover his duck and run for the throwing line after tagging a player, as he in turn may be tagged as soon as the new guard has placed his duck on the rock.

A stone that falls very near the duck rock without displacing the duck may also prove disastrous to the thrower. Should a stone fall within a hand span (stretching from finger tip to thumb) of the duck rock without knocking off the duck, the guard challenges the thrower by shouting "Span!" whereupon he proceeds to measure with his hand the distance between the duck rock and the stone. Should the distance be as he surmises, the thrower of the stone has to change places with him, put his own duck on the rock, and become the guard. This rule cultivates expert throwers.

When used in a gymnasium, this game may best be played with bean bags, in which case one bag may be balanced on top of an Indian club for the duck on the rock.

> The modern Greeks play this game with a pile of stones instead of the one rock or stake with the duck on top. The entire pile is then knocked over, and the guard must rebuild the whole before he may tag the other players. These variations make the game possible under varied circumstances, as on a flat beach, or playground where no larger duck rock is available, and add considerable to the sport.

Source: *Games For The Playground, Home, School and Gymnasium,*
        Jessie H. Bancroft, New York: The Macmillan Co. 1917.

Bibliography

Appletons' Cyclopedia of American Biography. New York: D. Appleton and Co., 1887.

Barron, Elizabeth Pitt, "Only Time Will Tell". Mill of Kintail, 1982.

CAHPER Journal, "R. Tait McKenzie Day Observances at the Mill of Kintail. Official Opening Speech in Remembrance of Robert Tait McKenzie." July-August, 1976.

Canada's Sports Hall of Fame, Naismith File.

Cosentino, F., M.Dinning, G. Malszecki, K. Jones, *A History of Physical Education*. Toronto:Captus Press, 1987

Day, James, "Robert Tait McKenzie: Physical Education's Man of the Century." *CAHPER Journal*, April/May, 1967

Dewar, John, "The Life and Professional Contributions of James Naismith". Ed. D. Thesis, Florida State University, 1965.

Encyclopedia Americana, New York: USA Book-Strafford Press Inc. 1953.

Hussey, Christopher, *Tait McKenzie: Sculptor of Youth*. London: County Life, 1929

Gerber, Ellen, *Innovators and Institutions in Physical Education*. Philadelphia Lea and Febiger, 1971.

Gosset, Jean. Operations Manager, The Dr. James Naismith Basketball Foundation, Almonte.

Graburn, Richard, *Robert Tait McKenzie, 1867-1938, Sculptor of Athletes*. Calgary: The Nickle Museum, 1988.

Journal of Health Physical Education and Recreation (JOHPER) Special memorial Issue on Robert Tait McKenzie, February, 1944.

Kozar, Andrew, *Robert Tait McKenzie, 1867-1938, Sculptor of Athletes*. University of Tennessee Press, 1975.

Kozar, Andrew, *The Sport Sculpture of Robert Tait McKenzie*. Champaigne: Human Kinetic Books, 1991.

Leonard, Fred and George Affleck, *A Guide to the History of Physical Education*. Philadelphia: Lea and Febiger, 1947.

McGill. Jean, *The Joy of Effort*. Bewdley: Clay Publishing Co., 1980

McGill University, *McGill News*, Fall, 1992.

Mill of Kintail, Carol Munden, Curator, Almonte, Ontario.

McKenzie, Robert Tait, Biographical notes, University of Pennsylvania Archives, Philadelphia, Pennsylvania.

Mitchelson, Barry, The Evolution of Men's Basketball in Canada, 1892-1936. A Paper presented to the first Canadian symposium on the History of Sport and

Physical Education, University of Alberta. 1970.

Naismith, James, *Basketball: Its Originns and Development.* New York: Associated Press, 1941.

Newspapers: *Globe and Mail*, Montreal *Gazette*, Ottawa *Citizen*, Almonte *Gazette*.

Riley, Douglas, "Art and Athletics: The Work of Robert Tait McKenzie." *Journal of Education*, McGill University, Spring, 1976.

Webb, B. L. *Two Peach Baskets.* Lafayette: Spider Press, 1991.

Webb, B. L. *Basketball Man.* Lawrence: University of Kansas, 1973.

Webb, B.L. *Little Basketball Man.* Lafayette: Spider Press, 1991.

Wise, S.F. and D. Fisher, *Canada's Sporting Heroes.* Don Mills: General Publishing Ltd. 1974.

ABOUT THE AUTHOR

This is Frank Cosentino's eleventh book on Canadian sport. He is a former quarterback in the CFL, having played for ten years, appearing in five Grey Cup games and winning two. He has coached football at York and the University of Western Ontario, where his teams won the Vanier Cup in 1971 and 1974. He has degrees from the University of Western Ontario (HBA 1960), McMaster (BPE 1967) and Alberta (MA 1969, PhD 1973).

Currently a Professor in the School of Physical Education at York University, he and his wife Sheila have four children.

Dr. Donald West has ....ced as a psychiatrist since 1951 specializing in the abnormalities related to criminal behavior, and he is on the staff of the Cambridge University Institute of Criminology. Here, with the same grasp and lucidity that he has shown in earlier books, he tackles in popular terms one of the biggest social problems of the day — crime among the young. The special nature and extent of youthful crime; the backgrounds of the offenders; the latest psychological theories; sex, drugs and violence; penal systems; and "some cautionary afterthoughts" — these are among the headings of his exhaustive survey.

He is cautious about generalizing from official statistics, unwilling to draw parallels between the delinquents of one country and another, and aware of the difficulties of translating successful new advances in treatment into standard institutional practice. It is a wise, dispassionate book which will suggest new perspectives and ideas even to those most closely concerned with the subject.

D. J. WEST

The Young Offender

D. J. WEST

The Young Offender

INTERNATIONAL UNIVERSITIES PRESS, INC.

First published 1967
by International Universities Press, Inc.
239 Park Avenue South, New York, New York

Manufactured in Great Britain

HV
9146
.W4
1967

Contents

12 Some Cautionary Afterthoughts

1 The Youthful Record of Crime

Crime today covers everything from the housewife who shakes her doormat in the street after 8.0 a.m. . . . to the robber who hits an old woman with a length of iron pipe.

Barbara Wootton (quoting Glanville Williams), *Social Science and Social Pathology* (1959). Allen & Unwin. p. 305.

All one really needs to start with is a first approximation sufficient to indicate what one is talking about; the fuller and more exact description should emerge later as the investigation progresses.

T.H.Marshall, *Class, Citizenship and Social Development* (1964). New York, Doubleday. p. 174.

What is meant by the 'young offender'

Defining offenders

The offences committed by young people differ in kind and in motive from the typical crimes of adults. Infants may steal things not knowing this is forbidden, older children may do so because they have not yet learned the self-restraint which normally develops with increasing years, and adolescents may break the law to show off their daring or to annoy their parents. Adults are more often credited with taking calculated risks for the sake of dishonest gains. The relevance of age to culpability and to methods of control is recognized in the statutes of every modern legal system, although the precise chronology differs from one country to another.

In England, criminal responsibility begins at the age of ten. (Before 1964 it used to be eight.) A child of this age is held to be capable of deliberate criminal intent, and liable to legal punishment, but up to the age of seventeen he is dealt with by special juvenile courts and protected from the full rigours of the criminal law. Even after that, and up to the age of twenty-one, the young offender receives some consideration for not having attained full adult status. Recent legislation, not yet in force, envisages that in future persons under twenty-one years of age will not normally be sent to prison, but will serve all custodial sentences separately from adults, in borstal institutions or detention centres.* In this book, the term young offenders covers all who are under twenty-one, which includes juveniles, who are those under seventeen, and children, who are those under fourteen. [91].

Text-books of criminology sometimes begin by emphasizing the limitation of their subject-matter to behaviour defined as criminal by the legal code of the day. Unfortunately nature takes no heed of academic or legal convenience, and to find out about the causes of delinquency one has to go further than court

* Except for re-convictions following release from borstals, or for long sentences of three years or more for serious crimes. Criminal Justice Act, 1961, s.3.

procedures. For instance, one cannot hope to elucidate how absence of a father, or mental dullness, may contribute to delinquent behaviour without also examining fatherless and mentally dull children who do not break the law.

Even where discussion is limited to persons convicted by the courts, it is not so easy to define precisely and comprehensively what is meant by a delinquent, especially in the case of juveniles. The familiar tags – 'a crime is what the law says it is' and 'a criminal is a person convicted of a crime' – are not such infallible guides as the text-books make out. For instance, how does one categorize the condition of being beyond the control of one's parents, or being 'in moral danger', or of failing to attend school – an offence under the Education Act of 1944 for which the parents may be convicted rather than the child? These matters have no parallel in the criminal code relating to adults. Official statistics often simplify matters by equating 'criminal' with 'convicted of an indictable offence' or an offence which would be indictable if committed by a person of seventeen or over.

The predominance of thieves

Generalizations about delinquents are subject to serious limitations. The legal process by which the group is defined produces a strange hotch-potch of characters, including anything from rapists to children who keep running away. Clearly they need to be sub-divided somehow, otherwise the search for common factors and predisposing causes is doomed to failure, and yet a great deal of research and comment refers to delinquency in the abstract, with never a hint that this label covers a multitude of things.

Fortunately, observations about delinquency in general, and statistical trends based upon the sum total of law-breakers, need not be written off completely. Although the Home Office classification of indictable offences lists ninety-nine separate categories, some with as many as twenty to thirty sub-divisions, in practice nearly nine out of ten convictions are for crimes of dishonesty – stealing, burglary or fraud – and among young persons the proportion is even greater. For 1965 the distribution of convictions was as in Table 1.

Table 1. Numbers of persons of all ages found guilty of indictable offences (England and Wales, 1965)*

Offence	Number (in thousands)	Percentage
Larceny	128.6	59
Breaking and entering	44.6	20
Receiving, frauds, false pretences	17.2	8
Violence against the person	15.5	7
Sexual offences	5.5	3
Unclassified	7.0	3
Total	218.4	100

In England (as in all the developed countries) 'crime', roughly speaking, means thieving. The persons who go in for crimes against property may be a somewhat heterogeneous collection of individuals, but at least their activities have something in common, and as a group they differ distinctly from the average of the population in age, sex distribution, social-class membership, and probably in temperament. Among persons convicted of indictable offences, they preponderate to such a degree that their activities determine all the statistical trends of crime, and their characteristics are reflected in all the statistical observations on offenders. And this is true for both young and old offenders. Therefore, when statements are made in this book or elsewhere about delinquents or criminals without further qualification, the reader must remember that to all intents and purposes this means thieves. All other types of offender must be isolated from the general mass and considered separately.

The use of statistics

Much of the raw material of researches into criminal behaviour at any age consists of figures of convictions and re-convictions, figures for the varying incidence of different kinds of crimes as reported by police and courts, and the break-down of these figures according to age, sex or social class of the offender, and the type of punishment or treatment awarded. Although many people interested in the individual criminal's motives find such figures boring, they provide a fund of background information essential to serious discussion.

* *Criminal Statistics, England and Wales, 1965*, Appendix I.

Owing to the difficulties in classifying crimes, in obtaining accurate records set out in comparable form, and in knowing whether all sections of the community have been subjected to the same degree of scrutiny, deductions from official statistics have to be made with great reserve. Whereas the number of officially recorded house-breakings or shootings to kill may give a reasonable picture of the incidence of these crimes, the frequency with which naughty boys are brought to court is likely to reflect the policy of parents, teachers and police in dealing with juvenile misconduct as much as the actual incidence of delinquency. The need for caution in this regard will appear more clearly in the next chapter in relation to actual instances in which figures have proved misleading. Comparisons between one country and another are particularly difficult because numbers of convictions take no account of the vastly different levels of defining, reporting, detecting and recording crimes which exist in different parts of the world.

Apart from the statistical complexities of cross-cultural comparisons, it is probably best, in the first instance, to study delinquency in one particular country (in this case England), since the offences committed and the motives involved are very closely tied to the social setting. It would be nonsensical to compare juvenile law-breakers in the East End of London with the activities of youth in the wild tribes of Borneo, and almost as unwise to equate the delinquency of an American city that has a large Negro and immigrant population and a national tradition of criminal gangs and firearms with the delinquency of an English provincial town, or with the delinquency of a country like Algeria which has recently undergone the upheaval of war and revolution.

The general outlook

The ages of convicted offenders

In England, about fifty per cent of the persons found guilty of indictable offences are in the age range ten to twenty-one, which is more than double the proportion of this age group in the population. (In 1965 approximately twenty per cent of males over ten were under twenty-one – *Criminal Statistics*, Appendix II.)

The incidence of convictions at various ages is shown in Table 2. Among males there is a steep rise in the frequency of convictions from the minimum age of ten years to a peak at fourteen, with a swift dwindling thereafter, so that at twenty-five it is only a half what it was at fourteen, and after sixty it is very small indeed. The trend among females, shown in the same table, is rather similar, and also shows a peak at fourteen, although the decline with age is less swift. The table also shows plainly that boys constitute the main problem in England, as in other countries. At the younger age levels the incidence of convictions of females is only about a tenth that of males. It has been pointed out with justification that troublesome boys go in for crime, whereas troublesome girls merely go with boys. At one time, when the school-leaving age was fourteen, the peak incidence of convictions for both sexes was at age thirteen. Some authorities confidently predict that the peak will occur at age fifteen when the school-leaving age is raised again.

Table 2. Numbers of persons of various ages convicted of indictable offences per thousand of population of the same age (England and Wales, 1965)*

Age	Males	Females
10	6.7	0.5
11	12.5	1.0
12	20.5	2.8
13	27.5	4.2
14	35.4	5.9
15	30.8	5.1
16	26.5	3.8
17	28.2	3.4
18	27.3	2.8
19	26.8	3.0
20	23.9	2.5
21–4	20.2	2.0
25–9	14.3	1.9
30–39	7.8	1.5
40–49	4.2	1.3
50–59	1.9	1.0
60 +	0.7	0.4
All ages	9.7	1.5

* *Criminal Statistics, England and Wales, 1965,* Appendix III (a).

Many people seem to have got the idea that the *Criminal Statistics, England and Wales*, show an ever-increasing proportion of young people among convicted persons, but this is incorrect. The total number of convictions has increased, but even before the war, in the year 1938, the same proportion of convicted offenders, about a half, were under twenty-one. The Home Office *Report of the Committee on Children and Young Persons* (1960, Appendix 1) gives graphs of the numbers per 100,000 of population of males in the age groups eight to thirteen inclusive, fourteen to sixteen inclusive, and seventeen to twenty inclusive who were found guilty of indictable offences in each year since 1938. In each age group, up to 1953, the general trend was towards a rise in incidence year by year, with the groups maintaining roughly the same position relative to each other, the highest incidence being in the fourteen to sixteen age range, the lowest in the seventeen to twenty range. Since 1953, there has been a noticeable change. In the youngest age group, the incidence has increased only slightly. In the other age groups it has increased more sharply, but especially so in the seventeen to twenty group, which now has much the biggest incidence of convictions, even though the actual peak still remains at age fourteen. The significant statistical change in recent years, therefore, has been in the redistribution of offenders within the youthful category, those in the seventeen to twenty range having increased much more than those under fourteen.

'Non-indictable' offences

The practice of dividing the *Criminal Statistics* into indictable crimes and non-indictable offences, the latter being considered in principle less serious and often ignored in discussions on crime trends, has the effect of exaggerating the contribution made by juveniles to the crime problem. The non-indictable offences are in fact more numerous, include some very serious infringements of the social code, and probably have more relevance to the behaviour of the average person than the more dramatic indictable offences. They include common assaults; drunkenness; malicious damage; taking away motor vehicles without the owner's consent; reckless, dangerous, and drunken driving; offences by prostitutes; and two of the largest categories of sexual offences, exhibitionism and homosexual importuning. Compared with their numbers in the population, young people are actually under-represented among those convicted of non-indictable crimes. This is because the enormous numbers of motoring offences which make up the bulk of this category are committed pre-dominantly by adults. Even excluding these, some of the other common offences in the non-indictable category, such as drunkenness or failure to take out licences for dogs, cars or wirelesses, are at least as frequent after twenty-one as before, if only because juveniles, at least, have so little opportunity to commit them.

In an article in *The Times** Michael Power, who was engaged in a survey of juvenile delinquency in east London, made the point that the practice of equating crime with indictable offences may lead to dubious conclusions, since some of the activities of the young which arouse most public concern, such as malicious damage, insulting behaviour, and taking away motor cars, are charged as non-indictable. Whereas younger children are respon-sible for large numbers of minor larcenies, which account for the peak of indictable offences at age fourteen, these other kinds of offences are commoner in youths, and account for the fact that more youths of sixteen than boys of fourteen actually appear before juvenile courts, although not necessarily charged with indictable crimes.

In this book, because of the lack of research studies on non-indictable offences, the usual practice has been followed, and, except where the contrary is stated, 'crimes' and 'convictions' refer to the indictable category only.

The situation in other countries

Although comparisons between the criminal statistics of different countries are open to fallacy, it is worth noting some apparent contrasts in the trends of convictions of young persons reported from a variety of places. In some countries, such as Japan, the United States and Sweden, criminal convictions, and especially convictions of young offenders, have been increasing rapidly ever

* 9 August 1962.

since the end of the last world war. The increase has been particularly noticeable in the more prosperous countries. In other countries, such as England, there has been a decline in convictions of juveniles, either immediately after the war or in the early 1950s, only to be followed by a sharp increase since. In many countries which have recently experienced rapid socio-economic changes (such as West Africa and Latin American states) published statistics suggest that a serious delinquency problem has arisen where it never existed before. In some cases this may be due simply to the introduction of official record keeping; but at least in those under-developed countries undergoing rapid urban growth, social observers confirm the appearance of new forms of delinquency in the new towns [39]. Areas in which delinquency statistics have remained at a negligibly low level seem to be limited to remote agricultural regions and island communities, such as St Helena or some of the Pacific Islands [160; 165].

Exceptions to the general trends are Denmark, where the juvenile delinquency figures have been going down ever since the war, and Italy, where they have also been going down until very recently. Since both these countries have enjoyed increasing prosperity, the association between this factor and rising juvenile crime statistics cannot be invariable.

Cross-cultural studies to discover the nature and possible causes of these different trends might well yield valuable insights; but the difficulty of carrying out such projects, and still more the difficulty of obtaining finance for them, has held back research. In my opinion, it is one of the drawbacks of the way modern social research is organized that the more important and fundamental issues tend to be neglected in favour of easy, short-term projects that satisfy the academic demand for quick results.

The expectation of becoming a criminal

On the fundamental question of how far the increasing volume of youthful crime results from a greater persistence on the part of established offenders, or a wider recruitment of first offenders, the statistics give no immediate answer. Although the number of convictions of young persons has increased dramatically, the high proportion of first offenders among all young persons found guilty has changed only slightly, from seventy-four per cent in 1952 to seventy per cent in 1962. An ingenious calculation by Alan Little of the London School of Economics [156], comparing the statistics of indictable crimes by young persons in the age range eight years up to twenty-one in the years 1952 and 1962, suggests that over this decade twenty-eight per cent of the increase was due to growth of population, forty-two per cent to increased numbers of first offenders, and only thirty per cent to increased recidivism – including recidivism of the additional first offenders. It seems clear that a wider recruitment of new offenders has made the major contribution to the increase in youthful convictions. In a sense this is an optimistic conclusion, since it is the recidivist who represents the real menace, whereas the first offender usually disappears from the statistics after either his initial or his second appearance.

Nevertheless, the stubborn fact remains that these days a very substantial section of the young male population have the experience of being convicted at some time. Taking as a base the statistics of year 1961 for convictions of males aged fourteen to twenty inclusive, and counting convictions for theft, sex offences, violence, drinking and disorderly behaviour (whether classed as indictable or non-indictable), G. Prys Williams [212] has made the following estimate. In England and Wales, of all boys aged fourteen in 1961, 'in the absence of spectacular improvement, about one boy in every five will be convicted before he is twenty-one'. A rather similar estimate, made by Rose and Avison [215], based upon the statistics of 1962, concluded that the risk for males of being convicted for an indictable offence was 12.4 per cent by the eighteenth birthday, and 29.5 per cent for a total life span.

The favourite crimes of youth

The substance of youthful offences

Figure 1, taken from the *Criminal Statistics, 1964*, shows how the convictions of males in different age groups are distributed according to type of (indictable) offence. The under-fourteen group has the highest proportion of convictions for larceny, the

fourteen to sixteen group has the highest proportion of breaking
and entering, the seventeen to twenty group has the highest
proportion of violence, while the twenty-one and over group has
the highest proportions of convictions in the sex and fraud
categories. The picture fits in with the general impression that
young men are responsible for most criminal violence, adolescents
for the cruder types of offences against property involving breaking into premises, and older persons for the more sophisticated
types of dishonesty. It is safe to say that, in England, although
young persons go in for crimes legally classified as serious, notably
breaking and entering, compared with older offenders their scale
of operations is usually more limited, their techniques more
primitive and their organization less professional, especially so
in the case of juveniles.

Former approved-school boys, being mostly recidivists, might
be expected to commit more serious crimes, but a recent follow-
up study of one such group showed that the bulk of the offences
they committed in the three years after release were rather
trivial. Three quarters consisted of minor thefts, traffic offences,
loitering, and similar charges [234]. One boy had been convicted
of the classic offence of cycling without a rear lamp, and another,
who was wearing a studded belt when the police raided a café,
was for this convicted of carrying an offensive weapon. There
were no crimes of violence in which the victim was killed or
detained in hospital, no firearms were carried, and there were no
offences involving narcotics. Only eight per cent of the offences
were distinctly serious, the worst being the rape of an unwilling
girl by a group of boys, and some skilful shop-breaking for
expensive goods.*

Youthful crimes of violence arouse particular concern. An
analysis by Charlotte Banks [13] of the substance of the violent
offences of a sample of over 900 young men under twenty-one
sentenced to imprisonment, detention, or borstal showed that
violence constituted no more than ten per cent of the total of
offences. Among these offences of violence, no more than six
per cent led to serious injury or death. The circumstances of the
offences divided into three groups of roughly equal number:
youngsters brawling among themselves, fights with the police in

* See also p. 26.

Figure 1. Males found guilty of indictable offences in the year 1964, by age and class of offence*

Type of offence	Males under 14 years	Males 14 – 16 years	Males 17 – 20 years	Males of all ages
Miscellaneous	2.4	2.1	3.0	3.2
Sex	0.8	2.2	2.7	3.1
Violence, robbery	1.5	5.4	11.9	8.3
Receiving, frauds	5.3	5.6	5.3	8.0
Breaking and entering	32.9	33.1	25.8	23.5
Larceny	57.1	51.6	51.3	53.9
Total of all offences	100%	100%	100%	100%

* *Criminal Statistics, England and Wales, 1964*, p. xiii.

the course of arrests, and attacks made on others in the course of thefts. In addition there were a few cases of family squabbles. In the bulk of offences the violence consisted of punching or pushing aside, and the injury was trivial or technical.

At the same time one must never lose sight of the fact that, though the majority of young offenders may not commit very serious crimes, a small minority are as dangerous as anyone can ever be, and are responsible for some of the most atrocious and brutal crimes on record. Robbery with violence is most frequent among young men in their late teens or very early twenties. In the case of murder, it is often pointed out that the majority of offenders are over thirty years of age and that most of them are ordinarily law-abiding citizens who have attacked one of their own family under the influence of insanity or severe mental stress. However, among predatory murderers, those who kill strangers in the furtherance of robbery or other crimes, some are boys of sixteen and seventeen, and altogether something like a half are under twenty-one, and a large majority have a previous criminal record [277].

In the female sex, the trends of indictable crime are rather different. For all ages, breaking and entering is unusual, representing only 3.9 per cent of the total convictions of females. Sexual offences are very rare (0.1 per cent), but larceny is particularly common (83.1 per cent). The difference in the distribution of female crimes at different age levels is relatively slight. Soliciting for prostitution is a common type of female offence, but being non-indictable it is not included in the above percentages.

Where the increases have been greatest

In recent years in England, as in most countries, there has been a substantial increase in numbers of convictions, but it has been by no means uniform for all categories of offences. Certain crimes, which are predominantly the work of youthful offenders, have increased more than most. Convictions for breaking and entering, for example, have actually doubled over the last ten years. About the steepest rise of all, however, has been in convictions for drinking offences by juveniles of fourteen to sixteen, both boys and girls, which more than trebled between 1955 and

1962, largely due to the number of reported transgressions of the licensing laws by people under age trying to obtain drinks in public houses.

Convictions for crimes of violence have been increasing for all age groups more rapidly than most crimes, but especially so among youths. In recent years, however, convictions for indictable offences of violence against the person have tended to stabilize as far as the age distribution is concerned, with about fifteen per cent of those convicted in the juvenile age range, and another twenty-seven per cent of young persons over sixteen but under twenty-one.

A significant part of the increase in crimes of violence is only apparent, and due to the policy of charging as indictable offences acts which used to be dealt with as non-indictable common assaults. Between 1938 and 1960 the increase in non-indictable assaults was less than the increase in the size of the population. If, instead of considering, as is customary, convictions for indictable crimes of violence only, the non-indictable convictions are added, then the increase in total incidence of crimes of violence is no more than the general increase for indictable crimes of all kinds [13].

F. H. McClintock [163] made an interesting analysis of the circumstances associated with indictable crimes of violence in London in the years 1950, 1957 and 1960. The annual number of convictions of persons under twenty-one almost trebled from 1950 to 1960, but the types of offence remained much the same. Violent sex offences formed 10.1 per cent of the total in 1950, 13.5 per cent in 1960. Domestic disputes were 11.8 per cent of the total in 1950, 8.3 per cent in 1960. The most noteworthy change was a relative decrease in attacks on the police (from 32.9 per cent to 15.4 per cent) but a corresponding increase in attacks committed in streets, public houses, cafés, etc. (from forty-five per cent to sixty-three per cent). The figures for convictions of adults differed from these most conspicuously in the much larger proportion of attacks arising from family disputes (about forty-one per cent), and the much smaller proportion of attacks occurring in public places. This provides some confirmation of the common observation that violence committed by young persons often takes the form of rowdyism and fighting around cafés, dance-halls and similar resorts frequented by teenagers. In order to see whether preference for this type of violent hooliganism has been increasing more than other kinds, McClintock used data from the years 1950 to 1957 to compare the following categories of indictable crimes of violence: (1) unprovoked attacks; (2) attacks on strangers following some slight dispute; (3) attacks on bystanders who had tried to remonstrate; (4) gang battles. Altogether, these four categories, corresponding to what most people would regard as hooliganism, formed in 1950 27.6 per cent, and in 1957 29.9 per cent, of the violent crimes for which persons under twenty-one were convicted. So during that period, at least, young hooliganism had not increased appreciably more than other types of violence.

Although convictions of young offenders for larceny have not been increasing so rapidly as convictions for drunkenness or violence, nevertheless certain types of theft have shown a particularly sharp increase, notably pilfering from motor vehicles and larceny from shops. These types of theft are the ones likely to be most influenced by the temptations presented by more and more cars without garages, and more and more goods displayed on open shelves in shops and supermarkets. Leslie Wilkins [282] has plotted on a graph the numbers of offences of larceny from motor vehicles in the years 1938 to 1961, and the numbers of private vehicles registered in the same years, and demonstrated a close correlation between the two curves.

The expectations of a delinquent career

The chances of re-conviction

The majority of offenders are never re-convicted after the first time, but, other things being equal, the younger the offender when first he is convicted, the greater the likelihood that he will be re-convicted. Home Office research [132] has shown that of all criminal first offenders only thirty-six per cent are re-convicted within five years, but for children under fourteen years of age the re-conviction rate is fifty-two per cent. The figure decreases sharply with increasing age: for first offenders aged fourteen to twenty years it is forty-two per cent, for those who have reached twenty-one but are still under thirty it is thirty per cent, for those of thirty to thirty-nine it is fifteen per cent, and for those of forty and over it is only nine per cent. Naturally the chances of re-conviction are proportionately greater for offenders who have been previously convicted, but the general rule still holds true that, for any given number of previous convictions, the expected re-conviction rate is greater the younger the offender. For instance, with three previous convictions, the approximate re-conviction rates of national samples are ninety per cent for juvenile offenders, seventy-five per cent for those aged seventeen to twenty-nine, and fifty per cent for those aged thirty and over. Incidentally, the use of a standard five-year period for the calculation of re-conviction rates is justified by the observation that, at all ages, only a small proportion of offenders are re-convicted after a lapse of more than five years free from convictions. Follow-up studies of borstal boys confirm that re-conviction rates are definitely worse for boys first convicted at an early age. In the famous Mannheim and Wilkins study [168] it was forty-six per cent for those first convicted at sixteen or later, but sixty-five per cent for those first convicted at eleven or earlier.

In case these figures present a too gloomy impression of the criminal tendencies of young people, it is only fair to look at the other side of the coin. The fact that the peak age for criminal convictions is fourteen, and that each successive age group thereafter contains a smaller and smaller number of persons convicted for current offences, can only mean that the general trend is towards greater social conformity as the young offender matures. The very young offender, although likely to be re-convicted in the short run, is also very likely to cease being convicted by twenty-one or soon after. In other words, delinquency is typically a youthful characteristic which may be expected to clear up in later years. For example, in a recent search of the criminal records of a group of married men, average age forty-two, living in London, I found that of those with any kind of criminal record only fourteen per cent had convictions both as juveniles and since reaching the age of twenty-one.

A somewhat similar observation was made in a well-known survey of the after-careers of a sample of Glasgow schoolboys which was reported by Ferguson and Cunnison [72]. Of a total sample of 568 males who were followed up to age twenty-two, seventy (or twelve per cent) were convicted before they were eighteen years of age. However, of these seventy, only twelve, or approximately one sixth, were re-convicted during the four years following their eighteenth birthday.

The long-term prospects

A recent study of the subsequent careers of borstal youths, by Gibbens and Prince [88], has shown that even though many of them had large numbers of previous convictions, or had passed through approved schools before coming to borstal, and even though the majority were re-convicted not long after release, still the fact remained that the delinquent careers of these persistent offenders mostly came to an end in their early twenties. Ten years or more after discharge from borstal, only one fifth of the group were persistent serious offenders, convicted for robbery, burglary and similar crimes. Forty-five per cent had had no convictions, or only minor convictions, since discharge. A further fifteen per cent, although re-convicted soon after discharge, had had no further convictions over the last five years or more. Five per cent were persistent petty offenders, mostly associated with alcoholism. The remaining fifteen per cent had sporadic convictions with very long intervals in between, but some of these were probably persistent offenders who had been relatively successful at evading capture.

A rather similar result emerged from the study by P.D. Scott [234], who followed the careers of 149 boys released at ages from fourteen to sixteen from an English approved school. Although sixty-seven per cent had a further court conviction within three years of release, there was clear evidence of some improvement with time. The frequency of convictions for the year following release was only about a third what it had been for the same group of boys during the year preceding their committal to the school. Furthermore, a large majority of the re-convicted boys committed more offences in the first eighteen months than in the second eighteen months of their period of release. The discouraging statistic of sixty-seven per cent re-convictions masks the tendency for delinquent behaviour to decrease with time, even among recidivists. Evidently youthful crime in England, notwithstanding the publicity it attracts, has not reached anything like the level of seriousness or persistency reported in some of the great cities of North America, where narcotic addiction and lethal violence among adolescents are relatively commonplace.

It is in fact the exception rather than the rule for a juvenile offender to become a persistent recidivist. Indeed, really persistent offenders, although they may be held responsible for a high proportion of recorded crimes, are relatively unusual among the population of convicted offenders. In England and Wales, less than two per cent of all adult males found guilty of indictable offences have a record of twenty or more previous convictions. Of all offenders with a previous record, a substantial majority have less than five previous convictions.

Similar findings have been reported elsewhere. Bovet [22], in a report for the World Health Organization, suggested that in most countries only about twenty per cent of those convicted as juveniles are later convicted as adults. Nils Christie [36] in Oslo, who surveyed the records of all males born in Norway in the year 1933, found that by the age of twenty-five, out of a total of 20,000 still alive and in Norway, about a thousand had been convicted of an offence sufficiently serious for their name to have been placed on the Central Criminal Register, but of these only twenty-two per cent had been re-convicted. In this Norwegian survey, as in England and American studies, it was those first convicted at an early age who carried the greatest risk of re-conviction, and in these cases the risk persisted for many years afterwards.

In the United States also, a number of large-scale follow-up studies have shown that only a minority of juvenile delinquents go on to become persistent adult criminals, although the chances of this outcome are higher in that country than in England. William and Joan McCord [164] studied a sample of Boston delinquents. These were boys from a working-class area (average age eleven in 1939) mostly selected by teachers as being potential delinquents, who were enrolled in the Cambridge–Somerville youth project, an experiment designed to test the efficiency of a programme of big-brother guidance in the prevention of delinquency.* Their criminal records were followed up to 1955, when their average age was twenty-seven.

Of the total of 104 convicted at some time during this period for an offence other than traffic violation, sixty-six per cent were convicted by the age of seventeen, a further twenty-four per cent from age eighteen to twenty-two, and only ten per cent were convicted for the first time after twenty-two years of age. Of the ninety-four cases first convicted under twenty-three years of age, three quarters were not re-convicted after attaining that age. The self-limiting character of the delinquent careers of most young offenders was clearly demonstrated.

In the famous studies of Sheldon and Eleanor Glueck [96], who also worked in Boston, the prospects of young delinquents were found to be much worse than this, but they were dealing with more serious cases. Nevertheless they noted the same tendency to reform on growing older. They began with a sample of 1,000 boys from the Boston Juvenile Court during the years 1917 to 1922. Followed up for five years after completion of their penal sentences, only 14.6 per cent were found to have been free from delinquent behaviour during this period. Since the delinquents chosen for the study were those whom the court had referred to the Judge Baker Guidance Center for a report, and since the clinic recommended removal from the parental home of more than half the children, the sample probably included many of the worst types of cases. Although of an average age only thirteen and a half, their average number of previous arrests was over two per boy. In eighty per cent of cases one or other parent was born outside the United States, in seventy-four per cent of the cases both parents were Catholic† (and this in Protestant Boston), and in eighty-six per cent of cases their homes were close to vice spots and in areas infested by gangs.

In spite of the generally unfavourable outlook, continued follow-up over two further periods of five years yielded progressively more encouraging results. After fifteen years the proportion of non-offenders was two and a half times larger, and the proportion of serious offenders smaller by a half, than after the first five years.

* See also pp. 71, 110, 161, 253.
† But see p. 74 for explanations.

Persistent adult offenders are not always juvenile delinquents grown up. A substantial proportion of recidivists start their criminal careers late in life. Of all offenders convicted for the first time for an indictable offence, two fifths are twenty-one years or over. Furthermore, Home Office research on the criminal records of persistent adult offenders, defined as those liable to preventive detention, showed that the majority – fifty-five per cent – had no history of being convicted as a juvenile, and thirty-one per cent were convicted for the first time after reaching twenty-one. The latter figure was the more convincing, since records of convictions as juveniles were not always complete [112].

Research into the personal characteristics of persistent offenders of mature years shows that they are largely recruited from the ranks of the mentally abnormal, being solitary, ineffectual, zestless, and recognizably neurotic personalities [276]. Some of these mental misfits are sadly and consistently wayward from a tender age, but others only take to crime when they reach years of maturity without being ready to meet the demands of adulthood. In either case, the typical adult recidivist has little in common with the typical young offender, whose potentialities are sound even though his energies are temporarily misdirected.

Summing up the situation

Criminal statistics are often quoted in support of the dismal view that crime is increasing all over the world, and that young people are responsible for this. Actually, the picture is more complicated. No one really knows how much of the increase in numbers is due to more diligent reporting and recording. Certainly, most convicted persons are young males, but that is nothing new. The fact that the peak age for convictions is as low as fourteen years and that the incidence gets less and less with increasing age means that for most offenders liability to convictions is a passing phase of youth. The boy who is first convicted at fourteen or earlier is especially likely to be re-convicted shortly, but the boy who goes on to become a persistent recidivist all his life is exceptional in the extreme, and in all probability differently constituted and motivated from the ordinary juvenile delinquent.

The criminal statistics are recording primarily offences of

dishonesty; everything else is in comparison rather unusual. A great deal of the crimes recorded consist of comparatively petty and unimportant incidents. Indeed, it has been a criticism of the way the statistics are presented in England that they allow all the more important matters to be submerged in the sea of petty larcenies.

Most of the offences of juveniles lack the gravity and substance, or the scheming and planning, which the public associates with crime. Even when one examines the crimes of boys from approved schools, many of whom are confirmed recidivists, it appears that their range is mostly limited to minor thefts and traffic offences, and that serious violence, sexual assaults and professionally organized crimes are most uncommon. A somewhat older age group, the late teens and early twenties, includes some of the most dangerously violent offenders in existence, but fortunately they are very rare, and have little in common with the general run of young thieves or sporadic hooligans. The over-all impression left behind from a cursory examination of the statistical trends is that though the numbers are enormous they mostly stand for minor offences. Like an attack of measles, a first conviction in a schoolboy, though it can be serious, does not usually portend a blighted future.

2 The True Extent of Youthful Crime

However valuable a 'virtue' may be as the name of a class of acts, it is
not apparent that it has any widespread concrete existence.
   Hugh Hartshorne, *Character in Human Relations* (1932). New York,
   Scribner.

The crime wave

Today's youth worse than ever?

Ever since statistics began to be kept they have been held to prove the increasing lawlessness of youth. The press and television, echoed all too often in official pronouncements by authorities who should know better, find news value in reports of a wave of crime and hooliganism concentrated among teenagers. Talk of the present 'wave' has been going on for at least twenty years, and yet in the perspective of history the present situation is mild. One is certainly much safer from molestation in the city streets today than a century back, and the recollections of older people tell of rowdyism and drunken violence in the poorer neighbourhoods of English industrial towns to an extent quite unfamiliar in today's tame subtopia.

Every age bemoans the follies of the younger generation. The following words appear in a report on the English scene published in 1818.

The lamentable depravity which, for the last few years, has shown itself so conspicuously amongst the young of both sexes, in the Metropolis and its environs, occasioned the formation of a Society for investigating the causes of the increase of Juvenile Delinquency.

A little further on the increase in juvenile delinquency is described as unprecedented in extent and 'still rapidly and progressively increasing' [221]. Thirty years later, another report, written in response to a prize offer of £100 for the best essay on the topic of the fearful and growing prevalence of Juvenile Depravity and Crime, quoted statistics for England and Wales.

The number of juvenile offenders has gradually and progressively increased. . . . Juveniles, aged 15 and under 20, form not quite one tenth of the population, but they are guilty of nearly one fourth of its crime. . . . The period which shows the blackest, whether we look at the proportionate amount of crime, or its progressive increase, is comprised between 15 and 20 years of age [290].

In point of fact, some real changes in social behaviour, especially delinquent behaviour, are extraordinarily hard to prove. Even according to official statistics, though fashions in crime may change, people are not necessarily in all respects more lawless today than they were in the last century. In 1895, about half a million convictions for all kinds of offences were recorded. In 1962, provided one excludes minor traffic offences (i.e. those dealt with summarily), there were still half a million convictions for all other offences, although in the meantime the size of the population had increased some fifty per cent. In 1895, there were considerably more convictions for drunkenness than there are today. Throughout the last half of the nineteenth century the proportion of the population incarcerated in English prisons was considerably higher than it is now; notwithstanding the fact that since the last war the numbers in prison have doubled.

Are the statistics realistic?

The total of convictions rises inexorably year by year, but this could mean no more than that each year a little more of a virtually limitless reservoir of crimes is tapped off and enshrined in official statistics. The larger and more active the police force concerned with detecting and recording, the more offences come to light. Between the years 1931 and 1932, for instance, a dramatic increase of 222 per cent in the total figure of indictable offences in the London area was brought about by the simple expedient of abolishing the book listing items 'suspected stolen' and entering these instead as 'thefts known to the police' [220]. One of the biggest increases in the juvenile crime statistics followed the passing of the Children and Young Persons Act, 1933, which encouraged people to bring to juvenile courts many children who would previously have been dealt with by unofficial warnings and parental discipline. When the level of unrecorded offences (what criminologists like to call 'the dark figure') greatly exceeds the numbers of known offences, slight changes of policy on the part of the police will produce remarkable fluctuations in the crime statistics. Ben Whitaker [278] in his book on the police quoted the example of male importuning in Manchester, for which there was less than one prosecution per year in the period 1955 to

1958. Then a new chief constable arrived, and prosecutions for this offence over the next four years steadily rose from thirty in 1959 to 216 in 1961.

In the year 1958, just before the introduction in England of severer penalties for soliciting under the Street Offences Act, convictions of girls of seventeen to twenty for offences connected with prostitution rose sharply and actually exceeded for the first time the incidence of convictions of girls for theft. Since then, the frequency of convictions of females for sexual offences has fallen to less than a tenth the incidence of convictions for larceny. Nobody believes that there has really been such an enormous fluctuation in the numbers of practising prostitutes. When the new act was under discussion, and the topic of prostitution was given great publicity, the police were doubtless unusually active in trying to clear the streets, hence the unusual frequency of convictions. Subsequently, the development of the call-girl system and other devices have moved the prostitutes off the pavements, without necessarily abolishing their trade.

Changes in the methods of classifying and recording crimes could make the official statistics more realistic as a measure of crime trends. What is needed is some kind of index of crime, analogous to the cost-of-living index, which could take account of the gravity of the offences committed as well as the total numbers recorded. Separate indexes would probably be needed for major categories, such as personal violence, large-scale thieving, vandalism and sexual offences, since these different forms of behaviour do not necessarily increase or decrease in unison.

A courageous attempt to produce a more realistic index of juvenile crime has been made by two American criminologists, Thorsten Sellin and Marvin Wolfgang [237]. A single criminal exploit, such as a 'job' of house-breaking, was defined as an 'incident'. They based their measures on the number of 'incidents' reported to the police, disregarding the number of different charges to which a single incident may have led, or the number of persons involved. Scores were allocated for each element of damage done in an incident (e.g. injury requiring hospital examination, plus theft of more than $250). The scores were derived by sampling the opinions of relevant groups in the community (e.g. police officers, juvenile-court judges) on the relative seriousness of a range of items of damage. Thus the ultimate criteria of seriousness were subjective opinions, which cannot be expected to remain consistent and unchanging. Even so, the Sellin–Wolfgang scale is probably a better measure of social damage than the total of indictable crimes recorded, the statistic upon which most public discussion is at present based. It has in fact been applied by an English psychiatrist P.D. Scott [234], to demonstrate differences in after-conduct of various groups of boys discharged from an approved school, differences which would not have become so readily apparent by the usual process of counting the numbers of re-convictions.

The use of crime indexes might go a long way towards settling the age-old question to what extent the amount of damage done by delinquent youngsters is really increasing. But the difficulty of compiling accurate and comprehensive records must not be under-estimated. If the value of the goods stolen were to be officially recorded against all convictions for larceny, it would not be sufficient to take the uncontested testimony of victims, especially where insurance claims were pending.

The deterioration in morals

The 'disintegration' of the family

The opinion has got about that community standards in England have deteriorated, that relaxation of the moral, religious and disciplinary precepts of former generations has led to weakening of family ties, to insurbordination and selfishness on the part of the younger generation, and that individual effort, self-reliance and sense of duty have been undermined by undue dependence on a state system to provide financial security. Statistics of divorce, illegitimacy, alcoholism, abortion, venereal disease, suicide and crime are often cited as indexes of this rapid degeneration. The motives behind such comments deserve some scrutiny, for in many instances the statistics do not in fact warrant so gloomy an interpretation [75].

In 1951, 38,382 petitions for divorce were filed in England and Wales. This figure was a considerable increase over previous years, and was undoubtedly the consequence of the financial help provided for the first time by the Legal Aid and Advice Act, 1949. By 1955 the number of petitions had stabilized, and was then 28,314. In 1962 it was 33,818. This increase of divorce petitions has to be viewed against a background of increasing population, increasing popularity of marriage (fewer single people), and increasing duration of marriage (marrying younger and living longer). Viewed in proper perspective, it is by no means certain that the average family is less stable and cohesive than formerly, or that the prevalence of working mothers and busy fathers leads to inadequacies in the care and supervision of children. Social change has on the whole operated in favour of a greater home-centredness among the working masses. Shorter working hours, better housing and an enormous increase in household goods mean greater home comforts than ever before, and more leisure to enjoy them. Break-down of the once rigid attitudes to the respective roles of mothers and fathers means that husbands take a more active interest in home and children, and many a public house has lost custom to the home-based television set and to the fascination of do-it-yourself home maintenance [293]. The modern army of health visitors, N.S.P.C.C. officers, school inquiry officers, care committees, marriage counsellors, child guidance centres, and not least the juvenile courts, who have the power to remove children from inadequate parents and place them in the care of the local authority, combine to protect the young against the gross cruelties, exploitations and neglect which were once so frequently the fate of those born into the large families of the urban poor. The low incidence of nutritional disease, the faster rates of growth and development of the modern child and the enormous diminution in infant mortality indicate a great improvement in the health and happiness of the younger generation which one would expect to increase rather than decrease the chances of a young person attaining mature social and moral standards.

Public and private immorality

J. B. Mays [174] has argued that evidence for a deterioration in moral standards is provided by such things as the increase in thefts from railways, hotels and public institutions; the evasion of regulations, which became so prominent in connexion with rationing and black market transactions in the last war; the spectacle of official denials by government spokesmen rapidly being exposed as lies; and the newspaper accounts of business and political scandals. It may be so, but one has to allow the possibility that an apparent increase of moral lapses may be simply the result of a blaze of attention and publicity, or that a real increase in petty thefts may be the result of exposing the same moderately dishonest public to more and more unguarded property.

A. Grimble [107], a venereologist from Guy's Hospital, London, has pointed out that increases in illegitimacy or in sexually transmitted infections do not necessarily support the common assumption that thoughtless youths have become suddenly more promiscuous. A revulsion against shot-gun weddings could produce more illegitimate births. Morally neutral causes, such as changes in the sensitivity of infecting organisms to antibiotics, are too easily forgotten. Guy's Hospital statistics showed that the proportion of males with venereal infections who were under twenty years old actually decreased between 1932 and 1962. Over the country as a whole, however, recent statistics show the increase most marked in the fifteen to nineteen age group. The percentage increase among girls of this age has been five times that among the boys [192].

The supposed sexual laxity and promiscuity of the average teenager, which has been given so much attention by the press and been used as a pointer to the deterioration of moral standards generally, received no confirmation whatever from a careful survey of the sexual behaviour of young people under twenty years carried out in England under the auspices of the National Council for Health Education. In fact, about two thirds of boys aged nineteen and three quarters of the girls of that age were found to be without experience of sexual intercourse. Only a small minority could be called promiscuous. Of all those in the sample of under-twenties who had had any experience of sexual intercourse, not more than a quarter of boys and less than five per cent of girls had had more than ten different sexual partners in their life, and only three per cent of the sexually experienced boys had been with prostitutes [228].

There is no factual reason to assume that changes in public sexual morality have any relevance to the incidence of dishonesty in young people. However, as a supposed worsening in the one respect is sometimes used to explain a supposed worsening in the other, it is worth pointing out that in neither case does the evidence establish any such alarming degree of deterioration as one might gather from the contentions of moral jeremiads.

The extent of unrecorded delinquency

Everyone admits to some delinquency

A good deal of evidence points to the conclusion that delinquent behaviour has always been more or less universal, and that most of the young offenders who come before the courts differ from the rest of the population only in the accidental misfortune that they have been caught and prosecuted and their activities subjected to public scrutiny. If so, belief in an unprecedented wave of criminality among modern youth becomes all the more difficult to sustain.

J. B. Mays [173], in a study of juvenile behaviour in a slum district in Liverpool, suggested that the average lad from a bad neighbourhood participates in delinquent acts because others do so and he dreads to be thought different.* Of eighty youths interviewed, very few gave trustworthy testimony to law-abiding habits. Thirty-four had already been, or were soon after, convicted, but a further twenty-two admitted committing offences for which they never appeared before the courts. They appeared to live the same kind of lives as the boys who were caught, and their offences were similar, namely shop-lifting, larceny from lorries and warehouses, and occasional breaking-in with intent to thieve. Like those who were caught, the majority tended to grow out of their delinquent habits as they passed the age of fourteen. When recalling their juvenile escapades, both the caught and the uncaught offenders described stealing as a natural part of life from which they got some kind of thrill. Most of their exploits were committed in groups, and the sporting and self-proving character of their activities was revealed by the frequency

* See also p. 37.

with which the plunder consisted of articles of no particular
interest to them, which they afterwards threw away. On reading
descriptions of this kind of delinquent-prone community, one
begins to wonder if the minority who are too timid to share the
joys of law-breaking are more likely than the delinquents to be
maladjusted individuals.

Similar impressions have been gained in surveys in different
parts of the world. Kerstin Elmhorn [58] questioned schoolchildren in Stockholm, and found that over a half of all boys
admitted having committed at some time one or more of a list of
specified offences, such as vehicle theft or damage, breaking and
entering, or robbery. In contrast, only 3.5 per cent of the boys
were actually known to the police as offenders. Nils Christie [35]
questioned samples of young men in various parts of Norway,
giving each a crime score according to the frequency and seriousness of their self-confessed infractions. Less than ten per cent
were crime-free with a score of zero, and the crime scores of those
from upper-class homes were as great as those from lower-class
homes.

Similar impressions have been gained in surveys elsewhere.
In the Cambridge–Somerville Youth Study in Massachusetts, in
which a group of potentially delinquent boys came under close
scrutiny by social workers, the number of boys who were known
to have committed offences without being reported to the courts
exceeded the number brought to court. In fact, the number of
violations of a not too serious kind committed by the uncaught
offenders was not much less than the number committed by the
official delinquents, but they committed serious offences less
often [195].

Wallerstein and Wyle [273] submitted a questionnaire to a
cross-section of the New York population asking about law-
breaking, and of 1,698 persons who replied, ninety-one per cent
admitted that they had committed one or more offences after the
age of sixteen for which they might have received penal sentences. Of the men who replied, eighty-nine per cent admitted
to larceny, seventeen per cent to burglary and eleven per cent to
robbery. Results in some ways even more startling were obtained
by Porterfield [210], who questioned students attending college
in Texas about their juvenile misconduct. They all admitted

having committed offences, and furthermore they admitted a
frequency of offences which greatly exceeded the frequency with
which a sample of official juvenile delinquents had been charged
with the same range of offences. Sex offences were especially
prevalent, 24.5 per cent of the male students admitting to in-
decent exposure and 5.5 per cent to attempted rape. Yet hardly
any of the students had ever been before the courts for any
offence except traffic violations.

Those repeatedly convicted are usually the worst offenders

Short and Nye [244] administered an anonymous questionnaire
to 3,000 adolescents attending American high schools, and to a
group of official delinquents attending a penal training school. On
the whole, larger percentages of the training-school inmates than
of high-school boys admitted having committed each of the
forms of misconduct specified. Thus ninety-two per cent of the
official delinquents admitted having stolen small items worth less
than two dollars, compared with sixty-one per cent of the high-
school boys. Many more of the official delinquents admitted
really serious offences. Thus sixty-eight per cent admitted robbery by force, compared with only six per cent of the high-school
boys. On the other hand, as in Porterfield's study, a large number
of sexual offences were admitted by the ordinary population.
Approximately the same proportion of both groups, eleven per
cent, admitted to homosexual relations other than masturbation.
Over half the high-school boys admitted to malicious damage to
property. On a scale of delinquent behaviour constructed from
their responses, there was a definite overlap, the worst fourteen
per cent of high-school boys producing scores indicative of worse
behaviour than the best fourteen per cent of the penal-school
inmates.

In some more recent American research in which 180 youths
aged fifteen to seventeen inclusive were interviewed confiden-
tially about their offences, Erickson [62] found that a group of
fifty boys who had never been before a court admitted a tremendous number of offences, ninety-nine per cent of which had
never been detected or at least never acted upon. Nearly all of the
officially 'non-delinquent' had been involved in relatively minor

offences, such as gambling and petty theft, and forty-six per cent of them had committed more serious offences such as breaking and entering, automobile theft, forgery and narcotic violations. In both the frequency of offences and the proportion of boys who engaged in them the officially 'non-delinquent' closely resembled the group of thirty boys who had been convicted only once. A group of one hundred recidivist offenders (fifty on probation and fifty in an institution), however, admitted to something like a ten times higher frequency of violation of the law than the officially non-delinquent, and in the range of more serious offences the difference was even more extreme. It was not that a higher proportion of their offences were detected and punished, but rather that they committed them so very persistently that penal action was inevitable.

These findings must be treated with caution, since one cannot place too much reliance on the accuracy and consistency of self-reporting of delinquency.* Nevertheless, they strongly suggest that the conventional division between delinquent and non-delinquent is misleading when applied to adolescent boys, for delinquent behaviour is a matter of degree, and many of those who come to court, especially first offenders, are no different in their behaviour from the majority of the so-called non-delinquents. In a statistical sense, a certain amount of delinquent misconduct is a normal feature of youth. It is the minority who keep getting brought back to court whose behaviour is significantly more criminal than their neighbours', and who may be suspected of being in some way different or abnormal.

Honesty non-existent?

Tests for dishonesty

The investigations so far mentioned were all dependent upon self-reporting, although of course each investigation included some check on the truthfulness of responses. For example Short and Nye included some buffer items to which the correct answer was already known to be 'yes' for the great majority of persons who answer truthfully. If a particular subject answered 'no' to

* See p. 60.

several of these items, this indicated that he was probably a pious fraud. Then again, if a particular group of subjects, all members of one school class for example, produce scores very different from the rest of the population, one suspects some deception. Nevertheless, any systematic tendency on the part of all young people to exaggerate or to minimize their delinquencies, which might be either a deliberate or an unconscious tendency, would be difficult to detect and allow for by these methods of indirect inquiry. Actual observation of behaviour in delinquency-inducing situations presents a more immediately convincing, and in many ways a more informative, method of studying the delinquent potential of normal people. The method makes great demands on the skill and ingenuity of the investigator, who has to contrive suitable situations and means of observing subjects without letting them know what is happening. The most important series of experiments of this kind were conducted many years ago by Hartshorne and May [115], who applied classroom tests to 8,000 American youngsters attending state and private schools and ranging in age from nine to eighteen years inclusive.

The observations of Hartshorne and May covered the forms of dishonesty which underlie the bulk of indictable crime, namely stealing, lying and cheating. They used a great variety of test situations, but one or two examples must suffice. In the magic square test the subjects were given a box containing a collection of coins of different denominations. The ostensible task was to fit coins into the circular slots which were of appropriately different sizes, so as to make the rows and columns all add up to the same figure. This gave the children the opportunity to pocket some surplus coins. The puzzle boxes were later returned to a pile with no obvious means of seeing which had been used by a particular child. The number of excess coins retained by each subject provided the measure of stealing in that situation. Cheating was measured by allowing the subjects to report their supposed scores in various tests, under circumstances in which the investigator had secret means of knowing what were the subjects' true results. Sometimes prizes were offered for particular levels of achievement. The dynamometer test of strength of grip made use of the fact that a sharp fatigue effect causes a loss

of force after a few quick repetitions of the squeeze. The subjects
were therefore given several practice trials under supervision,
during which the experimenter observed unobtrusively the
maximum figure reached on the dynamometer dial. They were
then required to try hard on their own and record their highest
score, while the experimenter placed himself so that the dial was
outside his view. Those who reported substantially higher scores
than in the practice trials were cheats.

Situation counts for more than character

The conclusions to be drawn from this research were important,
unexpected, and most revealing as to the origins of dishonesty.
The popular assumptions that young people can be divided into
groups of honest and dishonest types, that honest types will
remain so in all situations, that honesty will increase with age, or
that honesty is correlated with acceptance of moral principles on
a verbal level were shown to be almost completely mistaken. The
most striking conclusion that emerged was that dishonest behaviour was much more closely linked to the situation in which
the juvenile found himself than to any characteristic of the child
as an individual. Thus, the percentage of cheaters ranged from
five to ninety-five or more according to which school or which
classroom was under consideration. Whereas a fair degree of
constancy was found in an individual's cheating habits in some
very specific situation, say mis-reporting of scores on an arithmetic test, or stealing money during a party game, it was not
necessarily the same people who behaved dishonestly in these
different situations. Few youngsters were honest in all of
the situations investigated, and few cheated under all circumstances, the majority were moderately dishonest, that is prepared
to be dishonest in some situations but not in others. There was
no such thing as a fundamental trait of honesty manifest in all
situations.

Since no trait of general honesty could be identified, there was
no invariable rule about girls or older children or upper-class
children being relatively more honest. There was a slight over-all
tendency for older children to cheat more than younger ones, but
the frequency of stealing by older and younger children was

about the same in the situations tested. The influence of the group in which the child was placed, and in particular the relations between the class members and their teacher, was greater than the difference between individuals. Impersonal and authoritarian teachers provoked the most cheating.

It seemed a little surprising, in view of the reputation enjoyed by girls for better decorum, greater social conformity and less delinquency, that no consistent differences occurred in the amount of dishonesty by boys and girls. Indeed, in word tests which the children were allowed to complete at home, after receiving instructions not to use a dictionary or to seek advice, girls cheated much more than boys. The investigators thought that the probable explanation lay in the stronger motivation of girls to do well at school, hence their willingness to take the trouble to look up the answers, whereas the boys, on account of their relative unconcern about formal scholastic requirements, could not be bothered with the effort involved in cheating in this type of test. Such comparisons suggest that outward respectability, which girls adhere to more than boys, may in some circumstances go together with an increased tendency towards secret delinquencies, stimulated by the need to keep up appearances. In those tests of lying which were based upon the tendency to answer personal questions with an implausible number of claims to virtuous behaviour, girls scored more highly than boys.

The investigators also looked into the question to what extent honest, law-abiding behaviour reflects the youngster's degree of understanding of the moral precepts and codes of adult society. They applied tests to various samples of schoolchildren who had been subjected to special moral instruction, but found no improvement in honesty. In one school, which had optional membership of an organization for encouraging truthfulness and other virtues, boys who joined were more dishonest than those who did not, and the longer they remained in the honesty-promoting scheme the more dishonest they became in practice. Possibly the system failed because it rewarded those prepared to make hypocritical protestations of virtue and discouraged those who cared most for the genuine article. Increasing age, which one assumes corresponds with an advance in social and moral understanding, was not accompanied by generally improved honesty. Clearly, neither familiarity with moral principles nor willingness to profess adherence to them, were effective in promoting honest behaviour.

Is there a specially wicked minority?

The conclusion that most people's dishonest behaviour is largely specific to the situation in hand must not be taken to mean that general trends towards honesty or dishonesty do not occur in some unusual individuals. In fact, Hartshorne and May's own later analyses of integration of behaviour [116] showed that some individuals could be identified who were both unusually honest and unusually consistent in their reactions, and these individuals were also above the average in at least three respects in which delinquents are said to be below average, namely emotional stability, persistence, and resistance to suggestion. Conversely, although the trait of dishonesty was less readily discernible, since consistency was so conspicuously lacking in tests of lying and cheating, in so far as it was possible to identify a minority of children who displayed dishonest behaviour in unusually high frequency in a variety of situations, this group showed just those characteristics that have been repeatedly quoted in connexion with juvenile delinquents seen in remand homes and institutions. These included scholastic backwardness, emotional instability (as indicated by a psychological test), suggestibility, keeping company with other dishonest youngsters, membership of the lower classes (i.e. children of labourers, or others earning small wages) and unfortunate home circumstances (e.g. family discord, poor discipline, neglectful parents, or parents giving a bad example in themselves). Youngsters with an undue share of these handicaps were particularly prone to dishonesty. These findings suggest that the minority of habitually dishonest youngsters have much in common with the habitual delinquents who comprise the bulk of inmates of penal institutions. On the other hand, the majority of dishonest acts, and presumably also the majority of delinquent acts, are the work of more or less normal individuals who break the rules now and then when opportunity arises or occasion demands.

3 The Social Background of Offenders

Crime belongs exclusively to the lower orders. I don't blame them in the smallest degree. I should fancy that crime is to them what art is to us, simply a method of procuring extraordinary sensations.

The opinion of 'Lord Henry' in *The Picture of Dorian Gray*, by Oscar Wilde (1891).

Il était indulgent pour les femmes et les pauvres sur qui pèse le poids de la société humaine. Il disait: – Les fautes des femmes, des enfants, des serviteurs, des faibles, des indigents et des ignorants sont la faute des maris, des pères, des maîtres, des forts, des riches et des savants.

The attitude of the good bishop in *Les Misérables*, by Victor Hugo (1862). Chapter 1.

Every true man's apparel fits your thief.

The hangman's comment in *Measure for Measure*, by Shakespeare. IV. 2.

Criminals as creatures of circumstance

The response to opportunity and temptation

The sociologist seeks explanations of behaviour in terms of the situation in which a person is placed. The psychologist is more interested in the variations of personality which make individuals respond differently. In real life, the complex interaction between person and situation hardly permits a separation of the two elements, but in trying to analyse the causes of delinquency it is a useful simplification to think of these aspects one by one, and to consider first the environmental and social determinants.

The close dependence of delinquency upon contingent circumstances, which may sometimes over-ride all considerations of individuality, is a fact too easily lost sight of in discussions centred upon the psychology of the offender. In the last chapter, investigations were quoted to illustrate how widespread, almost universal, is delinquent behaviour, and how a youngster's honesty in various test situations depends more upon opportunity, incentives and traditions than upon individual character. Nevertheless, it is sometimes argued that conscience matures later on in life, and that except for a small minority of deviants, mature adults no longer succumb to temptation. Furthermore, some crimes, like murder, produce such a degree of moral revulsion in the average person that it seems they could be perpetrated only by seriously disturbed individuals. Unfortunately, neither of these propositions carries much conviction in the face of historical and social observations on the proliferation of crime wherever opportunity and temptation combine.

In relatively trivial matters, the high frequency of delinquent acts by ordinary, respectable adults can be to some extent measured in such occurrences as the disappearance of 'souvenirs' from restaurants and public places, the steady drain of small items of consumer goods from factories where work-people take things away, or the substantial losses of stock experienced by shops and supermarkets, or the noise of drinking drivers revving

up their cars outside pubs at closing time. A great many people
are deterred from worse behaviour only by the risk of detection.
Stephen Hurwitz [138], the Danish criminologist, noted the
effect of the deportation of the Danish police by the Germans
from September 1944 to the end of the wartime occupation in
May 1945. During this period, in spite of the establishment of
private security organizations, law enforcement was much impaired, with the result that the numbers of thefts and robberies
notified to insurance companies multiplied remarkably, although,
so far as was known, sex crimes and murders did not significantly
increase. Presumably it would need a more drastic and prolonged
change of circumstances to release serious violence among the
civilized Danes.

More serious effects have been frequently reported following
revolutions and great disasters. During the French revolution in
1789, when effective police protection was removed, Paris became
a centre of attraction for marauding ruffians, who terrorized the
citizens, relieving them of money and possessions on the
slenderest pretext of collecting for the national effort. Worse
still, hordes of casual labourers and vagabonds whose criminal
propensities were normally held in check blossomed into fanatic
murderers and pillagers [147]. Pinatel [206], the French criminologist, quotes a number of examples of this kind, including the
pillage of goods which quickly followed the destruction of central
Hiroshima by atomic bombing. More recently, in November
1965, a black-out from a failure in the electricity supply affected
the whole north-east of the United States. Within minutes,
youths in Harlem were smashing shop windows and looting,
while at a prison near Boston the failure was immediately
followed by a mass riot.*

Political and racial conflicts furnish the most blatant examples
of serious crimes incited by external conditions, but sometimes
less dramatic influences produce a similar result. In England in
the nineteenth century, the system of burial clubs, which insured
against funeral expenses in the event of a death in the family,
became all too popular among the poorer classes. Many infants
met untimely deaths, either from neglect or from actual violence,
at the hands of parents interested in securing the insurance

* *Guardian*, 10 November 1965.

money [119]. At that time dangerous opiates could be procured without restriction, and it was customary to use these to quiet fretful infants, so child murders by these means carried little risk of exposure, especially as the natural mortality of infants was high and inquests on infant deaths were exceptional. The death rate of girls, who were of little potential use to parents, was considerably higher than that of boys. The situation became so notorious that a Select Committee on *Friendly Societies* (1854), after hearing evidence that 'child murder for the sake of burial money prevailed to a fearful extent',* recommended that no burial money should be paid out in the absence of a medical certificate as to cause of death, and that a limit should be set to the total sum payable for a child's death.

Special circumstances and terrible reactions

Sharp contrasts in the types of conduct found acceptable in different cultures show how much depends upon the accident of a man's place of birth and upbringing. The Moslem's duty to kill a sister who has allowed herself to become pregnant, or the old custom of the Hindu widow allowing herself to be burned to death on her husband's funeral pyre, would be condemned as serious crimes of violence on Western standards. Love-making practices accepted in one country are found revolting or even criminal in another.

Even within the confines of a single more or less unified culture, namely that of the contemporary Western world, the worst crimes of all, those which many people would regard as beyond the scope of any normal person, do in fact take place with awe-inspiring frequency in special circumstances. The sanctioned killing of enemies in wartime is too commonplace a reversal of behaviour to strike the imagination, but the tortures and mass exterminations of Jews in Nazi concentration camps, to which activity many socially conforming and respectable persons contributed, still act as a chilling reminder of our latent propensities. The belated trials of some of these concentration-camp killers, arrested after twenty years of useful and respected family life in their communities, proves the social normality of many such

* Minutes of Evidence, 1045.

criminals. Likewise, Nils Christie's investigation of concentration-camp guards in Norway suggested that their inhuman
attitudes to their charges were a product of the special situation,
and not the reflection of a generalized lack of feeling. Similarly,
there is no reason to suppose that the supporters of cruel
apartheid policies in South Africa, however 'criminal' they may
appear to democratic observers, are in any way abnormal or
defective in social conscience in other respects.

The idea of a natural reservoir of anti-social energy forms the
theme of William Golding's imaginative novel *Lord of the Flies*.
It describes how a band of respectably reared British schoolboys,
stranded on an island, quickly regress from democratic orderliness to rampant barbarity and tyranny. In reality, children's
reactions to extreme neglect prove how dependent is law-abiding
behaviour upon consistent social training and control. A great
proportion of crime a hundred years ago was the work of bands
of homeless waifs who roamed the streets of industrial Europe
and America. Sutherland and Cressey [258] refer to 'Arab street
boys' of New York, forlorn offspring of drunken or vanished
parents, who banded together to save themselves and to prey
upon the community that had thrown them out. In the more
highly developed countries today, the floating population of
homeless children from which these gangs were recruited no
longer exists. It takes war or national disaster to create a
comparable situation. In the aftermath of the atomic destruction of Hiroshima, vividly described by Robert Jungk [144],
orphaned and abandoned children ran wild in gangs, learned
to live by their wits amidst the general chaos, and were ultimately persuaded back into civilized community only with
difficulty.

Experimental demonstrations of the release of criminal behaviour in normal subjects are understandably difficult to set up.
Stanley Milgram [179] of the Harvard Department of Social
Relations came close to succeeding in some tests of obedience.
Unsuspecting volunteers were told by an authoritative experimenter to administer to a fellow volunteer (actually an accom-
plice of the experimenter) electric shocks of increasing severity
every time he made a mistake in a learning task. The supposed
shock apparatus bore horrific labels ranging up to 'danger,

severe shock'. In some of these experiments the subjects could
hear from the adjacent room, where the victim sat in an 'electri-
fied' chair, cries of protests (actually tape-recorded). In other
experiments there was no audible voice but at 300 volts the
victim pounded on the wall, and then fell ominously silent. In
the stiffest test of all, subject and victim were together, and the
subject had to force the victim's hand on to the electric plate
when the voltage reached a level at which, apparently, the victim
could not bear to maintain the contact voluntarily. The proportion of subjects who obeyed the experimenter completely,
working up to maximum shocks, varied from thirty per cent
to sixty-six per cent, according to the conditions imposed.
The setting must have seemed frighteningly realistic, judging
by the sweating and trembling and anxious comments of the
volunteers, but they still continued to give painful and possibly
dangerous punishment to an unwilling and protesting stranger.
The experimenter's conclusion, that a relatively mild form of
authoritative persuasion suffices to overcome the scruples of
many normal adults, has implications at once frightening and
humbling.

Low social class

How many delinquents come from low-class homes?

Granted that we are all potential delinquents, what are the factors
liable to bring it out? Two of the most important, namely age
and sex, have been described in the first chapter, when it was
explained that the great majority of thieving and violence is the
handiwork of boys and young men. Other important factors are
low status in the social-class system, educational deficiency,
poverty, inadequate or broken home backgrounds, residence in a
bad neighbourhood, and belonging to a large family.

Although the links between these factors and delinquent
behaviour must be known to all, it is perhaps worthwhile, before
discussing the theories put forward to explain them, to give some
examples to illustrate how close are the associations revealed by
some research surveys. The matter is complicated, of course,
because the factors are not independent of each other. Thus,

among families of low occupational status, many reside in slums, do not limit the number of children they produce, and suffer from poverty and lack of education. In other words, adverse factors tend to occur in clusters and to interact to make a very potent crime-producing situation.

In England, social-class membership can be gauged in a rough and ready manner from one's occupation (or father's occupation in the case of young people), which may be placed into one of five groups according to the Registrar General's classification. The lowest, Class V, comprises unskilled manual workers and casual labourers. The solid middle-class occupations, like doctors, teachers and businessmen, belong to Classes I and II. Classes III and IV comprise the bulk of workers, the distinction being between skilled and semi-skilled respectively. This system of ranking goes more by the prestige of one's job than the level of earnings, although, of course, the two are highly correlated.

All investigators are agreed that persons from the lowest social class are over-represented, and persons from the middle classes under-represented, in samples of delinquents brought to justice, but the true extent of the class bias is not yet clear. Little and Ntsekhe [157] found that among 381 boys in a London remand home in 1957, twenty per cent came from Class V, approximately double the proportion in which this class occurs in the London population. Only 7.5 per cent came from Class I or II, less than half the proportion of these classes in the London population. In other words, the lower-working-class boy had at least four times as great a chance of being found delinquent as the middle-class boy. A similar, but slightly more extreme, trend was recorded by Gibbens [83], from a sample of London youths who were serving sentences of borstal training in 1953 and 1955. Of fathers with classifiable occupations, twenty-six per cent fell into Class V. In an earlier study A. Gordon Rose found that forty per cent of borstal youths who were released during the last war had fathers in unskilled occupations [223].

Differences considerably more extreme have been reported in other studies. Terence Morris [188], in a well-known survey in Croydon, found none at all from Classes I and II in a small sample of seventy-nine juvenile delinquents, and a great excess from Class V. In a study of juveniles before London courts in 1952 Mannheim and others [167] found about half came from Class V. Possibly the class bias of young offenders has become less extreme in recent years. Certainly the increasing number of young people brought before the courts means that whatever their relative proportions there must be substantial numbers from all classes. Even on Little's figures, which are already out of date, it appears that the majority of delinquents originate in the average working-class home which makes up the bulk of the population.

Grading people according to the nature of their job gives no more than a rough indication of the whole complex of attributes included in social class. Educational background, family contacts, social aspirations, leisure pursuits, choice of companions, type of upbringing, and the whole style of living and outlook on life are involved in the notion of social class. Any or all of these different things may have an influence upon potential delinquency. Resentment and self-consciousness on the part of those of inferior status is an aspect of social class very much emphasized in contemporary theories of delinquency. One of the ways in which this may operate in the development of juvenile delinquents was shown in a recent study in Flint, Michigan [100]. A sample of recidivist delinquent boys and a control sample of non-delinquents of similar age, race, intelligence and social class (rated on father's employment) were interviewed and questioned about attitudes to their parents. Among the delinquent group, those with fathers in lower-status occupations had less respect for their parents. Fewer of the low-status boys said they would talk to their parents about personal problems, or do things in the company of either parent, and relatively few of them felt that their father's decisions counted for more at home than their mother's, or that they wanted to become the kind of person their father was. This tendency for low-class fathers to be less attractive to and less influential with their sons was also present among non-delinquents, but to a lesser extent. The investigators concluded that parents of low status are at a disadvantage in trying to exert control over their sons, and that this factor aggravates the tendency for their sons to react to social frustrations in a rebellious and delinquent fashion.

The educational retardation of delinquents

Another feature of low social status, namely poor educational attainment, is one of the most prominent and characteristic features of juvenile delinquents. In most cases this does not arise from lack of intelligence, but it may be due to lack of opportunity. Although state education for all has reduced the grosser differences between social classes, the fact remains that dirty and uncouth children from poor-class homes are unpopular with teachers, don't get much encouragement from their parents to do well in school, and often play truant. On the other hand, individual as well as social troubles must also play some part, since the child misfit, whether he be a noisy rebel or an over-anxious conformist, does not concentrate so well or learn so rapidly as his better adjusted colleagues.

Whatever the explanation, the facts are sufficiently striking. Eilenberg [56], in a study of a sample of boys in a London remand home for juvenile delinquents in the year 1955, found that thirty-nine per cent were up to or above the population average on intelligence tests, but only ten per cent were up to or above the average in scholastic attainment. Only twenty per cent were substantially below average in intelligence (I.Q. less than 85), but sixty-four per cent were retarded educationally by three years or more. A similar but rather less extreme trend was recorded by Gibbens [82] in his study of youths in borstals. Only fifteen per cent were substantially below average on an intelligence test (i.e. Grade E, the lower tenth percentile and below on Raven's Matrices Test) but twenty-five to thirty per cent were in the corresponding range of retardation on verbal and spelling tests.

In Ferguson's survey [69] of Glasgow boys (in which he took an unselected sample of 1,349 boys leaving school in January 1947 at the earliest permissible age) poor scholastic performance was very closely associated with likelihood of being convicted, both while still at school and subsequently. Thus, among the ten per cent of school leavers who had the lowest scholastic assessments, the chance of being convicted before the age of eighteen was over five times what it was among the top ten per cent.

Low socio-economic status is not the sole reason for the educational retardation of delinquent groups. When delinquents and non-delinquents were first matched for social class and then compared, as was done in the Flint Youth Study [101], delinquents still appeared worse in scholastic performance. The Flint study also showed that the delinquents' awareness of their poor scholastic showing was accompanied by a depressingly low level of expectations and declared aspirations in regard to their own future employment careers. Thus it would appear that many delinquents show in more extreme form the patterns of discouragement and social alienation which are, in lesser degree, shared by the whole of the lower social classes.

Is the class bias spurious?

Some authorities have challenged the assumption that delinquent behaviour is more prevalent among lower-class youngsters, and explain their over-representation at the courts by the greater liability of the lower classes to be apprehended and brought to justice for misdemeanours which would be otherwise dealt with if committed by middle-class persons. Doubtless private schools are more likely than state schools to discipline their pupils caught stealing without calling in the police, and middle-class parents are more likely to protect their children by making good loss or damage so as to forestall complaints and prosecutions. Perhaps, also, the badly dressed, badly spoken urchin found by the police in equivocal circumstances stands a poor chance of avoiding official arrest. Support for this point of view comes from researches on undetected delinquency. Short and Nye's questionnaire [244], referred to in a previous chapter,* showed that, according to their own self-reporting, American high-school adolescents of differing socio-economic class behaved equally badly. R. L. Akers [5], in a later study of a thousand high-school students in Ohio, confirmed that no significant relationship existed between the incidence of confessed delinquency and socio-economic status as graded by the North-Hatt prestige-ranking scale applied to the father's occupation. E. W. Vaz [265]

* See p. 41.

came to similar conclusions from questioning 1,639 high-school boys in Canada.

The conclusions of these American questionnaire investigations must be treated with some reserve, since innumerable studies of the characteristics of impoverished and socially alienated sectors of the community suggest that these classes have a high incidence of persistent delinquents. While the work of Hartshorne and May, and many others, has demonstrated that occasional delinquency, mostly unrecorded and not very serious, is the rule among normal youngsters of every class, it is possible that real differences between classes occur in respect of boys who commit serious and repeated transgressions. The proportion of boys who have ever committed crimes is of less significance than the quality of the delinquency in different classes. Another complication in interpreting questionnaire findings is the greater verbal fluency, and readier adaptability to interviews and tests, displayed by middle-class children, which may have the effect that they report a larger proportion of their transgressions, and so put themselves in an unfavourable light in comparison with lower-class children who may be less ready to confide. Even though the class bias of apprehended delinquents may be largely a product of selective arrests, this does not invalidate the observation that captive delinquents, who, after all, are the people the penal system must cater for, are preponderantly lower-class.

This argument about the association between delinquency and social class illustrates a difficulty that constantly crops up when research workers try to demonstrate the peculiarities of samples of delinquents. One can range offenders along a scale of increasing seriousness, beginning with those whose activities are known only from confidential questionnaires, to those known only to teachers and parents, to those known to the police, to those brought to court, and finally to those sent to penal establishments. With each succeeding step along this scale, the selection processes tend to pick out the more deviant and troublesome individuals. The ones at the end of the penal line, who are most often sampled by research workers, are by and large extreme cases whose characteristics are likely to be exaggerated compared with those at the beginning.

Financial hardship

Absolute poverty

In considering the role of poverty in producing crime, the state of affairs today hardly compares with the situation in Western Europe in former times, or with the present situation in some undeveloped countries, where a large part of crime consists of thefts of the very necessities of life. In Victorian England sheer want was such an obvious cause of theft that it seemed plausible to expect that relief of poverty would bring about a dramatic reduction in delinquency. The *Second Report of the House of Commons Committee on the State of the Police in the Metropolis,* published in 1817, referred to 'this alarming increase of Juvenile Delinquency' which it was inclined to attribute to 'the existence of poverty and distress, unknown perhaps at any former period to the same extent. But your Committee hope, that with the gradual removal of these causes, their lamentable effect will cease'. The same Report also stated:

The condition of these poor children is of all others the most deplorable; numbers are brought up to thieve as a trade, are driven into the streets every morning, and dare not return home without plunder; others are orphans, or completely abandoned by their parents, who subsist by begging or pilfering, and at night sleep under the sheds, in the streets and in the market places; when in prison no one visits them ... [136].

Other careful observers shared the sentiments of this Committee. The *Fourth Report of the Committee of the Society for the Improvement of Prison Discipline and for the Reformation of Juvenile Offenders,* 1818 [221], referred to a cause of juvenile crime

which every humane mind must contemplate with deep regret and compassion; the strong temptation to dishonesty, which has too frequently of late years prevailed, from a want of the necessaries to support life. ... It not infrequently happens, that boys, committed to gaols for petty offences, are discharged upon the wide world, without any alternative, but plunder or starvation.

In England, in spite of numerous legal and social reforms designed to prevent the exploitation of workers and to protect their children, such was the plight of the urban poor during most of the nineteenth century that a high level of delinquency from want seemed almost inevitable. Worsley [291] described the 'jaded operative, his wife and children returning together from the factory to an unwholesome hovel, in which the very air is pestilential' to find 'his only solace in the delirium consequent upon dram-drinking'. He went on to criticize employers for exposing their child workers to 'a fermenting mass of sin and vice' in the factories, and to trace 'the causes of juvenile depravity' to 'intemperance, as a most prolific source, which ministers to, or originates almost every vice . . .'. Clearly, therefore, Worsley, who saw poverty at its worst, did not regard material want as the only cause of juvenile crime, but emphasized the association of poverty and other factors, such as parental example, and methods of child training and scholastic instruction.

Poverty, in the sense of lack of basic necessities, has undoubtedly been an important concomitant of juvenile delinquency up till quite recently, especially in economically depressed areas. Bagot [12], in a study of juvenile delinquency in Liverpool before the war, found a surprising concentration of serious want among the families of his sample. On the Rowntree Human Needs standard, thirty per cent of Merseyside families were then below the poverty line, compared with 85.7 per cent of the families of delinquents. Taking a more extreme definition of poverty, adapted from previous surveys of Merseyside, more than half of the families of delinquents were seriously poor compared with only sixteen per cent among the Merseyside population. Cyril Burt [26], in a survey in 1923, found that over a half of the juvenile delinquents in London, compared with less than a third of the general London population, came from poor homes. There was a high correlation (.67) between delinquency rate and percentage of poor homes in the various London boroughs.

Relative poverty and temporary unemployment

The general impression today seems to be that the English welfare state has abolished all but limited pockets of physical want, and that what remains is associated with particular groups in the community, such as aged social isolates, problem families incapable of managing on limited incomes, and fatherless families. Such special groups cannot account for the great bulk of young offenders. Indeed, interest in the question of family income in relation to delinquency has fallen to such a low ebb that not much hard data on the topic is available.

Nevertheless, though serious poverty no longer explains the majority of crimes, the influence of financial pressure is still perfectly apparent, even if nowadays the hire-purchase commitments on a motor cycle or a television set may have replaced lack of food as the typical precipitant. Comparisons of fluctuations of economic indices, such as unemployment rates or production figures, with changes in crime rates have revealed distinct correlations. Although there are many exceptions (especially if one considers small areas where local conditions may outweigh national economic changes), the general rule seems to be that crimes against property increase more than usual whenever national prosperity decreases, and this appears to hold true even though the depression may still leave the population comparatively wealthy. Glaser and Rice [93], in an extensive survey over a twenty-five-year period in the United States, found substantial positive correlations between unemployment rates and the rates of convictions of adults for crimes against property. On the other hand, the crime rates of juveniles showed either no such relationship, or else a slight paradoxical trend in the opposite direction, that is less crime during periods of economic depression. It is readily understandable that juveniles should be less directly affected by unemployment than their wage-earning fathers, and furthermore, if it is true that most juvenile offences today arise from youthful exuberance and desire for thrills, it is conceivable that unaccustomed hardship might have a sedative effect.

The effect of financial pressure upon individuals is shown in the work records of offenders, among whom temporary unemployment, and hence temporary shortage of the cash needed to maintain an accustomed style of life, increases the likelihood of criminal behaviour. In a survey of 4,000 borstal youths, Norwood East [54] found that only about thirteen per cent of their working lives was spent in a state of unemployment, which was not appreciably above the average at that period for the general population of young males. At the actual times when their last offences were committed, however, the incidence of unemployment was very high, from forty-five to fifty per cent. The clear inference was that these young men were much more prone to commit offences during periods of unemployment than at other times.

Today it is relative deprivation rather than absolute poverty that provides the stimulus towards crime. Rapid advance by the community as a whole, and the assumption that reasonable material standards should be within everyone's reach may lead to sharper awareness of contrasts between different sectors of the community, and correspondingly greater discontent.

The continued operation of economic pressures tends to be somewhat obscured by the steady increase in crime rates which has accompanied increasing affluence in industrial countries. Many authorities interpret this as cause and effect, since the enormous increase in volume of material goods, and the corresponding increase in the number of property transactions, both legitimate and illegitimate, must have added greatly to the opportunity for and the temptation to criminal activities.* However, a long-term trend towards increasing social wealth, accompanied by a gradual increase in crimes, does not preclude the existence of temporary economic recessions during which offences precipitated by hardship become apparent in unusually steep increases in crime rates. The lower classes are always the hardest hit by temporary increases in unemployment. Moreover, it is the offspring of the lowest classes who experience most acutely the dreary homes, lack of educational stimulus, and other handicaps which cut them off from the benefits of the affluent society. But of course many other matters besides level of earnings enter into these social-class differences.

Bad neighbourhood

In most countries, townspeople contribute more than countrymen to the total crime rate per head of population. England is no exception, although the contrasts are less striking than they once

---

* This interpretation fails to explain why crimes of violence and of sex should also have apparently increased with affluence, but that is another question.

were, probably because of the widespread infiltration of urban development and urban attitudes into rural areas. Thus the county police forces, which cover a more rural population than the various city police forces, record only about two fifths of the total of indictable crimes, although they actually serve about a half of the total population. (This generalization does not, of course, apply to every individual category of crime: certain sex offences, for instance, are substantially commoner in rural areas.)

Within the urban regions, slum districts and densely populated industrial areas contribute most to crime. Clifford Shaw *et al.* [238], in a classic survey of juvenile delinquency rates in various zones within the City of Chicago, was one of the first to document the magnitude of the variations, and to identify the characteristics of the high delinquency neighbourhoods. Dividing the city into concentric zones, it was found that the innermost circle had a delinquency rate more than five times that of the most peripheral zone, with the intermediate zones showing a steady increase as one approached the centre. This curiously regular distribution was no doubt due to the way the city had developed, with the more prosperous families moving out to newer homes on the outskirts, leaving the centrally situated homes dilapidated, cheaply rented, overcrowded, and largely populated by recent immigrants with nowhere better to go.

In England, slum districts inhabited by poverty-stricken families or poor-class coloured immigrants are less sharply delineated than in some American towns, but to some degree a similar situation prevails. Grunhut [108] found that areas with a high rate of juvenile delinquency usually have a high rate of adult crime as well. In spite of social changes, delinquent areas maintained some consistency. He showed that well-known juvenile trouble spots, such as Bootle and Birkenhead, had disproportionately high delinquency rates both before and after the war. Some recent work by Rodney Maliphant on the distribution of offenders in London has shown the persistence of high delinquency rates in the same areas that Cyril Burt had identified as the trouble spots of a previous generation. Areas of high juvenile delinquency rate tend to coincide with areas of overcrowding, poor housing, low rents and few owner-occupiers, and to be accompanied by high rates of illegitimacy, infant mortality, tuberculosis, alcoholism and suicide. Grunhut calculated the delinquency rates for juveniles in different areas of England in the years 1948 to 1950. Oxford City, for example, had double the rate of the predominantly rural Oxford County, and the predominantly working-class industrial town of Swansea had almost double again that of Oxford City. The mean rate for selected industrial areas was 10.8 per thousand, compared with a mean rate of 4.4 for rural areas.

Within the towns themselves, the areas where the majority of juvenile delinquents live can be mapped with some precision. In the desirable residential neighbourhoods, patronized by middle-class professional and clerical workers, the delinquents appear sparse; in the older, poorer and more densely populated regions occupied largely by unskilled labourers, delinquents appear in large numbers. Some local-authority development schemes, where former slum-dwellers are re-housed in modern blocks of flats, appear on maps as black islands in a white sea of sparse delinquency [140]. As T.P.Morris [187] pointed out in a well-known survey of delinquent areas in Croydon, the locations of black spots do not always coincide with the most physically dilapidated areas; some newer housing estates have higher delinquency rates than older and more densely populated central areas.

In some recent research into the court appearances of juveniles in east London, M. Power* has shown that, depending upon which secondary school they attended, anything from three up to twenty per cent of the population of boys aged twelve to fourteen are found guilty in any one year. Furthermore, whereas over the whole survey area about one boy in four was likely to be found guilty at some time before reaching seventeen years of age, in some notable black spots, which were quite narrowly localized, every other boy was likely to achieve a juvenile court record.

These comments apply to areas of residence and are not necessarily true of areas in which the crimes actually take place. Areas of well-stocked shops or warehouses, large transport termini, the dockland region, places of amusement and centres of city night life, are likely to have a high incidence of crimes committed, although the delinquents responsible may have been

* (1966) *Proceedings of the Royal Society of Medicine, 58,* 704–5.

drawn there from living quarters some distance away. On the whole, however, petty crime in one's own neighbourhood, like breaking open next-door's gas meter, is more typical of juveniles than ambitious excursions to residential areas to burgle the houses of the rich.

Race and colour

Racial affiliations have furnished a traditional hunting ground for American criminologists, who regularly discover enormous over-representations of Negroes, Italians, and Puerto-Ricans among their delinquents. Argument then arises on how far this may be due to some intrinsic quality of racial groups or cultures, or how far it simply reflects the under-privileged position of these minorities in the American socio-economic system or the experience of emigration and unsettling changes of habit to which the foreign-born and their offspring have been subjected.

In England, statistical data about race and delinquency are hard to come by, although everyone knows from experience that Jewish families are under-represented and Irish families over-represented among the clients of the juvenile courts. One would have thought that this experience might lead to a proliferation of research; but whether from distaste or discretion, English investigators have mostly fought shy of such topics. None of the three most modern English text-books of criminology [139; 166; 268] quote any investigations into the ethnic affiliations of English delinquents. Some of the findings of American research in this connexion have a special importance, not just because they probably apply to most other countries, to a greater or lesser extent, but because the general conclusions of such research have formed the basis for a good deal of sociological theory about crime causation.

In the United States, the reported crime rates are often ten times as high among Negroes as among whites. In order to find out if the high crime rate of Negroes was associated with their relative poverty, Earl R. Moses [193] carried out a classic sociological survey of contiguous areas in Baltimore inhabited by whites and Negroes respectively. The white and black areas were well matched in regard to age and sex distribution and density of population, size of households, type of housing, and the high proportions of the inhabitants belonging to the lower occupational and educational strata. In other words, on a number of objective social criteria the areas and their people were similar, apart from the matter of race. Nevertheless, the crime rates in the Negro areas were some six times as high as among the corresponding white areas, and crimes of serious violence were particularly common in the Negro areas.

Similar situations arise in connexion with other racial groups. In a study of crimes committed by Arabs in Metropolitan France, C. A. Hirsch [122] estimated that, of the total males in the Seine department in the age range eighteen to fifty years, only ten per cent were North Africans, whereas 15.6 per cent of offences were committed by North Africans. However, the situation varied with the type of crime. Relatively few North Africans committed frauds, false pretences, or offences against morality, whereas many were guilty of violence. Violence in personal relations, especially in avenging insults and marital infidelity, seems to be tolerated in places like Moslem Africa, Puerto Rica, and at one time in Sicily and Southern Italy, rather as motoring offenders are tolerated by the British and American public.

Explaining the statistics

Evidence suggests that the differences between crime rates of different races arise more from their cultural and social background than from any biological peculiarity. Some of the persons officially classed as American Negroes, and sharing the same behaviour patterns, are actually near-white in colour, and biologically closer to European than African stock. Races which are notably law-abiding in a primitive rural setting become rapidly delinquent when they migrate to industrial urban areas, either in their own country or abroad. Immigrant minorities, whatever their race, or whatever part of the world they settle in, are generally vulnerable to delinquency so long as they remain under-privileged minorities. They are also apt to bring with them habits at variance with those of the host country. Sutherland and Cressey [257], in their well-known text-book, quote the U.S. Prisons Report for 1933 showing that among inmates committed for serious violence, men born in Italy were over-represented by eight times their number in the general population. Men born in America but with one or both parents born in Italy were not over-represented, which suggests that fortunately such habits are not necessarily passed on to the next generation.

Although, as Moses [193] showed, the high crime rates of Negroes in America cannot be attributed solely to their immediate economic distress, many other forms of hardship, arising from the American caste system, weigh more heavily upon the Negroes. Segregation in poorer areas of the towns, enforced by custom if not by law, restrictions on range of employment, inferiority in the face of officialdom (revealed in such matters as the smaller proportion of accused Negroes allowed bail, and the heavier penalties awarded if a white person is involved as victim) must all aggravate the Negro's aggressiveness. Negro crime rates vary enormously according to the conditions of the area in which they live. The differences in crime rates between Negroes and whites in the same region are less than the differences between persons of the same race living in contrasting areas like Georgia and New England. L. Savitz [226], in a study of migration of Negroes into a high-delinquency area in Philadelphia, found that local-born Negroes had a higher juvenile delinquency rate than the children of Negro families coming in from less turbulent neighbourhoods. However, the longer the immigrant Negro children had lived in the area, the greater was their delinquency rate, thus confirming the effect of living in a bad neighbourhood.

Broken homes

How close is the connexion with delinquency?

The special liability of children from broken homes to become juvenile delinquents has been the starting point for a great many psychological theories about the effects of loss of parents, or separation from parents, upon character development.* However, the closeness of the association between delinquency and broken homes is sometimes overestimated. The incidence varies

* See p. 157.

according to the area and generation from which the sample of delinquents is taken, and whether they are recidivists, and whether they are in institutions.

In a survey based upon a sample of 500 youths discharged from English borstals during the years 1941 to 1944, A. Gordon Rose [223] found that at the time of being committed half of the boys were from homes permanently broken by parental death, desertion, separation or divorce. In the later survey by Gibbens [84] just over a third of borstal boys from the London area had experienced such a break before reaching the age of fifteen. In an unselected sample of 100 boys committed to approved schools and sent to Aycliffe for classification, J. Gittins [92] found that in half the cases either one or both parents were dead, or else they were separated, deserted or divorced, the latter categories being much the more numerous. In only one third of cases did the boys come from apparently normally constituted parental homes. In a sample of 300 boys in detention centres in 1961, Charlotte Banks [15] found that forty-four per cent were from broken homes.

Although these figures seem quite striking, they are difficult to interpret for two reasons. First, in the absence of control groups of non-delinquents of the same age and social class, one does not know the incidence of family breaks among non-delinquents. Second, among the inmates of institutions, an over-representation of boys from broken homes may occur as a consequence of the policy of the courts, who are more likely to commit a boy if he has no stable home.

This last objection could not apply to the results of the survey of 700 young soldiers in a disciplinary unit for delinquents by Trenaman [263]. In this case there was no question of preferential selection of those without homes, but nevertheless a history of broken homes occurred with approaching double frequency in the delinquents compared with the ordinary soldiers, and was cited by the investigator as a major causal factor. In another well-known survey by Carr-Saunders *et al.* [28], covering nearly 2,000 English schoolboy offenders, comparisons were made with an equal number of non-delinquents from the same schools. The proportion of delinquent cases in which one or other natural parent was missing was approaching double that of the control group: twenty-eight per cent and sixteen per cent respectively. The difference in incidence was mostly accounted for by the larger number of instances of parental divorce or separation in the delinquent group.

American research has in general confirmed the genuineness of the statistical association with broken homes, while demonstrating how the magnitude of the association may vary according to circumstances. In the Cambridge–Somerville sample studied by William and Joan McCord [164], only a fifth of the delinquents came from broken homes, but still this was significantly more than among non-delinquents of the same neighbourhood and social class. T.P.Monahan [184] made a survey of the family composition of first offenders under eighteen years of age appearing before the juvenile courts in Philadelphia during the years 1949 to 1954. For comparison, similar statistics relating to the same age group in the total population were obtained from a census taken in 1950. The Census revealed that seven per cent of white children and thirty-three per cent of non-white children were from broken homes, that is not living in census-classified husband-wife families. The comparative incidence of broken homes among the first offenders was twenty-two per cent for white boys and forty-nine per cent for Negro boys, forty-two per cent for white girls and sixty-eight per cent for Negro girls.

While this result demonstrated that in both sexes and both races the delinquents more often came from broken homes, the contrast between delinquents and non-delinquents in this respect was greater for girls than for boys, and greater for whites than for Negroes. The high incidence of broken homes in the Negro population as a whole to some extent masked the effect. This survey also investigated the incidence of broken homes among those committed to institutions, and showed, as many have suspected, that the delinquents sent to institutions included a greater proportion from broken homes than delinquents dealt with in other ways.

Separation has worse effects than bereavement

Homes can be 'broken' in various ways. Most surveys which have taken this into account suggest that breaks caused by parental

desertion or separation are more closely associated with delinquency than breaks due to parental deaths. In his borstal survey,
Gibbens [84] commented that the proportion of youths who had
lost a parent by death before they were fifteen was no greater than
in a sample of young men from the R.A.F. It was broken homes
from other causes, such as illegitimacy or desertion, which distinguished the delinquents. A similar observation was made by
Ferguson [70] from his follow-up study of boys leaving school
in Glasgow. He found that boys who had lost a parent by death
were no more liable to court convictions than other boys. On the
other hand, among the six per cent of the schoolboys who had
lost a parent from other causes before reaching fifteen years of
age, a disproportionately large number were subsequently
convicted. Charlotte Banks [15], who also divides the broken
homes of her delinquent boys in detention centres into those due
to deaths and those due to separations, compared her incidence
figures with those of a recent National Survey by J.W.B.
Douglas and others.* Whereas homes broken by deaths were
three times as frequent as in the normal fifteen-year-old population, homes broken by divorce or separation were five times as
frequent. The fact that bereavements seem less significant than
breaks occasioned by separation or divorce suggests that discord
between parents may be more closely associated with delinquency
than actual loss of a parent. The offspring of a stable marriage
can withstand the shock of a parent's death, especially if adequate
arrangements for continuity of care are made.

Two large-scale studies of earlier generations yielded somewhat different results. In their large American survey, Sheldon
and Eleanor Glueck [95] found that sixty per cent of delinquents,
twice as many as among the matched controls, had lost a parent
during the first ten years of life, and that all types of family
breach, including those produced by parental illness and death,
were more frequent in the histories of delinquents. Cyril Burt
[26], in his classic study of London delinquents, found that
maternal (but not paternal) death was commoner among delinquents than non-delinquents, although, as usual, the high
incidence of parental separations and desertions among the
delinquents provided the more striking contrast. Illness and

* See p. 160.

death of parents were certainly commoner and possibly more damaging under the social conditions prevalent in previous generations.

Another more recent American survey [251], of 1,000 first offenders coming before a juvenile court in New Jersey, found that thirty-one per cent came from broken homes. The investigators tried to see if those from broken homes tended to commit the more serious offences. They also inquired whether the kind of break – divorce or death – made a difference, and whether such matters as the number of years a home had been broken, or the presence of a step-parent, or the sex of the parent having custody of the child had any bearing upon the seriousness of the offences committed. Contrary to what might have been expected from previous work, the differences were mostly insignificant, and the author concluded that the broken home was not of very great importance in determining the severity of a boy's misbehaviour.

Without going to extremes of scepticism, it is plain that the broken home, like all the other factors discussed in this chapter, cannot be more than a contributory cause of delinquency. Even in bad neighbourhoods, delinquents from intact homes outnumber delinquents from broken homes.

Too big a family

Another point on which investigators all agree is that families with a large number of children contribute a disproportionately large number of juvenile delinquents. T. Ferguson [71] demonstrated this most convincingly with his sample of 1,349 Glasgow boys. Of those from families of not more than four children, eight per cent were convicted by eighteen years of age. Of those from families of more than four children, sixteen per cent were convicted. A similar finding was reported by Trenaman [262] from his sample of 700 young delinquent soldiers. Compared with a control sample of ordinary servicemen, the average size of the delinquents' sibling family was nearly twice as large, 6.3 compared with 3.6.

Of course, as has already been pointed out, size of family is strongly linked with other social factors, notably poverty and overcrowding. Ferguson's survey showed that boys from homes overcrowded to the extent of four or more persons per room had an expectation of being convicted three times as great as the boys from homes with less than two per room. When there are many children at home, an unskilled worker's earnings may be but little above the subsistence level allowed to such a family if they go on National Assistance. If the mother of a very large family happens to be a not particularly efficient manager, the children are likely to be deprived both physically and emotionally, meals become erratic, attention spasmodic, and the absence of clean clothes or dinner money may lead to staying away from school.

Size of family is also linked with social-class membership and religious and racial affiliations. Lower-class families and Roman Catholic families more often have a large number of children than middle-class or Protestant families. Trenaman noted that twenty per cent of his delinquent soldiers were Roman Catholics, twice the proportion to be found at a normal army intake. F.H. McClintock [162], in his survey of crimes of violence in London, found that over a quarter of convicted offenders were either immigrants from the Irish Republic or coloured persons from the Commonwealth, obviously an enormous over-representation compared with the numbers of such persons in the London population. This link between size of family and other things shows once again how consideration of any one of these social background factors leads to all the rest. From the familar conglomeration of social handicaps (labouring class, poverty, overcrowding, immigrant, Irish, Roman Catholic, bad neighbourhood, poor schooling, broken home and large family) it seems futile to single out any one as the prime factor in the development of juvenile delinquency.

Combinations of adversity

The characteristics of unrespectable, delinquent-prone families

In view of the clustering together of adverse social factors, and the impossibility of understanding the operation of one factor in isolation from the rest, a more realistic approach would be to start with the individual delinquent families and investigate the whole constellation of circumstances which differentiate them from the law-abiding members of the community. This was actually attempted some years ago by a research team from Nottingham University in one of the few really detailed studies of a high delinquency area so far undertaken in England [249]. They noted that in the working-class district of 'Radby', a mining town in the Midlands, five selected areas, which contained in total a third of the adult population, contributed sixty-three per cent of the adult offenders and seventy per cent of the juvenile delinquents. They also noted that these same areas had particularly high rates of infant mortality, divorce, tuberculosis notifications, and other indexes of social malaise.

Examining the situation more closely, they found that in some areas delinquency was concentrated in certain 'black' streets, and that neighbouring 'white' streets, inhabited by respectable working-class families, housed very few delinquents. They interviewed families and graded households on a five-point scale according to the degree of social competence and attitudes displayed. In the worst grade (I) they placed the real problem families, chronic social misfits who made no pretence of keeping up with accepted standards of honesty, hygiene or household management. Into the highest grade (V) they put the socially aspiring families, people who wanted to better themselves and openly condemned the fecklessness and immorality of their 'black' neighbours. The bulk of ordinary working-class families, who believed in 'live and let live', trying to preserve reasonable standards themselves while remaining on friendly terms with their neighbours, went into the middle grade (III). While some streets had an extraordinary conglomeration of families in the worst grades, and were readily identifiable as 'black', other streets had poor-grade households dotted about among rows of more respectable families. The variability from one house to the next in the same street was often greater than the difference between the average of one street and another, or one district and another. Something in the 'under the roof' culture of individual families was often more important than the effect of the place they were living.

The Nottingham workers tried to pinpoint the differences

between 'black' and 'white' families. In the former, juvenile delinquency was very much more frequent (fifteen instances among seventy-two families in Grades I and II, none at all among fifty-nine families in Grades IV and V), so was the number whose children had a bad educational record (twenty-two out of seventy-two compared with none out of fifty-nine), and the number of broken marriages (eight out of seventy-two compared with none out of fifty-nine in which the woman of the house was living with a man not her husband) and the number living in big families (forty-four out of seventy-two compared with twelve out of fifty-nine in households containing five or more persons). The 'black' families lived in an atmosphere of squalor; possessions were untidy and uncared for, and individual ownership was not prized. In the 'white' families people took a pride in their own things, and house and garden were carefully tended. In the 'black' families leisure was largely taken up with gambling, whereas among the 'whites' this was only a minor interest. In the 'black' homes irregular sexual unions were frequent and openly discussed, whereas the 'white' families, at least in public, adhered to the conventional code of sexual morality. Minor acts of physical aggression – mothers clouting children, boys hitting their sisters – occurred much more often among the 'blacks'; whereas 'white' mothers made deliberate efforts to refrain from hitting their children in temper. Since both sets of families belonged to the working class, differences between the 'blacks' and 'whites' in regard to occupational status and amount earned were relatively slight.

Some of the most conspicuous differences lay in the field of child care. In the 'black' homes, parents quarrelled openly and violently, whereas the 'whites' tried to conceal their disputes from their children. In the 'black' homes, only the mother showed concern for the children, whereas in 'white' homes responsibility was more often shared between both parents. In 'black' families, children were given pocket money casually to spend as they felt like; the 'white' parents usually made their children put away savings, and made an effort to train their children in thrift and the use of leisure. For instance they encouraged Sunday schools and youth clubs, whereas 'black' parents did nothing to persuade their children to attend organizations, and their children were apt to find such places over-disciplined or too 'stuck up'.

The poorest group of all

Another way of investigating the relation between adverse social factors and likelihood of juvenile delinquency is to identify the most unfortunate or vulnerable group within the community, and see to what extent delinquent habits prevail among them. Something of this kind was done in a study of juvenile delinquency in an English seaport by Harriet Wilson [287]. She selected a group of unfortunate children from families referred to welfare agencies on account of various indications of neglect, such as shortage of clothing, inadequate meals, being sent to school in a dirty condition, or being kept away from school. The family had to show a certain minimum number of these un-favourable features in order to be included in the survey. This method of selection produced a group conspicuous for the presence of a large number of factors known to be correlated with delinquency. Thus, the average size of family was very large (7.4 children per family) and there were many cases in which a fluctuating family income repeatedly fell below subsistence level. Partly owing to the housing policy of the local authority, many of these families, who often owed money and were regarded as unsatisfactory tenants, were accommodated in old council property in close proximity to other unsatisfactory tenants in a squalid neighbourhood that was notorious for stealing and violent quarrels. Over a third of the fathers had bad work records, which were usually associated with mental or physical disabilities, and only a small minority of the children attended school regularly.

A large majority of boys from this type of background became juvenile delinquents. Thus, eighty-five per cent of the boys aged seventeen had had one or more convictions. The delinquency rate for boys in the sample was some eight times that of the average for the total population of boys in the city. When compared with a control group of boys from the same bad neighbourhoods, the boys in the sample had a cumulative delinquency rate which, at every age level, was more than double. This finding suggests that, given a sufficient combination of adverse social factors, most boys will become juvenile delinquents. From a theoretical standpoint, and as an exercise in teasing out possible causes of delinquency, this result is most important, but of course one has to remember that the majority of boys who become delinquent do so without having been through anything like such extreme adversity.

Social pressures not the final answer

The level of crime in a community appears to be largely determined by external pressures. In Victorian times, the prevalence of poverty and poisonous medicines led to a high rate of child murder. Wars and social disasters release phenomena of looting, violence and racial murders, which are normally held in check by police and government authorities. It is hardly surprising, therefore, that social pressures such as unemployment, lack of education, disrupted homes, over-sized poor families, and run-down neighbourhoods are all found to be correlated with delinquency rates. At one time or another, every one of these factors has been heralded as a prime cause of crime. But this is out of fashion. Professor Radzinowicz wrote recently:

> I am strongly convinced that the unilateral approach, the attempt to explain all crime in terms of a single theory, should be abandoned altogether with such expressions as crime causation. The most we can now do is to throw light on factors or circumstances associated with various kinds of crime [216].

Multi-factorial explanations remain possible. Although no single type of hardship has a monopoly in relation to delinquency, it could be that delinquents experience an accumulation of adverse pressures which build up to the point where restraints are overcome and crimes occur. This way of looking at the matter fits in rather nicely with the results of surveys, like those of Sprott and Wilson, which reveal the thick web of misfortunes in which the highly delinquent problem families, or the rougher slum elements among the working class, seem to be enmeshed. Lack of education, poor health, broken homes, low earning capacity, slum housing, inadequate child-rearing techniques, and general social ineptitude are merely the constituent elements of a power-ful compound social handicap, which looks like the most important causal nexus in delinquency.

Unfortunately, things are not really so simple. Statistically speaking, though each factor of social-background adversity correlates positively with delinquency, none of the correlations is spectacularly large. Narrowing one's sights to the minority with a serious accumulation of adversities produces a very large correlation indeed, but in the process one has eliminated most of the population, and most of the delinquents as well. In other words, notwithstanding the great importance of these readily identifiable forms of social handicap, other factors must be operating. How else to explain the increasing numbers of apprehended delinquents who come from socially secure homes, or the fact that middle-class youngsters confess to as many unreported delinquencies as their working-class peers? Perhaps the secret will be found in more subtle social factors, or in different stresses operating in different social classes; or perhaps, after all, the psychological make-up of the individual youngster holds the answer.

4 Some Social Theories

Contrary to current ideas, the criminal no longer seems a totally unsociable being, a sort of parasitic element, a strange and unassimilable body, introduced in the midst of society. On the contrary, he plays a definite role in social life.

E. Durkheim, *The Rules of Sociological Method* (1895). Translated by J. Mueller, Glencoe, Ill., Free Press (eighth edition 1950).

If you steal what you want from the other, you are in control; you are not at the mercy of what is given.

R. D. Laing, *The Divided Self* (1960). Tavistock Publications; Penguin Books (1965). p. 62 (Penguin).

Schools of crime

Crime as a style of life

Modern sociologists follow Durkheim in interpreting the bulk of criminal behaviour as a normal response to a bad environment. Instead of singling out individual scapegoats for punishment or psychiatry, they advocate social reform as the best means of tackling the true causes of crime. In many departments of human activity, such as personal hygiene, eating habits, dress and language, conformity with social custom comes about for the most part without reference to criminal law by a gradual and largely unconscious absorption of conventions universally accepted in a particular community. Persons deviating too far from such conventions, even if not actually locked away as madmen, would soon find themselves rejected by family and by employers, and left without means of gaining food and shelter. Against criminal habits the taboo is less strong, and among certain groups and in certain circumstances law-breaking is recognized, even tolerated, as a possible style of life. Furthermore, the choice between criminality and conformity is not an 'all-or-none' decision. Selective disobedience to the law is rife. Many drivers who exceed speed limits, or get into their cars after drinking parties, many tourists who pass through customs with undeclared goods, many retailers who disregard the permitted hours for sales, and many business-men who fake expenses, or devise misleading advertisements, or take advantage of office facilities for private purposes, would never class themselves as criminals, although they soundly condemn the more overt dishonesty of the housebreaker. On the other hand, the common crimes against property incur less disapproval among rough working-class groups than they do among those of respectable middle-class standards. Much of the contemporary sociological theories of crime concern the ways in which particular groups within the community succeed in evading or rejecting some of the moral restraints accepted by the predominantly middle-class law-makers. Understandably, most of these theories have originated in the United States, where the flaunting of political and business corruption, the more or less open pursuit of profitable 'rackets', and the conflict of ideals between different segments of a complex and fluid society, present to the young a particularly wide range of good and bad choices.

In view of the multiplicity of social factors concerned, no single causative principle can ever hope to provide a satisfactory insight into crime. Unfortunately some theorists have a partiality for over-simplified versions of events which they build up into supposedly universal explanatory principles. If, instead, the theories about to be mentioned are regarded as descriptions of different aspects of the problem, their real worth can be better appreciated.

Differential association

Broadly speaking, most sociological theories start with the assumption that the criminal way of life is something that has to be learned from experience. Whether a youngster becomes a crook or a respected and honest citizen depends upon the environment in which he has grown up. This is the idea behind the theory of 'differential association' first put forward by Edwin Sutherland in the 1939 edition of his *Principles of Criminology*. It has been castigated by one psychologist as the most sterile theory of crime ever devised, and lauded by numerous sociologists as the starting point of the modern approach. Basically, i: consists of the simple principle of bad example. Young people develop into criminals by learning wrongful ways from bad companions, and by seeing powerful and successful adults breaking the law. Thus, the youngster from a bad school and bad neighbourhood comes into contact more often than not with older persons of confirmed anti-social attitudes, from whom he learns to reject law-abiding principles and acquires skill in rule-breaking and evasion. Everyone is to some extent exposed to conflicting possibilities, temptations and restraints, but where the young person perceives or experiences more in favour of crime than against it, he will become delinquent. On this theory, the budding criminal strives for money, status and happiness just like everyone else, but the attitudes with which he has come into contact, especially in his strongest personal relationships, have been such as to teach him unlawful rather than lawful ways of attaining his ends.

Sutherland himself recognized the existence of criminogenic factors other than association; for example the role of opportunity in the making of the embezzler, or the influence of poverty in making theft seem appropriate, so it is clear that the theory cannot provide a complete explanation. It explains the transmission of the criminal outlook, but says little about how antisocial attitudes originate. Furthermore, the assumption that all criminality is learned from others has been challenged by those who believe that, although social restraint has to be learned, aggressive and predatory behaviour comes all too naturally from the cradle. To make the theory workable, Sutherland had to accept that the age of the potential criminal, and the perceived importance and status of the persons whose example is being taken influences the learning that takes place; otherwise one might predict that prison officers, police and criminologists would become criminals by association.

Sutherland's views were much influenced by two sets of phenomena; career criminals and adolescent gangs. In the criminal records of burglars, for instance, it was sometimes possible to discern a progression 'from a sport to a business', from petty crimes committed on the spur of the moment to highly organized and skilfully executed professional operations carried out with the minimum of risk for the maximum reward. Such offenders learn their techniques from older and more experienced criminals, and gradually earn for themselves an accepted place in the society of professional crooks, whose self-justifying philosophy they adopt along with the tricks of their trade.

Gangs as training for the criminal career

Affiliation to neighbourhood gangs of adolescent delinquents has always been a particular feature of juvenile offenders in America. In his classic study of juvenile gangs in Chicago, F. M. Thrasher [260] saw gangs as a training ground for crime. First encouraged to join gang companions in truancy, then drawn into dare-devil adventures and the experience of getting a kick out of disobeying rules, a boy is led step by step into actual crimes. The gang provides a reservoir of technical knowledge 'how to procure junk, open merchandise cars, rob bread boxes, snatch purses, fleece a storekeeper, empty slot machines . . .' Along with demoralizing personal and sexual habits, it instils 'attitudes of irresponsibility, independence, and indifference to law' along with 'an attitude of fatalism, a willingness to take a chance – a philosophy of life which fits him well for a career of crime'. As they grow older, youths thoroughly schooled in criminal ways in their juvenile gangs gravitate readily to the hierarchy of professionals ranging from 'silk hat' bosses with impressive business and political interests, to the 'numerous bums, toughs, ex-convicts, and floaters who frequent underworld areas . . .'.

Later students of the Chicago scene such as F. Tannenbaum [259] and W. F. Whyte [279] saw delinquent gangs as the inevitable outcome of the failure of the community to provide reasonable and constructive outlets for spirited and frustrated youth. Such gangs always flourished in the worst slums, where street-corner society provided a refuge from miserable and overcrowded homes, and an opportunity for self-expression, leadership, excitement and *esprit de corps*, otherwise denied to the uneducated and impoverished segments of the community. Whyte, in his description of the Norton Street gang, was quite clear that in spite of its lawlessness the group performed a constructive social function through the mutual support and solidarity of its members in the face of the misfortunes of economic depression and unemployment.

Nevertheless, it is towards a criminal mode of adult living that American adolescent delinquent gangs set their sights. Block and Niederhoffer [20], who studied gangs in East Side New York, described how the adolescent Corner Boys emulated and tried to join up with the older Pirates, whose delinquent coups were more sagaciously planned and more successful. In turn, the older groups formed a training ground and a source of recruitment for the really professional adult racketeers and criminals. Such organized gangs thrive best in communities, like the Cornerville society described by Whyte, in which the rackets extend from top to bottom, and form a large part of the life of the district, with prominent members of the respectable business and political world participating at the higher levels. Under these conditions, the frustrated youngster from the slums who finds legitimate avenues blocked has the ready alternative of a career structure in crime, beginning on the street corner, and ending up a big-time operator.

From such observations Sutherland and later theorists of this same tradition derived the conclusion that young offenders are on the whole normal members of a sick society. They differ from respected citizens only because they have had the misfortune to be reared among a class of society in which the delinquent style of life is more accessible and more easily learned than conformity to middle-class ethics.

Social protest theories

Anomie

Whereas Sutherland emphasized the normality of delinquent behaviour, other sociologists have explained it as a sympton of frustration which is liable to become pronounced among groups undergoing special stress. Durkheim coined the word 'anomie' for a form of social malaise in which the regulating and control-ling pressures of accepted social custom are reduced, so that people find themselves without guidance or constraint, so that unrest and delinquency multiply. This is an opposite state of affairs to that of a tradition-bound culture where everyone knows his place, and where, though they may suffer poverty, discrimination, or even slavery, people accept their lot without protest. Industrial progress tends to destroy the stability of tradition. As social mobility increases, as goods appear in unfamiliar abundance and new career prospects open up, the individual no longer has any fixed limits of expectation with which to curb his appetites and ambitions. The greater the possibilities, the higher the sights are set and the more fluid the social situation, the greater the danger of dissatisfaction and disillusionment. Durkheim pointed out that too much freedom could have repercussions in private life no less than in business and public affairs, so that men without wives were more prone to suicide and mental illness. Modern freedoms have exposed the younger generation to greater opportunities both good and bad. An abundance of leisure, greater scope for getting about and meeting other young people, faster growth and earlier physical maturity, the extraordinary proliferation of products for youthful consumption (pop records, scooters, transistors, teenage fashions), and a growing tradition of free thinking and independence of the ideas of the older generation have brought increased opportunity for self-expression, but at the same time have also increased the temptations and chances to commit illegitimate acts.

The notion of social anomie and its dangers has been taken further by modern sociologists, notably R. K. Merton [176]. He redefined anomie as a form of cultural chaos due to an imbalance between the approved goals of society and the legitimate means of attaining them. He noted the tremendous emphasis in America on 'getting ahead', making money, and acquiring the trappings (mostly consumer goods) which symbolize status and success in contemporary society. While these goals are accepted by people in all walks of life, access to the socially approved means of attaining them varies. According to one's starting position in the social hierarchy, the social system can act as either a barrier or an open door. Young people with poor backgrounds and education are handicapped in the race towards success symbols, although they are under the same pressure to make good. Hence comes the temptation to take illegitimate short cuts. Merton and Durkheim agree about the danger of unleashing unrealistic aspirations, but Merton goes on to explain why this should happen especially among the lower classes. In effect, his theory suggests that by organizing itself so as to arouse and then to frustrate lower-class aspirations, society gets the criminals it deserves.

Merton described several types of response to anomie, of which perhaps the most serious is 'retreatism' or contracting out. This refers to persons who repudiate the whole frame of reference of conventional society, rejecting both the goals and the means. Beatniks, vagrants, drug addicts, and other self-determining outcasts fall into the category. The 'innovators' as Merton called them, the ones who twist the rules of the game so as to have a better chance of winning, are less personally maladjusted, but are labelled criminals. They mostly belong to classes of society where the chances of self-improvement in a conventional job cannot compare with the rewards of a criminal career. Another outlet Merton called 'ritualism', an over-valuation of the rules at the expense of the goal. Such people make a great show of 'playing the game', but the prize has faded into some unattainable distance. These are the assiduous bureaucratic form-fillers and report-compilers, the regular attenders who always make the right gestures and obedient noises, but their activity has become an end in itself, divorced from any realistic purpose.

Delinquent sub-culture

Merton's theories have inspired other writers to examine in more detail the reactions of those groups within society which deviate from or positively reject the morality of the majority. Such groups have come to be known as 'sub-cultures'. One of the most obvious examples of a criminal sub-culture is that of the delinquent gang. Albert Cohen [41] studied the social outlook and origins of members of delinquent gangs of juveniles, and produced some penetrating observations which he and others have elaborated into a general theory of delinquency causation. He observed that American juvenile delinquent gangs are recruited from working-class boys frustrated by lack of status. The emphasis among middle-class parents on self-discipline, planned ambition, and constructive use of leisure by their children paves the way to educational and social advancement; whereas the freer and more spontaneous, but less ambitious, attitudes of the working class leave their children less capable of benefiting from conventional opportunities for advancement. Lower-class boys find themselves at a disadvantage because success in business and education is largely reserved for those with middle-class ideas, values, skills and contacts. Being sensitive to their inferior status, and finding the effort to adopt middle-class standards too great, some of these boys react by repudiating middle-class values altogether, and holding up to ridicule conventional respectability and morality. The sub-culture thus formed stands in relation to dominant culture rather like a witches' coven in relation to orthodox Christianity; so that what was most condemned is now most admired. The boy who has made no headway among his more respectable peers now gains status by acts of aggression, theft and vandalism. By demonstrating his defiance and contempt for the authorities who have rejected him, he relieves his own feelings, and also wins the admiration of others. Wherever this reaction is commonplace, the affected individuals are likely to come together to form a group solution to their status discontent, each member of the group obtaining support and encouragement from others similarly placed and similarly motivated.

Cohen pointed out that his interpretation satisfactorily explained some otherwise puzzling aspects of juvenile delinquent behaviour. A lot of delinquent activity cannot be accounted for in terms of simple material gain, since very often great risks are taken and effort expended to steal articles which are so little valued by the thief that they are soon discarded or given away. Boys who like thieving often also like bullying better-behaved children who are not members of their gang, as well as playing truant, defying teachers and destroying property. The common motive behind all these forms of anti-social behaviour is malicious delight in annoying the representatives of respectability. A resentment against being pushed around and exploited by authorities also accounts for two prominent features of the gang ethos, hostility towards any form of outside control, and 'short-run hedonism'. Gang members are very resistant to efforts by teachers or social agencies to regulate their lives or supervise their leisure activities. They prefer to hang about idly, without set purpose but out for fun, until some impulse of the moment takes them off to a football game or a delinquent exploit. Gang members especially resent attempts by parents to control them, and in Cohen's view gang loyalties may contribute as much to the break-down of family life as family conflicts contribute to gang recruitment.

Advocates of the delinquent sub-culture theory argue that the reactions described are essentially normal and inevitable responses to a given set of social circumstances. Cohen himself, however, was willing to admit individual differences in type of reaction. Some boys, like Merton's 'retreatists', instead of transferring their allegiance to a sub-culture, simply gave up trying and lapsed into apathy. Despite the common core of motivation in the sub-culture, different individuals might come to join it for somewhat different reasons.

After Cohen, various writers have put forward variations on the delinquent sub-culture theme, but without much change in the basic concept. W. B. Miller [181] suggested that working-class sub-culture in America is such as to generate gang delinquency of itself, without any need for a reaction against middle-class ideas. The focal concerns of lower-class youth, toughness and masculinity, cleverness in making easy money and not being duped, excitement in chance and risk-taking, and the wish to be independent and not bossed about, encourage attitudes that are already half-way delinquent. The ideal of the super-manly fighting tough guy, intolerant of personal affronts, contemptuous of sentimentality, regarding women as objects of conquest and 'queers' as targets for abuse, has much in common with the traditional gangster hero. Skill in outwitting others in street-corner gambling and in exchanging insulting repartee brings increased status. Weekly 'binges', with the prospect of sexual adventures, brawls, and unrestrained excitement relieve an otherwise dreary and unrewarding routine. Resentment of coercion, exemplified by walking out on jobs, breaking away from homes and wives, or running away from penal institutions, may represent a compensation for dependency cravings, obliquely revealed by the compulsive way absconders seek out further 'trouble' and bring about inevitable re-commitment to institutional care.

The increasing rejection of deviants

Leslie Wilkins [282] has produced a theoretical model which seeks to explain further the social dynamics of delinquent sub-culture formation. He began by pointing out how much tolerance of deviant or undesirable behaviour varies according to the way a community is organized. In general, personal experience of individual variations leads to greater tolerance. In a village, where everybody knows the local idiot, and the local drunk, they are less likely to be shut away in institutions. In a tightly organized urban community, where ordinary persons are shielded from direct dealings with deviants by professional social and medical workers, personal experience and information about deviants will be rather small. Hence, any deviation that actually obtrudes will appear subjectively more unusual and extreme, and the reaction to it will also be more extreme and intolerant.

Referring back to the theories of the delinquent sub-culture, Wilkins noted that decrease in tolerance of deviation can lead to a vicious circle (or negative feed-back system, to use the modern idiom). The greater the pressure towards conformity, the greater the strain on the socially handicapped, and the more likely they are to react negatavistically and to seek solace in the delinquent sub-culture. Participation in the delinquent sub-culture in turn produces a sharp retaliation by authority, the effect of which is to aggravate still further the deviant's status frustration, and provoke still more hostility. And so round and round again.

In summary, the model proposed runs roughly as follows. Inadequate information leads to a wider range of acts being defined as intolerable. This means that larger numbers of individuals are cut off from social acceptance, and these people, perceiving themselves as outcasts, begin to develop their own deviant values. This leads to still further rejection, and to still greater emphasis on conformity by the community in general.

Coherent and incoherent forms of protest

D.J. Boruda [21] has put his finger on a curious feature of the modern theories of the delinquent sub-culture. Whereas Thrasher and the older exponents of gang dynamics admitted the exhilaration and satisfaction experienced by boys skipping school and being chased by coppers, the later theorists, such as Albert Cohen, depict boys driven by grim psychic necessity into rebellion. It seems that 'modern analysts have stopped assuming that "evil" can be fun and see gang delinquency as arising only when boys are driven away from "good"'. In this respect these modern social theorists have come closer to psychological theories, which regard delinquency, or at least persistent or compulsive delinquency, as a sign of personal maladjustment.

A survey of aggressive gangs in New York by Lewis Yablonsky [292] suggests that the modern gang is less well organized and socially purposeful than those of previous generations described by Whyte and Thrasher. The modern gangs indulge in brutality for no logical purpose except to boost a sinking morale. Youths embittered by personal inadequacies and social failures fulfil their fantasies of power and success by terrorizing others. Unlike the old gangs, which at least provided some elements of friendship, camaraderie and leadership, these groups lacked stability of membership, or any spirit of cohesion, acting in a mob-like fashion to relieve themselves in spontaneous bursts of irrational violence. In other words, these gangs had sunk to the level of loose collections of handicapped or inadequate individuals, and could hardly be looked upon as useful or coherent forms of protest against social injustice.

Cloward and Ohlin [40] have put forward an ingenious theory to explain the contrasts between the miserably frustrated delinquent sub-cultures, typified by Yablonsky's gangs, and the well-socialized delinquents marching up the ladder of a comfortable criminal career, as described by the earlier writers. They point out that a successful protest reaction against middle-class values depends upon the availability of opposing values and alternative courses of action. Illegitimate means as well as legitimate means vary in accessibility. Only those neighbourhoods in which a criminal community flourishes offer the youngster easy opportunity for learning the criminal role. In the heyday of the Chicago gangs, when at least the higher echelons of the criminal organizations were well integrated into normal business society, criminality offered a natural and rewarding career. In the more socially alienated type of slum, populated exclusively with the failures and outcasts from society, delinquency remains unsophisticated and impulsive, and professionally organized crime has no chance to develop, since the requisite links with the dominant culture do not exist. In the bad old days, lawless districts were relatively stable and cohesive, and people stayed there all their lives. In modern times, with greater social mobility, and massive housing projects, transience and instability are the chief features of slum life. The juvenile gangs in these areas have no opportunity for getting ahead by crime, so they can only work out their grudge against society in futile violence. In Merton's terms they are really retreatists from life, failures in both the criminal and the legitimate worlds. Hence the popularity of other retreatist reactions, notably drug-taking, which has become so prevalent among young people in America's urban slums.

When gangs dwindle away

In keeping with the assumption that delinquent sub-cultures are not so well developed in England, one finds that organized gangs of young delinquents do not flourish to anything like the same extent as in the United States. Dr Peter Scott [232], a psychiatrist at the London Remand Home for boys, made a special study of the habits of juvenile offenders in this regard. In the first place, he emphasized that the street-corner and coffee-bar groups, among whom so many adolescent youths spend their leisure hours, are not really much concerned with delinquency, and although their members may become offenders, they do so on their own initiative, and not as part of the group. Many juveniles committed offences on their own, but even when they offended in company their most frequent companions were their own brothers or regular friends. Such associations, not being ordinarily committed to delinquent activities, could not be called gangs. Indeed, delinquent gangs with a definite membership and a recognized leader were rather unusual, and apprehended juvenile offenders who had committed crimes as part of organized gang activities were quite exceptional. On the other hand, temporary associations between some three or four boys who committed their offences together were not uncommon, but these were often composed of personality-handicapped boys, whose emotional immaturity unfitted them for normal companionship.

When social conditions approximated more to those in America, as for instance in the slums of Liverpool a generation ago, juvenile gangs were more in evidence. When conditions change in such a way that the normal, average youngster no longer craves the support of an aggressive body of youths committed to social warfare, then the gangs dwindle away or change their character. One Liverpool student described vividly the transformation of adolescent gangs in Liverpool with the advent of the craze for beat music [74]. Boys who had previously spent their time fighting, or breaking into cigarette machines, got interested in forming themselves into musical groups, collecting equipment, practising, and attending dances. Belligerent and criminal gang leaders lost their sway, since the majority of the boys now had both the money and the aptitude for indulging this new interest. Adults might doubt the good taste of the product, but at least the activity was not inherently destructive, and in the form of Beatle exports was eventually to prove a national financial asset. Unfortunately, the poorer and less competent boys couldn't keep up with the new development. This hard core of misfits and criminals remained behind in the depleted gangs. It is always the weaker brethren, those least effective in social skills and manners, those most disliked by authorities, those most confused by faulty upbringing, who cling to the remnants of the protest group long after others have progressed to marriage or other interests.

Observations like these run counter to expectations based upon purely social factors, and draw attention to the importance of individual deficiencies and quirks of character in the development of persistent habits of delinquency. In the past, sociologists have tried to explain everything in terms of external pressures; but clearly individuals react differently, and one is not likely to get further towards understanding delinquency without some scrutiny of the offender as a person.

Second thoughts on the delinquent sub-culture

Delinquents not fully committed?

D. Matza [172] has called attention to the lack of factual support for the existence of the attitudes commonly imputed to delinquents. He points out that the sociological stereotype of a juvenile delinquent as a person committed to an oppositional culture does not ring true for most delinquents actually met and spoken to. For instance, when questioned in the abstract about offences like car theft or fighting with a weapon very few express approval or admiration for such violations. Their indignation if falsely accused of more offences than they have actually committed suggests that they share to some extent in the common feeling for justice and condemnation of wrongdoing. Likewise, they are insulted rather than flattered to have their mothers called immoral or their fathers described as rogues and criminals. If they really were fully conditioned to an oppositional system, they would hardly drop out of crime and 'go over to the enemy' in such large numbers on reaching the age of discretion. Except perhaps for some spies, the apprehended criminal does not usually feel a martyr to his cause (like members of persecuted political or religious minorities); instead he either admits to remorse or puts forward mitigating excuses like 'You have to defend yourself, don't you?' or 'What do you expect when there's nothing else to do?'

In Matza's view juveniles are less alienated from the wider society and not so uncompromising in their anti-social attitudes as the sociological theorists would have us believe. He thinks it implausible to credit children with the ability to initiate and promulgate an oppositional culture. After all, children still come under the influence of parents, and most parents strive to keep them law-abiding. Even in the most delinquent neighbourhoods one hardly ever finds parental Fagins setting out to teach their children the thieving arts. Most of the time delinquents behave just like everyone else, only now and then they have lapses from the accepted norm. Matza believes they evade rather than oppose the dominant morality, and they do this by selecting and extending trends that already exist in the wider culture. For instance, they may extend the accepted justifications for violence from protection against attack to protection against insult. They may extend a common disregard for the property rights of monolithic organizations to the idea that big stores are 'fair game'. Furthermore, the non-criminal American community is far from homogeneous, and in certain sectors of society attitudes flourish which have a strong affinity to those of the delinquent sub-culture. The cult of cowboy masculinity in the mass media, the 'freedoms' of Bohemia, and the fatalistic philosophy that puts down all individual badness to social causes, reflect and lend support to the cruder versions prevalent among delinquents.

Matza's criticisms do not really contradict the idea of a delinquent sub-culture, but they warn against exaggerating the power and consistency of the anti-morality and anti-establishment attitudes. Most observations on sub-cultures have been made in towns in the United States where social discrimination on racial and economic lines is in particularly blatant conflict with the American ideal. Under these conditions, protest reactions are intense and in some degree realistic. In England, with its more muted versions of social conflict, the delinquents' allegiances are likely to be more mixed and vacillating.

The stresses of an educational meritocracy

American literature on sub-cultures stresses the stark contrasts between rich and poor, or white and Negro. T. R. Fyvel [80], in a colourful description of some features of modern working-class youth in England and in some other European countries, has drawn attention to other kinds of class conflict which can equally well give rise to a class of aggressively disillusioned, socially alienated, and delinquent-prone youth. Fyvel points to the peculiarities of the English educational system as one of the worst sources of trouble. As the Crowther Report of 1960 pointed out, enormous numbers of fifteen-year-olds are released on to the labour market with insufficient training or preparation for anything but dead-end jobs. These hordes had been virtually condemned to second-class citizenship ever since the age of eleven when they were excluded from grammar school promotion and relegated to what were then called secondary modern schools. Finding themselves in boring jobs, but with more leisure and ready cash than their better-class peers, who were busily occupied in higher education or apprenticeships, these working-class youths, lacking the self-discipline necessary to organize their time constructively, remained bored and aimless. Having been turned off the middle-class ladder to success, and resenting their status as social failures, they tried to compensate by self-display, by extravagant spending on pop-music and exotic clothes. First the Teddy-boy outfits, then the Italian styles, then the long-haired, leather-jacketed Rockers spread across England in successive waves. The attractiveness of the new fashions to rebellious youth is doubtless much increased by the displeased reactions of teachers and authorities generally. Of course, fashions tend to spread in time throughout the population, and some are taken up by students at grammar schools as well as pop-art entertainers, but the delinquent groups are always way out at the current

D

extreme, as evidenced by the extraordinary wardrobes collected from boys entering remand homes.

Clothes are a harmless form of protest, but of course England's delinquents share, at least to some extent, many of the inverted ideals described by Cohen, especially the resentment of organization, the belief in living for the pleasure of the moment, and the importance of not letting a chance 'to get away with something' go by. One English writer of what might be called the social protest school, Alan Sillitoe, in his well-known short story (also filmed) *The Loneliness of the Long Distance Runner*, depicted his delinquent hero as being so deeply imbued with the idea that he was being pushed around and bamboozled by middle-class authorities that he deliberately let himself be overtaken in a race that he had worked hard to win rather than give the impression of cooperating. This hero's disillusionment with conventional morality is completely understandable, especially when he fumes against toleration of the atom bomb, or the combination of puritanical restrictiveness with the exploitation of sex and snobbery in commercial advertisements. Among sub-cultural delinquents in real life, the frustration and disillusionment are felt and acted upon in a confused way without any such attempt at intellectualization.

The class conflicts assumed to be responsible for delinquent sub-cultures may take different forms according to the nature of the dominant culture from which they derive. Fyvel contrasted the state of affairs in Moscow and London. Both cities have experienced growing social protest groups of delinquent-prone youngsters, but the precipitating stresses have been slightly different. In London inadequate guidance and training allows lower-class youngsters to drift into difficulties. In Russia, where the educational system is much more tightly organized and adolescents of all classes are directed and disciplined to a high degree, it is those who do not make the grade, and find themselves threatened with banishment to uninteresting menial jobs in far-distant places, who are liable to take to hooliganism, drunkenness, and social subversion. Thus American-style clothes and music may serve to symbolize rejection of an over-regimented meritocracy by those frustrated youngsters who suffer its restrictions without achieving the rewards that are supposedly open to all.

Choosing between the theories

An outstanding weakness of the social theories of delinquency is absence of factual evidence in support of any one in preference to the rest. The few hard facts that have been established, such as the social-class and neighbourhood distribution of offences, are for the most part consistent with all the theories. The different viewpoints represent more or less plausible intuitive interpretations, based upon general experience of offenders and their outlook. Criminological research findings on the attitudes and family backgrounds of offenders do have relevance, but researches planned specifically to test a particular theory are almost completely lacking.

The criminologist Nigel Walker [269] looks forward to the day when sociologists will select groups of people on the basis of the various social causes of delinquency to which they have been exposed or not as the case may be, and then compare their actual delinquency rates so as to get some measure of the practical importance of the causes in question. That day seems still far-off, and in the meantime one can do no more than appraise the merits of the theories in very general terms with reference to their compatibility with the results of delinquency surveys and with one's own experience.

All the social theories have one feature in common: they make no assumption about the supposed peculiarities of delinquency. They interpret delinquent behaviour as a natural response, sometimes even a constructive response, to the situation in which the youngsters find themselves. Since social circumstances vary so much from one country to another, it is only reasonable that sociological interpretations should vary also.

Whenever an urban society is so organized as to produce a ghetto situation, with an identifiable segment of the population condemned by educational and social disadvantages to slum life and third-class citizenship, then one finds delinquency highly concentrated in poorer neighbourhoods and closely associated with social deprivation and social protest. Where a well-established wealthy community attracts an influx of poor migrants, especially if the migrants are of a different race, religion and culture, class conflicts are exaggerated, and alienated groups of

socially handicapped and discontented youths come into prominence. In such situations, of which prime examples are to be
found in some large American cities, the formation of self-
assertive and rebellious 'sub-cultures' is both eminently understandable and rather patently obvious. An important point made
by the more recent sociological observers is that sub-cultures
may be, according to circumstances, relatively purposeful and
successful, as in the heyday of the Chicago gangs, or relatively
ineffective, frustrated and irrationally violent, as in the Yablonsky
type of gang.

It is open to question how far the delinquent sub-culture
theories apply to contemporary English society. Slum clearance,
and social welfare generally, have greatly reduced both the ghetto
situation and the sad inferiorities of dress and physical wellbeing
that at one time distinguished youngsters of the lower classes. On
the other hand, as Fyvel points out, an educational meritocracy
has developed that tends to relegate the less fortunately endowed
to an inferior status that is all the more humiliating because it
cannot so easily be attributed to wicked injustice. An interesting
implication of this view is that, after all, it may be personal inadequacies that are responsible for some individuals falling
behind in a competitive society and joining the ranks of the
socially inept and delinquent-prone.

Statistics suggest that delinquent habits are no longer limited
to the socially under-privileged, but are permeating upwards
through the class barriers. The Oxford sociologist B.R.Wilson
[286] has suggested that the contemporary emphasis on 'success',
based upon intellectual and material superiority, and widely
diffused via the mass-media, has the effect of inducing a sense of
frustration among the younger generation which is by no means
limited to the very poor. A further source of stress is the imper-
sonality of modern social organization and control, well exemplified by the anonymity of ownership of industrial concerns, which
does little to foster the old-fashioned virtues of individual
loyalty. Furthermore, while current ideas of child-rearing favour
a permissive, indulgent and affectionate attitude to children,
adolescents find themselves thrust abruptly into an impersonal
and demanding world. The modern youth culture, with its
rebellious, anti-establishment overtones, provides adolescents

with an alternative and self-comforting system of values and status. The pop-singer idols capture the imagination of the under-achievers, because they symbolize the fantasy of a meteoric rise to the top without visible effort or conventional virtue. While not overtly delinquent, the modern youth culture, in Wilson's opinion, by its emphasis on protest, excitement, kicks and short cuts to success, erodes moral restraints, and lowers resistance to delinquent temptations.

All this sounds very plausible; but as with so much of present-day theorizing, speculative interpretation has far out-distanced the facts of research.

5 The 'Bad' Seed?

Whence and what art thou, execrable shape?
Milton, *Paradise Lost*. Book II.

Everyone is as God made him, and often a great deal worse.
Miguel de Cervantes, *Don Quixote*. Part 2, Chapter 4.

The born criminal

The dubious concept of one criminal type

Even in neighbourhoods or social classes where the risks of delinquency are at their highest, not everyone takes to crime. Unless one believes the selection occurs by pure chance, it seems reasonable to look for the qualities which render certain individuals relatively vulnerable. Research on these lines has proved fascinating but very complex. At first, attention was directed more or less exclusively to individual weaknesses or pathology, to factors like ill health, mental subnormality or neurosis, but of course a delinquent response to a bad environment can be associated with more positive qualities, such as adventurousness, vigour, and self-assertion. Clinical studies of small groups of untypical offenders, for instance those whose anti-social outbursts are the result of epilepsy or of neurotic tensions, have led to dubious claims as to the relevance of such abnormalities to the generality of delinquency. Delinquent behaviour has a multiplicity of origins, and however closely tied it may be in a given case to an identifiable abnormality, it does not follow that the next case will show the same abnormality, or indeed any abnormality at all. Furthermore, the concept of delinquent susceptibility is itself an obvious over-simplication, for even when only thieving is under consideration it is likely that susceptibility to being caught once or twice at an early age is a different matter from susceptibility to becoming a recidivist. Likewise, susceptibility to delinquency probably means very different things in a person from a delinquent-ridden slum and in someone from a respectable middle-class environment. The dangers of generalizing too readily are very great.

Apart from the intrinsic complexities of the topic, research in this field also has to contend with strong emotional resistance to any findings which suggest that delinquent-prone individuals have identifiable psychological peculiarities. Sociologists are sceptical of the importance of individual differences in the face of massive social forces. Authoritarians don't want to know about anything that seems to provide excuses for bad behaviour. Lawyers don't like anything that detracts from the basic principles of self-control and personal responsibility upon which all justice rests. Yet it was in the relatively conservative atmosphere of the last century, and long before modern psychological ideas had taken root, that the most extremist of theories concerning the individual peculiarities of criminals gained widespread acceptance.

Nineteenth-century theorists believed that criminal habits signified some inborn moral deficiency. Some went so far as to suggest that criminals represented a reversion to an earlier stage of man's evolution, children with the mental endowment of primitive savages unluckily born into a civilized age. Others looked upon the criminal as a degenerate type, sharing with the mentally subnormal an incapacity to attain normal social standards because of some innate brain defect. This way of thinking lay behind the preoccupation with criminal anthropology, which in those days meant studying the bodily measurements, skull shapes and facial characteristics of criminals.

Alleged biological inferiority in criminals

As long ago as 1869, Dr G. Wilson read a paper to the British Association seeking to prove the moral imbecility of habitual criminals by showing that their skulls were smaller than average. The ultimate expression of this school of thought is to be found in the work of the Italian forensic psychiatrist, Dr Cesare Lombroso, whose investigatory zeal was stimulated through being called upon to carry out a post-mortem on the body of a famous brigand, during the course of which he came across a curious hollow on the man's skull which reminded him of similar features on the skulls of lower animals. Lombroso, in his famous treatise *L'Uomo delinquente*,* claimed that many criminals had physical anomalies bearing a striking resemblance to the physical features of primitive savages, apes, and in some cases to animals even lower in the evolutionary scale, such as the fierce carnivora. Thus, like apes, many criminals had an arm span

* Turin, 1895.

exceeding their height, a flat nose and sugar-loaf form of skull, and palms marked with few creases. Their lower face and jaw were often unduly developed and protuberant, in striking contrast to their narrow forehead and low skull vault. Tests revealed that their sensory powers were blunted, they could not interpret light touches on the skin as readily as the average, and a sharper stimulation was needed to produce any feeling of pain. Lombroso believed that the typical attitudes of criminals, their lack of moral sense, their immunity from remorse, their cynical attitudes, their impulsiveness and inability to restrain their passions, their violence and cruelty, were likewise attributes of a primitive constitution [73].

Today, such views seem quaint, and modern research has produced no support for Lombroso's ideas about the physical stigmata of criminality. Nevertheless, at the time, the work of the criminal anthropologists undoubtedly gave a boost to the popular notion that moral turpitude, feeble-mindedness, and coarse or deformed physique represent different aspects of degeneracy, and therefore tend to occur together in the same individuals. Belief in the existence of a congenital weakness of moral sense, analogous to or coincident with a congenital mental defect, led to the inclusion in the English Mental Deficiency Acts of 1913 and 1927 of a legal category of 'moral defectives' who were defined as persons 'in whose case there exists mental defectiveness coupled with strongly vicious and criminal propensities, and who require care, supervision and control for the protection of others'.

In point of fact, although modern evidence does not support the idea that either physical or mental defects are necessarily linked with immorality, it is true that the severer forms of mental subnormality are often accompanied by physical anomalies. In these cases, not only has there been gross interference with the growth of the brain and nervous system, but many other structures show signs of stunting or deformity. A brief walk round any hospital for the mentally subnormal should suffice to convince anyone of the prevalence among such patients of the stigmata that Lombroso associated with criminality. Indeed, one of the factors responsible for his results could well have been the number of mental defectives in the prison population in nineteenth-century Italy. In modern times, these people are sifted

out and cared for in hospitals instead of being allowed to sink
into destitution and crime.

Refutation of Lombrosian ideas

The most determined critic of criminal anthropology was an
English prison medical officer, Charles Goring [104], who published a survey of 3,000 prisoners, comparing them with a
control group from the normal population, from which he concluded that a physical type specific to criminals did not exist,
although he agreed that, as a group, criminals were physically
and intellectually below the average. Even this conclusion must
not be taken too seriously, since Goring compared his criminals
with quite different groups, particularly undergraduates, whose
racial backgrounds, level of nutrition during growth, exercise
habits and social advantages presented a marked contrast to
those of the average prisoner.

A brief recrudescence of Lombrosian ideas was produced by
Hooton [135], who compared American prisoners with samples
from among the general population. He found that white, native-
born American male criminals compared with white American
civilians were on average smaller (lighter and shorter, with smaller
heads) with a higher incidence of misshapen ears (one of the
Lombrosian stigmata), snubbed noses and narrow jaws. Dividing
the criminals according to the nature of their offences showed
that the differences between civilians and prisoners were practically the same regardless of the type of crime. Hooton concluded that 'the primary cause of crime is biological inferiority
– and that is exactly what I mean'.

As in so many researches in this subject, the fatal flaw in
Hooton's work probably lay in the manner in which he selected
the 'control group' with which to compare his prisoners. In the
case of his native-born whites, half of the controls consisted of a
group of firemen in Nashville, Tennessee, and the remainder
were drawn rather haphazardly in Boston from men found on
bathing beaches or attending hospitals or from soldiers at drill
halls, and were measured by a different observer. There was no
guarantee that these volunteers were truly representative of
Americans in general. Furthermore, since physique is known to

be linked with social class of origin and with choice of occupation, it is not established whether the alleged physical differences between prisoners and civilians had any connexion with the causes of their criminality, or were merely secondary consequences of the fact that the criminals belonged to a different range of social and occupational classes from that of the controls.

The dim-witted delinquent

Results of intelligence tests

One of the most constant of an individual's psychological qualities is intelligence. Barring accidents like brain injuries or disease, a child who ranks high among his contemporaries on the results of intelligence tests will usually continue to do so throughout life. Although the tests measure something surprisingly constant, the nature of intelligence eludes precise definition. Some psychologists dismiss the problem by saying that intelligence is whatever the tests measure – rather like the criminologists who say that a crime is whatever the courts declare a crime. Perhaps the nearest one can get to it is to say that intelligence tests measure general intellectual capacity for grasp and insight into new and puzzling situations and problems. The individual who lacks this capacity to a serious degree is recognizably dull and stupid in everyday life, and only those who achieve above average scores on intelligence tests are able to become successful students or pass examinations for professional careers.

At one time leading psychologists believed dullness of intellect to be the commonest characteristic of the criminal. In the early decades of this century, Goddard applied tests to various groups of American prisoners and declared anything from a quarter to nine tenths feeble-minded. More recently, Mary Woodward [289], in a comprehensive review of the results of intelligence tests applied to offenders, suggested that the average intelligence quotient of delinquent groups, both in England and America, was not more than eight points below that of the normal population.

Since samples of criminals, especially those taken from institutions, regularly include an over-representation of socially deprived and educationally backward persons, they will always be found to perform far below average on questions involving scholastic skills, upon which the older tests of 'intelligence' relied. In the more modern types of test, which involve non-verbal puzzles, like fitting shapes and patterns together, the un-educated are no longer at such a disadvantage, and when these tests are administered to samples of remand-home boys, borstal youths, or older prisoners, the intelligence scores obtained are not so very different from those of the normal population, except that there are relatively few really bright individuals, and an excess in the dull to average range [56].

Even this undramatic difference might melt away if, instead of comparing the delinquent groups with the average for the whole population, one compared them with a control group of non-delinquents of similar social background. This is not so easy to do in practice, because the commonly used criterion of socio-economic status, namely father's occupation, in the case of delinquent families may not provide a reliable guide to educational opportunity. In their analysis of the Cambridge–Somerville Youth Study, W. and J. McCord [164] were fortunate in having available a large sample of young working-class males who had been selected at the early age of eight years, for the most part because they were judged potential delinquency risks. Actually, forty-one per cent were convicted at least once during the ensuing seventeen years, and of those who were convicted there was indeed an over-representation (forty-two per cent) of individuals of rather dull intelligence, with quotients not more than 90. However, the unconvicted group had just as high a proportion (forty-four per cent) of individuals with the same range of intelligence scores. The excess of dullards in both groups was accounted for by the fact that the whole sample came from broken-down delinquent neighbourhoods, where the intelligence range of the population is generally depressed. The follow-up study showed very neatly that under these circumstances individual dullness bore no significant relationship to likelihood of a criminal conviction.

Previous work has not always yielded the same result. Cyril Burt [26], in his great study of London juvenile delinquents more than forty years ago, compared his delinquent group with non-delinquent children of the same age and social class, living usually in the same streets and attending the same schools. He found that both intellectual dullness and actual mental subnormality were three or more times as common among the delinquents. The improvements which have since taken place in the social and educational services may have prevented many dull children from lapsing into delinquency, and probably accounts for the fact that modern delinquents are not conspicuously duller than their social peers.

Types of intelligence and types of crime

A modified version of the theory that delinquents are intellectually inferior suggests that their main characteristic consists less in generalized dullness than in a selective lack of verbal skills compared with their relatively better performance on practical, manual tasks [211]. This suggestion seems plausible, because it fits in with the popular impression of the delinquent as a person who expresses himself more readily in action than in thought. However, it is singularly difficult to establish this as a characteristic peculiar to delinquents, since it has often been held to be typical of lower-working-class males in general, because of their traditional contempt for book-learning, abstract vocabulary, and middle-class subtleties of speech. Furthermore, as a recent review of research on the point has shown [196], actual findings have frequently failed to conform to the theoretical prediction. In fact, some recent research on English schoolchildren by P.E.Vernon [266], in which performance on a wide range of tests was related to the presence of environmental adversity, showed that children from homes of a low cultural level, where educational and linguistic stimulus was lacking, were as badly handicapped in practical-spatial tasks as in verbal comprehension or scholastic achievement.

It is sometimes suggested that criminals of above-average intelligence do not appear as often as they might in the criminal statistics because they use their intelligence to develop skills to evade being caught. By the nature of the case one can't know about those who have never been caught at all, but likelihood of re-conviction among those who already have a record bears no

significant relationship to intelligence. The prison psychologist
B. Marcus [170] reported on the re-convictions of 800 men
followed up for three years or more after discharge from Wakefield Prison. On average, according to their test scores in prison,
the ten per cent who were re-convicted during this period were
no less intelligent than those who stayed out of trouble. A
similar result in the case of juveniles was obtained by J. W.
Anderson [9], who compared first offenders and recidivists in a
sample of boys in the London Remand Home and found no
significant difference in intelligence scores.

   There is a demonstrable relationship, however, as Marcus and
others have shown, between the average intelligence scores of
those who commit different types of crime. As groups, sexual
offenders and those guilty of personal violence are on average less
intelligent than thieves, and of course considerably less intelligent
then embezzlers. This might well be the consequence of the
lowest social class, whose intelligence as a group is below average,
being relatively uninhibited in sexual and aggressive behaviour,
and so contributing large numbers of these types of offender.

Sub-cultural and pathological subnormality

When it comes to the minority who are sufficiently deviant to be
classed as mentally subnormal, a more definite relationship with
criminality emerges, although even then it is not so close as has
often been supposed, and may be due in large part to the methods
of selecting persons for legal ascertainment. The English Mental
Health Act, 1959, defines subnormality as 'a state of arrested or
incomplete development of mind ... which includes subnormality of intelligence and is of a nature and degree which
requires or is susceptible to medical treatment or other special
care of training of the patient'. Such a patient, if under twenty-
one years of age, may be compulsorily committed to a mental
hospital on the appropriate medical recommendations.

   In practice, persons whose scores on tests place them in the
bottom five per cent of the population on measurable intelligence
are liable to be admitted to institutions [30], but in fact this
happens to not more than one in a hundred among the dullest
five per cent. In spite of their intellectual disadvantage, the great

majority fit into the community in simple, undemanding jobs. However, those whose dullness is combined with a wayward temperament, or those whose training has been neglected on account of bad family backgrounds, find themselves in social difficulties, and are liable to be referred for examination and officially ascertained as subnormal. The selection process accounts for the fact that, among children below the age of puberty attending state schools for the educationally subnormal, boys invariably predominate. At this age, teachers find boys more often troublesome than girls, so boys are preferentially selected for disposal in special schools. Stein and Susser [250] demonstrated a great preponderance of lower-class, badly educated, and socially unaspiring families among those whose children were ascertained subnormal. In institutions, there is always a relatively large number of admissions of subnormals after adolescence, at an age when the guiding influences of school and parents begin to wane, and young persons are expected to assume some individual responsibility.

This way of looking at the problem emphasizes the cultural determinants of subnormality. Intellectually, subnormals fall on the dull side of the average, but most of them are within the natural range of variation, they have no obvious physical defects, and they generally come to notice on account of social as much as intellectual incompetence. The families least able to contend with difficulties, those in which the parents are themselves dim-witted, ineffectual or neglecting, and who often produce large numbers of children, are the ones least able to cope with the training of children of low intelligence. Hence the duller off-spring from such families are very liable to be ascertained sub-normal, thus perpetuating from one generation to the next a complex of social problems that is likely to include both sub-normality and delinquency.

There seems no doubt that the increasing complexity of urban civilization makes heavy demands upon the duller members, who find learning to read, write and calculate, learning to handle machines, use a telephone, drive a car, or master a trade, or learning the complicated array of attitudes and habits required by society comes less easily to them than to their brighter neigh-bours. Most instances of moderate subnormality result from a combination of below-average intellectual endowment and deprived upbringing, which has the effect of stunting mental growth and discouraging social learning. It was once popularly believed that intelligence, as measured by tests, was essentially a fixed, unalterable attribute, determined exclusively by hereditary endowment. Modern research suggests that not more than three quarters of the variation in intelligence between individuals is due to innate factors, and this leaves a lot of scope for environmental influences. Uninterested and neglectful parents, who are often dull themselves, give their offspring insufficient stimulation. They don't bother to talk to them or explain things, they don't give that loving encouragement which is an essential part of training, and as a result their children never learn to take things in properly. Extreme examples are on record of unwanted children, usually illegitimate, shut away in solitude in an attic. Such children, if they pass the critical age when social contacts and language are normally learnt, may remain permanently imbecilic. In less extreme cases, transfer to a good foster home, provided it takes place while mental growth is still possible, results in a considerable increase in test scores. Clarke and Clarke [38] studied the changes in intelligence quotient among subnormals which took place over a period of eighteen months following committal to an institution. The prospects of improvement with training were better with those from the worst homes, presumably because in their case environmental factors predominated. The subnormal children who came from very adverse backgrounds made an average increase of ten points of I.Q., compared with an increase of only four points in those from less bad homes. A follow-up investigation six years after first committal showed continuing improvement.*

Severe subnormality, legally defined as 'of such a nature or degree that the patient is incapable of living an independent life or of guarding himself against serious exploitation . . .', constitutes a different and more strictly medical problem. Most such persons give scores on intelligence tests worse than 99.8 per cent of the population, which means, in the case of adults, that they

---

* The difference between the changes in the two groups was the important finding. The statistical phenomenon of regression to the mean might explain some degree of apparent improvement on re-testing.

have a 'mental age' of less than six years. Most of them have demonstrable physical abnormalities, paralyses or deformities. In other words they are pathological cases in which, as for instance in the common 'Mongol' type, some developmental flaw (in this instance associated with an identifiable chromosomal abnormality) has prevented the normal development of the brain and nervous system. Many such unfortunates require skilled nursing care just to keep them alive. They contribute very little to crime statistics, partly because they are comparatively rare outside of institutions, and partly because their incapacities, both mental and physical, are too severe to allow much scope for criminal activities. They differ from the 'cultural' type of moderately subnormals in that they are as likely to appear in better-class homes as in the poorer homes [202], and they have not usually been deprived of affection or training.

Since there is such a clear association between social adversity and moderate subnormality officially ascertained, it is not surprising to find, in clinical surveys of mentally subnormal individuals, that those who have come from the worst environments are often the most unstable in behaviour. Dr Michael Craft [44] made an interesting comparison between a series of subnormals transferred to the special hospital at Rampton on account of their violent or obstreperous behaviour, and a control group of patients of similar grade of defect who remained in the ordinary hospital. The former group had a much higher incidence of unsatisfactory backgrounds as judged by interventions by the National Society for the Prevention of Cruelty to Children, the absence of one or both parents, or indications of severe poverty.

Subnormal offenders

East, in a survey of 4,000 youths examined at Wormwood Scrubs Prison as to their fitness for detention in borstals, found 3.5 per cent potentially certifiable as mentally subnormal [53]. In his smaller sample of 200 youths actually committed to borstals, T.C.N. Gibbens [82] found three per cent of unstable dullards whom he described as 'borderline defectives'. Although this is several times what one would expect of a normal young male population, subnormals obviously do not account for more than a small minority of the population of young criminals. However, it is of interest to isolate the subnormal group and consider their special characteristics.

Like any other under-privileged minority, mentally subnormal people, especially if they have been forcibly detained in institutions, may develop attitudes of resentment and revolt. They may also feel at a loss to make their mark among their peers, so when opportunity presents itself to participate in delinquent activities they are easily led into stupid exploits in the hope of winning acceptance. Sexually, they have normal physical and mental urges but often without the ability to make social contacts with the opposite sex and achieve their goal in a conventional manner. G. de M. Rudolf [225], in a survey of the incidence of crime among subnormals released from English hospitals, demonstrated that patients discharged or released on licence have a considerably higher incidence of criminal convictions than the population average. He noted that all kinds of offences of all degrees of seriousness were committed by subnormals, but that sexual crimes were particularly common. Liability to minor crimes seems to be rather widespread among subnormals. Nigel Walker [270] pointed out that of the 305 male offenders of seventeen years of age or more who were committed to hospitals by English courts on account of mental subnormality during the year 1961, as many as thirty-two per cent were guilty of sexual offences. (Of all males of seventeen or more convicted of indictable offences that year, only five per cent were convicted of sexual offences.) Crimes of serious personal violence, on the other hand, are not particularly characteristic of subnormals in general, and murder is rarely committed by them.

In subnormals, as in other types of mentally abnormal person, background and personality count for more than the degree of handicap in determining criminal habits. The general run of subnormals are not particularly criminal, but those with an intellectual handicap combined with temperamental aggressiveness or psychopathic disposition can be quite a menace.

Rudolf did not follow up his cases long enough to see if they gradually got adjusted to life outside the institution. The few long-term surveys that have been done tend to show that the ultimate prospects of mentally handicapped people are not so bad as one might expect, that very few commit serious crimes, and only a small minority become persistent offenders. Thus D. C. Charles [32], in a survey of 127 cases ascertained mentally retarded during their schooldays, and traced some twenty years later, found no very serious crimes had been committed, although sixty per cent of the men had been convicted on one or more occasions. Petty crimes, especially traffic violations and drunkenness, accounted for the great majority of convictions. At the other extreme a twenty-year follow-up of cases from two Danish island colonies for subnormals, which receive unruly or criminal patients, revealed a much more depressing picture [280]. Of fifty-eight men, eight had died, one while trying to escape from the mental institution, three by committing suicide. Two of the suicides occurred in prison, one by a man who had committed 400 burglaries, the other by a man who had committed murder. Of the fifty surviving at follow-up, about a half were 'managing decently' in the community. However, it was also about a half who had received one or more sentences for criminal offences, some of them of quite serious nature. Repeated thefts were the most frequent of their offences, but crimes of fraud, sex and violence were not uncommon.

The contrast between the ordinary harmless subnormals and the psychopathic types accounts for the fact that whereas serious crimes of violence are untypical of the general run of subnormals, nevertheless, among the minority of serious criminals, for instance those who commit murder, rape, and sexual assault with violence, a surprisingly high proportion are drawn from the ranks of the more unstable and aggressive subnormals. It seems that the conjunction of impulsiveness with lack of imaginative appreciation of the consequences or gravity of their acts makes a few subnormals a real danger.

The classification of subnormals into the more severe cases who are organically damaged, and the less severe cases, who are culturally deprived dullards, useful as it is in identifying general trends, cannot be applied in a hard and fast way to every individual case, since some people display varying mixtures of both kinds of handicap. The combination of social adversity and organic defect can sometimes produce quite monstrous and dangerous deformities of character.

Physical defects

Minor physical handicap

According to some theorists, people take to crime because they find difficulty in competing according to the rules. Hence, any kind of physical handicap or disease which interferes with social adjustment might be expected to predispose to delinquency. In practice, it has not been convincingly demonstrated that criminals as a group, and especially young criminals, are any less healthy than their non-delinquent peers. Earlier surveys often found a high incidence of physical disease and malnutrition among delinquents. In the 1920s, Cyril Burt [26] found that defective physical conditions were roughly one and a quarter times as frequent among delinquents as among non-delinquents. Nearly seventy per cent of his delinquents were suffering from some degree of bodily weakness or ill-health, and fifty per cent were in urgent need of medical treatment. With improved social conditions this no longer holds true. In a comparison of the medical records of delinquent boys in a London remand home in the years 1930 and 1955, Eilenberg [56] found that over this period serious physical disease and serious malnutrition had virtually disappeared as a feature of young delinquents. In fact the delinquent boys were slightly heavier than the average for London schoolboys. However, he did note a significantly higher incidence of minor physical ailments in the remand-home boys, including skin complaints, visual defects, ear discharges and deafness, and skeletal deformities. Some of these were treatable conditions that had been neglected.

The slightly raised incidence of physical anomalies among delinquents may be merely a feature of the social class from which they come. Larger studies, using control groups taken from the same social class, have not shown any consistent trend. Thus E. and S. Glueck [95] found that most of the defects which cause embarrassment, such as squints and genital peculiarities, were, if anything, commoner among the non-delinquents. W. and J. McCord [164], in their analysis of the Cambridge–Somerville youth project, found no correlation between general physical ill health and delinquency proneness. Ferguson [69], in his Glasgow survey, showed that boys from schools for the physically handicapped were no more frequently delinquent than those from ordinary schools – although those who were tended to be unusually persistent. A reaction of social withdrawal and shyness may possibly be more typical of the physically handicapped than one of rebellion and delinquency, although the rebellious reaction may be an important characteristic of certain handicapped individuals.

D. H. Stott [252] attempted to show that the more maladjusted among delinquents are more likely to have physical defects. Applying a maladjustment questionnaire addressed to school-teachers, he found that among a sample of 400 boys on probation in Glasgow, those rated 'maladjusted' had a much higher incidence of physical ailments. In order to see if this association was simply the consequence of both the socially maladjusted and the physically inadequate coming from the same poor backgrounds, he separated out a group from satisfactory homes and found that the relationship still held good even in the absence of obvious environmental adversity.

As usual, when one comes to consider special groups of offenders the incidence of abnormalities increases. Borstal youths are on the whole more serious and persistent delinquents, and come from worse backgrounds, than the average boy in a remand home, so it is not surprising to find that they have a larger proportion with physical defects. T. C. N. Gibbens [82] found that among his borstal sample double the expected proportion had been rejected on physical grounds when called up for military service.

Whatever one believes about the importance or otherwise of the presence of physical defects in fostering delinquent tendencies, clearly nothing but good can come from trying to correct them when their presence is detected. This was done, for instance, by Ogden [198], who arranged surgical treatment for borstal inmates with minor deformities, and showed that their reconviction rates appeared to decrease. He believed the procedure worked by liberating these youngsters from chronic embarrassments and irritations, and so rendering them more susceptible to training. In a more recent Canadian project [153], 450 young male prisoners who had disfigurements improved in behaviour after plastic surgery.

Brain damage and bad behaviour

A somewhat more subtle version of the physical-defect theory
has gained acceptance in recent years, based upon evidence that
relatively slight degrees of brain damage, sustained perhaps
during development in the womb or in the process of birth,
although insufficient to cause paralysis or other physical symptoms, may nevertheless result in emotional instability and possibly
delinquency. One of the best pieces of evidence for this view has
been produced in a Scottish survey by C.M.Drillien [50], who
followed up a sample of prematurely born infants, and, at the
age of seven years, had their teachers rate their behaviour on a
questionnaire designed to elicit signs of maladjustment (Stott's
Bristol Maladjustment Guide). Children who were maturely
born (i.e. over $5\frac{1}{2}$ lb. at birth), and without complications in
pregnancy or delivery, produced the fewest indications of
maladjustment. A history of premature birth, of complications of
delivery or pregnancy, or of family stress, each added a considerable increment to the maladjustment score. Such findings
lend support to the theory that a series of minor neurological
impairments can produce a cumulative deterioration of behaviour, and that individuals so affected are rendered particularly
vulnerable to adverse environmental influences.

Unfortunately, much of the evidence bearing upon this theory
is somewhat complex and equivocal. Clinical experience of
persons with epilepsy, head injuries, brain infections, or other
conditions liable to damage the brain shows that some of these
patients, especially if they are young and of unformed character
at the onset of the illness, afterwards become extraordinarily
irritable, aggressive and sometimes delinquent. However, the
outcome is very unpredictable, and large-scale surveys of the
after-careers of patients who have had encephalitis or epilepsy
have failed to confirm any conspicuous general trends towards
delinquency. For example, C.H.Alström [7], in a careful follow-
up study of 345 adult male epileptics over a ten-year period,
found crimes of violence recorded in seventeen per cent of the
sample compared with eleven per cent in a control group. There
were no instances of homicide, and nearly all the crimes were
minor, usually related to alcoholic abuses.

D.A.Pond [209] has pointed out that the over-activity and aggressiveness of epileptic and brain-damaged children brought to psychiatric clinics are very similar to the symptoms of children brought on account of purely emotional disturbance. Furthermore, the organically impaired children with behaviour problems usually came from broken or disturbed backgrounds such as are also associated with bad behaviour in organically sound children. He quoted in support a Swedish study by Dencker and Löfving, in which a large series of twins, one of each pair having sustained a serious head injury, were followed up years later. Often the uninjured twin showed similar symptoms, although in a milder degree. The work strongly suggested that the psychological disturbances following brain injury had more to do with the previous personality and background of the patient than the extent or nature of the injury. A fair statement of the position would seem to be that even minor degrees of neurological disease, injury, or congenital abnormality are liable to exaggerate the effects of an adverse environment or of underlying defects of personality; but that in the absence of these additional factors even very serious injuries may not produce any permanent deterioration in behaviour.

From a research standpoint, the difficulty of sorting out the effects of organic and environmental handicaps is greatly increased by their tendency to occur together in the deprived section of the community. Thus J.W.B.Douglas [47], in a national survey of all children born over a given span of time, found a very significant correlation between bad behaviour, as evaluated by primary-school teachers, and a history of premature birth. However, among the children of better-class mothers, the association between prematurity and bad behaviour no longer held true. He concluded that the connexion was not a matter of cause and effect, but was largely due to the high incidence of premature births among the unsatisfactory mothers who reared badly behaved children.

It seems clear that physical defect, either in general or more specifically neurological form, does not account for the bulk of delinquent behaviour, although it may be a contributory factor in many cases, and an important factor in a few.

Brain waves in delinquents

The electro-encephalograph, which records in wave tracings the electrical activity of the brain, might be expected to provide further evidence as to the neurological abnormalities of certain delinquents. Applied to persons of epileptic tendency, the instrument can be used to show that fits are associated with paroxysms of fast waves of high amplitude, indicative of numerous brain cells discharging in unison. When this abnormal rhythm spreads too far, generalized convulsions and loss of consciousness occur. Rather similar paroxysmal disturbances, but limited to areas of the brain where they do not cause convulsions, have been found in tracings obtained from individuals of abnormally aggressive temperament. This has led to the theory that explosive outbursts of rage may sometimes represent the 'equivalent' of an epileptic fit, a theory reminiscent of the traditional notion of a 'brain-storm'.

Apart from these paroxysms, a commoner indication of cerebral instability is the presence of waves slower than those which are usually found in the records of normal, wakeful adults. It is possible to classify people as 'normal' or 'abnormal' on their E.E.G. records according to generally agreed criteria, such as the system evolved by F.A.Gibbs, which depends upon counting the frequency of various types of deviant waves. Anything up to one fifth of the population may be classified as 'abnormal' on these grounds. When the same tests are applied to E.E.G. records taken from mental patients, a much greater incidence of abnormality has been found. Unselected groups of criminals, however, have shown no such trend [89], but of criminals classified as 'unstable and aggressive' or 'psychopathic' something like a half have been found to have 'abnormal' brain rhythms [57]. In one of the most famous investigations of this kind Hill and Pond [121] examined the records of a series of 105 English murderers, and found that of those who had committed clearly motivated crimes only ten per cent had abnormal E.E.G. records, but nearly all of the irrational murderers showed abnormalities.

In a more recent research by Loomis [159], who examined the E.E.G. tracings of 100 young delinquents (modal age fifteen to sixteen years) in an American reform school for boys, the proportion with specifiable abnormalities was no greater than that found in unselected school populations of similar age. On the other hand, among a group of fifty delinquents from the same reform school who had been specially selected for psychiatric examination on account of peculiarities noticed by the staff, the proportion with E.E.G. abnormalities was almost double the ordinary figure. Impulsive violence was only one among many symptoms displayed by the youths with abnormal E.E.G. recordings.

In so far as these abnormal tracings may be thought to signify the presence of a constitutional neurological defect, they provide another piece of evidence for innate delinquent propensities in some individuals. However, the findings refer only to specially selected groups of violent and peculiar offenders. E.E.G. abnormalities also occur in individuals of 'psychopathic' temperament who do not happen to have committed crimes. Individuals with abnormalities of the E.E.G. must not be regarded as doomed, for a great many improve or 'mature' with time. Judged on adult standards, the E.E.G. tracings of most normal children would be classed as abnormal. Among adults, the proportion found to be 'abnormal' decreases steadily with age. Curiously enough, Gibbens and others [86], in a follow-up study of a series of psychopathic recidivists, found that those with E.E.G. abnormalities on first examination did rather better than those with normal records. This confirms the impressions of other workers [55], who find that psychopaths with normal E.E.G. records are relatively more aloof and set in their ways, and more obviously strongly conditioned by a very bad social background; whereas those with abnormalities have slightly better backgrounds, more frequent histories of brain injury or disease, more signs of conflict within themselves about their behaviour, and a greater potentiality for change. Thus, the connexion in certain people between unstable and anti-social behaviour and E.E.G. abnormalities is beyond doubt, but the details of these relationships, and their meaning in regard to cause and effect, have yet to be worked out. Modern anti-convulsant drugs, which have a stabilizing effect upon brain rhythms, without actually putting the patient to sleep or causing too much drowsiness, have proved most effective in controlling epileptic attacks. The same drugs have been given to aggressive psychopaths in the hope of controlling their emotional outbursts, but on the whole without any great success, except in those cases associated with definite clinical epilepsy.

Insanity

Mental diseases, like manic-depressive psychosis and schizo-phrenia, which are probably due to some underlying but as yet not precisely identified organic defect are hardly worth mention-ing in connexion with young offenders, since their incidence is so small. Melancholia is a disease of middle age, and schizo-phrenia does not usually manifest itself before early adult life. Occasionally young schizophrenics under the influence of delusions of persecution or preoccupied with bizarre sexual impulses commit family murders or other atrocious acts of vio-lence, but fortunately such events are rare. Among young delinquents examined in remand homes, schizophrenia is rarely diagnosed, and probably no more often than might occur in routine examinations of a normal population during an army call-up.

The criminal physique

Sheldon's body types

In recent years techniques known as somatotyping have been developed whereby individuals may be classified according to their characteristic physique by measuring the relative size of the muscular, bony and fatty components of the body. The pioneer in this field was a psychiatrist, E. Kretchmer, who was interested in the observation that susceptibility to one mental disease or another was apparently associated with body build. He divided people into asthenic (the thin, lanky type), athletic (the muscular type), pyknic (squat, barrel type), and dysplastic (mixed) types, and found that the asthenics were prone to introverted temperament and schizophrenic illness, while the pyknics were more prone to mood fluctuations and manic-depressive psychosis. W.H. Sheldon [240] developed a method of rating numerically these various bodily elements by measuring the contours on photographs taken in the nude. He later introduced his system into the criminological arena by claiming that the physical types were related not only to temperament, but also to delinquent tendency.

On Sheldon's system each person receives three numerical ratings according to the strength of three primary bodily components called endomorphy, mesomorphy and ectomorphy. Although many people score equally on more than one rating, others show a predominance of a particular component. Endomorphs have large body cavities and viscera (barrel chests and pot bellies) with soft, rounded surface contours. Mesomorphs are solidly built and heavy, with a lot of muscle. Ectomorphs are light-weight skinny types with slender bodies. The names of the three body types were taken from the three layers of the developing embryo, which form respectively the viscera and body linings; the muscle, bone and connective tissue; and the nervous system and surface skin. The body types were thought to result from differential development of one or other of these fundamental tissue components. Whether the measurements used in Sheldon's system really do have these biological implications is doubtful. The Sheldon types correspond roughly, but not exactly, to Kretchmer's system, the endomorphs having much in common with the pyknics, the mesomorphs with the athletics and the ectomorphs with the asthenics.

Sheldon applied his typing system, using photographs, to 200 male students at a university and to another 200 youths resident in a Boston institution for difficult and delinquent boys. He found that whereas among the college males there were as many ectomorphs as mesomorphs, among the institutional youths there was a heavy preponderance of mesomorphs and few ectomorphs. The preponderance of sturdy mesomorphs was most noticeable among the healthiest of the institution youths, those who were simply delinquents without having any accompanying psychiatric or medical disabilities. Sheldon identified this type of physique with the boisterous, affable, out-going, yet fundamentally aggressive and undisciplined, temperament (Dionysian) that predisposes to a predatory rather than a subservient or docile attitude to life. He saw the delinquents as individually unsuccessful predators, whereas some political bosses and irresponsible jingoists in the community at large were examples of the same type who had won themselves social status. Sheldon thought selective breeding was a cause of the delinquency problem and eugenic measures a possible long-term remedy. He argued that 'our best stock tends to be outbred by stock that is inferior to it in every respect' [241]. The parents of the delinquents were producing many more offspring than the parents of college students. They were 'expending a greater proportion of their energies on uninhibited or irresponsible sexuality'. The predatory types were reproducing themselves at an alarming rate, thus causing a population explosion that could only end in a death struggle for survival.

Fortunately, an acceptance of some of Sheldon's research findings does not force one to share his alarming speculations about the deterioration of the race. Indeed it is arguable that the beefy, vigorous mesomorph is biologically an admirable type who is apt to become delinquent only under adverse conditions. The same type of youth in a different social class might be a successful rugger captain or rowing blue.

The physical and temperamental differences outlined by Sheldon are detectable from quite an early age, which is in keeping with the idea that these are largely inborn qualities. R. W. Parnell [200] found in a sample of Oxford schoolchildren of eleven a high positive correlation between ectomorphic physique and traits of meticulousness and susceptibility to anxiety and guilt feelings, which were assessed by psychological testing and psychiatric interviews. In contrast, 'muscularity' (Parnell's version of mesomorphy) correlated with traits of aggressiveness and restless or explosive behaviour.

Physical types among delinquents

The largest and most famous application of Sheldon's system to delinquents was made by S. and E. Glueck [97], who compared 500 delinquent youths attending two correctional schools in Massachusetts with 500 youths, who were believed to be non-delinquent, from state schools in Boston, who were matched with the delinquents for age, intelligence level, racial origin and residence in poor urban areas. The results confirmed Sheldon's claims. There were twice as many mesomorphs among the delinquents (60.1 per cent compared with 30.7 per cent) but less than half as many ectomorphs (14.4 per cent compared with 39.6 per cent). The matching procedure ensured that these findings were not due to differences in race or social class between the delinquents and non-delinquents. Assessments of the boys, made by means of psychiatric interviews and psychological tests, showed that, among both delinquents and controls, those of mesomorphic physique tended to be relatively more powerful and energetic, more apt to work off their tensions or frustrations in action, and less inhibited by feelings of inadequacy, submissiveness to authority or by sensitivity to conflict situations. It is easy to see how these traits might predispose to aggressiveness and delinquent behaviour, although of course only a minority of mesomorphs actually become delinquent.

In contrast, the ectomorph was characterized by greater liability to feelings of inadequacy and to emotional conflict, a more sensitive and imaginative turn of mind, and less out-going energy. These traits acted as a curb on aggressive impulses, so that frustrated ectomorphs tended to bottle up their emotions, and to react to difficulties by blaming their own inadequacies or by generating nervous symptoms, rather than by resorting to rebellion and delinquency.

Although the degree of vulnerability to delinquency varied, the Gluecks found that the adverse factors associated with the onset of delinquency (such as poor homes, bad relationships with parents, lack of self-control, undue suggestibility, and delinquency in other members of the family) were much the same in all types of physique. But the association between disharmony in the home and delinquency was closer in the case of ectomorphs than mesomorphs, presumably because ectomorphs are more sensitive to environmental conditioning, whereas mesomorphs, being more robust and self-assertive, become slap-happy delinquents without necessarily having a very disturbed background, or, in other cases, resist becoming delinquents in spite of bad home influences. Some of the most intractable delinquents, however, were mesomorphs with the aggressive drive typical of their physique, but unhappily coupled with emotional instability, mental conflicts and feelings of inadequacy such as more often occur in ectomorphs.

Sheldon's system of typing human physique has been subjected to considerable criticism in recent years. The shapes of
photographic silhouettes may not give the best indication of
physique. More recently other workers have used quite different
procedures, for example taking X-rays of limbs and counting the
ratio of muscle to bone at a particular level across the calf or
upper arm. Another way of estimating muscular development
uses strength of grip, as measured by squeezing a dynamometer
bulb. Sheldon hoped to eliminate the complicating factor of the
amount of fat present, which of course varies with age and feed-
ing habits, but in this he probably did not completely succeed.
Furthermore, it remains an open question at what stage of
growth the bodily configuration becomes stable and permanent.
Some authorities consider that the whole idea of dividing people
into types is misconceived, and that better correlations between
physique and behaviour might be had by using an array of
simpler variables such as height, weight and shoulder width.
Sheldon's types, although thought by their originators to arise
from genetic differences, may well be connected with other
factors. The muscular, hyper-masculine mesomorphic youth, for
example, may well owe the splendours of his physique largely to
his endocrines which are certainly prompted by nutritional and
environmental circumstances as well as by the genes.

These and many other technical difficulties serve to emphasize
the complexity of the relationships between physique and
temperament, but they in no way invalidate the fundamental
principle, pioneered by Sheldon, that the individual physical
constitution has an obvious bearing upon human behaviour, and
in particular upon delinquent behaviour. The measures relevant
in this context, such as height, weight and muscularity, are
variants of the normal, and in this respect quite unlike the
Lombrosian stigmata, which were thought to indicate degeneration or pathology. Nevertheless, they are measures which, to a
large extent, appear to be predetermined by inborn or hereditary
factors. Although it is highly unfashionable to suggest that
delinquent propensities may have some hereditary basis, research
evidence compels one to consider carefully some of the links that
have been discovered between delinquent behaviour and certain
physical and psychological traits presumed to be inherited.

Inherited criminality

Familial incidence of criminality

The individual qualities so far discussed as possibly related to criminal propensities have in common the factor of being supposedly determined to a large extent by heredity. Hence it seems relevant to mention at this point some attempts to obtain direct evidence for the inheritance of criminal tendency.

The first problem is whether in fact criminality does run in families from one generation to the next. If it does not, then the question of heredity hardly arises. If it does, then one has to try to sort out how far this can be accounted for by environmental factors, such as contamination through contact with criminal relatives, or adverse influences acting upon the whole family.

In countries like England, where for many years a central register of all convicted persons has been kept by the police at the Criminal Records Office, one might expect to have a lot of information available on the distribution of criminals between families from one generation to the next. It would be most interesting to know, for instance, whether the children of criminals, if they take to crime, have any tendency to commit the same kinds of offences as their parents. Does violence breed violence, or sex offences breed further sexual offences? Unfortunately, this type of investigation has been almost totally neglected.

Some studies of samples of young offenders have noted the presence or absence of criminality in their parents. Although these often rely on local police or probation reports rather than on a systematic name search, they are sufficient to demonstrate a high incidence of convictions among the parents and siblings of juvenile offenders. Nevertheless, surprisingly large numbers come from apparently law-abiding families, and in the case of those who commence a persistent criminal career only after reaching adult years, the presence of criminal convictions in their parents is the exception rather than the rule [276]. Such observations suggest that extraneous environmental influences are often more powerful than any direct transmission from parents to children, whether by bad example or bad heredity. All the same, as every probation officer or social investigator well knows, many notorious families exist among whom nearly every member is either a known criminal or a social menace in other ways. Where one member is alcoholic, another a prostitute, another a hospitalized mental patient, and the rest petty criminals, some familial weakness is obviously present, although criminality is only one of a number of ways in which it may manifest. The environment has to be suitable for bringing out such tendencies. No one is born a skilled safe breaker.

Seriously defective characters, with marked aggressive tendencies and shallow, callous emotional responses, who are diagnosed by psychiatrists as psychopaths,* may be suspected of having some innate abnormality. Franz Kallmann [145], who investigated the genetics of various human abnormalities, noted that psychopathy may be passed on through generations of disorderly families, but it was doubtful how far hereditary mechanisms were involved. The transmission did not follow the lines of closest blood kinship. The children of psychopaths showed a higher incidence of disorder than the brothers and sisters of psychopaths, which is what one would expect of a condition produced by faulty child-rearing rather than pure inheritance.

Twin studies

A classic method of sorting out the effects of heredity and environment makes use of comparisons between samples of identical and non-identical pairs of twins. Identical twins supposedly come about by the splitting of a single fertilized egg to produce two separate individuals with precisely the same genes. Since they have exactly the same hereditary endowment they are always of the same sex, blood grouping, eye colour and so forth. Any differences between them must be the result of environmental influence (although one has to remember that in this context environment begins in the womb). Non-identical twins come from different eggs, and from the physical standpoint are no more alike than ordinary brothers and sisters, except for being of the same age. Qualities like physique and intelligence, on which identical twin pairs are much more alike than non-

* See p. 150.

identical twins, can generally be assumed to be hereditarily determined. A complication arises, however, if one believes that identical twins actually experience more similar environments than non-identical twins, and that this might account for their more frequent concordance. Some identical twins look so alike and dress so alike that parents and others treat them with greater equality than if they had been non-identical. Thus, identical twins may to some extent generate their own similar environments. This argument cannot apply in the case of twins separated from birth or soon after and reared apart. Studies of twins have shown that in such matters as intelligence and extraversion the degree of concordance between identical twins is as great or almost as great when they are reared apart as when they are brought up together, and very much greater than the concordance between non-identical twins reared together [242].

In the 1930s, a number of large-scale surveys of twins were published, purporting to show that where one member of an identical twin pair was criminal the other usually was as well, but that non-identical twins were much less often concordant. This work has been reviewed by Slater [248]. The earliest, as well as the most startling, result was published in Germany by Lange in 1929, and subsequently translated under the dramatic title *Crime as Destiny*. He found that in ten out of thirteen pairs of identical twins, that is seventy-seven per cent, both members had a criminal record; whereas out of seventeen pairs of non-identical but same-sexed twin pairs only two, that is twelve per cent, both had criminal records.

In two later series of criminal twins, also German, smaller differences were reported. Stumpfl [255] found that of eighteen pairs of identical twins eleven, that is sixty-one per cent, had criminal records in both members, but, of nineteen same-sexed non-identical twin pairs, seven, that is thirty-seven per cent, both had records. H. Kranz found that fifty-five per cent of thirty-two pairs of identical twins were concordant on the possession of a criminal record, but so were fifty-three per cent of forty-three same-sexed non-identical twin pairs. However, both these investigators found a much greater concordance between non-identical twins on temperamental qualities like aggressiveness and social rebellion which underlie serious criminality.

Stumpfl noted that if he counted only the more serious or habitual criminals, the difference in concordance of identical and non-identical twins became much greater. In the case of juvenile twins, concordance on juvenile delinquency is greater than concordance between adult twins on adult criminality. However, the concordance is almost equally great for non-identical as for identical twins, thus confirming the common-sense view that juvenile misbehaviour for the most part reflects environmental influences.

The distinction between identical and non-identical twins may not always have been too certain in these earlier investigations, which used general physical resemblance as a criterion instead of more exact measures like blood groups and fingerprints. A more serious objection, however, concerns the method of selection. Unless one can be sure that all examples of twins in a particular population have been studied, those left out may bias the findings. In the case of criminal twins, for instance, identical brothers, being more noticeable and striking, might be more easily picked out in a search than non-identical twin brothers. For the reason that identical twins reared together may in effect have more similar environments than non-identical twins reared together, the most convincing observations are those made on twins who have been reared apart from an early age. There have been too few such cases in the studies of criminal twins to provide conclusive results. It is unfortunate that interest in the question of the hereditary element in crime has dwindled, and repetitions of earlier work using improved modern techniques have not been tried.

A conclusion

Although inherited attributes may favour a delinquent outcome, environmental circumstances finally bring it about. In observation of infant behaviour, certain primary patterns of reaction (e.g. active–lethargic, intense reactors–mild reactors) appear very early and persist through childhood. But the ultimate effect on social adjustment depends upon how these tendencies are absorbed or exaggerated by training and other social influences [34].

The upshot of all this work amounts to this: a strong case has been made out for the existence of an inherited factor contributing to the behaviour of some serious and persistent criminals. However, owing to technical imperfections in the evidence, resolute sceptics can still argue that the case has not yet been adequately established. Furthermore, in relation to most juvenile delinquency, and to the less serious types of occasional criminals, the influence of heredity seems negligibly small. Even in regard to the persistent criminality of pathological individuals, case histories of identical twins taking different paths demonstrate the importance of life experience in determining whether or not a particular predisposed individual will in fact turn into a criminal. Such case histories show that incidents like a minor brain injury in childhood or an unwise marriage serve to tip the balance and provoke a criminal pattern in the less fortunate member of a twin pair.

6 Some Psychological Theories about the Development of Criminals

(imitating judge)
'In the opinion of this court, this child is depraved on account he ain't had a normal home.'
'Hey, I'm depraved on account I'm deprived.'
'So take him to a head shrinker.'
    Leonard Bernstein and Stephen Sondheim, *West Side Story* (1957). London and New York, Chappell & Co.

A behaviouristic view of criminal traits

Psychomotor clumsiness

Psychologists of the behaviourist school believe in studying people's actions, which can be objectively observed and measured rather than their thoughts and feelings, which can only be deduced somewhat indirectly and inaccurately from what they are able to put into words. Behaviourists categorize people according to their measurable reactions to various set situations or stimuli. For instance, given a situation in which a reward is offered for solving a puzzle which is actually insoluble, some individuals, characterized by 'low frustration tolerance', will quickly lose patience and behave aggressively. By classifying people in such terms, some behaviourists believe they can identify personality traits which correspond to innate or constitutional differences in the physiological reactivity of the nervous system. In England, a leading exponent of this approach, Professor H. J. Eysenck [64], claims to have identified a constellation of traits characteristically associated with criminality, a constellation which he believes to be largely determined by heredity. Since the evidence for a connexion with criminality is better in the case of some traits than others, it will be convenient to consider them separately. One of the traits described by Eysenck, namely mesomorphic physique, has already been discussed in the preceding chapter.

Another trait is what might be called psychomotor style. This was discovered as long ago as 1914, when the American psychologist Porteus introduced a paper-and-pencil test of intelligence in which subjects had to trace their way through a series of printed mazes of increasing difficulty, being told to make one continuous pencil line from start to finish, not to lift their pencil until reaching the end, not to turn down any blind alleys, and not to cut or touch any of the lines marking the borders of the maze paths. Porteus found that subjects varied in the way they heeded or disregarded the test instructions. Persons who were swift and careless, and did not bother about cutting corners or touching edges, were particularly prevalent among delinquent types. Porteus developed a method of scoring based upon counting the number of careless errors, and this 'Q' score, as he called it, was used thereafter in many criminological researches. It invariably proved to be on average significantly higher among delinquents than among non-delinquent controls. In a survey of borstal youths from the London area, Dr T. C. N. Gibbens [82] confirmed that, compared with a control group of youths of similar age and social class attending a training establishment, a higher proportion of the delinquents had high 'Q' scores. He also confirmed Glueck's finding that the delinquent youths were more frequently of mesomorphic physique, very much more so than comparative groups of male undergraduates or officer cadets. Unfortunately, whereas virtually all the borstal youths produced maze scores, many of them had doubts about letting themselves be photographed in the nude, but the numbers were sufficient to show that high 'Q' score and mesomorphy tended to go together in the same individuals.

Several explanations of the connexion between 'Q' score and delinquency have been suggested, based upon the different types of error which make up the score. For instance, disobeying the test rules might indicate a defiant attitude typical of delinquents. On the other hand, a slovenly wavy pencil line that touches sides and cuts corners in a clumsy, careless manner might be a sign of poor muscular control. H. S. Anthony [10] tested the accuracy of movements of a sample of R.A.F. recruits, using an apparatus that had been developed for investigating accident proneness in Air Force pilots. She found that those young men who were subsequently convicted of offences differed from the rest in the poorer quality of their psychomotor performance. More recently, H. B. Gibson [90] compared a group of ordinary schoolboys aged about twelve with a group of boys in a remand home for delinquents. He used a refined form of printed maze consisting of a spiral track along which were scattered obstacles, in the form of a letter O in heavy type, round which the boys had to trace their way with a pencil, being told to go 'as quickly as you can'. The test gives two scores, time taken, and number of errors, the latter given by the number of 'collisions' with obstacles or sides. Those with large error/time ratios, that is the quick and careless types, were over-represented among the delinquents. Applying the same test to a large sample of young schoolboys, aged eight to ten, none of whom had yet been found guilty in the juvenile courts, he found a significant difference between a group classed by their teachers as well behaved and another group classed as poorly behaved. The naughty boys, like the delinquents, included a disproportionate number of quick and careless boys. This test probably identifies the type of person who can be easily induced to risk speeds beyond what his manual dexterity permits, and who remains undeterred by his own mistakes. This may be one reason why men convicted of offences against property have a much greater than average likelihood of also being convicted for motoring offences.

If this new development in research is confirmed, a quick-careless response on psychomotor tests at a relatively early age may prove to have some predictive value in identifying groups likely, in later years, to prove particularly prone to delinquency. Since psychomotor performance is closely bound up with the functioning of the nervous system, and probably derives more from constitutional differences than from social training, these results tend to support the unpopular view that an individual's inherent qualities count as much as his environment in determining whether he will become delinquent.

Resistance to conditioning

Another half-physiological, half-psychological attribute which Eysenck believes has a close connexion with potential delinquency is 'conditionability'. Experimental psychologists nowadays lay great emphasis on the factor of conditioning in habit-training and indeed in all aspects of learning. Pavlov started the whole idea with his famous dogs salivating at the sight of food. By ringing a bell just before he showed them the food, he found that the dogs soon responded by salivating automatically at the sound of the bell, even when no food followed. Their response had been linked with an associated or conditioned stimulus learnt by experience. Similar conditioned responses can be demonstrated in humans, for instance by blowing a puff of air at the eye and showing an ace of spades simultaneously. After a number of repetitions, the mere sight of the ace of spades becomes sufficient to elicit an automatic blink response. In humans, responses which are normally involuntary or automatic, such as the reflex contraction of the pupil of the eye when a bright light is shone into the face, are the ones which most easily become conditioned to extraneous stimuli, and, the link once established, the subject has no control over the automatic reaction.

One of the most powerful of our innate, automatic responses is the reaction of fear and avoidance of painful stimuli. According to one theory of learning, the infant acquires the self-restraint which underlies all social conformity by a process of conditioned avoidance. Certain situations and types of behaviour – for instance screaming, punching, urinating on the carpet – are swiftly followed by slaps or other punishments, which in turn cause fear and withdrawal. Thus, frequent repetition of punishment, by means of the conditioning mechanism, gradually establishes an automatic conditioned reaction of anxiety and withdrawal in the face of situations liable to provoke bad behaviour. The process is aided by a characteristic of conditioning, known technically as generalization, whereby avoidance responses readily become linked with a wide range of associated stimuli. Furthermore, in humans, because of the ability to increase associations by the use of language, and in this context to define a wide range of behaviour as bad, conditioned avoidance reactions can be greatly reinforced and extended.

This theory explains rather neatly the development of the conscience, in terms of a built-in, automatic avoidance of bad behaviour, which works independently of the chances of being observed or found out on any particular occasion. Positive items of conditioned behaviour, like the dog preparing for food at the sound of a bell, tend to disappear rather swiftly, if the bell sounds a few times and no food follows, but the extinction of conditioned avoidance behaviour is much slower. The child who has once been conditioned to avoid punching his sister may go on restraining himself indefinitely because the act of avoidance itself eliminates the possibility of experiencing loss of control without punishment.

The ease with which conditioned responses become established, and their persistence, differ from one individual to another. H. J. Eysenck [65] cites some amusing experiments by R. L. Solomon, at Harvard University, in which the investigators taught puppies that a particular dish of food was taboo by swatting them with a newspaper whenever they approached it. Later, with the experimenter absent but observing, the puppies were let into the room again. Some of them overcame the taboo without difficulty. Others dithered about and whined before taking the food. Others fasted so long they had to be rescued from the situation. Differences between individuals in respect of conditionability probably depend upon some innate quality of the nervous system. Long ago Pavlov demonstrated in conditioning situations that there was a varying balance of reactivity (excitation) and resistance (inhibition) demonstrable in the nervous system of dogs. The strength of a conditioned response is prevented from building up and up as stimuli are repeated by the development of an inhibitory or fatigue factor. After a rest pause, however, the inhibitory factor diminishes, so that when the stimulus reappears the response occurs more strongly than ever, even though no learning practice has taken place meantime. People differ in the degree to which they build up this physiological inhibition. A simple method of demonstrating this consists of recording electronically a subject's performance on a tapping test in which he has to keep on tapping a metal stylus on a plate as fast as possible. Every so often the fast sequence is interrupted by involuntary pauses as inhibition builds up. People who condition slowly (or are of extraverted temperament) produce more pauses.

In experiments with humans in which a noise and a puff of air to the eye are given together, the number of repetitions required to establish a blink reaction to the noise alone gives a measure of the speed of conditioning. To test Eysenck's theory, it needs to be shown that persons resistive to social learning are relatively slow on conditioning. Eysenck maintains that experiments with psychopaths, who represent the most extreme examples of badly behaved and socially unconforming characters, show that they are both slow on conditioning and high on tests of Pavlovian inhibition. The same is true of children with brain damage, who also tend to be badly behaved and resistant to social training. Gordon Trasler [261] has compared the main assumptions of

Eysenck's theory with descriptions of criminals and found that they fit rather well. In the first place, the disturbances of up-bringing which are so commonly found among the more serious and persistent of juvenile delinquents, as well as among adult psychopaths, are of just such a kind as would be expected to interfere with smooth social conditioning. Broken and dis-harmonious parental homes, erratic or inconsistent discipline, parental absence or neglect, are cases in point. Second, it has been frequently reported by clinicians that one of the most noteworthy features of the more unrepentant and unconforming types of offender is that they are strikingly untroubled by guilt, and that they have a slap-happy, devil-may-care attitude to life. This absence of anxiety and guilt is just what one would expect on the theory that these are individuals in whom, either on account of constitutional resistance, or through ineffective train-ing, or both, social conditioning has been inadequately estab-lished. Because training in honesty and conformity to legal requirements proceeds in infancy simultaneously with training in social skills generally, one might expect the individual who has failed in learning in one sphere to show incompetence in others. Studies of the personality and mode of life of habitual criminals strongly suggests that this actually happens, for a great many of them are described as socially immature and have enormous difficulty in fitting into any ordinary group, settling to work, or getting on with their wives. Since conditioned avoidance depends on situations provoking a certain level of tension or anxiety, any influence which damps down anxiety may be expected to reduce the avoidance response. Tension-relieving drugs, of which alcohol is the best-known example, in fact have just this effect. It has been shown in laboratory experiments with animals that alcohol makes their conditioned avoidance responses much less reliable, and it has been noted often enough that man's conscience is soluble in alcohol.

Extraversion

Extraversion–introversion is another important personal quality which is said to correlate with both conditionability and delin-quency potential. The terms were first introduced by Carl Jung

[143] in intuitively based clinical descriptions of two contrasting types of temperament, the introvert, who tends to be thoughtful, reflective, cautious, introspective and concerned about his own feelings, and the extravert, who is more out-going, sociable and more concerned with action and practical matters than with feelings and theory. In recent years, with the development of personality questionnaires, it has been confirmed, notably by Eysenck, that certain attitudes, collectively suggesting a sensitive, imaginative, reflective and somewhat inhibited temperament, tend to cluster together in the same individual; while another cluster, suggesting a cheerful, matter-of-fact person who adapts himself readily without much need for thought, occur together in individuals of opposite temperament. These clusters represent the opposite extremes of a continuous variation from predominantly introverted to predominantly extraverted individuals, with the majority falling somewhere in between.

Introversion–extraversion seems to be a very fundamental personality measure. In any given individual it remains surprisingly steady over years, and evidence has been adduced that it is to some extent an inherited attribute [67]. Furthermore, it is correlated with a large number of other measures, both psychological and physiological. For example, introversion correlates positively with being of ectomorphic physique, with quick conditioning, with high level of aspiration, with anxiety reactions and marked physiological changes in response to stress, with a high threshold to sedative drugs, and with certain perceptual habits (such as high degree of rigidity in seeing only one aspect of an ambiguous picture, and small figural after-effects). In contrast, below-average introversion (in other words above-average extraversion) is associated with mesomorphic physique, slow conditioning, low aspiration, low reaction to stress, low sedation threshold, low persistence, etc. [68].

Crucial to the present discussion, criminal types are said to be more predominantly extravert than law-abiding or socially conforming individuals, who are more often on the introverted side. Evidence for the extraverted characteristics of samples of criminals comes first from clinical experience, especially with young delinquents, among whom the sociable, adventurous, but relatively unreflective type of youth seems particularly common.

Systematic testing with questionnaires, for example in a survey of borstal inmates by Alan Little [155], has not always confirmed this impression, but Eysenck cites a number of confirmatory studies, including some work by F. Warburton in which a group of particularly recalcitrant inmates of Joliet Penitentiary in Chicago were found to be highly extraverted [64].

Neurotic extraverts

Another important dimension upon which individuals vary is in neurotic tendency or emotional instability. Eysenck and others have developed tests for grading people on this trait. Those who are prone, when under stress, to produce neurotic symptoms give high scores on these tests. Although, according to Eysenck, neurotic tendency and introversion are completely independent, the quality of neurotic reactions varies according to one's position on the extraversion–introversion continuum. Thus, the introvert who is also neurotic suffers from excessive anxiety, and sometimes from obsessional and phobic symptoms, and tends to be miserable, over-inhibited and self-punishing. In contrast, neurotic extraverts, whom clinicians identify as hysterics and psychopaths, are misfits who are apparently oblivious of their own peculiarities, and apt to attribute their difficulties to imaginary ailments or adverse circumstances for which they feel no personal responsibility. Tests given to psychopaths, whether they be patients in hospitals or criminals in prison (as for instance the Warburton investigation quoted above), confirm that as a group they tend to be both markedly neurotic and markedly extraverted. On the other hand, unstable introverts, because of their over-inhibited quality, are likely to be over-conforming rather than social rebels or delinquents. In a recent investigation in which the present writer was concerned, using a sample of schoolboys, it emerged that those graded unstable extraverts on psychological tests were significantly more often than the rest graded badly behaved by their teachers. Neurotic tendency, therefore, would seem not to be closely related to delinquent trends except when combined with a marked degree of extraversion.

Some confirmation of these ideas about the character traits of young delinquents was produced in an interesting project carried out by the psychologists Hathaway and Monachesi [117], who administered the questionnaire known as the Minnesota Multiphasic Personality Inventory to 4,000 children in the ninth grade of the state schools in Minneapolis. The youngsters, most of them were fifteen years old at the time of testing, were followed up for two years to see which of them appeared in the official records of the Juvenile Division of the Police Department. Of the boys, twenty-two per cent, and of the girls, eight per cent, were found to have police records. The sample was sub-divided into those who had not committed offences until after the time of testing (who were in the majority) and those who had already committed some offence, but since both these groups differed from the non-delinquent children in rather similar ways, the distinction can be ignored for present purposes. The non-delinquent males gave scores indicative of a greater degree of introversion than the delinquents. The delinquents' scores indicated greater sociability and a higher level of energy and enthusiasm. They showed no particular excess in emotional instability, in fact it was the non-delinquent males who, more frequently, gave scores indicative of depressive trends and femininity of interests. In particular, the neurotic introvert, the self-critical, inhibited type of personality, was more in evidence among the non-delinquents. Despite these trends, the findings were very variable, with numerous inconsistencies. The prediction of delinquency in an individual case is way beyond the scope of present questionnaire methods. In fact, the most significant difference statistically between delinquents and non-delinquents was the high scores given by the former on the validity scales which are meant to detect unreliability of response. An implausible excess of claims to virtue ('faking good') and a suspicious excess of self-denigrating responses ('faking bad') were both features of the delinquent group.

Conclusions still tentative

The cluster of traits identified by Eysenck as criminogenic, namely mesomorphic physique, poor conditionability, psycho-motor clumsiness, and emotional instability when combined with

extraversion, certainly presents a challenging subject for research, although the evidence on some of these points remains
weak. In particular, measures of conditionability applied to
humans are relatively new, and results are often inconsistent. The
techniques are not very easy, and many extraneous influences,
such as motivation, distractions, and physical fitness, may
possibly interfere with the responses. It has yet to be established
how far conditionability can be regarded as a unitary trait, or to
what extent a given individual varies in his speed of conditioning
according to the kind of situation in which he is placed. The
correlations emerging from this kind of research are usually
quite small, which means that the factors dealt with represent
only a small part of the total situation. Conditioning theory, at
least in the elementary form here described, seems to be a gross
over-simplification of the problem. The extraverted, slap-happy
personality, with a careless disregard for social rules, represents
a well-recognized type among criminals, but not by any means
the only type. He is probably most typical of the vigorous, unreflective, practical-minded youngster from the working class
who so often passes through a rebellious, delinquent phase on the
road to maturity. On the other hand, although persons of anxious
or introverted temperament do not ordinarily take to delinquency
at all readily, if they are serious social misfits, and if their circumstances are such as to bring crime into their ambit of personal experience, a minority of these people will take to thieving
as an escape from the difficulties of a more conventional adjustment. Such maladjusted introverts are most prevalent among
older recidivists, especially those commonly described as of
inadequate personality. Since these cases are so frequent among
the inmates of our prisons, they may account for surveys based
on prisoners not always showing the expected excess of extraverts
and poor conditioners [276]. Eysenck himself [66], in discussing
the varying response of different groups of criminals to the same
treatment régime, appears to recognize that an introverted group
exists for whom conventional penal discipline may be inappropriate treatment. Finally, some people find the conditioning
theory unconvincing because the picture it gives of an automatic
assimilation of good and bad reactions leaves out of consideration
the human qualities of thought and feeling. In the context of

child–parent relationships, where social learning takes place, love and hate still count in the estimation of many traditional psychologists.

Psychoanalytic theories about the origins of the anti-social character

The scope of psychodynamic interpretations

The evidence so far discussed suggests that inborn, constitutional features may predispose certain individuals to criminal behaviour, but many psychologists, particularly those of the psychoanalytic school, believe that more important distinguishing features of the criminal character derive from attributes of personality acquired, or at least emphasized, through early upbringing. For instance, whatever the explanation, it seems that children of cruel, rejecting parents are prone to develop undesirably aggressive traits [63; 158]. This kind of observation might furnish a link with sociological findings if it could be shown that the delinquent propensity of certain groups or cultures was due to their peculiar child-rearing practices. The psychodynamic theories, which interpret human character as the outcome of conflict of feelings, have a strong popular appeal. Everyone can understand theories about aggression born of fear, or hostility due to anticipation of rejection, since, in some degree, we have all felt that way ourselves. For scientific purposes, however, empathy is no substitute for objective verification.

Psychodynamic explanations of delinquent behaviour vary enormously in scope. Some refer to patterns commonly found among the generality of delinquents, others to behaviour unique to a particular person or to a specific type of offence. For example, compulsive stealing of women's underwear from clothes-lines is associated with a particular sexual perversion, which in turn is often associated with a recognizable personality type and pattern of upbringing, but it would be ridiculous to expect to find the same pattern among thieves in general. Stealing by small children from mother's purse may sometimes signify a feeling of deprivation of maternal love and attention, but although 'stealing love' by an emotionally deprived person may provide an unconscious motive, or part motive, for some adult larceny, this would be an implausible explanation in the majority of cases. On the other hand, the identification of a personality type who is impulsive, incapable of strong personal attachments, and unrestrained by guilt feelings might provide an explanation for the behaviour of a large proportion of persistent offenders. It is this theory of a recognizable personality type underlying a wide variety of delinquent behaviour, and supposedly attributable to a substantial proportion of delinquents, which needs to be considered first.

Neurotic conflicts in delinquents

Some of the most detailed and useful theories about the origins and significance of character traits derive from psychoanalytic studies. When the subject was first being developed by Freud, interest centred upon patients with neurotic complaints, such as irrational and excessive anxiety, phobias, obsessional habits and preoccupations, or aches and pains traceable to nervous tension rather than to organic disease. Exploration of the emotional life of such sufferers led to the theory of unconscious mental conflict, of individuals torn between the irreconcilable demands of instinct and the restraining forces of social conscience. Neurotic patients seemed to have developed super-sensitive consciences, especially in matters concerning sexual or aggressive feelings, which they could not experience without a strong sensation of guilt or worry. Many of these neurotics had been brought up by strict and repressive parents. Freud advanced the theory that the human conscience (or super-ego) derives from parental injunctions, which the small child incorporates at a very early age, often in somewhat distorted, primitive and literal forms. The child of repressive parents stands in danger of absorbing particularly rigid taboos, which handicap him permanently in his efforts to make a flexible and realistic adjustment to life's conflicting demands, rendering him a prey to paralysing anxiety or other crippling symptoms. The chief aim of early psychoanalytic treatment was liberation from inhibitions and guilt feelings by bringing the patient to recognize and accept his own nature, and to allow himself ordinary ways of fulfilment.

The bold and uninhibited young delinquent, who is conspicuously untroubled by guilt, remorse or nagging anxiety, presents a very different picture. Some psychoanalysts have tried to reconcile this stubborn fact with the contention that delinquents are neurotic by suggesting that their apparent unconcern masks serious mental conflicts which have been so deeply repressed that no trace of them remains in conscious thinking. Unless the existence of such conflicts can be demonstrated in some way, and this does not seem possible in most cases, the theory remains unconvincing.

The anti-social character

A more recent and more plausible psychoanalytic theory suggests that the typical delinquent deviates from the normal character in a direction opposite to that of the anxiety neurotic. Instead of being, like the neurotic, a prey to acute conflict between instinctual impulses and an uncompromisingly rigid super-ego, the delinquent has a very weak, unformed super-ego, which leaves his instinctive impulses unrestrained and unmodified by social considerations. On this theory, the anti-social character, who strikes observers as a self-centred, overbearing individual who must have his own wants satisfied immediately regardless of consequences to other people, becomes like this very early in life through failure to incorporate the inhibiting influences which, in the neurotic, are taken up and developed to excess. In this respect the anti-social character is correctly described as retarded or immature. Like the young infant, he cannot postpone immediate gratification, but gives free vent to his covetousness and aggression even when, in his own interests, self-restraint would be more advantageous. He cannot tolerate present frustration for the sake of future benefit, and so lacks the patience necessary to scholastic learning. Because he lacks the restraining force of a guilt-inducing conscience, he succumbs to the temptation of the moment, truanting, lying or stealing as occasion arises, and suffering no remorse afterwards. Furthermore, and this seems very fundamental, he seems to lack the capacity for forming those stable, loving attachments to others which, in adults, as well as children, provide the incentive for considerate and altruistic behaviour. Perhaps for this reason, even as a schoolchild, the anti-social character, despite the kudos associated with daring and rebellion, is not usually popular with his classmates.

Features of early upbringing cited by psychoanalysts as likely to interfere with super-ego formation centre upon the emotional tone of the child's earliest experience of other persons, namely his relationship first with his mother and later, and to a lesser extent, with father and other adults. Where the relationship is close and loving, this favours the process of identification, whereby the infant comes to develop a self-reference ideal based upon his image of the parent. A loving relationship acts as a powerful incentive to conformity, since rebellion or badness risks the withdrawal of love, upon which the child feels utterly dependent. When the maternal relationship is less close, as for instance if the parents are over-burdened, preoccupied, uninterested or neglectful, opportunity to learn and absorb the rules is correspondingly reduced, and the situation is worse still if the parents are inconsistent, sometimes condoning and sometimes punishing a particular act. If mother is positively hostile towards the child, the threat of further rejection loses its force, so the child obeys when under observation, but acquires no internal constraints. In short, unloving, erratic and neglectful parents, by failing to teach their babies to curb their impulses properly, and by failing to inspire a restraining ideal or super-ego, leave an indelible mark upon the character of their offspring, who risk growing up into anti-social adults with a permanent incapacity for love and kindness.

The anti-social character type as described by psychoanalysts is virtually the same as what psychiatrists commonly describe as a psychopath. The label psychopath, however, is usually reserved for particularly bad cases who are very set in their ways, and the term is sometimes used to imply the existence of inborn pathology. The psychoanalytic emphasis on the psychological determinants of the anti-social character seems to carry with it a relatively optimistic view as to the fluidity of the situation and the prospects of change for the better, and to avoid implying that normals and anti-socials are separated by any clear or fixed dividing line. Furthermore, the term psychopathy has come to be used with greater reserve since the English Mental Health Act, 1959, gave doctors the power to detain compulsorily in mental hospital anyone under twenty-one (or a person of any age convicted of an offence for which a prison sentence can be given) who is certified as suffering from 'psychopathic disorder'.

The psychoanalytic and the sociological viewpoints

It is not always easy to see clearly how psychoanalytic ideas differ from sociological theories of delinquency causation, since both seem to describe a similar situation in somewhat different language. The unusually lucid statement of the psychoanalytic theory of anti-social character formation put forward by the late Kate Friedlander [79] allows one to discern some of the points of contrast. Friedlander classed as secondary causes all those environmental factors which affect the child from the age of seven onwards, including the influence of companions, the use of leisure, the type of school and neighbourhood, and the experience of frustration or satisfaction in employment. In her view such factors can be very important in increasing the incidence of delinquency, but they affect only those youngsters who have some degree of pre-existing anti-social character formation. The important, primary causes operate in infancy, largely through the mother's handling of her child. Psychoanalysts do not deny the existence of constitutional differences – indeed Friedlander points out that with some children instincts are particularly difficult to bring under control – but they suggest that the outcome in any individual case can be greatly modified for better or worse by the type of upbringing received.

Apart from drawing attention to the temporal sequence of events, the psychoanalytic distinction between primary and secondary factors does not seem to have much practical value. The factors in infancy which make for anti-social character formation do not necessarily lead to actual delinquency unless the secondary environmental influences are present at a later stage, and, conversely, the secondary influences are relatively ineffective in the absence of the primary factors. The real difference between the psychoanalytic and the sociological viewpoints rests upon the emphasis placed by the analysts upon the very great importance of upbringing in the early years, and upon defective character formation as the essential precursor of chronic delinquency. If the analysts are right about all this, it should be possible to demonstrate objectively that the confirmed delinquent differs from the average youngster on specified traits of character, and that a close relationship exists between the events of early childhood and subsequent delinquent tendencies.

The 'neurotic' criminal

Franz Alexander [6], one of the first psychoanalysts to sub-divide criminal behaviour into distinct psychological groups, labelled one type the 'acting-out neurotic' criminal. Like many psychological terms, this has degenerated with popular usage, so nowadays it sometimes seems a mere synonym for a badly behaved person. Correctly used, it describes a person who as a result of mental conflict behaves badly in a particular sphere, although in other respects displaying a definite conscience. Un-like the psychopath, or the delinquent character described by Friedlander, whose childish unrestraint is a consistent feature, the acting-out neurotic, when closely observed, can be seen to be irrational and inconsistent, at times condemning or disowning his own actions, at other times behaving like an anti-social rebel. A classic example of acting-out neurotic behaviour is seen among certain opulent women shop-lifters, usually of mature age and respectable antecedents, who appear under a compulsion to steal (kleptomania), when they could with much less trouble buy what they need. Apart from their one anti-social gesture, which they cannot explain other than as an irresistible urge, they are generally law-abiding and conventional. In such cases strong but uncon-scious motives are at work. One such motive, identified by Freud, produces what he called the 'criminal from a sense of guilt'. Like all neurotics, these unfortunates have highly sensitive super-egos, and suffer chronic feelings of guilt, usually related to repressed sexual complexes. Unlike ordinary neurotics, whose tensions burst forth in symptoms, they relieve themselves in actions of a more or less reprehensible kind. This enables them to rationalize their feelings as legitimate remorse, and if their actions provoke punishment, so much the better, because thereby they assuage some of their guilt without needing to look closer into its origins. This explains the curious way in which many neurotic criminals persistently commit their offences under circumstances that invite detection. Unconsciously, they seek punishment, and if they bring down upon themselves the full rigours of the law, this enables them to displace their guilt from their private sin on to the publicly condemned act, and to obtain relief through the public atonement that follows. Although in behaviour they resemble the bold, carefree psychopaths, these guilt-ridden neurotic criminals have as much inner conflict as any ordinary neurotic, and clinical examination soon reveals their malaise.

Everyone with experience of forensic psychiatry can recall incidents and individuals conforming to this 'acting-out neurotic' pattern. Sometimes the psychological process seems quite transparent, and close to the surface of awareness. For example, one young man was referred to the present writer for a psychiatric examination after he had broken open a gas meter in a friend's house. He was not a habitual thief, and the police making inquiries had no particular reason to suspect him, but he almost insisted on confessing. He had had a strict religious upbringing, and he explained that he felt it would be good for him to tell all. On subsequent examination, it emerged that he was feeling very worried and ashamed about some irregular sexual behaviour, and was seeking reassurance that he was 'normal'. Where the acting-out behaviour appears irrational, as in the well-to-do thief, or the sexual fetishist or exhibitionist, the neurotic basis is obvious, but when, as usually happens, the crime serves the purpose of financial gain as well as an unconscious motive, one needs to study the offender's life history and personality before reaching a conclusion. Since this is done only exceptionally, many neurotically motivated offenders may escape notice. Alexander believed such persons to be quite common among criminals, but most modern penal experts would disagree.

The following chapter sets out the results of a number of psychological studies and indicates how far they go towards confirming the existence of the anti-social and the neurotic character types among delinquents, and their relation to disturbed upbringing. Clinical experience at child guidance clinics, remand

homes and prisons leaves no room for doubt that certain delinquents manifest in extreme and unpleasant form the character
traits described, and that in many instances their life histories
run monotonously along predicted lines. On the other hand, these
problem cases are preferentially selected for psychiatric examination, so the clinician may easily build up a mistakenly bad impression of what the majority of young delinquents are like.
Many youngsters caught by the police are perfectly ordinary
characters, no different from others of their age and class. The
important question is how many delinquents display neurotic or
psychopathic patterns. Part of the answer seems to be that these
patterns are most likely to occur among the more persistent and
troublesome offenders, the ones the penal authorities find most
difficult to cope with. Such patterns may also occur among unpleasant individuals who make a lot of trouble for their families
and associates without actually committing those particular acts
which would bring them under the jurisdiction of the criminal
law.

7 Verifying the Psychological Factors in Delinquency

The clinical contribution finished in a kind of intellectual shouting match, such as one might expect if a crowd of newspapermen invaded the affairs of the laboratory. . . .

By contrast, the scientific study of personality . . . has based its theories on actual behavioural measurements. Different laboratories can repeat them and statistical and mathematical treatments of these measurements can be applied by anyone who wishes to check.

Raymond B. Cattell, *The Scientific Analysis of Personality* (1965). Penguin Books.

Maternal deprivation and criminality

Bowlby's pioneer concept

Astute clinical observers, and particularly those of the psychoanalytic school, have furnished a wealth of impressions and theories; but for the most part have left to other workers the task of collecting objective evidence to confirm, refute or modify their ideas. One way of doing this is to take some relatively simple proposition from the psychoanalytic model and see how it works out in practice when large numbers of unselected cases are surveyed. For example, if the psychoanalysts are right about the crucial importance of the early mother–child relationship in determining character, it should be possible to show that persons who have experienced a serious interruption of maternal care during a critical phase of development are specially liable to personality disturbance in later years. The psychiatrist John Bowlby [24] has become known as the great protagonist of this chain of cause and effect. In his first research on the topic, entitled *Forty-four Juvenile Thieves*, Bowlby [23] matched forty-four children, seen at a child guidance clinic and reported as stealing, with forty-four others, of the same age and sex, who, although emotionally disturbed, were not thieves. He reported that seventeen of the young thieves had been separated completely from their mothers for six months or longer during their first five years of life, whereas only two among the control group had had this experience. Furthermore, fourteen of the thieves had a serious and distinctive disturbance of personality which he called 'affectionless character', and of these all but two had experienced separation from mother. Bowlby's affectionless characters corresponded to what most people call 'psychopaths'. They showed a marked disability for close relationships with others, and a consequential lack of motivation for considerate or socially constructive behaviour.

These pioneer observations were much too neat and simple to be true of the majority of delinquents. The crudities of this

first small study, and the over-ambitious conclusions it was made
to support, drew sharp fire from critics such as Barbara Wootton.
Nevertheless, Bowlby's work has born fruit in a mass of subsequent research, and, even if his initial views were exaggerated, the
central idea, that disturbance of the mother–child relationship
may sometimes produce lasting damage, has gained widespread
support. As can be seen from Mary Ainsworth's excellent review
[4] of the controversy, the chief points of dispute now concern
questions of detail, such as how specific or how general the dele-
terious effects of deprivation are, how far they may be made good
or reversed, how closely they are linked with delinquent behaviour, by what process they come about, what is the age at
risk, and how severe the deprivation has to be.

Effects of severe deprivation

In the discussion on mental subnormality, reference has already
been made to the effect of severe deprivation, especially if it
occurs during the first year, in retarding intellectual growth and
facility with language.* There seems little doubt that really
severe deprivation, such as was studied by Goldfarb [102], leads
to deep and lasting disturbance. He used a sample of babies
separated at about four months of age and placed for three years
in an institution which made little effort to replicate the personal
quality of normal mothering. Compared with babies placed in
foster homes, these children were noticeably retarded in intelligence and scholastic attainment, and most of them developed
into cold, unresponsive, detached personalities, who lacked the
capacity for sustained effort, and showed various kinds of
difficult and wayward behaviour.

Animal studies have also demonstrated sensitive periods of
development during which certain social responses have to be
acquired once and for all if they are ever to be learned properly.
The 'imprinting' of following responses in young birds was one
of the first examples to arouse scientific interest. Normally
young birds follow their mother instinctively, but if she is taken
away and some other moving object, even a human being, replaces her, the instinctive response attaches itself equally

* See p. 114.

strongly and lastingly to the substitute, provided always the substitution has taken place during a brief, critical phase of development. By interference with the normal mother–offspring relationship, the subsequent social behaviour of a bird can be utterly deranged, so that the creature makes courting gestures to humans, joins flocks of another species, or tries to copulate with inanimate objects. The possible implications for human affairs emerge still more plainly in experiments with animals closer to ourselves in evolution. A homely example derives from the training of guide dogs, who are more easily educated for human needs if they have been consistently kept with humans as puppies instead of being put into kennels. More dramatic and horrifying are the experiments with monkeys, started by Harlow [113; 114], which show that artificial deprivation of mothering during infancy leads to gross social maladjustment when the monkeys become adult, particularly noticeable in inability to care for their own offspring, and absence of heterosexual responsiveness.

These observations, though fascinating in themselves, are several steps removed from delinquency research. Nowadays, very severe deprivations, like the situations studied by Goldfarb, are rare. It is important, therefore, to know the effect of the lesser degrees of deprivation which are found more commonly among delinquents. It is also important to find out what constitutes deprivation: whether, for instance, it includes neglect without actual physical separation, or separations during which an adequate mother substitute is provided. Research findings so far give the general impression that parental indifference or neglect is as damaging as separation, and that the effects of separation are greatly mitigated by substitute mothering.

Separation without deprivation not so important?

As has been mentioned in Chapter 3, surveys of young delinquents have regularly produced 'broken homes' as a contributory factor in a substantial minority of cases. Analysis of the nature of the separations involved in these cases suggests that separation from father is at least as strongly associated with delinquency as separation from mother – although perhaps for different reasons – and that separations in childhood are of significance as well as

separations in infancy. Hilda Lewis [152], in her study of children
from disrupted homes, found a very high incidence of behaviour
problems, but concluded that delinquency was linked more closely
with parental neglect than with actual separation. C.J. Wardle
[274], in a study of children attending a child guidance clinic,
found that those children who were stealing or otherwise
behaving badly came significantly more often than non-delinquents from broken homes, had a higher incidence of separation
from mother of more than six months' duration, and more
frequently had parents who themselves came from broken
homes. On the other hand, a study by Naess [197] of a less
selected group of delinquents, matched against a control group
of their own non-delinquent siblings, found no greater incidence
of separations among the delinquents. Alan Little [154] tried to
test whether, among youths in borstal, those with a history of loss
of parents or separation from parents had a greater likelihood
of re-conviction. His conclusions were almost completely
negative. Although an unexpectedly high incidence of separations
was noted (over four fifths had experienced separation from one
or both parents in childhood) no significant connexions were
found between the presence, timing or severity of the parental
deprivations and the likelihood of re-conviction or the nature of
the offences committed.

Perhaps the most satisfactory approach for the purpose of
validating scientifically the ultimate effects of events in infancy
consists of long-term follow-up studies of unselected groups,
tracing the after-lives of children observed in early years, and
comparing outcome, as regards behaviour and social adjustment,
with the individual's early history of maternal care. One such
project is the National Survey being carried out in England by
J.W.B. Douglas and his collaborators. This began as a consequence of interest taken by the Royal Commission on Population. The sample consisted of all births which took place in
Great Britain in the first week of March 1946. The original
purpose was to study the circumstances of the confinements;
but, having obtained a sample that was fully representative of
children in all types of home and in all parts of the country, the
investigators saw that they had a unique opportunity. By following these children through their school years, recording any

firmed non-sexual delinquent. This is especially evident among those convicted of heterosexual assaults, although it may also be found in boys who experiment with a variety of deviant activities, perhaps one time stealing women's underwear, another time spying on women's lavatories or changing-rooms, or another time exposing themselves indecently.

Of course many young sex offenders are quite normal psychologically. A youth whose only offence consists in having been intimate with a girl under age, although she may have been as physically mature and as eager for the experience as himself, is often no different sexually or socially from many of his peers. On the other hand, many of the men who offend by making unwanted or aggressive sexual approaches to strange women, although not abnormal in the nature of their sexual inclinations, are often to some extent psychopathic, lacking in self-control in many other ways, and possibly unwilling or unable to submit to the constraints of marriage and family life. Some of them, on the other hand, may be shy, inadequate personalities who find difficulty in striking up normal social relationships with the opposite sex, and so feel sexually frustrated. Over half the males who come before the courts for sexual offences have committed sexually deviant acts, shocking women by a ritualistic display of the genitals (exhibitionists), indulging in sex play with pre-pubertal children (paedophiles), taking part in or proposing sexual acts with other males (homosexuals), or making obscene suggestions by telephone.

These deviant offenders are not all of them perverse to the extent of being unable to obtain sexual satisfaction normally. Some are young, immature characters groping their way by crude experiment towards a more realistic pattern. In the human species the sexual instinct has to be channelled in the right direction by learning, and although ideally this process should be completed by adolescence, it isn't always so. For instance, a certain amount of homosexual interest occurs so commonly at adolescence it is widely regarded as normal, and Kinsey's surveys [148] have shown that many young men of predominantly homosexual habits in early adult life develop later into well-adjusted heterosexuals. Some delinquent youths take advantage of their homosexual propensities and either prostitute themselves for

G

money or social gain, or else entice older men into compromising situations in which robbery, blackmail or extortion can be practised with relative impunity.

Prospects of re-conviction

Sex offenders, particularly young ones, should be handled sympathetically, since the expectation of future re-conviction is much smaller than in the case of thieves, and one does not want to do anything that will hinder socio-sexual learning and development still further. In the Cambridge survey of a sample of 2,000 convicted sex offenders [217], 82.7 per cent had never before been convicted of a sexual offence, and 84.5 per cent were not subsequently convicted of sexual crime during a follow-up period of four years in freedom. This surprisingly optimistic outlook has been confirmed by researches in other countries. In a twenty-year follow-up of 2,000 Danish sex offenders, Sturup [256] showed that only ten per cent were re-convicted of sexual crime. Nevertheless, some categories of sex offenders do have a higher re-conviction rate. The Cambridge survey showed that as many as twenty-seven per cent of men convicted of homosexual offences with boys under sixteen were re-convicted. By the end of the follow-up period, five per cent of the sample were recidivists with four or more convictions for sexual offences. This minority were mostly confirmed paedophiles, exhibitionists, or homosexuals addicted to importuning in public lavatories. They were a particularly abnormal group; for the most part they were men of mature age (forty per cent being over thirty when first convicted of a sexual offence), and over half of them had convictions for non-sexual offences as well.

Sexual assaults on children

Child-molesters or paedophiles, particularly homosexual paedophiles, arouse great disgust among parents, prisoners and judges, as well as fear for the harm they may do to the children by shocking and terrifying them, or by awaking in boys a taste for deviant sexuality. Actually, the dangers to children are less than popularly supposed. Most paedophiles are childish in their approaches, and go no further than the mutual display and fondling which small children might indulge in among themselves. Although this does not make the offence any less obnoxious, the fact is that the victims are not infrequently seductive, attention-seeking children who try to elicit interest from neighbours, relatives or strangers where they have not been able to get it from their own parents. A survey of a sample of child victims in London showed that two thirds of them had been sufficiently willing participants to cooperate in assaults more than once or by more than one assailant. The assailants were mostly relatives or neighbours, less commonly strangers [87]. Given a normal background, the experience itself is not likely to impair a child's emotional development [16], although the fuss and distress of subsequent court appearances can be harmful. In Schofield's recent study of homosexuals and a control group [229], neither in his own samples nor in his survey of other researches did he find any evidence that casual homosexual contacts with adults were liable to turn boys towards a homosexual orientation in later years. Indeed, the very fixed type of exclusive homosexual deviant, who has an ineradicable aversion to heterosexual contacts, is likely to have been sexually inhibited and inexperienced in his early years.

J. W. Mohr [183], in a careful study of paedophiles in Canada, found that these offenders tended to cluster into three age groups, with peaks of incidence at adolescence, at thirty-five, and again at about sixty years. Many of the first group were shy and socially retarded youngsters who might be expected to develop normally in time, given the right encouragement and opportunity. Among the older offenders, many had slowly developed a precarious sexual adjustment, which later gave way in the face of the stress of family or marital problems, or the feelings of loneliness and failing powers experienced at the onset of old age. Only a minority were sufficiently compulsive and persistent in their practices to warrant detention in close custody.

As has been shown by Schofield and other investigators, ordinary homosexuals do not go in for child-molestation, and are very different from the paedophiles in background and attitude. On the other hand, some homosexuals, although they have no interest in pre-pubertal children, have little scruple about activities with post-adolescent youths. Since the majority of the homosexual incidents which actually come to courts concern importuning or indecency in public places, or activities with youths, it is doubtful if the proposed reform of the law would result in any great change in the criminal statistics. There is no evidence of any increase in homosexual tendencies among young persons. In so far as homosexual fixations are based upon fears and inhibitions against normal sexuality instilled by a repressive upbringing, one would expect some decrease in incidence as a result of the more open and matter-of-fact approach to sex that has developed in recent years.

Sexual maladjustment can spoil all prospects of a happy life, or, by the ruin of an established marriage, damage the emotional development of children of the next generation. The courts are therefore performing a very useful social service if they see to it that young sexual deviants whose behaviour has come to light through police action are seen and treated psychiatrically whenever possible.

Girl delinquents

Why are girls less often delinquent than boys?

Various reasons have been put forward why crime is not a typically feminine habit. Perhaps it is partly a matter of opportunity. Men go out and about more, frequent bars more, and so have more chance to thieve at work, to commit business frauds, and to learn about criminal ways and means. In countries where, by tradition, women were kept to a purely domestic role, playing no part in the wider social and economic life, their crime rate was correspondingly tiny. It seems to be a general rule that, as women become emancipated, so the proportion of women among convicted persons increases. N. Walker [271] has contrasted the ratios of men to women among adults convicted of various offences in England. In larceny from unattended vehicles it is eighty to one, in assaults and woundings it is four to one, in drunkenness and disorderly behaviour it is fourteen to one, in larceny from shops it is one to two. Shop-lifting is a more typically feminine crime presumably because women have more opportunity for it.

Pollak [207] has suggested that the difference in crime rates between the sexes is exaggerated by a policy of not pursuing inquiries or pressing charges against women. Another suggestion is that women in our culture are brought up to be more passive and conformist than men, and so they are more likely to support morality and the *status quo*, and avoid crime. Men are expected to be more assertive, to compete, and to provide, and are therefore under greater temptation to dishonesty.

The misconduct of juveniles shows marked sex characteristics long before the age when economic pressures, or even differences in physical strength and agility, could plausibly account for it. School-teachers find girls more amenable, parents less often take their daughters to child-guidance clinics, and the number of places in remand homes or approved schools occupied by pre-pubertal girls is very small indeed. As the psychiatrist T.C.N. Gibbens [81] once said of girls:

... environmental stress is much more likely to produce shyness, timidity and inhibited neurotic behaviour of a sort which is less often complained of by parents because it causes less nuisance and more easily passes for normal. It is only a small proportion of girls who 'act out' their troubles by wayward, aggressive and defiant behaviour ...

Wayward girls are worse than delinquent boys

The small minority of girls who do become actively wayward generally present more difficult problems than boy delinquents, and they more often come from very disordered or conflict-ridden homes. Using data from the Flint, Michigan Youth Study,* Ruth Morris [186] compared matching groups of delinquent and non-delinquent boys and girls. She found that, to a significant extent, the delinquent girls had the highest incidence of broken homes, or of homes beset by quarrels and tensions, and they were more often untidy and neglected in personal appearance. Male delinquents often appear to be boisterous, exuberant boys who have found satisfaction among their more rebellious peers, but wayward girls are more often unhappy

* See p. 57.

misfits. Although admitted on the fringes of male gangs, girls have nothing like the same support from the delinquent sub-culture that boys can find.

Another big difference appears at puberty. Whereas the way-ward boy usually takes to stealing and breaking-in, and only exceptionally to sex offences, the wayward girl more often takes to sexual misconduct. The promiscuity of wayward girls serves as an effectively upsetting form of protest against the attitudes and restrictions of older relatives. Often, it also seems a way of searching for the affection which was wanting in an unhappy parental home. It would be wrong to suppose that all young girls who run away from unhappy homes into the arms of a lover are promiscuous. Some of them form emotional attachments as strong as they are unsuitable. As Gibbens [81] pointed out, even promiscuous girls are not necessarily bound for a career of pro-fessional prostitution. In his sample of 400 girls passing through a London remand home only about five per cent became prostitutes.

Girl thieves are often, but not always, sexual rebels. The two forms of behaviour are perhaps influenced by different factors. In a study of a sample of girls at an English approved school, the psychologist Elizabeth O'Kelly [199] contrasted the background of thieves and sexual delinquents. While both groups came mostly from disturbed homes, the thieves had more often suffered separation from or rejection by parents, while the sexual delin-quents more frequently had difficult relations with fathers, and mothers who were conjugally unstable.

Such surveys as have been done on older girls in borstal, who are mostly convicted for offences against property, or disciplinary offences, such as running away from approved schools or break-ing the conditions of probation, demonstrate very clearly the highly unstable character of the girls concerned, much worse than boys in borstals, and the continuance of problems of sexual promiscuity. Dr Epps [61], who studied 300 borstal girls of average age nineteen, found that thirty-seven per cent required treatment for syphilis or gonorrhoea or both, which was many times the rate of venereal infection among youths in borstals. About a third had experience of prostitution. Unhealthy homo-erotic behaviour was also a problem, not necessarily indicative of a real fixation, but due, Dr Epps thought, to the segregated environment and the instability of the inmate group. The incidence of neurotic symptoms, psychopathic traits and disordered homes was all greatly in excess of what has been reported of borstal youths.)

Legal control of promiscuous girls

The methods of dealing with troublesome girls are complicated by the double standard adopted by society, and by those who enforce the law, to the sexual behaviour of boys and girls. Staying out late in the company of the opposite sex, and actual or suspected sexual promiscuity are taken more seriously in girls, partly because of the risk of pregnancy, partly because it is considered particularly unseemly, leading as it does to loss of social status and to prostitution. Although, technically, it is the boy or man who commits an offence by having intercourse with a girl under sixteen, it is the girl who is the more likely to lose her liberty as a result. In England, juveniles up to the age of seventeen may be brought to court and dealt with as 'in need of care, protection or control' if they are 'falling into bad associations' or 'exposed to moral danger' or have been the victim of a sexual offence or are members of the household of a person convicted of a sexual offence against a child.* Alternatively, the parents may complain to the children's officer that they cannot control her conduct. In either case, the court frequently puts the girl under the care of the local authority, but may order supervision by a probation officer or commit her to an approved school. The population of approved-school girls has more 'protection' cases than official offenders.

According to the letter of the law, juveniles of either sex may be brought before the court on these grounds. In practice, boys who stay out late or get into bad company are not usually apprehended, but women police frequently take girls into custody if they are found in night clubs, or in the company of known prostitutes, or after running away from home with a lover. However, after reaching the age of seventeen, except if already under supervision, the girl can no longer be compulsorily

* Children and Young Persons Act, 1963, s.2.

controlled in this way unless she breaks the law, and in England prostitution itself (as opposed to soliciting in a public place, or benefiting from the prostitution of others) is not an offence.

The system whereby girls can be compulsorily segregated, and processed as if they were criminals, for sexual behaviour which is not in itself defined as illegal naturally produces resentment. Those committed to institutions, though protected temporarily from becoming pregnant, are exposed to the influences of an unstable and anti-social peer group, and are prevented from coming to terms with a normal social environment. On the other hand, if such girls are allowed to live outside, and then become pregnant, the consequences, both to themselves and others, can be still more distressing.

Youthful violence

Age and type of offence

Contrary to popular belief, there is a smaller proportion of youthful offenders among persons convicted of violence than among persons convicted of larceny or of breaking and entering. In the *Criminal Statistics, England and Wales, 1965*, fifty-eight per cent of those convicted of indictable crimes of violence against the person were aged twenty-one or more, compared with only twenty-nine per cent of those convicted of breaking and entering. Convictions for violence are uncommon under fourteen years of age, but quite common from fourteen to seventeen, and twice as common again from seventeen to twenty-one. It seems that adolescence is the time when some delinquent boys first begin to add violence to their repertoire of infractions. Up till then, their aggressive acts are usually limited to fighting among themselves in playgrounds and similar places, where such behaviour is widely tolerated, provided no one gets badly hurt. Occasionally, however, some police action is taken, as in a case recounted to me by a probation officer who was put in charge of four small boys, all aged under ten, after they had been convicted of robbery with violence. They had knocked down a school-mate, and then taken from him sixpence wrapped up in a handkerchief, thus transforming an incident of petty bullying into a grave criminal act.

The aggressive youth begins to appear in the criminal statistics when he gets involved in fights over girls at dance-halls, or teams up with a gang bent upon spoiling some rival social function, or gets quarrelsome after taking drink, or forces himself upon girls. As was shown in the study of violence in London by F.H. McClintock [162], relatively few of the incidents leading to indictable convictions involve serious injury, or the use of knives or guns, or are committed in connexion with other crimes, such as robbery, or resisting arrest. The typical act of youthful violence is one of quarrelsomeness or hooliganism, involving a punching attack in a pub, café, or in the streets, perpetrated in the heat of the moment, usually in a low-class neighbourhood by a low-class assailant against a person known to him. Although old ladies or other respectable and unprovocative citizens have been waylaid on the streets, this is a very uncommon event in England. The proportion of youths convicted for the first time for violence who have a previous record of conviction for an offence against property is much higher than the average for their age and sex, which confirms the common-sense view that delinquents are more prone to violence than non-delinquents.

More than most crimes, offences of violence are typically committed by lower-class persons. The lower-class culture affords the young male comparative freedom to express his aggressive feelings physically. Unfortunately many persistent delinquents seem to have an inordinate amount of aggression to express; indeed aggressiveness has always been thought one of the hallmarks of the psychopath. Middle-class people are much more restrained in their aggressiveness; but at the same time probably more effective in verbal attacks and in fighting through solicitors or by complaints to officials. The fact that girls are comparatively non-violent is probably due as much to cultural restraints as to physical incapacity. Females who have committed personal violence are not uncommon among borstal girls, and, as Wolfgang and Ferracuti [288] have pointed out, in Philadelphia coloured females have a homicide rate two to four times that of white males. These investigators have set out to demonstrate, in a study carried out at the University of Puerto Rico, that open

violence in particular circumstances can be normal, socially
supported behaviour in some sub-cultures. Where this state of
affairs is well established it will be reflected in the attitudes and
personalities of the people, and in the absence of guilt feelings
following acts of violence. The fact that the use of violence may
be restricted to one sex, or to a particular age group, may be
itself a cultural expectation rather than a biological phenomenon.
Among some aggressive American gangs, acts of violence help
individuals to prove 'heart' or to acquire 'rep', but even among
the wildest groups there are always some limits to the acceptable
degree or frequency of violence.

Origins of violence

According to some psychologists, aggressiveness results from
chronic frustration of instinctual satisfactions [18]. The child
deprived of parental love, the low-class person who is bossed
around and given small reward for any effort he may make, the
youngster who can only get what he needs at the risk of brutal
punishment, are so sensitized by their frustrating experiences
that the slightest provocation serves to elicit an aggressive reaction. If the frustrating agents are parents or vaguely identified
authorities responsible for social injustice, they are often too
powerful or too remote for direct attack, and then the aggression
tends to get displaced on to substitutes. Hence the popularity of
scapegoats, especially members of racial minorities, as targets for
seemingly wanton bullying.

Acts of malicious destruction may provide one substitute outlet for aggression against people. While it is inconvenient to have
one's car tyres cut with a razor, it is less so than having one's face
so treated. J.M.Martin [171], in a study of juvenile vandalism in
New York, came to the conclusion that such offenders were more
predominantly male, rather younger, and more prone to offend
in groups than the general run of young delinquents. He found
that some of these offenders were normal and usually law-abiding
boys who had been accidentally caught up in group exploits, but
more often they were either seriously disturbed individuals,
using the opportunity to hit out blindly, or else they were members of an aggressive sub-culture, living in bad neighbourhoods,

and participating in the marauding activities of local gangs. Some vandalism has a crude economic element, like tearing fixtures off walls and then selling them, and some is actuated by spite against the owner of the property, but more often vandalism is simply a satisfyingly aggressive mode of demonstrating delinquent prowess and contempt for authority. Many youngsters who take part in such destructive exploits have little experience in caring for property of their own and little appreciation of the consequences of their acts.

Violent tendencies in young men are not necessarily indicative of a poor outlook for the future. The spiritedly aggressive youth probably has a better potential for adjustment later on than the passive, discouraged type. T. C. N. Gibbens [85], in his survey of borstal lads, remarked that 'the outlook for rehabilitation often seems unusually good' in the case of those convicted for violence. On the other hand, a more diffuse kind of aggressiveness (corresponding to the Hewitt and Jenkins description of unsocialized aggressiveness), erupting in inappropriate situations, and manifest quite early in childhood, appears to be a bad sign. H. H. Morris *et al.* [185] followed up a group of children seen by psychiatrists on account of cruelty, destructiveness, defiance, tantrums or other aggressive behaviour. Open rejection by parents, and a high incidence of criminality and personality disorders among the parents were typical of the histories of these children. By the time they were young adults, only one fifth of this group had achieved a satisfactory adjustment. Some had become chronic mental cases, others were criminals, and a majority were leading irregular and disordered social lives.

Clinical examination of young men convicted of violence suggests no simple solution. A very few have identifiable neurological conditions, epilepsy, or mental subnormality, which might contribute to their aggressiveness. A minority are violent only when intoxicated, so that control of their drinking habits is the primary concern. Most of them present a mixture of individual character defects and low social standards. Except in some extremely volatile cases, tranquillizing drugs are not particularly successful. It appears that with this type of offender, as with many persistent offenders against property, there is no substitute for a thorough inquiry into the individual history and personal characteristics followed by a slow process of personal and social training.

The influence of television

It has been said that members of delinquent sub-cultures derive their deviant scale of values by selecting and exaggerating trends apparent in society as a whole. Delinquents need not look very far to find models for the violent anti-hero; he appears in comics, on television, in the cinema and in the popular press. Many commentators have criticized the mass-media, and especially the television authorities, for depicting crime and violence so much larger than life. It is claimed that by making criminal activity 'news', and by using crime as a recurrent theme for popular plays and films, journalists and broadcasters are holding up exaggerated models and distorted values which young people may emulate, and are diffusing information about criminal activities which some of them may then decide to try for themselves [285].

The long-term effects upon society of persistent exposure to spectacles of violence and crime are almost impossible to assess. However, the Television Research Committee, appointed in 1963 by the Home Secretary, found no direct evidence of a general increase of violence as a result of young people viewing television. On the other hand, evidence was forthcoming that potentially aggressive and maladjusted youngsters find violence on the screen particularly fascinating, but instead of obtaining vicarious satisfaction they are more likely rather than less likely to respond to a situation aggressively afterwards [111]. Just what ought to be done on the basis of such a finding is far from obvious. It is the old problem, which is common to the regulation of alcohol, pornography, loans, gambling, etc., whether to apply rigorous prohibitions to everyone for the sake of trying to shield the susceptible few.

9 The Penal System

Penal legislation hitherto has resembled what the science of physic must have been when physicians did not know the properties and effects of medicines they administered.

Sir Samuel Romilly (1811), quoted by L. Radzinowicz in *A History of the English Criminal Law* (1948). Stevens & Sons. Vol. 1, p. 396.

Every act of authority of one man over another, for which there is not an absolute necessity, is tyrannical.

Cesare Bonesana, Marchese de Beccaria, *Essay on Crimes and Punishment* (1764). (First American edition, New York, 1809, p. 12.)

Sentences for the young

Nineteenth-century reforms

Use of the grand title 'penology', or the euphemistic label 'treatment', cannot disguise the fact that the things done to offenders have scant scientific basis. If the causes of deviant behaviour are diverse and little understood, the means of controlling it have hardly reached the point where scientific scrutiny can begin. What happens to offenders in practice is an uneasy mixture of traditional punishment, segregation and discipline, diluted by humanitarian and psychological ideas about the importance of the sympathetic, personal approach.

Descriptions of the English penal system in operation, and of the laws which govern it, will be found in more authoritative works [77; 224; 268]. In England, rapid legislation and continuous political argument have put the contemporary system, at least in so far as it applies to young offenders, into such a state of flux that any detailed statement would soon be out of date. The brief sketch which follows is intended merely to give a little practical orientation so that it may be seen how far theories and proposals about treatment are just pie in the sky.

On the scale of history, methods of disposal of convicted offenders of any age other than by death, flogging or imprisonment under highly deprived conditions are quite recent developments. The hanging of small children used to be 'by no means unusual' in England [46]. In 1816, Samuel Romilly, in pleading unsuccessfully before the House of Commons for the abolition of hanging as a penalty for shop-lifting, mentioned the case of a ten-year-old boy at that very moment in Newgate Prison under sentence of death. In fact, since crime has always been a youthful activity, most of those hanged in the days when thieves were liable to execution were youngsters. The English Solicitor General, in 1785, noted that nine out of ten offenders hanged at that time were under twenty-one [214].

In the first part of the nineteenth century, in England as in

most other countries children and young persons, both those
convicted and those awaiting trial, were sent to the same appalling
prisons as adults, where no doubt they were quickly depraved
and brutalized by their experience. In 1817, the *Second Report of
the House of Commons Committee on the State of the Police in the
Metropolis*, reported that in the previous year the new prison at
Clerkenwell had received 399 felons aged from nine to nineteen,
and that young and old were mixed indiscriminately, regardless
of the nature or gravity of their offences. The report went on to
describe how petty street pilferers, many of whom might be
boys just starting a career of crime, were 'usually committed for
a short time to prison, sometimes severely flogged, and then,
without a shilling in their pockets, turned loose upon the world
more hardened in character than ever'. Sir Edmund Du Cane
[51], writing of the same period, 1816, noted that of the 3,000
prisoners in London aged under twenty a half were juveniles
under seventeen.

Separate arrangements for young prisoners were made for the
first time following the report of a Select Committee of the House
of Lords set up in 1835 to inquire into the state of the jails. One
of their recommendations was to open a penitentiary for juveniles. At that time, prisoners awaiting transportation were confined
aboard the famous convict hulks so vividly portrayed by Charles
Dickens. Since boys could not be transported until they reached
fourteen years of age, some of them had to remain as much as
five years on the hulks. On 21 July 1831, John Capper, Superintendent of the Convict Establishment, that is the hulks, giving
evidence before the Select Committee on Secondary Punishments, explained that the youngest of his charges was 'nine years
old and deemed incorrigible' and that 'it is quite melancholy to
see some of them; they can barely put on their clothes'. He
thought solitary confinement a more efficient punishment for
boys than whipping. Under the Parkhurst Act, 1838, an old
military hospital on the Isle of Wight (still one of our most
famous prisons) became for the next twenty-five years a prison
which received boys from ten to eighteen years of age. This
institution was criticized by the militant reformer Mary Carpenter, who preferred to see schools for delinquents privately run
by religious bodies [27]. She claimed that the use of leg irons,

armed guards, whipping, solitary confinement and a generally
tyrannical régime kept the boys in a desperate and unreformed
condition, ready to break out, plunder and kill if ever they got
the chance. Although certainly very harsh by modern standards,
the Parkhurst experiment represented an advance on the
previous system, and some of the men who ran the prison were at
least as enlightened in their understanding of juvenile troubles
as the staff at the private reformatories, at some of which
whippings were excessively frequent. The Youthful Offenders
Act, 1854, authorized the establishment of Reformatory Schools
run by voluntary agencies under the supervision of the Home
Secretary, as an alternative form of detention for juveniles,
although they had first to serve a short time in prison. The boys'
prison at Parkhurst finally closed in 1864.

The development of approved schools and borstals

The numbers of juveniles incarcerated in prisons with adults
gradually decreased, until the Children's Act of 1908 finally
abolished imprisonment for those under fourteen, and placed
restrictions on the imprisonment of those in the fourteen to
sixteen age group. The reform schools in England, and the houses
of refuge in the U.S.A., served to rescue young people from the
adult jails, and to give young paupers and criminals (at that time
these categories were scarcely distinguishable) a chance to learn
a job and earn their bread. These schools long preceded the
establishment of compulsory school attendance. They were the
precursors of the present-day approved schools, which are
institutions run by local authorities or private persons, 'approved'
and inspected by the Home Office. They receive delinquents sent
to them as compulsory boarders by order of the courts. At
present children aged ten and under seventeen may be sent to
approved schools, where they may be detained for up to three
years, but not after reaching the age of nineteen. For the two
years following release, but not after reaching the age of twenty-
one, they are legally under supervision, and can be recalled for
bad behaviour. The juvenile courts may also make Fit Person
Orders in respect of offenders, which have the effect of transferring parental rights and responsibilities to a guardian, usually

the local authority. The juvenile may then be sent to foster parents, a children's home, a boarding school for maladjusted children, or an approved school, according to his particular needs.

The institution of reformatories for children still left a large number of adolescent offenders mixed up with old lags in adult prisons. It was not until the end of the nineteenth century that some small-scale experiments with institutions specially designed for slightly older youths led to the development of the English system of borstals. Borstal detention (now called training) was first formally instituted in the Prevention of Crime Act, 1908, which provided a system of separate incarceration and training, as an alternative to imprisonment, for young persons. At present, delinquents aged fifteen and under twenty-one may be committed for borstal training for the same range of offences as adults may be imprisoned. The period of detention is from six months to two years, with a further two years under the supervision of a probation officer following release, during which time the offender may be recalled for another six months if he misbehaves.

In spite of the coming into existence of the borstal system, it was a long time before the idea became accepted that the majority of youngsters could be dealt with outside of the adult prison system. However, under s.3 of the Criminal Justice Act, 1961, no one under twenty-one should be committed to prison unless his offence warrants detention for three years or longer. A special section of the prison at Wakefield is reserved for youths serving long sentences.

Borstals differ from prisons not so much in the security precautions against escape (indeed the majority of borstals are 'closed' institutions) as in the comparative freedom and mobility of the offenders within the institution, in the assumption by the staff of a teaching and training role which brings them into constant functional contact with inmates, and in the concentration upon learning a job and using time constructively. In theory, at least, borstal training 'seeks the all-round development of character and capacities – moral, mental, physical and vocational'. In the case of ' young offenders for whom a long period of residential training away from home is not yet necessary, but who cannot be taught respect for the law by such measures as fines and probation' [126], the Criminal Justice Act, 1948, provided for the setting up of detention centres. These now receive offenders from fifteen up to twenty-one years of age, for a stay of three to six months, in 'secure establishments with strict control' where the régime is 'brisk and firm' with 'a strong emphasis on hard work' [132]. The intention is primarily deterrent, and the system was at first described as 'a short, sharp shock'. For boys, the medicine consists of an unremitting sequence of square bashing, P.T., and manual labour mostly performed at the double. It is said to be 'unsuited to those are are seriously handicapped physically or mentally'. Prisons, borstals and detention centres are at present all run by the Prison Department of the Home Office.

The *Report of the Departmental Committee on Corporal Punishment,* 1938, recommended the abolition of this penalty for both juveniles and adults, and in fact it came to an end with the Criminal Justice Act, 1948. It is retained in England (but not in Scotland) for male prisoners guilty of serious violence against a prison officer, although the 'cat-o'-nine tails' may not be used for the purpose on those under twenty-one. It is not permitted in detention centres, or borstals, but it is used to a limited extent in approved schools and remand homes. To all intents and purposes, however, torture by flagellation, once the most frequently used and highly regarded of English penal treatments, and stoutly defended by judges as a necessity for the protection of society, has now passed into disuse, and this in spite of an important and vocal section of public opinion still in favour of it. Flogging always had serious practical disadvantages. The tough young thug, well used to personal violence, was probably made still tougher and more determined to retaliate. More timid types, who might have been put off by it (the middle-aged shop-lifters for instance), were rarely considered suitable subjects. This leaves committal to a detention centre as the most overtly punitive of the measures open to the courts for most young offenders.

Non-custodial sentences

Attendance centres form a less important part of the penal establishments [161]. They also came into being with the Criminal

Justice Act, 1948. They are usually run by the police and serve offenders aged ten up to twenty-one, who are required to attend for hourly or two-hourly periods up to a maximum of twenty-four hours, during what would normally be their free time, usually Saturday afternoons. This punishment can be combined with probation or a fine if more than one offence has been committed, and it can be given for failure to comply with the requirements of probation. It is not meant for the more serious delinquents, and those previously sentenced to penal custody are not eligible. The régime consists of inspection for tidy appearance, P.T., 'chores' and instruction in carpentry or other useful skills.

Apart from attendance centres, the non-custodial measures for young offenders are much the same as for adults, namely, police cautions, conditional or absolute discharges, fines and probation orders. In the case of children the maximum fine is £10, or £50 for young persons under seventeen. It is the parent who must pay a child's fine, and a parent may be ordered to pay a young person's fine. Probation orders place the offender under supervision for a period of up to three years, during which he must comply with the requirement to report to, and receive visits from, the officer as directed, to lead a regular and industrious life, and to abide by any additional special requirements that may be written into the order, such as residing with a particular relative, staying at a special hostel for probationers, or undergoing psychiatric treatment. A breach of the requirements renders him liable to sentencing for the original offence, or he may be fined or sent to an attendance centre while the probation supervision continues. As with adults, a further conviction while on probation renders him liable to two separate sentences, one for the original offence, another for the latest offence. Since probation is technically non-punitive, with a possible sentence in abeyance, it cannot be combined with other penal measures. In respect of any one conviction, the offender who has paid a fine or gone to a detention centre cannot then have the benefit of probation. Those given probation or a conditional discharge can be ordered to pay for damages or compensation to victims.

Except in the case of certain serious crimes which must be

reported to the Director of Public Prosecutions, the English police exercise a discretion whether to bring an offender to court, or to dispose of the matter with an informal or formal caution, the latter being entered in their records. Something like a quarter of a million formal cautions are administered annually to traffic offenders. Formal cautioning is also very commonly used with juveniles, especially younger juveniles and first offenders, but practice varies from one police district to another, some forces hardly using the procedure at all, others applying it to nearly half the children apprehended.

In some areas, of which Liverpool is perhaps the best known, a system of police juvenile liaison has developed, whereby, with the consent of their parents, juvenile offenders who have been cautioned are subsequently visited in their homes by plain-clothes policemen, who talk to their parents, inquire after their welfare, and issue authoritative advice and warnings, after the manner of some probation officers. The police also attempt prevention, by visiting and advising children who have not got so far as to commit crimes under circumstances in which they could be convicted, but who are known to them for truancy, disorderly behaviour or keeping bad company. Judging by the low re-conviction rates of juveniles who have committed indictable offences but have been dealt with by the liaison officers, the scheme seems to have had a good effect. However, professional social workers tend to criticize the encroachment of amateurs on to their domain, and some legal authorities feel the system usurps the decision-making powers of the courts. The important issue is whether it really works, not whether a few sensitive toes may be stepped upon in the process [175].

The annual criminal statistics for England and Wales give data on the use made by the courts of the different sentences or orders available. In 1965, 25, 37 and 39 thousand persons were found guilty by magistrates courts of indictable offences in the age ranges ten to thirteen, fourteen to sixteen, and seventeen to twenty respectively. Taking the age groups in this order, fines were given to 18.5 per cent, 31.6 per cent and 53.5 per cent of offenders, probation to 33.3 per cent, 29.2 per cent and 17.4 per cent, and some form of detention to 5.4 per cent, 9.0 per cent

and 10.0 per cent [128]. The increasing use of detention and of
fines, and the decreasing use of probation continue after the age
of twenty-one. For non-indictable offences, the great majority, in
all age ranges, were fined.

Courts for the young

Special features of juvenile courts

Save in exceptional circumstances (as when a juvenile has been
involved together with an adult in committing an offence) all
persons under seventeen are tried summarily in special magistrates' courts for juveniles. At these courts, the magistrates, who
must include both a man and a woman at every session, are
supposed to be specially qualified for dealing with children. The
convictions and sentences they record are officially known as
'findings of guilt' and 'court orders', which technically do not
rank the same as criminal convictions. Unlike the ordinary
courts, they have a statutory duty, when making decisions, to
have regard to the welfare of the offender and when necessary to
take steps to remove him from undesirable surroundings and
secure a proper education and training, and they are obliged to
obtain reports on the social background of the offender. These
are usually furnished by the probation officers or by representatives of the local authority children's department, and by the
child's school. The juvenile courts can postpone their decision,
following a finding of guilt, and in the meantime send the offender
for a few weeks to a remand home, where he is kept in custody
and under observation while social reports on his background and
behaviour (and also psychiatric reports, if requested) are being
prepared. Although theoretically not intended as punishment, a
belief in the salutary effect of a short spell in a remand home may
not be without influence when magistrates decide upon this
course in preference to obtaining reports from probation officers
or clinics while the child is at liberty. On the other hand, it must
in fairness be pointed out that remand homes are geared to
producing psychological and medical reports for courts, when
these are needed, more swiftly and efficiently than most outside
clinics. Incidentally, the police use remand homes in place of

station cells when they do not think it wise to allow a juvenile to go home after he has been apprehended.

The juvenile courts are meant to be welfare agencies as well as dispensers of punishment, and they do in fact take into account a great deal more than just the nature of the offence that has brought a child before them. However, the most casual scrutiny of their decisions suffices to show that tariff justice remains a most potent consideration, so that trivial first offences usually lead to a fine or discharge, and subsequent or more serious offences to probation or custody. Presumably anything departing too far from this routine would shock the sense of justice of parent, child and magistrate alike.

In the juvenile courts certain rules that have to be followed in adult courts are waived. For example, although press representatives have to be allowed in, members of the public are not permitted to attend as casual observers, and the juvenile must not be identified by name in any report that may be published. The proceedings are meant to be relatively informal, but they vary a great deal in practice: anything can happen, from a confidential exchange of whispers between the child and the magistrate to a sternly formal session with child and parents stiffly at attention. The magistrates have the power to order a parent to attend with the child if they think it necessary. The child's rights to question witnesses and so forth have to be explained to him in suitable language, and his parents must be allowed to help him with his defence. In practice, juveniles are rarely legally represented in court, and a prosecution case is not often effectively challenged, so that occasionally technically innocent youngsters, especially if they are wearing the disapproved clothes of contemporary adolescent protest, risk being penalized for being at the scene of trouble when the police arrived [15]. Any attempt to make the proceedings more sophisticated or judicial, however, would be completely lost upon the majority of the delinquents. In the present writer's experience of examining many boys after their appearance in a juvenile court, few had remained calm enough to understand properly what was happening, and most were concerned only with whether they had 'got away with' probation or were to be 'sent away' [233].

The 'care, protection or control' process

Apart from hearing charges against children aged ten years or over, the juvenile courts also have to deal with children of any age who are 'in need of care, protection or control' or who are persistent truants from school. Such hearings are technically civil rather than criminal trials, and they may occur in a variety of circumstances. For instance, if it comes to the attention of the authorities (i.e. police or children's department) that a child is neglected or starving or cruelly treated or sleeping out, perhaps because a parent is alcoholic, in prison, a mental patient, a prostitute, or simply feckless and uninterested, then he may be brought to court as in need of more care and protection than his parents are providing. The parents themselves may have complained to the children's officer that their child is unruly, or sexually promiscuous or pregnant, and that they can no longer maintain proper control. A juvenile, even though not actually charged with an offence, may also be brought before the court because he or she has been involved in sexual irregularities, drunkenness, drug-taking, begging, gambling or other undesirable pursuits. The court has power to make a Fit Person Order, or an approved school committal, in all such cases. The distinction between official delinquents and children brought to court as being in need of care, protection or control is often more theoretical than practical.

In some countries the distinction between child offenders and children in need of care is not attempted, and all juvenile problem behaviour is dealt with by welfare or education departments instead of by courts of law, in which case the age of criminal responsibility and liability to criminal prosecution is not reached until around school-leaving age. This has been the accepted system in Scandinavian countries since the turn of the century [222]. Neglected, maltreated and badly behaved juveniles who cannot be handled by parents and teachers are dealt with by municipal welfare councils with power to remove a child from home and commit to foster homes or special institutions. The final outcome, therefore, is the same, the essential difference being that the decisions are taken by welfare agencies and social workers rather than by courts of law, so that the emphasis is presumably more upon dealing with a family situation and less upon fitting the punishment to the crime. The usual arguments against this type of system centre upon the risk of giving such powers to administrators, who are not subject to the same degree of public scrutiny or traditions of justice as the magistrates, and the inadvisability of contaminating the benign image of welfare workers by making them wield the big stick. Neither argument seems very cogent. It is a matter of opinion who is best qualified to make these decisions. Until a few years ago, doctors could not make compulsory admissions to mental hospitals without a magistrate's authority, but the removal of that protection hasn't led to any disaster. Probation officers have always had authority behind them, since non-cooperation on the part of their clients is a breach of the court's order, but they are not less successful than other social workers at dealing with delinquents. More to the point is the observation that juvenile courts deal with vast numbers of infractions of the law – such as travelling on buses and trains without tickets, riding bicycles without lights, pinching fruit off trees, behaving noisily in public places – which are not necessarily indicative of any need for social welfare, but are probably most effectively checked by sharp reminders, small fines, and the payment of the costs of damage [31].

Proposals for family councils and family courts

It has been proposed to introduce a Scandinavian-type system in England. In August 1965 the Home Office published the government's proposals for setting up family councils to replace the juvenile courts [131]. These would be recruited from social workers and others experienced in family problems, and they would be given similar resources for sending delinquents to detention centres or approved schools, and for arranging super-vision, observation in a remand home, or the payment of compensation for damage; but they would have power to act only with the parents' concurrence. Some of the institutions would undergo transformation, at least in name, the remand homes becoming observation centres, and all the approved schools being taken over by local authorities and run in conjunction with their other residential schools for maladjusted and homeless children. The family councils would have no power to impose fines, although that relatively harmless method of expressing official disapproval has long been used by the courts in some two fifths of juvenile cases. The task of supervising young delinquents, hitherto performed by the probation officers working with juvenile courts, would be taken over by officers of the local authority children's departments. These officers, who are busy providing care and foster placements for orphans, illegitimate babies and for the children of sick or neglectful parents, might find it difficult to cope with a large influx of rebellious delinquents.

In the minority of cases where the facts of the offence are likely to be disputed by child or parent, or if the parent cannot agree with the measures proposed by the family council, the case would be referred for adjudication to a family court. One of the purposes of the family council would be to enlist the cooperation of parents in discussing how best to deal with the children, but it is uncertain how many parents would try to fight the social workers by appealing to the court. These proposals virtually abolish the distinction between children in need of care and children who commit crimes. The family councils would use the same administrative mechanism for dealing with neglected, truanting, troublesome and delinquent children. While this may be helpful in removing the stigma of a criminal record, it remains to be seen how far it will affect the keeping of statistics of juvenile crime. A stroke of the administrator's pen could abolish juvenile offences along with the juvenile courts, and, while that might look good on paper, it would hamper study and research on juvenile delinquency.

The proposed family councils and courts would cope with children up to the age of sixteen. From sixteen up to the twenty-first birthday, offenders (except in the case of very serious charges, like murder, rape or robbery) would be dealt with by a specially constituted young offenders' court, which would be required, as are the juvenile courts at present, to have regard to the welfare of the offender, not merely to punish him for the crime. The approved schools for senior boys would be taken over by the Home Office and administered together with the borstals under the title of Youth Training Centres, where the offender would be sent for six months to two years, followed by a period of compulsory after-care during which he would be liable to recall 'if he were found to be conducting himself in a way which made this course desirable in his interests'.

The supporters of these new arrangements claim that they would make way for a more therapeutic approach to children than can reasonably be expected of a juvenile court modelled after the pattern of a criminal trial and sentence. For instance, it is argued that a family council's decisions would be more flexible and more easily modified in the light of a child's reactions, or in response to changed circumstances at home, than is the case when a court has pronounced an official order. However, it must be pointed out that a reshuffling of administrative responsibilities and a renaming of institutions do not in themselves meet the greatest need, which is for more skilled workers and increased facilities for treatment. Furthermore, many children who have committed minor public nuisances and are at present dealt with by judicial warnings and fines hardly need to be discussed and processed as if they were maladjusted, and might indeed be confused and resentful at this. The welfare role envisaged for the young offenders' court seems admirable in itself, but it leads one to question why all courts cannot be required to have regard to the welfare of the unfortunates who come before them. The proposals have stimulated so much adverse comment from persons working with delinquents that perhaps the government will have second thoughts.

Penal régimes

The punitive element

In the nineteenth century, harsh measures were thought the best means of reformation. Penal régimes were frankly and unashamedly made as disagreeable and degrading as possible, with the idea of frightening off potential malefactors, and making offenders think twice before reverting to crime and risking further punishment. Convict garb, enforced silence, separate confinement, the treadmill, and the lash were means to this end.

Strict enforcement of all these measures was strongly advocated in the *Report of the Select Committee of the House of Lords on Prison Discipline*, 1863 [137], which laid down 'hard labour, hard fare and a hard bed' as the essential ingredients of discipline. In the present century this has ceased to be the official policy of English prisons. In a stirring speech in the House of Commons in 1910, Mr Winston Churchill stated: 'The mood and temper of the public with regard to the treatment of criminals is one of the most unfailing tests of the civilization of any country.' He went on to urge upon those in charge of criminals 'tireless efforts towards the discovery of curative and regenerative processes; unfailing faith that there is a treasure, if you can only find it, in the heart of every man'. A decade later, Alexander Paterson, one of H.M. Prison Commissioners, coined the phrase that an offender comes to prison 'as a punishment, not for punishment'. Since then, the declared aim has been the training and treatment of prisoners 'to establish in them the will to lead a good and useful life on discharge, and to fit them to do so' (Prison Rules).

How far this admirable ideal comes over in practice is open to question. Very unpleasant features still exist in many prisons, particularly in the old local prisons, where everything is cramped behind the constricting walls of grim Victorian fortresses that were meant for a population half the size of what exists today. Slopping out, tobacco rationing, prison dress, limitation and censorship of letters, restricted and supervised and even caged visits, mail-bag sewing, under-paid labour, discharge with un-stamped employment cards, are all justified officially as necessary evils of security or lack of facilities, but to the outsider, and more especially to the prisoners themselves, they seem more like a continuation of the age-old policy of degradation and punishment.

Moral conviction that transgressors ought to suffer, and anxiety that unless they are made to suffer for their crimes they will not be reformed limit the extent to which the public will tolerate improved conditions in penal institutions. In so far as delinquents come from poor homes, even quite low standards of institutional comfort may exceed their customary experience. In the *Minutes of Evidence before the Select Committee of the House of Lords on the Execution of the Criminal Law*, 1847, a witness stated, with reference to the improved treatment of boys in prisons:

I am prepared to say that whenever a Boy goes into prison he can never come out, in point of Feeling, as the same Individual again. . . . In Nine Cases out of Ten, he finds his personal Comfort attended to much better there than at home; he finds the Prison clean and airy, and the Labour light, and he comes out with less Disinclination to go there again [124].

Another witness who came before the same Committee, Reverend Whitworth Russell, a prison inspector with twelve years' experience, gave a similar opinion on the ineffectiveness of imprisonment for juveniles. He said: '. . . I am confident that in the Great Majority of Cases the Juvenile Delinquent is rendered much worse, and much more dangerous to Society, by Imprisonment.' Asked about the great dread of being brought back to prison (Question 684), he replied:

Decidedly not, after they have been in it. I have visited Prisons when children have been brought in for the first time, and I have seen them overwhelmed with Fear and Distress, clinging with instinctive dread even to the Officer that brought them there; and I have seen those very children, three or four days afterwards, laughing and playing in the Prison Yard with the other Convicts, and I felt then that the Dread of a Prison was gone from those children for ever [124].

Similar considerations arise today. In the Bow Group pamphlet *Crime in the Sixties* [43], the authors refer to the argument that pampering criminals in prison leads to an increase of crime. The argument has particular application to open prisons, where the régime and the surroundings are comparatively pleasant. The authors counteract it by suggesting that 'Open prisons should only be used for those prisoners who would otherwise be likely to return to crime. If they are successful in this, the community has no cause for complaint'. The implication would seem to be that transgressors who can be dealt with harshly without risk to the community should be made to suffer.

Prisons

Certain basic facts about the régimes inside penal institutions, such as the numbers, qualifications and earnings of the staff, the rules enforced, the permitted range of punishments, the nature of the food and the sleeping accommodation, can all be gleaned from official publications, but these dry bones need something extra to make up a living reality. The policy pronouncements of government agencies about penal aims and methods are of limited help, since they are usually couched in very general terms and employ a euphemistic style and phraseology apt to mislead the unsophisticated. The official statement [125], with reference to prisons, that 'Methods of training have been progressively extended and improved, notably in the application of psychiatry and psychology . . .' is unassailably correct, but it leaves out the information that provisions are still so limited that not more than a tiny fraction of the potential clients can get help from them.

Detailed, critical appraisals of penal régimes in England are rather rare. One reason for this is that the people best informed, namely those who run the institutions, are traditionally precluded from free discussion and comment because they are government servants, and because their department's affairs are widely believed to be somehow specially protected by the Official Secrets Acts. Quite recently, the Home Office sanctioned publication of part of a study by two sociologists [189] of the régime at Pentonville Prison, London. A very depressing picture emerged, with officers disillusioned and sceptical of the value of any attempt to reform crooks, and the prisoners themselves resentful of the soul-destroying monotony and humiliation, and dominated by a spirit of mistrust and non-cooperation. A more general account of the varying conditions inside English prisons has been published by Hugh Klare [149], Secretary of the Howard League for Penal Reform.

For various reasons, young persons under twenty-one have been finding their way to prison in substantial numbers. However, when the provisions of the 1961 Criminal Justice Act, s.3., are brought into operation, only those given long sentences of three years or more, or those re-convicted after a previous term in borstal and sentenced to eighteen months or more, will be received into the prisons. Hence, in future, prisons will be receiving only the worst of the young recidivists, and those who have committed the most serious crimes. The conditions prevailing in prisons will not be particularly relevant to the generality of young offenders, except in so far as they illustrate the ambivalence of purpose underlying the approach to offenders of all ages.

Detention centres

Detention centres nowadays receive more young offenders than either approved schools or borstals. Although, as is true of any penal establishment, the majority of inmates of detention centres have been sent there for thieving, those committed for crimes of violence, traffic violations, and driving away other people's vehicles are found in considerably higher proportions than among the borstal population [130]. A sample of youths aged seventeen to twenty, inmates of detention centres, were studied and interviewed by the Oxford researchers, Dunlop and McCabe [52]. For most of these youths, the energetic, organized programme, starting at 6.15 a.m., with long periods of closely supervised hard work, and the enforcement of extreme orderliness and cleanliness, with frequent changing of clothes, showers, kit inspections, floor scrubbing, and parades, came as a new experience. Some affected indifference, like the boy who commented 'It's a lot of shouting, it can't hurt you . . .', but most of them expressed resentment at the physical hardship, the prohibition of smoking, and other restrictions. However, a large number seemed to become rapidly tolerant of the routine, and even to enjoy the exercise. Loss of liberty, however, was the one aspect of their punishment which they all felt acutely. In comparison with any delay in their date of release, all other disciplinary measures were felt as minor irritants. The existence of a system of promotion to higher grades for satisfactory work and obedience, although it involved extra privileges, had not much significance to the inmates apart from its influence upon the date of release.

The nature or number of previous convictions had little bearing upon the likelihood of a youth fitting into the routine and being regarded by the staff as a good trainee. Those with a facility for physical training were at some advantage, and so were some of those with previous experience of institutional life in children's homes or approved schools. Some of the youths committed for violence were amongst the most overtly obstreperous and defiant. However, a follow-up study produced no evidence for any connexion between satisfactory behaviour inside the detention centres and the likelihood of further convictions after release. Compliance with an enforced routine has little relevance to self-control in freedom.

Contrary to what might have been expected, the bitterness against the officers running the centres which was expressed by some inmates was not shared by the majority, who, in spite of a certain distrustful reserve, were prepared to concede that the staff behaved fairly. In spite of the limitation of free conversation between inmates to short set periods, and the patrolling of dormitories, the more important human contacts were between each other rather than between offenders and staff. The leadership of the more confident and aggressive, who were sometimes the most delinquent, was shown by the rapid assumption of criminal slang and verbal bravado by the previously unsophisticated. This contamination effect is likely to become increasingly damaging if all kinds and degrees of offender continue to be mixed up together in the same detention centre. Detention centres have been criticized as retrograde institutions, because the purpose is more obviously punitive than remedial. The things one intelligent ex-detainee recalled were being stripped of clothes and possessions, ordered about senselessly, set to scrub already clean floors, paraded in the snow, and made to shave with blunt blades. He summed it up as 'three months of blind obedience in digging holes, endless P.T. and continual unreasoning deprivation', and complained that the system merely exposed the power of the law without teaching the offender how to change himself in order not to get into trouble again [204].

Judged by the re-conviction rates of those passing through detention centres (more than a half re-convicted in the three years following release) the system is not particularly successful in deterring future criminality, but then neither are the approved schools and borstals, which give more prominence to reform by education, social training, and individual attention.

Borstals

The variety of régimes

The English borstals are difficult to describe because they are so varied. Some are run on sternly authoritarian, military-style discipline, others enjoy a comparatively relaxed atmosphere with a great deal of discussion between staff and inmates. Some are built in prison-fortress style and are closed 'security' institutions, others are wide open, with youths working in the surrounding fields or even going out to employment in the neighbourhood. In methods of discipline, in the organization of work and leisure activities, in the use of incentives and grades, and in the amount of personal attention paid to inmates as individuals, borstal governors and housemasters have considerable scope for initiative. Consequently, what happens in practice, and the impact of the experience upon inmates depend a great deal on the ideas and personality of those in charge. Unfortunately, these matters elude documentation, and the late Sir Lionel Fox summed it up justly when he wrote 'To find out what is going on in a borstal in any detail, the only safe plan is to go and see' [77].

In general, borstals lay great emphasis on training in habits of steady work, and on trying to arouse interest in a job. These aims are of course particularly appropriate to the large number of incompetent and work-shy youngsters with whom they have to deal. Everyone puts in a full day's work, and the tasks provided are useful and constructive, such as building, farming, carpentry and mechanics. Trade training courses, utilizing skilled instructors and impressive workshops, are given to those sufficiently able and conscientious to follow them. Athletics, team sports, camping expeditions and similar pursuits are special features in some borstals. Classroom teaching and coaching for illiterates are also provided. Social training takes place mostly through the natural interchange between youths and staff or instructors (who are often visitors from outside) in the course of their many practical activities. Inmates have to display some willingness and effort in order to earn promotion through the various grades and secure release more quickly. Some borstals pay more attention to personal and psychological factors, and staff are encouraged to have fairly intimate talks with the youngsters about their family problems, their worries for the future, and their attitudes to crime. A few establishments have group counselling, that is discussion sessions led by a staff member at which inmates are allowed to talk more or less freely about their personal problems or their feelings towards authority. On the whole, however, the borstal tradition is based upon the assumption that, given the right mixture of practical training and authoritative persuasion, the majority of normal youngsters will fall into line. When a more individual and exploratory approach is attempted, in order to find out why some people won't or can't fit in, then the staff have to face the inevitable conflict between condemning bad conduct and understanding it. As one governor is reported to have put it: 'The degree of honesty displayed by lads in their dealings with staff has produced several problems. . . . [We are] confronted with what appears to be self-condemning statements by lads. We have had to change our methods of evaluation . . .' [127].

Before admission to any particular borstal, the trainee spends some weeks at an allocation centre, where his background history and circumstances are reviewed, his behaviour watched, and where he receives psychological tests. Finally an allocation board considers all the information and decides to which institution to send him. The decision seems to be arrived at by a kind of intuitive consensus of opinion, with certain points of reference kept in mind [190]. Age and sex, of course, are prime determinants. After that, such things as interest in a particular trade, intellectual capacity (or lack of it), danger of absconding, advisability of being near to (or far away from) visiting relatives and religious affiliations may all be taken into account. More particularly, the allocation authorities try to envisage the most suitable social climate, whether, for instance, he needs 'a framework of support and "mothering" as opposed to a more rigorous, disciplined régime'. Certain borstals are meant to cater for the older and more sophisticated types, especially those whose attitudes have hardened against authority and who would be expected to be disruptive and contaminating influences in any institution run on democratic lines. Factors which limit choice also have to be faced, for instance whether there is an appropriate vacancy, whether the available range includes any régime likely to satisfy the needs of some difficult or exceptional youth, whether a particular borstal can handle any more problem cases than it has already got, or whether the need to separate an offender from his accomplices or fellow gang-members overrides other considerations.

Coping with the more difficult cases

Borstal staffs commonly complain of the ever-increasing proportion of feckless and hopeless types whom they are obliged to receive. A recent report by an allocation centre governor describes inadequate, insecure and unstable characters, with an increasing incidence of suicidal tendency and psychiatric referrals, who drift inevitably into trouble, yet remain cynical of advice and authority, and contemptuous of legal or moral restraints [127]. It may be true that young offenders today include more psychological misfits than when thieving was more a necessity and less an expression of personality. On the other hand, it could also be that a more sophisticated scrutiny of borstal inmates is bringing about a clearer recognition of their inadequacies. The more difficult types gravitate to the recall centres, which deal with those who have offended while out on licence, and those who, on account of absconding or misconduct, have to be removed from other borstals. The Home Office reports that about one third of the youths discharged from one of these centres in 1963 were homeless [127].

In the administration of borstals, the Prison Department cannot run too far ahead of popular opinion and parliamentary comment. The 1951 *Departmental Committee to Review Punishments in Prisons and Borstal Institutions* criticized the borstal policy of leniency, appeasement and soft treatment, and advocated a tightening of discipline.

What Roger Hood [134] has called the golden age of borstals has passed. At one time they admitted only the most promising and trustworthy cases, and all the rest went to prison. Consequently, the proportion re-convicted after release was small, and so was the number of abscondings. Now that the better types get probation, while the worst types get to borstal, success rates have dwindled, abscondings increased, and optimism about the effectiveness of reformative training on liberal lines has correspondingly decreased.

The attempt to treat a larger proportion of more difficult youths under open conditions means more chance to abscond; and by stealing vehicles to make a getaway, or by breaking into houses to find food and money, absconders provoke protests by local residents, and give the whole reformative system a bad public image. On the other hand, where security precautions and discipline by brute force are found necessary right up to the moment of discharge, this is a plain indication of the failure of the ideal of training the offender to fit him for life outside. The great difficulty is that a thorough-going application of individual treatment under ideal conditions demands more in time, attention, personal skill, tolerance of disturbance, and risk-taking than state institutions, under present-day conditions, are likely to provide. Unfortunately compromise solutions sometimes get the worst of both worlds. Forgoing harsh deterrents for the sake of a benign, but not particularly effective, paternalism may suffice for the more normal personalities, but is not likely to make much impression on seriously inadequate or psychopathic types.

In a recent follow-up of the after-careers of borstal inmates, Gibbens and Prince [88] remarked upon the lack of correspondence between performance in borstals and subsequent re-convictions. This was particularly noticeable among the previously institutionalized recidivists, who knew how to toe the line and keep out of disciplinary trouble while inside, but who quickly reverted to crime on release. Another group of outward conformists with bad subsequent records was made up of intelligent but markedly neurotic or unstable lads, who were able to conceal their problems while in the protected institution environment, but who soon broke down again outside. In spite of these exceptions, there does appear to be some connexion between behaviour outside and behaviour in borstal. A. G. Rose [223], in an analysis of the files of 500 borstal inmates, found that breaches of discipline, bad work habits, and poor progress in borstal training were associated with bad previous criminal and work records, and greater liability to subsequent re-conviction. He concluded that there was probably some continuing and therefore unchanged factor of personality manifesting itself in different ways in and outside the institutions.

Approved schools

The approved schools of England, perhaps soon to change their name and become a more integral part of the welfare services, are already more fully committed to an ideology of treatment than the institutions governed by the Prison Department. They have to deal with deprived children as well as official delinquents, and to receive many youngsters whose babyish ways and lack of social sense reflect the inadequacy of their home life. Their staffs are chosen for their experience in the control and education of difficult children. Like the borstals, they have the benefit of a system whereby the boys are observed for some weeks in a classifying school before being allocated to a particular institution. While personality and disciplinary needs feature in this allocation, limiting factors, such as religious attachments or the location of vacancies, also largely determine the choice of school. Educational retardation, and potential intelligence are also taken into account, and this is important since these children are still of an age to make up for lost time, although emotional turmoil or stubborn resistance often bars the way. The classifying schools also undertake interviews with parents and inquiry into home backgrounds, so that by the time a headmaster receives the boy he is accompanied by a bulky dossier setting out his life history, present circumstances, and outstanding personality problems. Incidentally, these descriptions are interpretative as well as factual. Examples have been published by the Home Office [92]. In one of these, a boy's defensive distrust and lying was traced to resentment against an uninterested step-father and a hostile, critical mother. Such evaluations provide a useful basis from which the approved school staff can get to know their charges, but sometimes an interpretation, once on record, may be echoed uncritically by teachers and social workers ever after.

Even more than at borstals, the heads of approved schools set the tone of their establishments, and determine the relative emphasis on deportment, obedience, scholastic instruction, constructive hobbies, vocational training, athletics, contact with parents, staff conferences, psychological interpretations, and the attention given to advice from a visiting psychiatrist. The minority of schools run by local authorities, which must heed public opinion and avoid scandal or adverse publicity at all costs, are likely to select more conservative and authoritarian heads for safety's sake. Individualistic and pioneering heads are more likely to be found for schools managed by philanthropic organizations, especially if the managers include persons professionally interested in psychology or child guidance [142].

As in all institutions for offenders, a certain conflict exists between staff members committed to understanding, tolerating, and sympathizing with the deprived children, and staff members of the older tradition who prefer to stamp out bad behaviour by force, and who have little sympathy with the poor standards revealed by children of the feckless lower classes. However it is handled, the approved schools' task is an exacting one. P. D. Scott [234], in a recent review, described the grossly disordered homes from which the majority of the children have come. In his sample, seventy-seven per cent had parents who were seriously anti-social or alcoholic or markedly hostile to each other, or grossly inconsistent in the disciplining of their offspring, and these features were often associated with a history of illegitimacy and of periods with foster parents or under the care of a local authority. In these cases, little support is to be expected from the parents, either during the child's stay at school or subsequently. Should some misfortune befall an inmate, however, such parents are the first to complain vociferously in their urge to displace blame on to the school authorities. The pressure of watchfully hostile parents, press, and public can dampen reforming zeal and discourage innovation.

Cause and moral responsibility are different categories. An Institute and Chair of Criminology have recently been established in this University. It would not, I feel sure, occur to any of those engaged in investigating the causes of crime to suppose that this committed them to a denial of the moral responsibility of the criminal.

E. H. Carr, *What is History?* (The G. M. Trevelyan Lectures, Cambridge, 1961). Penguin Books (1964).

For my own part I can see no real objection to an approach to criminal behaviour which treats this as an evil thing to be eradicated by the methods that experience suggests to be most effective, and which asks no questions as to the degree of responsibility of the offender for what he has done. . . .

Barbara Wootton, *Contemporary Trends in Crime and its Treatment* (The Nineteenth Clarke Hall Lecture, 1959). London.

Protection, detection and deterrence

The variety of controls

Different ways and means of preventing delinquency or of treating established delinquents are suggested by different criminological theories. By and large, the sociological school of thought, represented by such writers as Albert Cohen, favour social reforms in preference to attempts to rectify the supposed character defects of individual delinquents. If delinquents act as they do in fulfilment of a recognized role, which is sufficiently accepted in certain sectors of society to enhance their standing among their peers, as well as to bring monetary rewards otherwise impossible for members of their class to achieve, the answer would seem to lie in reforms aimed at a more egalitarian distribution of opportunity, and a general increase in legitimate means of gratification and advancement, so that the delinquent way of life loses its attractiveness and status. On the other hand, if delinquency is conceived as a blind hitting out at society on the part of individuals who have never learned to control their primitive emotions, attention to the mental health of the community and special provisions for children deprived of normal parental care would seem to be the best approach.

In real life, the situations leading to delinquency are so complex that many different lines of attack have to be tried. While one should be able to learn something from the outcome of preventive efforts, evaluation is difficult, since any one intervention is but a drop in the ocean in relation to the total situation. However, in human affairs one has often to act in advance of scientific knowledge, and attempts to combat the delinquency problem cannot wait upon the resolution of academic controversies or the uncertain results of long-term research. Although satisfactory scientific proof may be lacking, this does not necessarily mean that no practical benefits have been derived. For example, it is a reasonable, though unprovable, assumption that relief of poverty has reduced certain kinds of theft; but even if it had not had that effect, it would have been a worthwhile social measure for many other reasons.

Early social theorists, such as Bentham and Beccaria, fastened their attention upon the legal system as the most obvious force within society guiding and controlling the range of permissible behaviour. In his influential essay *Dei Delitti e delle pene,* first published in 1764, the Marchese de Beccaria argued that social conformity would be increased if punishments were made to fit the crime, that is to say of a severity proportionate to the harm done, instead of reflecting the capriciousness of judges or the social status of the offender. He thought that too harsh a punishment for lesser crimes impaired deterrence, since nothing worse was left in reserve for dealing with the more serious crimes. All that was necessary was a punishment just sufficiently severe for it to be not worth while taking the risk for the sake of the gains ensuing from the crime in question. His ideas never had any basis in factual observation, and after nearly two centuries of tariff justice in place of arbitrary punishment crime is still with us.

Some theorists have over-emphasized the part played by the criminal law in preventing delinquency. It needs pointing out that pressure of public opinion and the general expectations of a community regarding the behaviour of its members exert a powerful controlling force. In small primitive communities lacking a formal legal code, such pressure has often sufficed to preserve a quite rigid code of behaviour, and in our own society there remain large areas of conduct which seem not to require penal sanctions. For example, in the more highly developed countries, it has lately become such a matter of shame to fall below a given standard of personal hygiene that to appear in the streets in smelling rags is a sure sign of madness or intoxication. In other areas, although legal sanctions exist in the background, the function of law seems less a matter of prescribing punishments than formulating an agreed standard for the guidance of the community. This applies to a host of welfare regulations, such as restrictions on the employment of children, compulsory insurance, control of cleanliness in selling food, and safety measures in factories. Although all these things once gave rise to bitter political controversy, for the most part reminders and inspections serve to maintain conformity, without resort to prosecutions. The existence of a delinquency problem implies a failure of the normal processes of social control, and efforts to strengthen these controls should take priority over measures for dealing with individual law-breakers.

Protective and restrictive measures

Many measures are taken to render crimes more difficult to commit, and thereby to reduce the temptation to succumb on impulse. The use of locks and bolts, safes, burglar alarms, and street lighting, and of course the patrolling policeman, are well accepted customs. Other protective devices work more indirectly. Accountancy and banking systems discourage frauds, elaborate methods of printing bank-notes prevent easy forgery, the age and test qualifications required of drivers reduce traffic crimes due to ignorance and incompetence, control of the sale of firearms and poisons reduces impulsive murders, car registrations, passports and identity cards hinder secret journeys and impede the escape of known criminals, while the banning of young people from drinking bars and the high tax on alcohol doubtless prevents some disorderly behaviour.

Some measures work on the principle of encouraging constructive social habits. The no-claim bonus scheme in car insurance rewards the safe and presumably law-abiding drivers. Compulsory weekly deductions from wages for unemployment and pension benefits protect the thriftless from periods of destitution and severe temptation.

In practice, these protective devices could be indefinitely extended, although every extension involves a certain amount of expense and inconvenience. Academics, at least, would hardly support the construction of iron grilles to guard booksellers' shelves against shop-lifters; but many might favour a plan to penalize motorists who carelessly leave an ignition key in their parked car. The central agency which checks a shopper's credit-worthiness when he wants to buy something on hire purchase is a device which not only protects the store, but also protects the improvident from their own weakness, and indirectly reduces the risk of debts and frauds. Another helpful system practised in some countries is the use of token discs in place of ready currency in public telephones or gas meters.

Many conceivable methods of protection are objectionable because they infringe civil liberties, or have other undesirable consequences. Abolition of immigration might be advocated as a means of eradicating one of the social situations leading to crime, but many people would think such a measure too drastic to be justified on these grounds. Limitation of the number of children which parents with low income may be allowed to retain could be enforced by compulsory abortions or adoptions, but the ethics of such action would be open to question.

Many possible methods of protection would be impracticable in a democratic society. Prohibition of the sale of alcohol in the United States proved virtually unenforceable owing to lack of public support. Likewise, the use of doctors and medical records to check on law-breaking is open to criticism. Most patients believe they can safely tell criminal secrets to doctors, and indeed it is often essential they should do so in such matters as abortion, venereal disease, and injuries due to personal violence, to say nothing of psychiatric conditions, in which all causes for worry or stress have to be explored. In law, though not in present custom, information concerning felonies must be reported to the police. If this was really enforced, many people might die or remain sick or infectious for fear of confiding in doctors. Such consequences could hardly be justified for the sake of exposing and punishing guilty patients and their associates. Another questionable method of protection is telephone tapping and the interception of mail, which is considered by many people too heavy a price to pay for the sake of trapping criminal conspirators. With the use of computers for searching out a particular individual, a national register of fingerprints might become practicable, although, judging by the resistance of the English public to the use of identity cards, it might not be a popular measure. Probably more people would support a proposal to amalgamate the registers of a person's birth, marriages and death, which would at least discourage bigamy.

Countries differ greatly in the extent to which they enlist the active cooperation of the public in the apprehension and punishment of offenders. Although in England and America the public have a duty to report crimes, people often prefer to look the other way for fear of becoming embroiled in inconvenient legal proceedings, and it is only in times of national crisis that citizens band together to form special police or militia units to protect law and order. In some countries, however, these arrangements are commonplace. In the Soviet Union, employees elect their own comrades' courts, which have powers to control the conduct of members of their group. These courts issue reprimands, levy fines, or request a man's demotion; furthermore, they can consider matters affecting socialist morality, even though the undesirable behaviour in question does not amount to a formal breach of the law.

Punitive deterrents

Deterrence is a topic much discussed in criminological and legal texts. It is held to operate in two ways: by teaching the caught offender that it will not pay him to offend again, and by warning off the potential offender with an example of what may happen to him if he breaks the law. Other aspects receive less attention: but the need to reinforce public morals by the proclamation of legal sanctions, the need to allow aggrieved victims to feel that their hurt has been avenged, and the need to incapacitate the worst offenders by eliminating them from society are also mentioned occasionally. Deterrence is still the chief function the judges have in mind when passing sentence.

Closely allied to the philosophy of deterrence, and equally dear to the legal mind, is the concept of criminal responsibility. This means, in effect, that any sane person should be held accountable for his own misconduct and should receive his just deserts. Once admit the idea of adjusting the punishment on utilitarian grounds, and some people will get away with too mild a punishment, and others will get too much, not for what they have actually done, but perhaps for what some psychiatrist thinks they might do in future, unless they receive appropriate 'treatment'. Curiously enough, many lawyers are content to forgo this principle in the case of juveniles and see little harm in adjusting sentences to fit the needs of the particular child, but are loath to allow the same flexibility in the case of adults. The classical lawyer's viewpoint considers that society's best protection lies in a predictable scale of deterrents based upon the nature of the offence and the penalty attached to it in the legal code.

Hardly any scientific evidence is available on the effectiveness of punitive deterrents, and discussions on the topic tend to be abstractly philosophical and over-simplified, as if all forms of delinquency were similarly motivated and could be similarly controlled. The effect of punishment on the after-careers of caught offenders might be studied by comparing groups who have had light sentences and harsh sentences for similar offences. So far as I know, this has not been done, but even in the unlikely event that it could be established that some optimum level of fine or length of imprisonment was associated with significantly fewer re-convictions, this would tell one nothing about the general deterrent effect. What is needed to deter an individual from repeating his offence is unlikely to be the same as what is needed to deter potential imitators. Exemplary sentences of long imprisonment may be effective as a general deterrent, while actually making the individual punished worse than before, by unfitting him for life in freedom after release. Furthermore, public sentiment will not now permit violent deterrents, such as public hangings, or flogging, even if they could be proved effective. Democratic countries have no wish to imitate the systems of harsh, judicial coercion characteristic of dictatorships, even though history has shown that whole populations can be cowed into conformity by such means. Very likely, as Barbara Wootton has suggested, some petty offences, such as wrongful parking, in which the offender has little emotional or financial involvement, might be reduced by increased severity of punishment. In Scandinavian countries, where driving after drinking carries with it an automatic prison sentence, people are in fact much more careful not to go by car to drinking parties than they are in England or the United States, and the existence of this legal penalty has probably contributed to their restraint. But some difficulty arises in dealing with the more serious offences if the big guns have already been brought out to deal with more trivial matters. And anyway, where the stakes are high, or the need sufficiently pressing, people will risk the most extreme punishments. It is said that in the days when pickpockets were publicly hanged other pickpockets used to attend the executions and ply their trade among the watching crowds.

The risk of being found out

Possibly the potential offender's estimate of the risk of being caught acts as a more powerful deterrent than the severity of the punishment involved. Some work done in England by the Government Social Survey, questioning young people about their attitudes to delinquency, their own misconduct, and their anxieties about being caught and punished, seems to suggest that the unpleasantness of appearing publicly in court and the adverse reactions anticipated from family and friends loom larger in the minds of the young than the actual penalties likely to be imposed upon them.

Evidence exists that changing the likelihood of detection affects the incidence of law-breaking. Increases in crime due to reduced police supervision in times of crisis have already been commented upon.* An amusing example has been quoted by Professor J. Andenaes [8] in which a known increase in risk of detection served to deter young offenders from driving away other people's cars. At the time of the 1956 Suez petrol crisis, the Swedish government placed restrictions on the driving of private cars at weekends. This greatly increased the risk of drivers being stopped and questioned at these times. The result was a dramatic decrease in car-theft at weekends. Professor Andenaes drew the moral that 'even such a youthful and unstable group as automobile thieves react to an increase of risks when the increase is tangible enough'.

Organized, professional criminals are said to weigh up carefully the risks involved, and to avoid certain types of offence, such as shooting bank employees, because the penalties are too heavy [76]. However, such rational restraints hardly apply to impulsive crimes of violence committed in the heat of passion. In England, most murders are family affairs, and the majority of those who kill a member of their family kill themselves at the same time, so it hardly looks as if the prospect of penal sanctions has much

* See p. 52.

effect in those cases. On the other hand, the activities of young thugs are influenced by the mores of the criminal sub-culture. In England this sub-culture does not generally tolerate murderous violence, and it could be that the older, professional criminals, who have been rationally deterred from carrying firearms, may have helped to set the tone in this respect.

Welfare

Crime prevention may also be sought by more positive social measures, intended to relieve people of the necessity to obtain their ends illegitimately. A classic example is National Assistance and old-age pensions, which should remove the need for anyone to steal to eat. This represents but one of a host of sensible welfare measures which operate on the general principle of attacking the social evils which provoke offences. Such schemes have a long history, and in a changing and developing society the scope for them is constantly enlarging. In the nineteenth century, the realization that intolerable physical conditions of filth, pestilence and overcrowding provided breeding grounds for immorality and crime led to the establishment of state-financed systems of public health, sanitation and housing for the poor. In England, reformers like Lord Shaftesbury and Edwin Chadwick, who sat together on the first Board of Health, brought moral fervour to bear on drains and refuse disposal. The latter's *Report on the Sanitary Condition of the Labouring Population*, 1842, by drawing attention to the degrading conditions of the urban poor, and the inevitable effects on the health and character of their children, gave considerable impetus to the social welfare movement [283].

In modern times, a multitude of services for promoting the health and wellbeing of children are taken for granted. All births have to be reported immediately, and in England local authorities are empowered to send health visitors to private homes to see that babies are being properly cared for. At a later stage, children come under the surveillance of schools, and school medical services. The children's departments of each local authority watch over the whole, providing residential homes and other services for children whose parents are prevented by illness or other circumstances from giving adequate care. They also have the power, subject to court orders, to remove children forcibly from parents considered cruel, immoral or inadequate. By recent legislation,* they are required to seek out and advise parents of children who appear to be at risk of becoming delinquent.

In addition to the services which see to it that the elementary physical and moral needs of children are being met in their homes, the school and youth services outside provide essential training in literacy, in technical knowledge, and in social skills, without which no young person can fit in successfully with the requirements of modern society. Parent-teacher associations, the youth employment service, Sunday schools, Scouts, youth clubs, organized sports, to say nothing of the commercial enterprises which supply young people with meeting places, hobbies, pop music, public entertainments, motor scooters and interesting clothes, all help to lessen the incidence of disgruntled misfits and unemployables, and to combat idleness and boredom, and hence presumably contribute something to the prevention and control of delinquency. Criminologists, of necessity, concentrate upon the failures, and upon measures for improvement, but it is easy to forget how much advance has already been accomplished in a short time, and how much worse the situation would be without the existing services.

Naturally, no amount of welfare will provide an insurance against all forms of delinquency. However, there is little fear of reaching the point where further extension of welfare would bring little return, for the amount invested is always restricted by economic, political and moral considerations. Aid to the improvident, and to the actual or potential delinquent, is still limited by the fear that too lavish a provision for the undeserving might lower the incentive for the average man to work hard and stay honest. The wish to prevent wrongdoers escaping punishment sometimes stands in the way of effective counter-measures against particular abuses. For instance, one might expect to decrease the incidence of blackmail by giving immunity from prosecution to victims prepared to collaborate with the police in producing evidence to convict the blackmailers; but that would mean that the victim's crimes (most often deviant sexual misconduct) would go unpunished. In England, addicts can be

* Children and Young Persons Act, 1963, s.1.

given controlled supplies of their drug by doctors, but in the United States this is unlawful, and widely regarded as reprehensible, since it would mean allowing a forbidden gratification without penalty. This situation not only forces American addicts into worse crimes in their efforts to get money to pay the high price of smuggled drugs, it also profits the illicit narcotic traders, who are thus encouraged to push their drugs upon still more young people, so that they become 'hooked' and swell the numbers dependent upon the racketeers. The evils attendant upon self-attempted or back-street criminal abortions could be largely prevented if both girls and boys accepted, understood and had ready access to contraceptives, and if abortions could be performed lawfully in hospitals on social as well as medical grounds. In some countries, such as Canada, the official attitude finds either of these measures morally and legally intolerable. The fact is that once one leaves the abstract question of cause and examines the ramifications of crime prevention, one is immediately confronted by a host of unresolved social issues affecting everyday habits and beliefs.

The more potent schemes of prevention, especially those which involve intervention in the affairs of the adult community, naturally arouse the most opposition. Another limiting factor is the unfortunate side effect whereby more social action on one front usually means less action in some other direction. If too much money gets spent on education, there is less for pensions. If too much attention is given to helping the lame ducks to achieve a minimum standard of proficiency, there is risk of neglecting to draw out the potential talents of the gifted minority who might become valuable leaders and innovators.

Education

Improved teaching methods

Recent developments in prevention consist for the most part of attempts to make the welfare services more effective. The basic aims are to reduce the level of conflict and maladjustment in the population at large, and to provide special attention or help for those groups who, as a result of personal or economic handicaps, are specially vulnerable to delinquent temptations. In conformity with the view that delinquency arises from a multiplicity of interacting factors, the attack has to be mounted along a wide front, but the schools are perhaps better situated than any other service to bring influence to bear upon young people.

In the deliberations of the United Nations Congress on the Prevention of Crime [264] the role of education was given special prominence. It was pointed out that all kinds of improvements in educational methods have relevance, since they help to draw a larger proportion of pupils into effective participation in school life, and hence to reduce the numbers of the discontented and potentially delinquent. For instance, the identification of children with obscure disabilities of perception which interfere with reading, and the development of techniques to overcome this successfully bring in some pupils previously considered ineducable. The fostering of a democratic classroom atmosphere, in which children are helped to assume a rational attitude to their own moral and social responsibilities, the use of television and other aids for enhancing the interest and impact of what is taught, and the adjustment of the curriculum to suit the interests and social circumstances of the children in particular areas: all these help in overcoming the apathy and antagonism of the more difficult and socially alienated pupils. Schools which put too exclusive an emphasis on traditional academic subjects, neglect practical and manual activities, and fail to use models, films, drawing and other non-verbal methods of communication, aggravate the inferiority of the socially deprived, whose handicaps are generally most severe in reading and verbal facility. An understanding of the sort of jobs people do in trade and in the community services is more helpful to the practical minded youngster than learning scraps of a foreign language. The use of teaching machines and programmed learning allows the retarded pupil to proceed at his own pace without public exposure of his mistakes. Home visits by teachers enlist the interest and co-operation of apathetic parents. The promotion of hobby groups and discussion groups, the organization of holiday camps with additional instruction, the recruitment of teachers with special experience in handling lower-class children, the provision of expert counsellors for helping the teaching staff to cope with problem cases and the provision of pre-school nurseries for preparing small children to take part in classes have all been tried [103]. In Stockholm a practical enterprise of special relevance to delinquency prevention is the system of instructing schoolchildren in the functions of the police so as to counteract prejudice against the forces of law and order. Policemen come into the schools to talk about their jobs, and visits to police stations are arranged.

Concentration on the poor risks

Many schemes concentrate upon the children from poorer homes, since they supply so many of the scholastic failures and official delinquents. Methods have been introduced to try to combat the generally low motivation, poor concentration and social ineptitude prevalent among these children. If left to their own devices, such children become a nuisance in class, arouse the teacher's antagonism, and gradually fall further and further behind both academically and socially [48]. These school misfits are apt to seek in truancy, and in the thrills of delinquency, some compensation for their inability to compete in more acceptable ways. Teachers are usually able to identify such trouble-makers more easily than they can do anything to improve them. Since they are so unattractive and uncouth, at least on middle-class standards, teachers have to guard against showing contempt or class prejudice. Being aware of their inferiority, these children are on the look-out for slights and insinuations, and anything of this sort alienates them still more.

Some of the most determined attacks on the problem have been made in the United States as part of the national campaign against poverty and racial discrimination. The poorer and more delinquent-prone segment of the American school population is glaringly obvious, since most of the children in question are of distinctive ethnic background, that is Negro, Puerto-Rican, Mexican – anything other than the dominant white, protestant group to which most middle-class Americans belong. It has been proved that the poor performance of these under-privileged children is partly the result of educators accepting the low standard as inevitable, and failing to draw out such potential as exists.

In New York, the 'Higher Horizons Program' set out to give a community of under-privileged and retarded schoolchildren a vigorous educational campaign, which included exposure to music and cultural activities, remedial coaching for individuals, and much proselytizing among parents. Ambition was aroused so that the children began to aim for vocational and scholastic goals previously regarded as unrealistic. The outcome was a phenomenal increase in the pupils' attainments. The demonstration that poorer children perform better if they are stimulated more, or placed among better-class children of higher standards has led to another New York enterprise, a drive to break down the segregation of the worst pupils in the worst schools. Children are collected by bus and transported to schools in other areas where the population is more mixed and they can have the benefit of being among more civilized class-mates [239].

Educating the community

Naturally there are severe limits to what such schemes can accomplish. However enlightening the school day, the children have to go back to their homes at the end of it, and if the contrast between what they have learned at school and what they experience at home is too great, that in itself can be a source of misery and conflict. Where racial and economic handicaps have deadened the interests, ambitions and morals of the parents, the home situation will always be a hindrance to a child's social and academic progress. Forcing such children into open competition with those from better backgrounds may sometimes produce so much stress that learning is worse blocked than before. An alternative scheme, also tried in New York, consists of all-day Neighbourhood Schools in which activities continue after the normal school hours, drawing in parents and others for meetings and discussions on local issues. In this way, the educational programme seeks to influence children, their parents, and the community, all at the same time.

Schemes for extending services from the schools into the community, for organizing leisure time, for help in finding jobs, and for bringing in parents, have also been tried. In New York, the Columbia School of Social Work is associated with one of the most ambitious programmes of this kind. It goes under the stirring title of Mobilization for Youth Incorporated. The 1965 synopsis lists experiments with over fifty different methods of approach. These include special teaching techniques for use with discouraged and undisciplined children, the provision of facilities and helpers to encourage the completion of homework, vacation schools using unconventional instructional materials, and non-punitive c unsellors for tracking down and helping absentees from school. Other projects are concerned with extra-curricular instruction to improve employment prospects. Youngsters who have left school with no marketable skills are given aptitude tests and then introduced to schemes devised for coaching backward pupils in the specific tasks they might be called upon to carry out when they join offices or factories. One scheme goes so far as to set up actual work-places, repair garages, offices and so forth, where candidates can receive realistic training on the job. Another project concentrates on youngsters who have appeared before a juvenile court, arranging visits to their homes, and giving advice to their families on how to make the best use of the numerous social agencies available to them. Another project provides legal aid, teaching unsophisticated people how to exert their citizens' rights when in conflict with landlords, police, courts or welfare departments. Another organizes disgruntled young people into social action groups, diverting their attention from futile acts of rebellion to more constructive forms of democratic protests, such as forming committees, holding meetings, sending deputations to speak to officials, and producing pamphlets.

Capturing the audience

Bringing in the 'unclubbable' types

One of the greatest difficulties in operating schemes for delinquency prevention is that the boys who are most in need of help are hardest to reach. The wilder and more undisciplined boys are often uninterested in or ineligible for the clubs and activities arranged by voluntary and religious organizations, or else they are ousted from the clubs because they are too destructive or too great a nuisance. One trouble has been that official youth activities have perhaps tended to be rather too tame and over-organized to appeal to the dare-devil propensities of some of these youths. An effort to rectify this has been made in the Outward Bound courses which provide more adventurous expeditions and sports activities. At the same time, the Duke of Edinburgh Award scheme gives recognition to achievements in these activities, rewarding, for example, skills in rescue work. Numbers of boys from approved schools and borstals have been encouraged to join in these schemes, with promising results.

Unfortunately, a minority of socially inept and hostile youths is inevitably left out of any scheme which suits the normal youngster. Since it is from this hard core that recidivist delinquents are likely to be recruited, ways and means have been sought for making contact with them and trying to draw them into schemes for their social betterment. The social case-worker approach, based on the psychotherapeutic model, in which one waits for the client to give voice to his problem, simply doesn't work with youths who don't acknowledge that they have any personal problem, and who think that their troubles are all the fault of other people. More active or aggressive methods of approach have had to be used, and in effect some social workers have completely reversed their technique and become what amounts to missionaries trying to sell unpopular ideas to a resistant clientele.

In recent years so much has been reported along these lines that it is difficult to select any one example, but perhaps the activities of the Harvard team led by Ralph Schwitzgebel [231] will serve the purpose. He recruited clients by accosting likely-looking youths in the less pleasant parts of Boston and offering to pay them to come to his laboratory and talk into a tape-recorder. He was open with them about the general purpose, which was to help students of delinquency, although at first some of his clients thought that there must be more to it, and that they were actually being taken along for some dishonest or immoral purpose. He generally invited the youth to bring along a friend to look over the set-up, and gave them time to think over the proposition before deciding; a strategy opposite to that of the common con man, who tries to force an immediate commitment.

The talks into the recorder led gradually to the youths confiding in the researchers and participating in therapeutic discussions of their problems. At first they were encouraged to expound their own views on social questions, and to participate in philosophical discussions on delinquent conduct, before working round to a more personal angle. It was considered that having to reflect about such questions might in itself lead to more restraint in their behaviour.

The scheme depended upon continued regular attendance, and since the boys who took part were the sort who were unused to thinking ahead and keeping regular appointments they had to be trained in this by means of higher fees for prompt appearance, and by such powerful reminders as being collected by a large car with a pretty girl inside. They were also paid for carrying out practical tasks which were devised as a subtle and indirect means of controlling their conduct. For example, some of them were required to keep diagrammatic charts of their own behaviour, others were loaned cine-cameras for recording the activities of their gangs. In order to encourage the acquisition of driving licences, so that boys could borrow cars legitimately instead of stealing them, one of the tasks set and successfully completed was the revision and clarification of a driving instruction manual.

This particular programme of delinquency prevention included a follow-up of the subsequent convictions of the 'treated' group, and of a matched control group of similar delinquents who had not had the same attention. The numbers involved were small, but the experimenters calculated that the re-conviction rates of the boys taking part was significantly less than that of the control group, and also less than would be expected on the basis of the re-conviction rates of other samples of delinquents in Boston.

Street-corner research

The scheme just described concentrated on developing techniques for inveigling delinquents into attending what was in essence a slightly disguised treatment centre. Other workers have adopted the alternative strategy of going out to meet delinquents, and potential delinquents, on their own ground, making friends with them, even joining up with their gangs, in the hope that by infiltration from the inside they might subvert the influence of the more anti-social leaders, and persuade others into a frame of mind in which cooperation with social agencies becomes feasible. As the Roman Catholics found with their worker priests, social participation carries with it special dangers. Sometimes it becomes doubtful which side is doing the converting. If the 'detached worker', as he is called, becomes too much identified with the gang and its problems he may take their side against authority. Conflict may arise if the police come to feel that gangs are being stimulated and given added status by having a 'detached worker' allocated to them, or that the worker is forgetting his duty as a citizen when he fails to warn the police when he knows a crime is being planned, or that the worker is repeating damaging allegations about improper police methods.

Whatever may be the true extent of the detached workers' effect, or lack of effect, upon the incidence of delinquency, they have at least provided a rich source of descriptive material on life in the delinquent sub-culture. Mary Morse [191] has reported on a series of experiments in which young workers were sent out in different parts of England to try to make contact with young people who were not attached to any official youth organization, with a view to finding out how the existing facilities might be adapted to bring in these drifting isolates. Not all the groups studied were made up of potential delinquents, but one in particular, described as the Lymport coffee-bar youths, consisted mostly of delinquents who came from one of the poorer and drearier areas of the town. In that area, the police were treated with suspicion, even by adults, and certain offences, such as shop-lifting, were widely regarded as normal and justified. The young woman worker got to know the youths by dint of taking a job as a waitress in their favourite coffee bar. Although she did all she could to conceal her true purpose, she was regarded as an oddity, and was teased on account of her educated accent, and was even suspected by some of being a student observer, but in spite of all that she was sufficiently taken into their confidence to be able to make some astute comments on their attitudes and mode of life.

The group centred around a few popular and spirited young men who were unquestionably established delinquents. The loose collection of their friends and acquaintances who met in the coffee bar provided a source of ever-ready accomplices for planned house-breaking and similar activities. Most of them came from large, poor families, characterized by broken homes, marital infidelity, promiscuity and alcoholism. Once they had left school, their parents generally left them to get on with their own affairs, until such time as they provoked trouble with the police, when they would be threatened with being turned out of the house. Convictions, followed by incarceration in penal institutions, finally brought about the dissolution of the clique. Although some of these boys made occasional use of boxing or swimming facilities, formal attachments to youth clubs were avoided. Most of them claimed to see money-making as the chief goal of life, and they were both envious and suspicious of persons of substance. Their fantasies were of the get-rich-quick variety. Money was a perpetual problem, for though many were capable of earning high wages, this was offset by reckless drinking and spending at weekends, and in some cases by work-shyness or inability to stick at a job for any length of time. Indeed it was noticeable that in spite of high wages some youths got bored after their first few years experience of dead-end and uninteresting jobs, and joined the ranks of layabouts. At times the local pawnshop housed most of their clothes. Drunkenness, bravado in the face of threatened imprisonment, and delinquent escapades were all part and parcel of their image of manhood.

Perhaps the most important lesson to come out of these studies was that the supposedly unreachable youngsters were in fact approachable given an initially uncritical, undemanding and sympathetic approach on the worker's part. The obvious shortcoming of most youth organizations was in expecting too much of these young people too soon. No change is to be expected in morals or behaviour until a close and special contact has been built up with some responsible worker who can bridge the gap between disgruntled youth and uncomprehending authority. In the worst areas, such as Lymport, special clubs are needed if the unattached are to be catered for at all, for their behaviour would quickly ruin any normal club. A second point which emerged, none the less important for being trite and unexciting, was the need to tackle a constellation of social and personal factors simultaneously. The youth with a grievance based upon parental rejection or neglect was very likely also to be frustrated at work by the preferential treatment and apprenticeships awarded to those with a better education than himself. He was also likely to spend his leisure among those with similar problems and disillusionments, and so to have his anti-social attitudes continually reinforced.

Middle-class deviants

A further and rather more novel conclusion emerged as a result of studying a variety of groups and areas, namely that delinquent groups may show quite different kinds of social disturbance calling for different measures of prevention. Whereas the tribulations of the Lymport youths were exactly as described in all the texts on deprived delinquents, a more middle-class group of unattached young people, residing in the coastal resort of Seaport, presented a new set of backgrounds and problems. This group was studied by a young man who took a flat in the neighbourhood, patronized the coffee bar where they met, made friends with them, joined in their parties, and helped organize a drama group which became a focal meeting point. The members of this group came from relatively affluent homes, and their parents were mostly people who had made money and got ahead, at least economically, though not necessarily in social acceptance. The youngsters had commonly been to grammar schools or technical colleges. They were an unstable lot, with a poor showing in educational or vocational accomplishment. Although their aspirations were towards highly paid positions, such as actors or successful writers, they were incapable of sustained effort, and most of them had failed to get very far in the educational system and were drifting discontentedly and aimlessly from one job to another. It seemed that many had lacked warmth or consistent support from their preoccupied parents, and had become embittered by their failure to fulfil their own and their parents' ambitions for further social and educational advancement. Their unsettled and rebellious behaviour went beyond the limits of normal adolescence. They not only rejected parental injunctions and affected to despise the trappings of conventional respectability, they were contemptuous of other teenage groups as well. They hated the 'hearties', who offended by adopting conventional enthusiasms (the pipe-smoking young conservatives), and also the 'thicks', the tough working-class types of lesser education and cruder tastes. Their own preferences were for middle-class luxuries without middle-class effort. They liked to cadge lifts and favours, to use trains and visit cinemas without paying, and their favourite recreation was going to private teenage parties where sexual licence, rowdyism, heavy drinking, and sometimes illicit drugs, could all be indulged. They avoided youth clubs, which they considered dull and generally unsympathetic.

The companionship and mutual support of a group of fellow rebels and extremists helped to cover their individual insecurities and fear of commitment. Although some among them were officially convicted delinquents, this was less common than among the Lymport youths. Their illicit activities tended more towards getting away with something when the opportunity presented than to planning the old-fashioned crimes which so often lead to swift arrest. Under the influence of the social worker's prodding they succeeded in putting on a theatrical play, and this success, unexpected either by themselves or by their disillusioned parents, seemed to bolster their self-confidence and make them a little more amenable to normal society.

Evaluation of schemes for delinquency prevention

Helping potential delinquents

Social measures which impinge upon the whole community are very difficult to assess, because there can be no control group of untreated cases for comparison. If increasing welfare activity in the field of housing and education is followed by a decrease in juvenile delinquency, this is not necessarily a matter of cause and effect, since the statistics are subject to continuous and largely unexplained changes independent of any programme of prevention. However, where particular neighbourhoods are saturated with delinquency-prevention activities, as in the 67-block slum area of Manhattan covered by the Mobilization for Youth scheme, it should be possible in time to get a rough idea by comparing changes in the delinquency rates in the experimental area with changes in other similar neighbourhoods over the same period. But such evaluations will always be rather crude. For one thing, varying public interest and police activity affect the statistics, and this process may be considerably enhanced by the publicity attached to preventive programmes.

Programmes of treatment for individuals, which are directed at selected persons identified as potential delinquents, are in principle easier to evaluate, since there remains a body of un-treated cases for comparison. Since most such programmes have given disappointing results when subjected to statistical analysis, one must be clear that it is one particular type of prevention only that is being evaluated.

One of the best-known campaigns of this kind, which included a built-in system of evaluation, was the Cambridge–Somerville Youth Study.* Some 250 boys of average age eleven years, each one matched with a 'control' boy of similar age, social class, intelligence and high delinquency potential (as assessed impressionistically by teachers and social workers), were given the benefit of a fairly intensive and long-term programme of social treatment. Each boy was allotted a big brother or counsellor who was supposed to offer active advice and help. In point of fact, the counsellors succeeded in bringing most of the boys into contact with Scouts, Y.M.C.A., or other youth organizations, more than half of the boys received special scholastic tutoring, and a third had the benefit of direct counselling or psychotherapy for personal problems. Owing to wartime disruptions and other causes, the programme was not as consistently intensive as had been intended originally, but it was certainly far more than would have been got routinely from the educational and welfare services, which was all that the 'control' boys received. When the results were analysed, comparing the delinquency records of both groups over the next seventeen years, it was found that the treated group had just as many convictions as the untreated group, and that both the numbers and types of crimes were similar in the two groups [164]. A further comparison, to see if

* See pp. 28, 71, 110, 161.

those who had had more frequent contacts with counsellors did any better, likewise yielded no significant difference, although a dozen boys who received very intensive treatment did rather better than a dozen carefully matched controls.

Disappointing results

The disappointing outcome of the Cambridge–Somerville project has been experienced in other studies also. Two American psychiatrists, E. F. Hodges and C. D. Tait [123], have published the results of a similar project, begun in 1954, centred on the Second Police Precinct in Washington, an area which at that time included about seven per cent of the population of the District of Columbia, while contributing about eighteen per cent of the recorded crimes and sixteen per cent of the juvenile court cases. It was in fact a slum area characterized by low income, overcrowding, and dilapidated housing. Children from two elementary schools in the area served as subjects; 179 were referred for help on account of difficult behaviour at school, and of these seventy-three were considered to be potential delinquents in need of treatment. Of these thirty-seven received treatment, while the other half were left untreated for comparison. The majority of both the treated and untreated groups consisted of Negro boys. The chief service received by the treated group consisted of social casework, under the guidance of psychoanalytically trained psychiatrists, to the extent of about a dozen interviews with each mother, and a dozen interviews with each child, spread over a period of one to two years in most cases. The treatment was unsolicited by the families concerned, and their failure to keep appointments was a main cause of irregularity in number and frequency of interviews. In the course of time, the parents became less cooperative or receptive to the social workers, and the parents of children who became delinquent were significantly less often cooperative than the rest. This resistance to treatment appeared to stem from the mothers' handicaps of poverty, hours of work outside the home and limited intelligence.

Followed up eight years later, sixty-nine per cent of the treated children and sixty-three per cent of the untreated children had become official delinquents. Further comparisons of the treated and untreated groups on the basis of their delinquency potential as assessed by the Glueck prediction system* suggested that, if anything, the treatment group had started off in a slightly favoured position, with a slightly smaller antecedent likelihood of delinquency. This only served to emphasize the apparent failure of the traditional treatment approach as a means of preventing delinquency.†

Yet another study on similar lines with a similar result was reported by some investigators working for the New York City Youth Board [45]. They assembled two samples of potentially delinquent schoolboys, each consisting of twenty-two boys, matched for probability of delinquency on the Glueck system, as well as for age, intelligence level, and ethnic group. Agreement was reached with a child guidance clinic to undertake treatment for all boys in the first of these samples, with a view to lessening their delinquent tendencies. In fact, all but two of these treated boys were in contact with the clinic for at least thirty months, and two thirds for over four years. The other group of twenty-two boys received no treatment. Some ten years later the delinquency records of the two groups were compared, and exactly the same number (ten) official delinquents were found in both the treated and untreated groups. As the authors put it in a mild under-statement, the result offered no encouragement for the hope that child guidance therapy is effective in materially reducing the incidence of delinquency among a population of predisposed boys.

Another and larger-scale project was carried out with problem pupils at a New York high school in an attempt to demonstrate the effect of group discussions and individual counselling by the skilled professional caseworkers of a Youth Counselling Service in preventing delinquency and promoting social adjustment among teenage girls [177]. Some four hundred pupils were identified as potential problems on the basis of previous school reports. Such points as indiscipline in class, defiance, quarrelsomeness, tempers, dishonesty, unexplained absences, failure to perform up to the level of individual intelligence, moodiness and nervous habits were taken as indications of potential disturbance. Between

* See p. 165.
† But see p. 285.

a quarter and a third of the girl-pupil population were considered potential problems. The selection must have been valid, since records collected over subsequent years showed that the group identified as potential problems were consistently poorer in performance and social adjustment than the rest of the girls.

The main experiment consisted in picking at random a half of the potential problem girls, submitting these to a special treatment programme by the Youth Counselling Service, and then following the progress of the treated and untreated groups. Progress was assessed in various ways, by academic performance and conduct marks; by teachers' reports of work traits and character; by histories of truancy, of leaving school without graduation, of illegitimate pregnancy, of contacts with police or courts; and by self-rating questionnaires of social attitudes. On none of these criteria did the treated group appear different from the untreated group to any significant degree. And yet the treated group had been exposed to all the traditional resources of the casework approach. Individual therapy was attempted with 125 girls. Of these, a small minority proved unapproachable, owing to parental refusal of visits, running away, or premature removal from school. About a half of the girls failed to develop any very close involvement in the treatment, although many of them were seen a dozen or more times by the caseworker. The parents of these girls were usually uninterested or antagonistic in the face of the Youth Service's attempts to help. They included some of the most disturbed cases from the worst backgrounds. The group treatment programme fared better in securing and maintaining eager participation. Generally, both clients and caseworkers felt that the discussions, which concentrated on the difficulties and uncertainties of adolescence, had been of benefit in fostering confidence and social maturity. Nevertheless, judged by concrete results, the whole programme of preventive treatment was sadly ineffective.

Reasons for failure

One is forced to conclude from these studies that the commonly accepted treatments of individuals are not very useful in preventing delinquency. The conclusion is highly unpalatable to social caseworkers and child guidance therapists, whose minis- trations are made to seem futile. It also seems to imply that commonly held assumptions about the psychological determin- ants of delinquency, if not altogether mistaken, are of small value in the development of practical remedies. However, at the risk of appearing credulous, or of indulging in special pleading, it is necessary to point out that psychological treatment is not being given a fair trial unless it is firstly intensive and secondly applied to properly selected cases. Psychoanalytic literature, from which case-workers have taken their theoretical framework, emphasizes that successful therapeutic effects generally occur only after a long and intensive relationship between client and analyst. It is on the special quality of this relationship, and its power to affect all other relationships into which the patient may enter, that psychoanalysis depends. Indeed it could hardly be otherwise if the treatment is successfully to counteract habits conditioned by a lifetime of past experience plus the continued pressures of events outside the analytic hour. In practice, most clinic psychotherapy and social work based on the analytic model falls far short of this ideal; superficial contacts of thirty minutes or less once a fortnight being much more typical than the long and almost daily interviews associated with classic psychoanalysis. This could be one reason for the ineffectiveness of treatments as currently practised, but if so it is hard to see what to do about it, except perhaps to concentrate attention on a few at the expense of the many. Another and more promising possibility is that the conventional psychological treatment approach works with delinquents who have psychological dis- orders, but has a negligible or even harmful effect upon the majority, whose behaviour represents a natural response to social pressures. Finally, it could be that the individual approach commonly fails because those in greatest need are unapproach- able by traditional clinic methods. These suggestions are taken up more fully in the next chapter which deals with treatments for established delinquents.

1 The Treatment of Apprehended Delinquents

The possibility of analytic influence rests upon quite definite pre-conditions. . . . Where these are lacking – as in the case of children, of juvenile delinquents, and, as a rule, of impulsive criminals – something other than analysis must be employed. . . .

Sigmund Freud in a foreword to *Wayward Youth* by August Aichhorn (1925). (First English edition, Imago, 1951.)

We have no reason to consider the staff of the School Medical Service or of the Psychiatric Department of the hospitals or even the Child Guidance Clinic personnel so outstandingly successful in the treatment of young delinquents that we should all bow down in front of them in reverential awe!

J. B. Mays, *Sociological Review Monographs*, No. 9 (1965). Keele. p. 196.

From psychotherapy to therapeutic community

Resistance to traditional psychotherapy

Unlike the preventive social measures described in the last chapter, which apply to all and sundry, the attempt to treat apprehended delinquents rests on the assumption that they have something wrong with them, unless, of course, the word treatment is being used as a euphemism for detention in custody. In practice, most youngsters who get as far as being committed to approved schools do show signs of individual maladjustment, mostly in the form of some degree of anti-social or psychopathic distortion of character. The old-fashioned medicine for such bad characters is stiff, reformatory discipline; but psychoanalytic theories suggest that an opposite approach might be more effective.

Traditional psychoanalysis requires the client to ponder aloud upon his deepest feelings and motives, while the therapist prompts him if the flow stops or lapses into triviality. Now and then the therapist may interject challenging interpretations, but mostly the client has to work things out for himself, since self-realization is the essence of the process. This method, or modifications of it, was developed for the treatment of educated, middle-class anxiety neurotics. They cooperate readily, because their tensions impel them to unburden themselves, and they generally have an aptitude for introspection and verbalization. The typical delinquent character type seldom takes kindly to this procedure. By temperament and social background he is inclined to put his feelings into action rather than words, and to have little capacity for abstraction or introspection. Furthermore, on the surface at least, delinquent characters are often slap-happy, extraverted persons; their worries, if any, are not about themselves, but about externals, like what punishment they may get, or what injustices they have experienced. In classical psychoanalysis, the patient is told: 'The problem is in you, and you can solve it if you want.' If the patient doesn't turn up, or doesn't talk, that is 'resistance', a sign that he doesn't want to change. On this criterion, one would have to give up as untreatable the many delinquents who say: 'There's nothing wrong with me, I don't know why they sent me here.' This impasse goes a long way towards explaining the ineffectiveness of the efforts of clinics to change delinquents by traditional methods of individual psychotherapy. The old model doesn't fit, since the delinquent's conflict is with society not within himself, and the therapist's language and way of thinking are incomprehensible to him.

Reality therapy and group therapy

One way of adapting the treatment to suit the delinquent is for the therapist to become more active and directive, to confront the patient forcibly with the disasters his transgressions are likely to bring upon him, to hold up a metaphorical mirror to show him just where and how he goes off the rails. Schmideberg [227] has called this 'reality therapy'. Instead of waiting expectantly for the patient to work things out he is shown firmly, consistently and repeatedly the limits within which he must learn to live. Such treatment has something in common with plain old-fashioned moral training, except that the appeal is to the realities of the social situation rather than to an abstract religious ethic. In the hands of a skilled psychotherapist, who avoids personal recrimination or blame, and who understands the difficulty the delinquent finds learning to control his reactions, this can be a more powerful weapon than the conventional homily.

Another way to appeal to the delinquent's sense of realities is by conducting psychotherapy in a group setting: half a dozen or more patients meeting together with the therapist to discuss their life histories and problems. This technique, like psychoanalysis, developed as a method of treating neurotics, but it has a wider application. Some people are unable to look inwards and see themselves as others see them, but they can nevertheless observe and interpret other people's motives and behaviour quite astutely. In a therapeutic group they can see and learn from others with similar difficulties. Since they import into the group their own habitual patterns of reaction in social situations, they can also learn from the comments of their fellow members the sort of impact their behaviour produces. Clinical impressions suggest that the group experience makes a more vivid impression upon some delinquent characters than any amount of abstract discussion at individual interviews.

The therapeutic community

Daily life within a small community can be arranged like a therapeutic group, in which the participants can learn slowly, and profit from their mistakes, without too much harm to themselves or others. This is the ideal of the therapeutic community, and attempts have been made to organize reformatory institutions on this basis. Since the delinquent must learn through experience with other people, especially people of greater maturity than himself, his contacts with the staff of the institution have to be informal, and the general atmosphere needs to be friendly and intimate, in fact as close as possible to that of a healthy family, which is the natural setting for social learning. Too much regimentation, red tape, or the giving of peremptory orders merely strengthen the barrier of dislike and distrust with which the delinquent fends off the demands of authority; so the institution needs to be run on democratic lines, the inmates being given as much personal responsibility as they can cope with, being drawn into the process of rule making and enforcement, and being given ample opportunity for free discussion of public grievances and personal problems. Since the experience of cooperation in worthwhile enterprises develops social skills and social confidence, inmates need plenty of scope for self-expression in constructive and vocational activities. For some delinquents the experience of living for a time under such conditions may suffice to produce a beneficial change of attitude; for others it provides a necessary background support without which they could not be reached by individual treatment. The therapeutic community does not consist in any single method or programme so much as in a guiding philosophy according to which the facilitation of educative social interaction is an essential preliminary to psychological change.

The ideas and practices referred to are not really new, although the name for them has been taken up in a big way in recent penological writing. They first came to the fore in an educational context, notably in progressive boarding schools and in reform schools for wayward juveniles.

Early examples of therapeutic schools

Long before psychological theory lent support to such endeavours, humanitarian and religious motives inspired the foundation of homes for young delinquents where they might be trained and looked after in a manner approximating to the care provided by normal parents. A very early example was the school for depraved children at Neuhoff, Switzerland, founded in 1775 by Pestalozzi, whose name is remembered today in the international villages for refugee children. A pioneer of the use of small family groups living in separate units or cottages was J.H. Wichern, who opened the Rauhe Haus, near Hamburg, in 1833. The pattern was followed on a larger scale by the French judge F. A. De Metz in the Colonie Agricole at Mettrai, which began in 1840 and had considerable influence on the organization of other reformatories. Mary Carpenter [27] described Mettrai enthusiastically in terms which suggest an extraordinarily modern system. The boys were divided in separate houses, each under the care of its own housemaster and his assistants, so that they met together in the larger community only during work and recreations. Corporal punishment was forbidden, prison walls dispensed with, and discipline kept through the masters' constant association with their charges. The school also had what would nowadays be called a system of after-care. Jobs were found for the boys on leaving, and each was allocated a 'patron' for advice and supervision. Only a small percentage relapsed into crime. Another successful school was the reformatory at Saltley, near Birmingham, begun in 1853, where the superintendent, John Ellis, a former shoe-maker and a remarkable character, set up a system of self-government under which he cooperated with a committee of the boys in formulating and enforcing democratic rules. As so often happens, the venture passed into oblivion with the charismatic character who had sustained it.

Since then, other schools in different parts of the world have come and gone, each one in large measure repeating the experience of its predecessors, occasionally quite independently and in ignorance of what had gone before. Thus, at the turn of the century, William George set up a school in New York State, known as the Junior Republic, because it took as model the United States constitution, and had the boys form themselves into self-governing committees to learn in practice the arts and rewards of good citizenship. A follower of George, Homer Lane, came to England and set up in Dorset the Little Commonwealth, where children were made to work out their own system of self-government, and to form themselves into groups for discussion and mutual help. In Russia, in the aftermath of the Bolshevik revolution, the appearance of roving bands of homeless young thieves and robbers led to the establishment of colonies for juvenile's, organized by the pioneer Anton Makarenko. He was another to make full and successful use of the democratic approach, self-helping groups and informal discussions. The more recent examples in England and America are too numerous to mention. Significantly enough, several have come to an end through withdrawal of support by the responsible authorities [141; 243; 284].

For many reasons the ideal of the therapeutic community is difficult to translate into practice. One source of difficulty is the annoyance aroused in some administrators when the clear and orderly appearance of a respectable institution is sacrificed to the psychological needs of turbulent youth. The whole approach makes great demands upon the staff, who have to come off their pedestals and tolerate familiarity and personal criticism from uncongenial and frequently hostile inmates. It calls for personal qualities of democratic leadership in the staff, otherwise the relaxation of authoritarian control may lead to unhelpful chaos and confusion, or perhaps give a chance to the worst characters to bully and tyrannize the rest. The ideals are more readily put over in small groups, in which the individual enthusiast can exert a personal influence on all concerned, than in large institutions which have a way of encouraging bureaucracy and social distance. Perhaps just because they are so exacting, these ideals often get watered down and forgotten, only to be rediscovered and propagated again under another name by some new enthusiast of the next generation.

Mental-hospital experience

The idea of a therapeutic community has taken root most firmly in the mental hospitals. These institutions have many problems in common with penal establishments; both are dealing with deviant behaviour, both are trying to persuade their inmates into conformity. The old-fashioned hospital operated a severely authoritarian and custodial régime. Although fetters and whips went out long ago, locked wards, barred windows, padded cells, and hefty male nurses for the disturbed sections were nevertheless much in evidence until recently, as was a heavy emphasis upon the chain of command, with the patients at the lowest point of the pecking order. Under these conditions, some patients lost all initiative and lapsed into hopeless apathy. Others reacted with violence to the restraints that were meant to subdue them [99]. In the last twenty years, a great change has come about. Now the hospitals are proud of their open doors, and most patients come and go as they please without physical or legal restraint. Instead of being shut away or put to bed, patients are given responsibilities to the limits of their capacity, and encouraged to take part in work and social activities as well as in discussion groups with doctors and nurses. Admittedly, the use of new tranquillizing drugs has helped the process along, but even so it is clear that many patients were in the past restricted unnecessarily and to their detriment, and that much difficult and erratic behaviour can be kept in check by the influence of a favourable environment [37].

In England, the psychiatrist Maxwell Jones was one of the leading pioneers of the therapeutic community ideal. He provided a link between hospital and penal practice by developing an 'open' unit at Belmont Hospital (now the Henderson Hospital), which specialized in treating psychopathic and neurotic offenders. This is a largely self-governing patient community with group psychotherapy and communal work activities the main treatment resource.

Therapeutic communities in action

Aichhorn's school

The therapeutic community approach has also been tried in reformatory school projects for ordinary young delinquents who have not been diagnosed as neurotic or psychiatric cases. Three examples may be mentioned by way of illustration. The first was an experiment by an Austrian, A. Aichhorn [2], which has become a classic of penology and education. The second was a recent experiment in the rehabilitation of homeless borstal boys inaugurated by Frank Foster, then Director of Borstal After Care, and carried out with the help of Dr D. Miller, a practising psychoanalyst in London [180]. The last example, from the United States, was an instance of the failure of a would-be therapeutic community, as recorded by a participant sociological observer, H. W. Polsky [208].

Aichhorn began his experiment just after the First World War when he was put in charge of a residential institution for delinquent boys at Oberhollabrun. He had had long experience as a school-teacher, and an organizer of settlements for boys. He brought to his new task a burning conviction that the bad behaviour and character deformities of most delinquents were due to lack of consistent love and care during the formative years of childhood; that their aggressive and provocative attitudes represented their way of fighting back against a world which they had come to perceive as hostile and rejecting. He believed that continued punishment and coercion could only make them that much readier to take revenge upon society after release, and that the only hope of reclaiming them was to satisfy their frustrated craving for affection by an initial policy of unconditional acceptance, which could be followed later by a very gradual and tolerant programme of training to enable them to meet the demands of normal society. His ideas and the practices he introduced were the result of intuitive understanding, but when he became familiar with psychoanalytic theory he was able to interpret and explain his work in those terms.

In the management of reformatories he advocated breaking down inmates into small groups, with members not too diverse in character. As for the environment, he wrote: 'we felt intuitively

that above all we must see that the boys and girls from fourteen to eighteen had a good time . . . an environment must be
created in which they could feel comfortable' [3]. He depre-
cated the kind of establishment in which rows of beds were
ranked like soldiers, not an inch out of line, with covers folded
precisely at right angles. Such meticulous conformity, difficult
enough for the normal child to attain, could only be achieved
among dis-social children by brute force, and would disappear
once that force was left behind. He found that a policy of studied
tolerance, in which the staff allowed the youngsters to be as rude
and provocative as they pleased, without retaliation, generally
paid off in time. In the past, the children's chronic sense of
grievance had always been confirmed by automatic punishment,
but now, once they realized that the expected reaction was no
longer forthcoming, they experienced an upsurge of confusing
emotion which shattered their cold and sullen defensiveness,
brought out their yearnings for human attachments, and laid
them open to influence by friendly members of staff.

Aichhorn's faith in this non-punitive approach led him to
apply it even to those difficult cases whose quarrelsomeness and
defiance reached such extremes that they were not tolerated by
their fellow delinquents. A dozen such boys, every one of whom
had been brought up without affection in a broken or dishar-
monious home, were placed together and left to their own
devices, staff members intervening only when necessary to
prevent injury. Opportunities for play and interesting occupation were provided, but not obligatory. Before long the furniture
and windows were all broken, the place was a shambles, and boys
were taking their food in corners, like animals, rather than sit
together at the meal-table. Still Aichhorn persisted, feeling that
once their aggression had reached a certain pitch it would expend
itself and be replaced by other feelings. And so it turned out.
After their outbursts had subsided, or become less frequent, they
began to form attachments to the staff, and developed as much
dependency and jealousy of each other as one might have expected from nursery children. They were then moved to fresh
quarters, which they did not break up, and the slow process of
training these over-sensitive and childish youngsters could begin.
Aichhorn was aware that at this stage, in the slogan of a later

exponent of the reformative art, Bruno Bettelheim, *love is not enough*. Once the emotional ice had broken, and the youngsters had become amenable to influence, the staff had to apply gradually measured doses of frustration, discipline and restriction so as to train their charges to meet the demands of normal life. The therapeutic community provided an environment in which emotional ties could develop, and in which the youngsters could find comfort and support while being tamed and broken in to social control.

Limitations of the treatment

The ideal therapeutic community varies with the needs of the particular group under care. Aichhorn knew the foolishness of applying to everyone methods devised for the established delinquent character. A normal, well-socialized youngster does not need to be handled like a baby who hasn't yet learned to control his tantrums and elementary hate reactions, and the boy who merely joins in with illegal escapades because that is expected behaviour among his group does not need to be treated as if he had some serious defect of personality. On the other hand, although a great many apparently impossibly psychopathic youngsters will form a therapeutic attachment in time, given sufficient patient endurance on the part of the staff, a minority will always remain unamenable and require a different approach. The policy of patient expectancy assumes that a normal potential exists, despite the present distorted reactions, but in cases of brain damage or defect, for instance, this may not be the case. So-called autistic children, who seem incapable of perceiving the world around them sufficiently clearly to respond realistically, and who remain wrapped up in their own imaginings, would hardly be aroused by the sort of approach that works with ordinary children. After serious brain injuries, if certain areas are affected, some unfortunate people become emotional zombies whose feelings lack the intensity or the discrimination necessary for any great attachments. In rare cases, some severely psychopathic youngsters, especially those of the coldly withdrawn passive type, who may be intellectually dull as well, give a rather similar impression. Sometimes these characters have come from apparently normal homes. Although it is difficult to prove, it could be that some of them are suffering from a congenital brain defect which makes them unresponsive to normal socializing influences. If so, they are unlikely to be much improved by placement in a therapeutic environment suited to more normally constituted youngsters.

The Northways Home

Derek Miller, whose treatment project took place some quarter of a century after Aichhorn's, and was inspired by a more sophisticated level of psychoanalytic theory, came to many of the same practical conclusions as had earlier exponents of liberal reformatory régimes. Like Aichhorn, he emphasized the need to have a group of compatible and not too abnormal individuals. He selected his delinquents so that all of them were working-class youths from socially deprived backgrounds, but he would include only those of about average intelligence, and he would not admit those whose behaviour disturbance was so great as to presuppose some form of madness or brain damage, or to require hospital treatment. All of them were at least potentially capable of forming reasonable human relationships.

The essence of the treatment, as in other therapeutic communities, was to provide a situation in which the delinquent felt loved and understood, in which relationships could develop, in which the more destructive expressions of aggression were controlled, while at the same time the basic need of youth to be moderately defiant and assertive of masculinity was allowed for, and in which a gradual assumption of normal responsibilities was helped along by personal attention, advice, discussion and interpretation as occasion arose.

The clients in fact consisted of young men aged seventeen to twenty released on licence from borstals, and with no parental home to which they could return. They were seen by the psychiatrist while on leave from their institutions, shortly before release, and if considered suitable they were invited to visit the house, Northways, and offered a place there. Acceptance was voluntary, but the great majority came gladly. They were recidivist delinquents, with an average of four previous convictions, and an average of nine years spent in institutions by each boy.

The whole scheme was on a small scale, twenty-one youths being dealt with over a two-year period, with perhaps only half that number living in the house at any one time. A woman warden, a male assistant, and the visiting psychiatrist acted as therapists. Discussion sessions with the boys were held weekly by the psychiatrist. No topics were banned, and such difficulties as those due to epidemics of stealing in the home were openly discussed. At first the boys showed their distrust by making superficially obsequious and compliant noises, while concealing their true thoughts. Boys out of a job might leave the house at the usual time so as not to have to admit the fact. However, as time went on, the boys lost some of their distrust, they no longer needed to test the staff's sincerity by provocative actions, and as the atmosphere settled down it became possible for boys to spend more of their energy helping each other instead of fighting. In fact, the project demonstrated yet again that seemingly unapproachable and unresponsive characters can be brought into a therapeutic relationship given patience and restraint on the part of the staff, and a willingness to make allowances for the limitations and peculiarities of their charges.

One feature of these youths which had to be understood was their inability to express their feelings except by impulsive action. For example, following the arrest of one of their members the discussion group pointedly steered clear of reference to what had happened. Instead, they fell to grumbling about the uselessness of discussions, and started quarrelling and fighting. After the therapist had pointed out that they must be very worried about the arrested boy, they quietened down and were able to talk sadly about the situation. But in order to intervene at all effectively, the therapist had to be able to perceive the emotional pressures behind the boys' behaviour. Their demands upon the staff were enormous and childishly irrational, they competed for attention, they resented the staff attending to their own family concerns or having time off, they fantasied the psychiatrist as an enormously affluent person who could be asked for anything, and they tried to set one staff member against another.

While allowing a great deal more licence than is customary in institutions, the psychiatrist kept firmly to certain rules and limits, which the boys could not exceed if they wished to stay in the house. For example, if stealing from outsiders was reported or detected, he would report it to the police, and he would not allow them to shock the woman warden with crude sex talk or gestures. He would not intervene to protect the boys from the natural social consequences of bad behaviour, or from normal social responsibilities (such as reporting to the borstal after-care officers), since the object of the exercise was to help them to confront reality. Likewise, the conditions of the borstal licence and of their financial contribution to their stay in the house were used to circumvent deliberate unemployment, and the existence of trustees who would not permit rowdyism or nuisance to neighbours was exploited to reinforce the realities of the situation. A special effort was made to keep the boys' concerns and aspirations directed towards jobs, interests and friends outside, so that the training process would help them to integrate with the normal community instead of becoming dependent upon institutional life. The psychiatrist was also firm about stating when a boy had progressed sufficiently to make arrangements for leaving, and would not allow himself to be dissuaded from this decision by a flare-up of misconduct meant to demonstrate a need for further protection.

Within these wide limits the boys had freedom to express themselves and get in and out of difficulties. They had door keys to come and go as they wished, although they were expected to notify the warden if they intended to stay out for the night. Some care was taken not to make demands upon them that would be considered inappropriate for young men of their age and class; so washing up and feminine domestic tasks were done for them, but they had to work to help pay for it. Such demands as the boys were asked to meet were quite enough to reveal their social ineptitude in numerous ways, and to provide material for discussion and guidance. They were ignorant and confused about tax forms, unemployment benefit, National Health registration, and hire purchase charges. For want of initiative an inordinate proportion of their leisure time was spent watching television, and they talked about tidying up the garden without ever getting round to it. At work, they slacked off when unsupervised, but resented being ordered about. Their difficulties showed up particularly in their relations with girl-friends, whom they treated with extreme inconsiderateness, while at the same time making jealously possessive demands. Some of the boys were sexually very promiscuous, as if to repair their wounded masculinity, while others were fearful of intercourse.

The differences between Northways and ordinary penal treatment

Unlike the older treatment experiments, which traditionally relied upon clinical impressions to substantiate the value of the work, this project did include a control, a group of homeless borstal boys matched with the Northways inmates for age, intelligence and average number of previous convictions and time spent in institutions. The control group received only the usual borstal after-care services. The after-careers of the Northways boys, as regards re-conviction, settled marriages and employment records, were consistently better than the control group, although the numbers were too small for satisfactory statistical demonstration. There was also the complicating factor that the good offices of the Northways staff probably got their boys more consideration at the hands of employers, after-care officers, etc., so the whole of any good effect could not necessarily be attributed to the therapeutic experience itself.

One can see how difficult it would be to reproduce fully in a big institution the conditions exemplified by the Northways project. Sheer size would preclude the enormous amount of time and attention given to each boy, and administrative considerations would hamper flexibility. For example, Miller comments that in spite of effort and good will, the borstals could not provide discharged boys with a suit of clothes in a style they could wear without embarrassment. Similarly, the vocational training they had received in institutions did not prepare the boys for conditions in industry outside, and some of them had come away with silly notions of the extent of their skill or what they could earn in a normal labour market. On the psychological side, while some institutions subscribe to the therapeutic community theory, inadequate practice, with staffs not fully trained for the task, can bring a potentially effective technique into serious disrepute. An essential ingredient in all psychological treatment is a close and continued relationship between the therapist and his clients. In the special case of delinquents in custody the time of release into the world outside represents the most critical period, when they stand in greatest need of the help and support of their therapist. Unfortunately, in conventional penal institutions inmates are generally passed on to different after-care authorities the moment they leave.

Cottage Six

The next example is instructive because it shows how an attempt to produce a therapeutic community may fail despite the presence of a trained professional staff fully committed to putting it into practice. H. W. Polsky studied the work of Hollymeade, an American residential school for Jewish problem children, half of whom were sent by the courts. The school was committed to a therapeutic community ideal, and was an open institution, in so far as there was no enclosing security fence, although patrolling custodial officers were employed to try to prevent abscondings. Inmates were allocated to different residential cottages according to sex, age, social class and the nature of their delinquency. Cottage Six housed twenty of the older, tougher boys, placed under the care of a married couple, the house parents, who lived in the building. The boys attended school classes within the grounds, and also paid regular visits to a social caseworker for individual psychotherapy. Their progress with the caseworker was supervised by the staff psychiatrists. These interviews constituted the major therapeutic effort and the chief point of contact between the boys and the clinical staff. However, the professional clinical workers left the institution each evening and weekend, and so for the greater part of the time the boys were left with only the cottage parents. These were working-class people with no professional training, who were separated from the treatment staff by a considerable gulf of status, knowledge and function. This flaw in the system enabled the small cottage group to build up an inmate tradition at odds with the official values of the institution.

Inside the cottage, the stronger and more aggressive boys

boasted of their delinquency, bullied the weaker or more timorous, and established a pecking order by the use of threatening gestures, incessant comments of an insulting or teasing kind, and occasional beatings. The cottage parents unwittingly colluded in this anti-social behaviour by favouring the more aggressive boys because they were helpful in keeping order within the house. They also shared the aggressive delinquent's dislike and contempt for the weak and snivelling, the 'queers' and the 'bush boys'. Queers were the softer or more timorous types who were the butt of teasing and insinuations about being homosexual. Bush boys were weaklings who bitterly resented their low status and tried to make up for it by futile bickering and tantrums among themselves. In one striking incident a low-status boy turned on his tormentor in a violent assault, was beaten up by the others for his pains, and then transferred to a state mental hospital because his behaviour was so disruptive. In this subculture, newcomers were soon pressed into a professed admiration for delinquent skills, for the forbidden pursuit of the girls who inhabited neighbouring cottages, for success in 'sliming out' of classroom attendance, and for ability to manipulate and bully people, since all these things were synonymous with respect and privilege in the cottage environment. Boys who were taking their casework treatment seriously never referred to it in the cottage. Sometimes they kept themselves a little aloof, though apparently falling in with the mood and attitudes of the prevailing culture. The habit of protecting inner feelings by superficial conformity can work two ways, by playing bad to please peers, or by playing good to please authorities. Private talks with individual boys showed that some were less committed to the cottage values than appeared from their bravado in public.

The experience of Hollymeade shows how important it is to the proper functioning of a therapeutic community that the staff should not be divided against themselves, and that everyone should have a role in the treatment effort. The system whereby a professional staff of psychologists and social workers undertakes treatment, while the non-professional custodial staff looks after discipline and locking up, is quite inimical to the therapeutic community ideal. Within the staff hierarchy, the expert therapist's duty is to teach others to help him rather than to keep his own special relationship with inmates sacrosanct. As with many other requirements, this comes easier in institutions that are not too large.

Behaviour therapy

This is the name given to a series of techniques based upon the theories of learning and conditioning as exemplified in the writings of behaviouristic psychologists such as H.J.Eysenck.* Basically, they consist of training by a manipulation of rewarding and punishing stimuli. In a sense, all forms of education and child training do just this, but the experimental psychologists maintain that in ordinary life rewards and punishments are not applied sufficiently consistently or quickly to produce the best effect, and punishments are often unnecessarily severe and protracted.

In experiments with animals, situations can be rigged quite simply. Choosing the right path (literally) can be rewarded with food, or taking the wrong path can be punished with an electric shock, so that one can work out the optimum timing and severity of punishment, or the relative effectiveness of punishment or reward. Human behaviour is so much more complicated and difficult to keep under surveillance that results are less clear-cut, but similar general principles are believed to hold true.

Learning by 'conditioned avoidance' of unpleasant stimuli has already been mentioned.† This is the basis of aversion treatment, a method that has long been in use for alcoholics. The favourite tipple is given, followed at once by some unpleasant stimulus, usually an injection of emetic, although electric shocks or even a whip would presumably work just as well. The process is repeated again and again until the patient is too exhausted for it to be continued safely. After a few weeks' rest, he goes through the course again. Provided the timing of the stimuli is right, an automatic aversion reaction sets in, and the patient can't stand the thought or taste of alcohol, at least for the time being. The same technique has been used with sexual deviants, by first showing them pictures to evoke their illicit desires, and then

* See p. 137.
† See p. 140.

administering a shock or emetic to build up an aversion [78]. The temptation to commit forms of crime, such as burglary or violent robbery, is not so easily aroused to order, so aversion treatment has hardly been used in any systematic way for the generality of delinquents [110]. Moreover, aversion is less effective where the situation and the response are not very clear-cut and specific. It might discourage particular acts, like taking money from shop tills, without having much effect upon deceit and dishonesty in other situations.

The use of automatic rewards for correct behaviour (operant conditioning) has been tried, using money or gift tokens as the easiest means of quick gratification. Burchard and Tyler [25] claim to have produced remarkable improvement in the behaviour of a delinquent boy in a reform school by this means, when conventional methods of punishment had failed. In animal experiments in which food is offered to those who respond correctly, the gratification is more powerful and immediate, since they are starved for some time beforehand. The same effect can be obtained in humans by first placing them in a situation of discomfort, and then offering relief as a reward. A technique for the purpose has been described by a Canadian psychiatrist, P. M. Middleton [178], formerly consultant to a penitentiary. The discomfort is produced by injection of a paralysing drug, succinyl choline, which arrests breathing and produces asphyxia. The relief consists of whiffs of oxygen under pressure, given with an anaesthetic machine. Under these circumstances, delayed reward amounts to a quite impressive punishment, as the subject becomes asphyxiated. One drawback of the technique is the subject's inability to behave either correctly or incorrectly, since he is paralysed. This is overcome by the use of a pressure cuff around one arm to stop the drug reaching one hand. The subject, who is otherwise completely immobile, can use this hand to signal to the therapist. In treating a young delinquent, the therapist asks him to imagine himself reacting correctly to imagined situations, such as telling a friend who proposes to break into a shop that the idea is stupid. When he has the idea clearly in mind, he signals and gets the rewarding whiff of oxygen.

The techniques of behaviour therapy are anathema to some therapists because it seems like manipulating people against their will. A natural extension of behaviouristic principles could lead to brain-washing, with drugs given to increase conditionability or suggestibility, and a sophisticated alternation of torture and kindness used to batter down resistance. On the other hand, in extreme cases, where the actual alternative is fifteen years' preventive detention, or frequent condemnation to bread and water and solitary confinement, who is to say that a short spell of brain-washing might not be more humane – if only it worked.

Demonstrating results

Comparing re-conviction rates

The effectiveness of various methods of disposal of offenders in the penal system is hard to assess, since persons awarded different sentences for similar offences are not necessarily comparable. Moreover, when attempts have been made to examine approximately comparable offenders undergoing different penal régimes, the long-term outcome has usually been found much the same in both cases. Cynics can argue, therefore, that it makes no appreciable difference to re-convictions what sentence the courts decide upon.

An example of somewhat disappointing findings in relation to the effectiveness of more progressive penal measures is a research by Sir George Benson [17], who used the Mannheim–Wilkins prediction score* to identify comparable groups of young offenders who had been awarded sentences of borstal training and imprisonment respectively. He found no difference in outcome. More recently, Charlotte Banks [14], who analysed the re-convictions of samples of youths passing through prisons, borstals and detention centres, concluded that the important factor determining future outcome was the number of previous convictions. The type of penal institution to which a boy was sent appeared to have little influence.

In their 1964 handbook on sentencing for the use of the courts, the Home Office [132] tried to assess the effectiveness of different sentences by first calculating 'expected' re-conviction rates, taking into account age, class of offence and number of

* See p. 164.

previous convictions. Adjusting the 'expected' rates to 100 for arithmetical simplicity, it was found that, of a sample of juveniles convicted in the London Metropolitan Police District, first offenders discharged or fined had an actual re-conviction rate considerably lower than the expected figure of 100 (rates of 87 and 72 respectively), whereas those committed to approved schools had a re-conviction rate of 149, considerably higher than expectation. Similarly, among young first offenders of seventeen to twenty-one years of age, those discharged or fined did considerably better than expectation (rates of 89 and 75 respectively), whereas those given custodial sentences did worse, with a rate of 150.* The contrasts were much less striking, however, in the case of adult offenders, or offenders of any age who had been convicted previously.

Random allocation to different régimes

The figures just quoted must be treated with reserve, since the courts doubtless took into account when sentencing many factors of behaviour and social background not allowed for in these comparisons. Nevertheless, as far as they go, the figures do lend support to the many observers who claim that a young offender's first experience of penal custody is likely to have a bad effect upon him as an individual, and to render him more liable to re-conviction.

In theory, it should not be difficult to test scientifically the reformative effect of different methods of dealing with offenders who have been caught, since one has a ready-made criterion for comparison in the statistics of re-convictions following release. All one needs to do is to allocate a group of offenders at random between the different methods of disposal, and then wait to see if those awarded any particular punishment or treatment are less often re-convicted. Unfortunately, although many authoritative persons will fully admit in abstract discussion that they have no idea what works best, when it comes to making practical decisions about real people they are unable to leave matters entirely to chance. The Prison Department has power to send offenders to

---

* These conclusions were only tentative, however, since for some age groups the calculations were based upon small numbers.

open or closed prisons or borstals, but their decisions have to
take into account escape risks, the number of vacant places, and
whether a potential inmate will cause trouble in an open institution. The courts have power to choose between fine, probation
and confinement, but in so far as they must appear fair and just
they cannot do this completely at random. One way out of the
impasse is to make a random choice within specified limits. For
instance, magistrates could be asked to select some offenders
deserving of confinement, but not so bad that probation was out
of the question, and then to allow a flip of the coin to decide in
which cases to allow the more lenient course.

So far as I know nothing of this kind has been done by any
English courts. Some American investigators have been able to
compare the outcomes of different disposals of juvenile offenders
determined by a judge in Utah, who used random numbers to
make the selection [59; 60]. Originally, the pool of eligible
delinquents was meant to consist of relatively serious offenders,
who might be committed to reform school, awarded probation,
or given probation with the addition of intensive psychological
counselling and social work. However, Judge Paxman, the enlightened lawyer who collaborated in the scheme, found too few
cases suitable for committal, so the random choice had soon to be
reduced to one of probation or probation plus counselling. This
was a pity, since the greatest difference seemed to be in the boys
sent to institutions, who fared worse than the rest. However,
there was also a slight difference between the other two groups,
in that the boys who got special attention were less often
re-convicted.

Matched offenders on probation and in prison

Another method of evaluating different disposals makes use of
the arbitrary element already present in these decisions. Since
magistrates vary considerably in the severity of their sentences
[133], and the penal authorities often distribute similar offenders
between institutions operating different régimes, it is possible to
collect matching groups of similar offenders who have had
different treatments and to compare the results. One such
comparison, which was a model of carefulness and clarity, was

made by L. T. Wilkins [281] when he was at the Home Office Research Unit. He assembled matching pairs of offenders, the members of each pair being of the same age and sex, convicted of the same kind of offence, and having the same number of charges and offences taken into consideration and the same number of previous convictions. In each pair, one had been sentenced to imprisonment and the other put on probation. The big question was whether the probationers fared better or worse than the prisoners. The answer was that no significant difference in re-conviction rates was detectable.

Had this experiment produced a different result, favouring one form of treatment over the other, it could have been argued that the matching was imperfect. The weak point in all such experiments is that the matching process cannot take into account all of the factors which may have relevance. Supposing, for instance, that offenders who are polite in court have better prospects of freedom from future convictions, and also better chances of being awarded probation. This would mean that probationers would have a better record on follow-up because magistrates had selected the better types in the first place. Since politeness in court would not be visible in official records, it could not be taken into account in the matching process.

'Open' and 'closed' borstals

In a well-known English study of borstal boys, Mannheim and Wilkins [169] compared the outcome of two groups of institutions, the 'open' and 'closed' borstals. Generally speaking, the former are somewhat more relaxed in atmosphere, and the inmates are given more personal responsibility, while the latter have a stricter discipline, and opportunities for self-expression and non-conformity are fewer. The technique of comparison was different, though similar in fundamental principle. The investigators used extensive data on borstal boys to construct prediction tables indicating probability of re-conviction on release in any individual case. These were based on a few points in the boy's official record which experience had demonstrated to be highly correlated with subsequent re-conviction. The tables provided a basis for calculating the expected frequency of

future convictions allowing for the proportions of good and bad
risks in any particular group of borstal boys. The expected re-
convictions of groups of boys, allocated to open and closed
borstals respectively, could then be compared with their actual
re-convictions in order to see if these different treatments resulted in any significant deviation from the expected outcome.
The investigators concluded that open borstals had a better
success rate than closed borstals, even after all possible allowances
had been made for the fact that the youths sent to open borstals
were better risks. Those who believe that the more relaxed and
liberal training régimes are not only kinder and pleasanter but
also more effective can take some comfort from this result. But
of course, as in the comparisons by matching methods, the
possibility lurks in the background that some relevant factors
omitted from the expectancy calculations may account for the
differing re-conviction rates rather than the treatment itself.

Reasons for negative results

Uncertainty of interpretation hardly arises in many comparisons
of penal treatments, since the statistical results often show no
significant differences. Wilkins's comparison of sentences of
probation and imprisonment was a case in point. One can interpret such negative results in several ways. Nigel Walker [272]
points out that perhaps penal measures are for most offenders
interchangeable, so that those who would be discouraged from
repetition of offences by imprisonment could be equally discouraged by a fine. This explanation is supported by the fact that
re-conviction rates are so much more closely associated with the
type of offence, the number of previous convictions, and the
age of the offender than they are with the nature or severity of
the sentence awarded.

Another interpretation is that all the existing penal treatments
are equally futile, or at least negligible in their effects compared
with the other pressures that determine an offender's future
behaviour. Another and more likely explanation is that the concepts of 'offender' and of 'treatment' are too vague and all-
embracing to be workable. Different kinds of offenders, like
different types of sick persons, might benefit from different

treatments. Furthermore, the official label covers a wide range of actual treatment experiences. Probation can mean anything from cursory visits to intensive psychological probing, depending upon the competence and commitments of the officer in charge. In short, the apparent ineffectiveness of penal measures might be the fault of applying ill defined treatments indiscriminately to all and sundry.

Varying effectiveness according to type of offender

It has already been indicated in a previous chapter* that delinquents fall into groups of contrasting psychological make-up and differing treatment needs. This was neatly demonstrated at an American naval establishment, Camp Elliott, San Diego, in what has become a classic experiment in the treatment of delinquents by Grant and Grant [106]. The investigators had previously developed a system of classifying the personality of an offender according to what they called his level of maturity development, which is manifest in his manner of handling personal relationships. At the lowest level, 1, analogous to that of a small baby, other people are scarcely envisaged as separate entities. At level 2, other people are perceived as suppliers or withholders of his personal wants, but of no interest in themselves. At level 3, they are seen as objects which can be manipulated for his own purposes, but he still has little appreciation of others as individuals with thoughts and feelings in their own right. At level 4, he has developed a primitive conscience, and is capable of experiencing guilt, inferiority and admiration, but at this stage he has an undiscriminating black-and-white image of right and wrong derived from a crude perception of the feelings of parents and others. He is thus prone to neurotic conflict between his natural impulses and his unrealistic conscience. At level 5, he becomes more perceptive and flexible and can feel sympathy with others.

This classification has much in common with the stages of moral development described by Peck and Havinghurst [201], and still earlier by Piaget [205].† However, the point of interest

* See p. 173.
† See p. 180.

for the moment is that the Grants reported that delinquents of relatively high maturity level (4 or more) responded better to a psychological counselling approach the more intensively it was applied, whereas with increasingly intensive treatment those of less mature personality did worse and worse. (The criterion of success in this experiment was satisfactory return to military duties.) The implication would seem to be that, in order to benefit from treatment involving discussion and exploration of motives, the offender must have reached a certain maturity level, otherwise the therapeutic effort may make him worse rather than better.

Confirmation of this view was obtained in another Californian project, the Pilot Intensive Counselling Organization, known for short as the P.I.C.O. experiment [1]. Juvenile delinquents in an institution were divided prospectively into two groups considered likely to be 'amenable' or 'non-amenable' to treatment. The former group displayed more anxiety and readiness to accept help, and had a higher level of verbal intelligence than the latter. All offenders, regardless of their prospects, were then allocated at random for either intensive counselling or else for the ordinary institutional régime. Success was judged by frequency of arrests and subsequent penal confinements during a follow-up of several years after release. The amenables did better with counselling than without, but the non-amenables who got counselling did distinctly worse than those dealt with in a more traditional manner. Similar results were obtained when the same experiment was repeated in a second institution.

Since the Grants' pioneer experiment, the maturity scale classification has been used in a number of experiments, mostly in California, as a means of testing the value of different kinds of treatment régimes for different types of delinquents. The chief drawback of the classification has been that it is based upon interpretations of the offender's responses in the course of lengthy interviews, and of course skills and attitudes of the interviewer affect the reliability of the assessment. However, psychologists have now devised questionnaire style tests which appear to do the same job and to produce substantially similar results without the complicating factor of interviewer bias [105].

An evaluation of the usefulness of the maturity level classification in practice is now being made in the Community Treatment Project of the California Youth Authority [275]. Excluding a minority of serious offenders considered ineligible, a group of juveniles, sufficiently seriously delinquent to have been committed to the Youth Authority, were allocated at random either to the Authority's traditional institutional programme or to an experimental programme of Community Treatment. The average age of the offenders was fifteen years, and those sent to the Community Project were each placed under the supervision of an agent responsible for carrying out treatment. The agents had an average case load of only eight to ten delinquents each, and could therefore afford to give every one a lot of attention. Treatment was varied according to individual needs as gauged by maturity level, and ranged from temporary confinement, surveillance and firm discipline, or foster-home placement, through guided group activities to individual counselling and psychotherapy.

Failures over a span of fifteen months following release or termination of special treatment (revocation of parole or recommitment by the courts being counted as failure) were distinctly more frequent among the ordinary penal group than among the community treatment group – forty-eight per cent compared with twenty-nine per cent. Comparison of responses on the California Psychological Inventory before and after treatment by the two groups showed that the experimental subjects had more frequently changed towards a better social adjustment than had the control subjects. This kind of research represents a substantial step in refining both treatment method and evaluation to a point where statistical demonstration of effectiveness becomes a feasible proposition.

2 Some Cautionary Afterthoughts

Our state of ignorance

When I was writing this book, a list of questions was sent to me from a student struggling to write an essay on juvenile delinquency and wanting some short authoritative answers. 'Why is there an increase in delinquency?' 'Does it run in families?' 'Why is it so much more marked in boys?' 'How widespread is the gang system, and are most gangs delinquent?' 'Are delinquents usually characterized by variability of mood or lack of concentration?'

When I look back on these elementary questions, it occurs to me how disappointed this student and other readers may be to find so many of these basic issues discussed, and so few clear-cut answers provided. In truth, the subject of delinquency bristles with unanswerable questions. The more one sees of it, the less one sees through it. Delinquency, like ill health, consists of a vast conglomeration of different phenomena, and no simple explanation or cure will be found to fit more than a small segment of the whole. The problems are so many-sided, so changeable, and so complex in all their social and psychological ramifications that we have hardly got to the stage of stating the issues coherently, let alone resolving them.

The topics covered in this book were selected because they represent some of the traditional preoccupations of criminologists, and hence a body of research and literature exists upon which to draw. A great many important topics have been left out simply because of the lack of relevant facts or research findings. For instance, in the recently publicized episodes of rowdyism at seaside resorts, or the epidemic of telephone smashing, or the consumption of intoxicating drugs, one would like to know if these are the work of the traditional thieving delinquents, or if they herald the appearance of new types of offender as well as new types of offence. In view of the criticisms made about over-large school classes and lack of control by teachers, one would like to know how much difference it makes to the risks of becoming delinquent which school a boy attends. Many people would like to know about the effect, if any, of television and the mass-media, but a learned committee now looking into this question finds it easier to list the investigations that need to be carried out than to reach decisive opinions. Even on the more traditional research topics, such as the social-class distribution of delinquents or the true amount of the increase in youthful law-breaking, the available evidence, although voluminous, is often conflicting and inconclusive.

There are many reasons for our continued state of ignorance or uncertainty about the basic facts of the situation. Delinquent acts are secret and shaming, and investigators can more easily persuade people to confide their private sex lives than to give a truthful account of their crimes. Parents, education authorities and politicians are all sensitive about the topic, and sometimes give more lip-service than active support to research, especially when research threatens to invade privacy or reveal an unpalatable state of affairs. The officials who deal with apprehended delinquents, the police, the magistrates, and the staffs of penal establishments, have, on the whole, contributed comparatively little to the published research findings. Maybe they don't consider it their job, or maybe they are too preoccupied with routine matters to spare the time for surveys; but efficient commercial organizations would never allow far-reaching executive decisions to be made without collecting all the available information. The Home Office *Criminal Statistics* and *Supplementary Statistics* do, of course, provide, an invaluable guide, but how much more useful they would be if the obsessive head-counting gave way sometimes to an analysis of representative samples of police records. This would give more information on the social backgrounds of offenders, their companions in crime, and the nature and circumstances of their misdeeds than whole text-books of criminology. The enormous numbers of social and psychological examinations carried out by the Prison Department at remand centres and borstal allocation centres could be used much more for producing published findings on the characteristics of offenders.

One difficulty is that the enforced reticence of public servants acts as a brake, and not all that is known is necessarily published. Government agencies do carry out research for their own purposes. A most valuable study of the self-reported delinquencies and social attitudes of a national sample of youths has been carried out by the Central Office of Information. One hopes a published report will be forthcoming.

The phenomena of youthful crime

In spite of the uncertain state of empirical evidence, some attempt has been made in this book to look for general patterns in contemporary English delinquency that might help to elucidate its origins or to decide treatment strategy. To this end, numerous exceptions and anomalous minority groups have been neglected, so any generalizations one makes are sure to arouse controversy and be fraught with difficulties and reservations. Nevertheless, it may be worth while to recapitulate some of the tentative suggestions that have emerged.

Criminal statistics are dominated by their largest category, the offences against property, and generalizations about delinquents as a whole really refer to thieves. Regardless of age, most first offenders are not re-convicted, and the minority of young offenders who are convicted repeatedly nevertheless have a strong tendency to cease being convicted in their early twenties. Hence, as far as records of convictions go, it would appear that delinquent habits are for the most part only very sporadic, and that the great majority of young people grow out of them. The long-term criminal career is a statistical freak in comparison with commonplace delinquency of an occasional and not very serious kind. In spite of the publicity given to atrocious or brutal crimes, the fact is that the great majority of the offences committed by young persons are not very serious, not carefully planned or premeditated, and not part of a professional commitment to crime.

The opinion that most convicted youths are ordinary youngsters who are not going to become recidivists is supported by the results of surveys of self-reported delinquency. The findings suggest that many of those brought before the courts are no different in behaviour or social attitude from their peers, who have committed just as many delinquent acts, but without being caught. With these points in mind, it is not surprising to find that the general run of young offenders brought to court are mentally and physically fit, and come from backgrounds typical of the social class to which they belong. Since so many delinquents are quite ordinary youngsters, it is reasonable to suppose that their behaviour represents the normal response of their age group to everyday circumstances. Hence the plausibility of explanations for the increase in convictions which lay emphasis on the increased exposure of the younger generation to opportunities and temptations. In other words, simple things like the increase in unguarded cars and other property, and increased leisure and freedom, which enable adolescents to wander about and get into mischief, may have more to do with the bulk of the delinquency statistics than maternal deprivation or personal maladjustment or the supposed deterioration in moral standards or family stability.

In any case, no one really knows how much of the increase in convictions, especially for minor offences, is due to the authorities becoming more determined and more effective in their attack on adolescent misbehaviour. The reservoir of unreported offences is always enormous, and the harder the authorities work on it, the more they will dredge up.

It is only when one begins to isolate from the general mass the hard core of highly persistent delinquents with repeated convictions that a group emerges with noticeable social and psychological peculiarities. The characteristic social background of persistent delinquents (low class, low income, educational backwardness, broken home, over-large family, child neglect, poor neighbourhood) has been described *ad nauseam*. Wherever this cluster of social deprivations is prominent, the delinquency rate is very high. This seems to apply just as much today, when the deprivation consists of relative poverty and social ostracism, as it did when poverty meant rags and near-starvation. But social deprivation alone, although it remains the most readily identifiable factor in persistent delinquency, fails to account for the increasing numbers of offenders who come from more affluent homes.

Among those convicted of sexual crimes, or serious crimes of personal violence, there is a smaller proportion of youthful offenders than among persons convicted of larceny or breaking-in. Sexually deviant activities in particular bring adults to court more often than youths. In the criminal histories of persons convicted of crimes of violence or sex, convictions for property offences often occur as well. Nevertheless, many sex offenders are timorous, inhibited neurotic types, quite different from the ordinary boisterous young delinquent. Others suffer from subnormality or social clumsiness, handicaps which frustrate their efforts to obtain permitted sexual outlets. Likewise, among seriously violent offenders, some are much more seriously maladjusted and anti-social than the general run of ordinary offenders. Drug-takers, on the other hand, are not necessarily anti-social at all in other respects. Although addiction may lead weak characters into crimes and other disasters, many young people participate in the craze for trying out prohibited drugs without coming to serious harm.

Delinquency theories

According to one point of view, there is nothing very special to explain. Occasional acts of defiance or rebellion are, and always have been, normal features of the transition from youthful exuberance to manly restraint. The phenomenon has become more noticeable merely because the enormous size, and the complex and impersonal organization, of modern communities make them more vulnerable to youthful disruptions. The more unattended cars are left about, the more plastic telephones are waiting to be prised open, the easier it becomes for youths to travel and congregate at popular weekend resorts, the greater the scope for nuisance. Adults naturally react less tolerantly, and prosecutions spiral upwards.

The behaviour of the hard core of persistent offenders cannot be so easily dismissed. It appears to be both different in origin and more serious in effect. The offenders involved have a high incidence of broken homes, educational failures, and neglected or erratic upbringing. Sociological theories interpret their behaviour as a natural reaction, on the part of the less privileged and the less well endowed, to the frustrations they experience in their unsuccessful attempts to get on and get ahead in the modern rat race. The theories differ in emphasis more than in

fundamentals. The earlier writers, such as Thrasher and Sutherland, emphasized the effect of bad example, and the ease with
which criminal habits could be learned by youngsters in the
slums. Later theorists, like Merton and Cohen, emphasized the
factor of social injustice. Lower-class boys were said to turn sour
and rebellious because they were being made to conform to
middle-class rules, and jump through middle-class hoops, without benefit of middle-class rewards.

Psychologists, and especially psychoanalysts, stress the
characteristics of delinquents as individuals. They suggest that
insufficiency of love or of consistency in infant care is liable to
induce a permanent distortion of personality which paves the
way for delinquency in later years. The sociological and psychological views do not altogether conflict, since most of the features
of upbringing which the analysts find damaging (such as neglect
or rejection of children, erratic training, and separations at
critical phases of development) are just those features which the
sociologists find most prevalent in the socially deprived segments
of the community. But even though the general incidence of
family disturbance reflects social forces, the analysts believe that
it is the level of disturbance in his own family which affects most
the individual youngster. This is particularly obvious among
youths from materially secure homes who have nevertheless
become delinquent.

Modern sociologists take into account these psychological
ideas. L. Yablonsky argues that the kind of gang or sub-culture to
which a youth is drawn depends on his style of upbringing. If he
has been moulded into a disgruntled, suspicious psychopathic
personality, he will find himself at home only among gangs of
similar aggressive-minded misfits. When stable working-class
communities developed an ethos all their own, and poverty was
no disgrace, the effects on developing youth were less damaging
than in social situations in which the lowest social grades are
largely made up of families who have drifted downwards on
account of social incompetence, and whose child-rearing practices
are therefore particularly unsatisfactory.

The classification of offenders into 'types' helps to coordinate
the rival claims of psychological and social determinants. Large
numbers of sporadic offenders are 'normal' persons behaving

no differently from other persons in their social setting. Many persistent delinquents are anti-social characters, persons who have been damaged by social and family adversities. They are too aggressive, suspicious and impulsive to adjust to the ways of normal groups, although some may be 'pseudo-socialized' to the extent of being able to fit in with a gang of similar misfits. The disturbance is a matter of degree, and if very marked tends to be called psychopathic, although this does not mean it is irrevocable. Finally, a small minority of persistent delinquents are maladjusted in a different sense, being inhibited, conflict-ridden types analogous to the classic anxiety neurotic.

Research has gone some way towards confirming, by means of social surveys, testing techniques and clinical assessments, that many persistent delinquents really do display demonstrable psychopathic traits, such as impulsiveness, inability to postpone gratifications, lack of concern for others, and so on. There is also similar evidence for the existence of the sub-group of predominantly neurotic offenders. Some of the research on these lines has been concerned with traits believed to be largely inherited, such as body-build and motor coordination, both of which are demonstrably connected with the likelihood of becoming delinquent. Such research is a far cry from the nineteenth-century preoccupation with inborn moral degeneracy, but nevertheless the findings bring a sharp reminder that some of the individual characteristics which favour delinquent reactions may be due to biological differences as well as upbringing and other environmental influences. Many people, though disposed to accept biological factors as an explanation of the contrasts between male and female criminal propensities, maintain a somewhat illogical resistance to the idea that such factors may have a wider influence. Evidence from electro-encephalographic studies and other sources strongly suggests that subtle forms of brain damage, even though not always manifest in paralysis or other gross physical symptoms, may handicap an individual's chances of social adjustment. If combined with unfavourable social influences, these physical factors may contribute to very serious forms of psychopathy and criminal behaviour.

In short, in explaining persistent delinquency, as with all unusual behaviour patterns, one has to take into account a great

variety of factors: social, individual, biological and environmental. The simple answer is a myth.

Delinquency prevention and treatment

Reliable information about the phenomena of delinquency may
be hard to come by; but facts about remedies and their effectiveness are still more scarce. As Grygier put it:

> The field of penology has been full of good intentions and false
> hopes. We have built penitentiaries and expected people to repent;
> we have assumed that juvenile delinquents need training and will
> receive it, naturally, from 'training schools' . . . Only recently have
> we begun to have second thoughts on these matters and to take first
> steps in checking our preconceived notions in controlled experiments
> . . . [109].

Resistance to systematic experiment and assessment on the
part of sentencers and penal administrators largely accounts for
the sad fact that few data are available on the response of comparable groups of delinquents to different punishments or training methods. Such elementary comparisons as have been made
generally suggest that one kind of disposal is as good, or as bad,
as another.

There are some obvious reasons why present penal methods
may not be very effective. The bold, pioneer treatment endeavours of men like A. Aichhorn, who appeared to enjoy some
measure of success, are infernally difficult to put over in government institutions, where treatment needs must be watered down
to meet the exigencies of economy, uniformity, public opinion,
and the attitudes of custodial staff. Even in the most progressive
of open borstals, where a great deal of time and effort is spent
talking with boys and looking into family problems, an inmate
may find himself 'sentenced' to an extra month for slipping out
an extra letter to his mother beyond the stipulated ration. While
group discussions and a therapeutic community atmosphere have
seemed effective in intensive, psychiatrically directed projects
like that of Dr Miller, their worth depends upon great persever-
ance in establishing and maintaining close relationships with
difficult characters. The task of alleviating serious social handicaps and character defects calls for much more sophisticated

techniques of educational and psychological training than are generally available in most penal establishments. Institutions are too often run to suit the least disturbed, who are capable of responding favourably to ordinary methods, whereas of course it is the worst cases who should get the best attention.

At present, one of the most obvious shortcomings of the institutional treatment of persistent offenders, especially where it concerns the rehabilitation of the more severely maladjusted, is the necessity for transfer of care at the moment of discharge, when the offender stands most in need of the help and support of the caseworker who knows him. Another difficulty is the large number of employment prospects automatically closed to young men who have been in borstals. The armed services, who used to take them, no longer do so, and many other official bodies have similar policies. This kind of discrimination means that society as a whole has little faith in the reformative effect of penal treatment, and little sense of obligation to try to make a place for anyone marked out as an official delinquent. For the small minority whose personality defects are too severe to respond to any such methods, or who have medical or psychiatric disorders in addition, professional medical care in specialist hospital units is badly needed, and the health service should provide the facilities. At present, the courts all too often commit youths to borstals, knowing them to be too grossly disturbed to benefit from a régime designed for normal boys, simply because no suitable place can be found for them in hospitals. In spite of the provisions for compulsory hospital treatment for psychopaths under the Mental Health Act, 1959, doctors have a regrettable propensity to reject offenders of all ages if their defects are too troublesome or apparently unchangeable, and to cast them out of medical care into penal custody, as once lepers were cast untreated into colonies. Only in this instance the incurables don't languish and die; after their 'time' is done they return as harmful as ever.

Such contradictions highlight the ambivalence of purpose of present-day penal institutions, which in turn reflect the conflict of ideas in society as a whole. Another difficulty which besets our state institutions is the wide range of problems and types of person that they have to deal with. American research suggests

that the kind of régime best suited to one type of personality, or
one level of maturity, may be positively harmful to another. The
present methods of sentencing offenders make no allowance for
this sort of thing. If the present proposals for setting up welfare
boards, in the shape of family tribunals, for dealing with juvenile
delinquents leads to greater discrimination in disposal, and a
willingness to experiment and to check results, it would indeed
be a great advance.

In discussing treatment or training in custody, which is
regrettably necessary for some persistent delinquents, one must
remember that this applies to a minority only, and is not the
answer to the great bulk of sporadic offenders who appear once
or twice at court and never again. The general high level of
delinquency convictions is largely kept up by provocations,
opportunities and temptations acting upon the youthful population as a whole. Hence, preventive action, in the form of protective and detective devices to reduce opportunities, and social
welfare to reduce temptations, are much more likely to lower the
general delinquency rate than a proliferation of custodial
establishments. Furthermore, attention to the rudiments of child
care and mental health might forestall the development of some
of those warped and aggressive characters from whom persistent
delinquents are so often recruited.

For the majority of first offenders, sharp reminders that they
have transgressed the limits of tolerable conduct are often all that
is needed, and measures involving removal from a normal
environment and segregation among established social deviants
should be avoided as far as possible. Occasionally, the fact of
coming to court will bring to light circumstances requiring the
attention of the welfare services, and the opportunity to help
should not be missed. One of the advantages of having a probation officer concerned in such cases is that he should know the
right source of help, whether it be legal advice, psychiatry,
National Assistance or Alcoholics Anonymous. Unfortunately,
in practice the services needed are not always readily available or
easy to call upon where the problem concerns an offender.

Nobody expects any one explanation or treatment method to
solve all health problems. Advocates of a single cure-all for
delinquency, whether it be harsher punishment or more child

guidance, are equally unrealistic. An unremitting attack on a wide front, using different methods for different problems, holds out the best hope for progress. Above all, social and penal measures, which seek to change behaviour, should be securely based upon rational inquiry into the causal factors involved, and should include objective assessment of the results of different courses of action.

List of References

Unless otherwise stated, books are published in London.

1 cited on p. 284   Adams, S. (1962). 'The P.I.C.O. Project', in Johnston, N. B., *et al.*, *The Sociology of Crime and Delinquency*, pp. 213–24. New York, J. Wiley.

2 267   Aichhorn, A. (1925). *Wayward Youth.* (1st English edition Imago, 1951.)

3 268   Aichhorn, A. (1925). op. cit., p. 149.

4 158   Ainsworth, M. D. Salter (1965). 'Further research into the adverse effects of maternal deprivation', in Bowlby, J., *Child Care and the Growth of Love*, 1965 edition. Penguin Books.

5 59   Akers, R. L. (1964). 'Socio-economic status and delinquent behaviour'. *Journal of Research in Crime and Delinquency*, *1*, 38–46.

6 152   Alexander, F., and Staub, H. (1956). *The Criminal, the Judge and the Public : A Psychological Analysis.* Glencoe, Ill., Free Press.

7 120   Alström, C. H. (1950). 'A study of epilepsy in its clinical, social and genetic aspects'. *Acta Psychiatrica*, Suppl. 63. Copenhagen.

8 239   Andenaes, J. (1965). 'Punishment and the problem of general prevention'. *Fifth International Congress of Criminology.* Montreal.

9 112   Anderson, J. W. (1958). 'Recidivism, intelligence and social class'. *British Journal of Delinquency*, *8*, 294–7.

10 138   Anthony, H. Sylvia (1959). 'Association between psychomotor behaviour and delinquency'. *Nature, 183*, 343–4.

11 170   Argyle, M. (1961). 'A new approach to the classification of delinquents with implications for treatment'. *California Board of Corrections*, Monograph No. 2, 15–26.

12 62   Bagot, J. H. (1941). *Juvenile Delinquency.* Jonathan Cape.

13 20, 23   Banks, Charlotte (1962). 'Violence'. *The Howard Journal*, 9, 1–13.

14 278   Banks, Charlotte (1964). 'Reconviction of young offenders'. *Current Legal Problems*, Vol. 17. Stevens & Sons.

15 70, 72, 215   Banks, Charlotte (1965). 'Boys in detention centres', in Banks, C., and Broadhurst, P. L. (eds.), *Studies in Psychology*. London University Press.

16 195   Bender, L. (1965). 'Offender and offended children', in Slovenko, R. (ed.), *Sexual Behaviour and the Law*. Springfield, Ill., C. Thomas.

17 278   Benson, G. (1959). 'Prediction methods and young prisoners'. *British Journal of Delinquency*, 9, 192–9.

18 202   Berkowitz, L. (1962). *Aggression*. New York, McGraw-Hill.

19 187   Bewley, T. (1965). 'Heroin addiction in the United Kingdom (1954–1964)'. *British Medical Journal*, 2, 1284–6.

20 86   Bloch, H., and Niederhoffer, A. (1958). *The Gang : A Study in Adolescent Behaviour*. New York, Philosophical Library.

21 92   Boruda, D. J. (1961). 'Prediction and selection of delinquents', in *Juvenile Delinquency Facts and Facets*, No. 17. U.S. Children's Bureau.

22 27   Bovet, L. (1951). *Psychiatric Aspects of Juvenile Delinquency*. W.H.O. Monograph No. 1.

23 157   Bowlby, J. (1946). *Forty-four Juvenile Thieves*. Baillière, Tindall & Cox.

24 157   Bowlby, J. (1953 etc.). *Child Care and the Growth of Love*. Penguin Books.

25 277   Burchard, J., and Tyler, V. (1965). 'The modification of delinquent behaviour through operant conditioning'. *Behaviour Research and Therapy*, 2, 245–50.

26 62, 72, 110, 118   Burt, C. (1925). *The Young Delinquent* (4th edition 1944). London University Press.

27 208, 264   Carpenter, Mary (1851). *Reformatory Schools for the Children of the Perishing and Dangerous Classes and for Juvenile Offenders*.

28 70 Carr-Saunders, A. M., *et al.* (1942). *Young Offenders*. Cambridge University Press.

29 190 Casriel, D. (1963). *So Fair a House: The Story of Synanon*. New York, Prentice-Hall.

30 112 Castell, J. H. F., and Mittler, P. J. (1965). 'Intelligence of patients in sub-normality hospitals'. *British Journal of Psychiatry*, *3*, 219–25.

31 217 Cavenagh, W. E., and Sparks, R. F. (1965). 'Out of Court?'. *New Society*, 15 July.

32 117 Charles, D. C. (1953). 'Ability and accomplishment of persons earlier judged mentally deficient'. *Genetic Psychological Monographs*, *47*, 3–71.

33 187 Chein, I., *et al.* (1964). *Narcotics, Delinquency and Social Policy*. Tavistock Publications.

34 132 Chess, S., *et al.* (1960). 'Implications of a longitudinal study of child development'. *American Journal of Psychiatry*, *117*, 434–41.

35 40 Christie, Nils, *et al.* (1965). 'A study of self-reported crime'. *Scandinavian Studies in Criminology*, *1*, 86–116.

36 27 Christie, Nils (1960). *Unge Norske Lovertredere*. Oslo.

37 266 Clark, D. H. (1965). 'The Therapeutic Community – concept, practice and future'. *British Journal of Psychiatry*, *111*, 947–54.

38 114 Clarke, A. D. B., and Clarke, A. M. (1954). 'Cognitive changes in the feeble-minded'. *British Journal of Psychology*, *45*, 173–9.

39 18 Clifford, W. (1965). 'Problems in criminological research in Africa south of the Sahara'. *International Review of Criminal Policy*, *23*, 11–17.

40 93 Cloward, R. A., and Ohlin, L. E. (1961). *Delinquency and Opportunity: A Theory of Delinquent Gangs*. Glencoe, Ill., Free Press.

41 89 Cohen, A. K. (1955). *Delinquent Boys: The Culture of the Gang*. Glencoe, Ill., Free Press.

42 188 Connell, P. H. (1965). 'The assessment and treatment of adolescent drug takers'. *Proceedings of the Leeds Symposium on Behavioural Disorders*. Dagenham, May & Baker.

43 221 Cooper, Beryl, and Nicholas, G. (1963). *Crime in the Sixties*, p. 29. Bow Group.

44 115 Craft, M. J. (1959). 'Personality disorder and dullness'. *Lancet*, 25 April, 856–8.

45 255 Craig, Maude M., and Furst, P. W. (1965). 'What happens after treatment'. *Social Service Review*, *39*, 165–71.

46 207 Cristoph, J. B. (1962). *Capital Punishment and British Politics*. Allen & Unwin.

47 121 Douglas, J. W. B. (1960). '"Premature" children at primary schools'. *British Medical Journal*, *1*, 1008–13.

48 244 Douglas, J. W. B. (1964). *The Home and the School*. MacGibbon & Kee.

49 161 Douglas, J. W. B., and Blomfield, J. M. (1958). *Children Under Five: the Results of a National Survey*. Allen & Unwin.

50 120 Drillien, C. M. (1964). *The Growth and Development of the Prematurely Born Infant*. E. & S. Livingstone.

51 208 Du Cane, E. F. (1885). *The Punishment and Prevention of Crime*, p. 200.

52 223 Dunlop, A. B., and McCabe, S. (1965). *Young Men in Detention Centres*. Routledge.

53 115 East, W. Norwood, *et al.* (1942). *The Adolescent Criminal*. Churchill.

54 63 East, W. Norwood, *et al.* (1942). op. cit., Tables 63 and 64.

55 123 Ehrlich, S. K., and Keogh, R. P. (1956). 'The psychopath in a mental institution'. *Archives of Neurological Psychiatry*, *76*, 286–95.

56 58, 110, 118 Eilenberg, M. D. (1961). 'Remand home boys: 1930–1955'. *British Journal of Criminology*, *2*, 111.

57 122 Ellingson, R. J. (1954). 'The incidence of EEG abnormality among patients with mental disorders of apparently non-organic origin: a critical review'. *American Journal of Psychiatry*, *111*, 263–75.

58 40 Elmhorn, K. (1965). 'Study in self-reported delinquency among school-children in Stockholm'. *Scandinavian Studies in Criminology*, *1*, 117–46.

59 280   Empey, L. T., *et al.* (1961). 'The Provo Experiment in delinquency rehabilitation'. *American Sociological Review*, *26*, 679–96.

60 280   Empey, L. T., *et al.* (1964). 'The Provo Experiment'. *California Board of Corrections*, Monograph No. 4.

61 198   Epps, Phyllis (1951). '300 female delinquents in borstal'. *British Journal of Delinquency*, *1*, 187–97.

62 41   Erickson, M. L., and Empey, L. T. (1963). 'Court records, undetected delinquency and decision making'. *Journal of Criminal Law, Criminology and Police Science*, *54*, 456–69.

63 147, 171   Eron, L. D., *et al.* (1963). 'Social class, parental punishment for aggression and child aggression'. *Child Development*, *34*, 849–67.

64 137, 144   Eysenck, H. J. (1964). *Crime and Personality*. Routledge.

65 141   Eysenck, H. J. (1964). op. cit., p. 117.

66 146   Eysenck, H. J. (1964). op. cit., p. 160.

67 143   Eysenck, H. J. (1959). 'The inheritance and nature of extraversion', in Halmos, P., and Iliffe, A. H. (eds.), *Readings in General Psychology*. Routledge.

68 143   Eysenck, H. J., *et al.* (1960). *Behaviour Therapy and the Neuroses*. Oxford, Pergamon.

69 58, 118   Ferguson, T. (1952). *The Young Delinquent in his Social Setting*. Oxford University Press.

70 72   Ferguson, T. (1952). op. cit., p. 22.

71 73   Ferguson, T. (1952). op. cit., p. 21.

72 26   Ferguson, T., and Cunnison, J. (1956). *In Their Early Twenties: A Study of Glasgow Youth*, Table 24, p. 76. Oxford University Press.

73 107   Ferrero, G. L. (1911). *Criminal Man: According to the Classification of Cesare Lombroso.*

74 94   Fletcher, C. (1964). 'Beat and gangs on Merseyside'. *New Society*, 20 February.

75 36   Fletcher, R. (1962). *The Family and Marriage in Britain*. Penguin Books.

76 239   Fordham, Peta (1965). *The Robbers' Tale*. Hodder & Stoughton.

77   207, 225   Fox, L. W. (1952). *The English Prison and Borstal System*. Routledge.

78   277   Freund, K. (1960). 'Some problems in the treatment of homosexuality', in Eysenck, H. J. (ed.), *Behaviour Therapy and the Neuroses*. Oxford, Pergamon.

79   151   Friedlander, Kate (1947). *Psycho-analytic Approach to Juvenile Delinquency*. Kegan Paul.

80   97   Fyvel, T. R. (1961). *The Insecure Offenders*. Chatto & Windus; Penguin Books (1963, revised).

81   197, 198   Gibbens, T. C. N. (1958). 'Psychiatry in remand homes for wayward girls'. *Actes du cinquième congrès international de défense sociale*, pp. 579–88. Stockholm.

82   58, 115, 119, 138,   Gibbens, T. C. N. (1963). *Psychiatric Studies
     169   of Borstal Lads*. Maudsley Monographs No. 11. Oxford University Press.

83   56   Gibbens, T. C. N. (1963). op. cit., p. 62.
84   70, 72   Gibbens, T. C. N. (1963). op. cit., p. 69.
85   203   Gibbens, T. C. N. (1963). op. cit., p. 17.
86   123   Gibbens, T. C. N., *et al.* (1959). 'A follow-up study of criminal psychopaths'. *Journal of Mental Science*, *105*, 108–15.

87   195   Gibbens, T. C. N., and Prince, Joyce E. (1963). *Child Victims of Sex Offences*. I.S.T.D.

88   26, 228   Gibbens, T. C. N., and Prince, Joyce E. (1965). 'The results of borstal training', in Halmos, P. (ed.), *Sociological Review Monograph*, No. 9. Keele.

89   122   Gibbs, F. A., and Bagchi, B. K. (1945). 'Electroencephalographic study of criminals'. *American Journal of Psychiatry*, *102*, 294–8.

90   138   Gibson, H. B. (1964). 'The Spiral Maze: a psychomotor test with implications for the study of delinquency'. *British Journal of Psychology*, *54*, 219–25.

91   11   Giles, F. T. (1959). *The Child and the Law*. Penguin Books.

92   70, 229   Gittins, J. (1952). *Approved School Boys*. H.M.S.O.

93	63	Glaser, D., and Rice, K. (1959). 'Crime, age, and employment'. *American Sociological Review*, *24*, 679–86.
94	166	Glueck, Eleanor T. (1964). 'Identification of potential delinquents at 2–3 years of age'. *International Journal of Social Psychiatry*, *12*, 5–16.
95	72, 118, 165	Glueck, S., and Glueck, E. T. (1950). *Unravelling Juvenile Delinquency*. New York, The Commonwealth Fund.
96	28	Glueck, S., and Glueck, E. T. (1940). *Juvenile Delinquents Grown Up*. New York, The Commonwealth Fund.
97	126	Glueck, S., and Glueck, E. T. (1956). *Physique and Delinquency*. New York, Harper.
98	165	Glueck, S., and Glueck, E. T. (1964). *Ventures in Criminology*. Tavistock Publications.
99	266	Goffman, E. (1961). *Asylums*. New York, Doubleday Anchor.
100	57	Gold, M. (1963). *Status Forces in Delinquent Boys*. Ann Arbor, Michigan University Press.
101	59	Gold, M. (1963). op. cit., p. 173.
102	158	Goldfarb, W. (1943). 'Infant rearing and problem behaviour'. *American Journal of Orthopsychiatry*, *13*, 249–65.
103	244	Gordon, E. W. (1965). 'A review of programs of compensatory education'. *American Journal of Orthopsychiatry*, *35*, 640–51.
104	108	Goring, C. (1913). *The English Convict*. H.M.S.O.
105	284	Gottfredson, D. M., and Kelley, B. B. (1963). 'Interpersonal maturity measurement by the California Psychological Inventory'. *Institute for the Study of Crime and Delinquency*, *Report 1*. California.
106	283	Grant, J. D., and Grant, M. Q. (1959). 'A group dynamics approach to the treatment of nonconformists in the navy'. *Annals of the American Academy of Political and Social Science*, *322*, 126–35.
107	38	Grimble, A. (1965). 'Morality and venereal disease'. *Excerpta Criminologica*, *5*, 383–406.

108 65 Grunhut, M. (1956). *Juvenile Offenders Before the Courts*. Oxford, Clarendon Press.

109 296 Grygier, T. (1965). In *Criminology in Transition*. Tavistock Publications.

110 277 Gwynne Jones, H. (1965). 'Behaviour and aversion therapy in the treatment of delinquency'. *British Journal of Criminology*, 5, 355–65.

111 204 Halloran, J. D. (1964). *The Effects of Mass Communication*. Leicester, University Press.

112 29 Hammond, W. H., and Chayen, E. (1963). *Persistent Criminals*, p. 26. H.M.S.O.

113 159 Harlow, H. F. (1961). 'The development of affectional pattern of infant monkeys', in Foss, B. (ed.), *Determinants of Infant Behaviour*. Methuen.

114 159 Harlow, H. F., and Harlow, M. (1962). 'Social deprivation in monkeys'. *Scientific American*, 207, 136–46.

115 43 Hartshorne, H., and May, M. A. (1928). *Studies in Deceit*. New York, Macmillan.

116 46 Hartshorne, H., and May, M. A. (1932). *Studies in the Organization of Character*. New York, Macmillan.

117 145, 170 Hathaway, S. R., and Monachesi, E. D. (1956). 'The M.M.P.I. in the study of juvenile delinquents', in Rose, A. M., *Mental Health and Mental Disorder*. Routledge.

118 169 Hathaway, S. R., and Monachesi, E. D. (1953). *Analysing and Predicting Juvenile Delinquency with the M.M.P.I.* Minneapolis, Minnesota, University Press.

119 53 Havard, J. D. J. (1960). *The Detection of Secret Homicide*, pp. 51–60. Macmillan.

120 173 Hewitt, L. E., and Jenkins, R. L. (1946). *Fundamental Patterns of Maladjustment*. Michigan, State of Illinois, D. H. Green.

121 122 Hill, D., and Pond, D. A. (1952). 'Reflections on 100 capital cases submitted to electroencephalography'. *Journal of Mental Science*, 98, 23–43.

122 68 Hirsch, C. A. (1953). 'La criminalité des

Nord-Africains en France'. *Revue internationale de criminologie*, 298–302.

123	254	Hodges, E. F., and Tait, C. D. (1965). 'A follow up study of potential delinquents'. *American Journal of Psychiatry*, *120*, 449–53.
124	221	Home Office (1847). *Reports of Committees*, Vol. VII (3), pp. 297, 79.
125	222	Home Office (1959). *Penal Practice in a Changing Society*, Cmnd 645. H.M.S.O.
126	211	Home Office (1960). *Prisons and Borstals: Statement of Policy and Practice* (4th edition), p. 57. H.M.S.O.
127	226, 227	Home Office (1964). *Prisons and Borstals 1963*, Cmnd 2381, pp. 26, 29, 33. H.M.S.O.
128	214	Home Office (1966). *Criminal Statistics, England and Wales, 1965*, Cmnd 3037, pp. xxiii, xxvi. H.M.S.O.
129	192	Home Office (1966). *Criminal Statistics, England and Wales, 1965*, Cmnd 3037, paragraph 14, p. xiii; Table IV (a), p. 188. H.M.S.O.
130	223	Home Office (1965). *Prisons and Borstals, 1963, Statistical Tables*, Cmnd 2630, Tables D.9 and D.15. H.M.S.O.
131	217	Home Office (1965). *The Child, the Family and the Young Offender*, Cmnd 2742. H.M.S.O.
132	24, 211, 278	Home Office (1964). *The Sentence of the Court*. H.M.S.O.
133	280	Hood, R. (1962). *Sentencing in Magistrates' Courts*. Stevens & Sons.
134	227	Hood, R. (1965). *Borstal Reassessed*. Heinemann.
135	108	Hooton, E. A. (1939). *The American Criminal: An Anthropological Study.* Cambridge, Mass., Harvard University Press.
136	61	House of Commons (1817). *Second Report of the House of Commons Committee on the State of the Police in the Metropolis.*
137	220	House of Lords (1863). *Report of the Select Committee of the House of Lords on Prison Discipline.*

138 52   Hurwitz, S. (1952). _Criminology_, p. 393. Copenhagen and London, Allen & Unwin.

139 67   Jones, Howard (1956). _Crime and the Penal System_. University Tutorial Press.

140 66   Jones, Howard (1958). 'Approaches to an ecological study'. _British Journal of Delinquency_, _8_, 277–93.

141 265   Jones, Howard (1960). _Reluctant Rebels_. Tavistock Publications.

142 230   Jones, Howard (1965). 'The approved school: a theoretical model', in Halmos, P. (ed.), _Sociological Review Monographs_, No. 9. Keele.

143 143   Jung, C. G. (1923). _Psychological Types_.

144 54   Jungk, R. (1961). _Children of the Ashes_ (trans.). Heinemann; Penguin Books (1963).

145 130   Kallman, F. J. (1938). _The Genetics of Schizophrenia_. New York, Augustin.

146 190   Kessel, N., and Walton, H. (1965). _Alcoholism_. Penguin Books.

147 52   Kinberg, O. (1935). _Basic Problems of Criminology_, pp. 130–36. Copenhagen, Levin and Munksgaard.

148 193   Kinsey, A. C., _et al._ (1948). _Sexual Behavior in the Human Male_. Philadelphia, Saunders.

149 222   Klare, H. J. (1962). _Anatomy of Prison_. Penguin Books.

150 180   Kohlberg, L. (1964). 'The development of moral character', in Hoffman, M. L., _et al._ (eds.), _Child Development_, Vol. 1. New York, Russell Sage Foundation.

151 169   Kvaraceus, W. C. (1961). 'Forecasting delinquency'. _Exceptional Children_, _27_, 429–35.

152 160   Lewis, Hilda (1954). _Deprived Children_. Oxford University Press.

153 119   Lewison, E. (1965). 'An experiment in facial reconstructive surgery in a prison population'. _Canadian Medical Association Journal_, _92_, 251–4.

154 160   Little, A. (1965). 'Parental deprivation, separation and crime'. _British Journal of Criminology_, _5_, 419–30.

155 144   Little, A. (1963). 'Professor Eysenck's theory of crime: an empirical test on adolescent

offenders'. *British Journal of Criminology*, 4, 152–63.

156 19 Little, A. (1965). 'The increase in crime 1952–1962: an empirical analysis on adolescent offenders'. *British Journal of Criminology*, 5, 77–82.

157 56 Little, W. R., and Ntsekhe, V. R. (1959). 'Social class background of young offenders from London'. *British Journal of Delinquency*, 10, 130–35.

158 147, 171 Loban, W. (1953). 'A study of social sensitivity among adolescents'. *Journal of Educational Psychology*, 44, 102–12.

159 122 Loomis, S. Dale (1965). 'EEG abnormalities as a correlate of behaviour in adolescent male delinquents'. *American Journal of Psychiatry*, 121, 1003–6.

160 18 Lunden, W. A. (1961). *Statistics on Delinquency*. Iowa, State University Press.

161 211 McClintock, F. H. (1961). *Attendance Centres*. Macmillan.

162 74, 201 McClintock, F. H. (1963). *Crimes of Violence*. Macmillan.

163 23 McClintock, F. H. (1963). op. cit., Appendix XI.

164 27, 71, 110, 118, 161, 253 McCord, W., and McCord, Joan (1959). *Origins of Crime*. New York, Columbia University Press.

165 18 McQueen, A. J. (1960). 'A comparative perspective on juvenile delinquency', in *Delinquency, Patterns, Causes, Cures*. Ann Arbor, University of Michigan.

166 67 Mannheim, H. (1965). *Comparative Criminology*. Routledge.

167 57 Mannheim, H., Spencer, J., and Lynch, G. (1957). 'Magisterial policy in the London juvenile courts'. *British Journal of Delinquency*, 8, 13–33.

168 25, 164 Mannheim, H., and Wilkins, L. T. (1955). *Prediction Methods in Relation to Borstal Training*. H.M.S.O.

169 281 Mannheim, H., and Wilkins, L. T. (1955). op. cit., Table 54.

170 112   Marcus, B. (1956). 'Intelligence, criminality and the expectation of recidivism'. *British Journal of Delinquency*, 6, 147–51.

171 202   Martin, J. M. (1961). *Juvenile Vandalism.* Springfield, Ill., C. Thomas.

172 95   Matza, D. (1964). *Delinquency and Drift.* New York, J. Wiley.

173 39   Mays, J. B. (1954). *Growing Up in the City*, p. 25. Liverpool, University Press.

174 37   Mays, J. B. (1963). *Crime and the Social Structure.* Faber.

175 213   Mays, J. B. (1965). 'The Liverpool Police Juvenile Liaison Officer Scheme', in Halmos, P. (ed.), *Sociological Review Monographs*, No. 9, Keele.

176 88   Merton, R. K. (1957). *Social Theory and Social Structure.* Glencoe, Ill., Free Press.

177 255   Meyer, H. J., Bargatta, E. F., and Jones, W. C. (1965). *Girls at Vocational High.* New York, Russell Sage Foundation.

178 277   Middleton, P. M. (1964). 'Motor deprivation or paralysed awareness in the treatment of delinquency'. Paper read at the International Congress of Social Psychiatry, London.

179 54   Milgram, S. (1965). 'Some conditions of obedience and disobedience to authority'. *Human Relations*, 18, 57–76.

180 267   Miller, D. (1964). *Growth to Freedom.* Tavistock Publications.

181 91   Miller, W. B. (1958). 'Lower class culture as a generating milieu of gang delinquency'. *Journal of Social Issues*, 14, 5–19.

182 188   Ministry of Health (1965). *Drug Addiction: The Second Report of the Interdepartmental Committee.* H.M.S.O.

183 195   Mohr, J. W., Turner, R. E., and Jerry, M. B. (1964). *Pedophilia and Exhibitionism.* Toronto, University Press.

184 71   Monahan, T. P. (1957). 'Family status and the delinquent child: a re-appraisal and some new findings'. *Social Forces*, 35, 250–59.

185 203   Morris, H. H., *et al.* (1956). 'Aggressive

behaviour disorders of childhood'. *American Journal of Psychiatry, 112,* 991–7.

186 197 Morris, Ruth R. (1964). 'Female delinquency and relational problems'. *Social Forces, 43,* 82–9.

187 66 Morris, T. P. (1957). *The Criminal Area.* Routledge.

188 56 Morris, T. P. (1957). op. cit., p. 166.

189 222 Morris, T. P., and Morris, Pauline (1963). *Pentonville.* Routledge.

190 226 Morrison, R. L. (1957). 'Borstal allocation'. *British Journal of Delinquency, 8,* 95–105.

191 249 Morse, Mary (1965). *The Unattached.* Penguin Books.

192 38 Morton, R. S. (1966). *Venereal Diseases.* Penguin Books.

193 67, 69 Moses, Earl R. (1947). 'Differentials in crime rates between negroes and whites'. *American Sociological Review, 12,* 411–20.

194 167 Mulligan, D. G., Douglas, J. W. B., Hammond, W. A., and Tizard, J. (1963). 'Delinquency'. *Proceedings of the Royal Society of Medicine, 56,* 1083–4.

195 40 Murphy, F. J., *et al.* (1946). 'The incidence of hidden delinquency'. *American Journal of Orthopsychiatry, 16,* 686–96.

196 111 Naar, R. (1965). 'A note on the intelligence of delinquents'. *British Journal of Criminology, 5,* 82–5.

197 160 Naess, S. (1959). 'Mother–child separation and delinquency'. *British Journal of Delinquency, 10,* 22–35.

198 119 Ogden, D. A. (1959). 'Use of surgical rehabilitation in young delinquents'. *British Medical Journal, 2,* 432–4.

199 198 O'Kelly, Elizabeth (1955). 'Delinquent girls and their parents'. *British Journal of Educational Psychology, 28,* 59–66.

200 126 Parnell, R. W. (1958). *Behaviour and Physique,* p. 61. Arnold.

201 180, 283 Peck, P. F., and Havinghurst, R. J. (1960). *The Psychology of Character Development.* New York, J. Wiley.

202 115   Penrose, L. S. (1964). *The Biology of Mental Defect* (3rd edition), p. 44. Sidgwick & Jackson.

203 172   Peterson, D. R., and Quay, H. C. (1961). 'Personality factors related to juvenile delinquency'. *Child Development, 32,* 355–72.

204 224   Pharoah, N. (1963). 'The long blunt shock'. *New Society,* 26 September.

205 179, 283   Piaget, J. (1932). *The Moral Judgment of the Child* (trans. M. Gabain). Routledge.

206 52   Pinatel, Jean (1963). *Criminologie,* p. 108. Paris, Dalloz.

207 197   Pollak, O. L. (1950). *The Criminality of Women.* Philadelphia, Pennsylvania State University Press.

208 267   Polsky, H. W. (1962). *Cottage Six: The Social System of Delinquent Boys in Residential Treatment.* New York, Russell Sage Foundation.

209 121   Pond, D. A. (1961). 'Psychiatric aspects of epileptic and brain-damaged children'. *British Medical Journal, 2,* 1377–88, 1454–9.

210 40   Porterfield, A. L. (1946). *Youth in Trouble.* Fort Worth, Texas.

211 111   Prentice, N. M., and Kelly, F. J. (1963). 'Intelligence and delinquency: a reconsideration'. *Journal of Social Psychology, 60,* 327–37.

212 19   Prys Williams, G. (1962). *Patterns of Teenage Delinquency,* p. 19. Christian Economic and Social Research Foundation.

213 173   Quay, H. C. (1964). 'Personality dimensions in delinquent males as inferred from the factor analysis of behaviour ratings'. *Journal of Research in Crime and Delinquency, 1,* 33–7.

214 207   Radzinowicz, L. (1948). *A History of the English Criminal Law,* Vol. 1, pp. 14, 523. Stevens & Sons.

215 19   Radzinowicz, L. (1966). *Ideology and Crime.* Heinemann.

216 78   Radzinowicz, L. (1966). op. cit., p. 99.

217 194   Radzinowicz, L., ed. (1957). *Sexual Offences.* Macmillan.

218 169 Reiss, A. J. (1951). 'Delinquency as the failure of personal and social controls'. *American Sociological Review, 15,* 196–207.

219 175 Reiss, A. J. (1952). 'Social correlates of psychological types of delinquency'. *American Sociological Review, 17,* 710–18.

220 34 *Report of the Commissioner of Police of the Metropolis for the year 1932,* Cmnd 4294, p. 16.

221 33 *Report of the Committee of the Society for the Improvement of Prison Discipline and for the Improvement of Offenders* (1818), pp. 11, 13.

222 216 Romander, H. (1965). *The Child Welfare Act of Sweden.* Stockholm, Ministry of Justice.

223 56, 70, 228 Rose, A. G. (1954). *Five Hundred Borstal Boys.* Oxford, Blackwell.

224 207 Rose, (A.) G. (1961). *The Struggle for Penal Reform.* Stevens & Sons.

225 116 Rudolf, G. de M. (1961). 'Crime amongst the unsupervised mentally sub-normal'. *Medical Press, 245,* 466–72.

226 69 Savitz, L. (1962). 'Delinquency and migration', in Wolfgang, M. E., *et al.* (eds.), *The Sociology of Crime and Delinquency.* New York, J. Wiley.

227 262 Schmideberg, Melita (1960). 'Making the patient aware'. *Crime and Delinquency, 6,* 255–61.

228 38, 192 Schofield, M. (1965). *The Sexual Behaviour of Young People,* pp. 88–9. Longmans.

229 195 Schofield, M. (1965). *Sociological Aspects of Homosexuality,* p. 154. Longmans.

230 170 Schuessler, K. F., *et al.* (1950). 'Personality characteristics of criminals'. *American Journal of Sociology, 55,* 476–84.

231 247 Schwitzgebel, R. (1964). *Streetcorner Research.* Cambridge, Mass., Harvard University Press.

232 94 Scott, P. D. (1956). 'Gangs and delinquent groups in London'. *British Journal of Delinquency, 7,* 4–26.

318 *The Young Offender*

233 215 Scott, P. D. (1959). 'Juvenile courts: the juvenile's point of view'. *British Journal of Delinquency*, 9, 200–209.

234 20, 26, 36, 230 Scott, P. D. (1964). 'Approved school success rates'. *British Journal of Criminology*, 4, 525–56.

235 188 Scott, P. D., and Willcox, D. R. C. (1965). 'Delinquency and amphetamines'. *British Journal of Psychiatry*, 111, 865–75.

236 171 Sears, R. R., MacCoby, E. E., and Levin, H. (1957). *Patterns of Child Rearing*. New York, Row, Peterson & Co.

237 35 Sellin, Thorsten, and Wolfgang, Marvin E. (1964). *The Measurement of Delinquency*. New York, J. Wiley.

238 65 Shaw, R. Clifford, and McKay, Henry D. (1942). *Juvenile Delinquency and Urban Areas*. Chicago, University Press.

239 245 Sheldon, E. B., and Glazier, R. A. (1965). *Pupils and Schools in New York City*. New York, Russell Sage Foundation.

240 124 Sheldon, W. H., *et al.* (1949). *Varieties of Delinquent Youth*. New York, Harper.

241 126 Sheldon, W. H., *et al.* (1949). op. cit., p. 836.

242 131 Shields, J. (1962). *Monozygotic Twins*. Oxford University Press.

243 265 Shields, R. W. (1962). *A Cure of Delinquents*. Heinemann.

244 41, 59 Short, J. F., and Nye, F. I. (1958). 'Extent of unrecorded juvenile delinquency'. *Journal of Criminal Law, Criminology and Police Science*, 49, 296–302.

245 170 Silver, A. W. (1963). 'TAT and M.M.P.I. psychopath deviant scale differences between delinquent and non-delinquent adolescents'. *Journal of Consulting Psychology*, 27, 370.

246 185 Sington, D., ed. (1965). *Psycho-social Aspects of Drug-Taking* (Proceedings of Conference at University College, London), p. 40. Oxford, Pergamon.

247 188 Sington, D., ed. (1965). op. cit., p. 39.

248 131 Slater, E. T. O. (1953). *Psychotic and Neurotic Illnesses in Twins*. H.M.S.O.

249 75   Sprott, W. J. H. (1954). *The Social Back-ground of Delinquency*. Nottingham, University Press.

250 113   Stein, Z., and Susser, M. (1960). 'Families of dull children'. *Journal of Mental Science*, *106*, 1296–319.

251 73   Sterne, R. S. (1964). *Delinquent Conduct and Broken Homes*. New Haven, Conn., College and University Press.

252 119   Stott, D. H. (1962). 'Evidence for a congenital factor in maladjustment and delinquency'. *American Journal of Psychiatry*, *118*, 781–94.

253 168   Stott, D. H. (1963). *The Social Adjustment of Children*. London University Press.

254 168   Stott, D. H. (1964). 'Sociological and psychological explanations of delinquency'. *International Journal of Social Psychiatry* (Congress edition, No. 4), 35–43.

255 131   Stumpfl, F. (1936). *Die Ursprünge des Verbrechens dargestellt am Lebenslauf von Zwillingen*. Leipzig.

256 194   Sturup, G. K. (1960). 'Sex offenses: the Scandinavian experience'. *Law and Contemporary Problems*, *25*, 361–75.

257 68   Sutherland, Edwin H., and Cressey, Donald R. (1955). *Principles of Criminology* (5th edition, revised). Chicago, Lippincott.

258 54   Sutherland, Edwin H., and Cressey, Donald R. (1955). op. cit., p. 163.

259 86   Tannenbaum, F. (1938). *Crime and the Community*. New York, Columbia University Press.

260 85   Thrasher, F. M. (1927). *The Gang*. Chicago, University Press.

261 141   Trasler, G. B. (1962). *The Explanation of Criminality*. Routledge.

262 73   Trenaman, J. (1952). *Out of Step*. Methuen.

263 70   Trenaman, J. (1952). op. cit., p. 195.

264 243   United Nations (1965). 'Social forces and the prevention of criminality'. *Third Congress on the Prevention of Crime and the Treatment of Offenders*. Stockholm.

265 59   Vaz, E. W. (1966). 'Self-reported juvenile delinquency and socio-economic status'. *Canadian Journal of Corrections*, 8, 20–27.

266 111   Vernon, P. E. (1965). 'Environmental handicaps and intellectual development'. *British Journal of Educational Psychology*, 35, 1–22.

267 166   Voss, H. L. (1963). 'The predictive efficiency of the Glueck Social Prediction Scale'. *Journal of Criminal Law, Criminology and Police Science*, 54, 421–30.

268 67, 207   Walker, N. (1965). *Crime and Punishment in Britain*. Edinburgh, University Press.

269 99   Walker, N. (1965). op. cit., p. 103.

270 116   Walker, N. (1965). op. cit., p. 59.

271 196   Walker, N. (1965). op. cit., Table 34, p. 296.

272 282   Walker, N. (1965). op. cit., p. 257.

273 40   Wallerstein, J. S., and Wyle, C. J. (1947). 'Our law-abiding law-breakers'. *Probation*, 25, 107–12.

274 160   Wardle, C. J. (1961). 'Two generations of broken homes in the genesis of conduct and behaviour disorders in children'. *British Medical Journal*, 5 August, 349.

275 285   Warren, M. Q., and Palmer, T. B. (1965). 'Community Treatment Project. Fourth progress report'. *California Youth Authority, CTP Research Report*, No. 6.

276 29, 129, 146   West, D. J. (1963). *The Habitual Prisoner*. Macmillan.

277 22   West, D. J. (1965). *Murder followed by Suicide*. Heinemann.

278 34   Whitaker, Ben (1964). *The Police*. Penguin Books.

279 86   Whyte, W. F. (1943). *Street Corner Society: The Social Structure of an Italian Slum*. Chicago, University Press.

280 117   Wildenskov, H. O. T. (1962). 'A long-term follow-up of subnormals originally exhibiting severe behaviour disorders or criminality'. *Proceedings of the London 1960 Conference on the Scientific Study of Mental Deficiency*, 217–22. Dagenham, May & Baker.

281 281   Wilkins, L. T. (1958). 'A small comparative

study of the results of probation'. *British Journal of Delinquency*, 8, 201–9.

282 24, 91 Wilkins, L. T. (1964). *Social Deviance*. Tavistock Publications.

283 240 Williams, E. N. (1965). *A Documentary History of England*, Vol. 2. Penguin Books.

284 265 Wills, W. D. (1964). *Homer Lane: A Biography*. Allen & Unwin.

285 204 Wilson, B. R. (1961). 'Mass media and the public attitude to crime'. *Criminal Law Review*, 376–84.

286 100 Wilson, B. R. (1965). *The Social Context of the Youth Problem*, Thirteenth Charles Russell Memorial Lecture. 17 Bedford Square, London w.c.1.

287 77 Wilson, Harriet C. (1962). *Delinquency and Child Neglect*. Allen & Unwin.

288 201 Wolfgang, M. E., and Ferracuti, F. (1964). 'Violent aggressive behaviour as a socio-psychological phenomenon'. *International Journal of Social Psychiatry* (Congress edition, No. 4).

289 109 Woodward, Mary (1955). *Low Intelligence and Delinquency*. I.S.T.D.

290 33 Worsley, Henry (1849). *Juvenile Depravity*. Charles Gilpin.

291 62 Worsley, Henry (1849). op. cit., pp. 90, 246.

292 92 Yablonsky, L. (1962). *The Violent Gang*. New York and London, Macmillan.

293 37 Young, M., and Willmott, P. (1957). *Family and Kinship in East London*. Routledge; Penguin Books (1962).

Indexes

General Index

Index of Persons

formatio
TRADITION. EXPERIENCE.
TRANSFORMATION.

Formatio books from InterVarsity Press follow the rich
tradition of the church in the journey of spiritual formation.
These books are not merely about being informed, but about
being transformed by Christ and conformed to his image.
Formatio stands in InterVarsity Press's evangelical publishing
tradition by integrating God's Word with spiritual practice
and by prompting readers to move from inward change to
outward witness. InterVarsity Press uses the chambered nau-
tilus for Formatio, a symbol of spiritual formation because of
its continual spiral journey outward as it moves from its center. We believe that each of us is made with a deep desire to
be in God's presence. Formatio books help us to fulfill our
deepest desires and to become our true selves in light of
God's grace.

Also Available:

Hearing God DVD
produced in cooperation with Renovaré

Six thirty-minute sessions featuring Dallas Willard,
Richard Foster and John Ortberg

ISBN 0-8308-3568-7

DALLAS WILLARD

❖❖

Hearing God

DEVELOPING A CONVERSATIONAL
RELATIONSHIP WITH GOD

Updated & Expanded by Jan Johnson

IVP Books

An imprint of InterVarsity Press
Downers Grove, Illinois

InterVarsity Press
P.O. Box 1400, Downers Grove, IL 60515
World Wide Web: www.ivpress.com
E-mail: mail@ivpress.com

Previously published under the title In Search of Guidance *in 1984 by Regal Books (first edition) and in 1993 by HarperSanFrancisco (second edition). All rights reserved.*

InterVarsity Press® is the book-publishing division of InterVarsity Christian Fellowship/USA®, a movement of students and faculty active on campus at hundreds of universities, colleges and schools of nursing in the United States of America, and a member movement of the International Fellowship of Evangelical Students. For information about local and regional activities, write Public Relations Dept., InterVarsity Christian Fellowship/USA, 6400 Schroeder Rd., P.O. Box 7895, Madison, WI 53707-7895, or visit the IVCF website at <www.intervarsity.org>.

Cover design by Cindy Kiple
Cover photograph: © Odilon Dimier/ZenShui/Corbis/Glow Images
Interior design by Beth Hagenberg

ISBN 978-0-8308-3569-0

Printed in the United States of America ∞

Library of Congress Cataloging-in-Publication Data

Willard, Dallas, 1935-
 [In search of guidance]
 Hearing God : developing a conversational relationship with God /
Dallas Willard. — Updated and expanded / by Jan Johnson.
    p. cm.
 Includes bibliographical references (p.   ) and index.
 ISBN 978-0-8308-3569-0 (pbk. : alk. paper)
 1. Spiritual life—Christianity. 2. God (Christianity)—Will. I.
Johnson, Jan, 1952- II. Title.
  BV4501.3.W5439 2012
  231.7—dc23

2012005244

P	18	17	16	15	14	13	12	11	10
Y	27	26	25	24	23	22	21	20	19

2

To Jane Lakes Willard

Sweet lady, Good soldier,
Faithful companion on the way

Contents

A Word from the Author

*M*any people feel confused and deficient when it comes to hearing God. In chapter one you'll meet my wife's grandmother ("Mema" to us all) who was one of these. I knew that her experiences with God were not lacking and that she lived a richly interactive life with God. Yet the language of "hearing God" made her feel like an outsider looking in. I have come to believe that there are many like this dear woman, befuddled by the descriptions others make—which in many cases may actually involve reducing the intimacy of communion which God desires to the notion of straining for the sound of an audible voice or "getting a word" after letting a nearby Bible fall open.

Being close to God means communicating with him, which is almost always a two-way street. In our ongoing friendship with God we tell him what is on our hearts in prayer and learn to perceive what he is saying to us. It is this second part of our conversation with God that is found by many to be so difficult or even unapproachable. How can you be sure God is speaking to you? The answer is that we learn by experience. The key is to focus more on building our personal relationship with our Creator and less on individual actions and decisions. Hearing God's directions is only one dimension of a rich and interactive relationship. Obtaining specific guidance is but one facet of hearing God.

Ultimately, we are to move *beyond* the question of hearing God and *into* a life greater than our own—that of the kingdom of God. Our concern for discerning God's voice must be overwhelmed by and lost in our worship and adoration of him and in our delight with his creation and his provision for our whole life. Our aim in such a life is to identify all that we are and all that we do with God's purposes in creating us and our world. Thus we learn how to do all things to the glory of God (1 Cor 10:31; Col 3:17). Learning the two-way communication between us and God will develop as a natural part of such a life.

It is very important to remember and to always keep before your mind this fact: You are an unceasing spiritual being, created for an intimate and transforming friendship with the creative Community that is the Trinity. Learning to hear God is much more about becoming comfortable in a continuing conversation, and learning to constantly lean on the goodness and love of God, than it is about turning God into an ATM for advice, or treating the Bible as a crystal ball. My hope is that this book will help you develop an ongoing relationship with God that will involve conversation, communion and consummation.

Dallas Willard, 2012 Expanded Edition

Preface

*H*earing God? A daring idea, some would say—presumptuous and even dangerous. But what if we are made for it? What if the human system simply will not function properly without it? There are good reasons to think it will not. The fine texture as well as the grand movements of life show our need to hear God. Isn't it more presumptuous and dangerous, in fact, to undertake human existence *without* hearing God?

Among our loneliest moments is the time of decision and the need for guidance. The weight of our future life clamps down upon our hearts. Whatever comes from our decision will be our responsibility, our fault. Good things we have set our hearts on become real only as we choose them. But those things or other things yet undreamed of may be irretrievably lost if our choices are misguided. We may find ourselves stuck with failures and dreadful consequences that we must endure for a lifetime.

Then quickly second thoughts dog us—and third, and fourth: Did I do the good and wise thing? Is it what God wanted? Is it even what *I* wanted? Can I live with the consequences? Will others think I am a fool? Is God still with me? Will he be with me even if it becomes clear that I made the wrong choice?

While we are young, desire and impulse and personal associations may carry us through choices that would paralyze us ten years later. In the bloom of youth we just do what we have to do or whatever turns us on. How simple it seems! Often we are not even conscious of having chosen anything. After collecting a few disasters and learning that actions are forever, that opportunities seldom return and that consequences are relentless, we hungrily cry to God, "Thy will be done on earth as it is in heaven!" More than reflecting a mere general concern for world affairs to conform to his will, our prayer expresses the burning need for God to be a constant guiding presence in our individual lives.

God has created us for intimate friendship with himself—both now and forever. This is the Christian viewpoint. It is made clear throughout the Bible, especially in passages such as Exodus 29:43-46, 33:11; Psalm 23; Isaiah 41:8; John 15:14 and Hebrews 13:5-6. As with all close personal relationships, God can be counted on to speak to each of us when and as it's appropriate. But what does this really mean? And how does it work in practice? I hope in the following pages to give a clear and workable answer to these questions.

We need accurate information about this because it isn't enough to "mean well." We truly live at the mercy of our ideas; this is never more true than with our ideas about God. Those who operate on the wrong information aren't likely to know the reality of God's presence in the decisions that shape their lives, and they will miss the constant divine companionship for which their souls were made.

> *God has created us for intimate friendship with himself—both now and forever.*

My strategy has been to take as a model the highest and best type of communication that I know of from human affairs and then place this model in the even brighter light of the person and teaching of Jesus Christ. In this way it has been possible to arrive at an ideal picture of what an intimate relationship with God is meant to be and also come to a clear vision of the kind of life where hearing God is not an uncommon occurrence.

To take this ideal picture seriously is to exclude all tricks, mechanical formulas and gimmickry for finding out what God wants us to do. We cannot reduce it to a device that we use to make sure we are always right. Indeed, I hope to make it clear that the subject of hearing God cannot be successfully treated by thinking only in terms of what God wants us to do if that automatically excludes—as is usually assumed—what *we* want to do and even what *we* want *God* to do. *Hearing God is but one dimension of a richly interactive relationship, and obtaining guidance is but one facet of hearing God.*

It may seem strange but doing the will of God is a different matter than just doing what God wants us to do. The two are so far removed, in fact, that we can be solidly in the will of God, and know that we are, without knowing God's preference with regard to various details of our lives. We can be in his will as we do certain things without our knowing that he prefers these actions to certain other possibilities. Hearing God makes sense only in the framework of living in the will of God.

When our children, John and Becky, were small, they were often completely in my will as they played happily in the back garden, though I had no preference that they should do the particular things they were doing there or even that they should be in the back garden instead of playing in their rooms or having a snack in the kitchen. Generally *we are in God's will whenever we are leading the kind of life he wants for us.* And that leaves a lot of room for initiative on our part, which is essential: our individual initiatives are central to his will for us.

Of course, we cannot fail to do what he directs us to do and yet still be in his will. And, apart from any specific directions, there are many ways of living that are clearly not in his will. The Ten Commandments given to Moses are so deep and powerful on

> *Generally we are in God's will whenever we are leading the kind of life he wants for us.*

these matters that if humanity followed them, daily life would be transformed beyond recognition and large segments of the public media would collapse for lack of material. Consider a daily newspaper or television newscast, and eliminate from it every report that presupposes a breaking of one of the Ten Commandments. Very little will be left.

Yet even if we do all the particular things God wants and explicitly commands us to do, we might still not be the person God would have us be. It is always true that "the letter kills, but the Spirit gives life" (2 Cor 3:6). An obsession merely with *doing* all God commands may be the very thing that rules out *being* the kind of person that he calls us to be.

Jesus told a parable to make clear what God treasures in those who intend to serve him:

> Who among you would say to your slave who has just come in from plowing or tending sheep in the field, "Come here at once and take your place at the table"? Would you not rather say to him, "Prepare supper for me, put on your apron and serve me while I eat and drink; later you may eat and drink"? Do you thank the slave for doing what was commanded? So you also, when you have done all that you were ordered to do, say, "We are worthless slaves; we have done only what we ought to have done!" (Lk 17:7-10; cf. Mt 5:20)

The watchword of the worthy servant is not mere obedience but *love*, from which appropriate obedience naturally flows.

Much of what you will read here is only elaboration on this parable. Certainly I do hope to be helpful to those who think just in terms of *doing what they are told to do*. But in spite of the good in that attitude, it remains the attitude of the unprofitable servant. And it severely limits spiritual growth, unlike the possibilities of a life of free-hearted collaboration with Jesus and his friends in the kingdom of the heavens.

Furthermore, if we are firmly gripped by a true picture of life with Jesus and are moving by experience deeper and deeper into its reality, we will be able to resist strongly but calmly the mistakes and abuses of religious authority. From the local congregation up to the highest levels of national and international influence, we hear people and groups claiming that they have been divinely guided as to what *we* are to do. This is sometimes benign and correct, both in intention and outcome. But this is not always the case.

Those who understand how individualized divine guidance, on the one hand, and individual or corporate authority, on the other, meld together in Jesus' community of transforming love will know how to respond appropriately to misuse of religious authority. Today there is a desperate need for large numbers of people throughout various arenas of life to be competent and confident in their practice of life in Christ and in hearing his voice. Such people would have the effect of concretely redefining Christian spirituality for our times. They would show us an individual and corporate human existence lived freely and intelligently from a hand-in-hand, conversational walk with God. That is the biblical ideal for human life.

In the pages that follow I deal with hearing God as it relates to living a *whole life* in the will of God: the question of *who* God wants us to *be* as well as what he wants us to do (where appropriate). What he wants us to do is very important, and we must be careful to learn how to know it and do it. But knowing what God wants us to do is never enough by itself to allow us to understand and enter the radiant life before the shining face of God that is offered to us in the grace of the gospel. Such a life is pleasing to him, one in which he can say to us, "This is my beloved child, in whom I am well pleased."

Chapter one clarifies the tension in which Christians live, believing that hearing God is very important to our walk with him but at the same time lacking a confident understanding of how it works in practice. Chapter two removes some common misunderstandings about God's communications with us. Chapter three explains the various ways in which he is with us. Chapter four examines some objections to the very idea of God's communicating with individuals. Chapter five deals with the various ways in which he communicates and explains and defends the centrality of the "still, small voice." Chapters six and seven discuss the centrality of God's speaking—God's Word—to his creation and to the process of redemption. The Word of God is not foreign to routine reality; it is at the very heart of it. Chapter eight clarifies how we can be sure that we are hearing God. Finally, chapter nine deals with what to do on those occasions, sure to come, when God is not speaking—or at least when we are not hearing him. Some of the Scripture translations throughout are paraphrases I have offered, and they are indicated by the word "paraphrase."

Sprinkled throughout these pages are six exercises called "Hearing God in Scripture," which offer guidance through key biblical texts in this book that help us meditate on the idea of hearing God. These have been written by Jan Johnson.

To deal effectively with hearing God as part of a life within his will, it's necessary to consider some deeper issues about what he intends for us and about the nature of the world in which he has placed us. From time to time, difficult subjects will be discussed. But my hope is to leave you with a clear sense of how to live confidently in a personal walk that is complemented by an ongoing conversational relationship with God.

For a presentation of the larger picture of life with Jesus Christ in the kingdom of God, of which hearing God is only one part, I refer readers to my books *The Spirit of the Disciplines* and *The Divine Conspiracy*.

Thanks to Raymond Neal, Beth Webber, Lynda Graybeal and Tom Morrissey for their indispensable assistance with this book at various points in its development.

1

A Paradox About Hearing God

There is not in the world a kind of life more sweet and delightful than that of a continual conversation with God. Those only can comprehend it who practice and experience it; yet I do not advise you to do it from that motive. It is not pleasure which we ought to seek in this exercise; but let us do it from a principle of love, and because God would have us.

Brother Lawrence, *The Practice of the Presence of God*

Sunday dinner was finished, but we lingered around the table, savoring the good food and reflecting on the morning's service at church. The congregation—where I then served as a very young (and very green) assistant pastor—was excited about its plans for a new sanctuary to replace its old building, which was much loved but long overused and outgrown.

The morning message had focused on the plans for the new building. Our pastor spoke of his vision for the church's increased ministry. He indicated how strongly he felt God's guidance in the way the congregation was going, and he testified that God had *spoken* to him about things that should be done.

My wife's grandmother, Mrs. Lucy Latimer ("Mema" to us all), seemed deep in thought as we continued to chatter along. Finally, she said quietly, "I wonder why God never speaks to me like that."

This simple comment, which came like a bolt out of the blue from the heart of this woman of unshakable faith and complete devotion, forever changed my attitude toward glib talk about God's speaking to us or about divine guidance. Through her words—in a way I came to understand only later—God spoke to me.

I was given a vivid realization, which has never left me, of how such talk places many sincere Christians on the outside, looking in. They are not necessarily lacking the experience of hearing God, but they do not understand the language or how their experience works. This leaves them feeling confused and deficient, and may lead them to play a game that they do not really understand and that rightly makes them very uncomfortable. It undermines their confidence that they are fully acceptable to God.

Mema, in fact, had a richly interactive life with God, as we all knew. But for whatever reasons, she had not been able to relate her experience of God's presence in her life—of which she was completely certain—to the idea of God's speaking with her. This left her at a loss for how to deal with the *conversational* side of her friendship with God.

Up to that point I had rashly assumed that if you were really a Christian, then God spoke to you as a matter of course and you knew it. I was sure that he spoke individually and specifically about what he wanted each believer to do and that he also taught and made real to individuals the general truths all must believe in order to enter into life with him.

The Moving of God
Later I came to realize that my confidence was not based on genuine understanding. It came from my experiences in a series of revival meetings in which I was immersed as a young man. During those meetings I became accustomed to interacting with a charac-

teristic type of thought and impulse, which was to me God moving on my mind and heart. This experience was clearly marked out for me and it guided my actions, though I held no theory or doctrine about it.

Then as I subsequently grew into the ministry, I learned to wait upon "the word of God" to come to me. In the most primary of senses the word of God is simply *God's speaking.* I also learned to expect his speaking to come through me to others. Experience taught me the remarkable difference between when it was "just me" talking, or even "just me" quoting and discussing Scripture, and when a certain something more was taking place.

Through their writings, great Christians of the past such as John Calvin and William Law offered what we might call "the ministry of Eli" to me (see 1 Sam 3:8-9).[1] They gave me further insight into what was happening in my experiences and why it was happening.

> *In the most primary of senses,*
> *the word of God is*
> *simply* God's speaking.

They helped me to identify and respond to experiences of God's speaking, just as Eli helped Samuel in the biblical story.

They also assured me that the same Spirit who delivered the Scriptures to holy men of old speaks today in the hearts of those who gather around the written Word to minister and be ministered to. And they warned me that *only if* this happened could I avoid being just another more or less clever letter-learned scribe—trying to nourish the souls of my hearers out of the contents of my own brain, giving them only what *I* was able to work up through my own efforts from the Bible or elsewhere.

It was not easy, however, for me to see that our most sacred experiences often blind us. The light that makes it possible for us to see may also dazzle our eyes to the clearest of realities and make it impossible for us to see what lies in a shadow. Caught up in my own experiences of the workings of God's voice, I did not

really understand it at all. I only knew its reality, and I thought-
lessly assumed it was a functioning, intelligible fact in every believer's life. Obviously, I had a lot to learn.

So for a long while I was unable to appreciate the huge problems that the idea of God's speaking to us created for some of the
most faithful adherents of the church—not to mention those entirely outside it. When someone seemed to have difficulty with
hearing God, I simply passed it off as a sign of weakness of faith
or even rebellion on their part. Yet I could not entirely avoid being
aware that many faithful, devout Christians can make no sense of
being guided by God—except perhaps as it comes in the form of
outright necessities imposed by force of circumstances.

I saw them driven to turn all guidance into blind force—rigidly
controlling guidance—and to treat God's will as nothing but fate.
And I was distressed at how often people identified some brutal
event as God's will—even when it clearly came from a decision
made by human beings. They then easily moved on to the faith-
destroying, even blasphemous idea that everything that happens
in this world is caused by God.

The Ongoing Conversation

Today I continue to believe that people are meant to live in an ongoing conversation with God, speaking and being spoken to. I believe
that this can be abundantly verified in experience when rightly understood. God's visits to Adam and Eve in the Garden, Enoch's
walks with God and the face-to-face conversations between Moses
and Jehovah are all commonly regarded as highly exceptional moments in the religious history of humankind. Aside from their obviously unique historical role, however, they are not meant to be exceptional at all. Rather, they are examples of the normal human life
God intended for us: God's indwelling his people through personal
presence and fellowship. Given our basic nature, we live—really
live—only through God's regular speaking in our souls and thus

"by every word that comes from of the mouth of God."

During the time I spent writing this book, I made a special point of drawing others out in conversation concerning their experiences of hearing God. When they sensed a spirit of acceptance and

> *People are meant to live in an ongoing conversation with God, speaking and being spoken to.*

understood the topic is to be dealt with seriously, then their stories began to flow. And as understanding and confidence grew, other cases came to mind that they saw to be or to contain a word from God to the individual. Many might be surprised to discover what a high percentage of serious Christians—and even non-Christians—can tell of specific experiences in which they are sure God spoke to them.

Of course, talking *to* God is an almost universal practice. The words "Talking to God: An Intimate Look at the Way We Pray" covered the front of *Newsweek*'s issue for January 6, 1992. The main article was devoted to some sociological studies of the practice of prayer undertaken in the United States. "This week," the article said, "more of us will pray than will go to work, or exercise, or have sexual relations. . . . 78 percent of all Americans pray at least once a week; more than half (57 percent) report praying at least once a day. . . . Even among the 13 percent of Americans who are atheists or agnostics, nearly one in five still prays daily."

As these studies also found, it is widely recognized that a major part of prayer is listening to God and letting God direct us. But those who experience a directing word from God rarely speak about it. Often they have never spoken of it at all, even to their closest friends.

The UFO Syndrome

Is it not with good reason that we hesitate to speak about experiences we regard as God's speaking to us? Similarly, those who think they have sighted a UFO or those who have had the much discussed near-death experiences soon learn to keep their mouths shut. They know that they may single themselves out for unwanted attention if they are not very careful.

Perhaps they will be regarded as eccentric or even crazy. And since those experiences are strange and hard to interpret, these people genuinely fear being misguided. They do not wish to go public with something that might be a mistake on their part. They also fear being thought of as arrogant, as taking themselves to be special or, to borrow language the apostle Paul used about his own experiences, as being "too elated by the abundance of revelations" (2 Cor 12:7 RSV).

Similar doubts and hesitations justifiably trouble those who feel they are spoken to by God. "Why is it," comedian Lily Tomlin asks, "that when we speak to God we are said to be praying but when God speaks to us we are said to be schizophrenic?" Such a response from ourselves or others to someone's claim to have heard from God is especially likely today because of the lack of specific teaching and pastoral guidance on such matters. Indeed, like the Sadducees of old, many church leaders discourage the idea that God *would* speak to the individual. And some leaders obviously prefer that God speak only to them and not to their flock. After all, it is well known that people go off into all sorts of errors and become quite unmanageable once God starts "talking" to them.

Our Leaders Hear from God

Faced with such inner fears and lack of teaching or even with explicit denial or discouragement, disciples of Christ today may be somewhat encouraged by another message that emanates from their fellowships. For we are also constantly confronted with suggestions or implications that ideally we *should* be engaged in communications with God, just like our leaders.

Certainly our Christian leaders commonly indicate that God has spoken to them. And precisely because they are our leaders, there is a strong suggestion that we should strive to be like them. Here are a few random cases.

In a television interview Dr. Ken Taylor, who produced the widely used version of the Scriptures known as the Living Bible and the New Living Translation, told how he had been concerned about children having a Bible they could easily understand. According to his statement, one afternoon "God revealed" to him "the idea of a thought-for-thought translation instead of word-for-word." This idea worked so well that such versions have now been published in many languages around the world and newer paraphrases abound.

Often it is in times of great inward distress that we hear the voice of God directed specifically to us. In the 1640s George Fox, founder of the Friends or Quaker movement, wandered the fields and byways of the English countryside, seeking someone who could show him the way to peace with God. He finally became convinced that

> there was none among them all that could speak to my condition. And when all my hopes in them and in all men were gone, so that I had nothing outwardly to help me, nor could I tell what to do; then, oh! then I heard a voice which said, "there is one, even Jesus Christ, that can speak to thy condition"; and when I heard it, my heart did leap for joy. Then the Lord did let me see why there was none upon the earth that could speak to my condition, namely, that I might give him all the glory.[2]

In book eight of his *Confessions,* St. Augustine (A.D. 354-430) tells how in a similarly distraught condition he "heard from a neighboring house a voice, as of boy or girl, I know not, chanting, and oft repeating, 'Take up and read. Take up and read.'" He could remember no child's game with these words. "So, checking the torrent of my tears, I arose; interpreting it to be no other than a command from God, to open the book, and read the first chapter I should find." Thus he came upon Romans 13:13-14. His condition was immediately transformed, as was Fox's centuries later, and one of the greatest and most influential of all Christians entered the kingdom of the heavens.

Quite characteristically, a weekly publication from a large local church states that the pastor "has been given a bold vision by our Lord." The vision is that every person in the entire geographical area where the church is located should be called to Christ in a one-year period by a telephone call from some person in the church. Notice this is not described as a bright idea that struck the pastor, but as a vision communicated to him by God. And of course that makes all the difference in the world in its meaning for the congregation that the pastor leads.

I cite these cases here not because they are exceptional but precisely because they are so common. There is a practically endless supply of such stories. They vary in detail from one denominational tradition to another, but they are present in all Christian communions to some significant degree, except those that have moved beyond theological liberalism into simple humanism.

Should we expect anything else, given the words of the scriptural record and the heritage of the Christian church? As Christians we stand in a millennia-long tradition of humans who have been addressed by God. The ancient Israelites heard the voice of their God speaking to them out of the midst of fire (Deut 4:33). A regular place of communion and conversational interchange between the high priest and God was established in the mercy seat over the ark of God (Ex 25:22; see also Lk 1:11-21).

But the *individual person* with faith among the Israelites also cried out expectantly to be taught by God:

> Teach me to do your will,
>   for you are my God.
> Let your good spirit lead me
>   on a level path. (Ps 143:10)

Israel's experience led the prophet Isaiah—who also had firsthand experience of conversing with God (Is 6)—to describe conditions of the faithful this way:

> Then you shall call, and the LORD will answer;
>   you shall cry for help, and he will say, Here I am. . . .
> The LORD will guide you continually. (Is 58:9, 11)

Abiding Includes Conversing

On the evening before his crucifixion, Jesus assured his little band of followers that although he was leaving them, he would continue to manifest himself to all who loved him. Judas who was also called Thaddaeus then asked just the right question: *How* would this manifesting take place? Jesus' reply was that he and his Father would "come to them and make our home with them" (Jn 14:22-23).

Certainly this abiding of the Son and the Father in the faithful heart involves conscious communication or conversation in a manner and a measure our Lord himself considers to be appropriate. It is simply beyond belief that two persons so intimately related as indicated in Jesus' answer to Thaddaeus would not speak explicitly to one another. The Spirit who inhabits us is not mute, restricting himself to an occasional nudge, a hot flash, a brilliant image or a case of goose bumps.

> *The Spirit who inhabits us is not mute, restricting himself to an occasional nudge, a hot flash, a brilliant image or a case of goose bumps.*

Such simple reasonings add further weight to the examples set by well-known Christians that confirm the thought that ideally we should be engaged in personal communion with God. We might well ask, "How could there be a personal relationship, a personal walk with God—or with anyone else—*without* individualized communication?"

Sometimes today it seems that our personal relationship with God is treated as no more than a mere arrangement or understanding that Jesus and his Father have about us. Our personal relationship then only means that each believer has his or her own unique account in heaven, which allows them to draw on the merits of Christ to pay their sin bills. Or possibly it means that God's general providence for his creation is adequate to provide for each person.

But who does not think there should be much more to a personal relationship than that? A mere benefactor, however powerful, kind and thoughtful, is not the same thing as a *friend*. Jesus says, "I have called you friends" (Jn 15:15) and "Look, I am with you every minute, even to the end of the age" (Mt 28:20, paraphrase; cf. Heb 13:5-6).

One-to-One with God

God walks and talks in our midst as part of how the kingdom of God is in our midst (Lk 17:21). Our relationship with God is not a consumerist relationship; nor do Christians understand their faith to be a consumer religion. We don't consume the merits of Christ or the services of the church. We are participants, not spectators. Accordingly, we seek to interact with God in a relationship of listening and speaking. Notice the interaction: "If my people who are called by my name humble themselves, pray, *seek my face* and turn from their wicked ways, then *I will hear* from heaven, will forgive their sin and heal their land" (2 Chron 7:14, emphasis added). If we humble ourselves and seek God, he will respond. Such interaction is part of our friendship with God.

In the last analysis, nothing is more central to the practical life of the Christian than confidence in God's individual dealings with each person. The individual care of the shepherd for his sheep, of the parent for the child and of the lover for the beloved are all biblical images that have passed into the consciousness of Western humanity. They pervasively and essentially mark our art and general culture as well as our religion. Not only conservative and liberal Christians, high-church and Pentecostal, but also Christian and Jew, and even Jew and Muslim, come together in saying, "The Lord is *my* shepherd, *I* lack for nothing. *He* makes *me* lie down in green pastures, *he* leads *me* beside still waters" (Ps 23:1-2, paraphrase).

The biblical record always presents the relationship between God and the believer as more like a friendship or family tie than merely one person's arranging to take care of the needs of another. If we consider that startling array of biblical personalities from Adam to the apostles Paul and John, we behold the millennia-long saga of God's invading human personality and history on a one-to-one basis. There is nothing general or secondhand about the divine encounters with Abraham, Moses, Isaiah, Nehemiah, Mary or Peter.

> *Nothing is more central to the practical life of the Christian than confidence in God's individual dealings with each person.*

The saga continues up to our own day in the lives of those recognized as leaders in the spiritual life. When we consider, coming through the ages, St. Augustine, Teresa of Ávila, St. Francis of Assisi, Martin Luther, George Fox, John Wesley, C. H. Spurgeon, Phoebe Palmer, D. L. Moody, Frank Laubach, A. W. Tozer or Henri Nouwen, we see in each case a person who regards personal communion *and* communication with God both as life-changing episodes and as daily bread. These are people who seek to focus their minds on God, to pray moment by moment. Untold thousands of humble Christians whose names will never appear in print—who will never preach a sermon or teach a class—can testify equally well to the same kinds of encounters with God as are manifested by the great ones in the Way.

Robert C. McFarlane was a well-known businessman in the Los Angeles area. He had moved to California from Oklahoma in 1970, and within just a few days of his arrival—due to a disastrous misunderstanding with a close friend—he had to take control of an insurance agency. He did not want it, but he had to make it succeed in order to save the large amount of money he had invested in it.

By the spring of 1973 he was in the third year of constant strain and stress in the operation of the business. He had recently been converted through the influence of the Rolling Hills Covenant Church in Southern California, and in answer to the prayers of his wife, Betty, and her many Christian friends.

One day that spring the continual danger of defeat, the daylight and dark hours of effort, the frustration at every turn and the hardened memories of the cause of his financial difficulties came upon him with special force. Robert drove toward his office, facing yet another day of futility and failure but having to accomplish the absolute necessities to keep the business afloat.

Suddenly he was filled with a frantic urge to turn left onto the road out of town—and just disappear. Afterward he always felt he was going to make that turn. How far he would have gone is, of course, unknown. But into the midst of his inner turmoil there came a command: "Pull over to the curb."

As he relates it, it was as if the words were written on the windshield. After he pulled over, there came to him, as though someone with him in the car said these words: "My Son had strains that you will never know, and when he had those strains he turned to me, and that's what *you* should do."

After hearing these words Robert sat at the wheel for a long time, sobbing aloud. He then drove on to his Long Beach office, where he faced twenty-two major, outstanding problems. All the most significant problems—whether they concerned company disagreements, clients' deciding to remain with his agency, payments by clients of sizable, late premiums or whatever—were substantially resolved by that day's end.

Wilhelm Hermann, a great theologian of the late nineteenth century, goes so far as to mark the Christian out in terms of a personal communion with God. "We hold a man to be really a Christian when we believe we have ample evidence that God has revealed himself to him in Jesus Christ, and that now the man's inner life is taking on a new character through his communion with the God who is thus manifest."[3] Spiritual formation into Christlikeness—true change of character—comes from living in relationship to God.

More recently the English philosopher and theologian John Baillie wrote, "Our knowledge of God rests on the revelation of his personal presence. . . . Of such a presence it must be true that to those who have never been confronted with it argument is useless, while to those who have, it is superfluous."[4]

The faith in a God who speaks personally to the soul is nowhere recorded more plainly than in the hymns of the church, from all ages, sung week by week by the church as it congregates and day by day by Christians as they go about their lives at work, at home, at play: "Savior, Like a Shepherd Lead Us," "All the Way My Savior Leads Me," "Lead On, O King Eternal," "Where He Leads Me," "Lead Kindly Light," "He Leadeth Me," "Holy Spirit, Faithful Guide," "Jesus Savior, Pilot Me," "If Thou But Suffer God to Guide Thee," "Guide Me, O Thou Great Jehovah" and "Jesus, Still Lead On." This brief list hardly begins to mention all the hymns devoted to personal divine guidance and the conversational communion of the soul with God. The words of these hymns follow a familiar pattern:

He walks with me, and He talks with me,
And He tells me I am His own,
And the joy we share as we tarry there,
None other has ever known.[5]

The Paradox

In the light of all this it is not an exaggeration to speak of a *paradox* in the contemporary experience and understanding of hearing God. This paradox seriously hinders our practical faith.

On the one hand, we have massive testimony to and widespread faith in God's personal, guiding communication with us—far more than mere providential and blindly controlling guidance. This is not only recorded in Scripture and emblazoned upon church history, but it also lies at the heart of our worship services and our individual relationships with God.

Receiving guidance from God actually serves as the basis of authority for our teachers and leaders. Rarely do people profess to teach and lead the people of God on the basis of their education, natural talents and denominational connections alone. Authority in spiritual leadership derives from a life in the Spirit, from the leader's personal encounter and ongoing relationship with God.

On the other hand, we also find a pervasive and often painful uncertainty about how hearing God's voice actually works today and what its place is in the church and in the Christian's life. Even those who firmly believe that they have been addressed or directly spoken to by God may be at a loss to know what is happening or what to do about it. In the Bible, poor flustered Gideon said to the Lord, who in some fashion stood before him, "Do something to prove that you are the one who is speaking to me!" (Judg 6:17, paraphrase).

Even if we were to beg for a word from God, we may have so little clarity on what it should be like and so little competence in dealing with it, that when it comes it will only add to our confusion. I believe that this is one reason such a word may be withheld from us by God when it would otherwise be appropriate and helpful.

Our need for understanding is clearly very great. We are all too familiar with the painful confusion of individuals who make huge efforts to determine God's will for themselves—people who are frequently very sincere and devout. We see them make dreadful errors by following a whim or chance event that, because of their desperation, they *force* to serve as a sign from God. We see them sink into despair, skepticism, even cynicism, often accompanied by a continuation of religious routine that becomes utterly mechanical and dead. They "know," on the basis of what has happened to them, that for all practical purposes they are simply "on their own."

We are also all too familiar, even if only though newspaper accounts, with the tragic domination of groups by those who lay claim to a special sign or word from God. Religious dictators are in unceasing supply and show up in surprising guises and places. Often they are not effectively resisted precisely because the other members of the group have no clear idea, tested and proven in experience, of how such a word from God really works. They are vulnerable to madness in the name of God.

First Steps Toward a Solution
As disciples of Jesus Christ, I believe we cannot abandon faith in our ability to hear from God. To abandon this is to abandon the reality of a personal relationship with God, and that we must not do. Our hearts and minds, as well as the realities of the Christian tradition, stand against it.

The paradox about hearing God's voice must, then, be resolved and removed by providing believers with a *clear understanding* and a *confident, practical orientation toward God's way of guiding us and communicating with us*, which is the aim of the chapters that follow. But before we can even begin working on this task, there are three general problem areas that must be briefly addressed.

First, *we need to understand that God's communications come to us in many forms.* What we know about guidance and the divine-human encounter from the Bible and the lives of those who have gone before us shows us that. We should expect nothing else, for this variety is appropriate to the complexity of human personality and cultural history. And God in redeeming humanity is willing to reach out in whatever ways are suitable to its fallen and weakened condition. We should look carefully at these many forms to see which ones are most suited to the kind of relationship God intends to have with his people. If we give primacy to forms of communication that God does not on the whole prefer in relation to his children, that will hinder our understanding of and cooperation with his voice—perhaps even totally frustrating his will for us. One of the main tasks of the chapters that follow is to prevent this.

Second, *we may have the wrong motives for seeking to hear from God.* We all in some measure share in the general human anxiety about the future. By nature we live in the future, constantly hurled into it whether we like it or not. Knowing what we will meet there is a condition of our being prepared to deal with it— or so it would seem from the human point of view. Francis Bacon's saying that knowledge is power is never more vividly realized than in our concern about our own future. So we ceaselessly inquire about events to come. The great businesses and the halls of government are filled today with experts and technocrats, our modern-day magicians and soothsayers. A discipline of "futurology" has emerged within the universities. The age-old trades of palm reading and fortune telling flourish.[6]

Within the Christian community this leads to a prominence of teaching on the will of God and how to know it. Russ Johnston draws upon his own wide experience to remark how this continues to be one of the most popular subjects,

A certain church I know has elective Sunday School classes for their adults. Every three months they choose a new topic to study. The pastor tells me that if they can have someone teach on knowing God's will, they can run that class over and over, and still people sign up for it in droves.

I've spoken at many conferences where part of the afternoons are set aside for workshops on various topics. If you make one of the workshops "Knowing the Will of God," half the people sign up for it even if there are twenty other choices.[7]

But a self-defeating motive is at work here. Seeking to know the future causes people to take these classes and workshops over and over without coming to peace about their place in the will of God.

I fear that many people seek to hear God solely as a device for obtaining their own safety, comfort and sense of being righteous. For those who busy themselves to know the will of God, however, it is still true that "those who want to save their life will lose it" (Mt 16:25). My extreme preoccupation with knowing God's will for me may only indicate, contrary to what is often thought, that I am overconcerned with myself, not a Christlike interest in the well-being of others or in the glory of God.

Frederick B. Meyer writes, "So long as there is some thought of personal advantage, some idea of acquiring the praise and commendation of men, some aim of self-aggrandizement, it will be simply impossible to find out God's purpose concerning us."[8] Nothing will go right in our effort to hear God if this false motivation is its foundation. God simply will not cooperate. We must discover a different type

> *I fear that many people seek to hear God solely as a device for obtaining their own safety, comfort and sense of being righteous.*

of motivation for knowing God's will and listening to his voice.

Closely aligned to wanting to hear God only to know the future, some people want to have God's distinct instructions so they will not have to be responsible for their actions. But responsibility and initiative are the heart of our relationship with God. We are not robots, and he does not work with robots.

Third, *misconceiving the nature of our heavenly Father and of his intent for us creates a truly overwhelming problem* to block our understanding of God's communication with us as his redeemed children and friends. From this then comes a further misunderstanding of what the church, his redemptive community, is to be like and especially of how authority works in the kingdom of the heavens. Indeed, all human troubles come from thinking of God wrongly, which then means, thinking about ourselves wrongly.

God certainly is not a jolly good fellow, nor is he our buddy. But then neither are we intended by him to be robots wired into his instrument panel, puppets on his string or slaves dancing at the end of the whiplash of his command. Such ideas must not serve as the basis for our view of hearing God. As E. Stanley Jones observed,

> Obviously God must guide us in a way that will develop spontaneity in us. The development of character, rather than direction in this, that, and the other matter, must be the primary purpose of the Father. He will guide us, but he won't override us. That fact should make us use with caution the method of sitting down with a pencil and a blank sheet of paper to write down the instructions dictated by God for the day. Suppose a parent would dictate to the child minutely everything he is to do during the day. The child would be stunted under that regime. The parent must guide in such a manner, and to the degree, that autonomous character, capable of making right decisions for itself, is produced. God does the same.[9]

A Conversational Relationship

The ideal for hearing from God is finally determined by who God is, what kind of beings we are and what a personal relationship between ourselves and God should be like. *Our failure to hear God has its deepest roots in a failure to understand, accept and grow into a conversational relationship with God*, the sort of relationship suited to friends who are mature personalities in a shared enterprise, no matter how different they may be in other respects.

It is within such a relationship that our Lord surely intends us to have, and to recognize readily, his voice speaking in our hearts as occasion demands. I believe that he has made ample provision for this in order to fulfill his mission as the Good Shepherd, which is to bring us life and life more abundantly. The abundance of life comes in following him, and "the sheep follow him because they know his voice" (Jn 10:4).

The next chapter begins to deal with these problem areas that confront our search for God's voice by looking at some general but essential preliminary guidelines.

Some Topics for Reflection

1. Can a person be sure that God has not spoken to them? What events in your past life *could* have been messages from God? Reflect on the details of some of these events.

2. What is the paradox about hearing God discussed in this chapter? Do you find that the tension it sets up is present in your life and the lives of religious people around you?

3. What might be the drawbacks of having a conversational relationship with God? What kind of person would you expect to be less than enthusiastic about living in such a relationship?

4. What does it say about someone's view of God that he or she uses the term *personal relationship* but there are no specific communications?

5. Should a leader who claims to have been spoken to by God ever be questioned about it? How might one intelligently go about this in a spirit of love?

6. Everything considered, would you *really* like to be spoken to by God?

2

Guidelines for Hearing from God

He brought me to the banqueting house,
and his banner over me was love. . . .
Eat, O friends; drink, yea, drink abundantly, O beloved.

Song of Solomon 2:4; 5:1 KJV

Those possessed of genuine love have God's life in them
and are well acquainted with him. Those who are not
have no knowledge of him, for God is love.

1 John 4:7-8, paraphrase

You may have seen the film *The Stepford Wives*.[1] It is the story of a couple, probably in their early or mid-thirties, who move into the upper-middle-class community of Stepford, where the men are mostly workers in high-tech industries and businesses, and the women stay at home.

The woman in the couple soon notices that most of the other Stepford wives uniformly exhibit very strange behavior patterns. They are continually ecstatic about cleaning their houses and baking. When they get together they mainly trade recipes, make crafts, or coo over their clean floors and their latest triumphs in making their husbands' lives more comfortable. They never fight, nor are they unpleasant to anyone—especially not to their husbands—and they have no opinions or interests that reach beyond their family, home and club.

Just a few remain on the feisty, individualistic side. But they each suddenly change to become just like the rest.

When this happens to the best friend of our most recent Stepford wife—who is already very suspicious about what is going on—she becomes desperate as her friend's hand rests within the flame on the stove, but is not burned. And the friend doesn't notice. Instead she simply mouths the same inane niceties over and over, while our main character backs away and runs out of the door.

By this time, however, the men's club has planned her "transformation." She pretends to become a sweet, sweet, *sweet* totally controlled wife, but she and her husband outwit them and expose the scheme.

Aside from its social agenda *The Stepford Wives* sends a message that is obvious and important. But it is one that is too often forgotten. *In close personal relationships, conformity to another's wishes is not desirable, be it ever so perfect, if it is mindless or purchased at the expense of freedom and the destruction of personality.* This is a point that must be grasped firmly as we come to think about God's relationship with his human creation and about what his love for us means.

God could have created a world of robots, instead of free people who love him and understand his participation in the kingdom and their work. But then there would be no conversations. There would simply be direction and conformity. That picture robs people of initiative and freedom that goes into true friendship with God—cooperative creativity. Is there subordination to God? Yes, but not forceful direction that leaves no possibility of initiative on the person's part.

When you surrender initiative, you make prayer meaningless.

It lifts your spirits, but does not influence what God is going to do. God has purposes and will accomplish these purposes, but he develops people who do those things. That is one reason it is hard to get people to pray at church and why prayer meetings are often dead. People don't see that prayer—real, two-way conversation with God—makes any difference. If you interpret the conversation simply as God telling you what to do, you don't see the importance of talking with and hearing God.

But prayer is an honest exchange between people who are doing things together. God and I work together, and I need to invoke his power in that activity. Joint activity is a key to understanding how conversation flows.

In such conversations we also talk about other things besides what God wants done today. We talk about what is happening, what is interesting or what is sad. Most conversation between God and humans is to help us understand things. God relates to his people in a way to help them grow and develop. We are not Stepford wives.

Specifically, in our attempts to understand how God speaks to us and guides us we must, above all, hold on to the fact that learning how to hear God is to be sought *only as a part of a certain kind of life*, a life of loving fellowship with the King and his other subjects within the kingdom of the heavens. We must never forget that God's speaking to us is intended to develop into an intelligent, freely cooperative relationship between mature people who love each other with the richness of genuine *agape* love. We must therefore make it our primary goal not just to hear the voice of God, but to be mature people in a loving relationship with him.

> *We must make it our primary goal not just to hear the voice of God, but to be mature people in a loving relationship with him.*

Only in this way will we hear him rightly. This is our *first* general guideline.

Guideline One: Love God with All Our Being

When we love people, we want to please them. We don't want this only in order to avoid trouble or to gain favor; it is our way of being with them, of sharing their life and their person. The gushing pleasure of small children as they help their parents comes from the expansion of the child's little self through immersion in the life of a larger self to which the child is lovingly abandoned. *With* their parents, children do big things they cannot undertake alone. But they would have no interest in doing these things apart from the parent's interest, attention and affection that comes along with the task.

Adults also get a sense of this larger power and larger life when they enjoy requited love. When, in the manner appropriate to the people involved, two become one, they identify with one another, expanding their selves and their world. The beloved, who both loves and is loved, does not want to order the lover about; instead the beloved desires that the lover understand what is needed so that no orders are necessary. Love is designed to be our primary way of "being with" others.

In this union of souls—in the conscious delight and rest in one another that is the highest and most exalted relationship possible between two persons—it is not right for one person to always tell the other what to do. And so it is in our union with God, a person both loving and beloved. He does not delight in having to always explain what his will is; he enjoys it when we understand and act upon his will. Our highest calling and opportunity in life is to love him with all our being.

God as Taskmaster

Far too commonly, no doubt, we think of God as did the man in the parable of the talents who regarded his lord as "a harsh man." He was, accordingly, afraid of his master and, proudly, in his blindness, gave him back exactly what "belonged" to him (Mt 25:14-30).

Such a person could not "enter into the joy of [his] master" because—misconceiving their relationship as he did—he could neither enter into his lord's mind and life nor open his own life to his lord. He actually abused his lord by taking him to be interested only in getting his own back, while the lord for his part was really interested in sharing his life and goods with others.

The point of the parable is the conversational nature of our relationship with God. The ten-talent man took initiative; he did not wait to be told what to do with it. This one-talent man had the wrong view of God. As he spoke, saying, "Master, I knew that you were a harsh man, reaping where you did not sow, and gathering where you did not scatter seed; so I was afraid, and I went and hid your talent in the ground. Here you have what is yours" (vv. 24-25), he seemed to be thinking: *I didn't do anything wrong.* In doing no wrong, he did the biggest wrong of all by not taking initiative, not taking part in what the Master was doing.

The role of taskmaster, whether a pleased one *or* an angry one, is a role that God accepts only when appointed to it by our own limited understanding. He thus often condescends to us because our consciousness cannot rise any higher (clouded as it is by our experiences in a fallen world with our superiors, whether they be parents, bosses, kings or those who stand over us in manipulative "love"). And the rule then, as always, is: "Let it be done for you according to your faith" (Mt 8:13). Well, no doubt it is better that we have *some* relation to God than no relation at all!

In the same way, we demean God immeasurably by casting him in the role of the cosmic boss, foreman or autocrat, whose chief joy in relation to humans is ordering them around, taking pleasure in seeing them jump at his command and painstakingly noting any failures. Instead, we are to be God's friends (2 Chron 20:7; Jn 15:13-15) and fellow workers (1 Cor 3:9 NASB).

When we come to learn how we can hear God and what divine guidance *really* is, we must be sure to do justice to the revelation of God in Christ. Hearing God and seeking guidance, as I showed in chapter one, are an almost universal human preoccupation. It is hard, however, to cleanse our minds of those motives, images and concepts that would brutalize the very God whom we hope to approach.

In the primitive rituals and the "Bible roulette" (picking verses at random for guidance) frequently practiced by present-day believers, we see both the desperate urgency and the superstitious character of human efforts to get a word from God, especially a word on what is going to happen and what we should do about it. If necessary, some people are prepared to *force* such a word from him or someone else. Like King Saul, many of us have our own versions of a witch of Endor (1 Sam 28).

Hearing God cannot be a reliable and intelligible fact of life except when we see his speaking as one aspect of his presence with us, of his life in us. Only our *communion* with God provides the appropriate context for *communications* between us and him.

> *Only our* communion *with God provides the appropriate context for* communications *between us and him.*

And within those communications, guidance will be given in a manner suitable to our particular lives and circumstances. It will fit into our life together with God in his earthly and heavenly family. Again, this is our *first* preliminary insight to help us in our learning to discern God's voice.

 ## Guideline Two: Mere Humans Can Talk with God

A *second* truth that is preliminary to any successful attempt on our part to hear God's voice concerns the relationship of our personal experience to the contents of the Bible and, by extension, to the lives of the saints and heroes of the faith throughout the ages.

When the crowds saw what Paul had done, they shouted,

> . . . "The gods have come down to us in human form!" . . .
> [A]nd the crowds wanted to offer sacrifice. . . . When the
> apostles Barnabas and Paul heard of it, they . . . rushed out
> into the crowd, shouting, "Friends, why are you doing this?
> We are mortals just like you." (Acts 14:11, 13-15)

The above scene from the book of Acts portrays the common
human response to people who are living in such a close relationship with God that special manifestations of his presence stand
out in their lives. We immediately think, *They just aren't human!*
By this we mean that their experience—including their experience of God—is not like ours and perhaps that they are even
some special kind of people, *so our experience of God could never
be like theirs.*

No doubt it is hard to believe that someone clearly manifesting a
transcendent life could still be human. One of the most serious and
severe doctrinal struggles in the early church was over the question
of whether Jesus was authentically human. A primary function of
the doctrine of the virgin birth, when first introduced, was to fix
firmly in people's minds the fact that Jesus really did have a human
body, since he was literally born of a woman. His body came forth
from a womb.[2] Still earlier, in "the days of his flesh," when his humanity was quite visible through his literal bodily presence and
processes, his closest friends and associates apparently could not
see his divinity. Philip, as the end drew near, said, "Lord, show us
the Father, and we will be satisfied." Jesus could only reply, "Have I
been with you all this time, Philip, and you still do not know me?
Whoever has seen me has seen the Father" (Jn 14:8-9).

Jesus was human, yet divine; divine, yet human. We must understand this precarious balance if we are to do justice to the realities of Jesus' redemptive presence in history. It is fairly easy to
state, but only the gracious inward assistance of God will enable
us to base our lives on it.

This problem of uniting the life of God with the life of humanity continued to bother the early believers. Elijah was cited by
James, the Lord's brother, as a case well known in this respect,
which could help the believers understand their own experience
and its possibilities. The story of Elijah's terror before Jezebel, his
running for his life and his dissolving into a mass of righteous
self-pity (1 Kings 19), shows clearly that he really was human. He
was, after all, "a human being like us" (Jas 5:17), regardless of his
occasional fantastic feats in the power of God.

The humanity of Moses, David and Elijah, of Paul, Peter and
Jesus Christ himself—of all that wonderful company of riotously
human women and men whose experience is recorded in the Bible
and in the history of the church—teaches us a vital lesson: *Our
humanity will not by itself prevent us from knowing and interacting
with God just as they did.*

How to Believe the Bible Stories
Conversely, if we are really to understand the Bible record, we must
enter into our study of it on the assumption that the experiences
recorded there are basically of the same type as ours would have
been if we had been there. Those who lived through those experiences felt very much as we would have if we had been in their
place. Unless this comes home to us, the things that happened to
the people in the Bible will remain unreal to us. We will not genuinely be able to believe the Bible or find its contents to be real, because it will have no experiential substance for us.

Failure to read the Bible in this realistic manner accounts for
two common problems in Christian groups that hold the Bible
central to their faith. *The first problem is that it becomes simply a
book of doctrine*, of abstract truth about God, which one can search
endlessly without encountering God himself or hearing his voice.
This same attitude led the religious authorities of Jesus' own day
to use the Scriptures for the very purpose of avoiding him. They

searched the Scriptures fervently, yet Jesus said of them, "you do not have his word abiding in you" (Jn 5:38). A. W. Tozer has pointedly remarked, in this connection, that

> it is altogether possible to be instructed in the rudiments of the faith and still have no real understanding of the whole thing. And it is possible to go on to become expert in Bible doctrine and not have *spiritual illumination*, with the result that a veil remains over the mind, preventing it from apprehending the truth in its spiritual essence.[3]

The other problem is that we simply stop reading the Bible altogether when we do not understand the experience of biblical characters in terms of how we experience life's events. Or else we take it in regular doses, choking it down like medicine, because someone told us that it would be good for us—though we really do not find it to be so.

The open secret of many "Bible-believing" churches is that only a very small percentage of their members study the Bible with even the degree of interest, intelligence or joy that they bring to bear upon their favorite newspaper or magazine. In my opinion, based on considerable experience, this is primarily because they do not know and are not taught how to understand the experience of biblical characters in terms of how they experience life.

Perhaps they are even warned *not* to understand it in this way, told that it is dangerous to do so. But the Bible itself teaches that we are to understand it in terms of our own experience when it says that Paul, Barnabas and Elijah were human beings like us and that Jesus knows how we feel in our weaknesses because he himself "in every respect has been tested as we are" (Heb 4:15). It means that *their experience was substantially like our own.*

If we are to hear God's voice ourselves and on an individual basis, we must, above all else, observe how his word came to those people described in the Scriptures. How did they experience God's communication? What was it like for them to hear God? We must prayerfully but boldly use our God-given imaginations as we read the stories of people who encountered God. We must ask ourselves what it would be like if *we* were Moses standing by the bush (Ex 3:2), little Samuel lying in his darkened room (1 Sam 3:3-7), Elisha under inspiration from the minstrel (2 Kings 3:15), Ananias receiving his vision about Paul (Acts 9:11) or Peter on his rooftop (Acts 10:10). We must pray for the faith and for the experiences that would enable us to believe that *such things could happen to us.* Only then will we be able to recognize, accept and dwell in them when they come. This is our *second* general guideline.

Humble Arrogance: Who, Me, Lord?

> Nevertheless, do not rejoice at this, that the spirits submit to you, but rejoice that your names are written in heaven. (Lk 10:20)

Richard Attenborough's movie *Gandhi* has a scene set in South Africa where the young Indian lawyer and a white clergyman are walking together on a boardwalk, contrary to South African law at the time. They are accosted by some brutish-looking young white men who seem about to harm them. But the mother of the ringleader calls from an upstairs window and commands him to go about his business.

As they walk on, the clergyman exclaims over their good *luck.* Gandhi comments, "I thought you were a man of God."

The clergyman replies, "I am, but I don't believe he plans his day around me!"

The audience laughs, of course. A cute point indeed! But beneath it lies an attitude and a set of beliefs that may make it impossible for us to take seriously the possibility of divine guidance. And if we do not take it seriously, then of course we shall not be able to enter into it.

To the statement made earlier—that we must think of ourselves as capable of having the same kinds of experiences as did Paul, Barnabas or Elijah—many will spontaneously reply, "But who am I to put myself in the place of these great ones? Who am I even to suppose that God might guide me or speak to me, much less that my experience should be like that of a Moses or Elisha?"

One who has such a reaction often presumes that it honors the greatness of God. In fact, it contradicts what God has taught about himself in the Bible and in the person of Christ. *His greatness is precisely what allows him to "plan his day" around me or anyone and everyone else, as he chooses.*

> ✓ *We must think of ourselves as capable of having the same kinds of experiences as did Elijah or Paul.*

Those spoken to by God in the scriptural record, such as Moses or Gideon, often tried to plead unworthiness or inadequacy. While such responses are in a sense fitting, they are also beside the point. They are irrelevant, as God makes perfectly clear in the stories concerned.

We might even find it hard to believe it if we were told that a high government official or some other important, though merely human, dignitary had called to talk to us. We might think, on the one hand, that we are not that important and, on the other hand, that such a communication might seem to *make* us important. Similar thoughts may be stirred up at the suggestion of God's talking to us. But these thoughts are simply irrelevant to his purposes in dealing with us. Furthermore, they contain tragic misconceptions that have the power to shut us off from the individualized word of God.

In the first place, we *are* that important. We were important enough for God to give his Son's life for us and to choose to inhabit us as a living temple. Obviously, then, we are important enough for him to guide us and speak to us whenever that is appropriate.

In the second place, *his speaking to us does not in itself make us important.* Just as when he spoke to the ancient people of Israel, his speaking to us only gives us greater opportunity to be and to do good and to have greater responsibility for the care and guidance of others. But if we allow God's conversational walk with us (or anything else) to make us think we are people of great importance, his guidance will certainly be withdrawn. For we cannot be trusted with it. Under the kingdom of the heavens, those who exalt themselves will be abased, as Jesus taught, and pride is the condition that comes right before a fall.

◇◇

Hearing God in Scripture

1 Kings 19:2-18

Before doing this lectio divina exercise, you might wish to review the last three sections about Elijah and his experience. (Begin at "Guideline Two: Mere Humans *Can* Talk with God" and skim up to this point.) This will help you enter into Elijah's experience in an informed, picturesque way.

To prepare to read this passage in order to receive from God, please set the book or electronic reader down for a minute. Close your eyes and breathe out slowly. Ask God to give you an openness to hear whatever the Spirit wishes to bring to you today.

> **Read—*lectio***
>
> Read the passage slowly, considering the invitation that reading Scripture is "encountering God himself or hearing his voice."
>
> *Jezebel sent a messenger to Elijah, saying, "So may the gods do to me, and more also, if I do not make your life as the life of one of them by tomorrow about this time." And when he saw that, he arose and ran for his life. . . . [He] went a day's journey into the wilderness, and came and sat down under a broom tree. And he prayed that he might die, and said, "It*

is enough! Now, LORD, take my life, for I am no better than my fathers!"

Then as he lay and slept under a broom tree, suddenly an angel touched him, and said to him, "Arise and eat." Then he looked, and there by his head was a cake baked on coals, and a jar of water. So he ate and drank, and lay down again. And the angel of the LORD came back the second time, and touched him, and said, "Arise and eat, because the journey is too great for you." So he arose, and ate and drank; and he went in the strength of that food forty days and forty nights as far as Horeb, the mountain of God.

And there he went into a cave, and spent the night in that place; and behold, the word of the LORD came to him, and He said to him, "What are you doing here, Elijah?"

So he said, "I have been very zealous for the LORD God of hosts; for the children of Israel have forsaken Your covenant, torn down Your altars, and killed Your prophets with the sword. I alone am left; and they seek to take my life."

Then He said, "Go out, and stand on the mountain before the LORD." And behold, the LORD passed by, and a great and strong wind tore into the mountains and broke the rocks in pieces before the LORD, but the LORD was not in the wind; and after the wind an earthquake, but the LORD was not in the earthquake; and after the earthquake a fire, but the LORD was not in the fire; and after the fire a still small voice.

So it was, when Elijah heard it, that he wrapped his face in his mantle and went out and stood in the entrance of the cave. Suddenly a voice came to him, and said, "What are you doing here, Elijah?"

And he said, "I have been very zealous for the LORD God of hosts; because the children of Israel have forsaken Your covenant, torn down Your altars, and killed Your prophets with the sword. I alone am left; and they seek to take my life."

Then the LORD said to him: "Go, return on your way to the Wilderness of Damascus; and when you arrive, anoint Hazael as king over Syria. Also you shall anoint Jehu the son of Nimshi as king over Israel. And Elisha the son of Shaphat of Abel Meholah you shall anoint as prophet in your place. It shall be that whoever escapes the sword of Hazael, Jehu will kill; and whoever escapes the sword of Jehu, Elisha will kill. Yet I have reserved seven thousand in Israel, all whose knees have not bowed to Baal, and every mouth that has not kissed him." (NKJV)

Now that the words are familiar to you, please read it again, remembering that "those who lived through those experiences felt very much as we would have if we had been in their place."

Also, listen with the ear of your heart for one of the following:

- A word or phrase, a detail or a special moment of the story that shimmers or stands out to you.

- Where you find yourself in the passage: in the person of Elijah or Jezebel or the angel; perhaps you identify with the cave or the baked goods, or even the earthquake, wind and fire. That's not silly or unusual. Just go with it.

In any case, do not choose this yourself. Let the Spirit bring it to you. Even if you don't like it, try to welcome it with meekness and see what happens (Jas 1:21). *the implanted word is able to save your soul - Receive with meekness*

Reflect—*meditatio*

Read the passage again slowly. As you do so and for a few minutes afterward, reflect on one of the following:

- The word or phrase that stood out to you. Why do you think these words resonated with you?

- Who or what you found yourself to be in the passage. How does it feel to be this person or object? What draws you? What are you thinking or feeling about God?

Give yourself a few minutes to do this.

Then ask God, How does this connect with my life today?

What do I need to know or be or do?

Respond (Pray)—*oratio*

After reading the passage one last time, talk to God about what you think the Spirit might have said to you or what came to you.

Pray in whatever way you are led. You might thank God for something or ask God for something.

Rest (Contemplation)—*contemplatio*

Do as you are led. You may wish to wait on God—to simply *be with* God. You may wish to pay attention to God, pondering especially, How did God *seem* in the passage? What about God makes you want to worship him, or at least *be with* him? Sit in the companionship of God—the one who invites you to come away and be with him.

The Strength of True Meekness

In seeking and receiving God's word to us, we must also seek and receive the *grace of humility*. Our being humble allows God to speak to us because he knows we will not misuse his word. Lack of humility creates problems. People have gifts of the Spirit without the fruit of the Spirit. God reproached Miriam and Aaron:

> Miriam and Aaron spoke against Moses because of the Cushite woman whom he had married (for he had indeed married a Cushite woman); and they said, "Has the LORD spoken only through Moses? Has he not spoken through us also?" And the LORD heard it. Now the man Moses was very humble, more so than anyone else on the face of the earth. (Num 12:1-3)

Miriam and Aaron wanted God to legitimize their position, insisting that he spoke to them also. But they weren't in tune with what God wanted done, but only with what they wanted done.

In this passage God explained his policy about humility and hearing him. Humility is a quality that opens the way for God to work because God resists the proud (1 Pet 5:5). Moses was one of the most humble, least presumptuous human beings who ever walked the earth. And Moses also may be the all-time record holder for lengthy conversations with God. If there were such a category in the *Guinness World Records* books, Moses would certainly head the list. Certainly a connection existed between his meekness and his close working and talking relationship with God. Psalm 25:9 says of God, "He leads the humble in what is right, and teaches the humble his way."

In his book *George Mueller of Bristol*, A. T. Pierson comments on this verse from the Psalms in a way that both elaborates the present point and will prove highly useful later in this book:

> Here is a double emphasis upon *meekness* as a condition of such guidance and teaching. *Meekness is a real preference for God's will.* Where this holy habit of mind exists, the whole being becomes so open to impression that, without any *outward* sign or token, there is an *inward* recognition and choice of the will of God. God guides, not by a visible sign, but by swaying the judgment. To wait before him, weighing candidly in the scales every consideration for or against a proposed course, and in readiness to see which way the preponderance lies, is a frame of mind and heart in which one is fitted to be guided; and God touches the scales and makes the balance to sway as he will. *But our hands must be off the scales*, otherwise we need expect no interposition of his in our favor.[4]

God will gladly give humility to us if, trusting and waiting on him to act, we refrain from *pretending* we are what we know we are not, from *presuming* a favorable position for ourselves and from *pushing* or trying to override the will of others. (This is a fail-safe recipe for humility. Try it for one month. Money-back guarantee if it doesn't work!)

Guideline Three: Hearing God Doesn't Make Us Righteous

This subject of humility brings us to the *third* preliminary truth that we must keep constantly before us in our search for a word from God: When God speaks to us, *it does not prove that we are righteous or even right*. It does not even prove that we have correctly understood what he said. The infallibility of the messenger and the message does not guarantee the infallibility of our reception. Humility is always in order.

This is an especially important point to make since the
appeals "God told me" or "the
Lord led me" are commonly
used by the speaker to prove

> *The infallibility of the messenger and the message does not guarantee the infallibility of our reception.*

that "I am right," that "*you* should follow *me*" or even that "*I* should get *my* way." Once and for all let us say that no such claim is automatically justified.

This is such a common misunderstanding for seeking divine instruction that some may say, "What is the use of it then? Why should God speak to me, or I listen, if it will not give me unquestionable authority and absolutely ensure that I am on the right track?"

In the chapters that follow I hope to offer a fully satisfactory response to this question. We shall then have to examine the issue of authority and of being "right" in relation to hearing God's voice. But in our efforts to comprehend what an individual word from God is and how it works, we must never lose sight of the fact that God's purposes are *not* merely to support us or make us look and feel secure in our roles or to make sure that we are right.

Indeed, being right is one of the hardest burdens humans beings have to bear, and few succeed in bearing up under it gracefully. There is a little placard I have seen that reads, "Lord, when we are wrong, make us willing to change, and when we are right, make us easy to live with!" A very wise prayer.

Paul the apostle has warned us that knowledge puffs up, whereas love builds up, and that no one knows anything as well as they ought to know it (1 Cor 8:1-2). This is so, it seems, even if we are hearing God. The voice of God we seek to hear in the Way of Christ is only *one* part of a life of humility, power, faith and hopeful love, whose final overall character is life with God in the embrace of "the everlasting arms" (Deut 33:27 KJV).

Chapter three will offer a clearer picture of what the experience of that life is like—of how it is that we are to be with God and God with us.

Some Topics for Reflection

1. Why does the *Stepford Wives* robotlike model of human relationships seem attractive to some people? What are its strengths and weaknesses?

2. Does the picture of love as a way of "being with" fit into what you have experienced in your life? Think of all the types of relationships in which love plays a role.

3. Discuss or reflect privately on the idea that one of God's main tasks is to see to it that no one gets away with anything (a taskmaster).

4. What is the relationship between communion, communication and guidance in human affairs—say, between a mother and daughter, or between friends? To what extent would this carry over or not carry over to God and his children?

5. Do you see inherent conflicts between being spoken to by God

and meekness or humility? What must be understood in order to resolve those conflicts?

6. Which of the three general guidelines for hearing from God in this chapter helps clear up any questions or doubts or misunderstandings you may have had?

Guide line 2 - Mere Humans can talk to God

3

Never Alone

Then the Lord God said, "It is not good
that the man should be alone."

Genesis 2:18

Look, the young woman is with child and shall bear a son,
and shall name him Immanuel.

Isaiah 7:14

I am with you always, to the end of the age.

Matthew 28:20

A little group from a college that I attended used to hold religious services on Thursday evenings for the inmates at a county jail located about thirty miles east of Chattanooga, Tennessee. The people imprisoned there were not hardened criminals but quite ordinary men who were serving short sentences of several months to a year for minor offenses. Isolation from their friends and families caused them to suffer acutely.

They really seemed to look forward to our weekly visits, perhaps more for the singing than anything else. In our group was a young lady who was a beautiful Christian as well as a fine musician. She would play the accordion and the men would join in enthusiastically with the songs and hymns. There was one song in particular that they rarely if ever failed to request:

I've seen the lightning flashing,
I've heard the thunder roll;
I've felt sin's breakers dashing,
Trying to conquer my soul.

I've heard the voice of Jesus,
Telling me still to fight on.
He promised never to leave me,
Never to leave me alone.

Then the inmates would swing into the chorus with all the pathos of desperate men contemplating their last hope on earth:

No, never alone; no, never alone!
He promised never to leave me,
Never to leave me alone.[1]

There is so much loneliness all around us. I once found myself in London with several days on my hands while waiting for a flight back to the United States. I spent a great deal of my time in Westminster Cathedral (not Westminster *Abbey*) in meditation and prayer. In the abbey one senses the great past—the majestic history of the English people and of God's dealings with them. In the cathedral, by contrast, which is some distance up from the abbey toward Victoria Station, there is a divine presence beyond all national histories. Something about the vast, obscure interior of that building impresses me with the nearness of God.

In front of the cathedral is a square with benches, some tables and off to one side a religious bookstore and a McDonald's— golden McArches and all. Here street people of London come to sleep safely in the morning sun, if it is shining, and to glean scraps of *haute cuisine* left by those who dine with McDonald.

I recall watching one woman in particular on several occasions as she slept, with children and pigeons flocking around her. She was blond, a little heavyset and about middle-aged. While she showed the marks of street life, she looked very much like many a woman at the center of a happy family. And I thought, *Whose daughter is she? Whose sister, or mother, or neighbor or classmate? And here she is, alone, alone, alone!*

A similar but even more profound feeling had come over me when our first child was born. I realized painfully that this incredibly beautiful little creature we had brought into the world was utterly separate from me. Nothing I could do would shelter him from his aloneness in the face of time, brutal events, the meanness of other human beings, his own wrong choices, the decay of his own body and, finally, death.

It is simply not within human capacity to care effectively for others in the depths of their life and being or even to be *with* them in finality—no matter how much we may care about them. If we could only really *be with* them, that would almost be enough, we think. But we cannot, at least in a way that would satisfy us. For all of us the words of the old song are true: "You must go there by yourself."

That would be the last word on the subject but for God. He is able to penetrate and intertwine himself within the fibers of the human self in such a way that those who are enveloped in his loving companionship will never be alone. This, surely, is the meaning of the great affirmations at the end of Romans 8:

> Then what can separate us from the love of Christ? Can affliction or hardship? Can persecution, hunger, nakedness, danger, or the sword? . . . [I]n spite of all, overwhelming victory is ours through him who loved us. For I am convinced that there is nothing in death or life, in the realm of spirits or superhuman powers, in the world as it is or the world as it shall be, in the forces of the universe, in heights or depths—

nothing in all creation that can separate us from the love of God in Christ Jesus our Lord. (vv. 35, 37-39 NEB)

Even our anguish over those dear to us can be completely put to rest when we see they are living in the presence from which nothing can separate them. The complete and ultimate blessing and highest good, the *summum bonum* of

> *God is able to penetrate and intertwine himself within the fibers of the human self in such a way that those who are enveloped in his loving companionship will never be alone.*

humankind, comes to those with lives absorbed in the Way of Christ—life in the presence of God. The completely adequate word of faith in all our sorrows and all our joys is "Immanuel, God with us!" Thus we sing:

Where'er Thou art may we remain;
Where'er Thou goest may we go;
With Thee, O Lord, no grief is pain,
Away from Thee all joy is woe.

Oh, may we in each holy tide,
Each solemn season, dwell with Thee!
Content if only by Thy side
In life or death we still may be.[2]

"In your presence," the psalmist says, "there is fullness of joy; in your right hand are pleasures forevermore" (Ps 16:11). Even in the valley of the shadow of death there is nothing to fear. Why? Because "you are with me" (Ps 23:4).

On the other hand, the fact that only God can take away our aloneness by his presence explains why the ultimate suffering and punishment is separation from the presence of God. The psalmist cries out in terror, "Do not cast me away from your presence, and do not take your holy spirit from me" (Ps 51:11).

The Giver and His Gifts

It is true of course that the person and presence of God with us is sought in part for its external effects. In many of this world's religions, the favor of the gods is mainly or totally sought simply because of its advantages. The psalmist, once again, describes the presence of God as a place to hide from the pride of man (Ps 31:20; see also 27:5; 32:7). After refusing to enrich and fortify himself with plunder from his victory over the kings (Gen 14:22-24), Abraham, father of the faithful, is given a vision of God saying to him, "Do not be afraid, . . . I am your shield; your reward shall be very great" (15:1).

When Jehovah was angered by the sins of the Israelites on their journey to Canaan and seemed about to desert them, Moses prevailed upon him by saying, "How shall it be known that I have found favor in your sight, I and your people, unless you go with us? In this way, we shall be distinct, I and your people, from every people on the face of the earth" (Ex 33:16).

Yet trying to control our circumstances by means of the presence of God is not what we rest in as disciples of Jesus. We are told to "be content with what you have; for he has said, 'I will never leave you or forsake you.' So we can say with confidence, 'The Lord is my helper; I will not be afraid. What can anyone do to me?'" (Heb 13:5-6). The promise here is not that God will never allow any evil to come to us, but that no matter what befalls us, we are *still* beyond genuine harm due to the fact that he remains with us and his presence is utterly enough by itself.

Our contentment lies not in his *presents* but in the *presence* of the One whose presents they are. In all our trials we are more than conquerors because, as we have seen, nothing shall be able to "separate us from the love of God in Christ Jesus our Lord" (Rom 8:39).

Thomas à Kempis speaks for all the ages when he represents Jesus as saying to him, "A wise lover regards not so much the gift of him who loves, as the love of him who gives. He esteems affection rather than valuables, and sets all gifts below the Beloved. A noble-minded lover rests not in the gift, but in Me above every gift."[3] Through the ages, the sustaining power of the Beloved Presence has made the sickbed sweet and the graveside triumphant; transformed broken hearts and relationships; brought glory to drudgery, poverty and old age; and turned the martyr's stake or noose into a place of coronation.

As St. Augustine has written, when we come to our final home "there we shall rest and see, see and love, love and praise. This is what shall be in the end without end."[4] It is this for which the human soul was made. It is our temporal and eternal calling: "Man's chief end is to glorify God and enjoy him forever."[5]

But now loneliness is loose upon the landscape. It haunts the penthouse and the rectory, the executive suite and the millionaire's mansion, as well as the barren apartment, the assembly line, the cocktail bar and the city streets. It is, as Mother Teresa of Calcutta once said, the leprosy of the modern world. A popular song of some years back deplored the fate of Eleanor Rigby and exclaimed over "All the lonely people! Where do they all come from?"[6]

There is a simple, correct answer to this question: the lonely people live apart from God. They live "without hope and without God in the world" (Eph 2:12 NIV). Their many experiences of alienation are rooted in their alienation from God.

Is it possible to make clear what a life *with* God is like, a life in which one is never alone? Is it at least feasible to explain the with-God life in terms that would enable an honest and open-minded person to approach the possibility of entering into it? We will be looking at concrete ways of understanding our "with" relationship to God, in which we are forever done with isolation and loneliness. The following words from Scripture provide some intriguing suggestions:

You shall be for me a priestly kingdom and a holy nation.
(Ex 19:6)

To him who loves us and freed us from our sins by his
blood, and made us to be a kingdom, priests serving his
God and Father, to him be glory and dominion forever and
ever. (Rev 1:5-6)

The basic idea here is that God calls us to a direct and fully self-
conscious, personal relationship with him (as priests) in which we
share responsibility with him (as kings) in the exercise of his authority. Exactly what does this involve, and how do we experience
it? There are a number of forms and phases involved, as I've described below.

Called to a Relationship with God

Blind faith. First of all, what we may call "blind" faith is a valid,
though very minimal, way of God's being with us. Here we find
ourselves believing in God and really believing that he is with us.
Perhaps we believe because of past experiences, or because we
have faith in the faith of others, or even because of abstract reasonings that tell us he simply *must* be here. But the only way that he is
present in our lives is our conviction—almost a mere will that it
shall be so. We have no *awareness* of his being here with us at all
and no *evidence* of his action in or around us. Still we believe. Still
we are faith-full.

Although this kind of faith is not to be despised—far from it—
the human heart can never be content to treat God's being with us
merely as a matter of blind faith with nothing else to go on. Abstract reasoning from the doctrine of God's omnipresence, mental
assent to the dogma that God must be with the believer, faith in
the faith of others, even remembrance of past experiences of
God—none of these can be an adequate foundation for sustained
spiritual growth.

Those who understand God's presence only in these ways must be encouraged to believe that there is much more for them to know and receive. Otherwise they will never enter into their capacities as kings and priests, never "reign in life through the one man, Jesus Christ" (Rom 5:17 NIV).

Sensing God's presence. Perhaps the next step beyond mere faith that God must be here is an imprecise but often very powerful sense, feeling or impression of God's presence. As is the case in our discerning the *voice* of God (to be discussed later), we need considerable experience in order to learn how to accurately recognize and assess the meanings of such impressions. Yet a sense of God's presence is frequently verified through the judgment of the worshiping community, and this serves as a basis for intelligent appraisal by, and cooperation among, individuals in the group. Different people simultaneously sense that certain things are to be done—that God is here and is moving in *that* direction.

This *corporate sensing* is a well-known phenomenon. Experienced pastors and laypeople frequently find they have synchronized their activities in a gathering or form of service through their sense of God's presence and intention for the particular occasion. It is something they come to expect and to rely on. And those who sense God's presence while alone in prayer, service, meditation or study find easy communication with multitudes of others who have had similar—or even seemingly identical—experiences. They talk a common language, based on the sameness of their individual experiences.

Such a strong sense of the presence of another also occurs at a purely secular level, where the "other" is a human being. We may have the distinct impression that someone is looking at us or listening to us, only to later learn that in fact a certain person *was* looking intently at us or listening to us at that time. It is not an uncommon occurrence.

There are those who are able to attract the attention of another person (across a large hall, for example) merely by staring intently at the back of that person's head. Some "smart" weapons of warfare are able to detect when they are being "watched" by radar, and perhaps we are not altogether unlike them. Some people seem more sensitive than others to such things, just as some have better eyesight or more acute hearing than others have.

It is clear that *one person's conscious concentration on another frequently evokes a reciprocal awareness.* Since this is known to be true among human beings, we should not be surprised that God's attention to us should result in our reciprocal awareness of God's presence.

Sometimes, of course, the sense of God with us becomes much more distinct. My oldest brother, J. I. Willard, served for over thirty years as a minister under the blessing of God. But his entry into the ministry came through long and intense struggles with personal and financial issues.

One evening he faced a major decision that had to be made the next day, a decision that would commit him for years into the future. He prayed long into the night, falling asleep at around 1:30 a.m. But, he relates, at 2 a.m. "that room lit up with the glory of God. I saw a figure. I did not see a face, but I recognized it to be the person of Christ. I felt a hand on my shoulder, and I heard a voice that said, 'Feed my sheep.'"

The presence of God almost overwhelmed his consciousness (as has been the case for many others who have been given such experiences), and it also transformed various aspects of his personality. He was suddenly living in the study of the Bible, memorizing much of it without trying to do so, even though his days were spent in hard physical labor. He had been painfully addicted to tobacco all of his adult life; desire for it was removed without his asking. According to him, the "aroma" of that room full of the presence of God has stayed with him ever since. Many others would testify that this was so.

The God who acts. The sense of God's presence in Christian experience is sometimes accompanied by extraordinary events or powerful effects not easily attributable, if attributable at all, to merely natural causes. This range of effects is a third form taken by God's presence with us, and the sense of his presence is by no means essential to it. The mark of the working of God's Spirit with us is the *incommensurability* of the effects with our merely human powers. The outcome is beyond natural powers to accomplish. Such humanly unaccountable results fit into and even certify the principles and purposes of the rule of God in human history, as manifested in the works of Christ and the Scriptures generally.

After many years of highly successful ministry, Dwight Lyman Moody had an experience of which he himself said,

> I cannot describe it, I seldom refer to it, it is almost too sacred an experience to name. . . . I can only say God revealed Himself to me, and I had such an experience of His love that I had to ask Him to stay His hand. I went to preaching again. The sermons were not different; I did not present any new truths; and yet hundreds were converted. I would not now be placed back where I was before that blessed experience if you should give me all the world; it would be as small dust in the balance.[7]

In his day, Moody was a constant source of wonder precisely because the effects of his ministry were so totally incommensurable, even incongruent, with his obvious personal qualities. He was a man of very ordinary appearance, unordained by any ecclesiastical group and quite uncultured and uneducated—even uncouth and crude to many.

At the height of Moody's effectiveness, between 1874 and 1875, Dr. R. W. Dale, one of the leading nonconformist clergymen in England, observed Moody's work in Birmingham for three or four days. He wanted to discover the secret of Moody's power. After his

observations were completed, he told Moody that the work was
most plainly the work of God, for he could see no relation between
Moody personally and what he was accomplishing. A smaller person might have been offended at this, but Moody only laughed and
replied that he would be very sorry if things were otherwise.[8]

In the Bible, Abraham fathered Isaac—the son of promise and
spirit—with Sarah, *contrary* to nature. It was achieved through
the energy of the Spirit, altogether beyond Abraham and Sarah
alike. But at an earlier point Abraham and Hagar were quite competent to beget Ishmael through the mere energies of their bodies
(Gal 4:22-28). Life with results beyond the natural *always* depends
on intimate interactions between us and God, who is therefore
present. These results could
never come from you alone.

> *Life with results beyond*
> *the natural* always *depends*
> *on intimate interactions*
> *between us and God, who is*
> *therefore present.*

When Paul and Barnabas set
out on their first missionary
journey (Acts 13–14), they moved
at every turning point in a power
that was far beyond themselves.
The result was an astonishing series of events, establishing communities of believers in Christ throughout central Asia Minor.
When they returned to their home in Syrian Antioch, they brought
the community of believers together and matter-of-factly "reported everything that God had done *with them,* and how *he* had
opened the door of faith to the Gentiles" (Acts 14:27, paraphrase).
There was no doubt of God's presence with them, because it was
he who energized their activities with a power beyond their own.
The fulfillment of Jesus' words concerning the divine Helper—"he
abides with you, and he will be in you" (Jn 14:17)—was to them
the most obvious fact of their lives. "The Spirit of him who raised
Jesus from the dead dwells in you, he who raised Christ from the
dead will give life to your mortal bodies through his Spirit that
dwells in you" (Rom 8:11; also Eph 1:19-20).

Conversational relationship. Brother Lawrence tells us,

I make it my business to persevere in his Holy presence, wherein I keep myself by a simple attention and a general fond regard to God, which I may call an ACTUAL PRESENCE of God; or, to speak better, an habitual, silent, and secret conversation of the soul with God, which often causes me joys and raptures inwardly, and sometimes also outwardly, so great that I am forced to use means to moderate them and prevent their appearance to others.[9]

So far we have considered three forms or aspects of God's presence with us: (1) when he is indeed close to us, but we are not aware of him or his effects, having only blind faith or abstract reasoning to turn us toward him; (2) when he is sensed, or there is a strong impression of his presence; and (3) when he acts in conjunction with our actions to change our surroundings in ways beyond our own powers.

Many who would agree with these three points might wish to accept what has been said so far as a complete account of the forms of God's presence with us. But Brother Lawrence has something more in mind, and I believe he is right. To stop now would be to omit what is most important in the ongoing relationship between human beings and God. It would rob the biblical idea of the *priesthood* and the *royalty* of the believer of its substance. It would leave our interaction with God too close to the level of vague feelings, the Ouija board and even superstitious conjecture.

How can we be friends of God if this is all there is to it? How is the rich conceptual content and knowledge found in the Bible to be understood as something communicated to us in revelation if the three forms of presence so far discussed are the totality of human interaction with God? Why, if God is personal, would he not also *talk* with us?

So we must add to the above that God is also with us in a conversational relationship: he speaks with us individually as it is appropriate—which is only to be expected between persons who know one another, care about each other and are engaged in common enterprises.

It is just such a conversational manner of presence that is suited to the personal relationship with God so often spoken of in the Christian community. This turns Paul's statement that "all who are led by the Spirit of God are children of God" (Rom 8:14) into a *framework for personal development*. Being "led by the Spirit of God" is neither blind, robot-style obedience nor feeling stuck interpreting vague impressions and signs.

Two Types of Guidance

Before going any further we should note that two types of guidance are commonly found in life. One is the *mechanical* variety that is involved in driving a car or in the remote electronic control of a model airplane or space probe. We guide something in this sense whenever we consciously cause it to proceed in a certain way we prefer. The simplest and clearest cases of this fall within the area of mechanical guidance.

But there is also *personal* guidance. Here too we wish to bring events to proceed in a certain way, but now we are dealing with people. They have a mind with which to consider matters on their own and a will concerning what is to be done. Ideally, personal guidance brings things to the desired outcome but, at the same time, allows the other person's mind to be guided to its fullest capacity without coercing that person's will. Thus the outcome is the work of both the individual being guided and the one who is guiding.

The individual's uniqueness counts before God and must not be overridden. It remains your life since you have been guided only through your own understanding, deliberation and decisions.

For this purpose God must *communicate* with you, the one who is to be guided. This is the only means by which God can have an impact on you and yet still leave you with the mental and spiritual space to retain integrity as a free personality. You can live as God's friend yet also govern your own life.

God generally deals with nonhuman or nonpersonal creation as one guides a car: by a causal influence mediated through physical reality that he has ordained in his creation. But God's *personal* creatures, whether angelic or human, are also guided by his communicating his intentions and thoughts. Personal creatures are *addressed* by him. In Psalm 32:9 we are admonished, "Do not be like a horse or a mule, without understanding, whose temper must be curbed with bit and bridle." We are to be led by—guided by— reasonable, intelligible communication, not by blind impulse, force or sensation alone.

Communicating with Words

This reasonable, intelligible personal communication may occur in one of two ways. First, God communicates through what we recognize as a voice or as words addressed to—or even through—us. The primary manner of communication from God to humankind is the Word of God, or God's speaking. The Bible itself is God's speaking preserved in written form. God spoke directly to Moses, to Ezekiel, to Paul and to many others. Through them he spoke indirectly to the people of Israel and to the church, and now—in the Bible—he speaks to world history.

In Acts 9:10-16, for example, we have the story of a man named Ananias. The events here immediately follow Paul's being struck down as the risen Christ addressed him on the road to Damascus. Paul went into seclusion in Damascus, where he fasted and prayed for three days. Apparently, around the end of that time, the Lord appeared to Paul's fellow believer Ananias of the same city and told him that he should go and speak to Paul (then called Saul). Thus Paul was put in touch with and ministered to by the believers in Damascus.

God's communication here is not a matter of theoretical argumentation, strong impressions or baffling events. The same is true for Peter's experience on the rooftop in Joppa (Acts 10), before he was called to preach the gospel in the house of Cornelius, the Roman.

According to the records we have, such guiding events happened to Paul over and over. He was about to go into Bithynia, on his second missionary journey. Somehow, as we are told in Acts 16:6-9, the Holy Spirit would not let him go. Then, as he waited at Troas, he had a dream that he should take a radically new direction and enter Europe instead of staying on his home territory in Asia Minor. In the dream a man from Macedonia called to him, saying, "Come over . . . and help us."

These purposeful, conscious communications by words seem to have been quite normal experiences for the early Christians. If we look at the advice on how the meetings of the church were supposed to proceed as given in 1 Corinthians 14, we see that they assumed that numerous people in the congregation were going to have some kind of communication from God which they would be sharing with the others in the group: "When you come together, each one has a hymn, a lesson, a revelation, a tongue, or an interpretation. Let all things be done for building up" (1 Cor 14:26).

The ancient prophecy of Joel was fulfilled in the early church: "Your sons and your daughters shall prophesy, and your young men shall see visions, and your old men shall dream dreams" (Acts 2:17; cf. Joel 2:28-32). The wish of Moses "that all the LORD's people were prophets, and that the LORD would put his spirit on them" (Num 11:29) is substantially granted in the church of Jesus Christ when it functions as its Lord intended.

Communicating Through Shared Activity

The second way God's intentions and thoughts are communicated to those who are with him involves a more active role by the recipient. It is very common among those who are most mature in his family or kingdom. Here we come to understand what God wants us to understand through *immersion with him in his work*. We understand what he is doing so well that we often know exactly what he is thinking and intending to do.

I believe that this is a great part of the condition described by the apostle Paul as *having the mind of Christ:* "Those who are spiritual discern all things, and they are themselves subject to no one else's scrutiny. 'For who has known the mind of the Lord so as to instruct him?' But we have the mind of Christ" (1 Cor 2:15-16).

Psalm 32 has an interesting statement in relation to this way of being with God. The psalmist here says, "I will instruct thee and teach thee in the way which thou shalt go: I will guide thee with mine eye" (v. 8 KJV). Newer versions generally say something like, "I will guide you with my eye upon you."

In two distinct types of human experience, one person is guided by the eye of another. First, very few husbands, wives or children have not occasionally been forcibly guided by the stare of their partner or parent. The fatherly or motherly eye on the child speaks silent volumes of profound instruction at a moment's notice.

There is, however, a second and even more important way in which we are guided by the eye of another. This happens when we work or play closely with another and know the intentions and thoughts of the other's mind *by our awareness of what they are focused on*. Someone else can work with me effectively only if they can see what I am doing *without having to be told* what I am thinking and what they should do to help. Model employees, for example, are by no means those who stand waiting for someone to tell them what to do. Everyone breathes more easily when the new person on the job no longer has to be told what to do at every stage.

Earlier we referred to the parable about the servant who obeys out of love. Jesus said that if you as the master asked your servant to prepare a meal, and your servant does what you tell him to do, you don't thank him. If a servant does *only* what he is told

to do, he is an unprofitable servant (Lk 17:7-10). The worthy, useful servant—much like a coworker—sees what needs to be done
and simply does it. We become so close to God that we do not
have to wait to hear his words. We don't have to be asked but are
engaged in free-hearted collaboration with Jesus and his friends
in the kingdom.

A similar distinction can be drawn with respect to levels of
friendship. In *The Transforming Friendship*, Leslie Weatherhead
describes a kind of friendship interaction that is cognitive but occurs beyond words:

> If my friend's mother in a distant town falls ill and he ur-
> gently desires to visit her, which would reveal deeper friend-
> ship—my lending him my motor-bike in response to his re-
> quest for it, or my taking it to his door for him as soon as I
> heard of the need, without waiting to be asked? In the first
> case there has to be a request made with a voice. But in the
> second the fact of the friendship creates in me a longing to
> help. The first illustrates the communion between two per-
> sons on what we might call the level of the seen; but the
> second illustrates the communion, at a deeper level, of two
> persons on what we may call the level of the unseen.[10]

In many cases our need to wonder about or be told what God
wants in a certain situation is a clear indication of how little we
are engaged in his work.

A coworker sees what needs to be done and simply does it. We become so close to God that we do not have to wait to hear his words. We don't have to be asked.

On one sabbath Jesus came upon a man with a withered hand
in the synagogue (Mk 3:1-5). He called him out and asked the peo-
ple gathered around whether one should do good on the sabbath (heal the man) or do evil (leave
him in distress). Their silence declared loudly and eloquently their

condition. They did not know what God would want or what to do! "They were silent" (v. 4).

After he had healed the man, however, they thought it right to make plans to kill Jesus. This was only another destructive fruit of the same hearts that *could* wonder whether or not the man should be healed. But Jesus knew what God wanted done in this case because *he knew the mind of God generally*. On another occasion when he was denounced for healing on the sabbath he calmly replied, "My Father is still working, and I also am working" (Jn 5:17).

Friends Have Shared Understanding

Jesus calls us friends if we do what he commands (Jn 15:14). As God's friends we always want to be asking God what he is doing and how he wants us to work with him. God's desires are important to us. Friends are people who understand one another, and so as friends of Jesus we obey because we understand what God, our intimate Friend, is doing. Intimacy with God grows from and creates further shared understanding.

Many cannot progress in their relationship with God because they focus solely on what they think God might be telling them to do. In these cases, the friendship aspect of the relationship is missing. Things are as they should be when we don't have to be told what to do.

Because we are God's colaborers, our wants and desires are also important to God and God's plan for us (1 Cor 3:9 KJV). His intent for us is that we would grow to the point we would do what we want because what we want is part of that shared understanding with God, our friend.

It's true that God sometimes tells us what to do, but we are not simply in a relationship of master and slave. Paul described himself as God's slave, but he didn't begin as God's slave. We are not driven to servanthood, but drawn to it. We, like Paul, move into complete service as free people under Someone who respects our wants and wills and helps us become the persons we want to be.

Saints who have been drawn into this friendship and single-focused service (slavery) become something no one has ever seen before. They become true individuals who are unique because God has shaped their hearts and their wills (Prov 3:5-6). Their desires match up with God's desires, and they are empowered to do what they and God want. (On the other hand, sinners are boringly predictable because there is nothing unique in what they live for. People who are enslaved to their desires are all similar.)

Shared Work for Good

God gives us as his colaborers the power of creativity, and we delight in our creativity. That shared understanding and creative activity is spelled out in Genesis 1:26, where we are given responsibilities so that we share in carrying out creative responsibilities with him: "Let us make humankind in our image, according to our likeness." What does that mean? Look at the next few words: "and let them *have dominion* over the fish of the sea, and over the birds of the air, and over the cattle, and over all the wild animals of the earth and over every creeping thing that creeps upon the earth." God is trying to create the greatest possible good and gives us the responsibility to exercise dominion to do good, using the powers that we have to do good.

I try to do physical labor from time to time. I like to work with brick and mortar and to pour concrete. Even though it's not very good quality work, I have to go back, look at it and enjoy it within just a few hours. That is how the dominion idea of Genesis 1:26 is built into us.

And yet even as we exercise dominion, we are working out the desires of our hearts within the boundaries of the divine conversation. That conversational relationship we carry on with God creates our unique life. And that is how God wants things to be.

As we do the work God has laid out for us, we always work within the larger framework of the community and fellowship we are a part of. We do not go off in a corner and do something creative. The dominion mentioned in Genesis 1:26 is meant to be exercised in a community of love, not in individual dominion. We find our delight in our friendships with other people, which moves us toward the trinitarian nature of human community. The Trinity is the model of life as it is intended to be in human existence, the basis for Christian community. We are invited to help heal broken relationships and bring them into dominion under God. Though the world's problems will not be solved this side of heaven, resolution of the problems of the world is meant to be begun now (Col 1:19-29).

In this life with God, his presence banishes our aloneness and makes real the meaning and full purpose of human existence. This union with God *consists chiefly in a conversational relationship with God while we are consistently and deeply engaged as his friend and colaborer in the affairs of the kingdom of the heavens.*

Becoming Temples of God

I want to emphasize that there is an important place for the first three forms or phases of being "with" God: blind faith in God's presence, the feeling or sense that he is near, and a display of the supernatural effects of his presence. But no amount of these can take the place of intelligible communication from God through word and shared activity.

When all of these types of presence are in place, then the royal priesthood of the believer (Ex 19:6) is realized as it should be. It is then that having a personal relationship with God becomes a concrete, commonsense reality rather than a nervous whistling in the spiritual dark.

God does indeed guide us in many ways, by special acts of intervention in our lives as well as by general providential ordering of the world. But his direct communication with us, by word and by shared activity, is the most important part. This is because we are to become the temple of God, one that actively understands and cooperates with God's purposes, one that is inhabited through a willing, clear-eyed identification of ourselves with Jesus Christ.

That's why it is Christ *in us* that is our hope of glory (Col 1:27). Paul attempts to capture this paradoxical reality in the following well-known statement: "I have been crucified with Christ; and it is no longer I who live, but it is Christ who lives in me. And the life I now live in the flesh I live by faith in the Son of God, who loved me and gave himself for me" (Gal 2:19-20).

The interpretation of these and similar passages from Scripture given earlier is not something that has only recently come to light. Such an understanding is not my solitary brainstorm. It represents the mainstream of Christianity throughout the ages, though this understanding must be renewed constantly. You may wish to compare what you have just read to the section "Several Manners of Divine Presence" in Jeremy Taylor's *The Rule and Exercise of Holy Living*, which will give a sense of the solidity of what I have said here with what has been taught in past times.[11]

Mistaken Views of How God Speaks to Us

To conclude this chapter, let us examine three commonly accepted interpretations of how God speaks to us (including how he gives us guidance) that are surely mistaken. They are harmful to our efforts to live a life in which we hear God and receive his guidance.

A message a minute. According to the first view, God is either telling you what to do at every turn of the road *or* he is at least willing and available to tell you if you would only ask him.

I do not believe that either the Bible or our shared experience in the Way of Christ will substantiate this picture. There is no evidence in the life of Peter or Paul, for example, that they were *constantly* receiving communications from God.

The union Christ had with the Father was the greatest that we can conceive of in this life—if indeed we can conceive of it. Yet we have no indication that even Jesus was constantly awash with revelations as to what he should do. His union with the Father was so great that he was at all times obedient.

This obedience was something that rested in his mature will and understanding of his life before God, not on always being told "Now do this" and "Now do that" with regard to every detail of his life or work.

Putting it this way returns us to the idea that *God speaks ultimately to the mature Christian.* This is not to say that people at the time of conversion—or as they first enter the church or begin to come alive in their experience of God—do not receive words from him. God meets us where we are. Yet God's working through the Holy Spirit and the indwelling Christ to speak to us is not to keep us constantly under his dictation. Too much intrusion on a seed that has been planted, as on the life of a plant or a child, simply makes normal, healthy growth impossible.

Thus E. Stanley Jones helpfully observes,

> I believe in miracle, but not too much miracle, for too much miracle would weaken us, make us dependent on miracle instead of our obedience to natural law. Just enough miracle to let us know He is there, but not too much, lest we depend on it when we should depend on our own initiative and on His orderly processes for our development.[12]

A redemptive community consists not of robots but of mature people who know how to live together and who know how to live with God. For that reason I think this model of a message a minute is mistaken and very harmful in our efforts to hear God. Extensive observations of individuals who *try* to live with this model, or at least profess to, show that they simply cannot do it and that any sustained effort to do so leads quickly to disaster.

Of course, the question is not whether God *could* give a message every minute. Surely he could do that. He could give ten or a thousand messages a nanosecond—even more, if that would suit his purpose of bringing forth the cosmic family of God. But it does not. Sometimes we get caught up in trying to glorify God by praising what he can do, and we lose sight of the practical point of what he actually does do.

> The Bible will not tell you which song you are supposed to sing next Sunday.

All of this must be kept in mind as we develop educational programs and worship services, and carry on the other activities of the church. In our services and in our models both of ministry and of pastors, we must remember that we are not making robots who sing, clap, pray, give and show up for meetings when they are supposed to. We are bringing forth the sons and daughters of God to live their unique lives in this world to his glory. We must do all we can to suit the means we employ to that end.

It's all in the Bible. I believe this second view, that it is all in the Bible, is seriously misguided and very harmful. It intends to honor the Bible, but it does so with a zeal that is not according to knowledge (Rom 10:2).

The Bible gives direct instructions about many situations in our lives. We do not need to make long inquiries into God's will in order to know whether we should worship an idol, take something that is not ours, engage in illicit sex or mistreat our parents. But other questions force us to realize that many of life's specific circumstances are not dealt with in the Bible.

The Bible will not tell which song you are supposed to sing next Sunday or which verse you should take as a text for a talk or a sermon. Yet it is very likely that God's special leading is claimed for nothing more frequently than for the selection of texts and sermon topics.

Neither will the Bible tell you what to do with most of the details of your life. Suppose you want to know how to raise your children. It will tell you some very important things but not everything you need and want to know on that subject. Your family, your work and your community will present you with many choices and issues about which the Bible simply says nothing.

The *principles* are all there, however. I happily insist that the Bible says all that needs to be said or can be said, so far as principles are concerned. But the principles have to be applied before they can be lived out, and it is largely at the point of application that almost everything imaginable has been "proven" from the Bible. In these instances people have found applications they desperately desire by scandalously loosening principles of proof.

Our reverence for and faith in the Bible must not be allowed to blind us to the need for personal divine instruction *within* the principles of the Bible yet *beyond* the details of what it explicitly says. A distinguished minister once said on television that if we would only accept the Bible as the Word of God, all differences between Christians would be resolved. But in fact it is Bible-believing Christians who disagree with each other most often and most heatedly.

Nearly every faction in Christendom claims the Bible as its basis but then goes on to disagree as to what the Bible says. An exalted view of the Bible does not free us from the responsibility of learning to talk with God and to hear him in the many ways he speaks to humankind.

A misguided expectation of the Bible's ability to speak specifically to an individual or a situation leads some people to play the Bible roulette mentioned earlier. They allow the Bible to fall open where it will and then stab their finger at random on the page to see which verse it lands on. Then they read the selected verse to see what they should do. This is trying to force God to give you a message.

Despite the fact that some great Christians have used this technique, it is certainly not a procedure recommended *by* the Bible, and there is no biblical reason why one might not just as well use a dictionary, the *Encyclopedia Britannica* or the newspaper the same way or simply open the Bible and wait for a fly to land on a verse.

A novel approach was recently suggested by a minister who stated in all seriousness that we should look up the year of our birth to cast light on what we should do. Unless you were born in the first half of the twentieth century (the earlier the better), this method will do you no good, since there are few verses numbered beyond 20 or 30. I was born in 1935, so I thought I would see what direction I could get from Genesis 19:35. I will leave it to your curiosity to see what that verse says, but I shudder to think what instruction might be derived from this method.

Of course, God is so great that he sometimes does use almost anything you can imagine for his purposes in the life of a person who sincerely seeks him. Even truly superstitious methods are not beyond his forbearance and use. But that does not certify them as methods chosen by him for the spiritual life.

In the upper room, lots were cast—akin to flipping a coin or drawing straws—to determine who would replace Judas among the twelve apostles (Acts 1:26). This method was often used in biblical times, and Proverbs 16:33 assures us that while the lot is cast into the lap, "the decision is the LORD's alone." Even the most biblically oriented churches of today would not think of rolling dice or flipping a coin to determine a policy for the church or to settle an issue in someone's life. This is true even though all might agree that God *could* determine the coin or the dice to come out as he wished.

So we have made some progress. Nevertheless, you hear people tell of opening the Bible at random and reading a verse to decide whether to undertake some enterprise or move or to marry a certain person. Many devout people will do such things to hear God because their need and anxiety to hear God is so great—though they may later try to hide it or laugh at it when revealed. Worse still, many actually act on the fruit of this "guidance" to the great harm of themselves and others. They are the losers at Bible roulette. What a stark contrast to this unhappy condition is the simple word of Jesus: "My sheep hear my voice. I know them, and they follow me" (Jn 10:27). We have problems when we try to force God to tell us something. We don't force a conversation. We respect and wait and listen.

Whatever comes is God's will. This third mistaken view of how God speaks is commonly adopted and has much to recommend it in terms of the peace of mind and freedom from struggle that it provides. But, in fact, it amounts to giving up any possibility of a *conscious* interchange between God and his children.

The view even shows up in some beloved hymns such as "If Thou but Suffer God to Guide Thee." It may seem to be about exactly what we are talking about: allowing God to guide us. But when we study the hymn closely we find it counsels us to accept *everything* that happens as the guidance of God.

If you wish to know what God would have you do, it is no help at all to be told that whatever comes is his will. For you are at that moment in the position of deciding what *is* to come. Does it mean that *whatever* you do will be God's will? I certainly hope not.

If Moses had accepted this view, there would have been no nation of Israel. Perhaps there would have been a nation of "Mosesites" instead. When the people made and worshiped the golden calf while Moses was on Sinai receiving God's commandments, God said to him, "Now let me alone, so that my wrath may burn hot against them and I may consume them; and of you I will make a great nation" (Ex 32:10). Not only did Moses not accept whatever came, he actually and successfully withstood God's own declared intent in the matter, appealing to God's reputation before the surrounding nations and to his friendship with Abraham. "And the LORD changed his mind about the disaster that he had planned to bring on his people" (Ex 32:14).

Many things that happen are not the will of God, although he obviously does not act to stop them. For example, "the Lord is . . . not wanting any to perish, but all to come to repentance" (2 Pet 3:9). Nevertheless countless people do perish and fail to come to repentance.

God's world is an arena in which we have an indispensable role to play. The issue is not simply what God wants, but also what we want and will. When we accept whatever comes we are not receiving guidance. The fact that something happens does not indicate that it is God's will.

With respect to many events in our future, God's will is that *we* should determine what will happen. What a child does when *not* told what to do is the final indicator of what and who that child is. And so it is for us and our heavenly Father. (We shall return to this point in chapter nine.)

> When we accept whatever comes we are not receiving guidance. The fact that something happens does not indicate that it is God's will.

In opposition to these three mistaken views of discerning God's voice we have the *conversational* view. We shall explore further how we can receive appropriate, clear, specific communication from God through conscious experience within the context of a life immersed in God's kingdom.

> Then you shall call, and the LORD will answer;
>   you shall cry for help, and he will say, Here I am. . . .
> The LORD will guide you continually,
>   and satisfy your needs in parched places,
>   and make your bones strong;
> and you shall be like a watered garden,
>   like a spring of water,
>   whose waters never fail. (Is 58:9, 11)

Many may still wonder whether we really do live in a universe where this could happen. Does the human and physical reality of our universe call for it? Does it even allow it? This is the issue to which we must now turn.

Some Topics for Reflection

1. Have you known people who were so close to God that they were never lonely? What do you think of the prospects of such a relationship for you? For others in the contemporary world?

2. Do the four basic forms of our being with God and God's being with us adequately cover that relationship (simple trust that God is present even though we are not aware of anything unusual; a strong impression of God's presence; extraordinary events or powerful effects that occur that are beyond our powers; conversational relationship in which God speaks with us individually)? What would you add? Or take away?

3. How important do you think blind faith (without evidence or even an awareness of God) is to the stability of the Christian's walk?

4. Discuss or reflect on some instances where you are sure God *acted* with you. How can you learn more about this from experience?

5. Can you explain to someone else the two main types of guidance (mechanical and personal)? Or the two aspects of personal guidance (spoken words and shared understanding or oneness of mind)?

6. Do you think that the critiques of the three views of hearing God said to be mistaken are sound? What would you disagree with in these critiques?

4

Our Communicating Cosmos

Earth's crammed with Heaven,
and every common bush afire with God;
but only he who sees takes off his shoes.

Elizabeth Barrett Browning

In him we live, and move, and have our being.

Acts 17:28

One can find a practically endless supply of stories about people hearing God, and each is of considerable interest in its own right. I love to dwell on them and I have noticed that other people rarely tire of hearing them, even when they do not entirely believe them. Although none of these stories is to be treated as "canonical," taken together they serve as an essential point of reference for research into divine guidance and hearing God.

One remarkable illustration concerns Peter Marshall, the Scot who in the middle of the twentieth century became one of America's most widely acclaimed ministers. Through his outstanding qualities as a man and a leader, he brought the office of the chaplain of the United States Senate to a new level of prominence.

Back in Britain, on one foggy, pitch-black Northumberland night, he was taking a shortcut across the moors in an area where there was a deep, deserted limestone quarry. As he plodded blindly forward, an urgent voice called out, "Peter!" He stopped and answered: "Yes, who is it? What do you want?" But there was no response.

Thinking he was mistaken, he took a few more steps. The voice came again, even more urgently, "Peter!" At this he stopped again and, trying to peer into the darkness, stumbled forward and fell to his knees. Putting down his hand to brace himself, he found nothing there. As he felt around in a semicircle he discovered that he was right on the brink of the abandoned quarry. Taking one more step would certainly have killed him.[1]

Many widely read religious magazines and Internet sites, from almost every denomination and theological persuasion, provide us with a constant stream of such stories. In his book *Does God Speak Today?* David Pytches compiled "real-life accounts" of "words" given to disciples of Jesus in modern times. He adds fourteen cases of what are pretty clearly *mistaken* claims of hearing from God.[2] It is useful to study these latter cases when it comes to understanding how God speaks. We need to know both what it is and what it is not.

The Limits of Signs

It is important, however, to recognize that there is a limit to how much our faith can grow by contemplating such stories—no matter how well attested they may be, no matter how reliable the minds and characters of the people involved. And this limit is not neglected in the teachings of the Bible itself.

Jesus tells of father Abraham's words to the rich man in hell, that if the rich man's brothers still on earth "do not listen to Moses and the prophets, neither will they be convinced even if someone rises from the dead" (Lk 16:31). This fits in with Jesus' refusal to do religious stunts, or signs, for those who demanded them (Mt 12:39-40; Mk 8:11-12; Lk 23:8-9; Jn 2:18; 6:30). I believe he refused because he knew that such deeds, no matter how wondrous, would be fruitless against the false ideas and mindsets of the observers. I cannot imagine that he would have withheld signs if they truly could have helped people to have genuine faith in him.

The signs, however, could not help. Our preexisting ideas and assumptions are what actually determine what we can see, hear or otherwise observe. These general ideas—which so often we hold because they express how we want things to be—determine what stories can mean to us. Our beliefs and opinions cannot, therefore, be changed by stories and miraculous events alone, since they prevent a correct perception of those very stories and events.

Agnes Sanford relates how, as the young wife of an Episcopal minister, her child came down with a serious ear infection. It lasted for six weeks while she prayed fearfully and fruitlessly. Then a neighboring minister called to see her husband and learned that the child was sick. Quite casually, though intently and in a businesslike manner, he prayed for the little boy, who immediately shut his eyes, lost his fever flush and went to sleep. When the boy awoke, his fever was gone and his ears were well. Sanford remarks,

> The strange thing is that this did not immediately show me a new world. Instead, it perplexed me greatly. Why did God answer the minister's prayers when He had not answered mine? I did not know that I myself blocked my own prayers, because of my lack of faith. Nor did I know that this [successful] prayer could not come from resentment and darkness and unhappiness, as a pipeline can be clogged with roots and dirt. This doubt and confusion remained in my mind, even though the child himself, whenever he subsequently had a bit of an earache, demanded that I pray for him.[3]

Necessity of General Understanding of God

Such a failure to see a new world is not strange, because it illustrates a fact about how our minds work. Witnessing God's specific interventions in our lives—whether to guide us, speak to us or perform saving deeds on our behalf—does not automatically clear up our confusions or straighten out the entanglements of our hearts. Such events may in fact only entertain or confuse us. They *may* stimulate us to seek understanding; but they do not of themselves *give* us faith and understanding.

Our understanding must grow *before* we can have any significant appreciation of what we are experiencing on occasions when God intervenes in our lives. We must have a correct general understanding of God and his ways. That is why the rich man was told, "Let them hear Moses and the prophets."

The role of the Scriptures and of scriptural interpretation is to provide us with a general understanding of God and to inspire and cultivate a corresponding faith. The power of stories alone to generate life-changing faith is overestimated today. Lack of general understanding may also limit the effects of a word truly given by God to the individual. Very often, in my experience, the word given *to* me is actually spoken *by* me. It simply comes out with no preliminaries. I have come to recognize this through repeated occurrence. I do not, however, always understand its true significance at the time. Many others have the same experience.

This is exactly what happened to Peter on the occasion of his great confession: "You are the Messiah, the Son of the living God" (Mt 16:16-17). Notice what followed in Peter's case. First, Jesus authenticated that this word given to Peter was indeed from his Father in the heavens. Then he began to explain further what was going to happen to him—persecution, death, resurrection.

> *In my experience, the word given* to *me is actually spoken* by *me. It simply comes out with no preliminaries.*

Immediately Peter showed that he did not understand what he himself had just said. God had enabled Peter to recognize Jesus as the Christ, but Peter still did not know what the Christ would be. Consequently he tried to cast Christ in a strictly human role. Jesus had to tell Peter to get out of his way, because he had his mind in the wrong place and was actually playing the role of adversary (Satan).

God is always trying, in many ways, to teach us about himself. He will certainly meet us with inward illumination as we study and strive to understand:

> If you cry out for discernment
> and invoke understanding,
> if you seek for her as for silver
> and dig for her as for buried treasures,
> then you will understand the fear of the LORD
> and attain to knowledge of God. (Prov 2:3-5 REB)

All of this must be kept clearly in view as we go on now to consider the basic questions: *What kind of world do we live in?* and *How does God relate to us, confined as we are within it?* Admittedly, we are entering an intellectual and spiritual hardhat area, where many have received injuries to their practical faith in God. We must deal with a number of difficult problems that trouble many thoughtful Christians and non-Christians alike: problems about the *very idea* of our being in a conversational relationship with God. The Bible has been given to us to help us with these problems, but we still have to work hard to resolve them.

If you are one who has no difficulty in this respect, perhaps you should just count your blessings and immediately skip to chapter five, which deals with the various ways God communicates personally with us. But if you find that you do not have any real confidence that God *would* or *could* speak to you and guide you, this chapter is designed to help. Put on your hardhat, your hard nose and your best brains, and prayerfully dig in.

Many people's honest response to the idea that God desires to interact with people in a conversational relationship will be:

1. that God *would not* communicate with run-of-the-mill human beings by surrounding them with his presence and speaking to them

2. that he *does not* communicate with *them* in that way

3. that he *cannot* do so

4. that God *should not* communicate with individuals (motivated by the need to control the divine presence and word for what they sincerely regard as proper purposes)

I offer the following replies to these four negative responses.

Truth 1: God Would

When considering whether God would be with ordinary human beings in a conversational relationship, we must remember not to think of him in the likeness of any human dignitaries we know. The rich, the famous and the great among humanity are still severely limited in their powers of communication by the fact that they are merely human. They are narrowly limited in their ability to interact personally with others. So it is possible for them to be in intimate contact only with a small number of other people—even with all the wonders of modern communications technology. Their span of consciousness, their capacity to pay attention and the scope of their willpower permit nothing more.

Beyond such factual limitations, human greatness is often taken to mean, and essentially to *require*, having nothing to do with just ordinary people. This sort of greatness is seen as involving a certain exclusiveness, insularity or snobbishness. If we cannot clear our minds of such associations with greatness, we won't be able to imagine that the great God would talk to *us*. We will think of him as a dignitary who is too busy, too conscious of his status or too high up to communicate with us.

How hard it is for us to come to an adequate conception of the *lowliness* of God—of how his greatness is precisely what makes him able, available and ready to hear and speak personally with his creatures!

This lowliness was at the very center of Jesus' teaching about God. In his actions and words Jesus made clear how totally accessible God is to the weak, to the downtrodden and castaway, to little children. "Let the children come to me, and do not stop them; for it is to such as these that the kingdom of heaven belongs" (Mt 19:14). Our Lord's phrase "such as these" includes many characteristics of children, but here I want to stress the element of unimportance. The humanly unimportant ones are important to God. God being who he is, and now revealed in the person of Jesus Christ, *we should be surprised if he does not speak to us.*

E. Stanley Jones has asked,

> Does God guide? Strange if he didn't. The Psalmist asks: "He that planted the ear, shall he not hear? He that formed the eyes, shall he not see?" (Ps. 94:9). And I ask: "He that made the tongue and gave us power to communicate with one another, shall he not speak and communicate with us?" I do not believe that God our Father is a dumb, noncommunicative impersonality.[4]

Truth 2: God Does

What about those who believe that God just simply does not speak to *them?* Here we must consider, I believe, two separate lines along which the cause of their difficulty may be found.

Are we "in tune"? First of all, *the fact that we do not hear God does not mean that God is not speaking to us.* Even at our human level it is common for us not to hear those who speak to us. It has probably happened to most of us this very day. Someone spoke to us, but we did not know it, did not hear it. Moreover, we know that messages from radio and television programs are passing through our bodies and brains at all hours of the day: messages that an appropriately tuned receiver could pluck from the air we breathe.

What an apt picture this is of human beings in relation to God: we are showered with messages that simply go right through or past us. We are not *attuned* to God's voice. We have not been taught how to hear it sounding out in nature—for as we read in Psalm 19, "The heavens announce the glory of God"—or in a special communication directed by God to the individual.

Some of Jesus' deepest teachings are about hearing. He taught in parables so that those who did not really want to hear the truth could avoid it. He realized that not everyone has ears for the straightforward purpose of hearing but that some use their ears to sift out only what they want to hear, leaving the rest aside. One of his most repeated sayings was, "If anyone has ears to hear, let him hear." But he also urged his hearers to make a great effort to hear, assuring them that what they received would be proportional to their desire and effort (Mk 4:23-24).

Are we ready vessels? This brings us to the second source of difficulty for those who say, "God just doesn't speak to me." Here a bit of honest soul-searching may be required. Possibly they are being spoken to and do not hear. It may also be that *they could make no good use of a word from God because of how they are living.*

Do they stand ready to obey and change if God directs that? Do they *want* to know if they are on a wrong path? In general it is a good thing for God to speak to us, but in individual cases there may be reasons it would be best for God to speak very little or even not at all. If it is true that God does not speak to me, then I must inquire whether I am such a case.

The question must be asked, To what use would I try to put a word from God? God is not a snob, and he is not far away: "See, the LORD's hand is not too short to save, nor his ear too dull to hear" (Is 59:1). But when he speaks, it is to accomplish his good purposes in our lives and through his creation.

God's guidance is not a gimmick that we can keep on tap for

our gain. It is not there to enable us to beat our competitors. We cannot invoke it to help us win bets on football matches or horse races or to prove that something is theologically correct. While it is available to every person who walks with God, it is not *at our disposal as we see fit* without regard to the purposes of God's government. Nor should it be, for that would be very dangerous.

We pray, "Our Father which art in heaven, hallowed be thy name; thy kingdom come, thy will be done on earth as it is in heaven." This preamble to the Lord's Prayer beautifully expresses the purpose of all God's activities in us: "Hallowed be *thy* name. *Thy* kingdom come. *Thy* will be done." Hearing God is a reliable, day-to-day reality for people with good sense; it is for those who are devoted to the glory of God and the advancement of his kingdom. It is for the disciple of Jesus Christ who has no higher preference than to be like him.

Are we ready to be in business with God? If you find yourself in a position where you can honestly say, "God has never spoken to me," then you might ask yourself, *Why should God speak to me? What am I doing in life that would make speaking to me a reasonable thing for him to do? Are we in business together in life? Or am I in business just for myself, trying to "use a little God" to advance my projects?*

When our lives are devoted to the will of God, he has reason to speak to us. If our lives are not devoted to his purposes, he may still speak to us and even use us for his purposes if we are strategically placed. After all, we are his creatures, no matter how misguided or rebellious. But for a willing walk in conscious, loving cooperation with God, we must come to grips with the issue *What are we living for?* We must face it clearly.

It may be that I have never come to the place where I can truly say, "I am living for one thing and one thing only—to be like Christ, to do his work and live among his people and serve them and him in this world. My life is to bless others in the name of God." If we have not come to that place, then the question that normally arises as, How do we hear the word of God? is replaced for us by the prior question, What would we do if we heard the word of God?

G. Campbell Morgan has a few incisive words to say on this point. Having mentioned that when God speaks to us his word comes as a disturbing element into our lives, he continues,

> You have never heard the voice of God, and you say: "The day of miracles is past. I am never disturbed. I make my own plans and live where I please and do as I like. What do you mean by a disturbing element?" . . . Beloved, you are living still among the fleshpots and garlic of Egypt. You are still in slavery. . . . You know no disturbing voice? God never points out for you a pathway altogether different from the one you had planned? Then, my brother, you are living still in the land of slavery, in the land of darkness.[5]

Perhaps we do not hear the voice because we do not expect to hear it. Then again, perhaps we do not expect it because we know that we fully intend to run our lives on our own and have never seriously considered anything else. The voice of God would therefore be an unwelcome intrusion into our plans. By contrast, we expect great spiritual leaders to hear that voice just because we see their lives wholly given up to doing what God wants.

Frank Laubach tells of the immense change that came over his life at the point when he resolved to do the will of God:

> As for me, I never lived, I was half dead, I was a rotting tree, until I reached the place where I wholly, with utter honesty, resolved and then re-resolved that I *would* find God's will, and I *would* do that will though every fiber in me said no, and I *would* win the battle in my thoughts. It was as though some deep artesian well had been struck in my soul. . . . You and I shall soon blow away from our bodies. Money, praise, poverty, opposition, these make no difference, for they will

all alike be forgotten in a thousand years, but this spirit which comes to a mind set upon continuous surrender, this spirit is timeless.[6]

Truth 3: God Certainly Can

Many fear that the physical universe, being what it is, makes communication with God impossible. It puts him too far away. Even some who understand both the lowliness of God's greatness and the greatness of God's lowliness and who really live to do the will of God are still troubled by the thought that brutal nature interposes itself as a barrier between us and him.

The poet Alfred, Lord Tennyson, after the death of his close friend A. H. Hallam, writes as if he were addressed by the personage of Sorrow:

"The stars," she whispers, "blindly run";
A web is woven across the sky;
From out waste places comes a cry
And murmurs from a dying sun.[7]

The face of nature—especially in times when the word of God does not come and we are not at peace with him—becomes cold, hard and forbidding: "I will break down your stubborn pride. I will make the sky above you like iron, the earth beneath you like bronze. Your strength will be spent in vain; your land will not yield its produce, nor the trees of the land their fruit" (Lev 26:19-20 NEB). "May the skies above you be brazen, and the earth beneath you iron. May the LORD turn the rain upon your country to fine sand, and may dust come down upon you from the sky until you are blotted out" (Deut 28:23-24 NEB).

The "warfare" between science and theology. Even beyond such experiences of nature's seemingly godless course (common through all generations of humanity), there is a special burden of unbelief that has been borne by Western civilization for the last several hundred years—the idea that it is *unscientific* to believe that God could speak to us or guide us. Today it is simply assumed that scientific knowledge excludes the presence of God from the material universe, of which we human beings are supposed to be a pitifully small and insignificant part.

The discoveries of the immensity of space and of the forces of nature—which appear to determine everything that happens and *seem* to run their course with no assistance from the hand of a personal God—can be quite overwhelming. When the great French mathematician and astronomer Pierre Simon de Laplace presented Emperor Napoleon with a copy of his book on celestial mechanics, the emperor asked him where God fit into his system. Laplace indignantly drew himself up and replied, "Sir, I have no need of any such hypothesis!"

According to the current model of the natural sciences, nature proceeds without invoking God. You will not find any laboratory manual, any statistical analysis of social processes—even in a Christian school or college!—that introduces God *as a factor* in its calculations.

The social institution of higher education, the university system, stands in world culture as the source of unquestioned authority so far as *knowledge* is concerned. Without going into detail, we must acknowledge that it currently throws its weight behind a picture of reality without God, a picture in which human beings are entirely on their own. Regardless of what the recognized system of education might say of itself for public relations purposes, it presumes in its processes that *you can have the best education possible and be ignorant of God.*

Thus we may seem to have imposed on us a picture of reality in which humanity is encapsulated within a material world. God, if he really exists, is pictured as being wholly *beyond* that material world, which for its part, seems to run without God. Given such a view of things, one of the most difficult issues we face in trying to think about hearing God concerns the "how" of it all.

For example, if you want to talk to someone in another country, you will have to put into action a chain of events in the physical substance, the inorganic matter, between here and there. You will perhaps begin by entering a number on your telephone. This will cause electrical impulses to propagate themselves by various means across the intervening space. A physical apparatus located at the other end will be sensitive to those impulses and will convert them into a form that your faraway friend can hear or see and understand.

The point is that to communicate across such a distance, *we must go through an intervening physical reality.* Even if I wish to speak directly to you as you stand here with me, I must do the same thing. I make some sort of noise with my vocal cords that strikes your eardrum, which somehow—in a way no one fully understands—causes you to think of specific things or events. I *bring about* your thinking, and that is what my communication with you comprises.

Given such a picture of communication, the questions we must now face are as clear as they are compelling: Is this the *only way* in which God can communicate with us? Does God always have to go *through* physical substance? Does the entire realm of organic and inorganic matter stand *between* us and God? *Where* is God in relation to that realm? How does God relate to us if he is far off from us?

Not all of reality involves space. For many, these will be the most difficult questions in this chapter, perhaps even in the whole book. So I shall hasten to remind you that God does *not* have to go through physical intermediaries of any sort to reach us—though on some occasions he obviously chooses to do so. The material world in which we are placed by God permits him to be nearer to us even

> The material world in which we are placed by God permits him to be nearer to us even than our own eyes, ears and brain are near.

than our own eyes, ears and brain are near. It is "in him" that we "live, and move, and have our being" (Acts 17:28).

Conversational life with God—or prayer—is not hindered by space and distance. When you speak to God, it is like speaking to someone next to you. Spirit is unbodily personal power. Our conversation is not limited by space, time or matter. God is looking for those who will worship him in spirit and in truth. You don't need a holy place, as the woman at the well learned when she asked, "Where is the holy place—on this mountain or in Jerusalem?" (Jn 4:19, paraphrase). God is not looking for a holy place. Places are holy because God is there.

Our faith may easily fall victim to our mind's tendency to *spatialize* everything. If we think of God as being literally outside the physical realm, then it will seem as if he is utterly out of reach for us and we out of reach for him. The edge of the known universe is now thought to be something like forty-six to forty-seven billion light-years away. Beyond that, even light waves, traveling at the speed of 186,284 miles per second, can never reach us! How then can we reach God or he us if he is out there?

The great scientist and Christian Blaise Pascal wrote,

> When I see the blind and wretched state of man, when I survey the whole universe in its dumbness and man left to himself with no light, as though lost in this corner of the universe, without knowing who put him there, what he has come to do, what will become of him when he dies, incapable of knowing anything, I am moved to terror, like a man transported in his sleep to some terrifying desert island, who wakes up quite lost and with no means of escape. Then I marvel that so wretched a state does not drive people to despair.
>
> I see other people around me, made like myself. I ask them if they are any better informed than I, and they say they are not. Then these lost and wretched creatures look around and

find some attractive objects to which they become addicted and attached. For my part I have never been able to form such attachments, and considering how very likely it is that there exists something besides what I can see, I have tried to find out whether God has left any traces of himself.[8]

The traces of God that have always been obvious to the earnest seeker (Rom 1:19) are found in the purposeful order that appears within nature and history as well as in the purposeful interventions that seem to show up in history and in our individual lives. It is impossible to develop this point fully here, but the *order* of events large and small throughout our world strongly suggests to an unbiased observer that there is a providential and personal oversight of our world and our lives.

This is what the apostle Paul has in mind when he says, in his sermon on Mars Hill in Athens, that God has so arranged our world that we should seek the Lord and—as the Jerusalem Bible nicely translates it—"by feeling [our] way toward him, succeed in finding him. Yet in fact he is not far from any of us, since it is in him that we live, and move, and exist" (Acts 17:27-28). Since God is not far, God hears us when we speak. When he speaks, we can hear him.

The New Testament presents Christ the Son as continuously "sustain[ing] all things by his powerful word" (Heb 1:3) and as the very glue of the universe. "In him all things hold together" (*synistemi*, Col 1:17). A. H. Strong spells this out:

> Christ is the originator and the upholder of the universe. . . .
> In him, the power of God, the universe became an actual, real thing, perceptible to others; and in him it consists, or holds together, from hour to hour. The steady will of Christ constitutes the law of the universe and makes it a cosmos instead of a chaos, just as his will brought it into being in the beginning.[9]

Hints from current physics. Now we come to a most important point for our present concerns. The current state of the physical sciences, in opposition to the crudely mechanical view that was dominant in some previous centuries, is very congenial to the view of God's presence in his world that we find in the New Testament. Sir James Jean interpreted the result of developments in physics during the first part of the twentieth century as follows:

> Today there is a wide measure of agreement, which on the side of Physics approaches almost to unanimity, that the stream of knowledge is heading towards a non-mechanical reality; the universe begins to look more like a great thought than like a great machine. Mind no longer appears as an accidental intruder into the realm of matter; we are beginning to suspect that we ought rather to hail it as the creator and governor of the realm of matter.[10]

More recently, in his essay "Remarks on the Mind-Body Question," Nobel laureate Eugene Wigner has pointed to a general recognition among physicists that thought or the mind is primary to physical reality: "It is not possible to formulate the laws of quantum mechanics in a fully consistent way without reference to consciousness." Princeton physicist John A. Wheeler even goes so far as to hold that subjective and objective realities, consciousness and matter, mutually create each other. Another leading physicist, Jack Sarfatti, remarks that "an idea of the utmost significance for the development of psycho-energetic systems . . . is that the structure of matter may not be independent of consciousness."[11]

I do not wish to make more of these interpretations of physics than is strictly warranted. In particular, no suggestion is offered here that physics proves any theological position or even that it proves matter to be dependent on mind, as the New Testament teaches. My sole point is that according to some influential contemporary views of physical reality, there is, so to speak, an inside—or better, a *nonside* or an unside—to matter that allows for a nonspatial and yet causal dimension to be in action within the physical world. This dimension accommodates very well the biblical view of God's omnipresent relation to his world in its creation and continued sustenance. The mental or spiritual side of reality does not traverse space to have its effects, any more than one of our own thoughts has to traverse space to influence another person or to influence our emotions or actions.

The crucial point in all this is that there is no reason in the established truths of science to suppose that God cannot reach us and be with us in order to guide and communicate with us. There is plenty of room left for God in the picture of the world presented to us by contemporary science. We can be comfortable, then, with the view that we live in the kind of material universe in which hearing directly from God is possible. This view is expressed in the Bible—in John 1, Hebrews 1 and so on. Since it is the nature of mind, always and everywhere, to guide, is it not therefore reasonable to *expect* guidance and communication from God?

This could never be learned from examining matter itself or the material universe by merely human abilities. The possibilities of physical matter are to be fully revealed only from the mind of its Maker. Archbishop William Temple has written with insight on this subject:

> *There is no reason in the established truths of science to suppose that God cannot reach us and be with us in order to guide and communicate with us.*

> We do not know what Matter is when we look at Matter alone; only when Spirit dwells in Matter and uses it as a tool do we learn the capacities of Matter. The sensitiveness of eye and ear, the delicacy of the artist's touch, are achievements which we could never anticipate from the study of the lifeless. So, too, we do not know what Humanity really is, or of what achievements it is capable, until Divinity indwells in it. . . . We must not form a conception of Humanity and either ask if Christ is Human or

insist on reducing Him to the limits of our conception; we must ask, "What is Humanity?" and look at Christ to find the answer. We only know what Matter is when Spirit dwells in it; we only know what Man is when God dwells in him.[12]

Perhaps the most profound revelation of the nature of physical matter to appear so far in human history is the body of Jesus Christ in his transfiguration and resurrection.

Such explorations clarify faith. It would be a great mistake to think that the previous discussions are irrelevant to the question of having confidence in hearing God's voice. There is a lyric that says, "When you believe in things that you don't understand you will suffer!"[13] Over and over humanity has proven this true. Perhaps the song oversimplifies things, but the human heart *is* largely dependent on the head. A lack of understanding *does* weaken faith and misdirect life—sometimes disastrously.

Even though it surely is not possible to understand everything, our faith will be strengthened by whatever understanding we can acquire. Science, vaguely understood, is a power in our age, a weighty authority, whether we like it or not. If you really do believe that the idea of hearing from God is *unscientific* in the world in which you live, you are going to have great difficulty in making enough sense of it to deal with it in practice or even to be open and intelligent concerning it. This is precisely where many people now stand, in bewilderment between their education and their faith. To the degree that you come to understand that the whole of reality is something penetrated through and through by God, you can begin to open yourself up to the possibility of receiving a direct communication from him.[14]

A comparison may help. God's relation to the world is similar—though not identical—to your relation to your body. You inhabit your body, yet it is not possible to locate or physically identify you—or any act of your consciousness or any element of your character—at any point in your body. God inhabits space, though he infinitely exceeds it as well (1 Kings 8:27). "The whole earth is full of his glory" (Is 6:3). The heavens are the throne of God, and the earth is his footstool (Is 66:1; Mt 5:34; 23:22). Your whole body is accessible to you, and you are accessible through it. As your consciousness plays over and through your whole body, so in a similar—though of course not identical—fashion, "the eyes of the Lord range throughout the entire earth, to strengthen those whose heart is true to him" (2 Chron 16:9).

We live in a world much too obsessed by practical concerns and governed by a fallen ideology—in part the ideology of the scientific—and it shapes our minds away from God. In our "existence as usual" we are like Jacob, wearily asleep on a rock in a desert ravine. He went to sleep in his sorrow, alienation and loneliness, seeing only the physical landscape. In his dream—or was he only then truly awake?—he beheld God's interaction with the place he was in. Awakening, he cried out, "Surely the Lord is in this place—and I did not know it! . . . How awesome is this place! This is none other than the house of God, and this is the gate of heaven" (Gen 28:16-17).

> The angels keep their ancient places;
> Turn but a stone, and start a wing!
> 'Tis ye, 'tis your estranged faces,
> That miss the many-splendoured thing.[15]

This sort of thing is a part of the very life of the Bible. If we cannot make sense of such things in terms of what experiencing them would be like for us, then—to reemphasize an earlier theme—we will not be able to believe it, *really* believe it. Our very reading of the Bible may force us into skepticism about what is most important: a genuine, living relationship with God.

We need to have done for our understanding what Elisha did for his young assistant on one occasion when they were in great danger.

Chariots of fire. The king of Syria was at war with Israel, but every time he laid his battle plans, Elisha would tell them to the king of Israel. The king of Syria naturally supposed that there was an Israelite spy among his confidants, but his aides all denied it.

> The mind of the king of Aram was greatly perturbed because of this; he called his officers and said to them, "Now tell me who among us sides with the king of Israel?" Then one of his officers said, "No one, my lord king. It is Elisha, the prophet in Israel, who tells the king of Israel the words that you speak in your bedchamber." (2 Kings 6:11-12)

The king of Syria did believe this and went right to the heart of the problem: "Get Elisha!"

> He said, "Go and find where he is; I will send and seize him." He was told, "He is in Dothan." So he sent horses and chariots there and a great army; they came by night, and surrounded the city.
>
> When an attendant of the man of God rose early in the morning and went out, an army with horses and chariots was all around the city. His servant said, "Alas, master! What shall we do?" He replied, "Do not be afraid, for there are more with us than there are with them." Then Elisha prayed: "O LORD, please open his eyes that he may see." So the LORD opened the eyes of the servant, and he saw; the mountain was full of horses and chariots of fire all around Elisha. (2 Kings 6:13-17)

◇◇

Hearing God in Scripture
2 Kings 6:11-17

Prepare yourself to *receive from God*. Close your eyes and breathe out slowly. Ask God to give you an openness to hear whatever the Spirit wishes to bring to you today.

Read—*lectio*

Before rereading the Scripture paragraphs about Elisha, consider Dallas Willard's meditation on what happened to Elisha's servant.

> *What* did the young man see? Spiritual or personal reality is a type of reality that does not necessarily reveal itself to good eyesight. This is also true in some measure of the spiritual side of you and me. God enabled the young man to see the powers of his realm that totally interpenetrated and upheld all the normal, visible reality around him (even the Syrian army itself). Every working of visible reality is a movement within the encompassing *Logos*, the sustaining Word of God, and it rests on nothing else but God through his Son, who was and is the "reflection of God's glory and the exact imprint of God's very being, and he sustains all things by his powerful word" (Heb 1:1-3).
>
> How we need our Elishas today who, by life and teaching as well as by prayer, might open our eyes to see the reality of God's presence all around us, in every bit of matter as well as beyond!

Now reread 2 Kings 6:11-17 (p. 103), allowing yourself to be immersed in the situation. Remember that "those who lived through those experiences felt very much as we would have if we had been in their place" (see p. 44).

Also listen with the ear of your heart for

- a word or phrase, a detail of the story that shimmers or stands out to you

- where you find yourself in the passage: one of the Syrian soldiers coming after Elisha (perhaps watching the terrified servant), the servant, Elisha, one of the fiery chariots or horses, a fly on the wall watching it all happen

In either case, do not choose this yourself. Let the Spirit bring it to you.

Reflect—*meditatio*

As you reflect on this passage, consider one of the following:

- The word or phrase that stood out to you. Why do you think these words resonated with you?

- Who or what you found yourself to be in the passage. How does it feel to be this person or object? What draws you? What are you thinking or feeling about God?

Give yourself a few minutes to ponder all this.

Then ask God, How does this connect with my life today? What do I need to know or be or do?

Respond (Pray)—*oratio*

Read the words in verses 15-17 one last time, preparing yourself for what you want to say to God about what you think the Spirit might have said to you or what came to you.

Pray whatever you need to pray. You might thank God for something or ask God for something.

Rest (Contemplation)—*contemplatio*

Do as you are led. You may wish to wait on God—to simply *be with* God. You may wish to pay attention to God, pondering especially, How did God *seem* in the passage to Elisha, to the servant, to you? What about God makes you want to worship him or at least *be with* him? Sit in the companionship of God—the one who shows up and can be seen.

Truth 4: And God Should!

From the humility and generosity of his great heart, Moses said, "Would that all the LORD's people were prophets, and that the LORD would put his spirit on them!" (Num 11:29). But this might be a mixed blessing, for one further serious objection to individual believers' living in a conversational relationship with God comes from a feeling that *this would lead to chaos in the church*, the community of believers. Therefore it should not happen.

Many beleaguered pastors will understand this. Perhaps the last thing they would hope for in their congregations is that people should be able to contradict and criticize their leaders—or one another—on the basis of their own private "conversations" with God.

Leaders with thoughts like these will feel the weight of a logic that objects to the essence of the Protestant (as in "protest") movement—a movement that continues apace today in an ever-increasing number of sects emerging within and upon the fringes of Christendom. Such logic drives toward a hierarchy of authority and subordination and naturally results in *one person's speaking for God and thus enforcing conformity.*

What is in question here is nothing less than the model of leadership and authority that is suitable for the redeemed community, which is living out the good news of God's reign in the context of human life. "Living stones" (1 Pet 2:5) in conversation with God himself begin to look much better, despite all their problems, once we compare them to the alternative—dead stones.

Sheepdogs or shepherds? In our examples and training for Christian leadership, we too often emphasize getting others merely to do as they are told. In this way the church largely conforms to the leadership structures of the world. Indeed, *leadership* is normally an empty euphemism when applied to our standard communal efforts, whether in a church or outside it.

To manipulate, drive or manage people is not the same thing as to *lead* them. The sheepdog forcibly maneuvers the sheep, whereas the biblical shepherd simply calls as he calmly walks ahead of the sheep. This distinction between the sheepdog and the shepherd is profoundly significant for how leaders of Christ's people think of their work. We must ask ourselves frequently which role we are fulfilling and constantly return ourselves, if necessary, to the practice of the shepherd.

> *To manipulate, drive or manage people is not the same thing as to* lead *them.*

When we lead as shepherds, our confidence is in only one thing: the word of the Great Shepherd, coming through us or, otherwise, to his sheep. We know that they know his voice and will not follow another (Jn 10:1-16). We do not *want* them to follow another, even if we ourselves are that "other." Only this supreme confidence frees us to be true ministers of Christ. We are then sure that "every plant that my heavenly Father has not planted will be uprooted" (Mt 15:13). And we have heard the Master say, "Everything that the Father gives me will come to me, and anyone who comes to me I will never drive away" (Jn 6:37).

Following the practice of the shepherd, we would never stoop to drive, manipulate or manage, relying only on the powers inherent in unassisted human nature (see 1 Pet 4:11). Not only that but the undershepherds (pastors under God) count on their flock to minister the word of God—along with "all good things" (Gal 6:6)—to *them*. Ministry of the word is never a one-way street when it is functioning rightly in any group. "A redemptive teaching relationship," as Henri Nouwen has said, "is bilateral. . . . The teacher has to learn from his student. . . . Teachers and students are fellowmen who together are searching for what is true, meaningful, and valid, and who give each other the chance to play each other's roles."[16]

It is at this point, however, that we must abandon the metaphor of sheep, lest they become sheep for slaughter. We are to lead "willingly," not "for sordid gain. . . . Do not lord it over those in your charge, but be examples to the flock" (1 Pet 5:2-3). We are indeed to be "the servant of all" (Mk 9:35); redemptive mutual submission (Eph 5:21) is achieved in this way.

So much current religious work is desperately out of line with these scriptural injunctions. This is bound to be so if those who lead do not rely intelligently on Christ's power and readiness to govern and guide his people effectively. They will invariably turn to controlling the flock through their own abilities to organize and drive, all suitably clothed in a spiritual terminology and manner. As their faith is, so shall it be. It will be in fact "my church" and "my ministry"—this is often explicitly said—and the flock will never experience how completely and in what manner *God* is Lord of *his* church.

Leadership: Cultic or Christlike? Spokespeople for the Christian community as well as the general public are frequently heard to lament the way in which cults turn their adherents into mindless robots. In our highly fragmented society that is dominated by gadgetry and technology, lonely and alienated people are ready prey for any person who comes along and speaks with confidence about life and death—especially when that person has some degree of glamour and professes to speak for God.

There are now more than two and a half thousand distinct cults active in the United States alone, most based on the premise that God speaks to one or several central people in the group in a way that he does not speak to the ordinary members. These members are taught not to trust their own minds or their own communications with God except within the context of the group, with all its pressures toward conformity to the word from on high. Frequently, adherents are taught to accept pronouncements that are self-contradictory and fly in the face of all common sense if the leader says they must.

These are common factors among many cults, even the more extreme groups that form around personalities such as Jim Jones and Charles Manson. But the more "mainline" religious groups, if they would be honest, might find that their *own* models of leadership actually prepare the way for cult phenomena because they too use these methods to some extent. I must ask *myself*, as a Christian minister, to what extent *I*, in order to secure enough conformity and support to maintain and enlarge *my* plans, might be prepared to have people put away their minds and their own individual experiences of guidance and communication with their Lord.

A great minister speaks. In contrast to the cultish mentality, consider the immense spiritual healthiness of that good man Charles Haddon Spurgeon:

> For my part I should loathe to be the pastor of a people who have nothing to say, or who, if they do say anything, might as well be quiet, for the pastor is Lord Paramount, and they are mere laymen and nobodies. I would sooner be the leader of six free men, whose enthusiastic love is my only power over them, than play the director to a score of enslaved nations.
>
> What position is nobler than that of a spiritual father who claims no authority and yet is universally esteemed, whose word is given only as tender advice, but is allowed to operate with the force of law? Consulting the wishes of others he finds that they are glad to defer to him. Lovingly firm and graciously gentle, he is the chief of all because he is the servant of all. Does not this need wisdom from above? What can require it more? David when established on the throne said, "[It is the Lord] who subdueth my people under me," and so may every happy pastor say when he sees so many brethren of differing temperaments all happily willing to be under discipline, and to accept his leadership in the work of the Lord. . . . Brethren, our system will not work without the Spirit of God, and I am glad it will not, for its stoppages and

breakages call our attention to the fact of His absence. Our system was never intended to promote the glory of priests and pastors, but it is calculated to educate manly Christians, who will not take their faith at second-hand.[17]

What, then, are we to say? Without doubt, having everyone personally confer with God does risk disagreements and uncooperativeness. If the spirit of the prophets is subject to the prophets, individual prophets may from time to time find themselves earnestly questioned and examined—perhaps overturned—by those they are appointed to lead. These leaders will then require a real security before other human beings, as well as a genuine authority from the Lord, to succeed in leading; they will also need a true humility—everyone thinking others better than themselves (Phil 2:3)—for them to carry on with their work.

Leading as Jesus led. How, though, could we ever have thought that anything other than this was required of a minister of the kingdom of God? For my part, I can only say this is exactly what we want to see in our leaders of the church of the Lord Jesus Christ. It is exactly the spirit in which *he* led. The spirit and the manner of the Chief Shepherd should be the one adopted by the undershepherds. We can minister Christ only as we teach what he taught in the manner in which he taught it.

If the leaders have this spirit of Christ, the individuals of the fellowship will have a correct and formative model of how they should respond to and bear their communications with God. Of course there *is* a subordination within the fellowship of believers, but it is not one that comes from a clever or crude struggle for ascendancy. Rather, it stems solely from authority given by experience in the Way and by the speaking of what is truly God's word. If we count on Christ (whose church it is) to bring about the *right* kind of subordination, we shall see the true unity and power of the glorious body of Christ, the living temple inhabited by God.

Fully realized, this unity is the light of the world, the end and aim of all human history.

Keeping a balance. We must never forget, however, that the social and outward dimension of the church is not the whole—nor ultimately even the basic dimension—of redemption. The social dimension, in all its glory, is derived only from the *individual's communion* with God.

The advice of St. Francis de Sales to his student Philothea gives a proper practical balance between the individual and social dimensions of our life in Christ. Describing as "inspirations" all of "those interior attractions, motions, reproaches and remorses, lights and conceptions which God excites in us," he directs her as follows:

> Resolve, then, Philothea, to accept with a ready heart all the inspirations it shall please God to send to you. When they come, receive them as ambassadors sent by the King of Heaven, who desires to enter into a marriage contract with you. Attend calmly to His proposals, think of the love with which you are inspired, and cherish the holy inspiration. Consent to the holy inspiration with an entire, a loving and a permanent consent.[18]

Then St. Francis wisely directs his friend back into the fellowship of the church, saying, "but before you consent to inspiration in things which are of great importance, or that are out of the ordinary way, always consult your advisor."[19]

Joyce Huggett passes on similar advice, which she received from her friend Jean Darnall: "If you believe God has told you to do something, ask him to confirm it to you three times: through his word, through circumstances, and through other people who may know nothing of the situation."[20] This precept of three witnesses is not a law, but it is a good rule of thumb in an area where rules of thumb are badly needed.

No man or woman is an island, though we always remain much more than the sum of our relationships to others—even in the Christian community. Our relationships to others, essential and helpful as they may be, must rest finally on our personal relationship to God himself. When *both* relationships are right, we find perfect safety, and

> this full and perfect peace!
> Oh, this transport all divine!
> In a love that cannot cease,
> I am His and He is mine.[21]

Some Topics for Reflection

1. Do you agree with what has been said about the limited ability of stories and signs to increase our faith, whether in guidance or elsewhere? If so, why do you think this is true? If not, why?

2. Do you have any problems with the following statement?

   We *mistakenly* try to think of God's dignity in terms of what we see in the experience of the "great ones" among human beings [perhaps a certain exclusiveness, insularity or snobbishness]. But God's dignity and greatness are seen precisely in his lowliness and accessibility to all.

   How do you respond to this idea of the lowliness of God?

3. What is it about persons that makes them attuned to God or to be ready vessels to act on what they hear from God?

4. Do you personally think that science makes the idea of hearing God questionable? Can you trace out your thinking on this matter in detail? Or can you articulate the thinking of someone you know well on this matter?

5. What are the main characteristics of a cultic style of leadership? Have you noticed any cultic behavior in the religious groups you are associated with or informed about? What would it cost

organized religious groups to give up such behavior?

6. How do you think you should relate your private experiences of God's speaking to your present fellowship and its leaders?

5

The Still, Small Voice and Its Rivals

Then Eli perceived that the LORD was calling the boy.
Therefore Eli said to Samuel, "Go, lie down; and if he calls you,
you shall say, 'Speak, LORD, for your servant is listening.'"

1 Samuel 3:8-9

And, behold, the LORD passed by, and a great and strong wind
rent the mountains, and brake in pieces the rocks before the LORD;
but the LORD was not in the wind: and after the wind an earthquake;
but the LORD was not in the earthquake: and after the earthquake a fire;
but the LORD was not in the fire: and after the fire a still small voice.

1 Kings 19:11-13 KJV

◆◆◆

*O*ne aspect of hearing God is receiving his guidance. As previous chapters have established, guidance is a process where some person, thing or sequence of events is brought to follow a definite course.

In the most inclusive sense the train is guided by the rails upon which it runs, the driver guides the car, the writer guides the pen or keyboard, the radar guides the airplane, the stars guide the ship, the teacher guides the class, and the parent guides the child. God could, certainly, *determine* the course of our lives by manipulating our thoughts and feelings or by arranging external circumstances—what is often called the "closing" and "opening" of doors in the "sovereign will" of God. But he can and does also guide us by *addressing* us. Humanity's actual experience of God, profusely documented in history, shows this.

God addresses us in various ways: in dreams, visions and voices; through the Bible and extraordinary events; and so forth. Once again, this is obvious in humanity's experience of God in general. It is also clearly marked out within the biblical accounts. But those who seek to live a life within God's will can be confused about the *significance* of the various ways God speaks with us.

Each way God communicates with us has its own special uses, but all the ways are not equally significant for our life with him. In terms of overall importance, the written Word and Jesus, the living Word, aren't to be compared to a voice or vision used by God to speak to an individual. And from among the individual's experiences of hearing God, the "still, small voice" has a vastly greater role than anything else.

What is this still, small voice? The phrase is taken from the story of Elijah quoted at the beginning of this chapter (see also the *lectio divina* exercise on pp. 48-50 in chapter two). The translation might just as well read "a gentle whisper of a voice" or "a gentle whispering." Each expression places the emphasis on the *unobtrusiveness* of the medium through which the message came. They are all seemingly unremarkable, inconspicuous, unassuming and perhaps not immediately noticed.

In the still, small voice of God we are given a message that bears the stamp of his personality quite clearly and in a way we will learn to recognize. But, in contrast with other cases, the *medium* through which the message comes is diminished almost to the vanishing point, taking the form of thoughts that are our thoughts, though these thoughts are not *from* us. In this way, as we shall see, the human spirit becomes the "candle of the LORD" (Prov 20:27 KJV).

Unfortunately, this gentle low-key word may easily be overlooked or disregarded, and it has even been discounted or despised by some who think that only the more explosive communications can be authentic. For those who follow this view, a life of hearing God must become a life filled with constant fireworks from heaven. But that does not square with the actual course of daily life. This has, in turn, led many to attack dramatic visions and the like as illusions or even as automatically satanic. A cloud of confusion and mistrust spreads over the whole issue of hearing God's voice. We can dispel that cloud if we examine and understand the many forms of God's speaking in relation to each other.

A Personal Appearance of Jesus?

A letter sent out by the *Guideposts* magazine staff tells of an ordinary suburban woman who one day, for reasons unknown to her, began to weep and continued weeping for four days.

> On the morning of the fourth day, alone in her living room, there was a sudden hum and crackle in the air. She saw a ball of white light through a window, spraying showers of multicolored light in its wake and approaching her with amazing speed. Then it was right there, beside her, and as she looked at it she saw a face.
>
> *He is perfect*, was her first thought. His forehead was high. His eyes were large, but she could not fix their color any more than she could the color of the sea. His features were lost in the overwhelming impression of life brimming over with power and freedom.
>
> Instantly she knew this was Jesus. She saw his utter lack of condemnation, that nothing she had ever done or would

ever do could alter the absolute caring or the unconditional love in his eyes.[1]

According to her account, Jesus was present with her in this way for three months, and then his presence began to fade. When this woman, Virginia Lively, last saw him, he said to her, "I will always be with you." She, like Thaddaeus (Jn 14:22), asked Jesus *how* she would know it, if she could no longer see him. He replied, "You will see me," and then he was gone. Some years later, while speaking to a church group, she found his eyes looking into hers again—but the eyes belonged to a woman in the second row. "And suddenly she saw his eyes looking at her from the eyes of every person in the room."[2]

Certain reactions to stories such as Ms. Lively's are common. Some people immediately conclude that the whole thing is of the devil, because "even Satan disguises himself as an angel of light" (2 Cor 11:14), and we cannot simply dismiss their concern. In fact, such experiences are always dangerous for various reasons. But we must also not overlook the fact that light serves as Satan's disguise because God really *is* light (1 Jn 1:5), because we are children of light (Eph 5:8) and saints in light (Col 1:12) and because God "maketh . . . his ministers a flaming fire" (Ps 104:4 KJV). But it would be strange if we came to shun the genuine simply because it resembled the counterfeit.

Some will suppose that Ms. Lively hallucinated or perhaps suffered an emotional collapse due to some stress she could not cope with or even face. Others may simply be at a loss to explain what happened, yet they remain unconvinced by her claim that Jesus Christ himself came to her.

At the other end of the spectrum are those who will consider her to be especially favored by God, placed above all those who haven't had such an experience. They may go so far as to confuse the medium with the message and will worship the experience rather than the One who, supposedly, was present through it. These people often feel spiritually inferior until something similar happens to them.

This insecurity is one of the dangers of religious groups that insist their members must reproduce the experiences of their leaders. In this situation, members will be tempted to try to *make* the great event happen, in whatever specific form it must take, and may even deceive themselves or pressure others into faking it. They may judge those without the required experience to be incapable of any significant spiritual ministry or service to God or even incapable of being received into heaven when they die.

Unusual experiences, like the one described by Ms. Lively, clearly pose problems for our understanding of guidance and for our understanding of the spiritual life in general.

The Primacy of the Inner Voice

Far be it from me to deny that such spectacular experiences occur or that they are, sometimes, at least, given by God. But a major point of this book is that the still, small voice—or the interior or inner voice, as it is also called—is the preferred and most valuable form of individual communication for God's purposes. God usually addresses individually those who walk with him in a mature, personal relationship using this inner voice, showing forth the reality of the kingdom of God as they go. We must therefore compare and contrast it to the other, more dramatic ways in which God encounters human beings.

It is important to bear in mind that you may not be very aware of hearing the voice; it need not force itself to the front of your thoughts. And one need have no theory or doctrine *about* this voice in order to hear it. When the voice came to little Samuel (1 Sam 3), he didn't know what it was or even that there was such a thing. So when you hear God's voice, you do not automatically know it is God's voice. Indeed, I believe it is possible for someone who regularly interacts with the voice of God not even to recognize it as something special. The Scripture teaches that the *less dramatic the message*, the *fuller the content* and the *more advanced the person who is receiving the message*. If you study the lives of Moses and Abraham, you will see that this is true.

In contrast to those who have some of the more spectacular experiences, those most adept at the divine-human conversation are often reluctant to speak much about the inner voice. And that is completely as it should be. God's communication with the individual is not for show-and-tell any more than intimate interchanges between two people generally are.

If, however, we are seeking to understand how God's speaking works, a discussion of the voice is indispensable. We need to consider the various ways God addresses men and women. For only then can we hope to gain a better understanding of the nature and function of the way that is most common and most suited to communion between God and humankind: his still, small voice. To begin with, I would like to take a look at a brief catalog of encounters with God, taken chiefly from the Bible. Most of these are like those reported in extrabiblical and even non-Christian sources, but the biblical accounts should be regarded as normative.

Reaffirming Our Participation in Biblical Experience

First, however, it is worth reminding ourselves to read the biblical accounts as if what is described is happening to *us*. We must make the conscious effort to think that such things *might* happen to us and to imagine what it would be like if they were to happen.

This will be difficult at first, for most people have become accustomed to thinking that God does such marvelous things only with *other* people. But remember what I wrote earlier (in chapter two) about how Elijah, Moses and Paul were people just like us, subject to like passions as we are. When misunderstood or mistreated, they felt as we would in the same situation. They experienced hunger, weariness, nervousness, confusion and fear just as we do. They doubted their abilities and self-worth just as we do. Just like us—witness Moses and Gideon—they often said, "Oh, no! Not *me*. I can't do it."

Generally speaking, God will not compete for our attention. Occasionally a Saul gets knocked to the ground and so on, but we should expect that in most cases God will *not* run over us. We must be open to the possibility of God's addressing us in whatever way he chooses, or else we may walk right past a burning bush instead of saying, as Moses did, "I must turn aside and look at this great sight, and see why the bush is not burned up" (Ex 3:3). I say in all seriousness that we may mistake the voice of God for the sound of someone's radio turned up too loudly, for some accidental noise or—more likely still—for just another one of our own thoughts.

> *God will not compete for our attention. In most cases God will* not *run over us.*

The reality of God's voice does not make seeking for it unnecessary. When I seek for something, I look for it everywhere. It's when we *seek* God earnestly, prepared to go out of our way to examine anything that might be his overture toward us—including obvious things like Bible verses or our own thoughts—that he promises to be found (Jer 29:13). But we'll be able to seek him only if we honestly believe that he might explicitly address us in ways suitable to his purposes in our lives.

Biblical Stories of People Who Hear God

Remembering that we need to use our imagination to identify with biblical experiences, we turn now to six ways God addresses people within the biblical record:

- a phenomenon plus a voice

- a supernatural messenger or an angel
- dreams and visions
- an audible voice
- the human voice
- the human spirit or the "still, small voice"

A phenomenon plus a voice. This first category of divine-human encounter is richly represented in the events of Scripture. God's covenant with Abraham, a major foundation of the Judeo-Christian tradition, was solemnized on just such an occasion. Fire from God passing through the air consumed the sacrifice Abraham had prepared, while God intoned the promise to Abraham and his seed (Gen 15:17-18).

Moses received his call to deliver Israel from Egypt by the hand of God while he stood before the bush that was burning yet unburned, and from which God spoke (Ex 3:3-6). The nation of Israel as a whole was called to covenant by God's voice from within a mountain on fire, pulsating with the energy of his presence (Deut 5:23). Ezekiel was addressed in the context of a meteorological display that defies all but poetic description (Ezek 1–2).

At Jesus' baptism the heavens appeared to open up, and the Spirit visibly descended upon him in conjunction with a voice from heaven that said, "This is my Son, the Beloved, with whom I am well pleased" (Mt 3:17). Saul's encounter with Christ on the road to Damascus involved a blinding light from heaven and an audible voice heard not only by Saul but also by those with him (Acts 9:3-8).

A supernatural messenger or an angel. In his book on angels Mortimer J. Adler, a distinguished philosopher and a historian of ideas, describes the opposition he received from his scholarly colleagues when he wished to include *angels* among the great ideas of Western humanity in a major publication.[3] There is no doubt that angels deserve the place in Western civilization assigned to them by Adler because of the attention they have received not only in religion but also in art, literature and philosophy. And it is certainly appropriate to describe the Bible itself as a book full of angels, from Genesis 16:7 onward.

Strictly speaking, the word *angel* means "emissary" or "messenger," but it is normally understood that such messengers, while they are persons, are not mere human beings. They are supernatural beings on a divine mission. God addresses humans through them, though they do not always reveal their identity.

Sometimes in the biblical record it is difficult to determine whether an angel or the Lord himself is on the scene. In Genesis 18, for example, we have an account of three men appearing at the door of Abraham's tent. In the middle of this chapter the text casually shifts from "they" and "the men" to "the Lord." This is then followed by the well-known dialogue between Abraham and the Lord concerning the fate of Sodom.

Strangely, at the opening of Genesis 19 only two angels appear to Lot in Sodom to finish off the episode. (The three men of Genesis 18 were apparently two angels accompanied by the Lord.) Hebrews 13:2 is taken by some as referring back to this story in Genesis when it exhorts, "Do not neglect to show hospitality to strangers, for by doing that some have entertained angels without knowing it."

In front of the city of Jericho, Joshua encounters "a man standing before him with a drawn sword in his hand," who has come to help as "commander of the army of the Lord" (Josh 5:13-15). He directs Joshua to take off his shoes because the ground he stands on is holy. The "army of the Lord" here consists mainly of angels, no doubt the same as the legions that became visible in 2 Kings 6:17, as was discussed in chapter four, and that later stood at the beck and call of our incarnate Lord (Mt 26:53). ("Lord of hosts" becomes a primary name for God as redemptive history progresses through the Old Testament; see, for example, Ps 24:10; 46:7; 59:5.) A few verses later, at Joshua 6:2, the commander now seems to be the Lord himself, explaining that famous and unorthodox military strategy whereby the walls of Jericho were to be brought down.

Human beings are so commonly addressed by angels in Scripture that I shall list only a few more of the outstanding cases: Balaam (Num 22:22-35), Gideon (Judg 6:11-24), the parents of Samson (Judg 13), Isaiah (Is 6:6-13), Daniel (Dan 9:20-27), Joseph (Mt 1:20-25), Zacharias (Lk 1:11-20), Mary (Lk 1:26-38), the women at the empty tomb (Mt 28:2-7), Peter (Acts 5:19-20) and Paul (Acts 27:23-26).

We should take note that these people encounter angels in an otherwise normal state of mind, as distinct from encountering them in dreams and visions, although the content of the conversations recorded sometimes suggests (as with Gideon, Samson's parents and Zacharias, for example) that the people involved felt things were more than a little strange.

Dreams and visions. These two categories of divine communication—dreams and visions—can be treated together here, since our purposes do not require scholarly depth and precision. Sometimes the two seem to coincide, perhaps because they often come at night and the recipients may have been uncertain whether they were awake or asleep. So it was with Paul: "During the night Paul had a vision: there stood a man of Macedonia pleading with him and saying, 'Come over to Macedonia and help us'" (Acts 16:9; see also Acts 18:9; 2 Cor 12:1). Both visions and dreams involve some degree of a trancelike condition, a certain detachment from the person's actual surroundings, which marks them off from ordinary waking consciousness.

On the other hand, some visions are clearly not dreams, as with Ananias, to whom the Lord spoke in a vision (Acts 9:10-13), and Peter in his rooftop trance, which is also specifically called a vision (Acts 10:9-19). Many dreams are not visions, as was the case with Jacob (Gen 28:11-17), Joseph (Gen 37:5-9), Joseph's jail mates (Gen 40:5-19), Pharaoh (Gen 41:1-7) and Nebuchadnezzar (Dan 4:4-18).

Gustave Oehler points out that the difference between a dream and a vision is not sharply marked out in the Bible.[4] But he does concede that the dream is regarded as a lower form of communication from God than a vision. Both are unusual states of consciousness, but the dream characteristically requires greater interpretation, often with considerable difficulty, in a manner that the vision does not. (Consider Joseph and Daniel's special wisdom in interpreting dreams.)

By the time of Jeremiah the understanding of the ways in which God speaks had progressed to the point where the dreaming prophet was treated with some disdain. The dream is like straw or chaff when compared to the wheat of God's *word* (Jer 23:25-32). His word is like fire, like a hammer that crushes the rock. The dream has no comparable power.

Oehler sees emerging here "the principle that a clear consciousness when receiving revelation is placed higher than ecstasy or other abnormal states of mind."[5] This is a vital point to keep in mind as we attempt to understand our *own* experiences of God's communications and the significance of the different ways in which he meets us today.

An audible voice. It is clear that on some occasions God has addressed human beings through what was experienced as an audible voice alone.[6] Something like this, though involving an angel from heaven, seems to have occurred with Abraham on Mount Moriah, as he was about to sacrifice his son Isaac (Gen 22:11-12, 15-18).

A most touching, informative and profound story is that of the child Samuel as he learns to recognize God's voice, which he clearly experienced as an audible voice (1 Sam 3). As this young boy lay on his pallet in the temple one night, he heard someone calling his name. He rose and ran to his old master, Eli, thinking that it was he who had called. This was during a period in Israel's history when God rarely spoke and gave no visions. Such things as voices and visions weren't commonly discussed at that time.

Hence, "Samuel did not yet know the LORD, and the word of the LORD had not yet been revealed to him" (1 Sam 3:7).

The third time Samuel came to Eli, saying, "Here I am, for you called me," Eli finally recognized what was happening. He told Samuel to go back and lie down, and he said, "If he calls you, you shall say, 'Speak, LORD, for your servant is listening' " (1 Sam 3:9-10). And so it happened. With this incident there began one of the most remarkable careers of any person who has ever lived before the Lord, fully justifying the use of the phrase "conversational relationship."

That brings us to the two most important ways in which God speaks to us: (1) in conjunction with the language of human beings, and (2) through the inner voice of our own thoughts. These two ways are the most suited to God's presence in our lives as a close personal friend, a presence shared by the whole Christian community. They are also most appropriate in working out the development of our individual personalities into his likeness.

The human voice. We have seen that an audible voice coming from no visible speaker was present with the boy Samuel, at the baptism of Jesus and on the road to Damascus. But no means of communication between God and us is more commonly used in the Bible or the history of the church than the voice of a definite, individual human being. In such cases God and the person he uses speak *conjointly*—God's speaking *along with* human beings. It may be that the one spoken *to* is also the one spoken *through*. It is frequently so with me. In this case the word is at once the word of God, God's message, and the word of the human being who is also speaking.

The two do not exclude each other any more than humanity and divinity exclude each other in the person of Jesus Christ. We can say that God speaks through us, as long as this is not understood as automatically ruling out *our* speaking *with* God and even, in an important sense, *through* God. The relationship must *not* be understood as an essentially mechanical one, with God simply using us as we might use a telephone. No doubt that would be

God's option should he choose, but usually he does not.

Samuel Shoemaker has written this excellent description of our experience of God in this respect.

> Something comes into our own energies and capacities and expands them. We are laid hold of by Something greater than ourselves. We can face things, create things, accomplish things, that in our own strength would have been impossible. . . . The Holy Spirit seems to mix and mingle His power with our own, so that what happens is both a heightening of our own powers, and a gift to us from outside. This is as real and definite as attaching an appliance to an electrical outlet, though of course such a mechanical analogy is not altogether satisfactory.[7]

I believe I can say with assurance that God's speaking in union with the human voice and human language is the primary *objective* way in which God addresses us. That is, of all the ways in which a message comes from *outside* the mind or personality of the person addressed, it most commonly comes through a human being.

> *God's speaking in union with the human voice and human language is the primary objective way in which God addresses us.*

This is best suited to God's purposes precisely because it *most fully engages the faculties of free, intelligent beings who are socially interacting with agape love in the work of God as his colaborers and friends.* This is obvious from the contents of the Bible. And of course the Bible is itself a case of God's speaking along with human beings—usually so in the process of its delivery to humankind and as it continues to speak to us today.

When God speaks in union with human beings, he often seems to purposely choose weaker vessels. In Moses' encounter with God through the burning bush, Moses' last line of protest against the assignment that God was giving him was that he didn't speak well: "O my Lord, I have never been eloquent, neither in the past nor even now that you have spoken to your servant; but I am slow of speech and slow of tongue" (Ex 4:10). The Lord's reply was that he, after all, had made human mouths and presumably could assist them to accomplish his assignments: "Now go, and I will be with your mouth and teach you what you are to speak" (Ex 4:12).

When Moses still begged God to send someone else, God angrily gave him Aaron as *his* spokesman:

> You shall speak to him and put the words in his mouth; and I will be with your mouth and with his mouth, and will teach you what you shall do. He indeed shall speak for you to the people; he shall serve as a mouth for you, and you shall serve as God for him. Take in your hand this staff, with which you shall perform the signs. (Ex 4:15-17)

Some New Testament passages suggest that the apostle Paul was not an eloquent man either. We know from his own statements that, whether by choice or necessity, he did not come among the Corinthians "proclaiming . . . in lofty words or wisdom"; rather he came "in weakness and in fear and in much trembling. My speech and my proclamation were not with plausible words of wisdom, but with a demonstration of the Spirit and of power, so that your faith might rest not on human wisdom but on the power of God" (1 Cor 2:1-5). Paul's only confidence was in God speaking *with* him, electrifying his words, as it were, when he spoke.

It is significant, I believe, that those the Lord chose to bear his message and carry on his work were for the most part "uneducated and ordinary" people (Acts 4:13). The pattern seems to prove amply that in God's selecting them there would be no mistake as to the source of their words and authority. God would use ordinary human beings and would dignify them by their association with him. But just as this is wholly suitable to his redemptive purposes, so it is wholly appropriate that everyone (especially the individuals involved) should be clear about the source of the power manifested.

There must be no misallocation of glory, not because God is a cosmic egotist but because that would destroy the order that's in the blessedness of life in Christ. It would direct us away from God. Hence Paul writes, "Let the one who boasts, boast in the Lord" (1 Cor 1:31). The success of the redemptive plan therefore requires that "not many of you were wise by human standards, not many were powerful, not many were of noble birth" (1 Cor 1:26). Moses and Paul, two of the people most responsible for the human authorship of the Bible, were, accordingly, weak with words so that they might have the best chance of clinging constantly to their support in God, who spoke in union with them, and so that they might unerringly connect their hearers with God.

Does the word of God then literally overpower us? In some parts of the Bible record, those who speak with God seem compelled by force, as we see in the case of Balaam. Balak, king of Moab, offered Balaam great riches and honor if he would curse Israel. He knew that Balaam spoke in unison with God— "whomever you bless is blessed, and whomever you curse is cursed" (Num 22:6). Balaam was obviously greatly tempted by the offer. Even after God told him not to go to Balak and not to curse Israel because Israel was indeed blessed (Num 22:12), Balaam kept toying with the idea. Eventually he thought that he had God's permission at least to go to Balak (Num 22:20). But even while he was in Balak's camp he was simply *unable* to curse Israel. He explained to Balak that he did not have any power at all to say anything: "The word God puts into my mouth, that is what I must say" (Num 22:38). When the moment came for him to curse Israel, after elaborate preparations, only a stream of blessings came forth (Num 23:7-10), to the exasperation of Balak.

It would be a great mistake, however, to take these and similar cases to mean that the person who speaks with God, and thus speaks the word *of* God, literally cannot help speaking. Perhaps this is true in some cases. It is certainly true that people cannot force *God* to speak with *them*. But the compulsion on the individual to speak, though often great, is normally still resistible. Human beings are not mere tools.

Yet people who understand what it is to speak for and with God have entered into the following experience of Jeremiah innumerable times. Speaking God's word had made him a laughingstock among those who knew him, so he resolved to speak no more for the Lord but could not keep that resolution:

> If I say, "I will not mention him,
>   or speak any more in his name,"
> then within me there is something like a burning fire
>   shut up in my bones;
> I am weary with holding it in,
>   and I cannot. (Jer 20:9)

The prophets often treat the word of the Lord as a *burden*. Later, in his sermon against the false prophets, Jeremiah cries,

> My heart is crushed within me,
>   all my bones shake;
> I have become like a drunkard,
>   like one overcome by wine,
> because of the LORD
>   and because of his holy words. (Jer 23:9)

The prophet may also exult in the power he feels surging within him, as Micah did:

> But as for me, I am filled with power,
>   with the spirit of the LORD,
>   and with justice and might,
> to declare to Jacob his transgression
>   and to Israel his sin. (Mic 3:8)

Jeremiah also experienced God's word to be of great power, like a fire that scorches and like a hammer that breaks rocks. J. B. Phillips said somewhere that, while he was doing his well-known translation of the New Testament, he often felt like an electrician working on the wiring of a house with the power on.

Later in this book we will explore in detail the idea of the word of God as a substantial power in the cosmos and in human affairs: an agency that could come "to John . . . in the wilderness" (Lk 3:2), have dominion over unclean spirits (Lk 4:33-36), be like the finger of God (Lk 11:20), be spirit and life (Jn 6:63, 68), increase (Acts 6:7), grow and multiply (Acts 12:24), not be bound in prison (2 Tim 2:9), function as the sword of the Spirit (Eph 6:17)—being more dexterous and powerful than any mere two-edged human sword, since it has a life of its own and is so acute that it can dissect thoughts and intentions (Heb 4:12)—and simultaneously hold all of creation together (Col 1:17). This complex picture of the word of God must be examined closely before we conclude our study. For the time being, however, we rest with the fact that that word can and does come to us through the living personalities, minds and bodies of other human beings as they speak to us in unison with God.

The human spirit or the "still, small voice." The final means through which God addresses us is our own spirits—our own thoughts and feelings toward ourselves as well as toward events and people around us. This, I believe, is the primary *subjective* way that God addresses us. Of all the ways in which a message comes from *within* the experience of the person addressed (such as dreams and visions or other mental states), the form of one's own thoughts and attendant feelings is the most common path for hearing God for those who are living in harmony with God. Of all the possible subjective routes, this mode is best suited to the redemptive purposes of God because, once again, *it most engages the faculties of free, intelligent beings involved in the work of God as his colaborers and friends.*

Thus the familiar King James Version of Proverbs 20:27 says, "The spirit of man is the candle of the LORD, searching all the inward parts of the belly." This is possibly better put in the Jerusalem Bible: "Man's spirit is the lamp of Yahweh, searching his deepest self."

In a passage of great importance to our exploration here, the apostle Paul makes a comparison between humans and God regarding self-knowledge: "For what human being knows what is truly human except the human spirit that is within? So also no one comprehends what is truly God's except the Spirit of God" (1 Cor 2:11). Paul then points out that we have received the Spirit of God and concludes that we can therefore search out and know the very mind of God by means of his Spirit—in contrast to the proverb quoted earlier, which emphasizes *the Lord's* use of *our* spirit. After quoting the question from Isaiah 40:13, "Who has directed the spirit of the LORD, or as his counselor has instructed him?" the apostle replies, "But we have the mind of Christ" (1 Cor 2:16).

So God uses our self-knowledge or self-awareness, which is heightened and given a special quality by his presence and direction, to search us out and reveal to us the truth about ourselves and our world. And we are able to use his knowledge of himself—made available to us in Christ and the Scriptures—to understand in some measure *his* thoughts and intentions toward us and to help us see his workings in our world.

◇◇

Hearing God in Scripture
Proverbs 20:27; 1 Corinthians 2:9-13, 15-16

Before doing this *lectio divina* exercise, take a minute to review what was written about this passage in the three previous paragraphs.

You may also recall from chapter three that a great part of having the mind of Christ is about working together with God in shared activity. Colaborers easily share thoughts with little effort because they're focused on the same people, tasks and goals. These ideas about how the still, small voice works will help you settle into the Scripture passage in a simple, informed way.

To prepare to read in order to receive from God, please set the book or electronic reader down for a minute. Close your eyes and breathe out slowly. Ask God to give you an openness to hear whatever the Spirit wishes to bring to you today.

Read—*lectio*
Read the passage slowly.

Man's spirit is the lamp of Yahweh [candle of the LORD], searching his deepest self. (Prov 20:27 JB)

"What no eye has seen, nor ear heard,
*   nor the human heart conceived,*
what God has prepared for those who love him"—

these things God has revealed to us through the Spirit; for the Spirit searches everything, even the depths of God. For what human being knows what is truly human except the human spirit that is within? So also no one comprehends what is truly God's except the Spirit of God. Now we have received not the spirit of the world, but the Spirit that is from God, so that we may understand the gifts bestowed on us by God. And we speak of these things in words not taught by human wisdom but taught by the Spirit, interpreting spiritual things to those who are spiritual.

Those who are spiritual discern all things, and they are themselves subject to no one else's scrutiny.

For who has known the mind of the Lord
*   so as to instruct him?*

But we have the mind of Christ! (1 Cor 2:9-13, 15-16)

Now that the words are familiar to you, please read them again. This time, also listen with the ear of your heart for a

9

word or phrase that shimmers or stands out to you. Do not choose this yourself. Let the Spirit bring it to you. Welcome it with meekness and see what happens (Jas 1:21).

Reflect—*meditatio*

Read the passage again slowly. As you do so, and for a few minutes afterward, reflect on the word or phrase that stood out to you. Why do you think these words resonated with you? Give yourself a few minutes to do this.

Then ask God, How does this connect with my life today? What do I need to know or be or do?

Respond (Pray)—*oratio*

Read the passage one last time, preparing yourself for what you want to say to God about what you think the Spirit might have said to you or what came to you.

Pray in whatever way you are led. You might thank God for something or ask God for something.

Rest (Contemplation)—*contemplatio*

Do as you are led. You may wish to wait on God—to simply *be with* God. You may wish to ponder, How did God *seem* in the passage? Close or distant? Caring or detached? What about God makes you marvel, or at least want to *be with* him? Sit in the companionship of God—the one who seeks you and is glad to do that.

Growing in Oneness of Mind

In the union and communion of the believer with God, their two beings are unified and inhabit each other, just as Jesus prayed: "I ask . . . that they may all be one. As you, Father, are in me and I am in you, may they also be in us, so that the world may believe that you sent me" (Jn 17:20-21). As we grow in grace, God's laws increasingly form the foundation of our hearts; his love is our love, his faith our faith. Our very awareness of our actions, intentions and surroundings then bears within it the view that God takes, bringing things into the clarity of *his* vision just as a candle might illuminate what is on our dinner table.

The spirit of the individual truly is, therefore, the "candle of the LORD," in the light of which we see ourselves and our world as God sees. In this way we are addressed by him, spoken to by him, through *our own thoughts*. This is something you can and should test by experiment. Those who begin to pray that God will enlighten them as to the nature and meaning of the processes that go on in their own soul will begin to understand. They will begin to see their spirit functioning as the candle of the Lord.

The soul's self-awareness applies to every part of the self: it touches upon one's family, possessions, profession and health; it reaches to one's fear of death, attitudes toward God, sexuality, preoccupation with reputation, concern with appearance and countless other areas of one's life. Our spirit, as a candle in the Lord's hands, may shed light on many other things apart from our own internal condition, although the primary point of the passage from Proverbs is the illumination of the inner life. Russ Johnston points out the importance of *recurrent thoughts* in God's communication with his children:

> We would see wonderful results if we would just deal with the thoughts that continue in our minds in a godly manner. But most people don't. . . . As thoughts come into your mind and continue, ask God, "Do you really want me (or us) to do this?" Most of us just let those thoughts collapse—and God looks for someone else to stand in the gap.[8]

But aren't all our thoughts inherently bad? This well-intended but mistaken teaching about our thoughts has harmed our understanding of hearing God's voice.

The great Puritan minister Thomas Goodwin wrote a powerful discourse titled *The Vanity of Thoughts*, taking as his text Jeremiah 4:14 (KJV): "How long shall thy vain thoughts lodge within thee?" Goodwin is careful and helpful in the way he describes these "vain" thoughts, but he leaves an impression, which is widely shared and emphasized, that if a thought is *our* thought, it could not possibly be trusted.[9] Doesn't God say in Isaiah 55:8, "My thoughts are not your thoughts"? And doesn't Jeremiah tell us that our hearts are desperately wicked, beyond our powers of comprehension (Jer 17:9)?

Of course there is an important point in all of this that stresses the difference between God's view of things and the view of the normal person apart from God. But this point must not obscure the simple fact that God comes to us precisely in and through our thoughts, perceptions and experiences, and that he can approach our conscious life *only* through them, for they are the substance of our lives. We are, therefore, to be transformed by the *renewing of our minds* (Rom 12:2). God's gracious incursions into our souls can make our thoughts his thoughts. He will help us learn to distinguish when a thought is ours alone and when it is also his.

Chapter eight will deal at length with the question of how we can know which thoughts are from God. But for now, just keep this practical advice in mind: when thoughts recur, always stop prayerfully to consider whether this may be an appearance of the Lord's "candle" or whether the thoughts may have some other significance. Although reoccurring thoughts are not *always* an indication that God is speaking, they are not to be lightly disregarded.

So the thoughts and feelings in the mind and spirit of one who is surrendered to God should be treated as if God were walking through one's personality with a candle, directing one's attention to things one after the other. As we become used to the idea that God is friendly and helpful, that he desires to straighten, inform and correct for our good as well as to comfort and encourage and that he really does love us, then we can begin to pray heartily with the psalmist, "Search me, O God, and know my heart; test me and know my thoughts" (Ps 139:23).

As we do this we are asking God, "Bring the light to bear upon my life, please," just as we might go to a dentist or doctor and say, "Examine me, please, and see if corrections to my physical condition are needed. Find out what is wrong and repair it." One's own spirit can then work together with the Almighty God, using one's thoughts and feelings to bring the truth of his word and his understanding to bear upon one's heart, life and world.

Having looked at the major ways in which God in the biblical record addressed the conscious mind and will in order to inform and guide, let us now give some thought to their meaning for our own quest to hear his voice.

God Speaks Today

Perhaps the first thing to say is that nothing in Scripture, in reason or in the very nature of things asserts *why any or all of these types of experience might not be used by God today.* No one should be alarmed or automatically thrown into doubt by such experiences coming to them or by reports that other people have experienced them. As always, we should simply follow Paul's admonition in 1 Thessalonians 5:19-22: "Do not quench the Spirit. Do not despise the words of prophets, but test everything; hold fast to what is good; abstain from every form of evil."

It is true that the existence and history of the church and the presence of the full written Scripture change the circumstances of and give new dimensions to the way in which God deals with human beings. But there is nothing *in* Scripture to indicate that the biblical modes of God's communication with humans have been superseded or abolished by either the presence of the church or the close of the scriptural canon.

This is simply a fact, just as it is simply a fact that God's children up to the present age have continued to find themselves addressed by God in most of the ways he commonly addressed biblical characters. The testimony of great Christians throughout the ages—those who are generally admitted to be honest, clear-minded and devout—should not be discarded in favor of a blank, dogmatic denial. Of course, at any time there may be some degree of fakery and confusion, well-intended or not. But such a blank denial has no scriptural foundation. Furthermore, it is often an attempt to substitute safety and deadness for living communications from God, or to look to the ponderous scholars or letter-learned scribes for their interpretation of God's word rather than hearing for ourselves the voice that is available to the plainest of people, or to resign ourselves to hear only what God has said in Scripture rather than to listen for the specific word he might have for us today.

The close of the scriptural canon marks the point in the (still ongoing) divine-human conversation where the principles and doctrines that form the substance of Christian faith and practice are so adequately stated in human language that nothing more needs to be said *in general*. Biblical Christians believe that nothing further will be said by God to extend or contradict those principles. But biblical Christians are not just people who hold certain beliefs *about* the Bible. They are also people who *lead the kind of life demonstrated* in the Bible: a life of personal, intelligent interaction with God. Anything less than this makes a mockery of the priesthood of the believer.

Surely one of the most damaging things we can do to people's spiritual prospects is to suggest that God will *not* deal with people specifically, personally, intelligibly and consciously. Or that they cannot *count on* him to do so, as he knows best. Once we have conveyed this idea to people, it makes no sense to attempt to lead them into a personal relationship with God.

Conversing with God

Rosalind Rinker relates how, after years of service on the mission field and many fruitless efforts at a satisfactory prayer life, she found herself rebellious and spiritually empty. Then, through a serious illness and other grave difficulties, "God began to take care of my rebellions through his great love. He began to teach me to listen to his voice."[10]

Almost by "chance," as she was praying with a friend for some of their students, she interrupted her friend's prayer with thanksgiving on a point that was being prayed for. After a moment of awkward silence and after they had sat back and laughed with great relief, they settled down again to prayer but now "with a sense of joy, of lightness, of the Lord's presence very near."

They then asked if the Lord was trying to teach them something about prayer. "Should we give Thee more opportunity as we are praying to get Thy ideas through to us? Would that give the Holy Spirit more opportunity to guide us as we pray?" Then Rinker stopped praying and said to her friend, "Do you know what? I believe the Lord taught us something just now! Instead of each of us making a prayer-speech to Him, let's talk things over with Him, including Him in it, as we do when we have a conversation."[11]

I recall very clearly the effect of her book *Prayer: Conversing with God* when it arrived on the scene in the United States. Group after group were brought to life as they learned to listen to God as well as "make prayer-speeches" at him. Their talk of "a life with God" now had real, objectively shareable content.

Silence Is Not an "Answer"

Nowhere is it more important to be in a conversational relationship with God than in our prayer life. Often God does not give us what we ask for, but I believe that he will always answer, always *respond* to us in some way. It is interesting that we commonly speak of answered prayer only when we are *given* what we request. When a request is denied, does this then mean that there has been no response?

Some people say that God's silence is an answer in these cases. But I think that if we know how to listen, God will normally *tell* us something when he does not give us our requests. We will hear it and grow through it if we have learned to recognize and acknowledge his voice.

> *If we know how to listen, God will normally tell us something when he does not give us our requests.*

This was certainly true in the case of Paul's famous "thorn in the flesh," which he begged the Lord to remove from him three times (2 Cor 12:7-8). God was not silent, even though he turned down Paul's request: "*But his answer was:* 'My grace is all you need; power is most fully seen in weakness'" (2 Cor 12:9 REB, italics added).

God is not impassive toward us, like an unresponsive pagan idol; he calls us to grow into a life of personal interchange with him that does justice to the idea of our being his children.

Do We Need Anything More Than the Bible?

Do we need anything more than the Bible? To many this is an inflammatory question, but it is one that must be posed. One of the arguments for disallowing any significant continuing use of voices, visions, dreams, prophetic people or individual thoughts as communications from God is that these, allegedly, are no longer "needed." "We have the Bible, and we have the church. Let *them* speak for God," runs the argument. A number of things should be said in response to this.

First of all, if by what is "needed" we mean what is minimally required to enable human beings to know God, this—according

to the Bible itself—is available independently of the Bible and the
church. Hence they too would not be "needed"—yet here they are.
For as Paul states in Romans 1:19-21:

> What can be known about God is plain to them, because
> God has shown it to them. Ever since the creation of the
> world his eternal power and divine nature, invisible though
> they are, have been understood and seen through the things
> he has made. So they are without excuse; for though they
> knew God, they did not honor him as God or give thanks
> to him.

However, if by what is "needed" we mean what is required for a
truly redemptive, personal *relationship* between God and the individual, then the existence of the Bible and the church is certainly
not enough. In addition to merely being there, they must at least
have an individualized function in the life of each person. And in
order for this to happen they—both the church and the Bible—
must become the means through which God personally and
uniquely addresses each individual.

Referring to the question, "Were not the miracles and gifts of
the Spirit only for the apostolic church?" Andrew Murray replied,

> Basing my views on scripture, I do not believe that miracles
> and the other gifts of the Spirit were limited to the time of
> the primitive Church, nor that their object was to establish
> the foundation of Christianity and then disappear by God's
> withdrawal of them. . . . The entire scriptures declare that
> these graces will be granted according to the measure of the
> Spirit and of faith.[12]

Murray further dismisses the idea that such a particularized
presence of the hand of God was necessary only in the early days
of Christianity: "Ah, no! What about the power of heathenism
today wherever the gospel seeks to combat it, even in our *modern*

society, and in the midst of the ignorance and unbelief which reigns even in the Christian nations."[13]

One of the most amazing conceits that creeps into the Western branches of the church from time to time is the following attitude: "We are so much better now than in more primitive times that it is enough to have a written Word of God without the kind of divine presence and interaction with humanity described in that written Word." How obviously mistaken this is now in postmodern times as biblical truth and ideas guide the course of human events less and less and as service to the old gods and goddesses of the pre-Christian world is explicitly reasserting itself in the highest levels of culture.

With such ideas of "progress" we shut ourselves off from God's resources for life and ministry in the present. C. H. Spurgeon is right on the mark with his comments on Psalm 103:2 (about not forgetting the Lord's benefits).

> Ought we not to look upon our own history as being at least as full of God, as full of His goodness and of His truth, as much a proof of His faithfulness and veracity, as the lives of any of the saints who have gone before? We do our Lord an injustice when we suppose that He wrought all His mighty acts, and showed Himself strong for those in the early time, but doth not perform wonders or lay bare His arm for the saints who are now upon the earth. Let us review our own lives. Surely in these we may discover some happy incidents, refreshing to ourselves and glorifying to our God. Have you had no deliverances? Have you passed through no rivers, supported by the divine presence? Have you walked through no fires unharmed? Have you had no manifestations? Have you had no choice favours? . . . Surely the goodness of God has been the same to us as to the saints of old.[14]

Bible Deism

Today something that could aptly be called "Bible deism" is prevalent, particularly in conservative religious circles. Classical deism, associated with the extreme rationalism of the sixteenth to eighteenth centuries, held that God created his world complete and perfect and then went away, leaving humanity to its own devices. God no longer offered individualized intervention in the lives of human beings, no miracles. Bible deism similarly holds that God gave us the Bible and then went away, leaving us to make what we could of it, with no individual communication either through the Bible or otherwise.

Bible deism is like the Sadducean doctrine current in the time of Jesus and Paul which taught that God stopped speaking when he finished speaking with Moses and that no alleged communications via angels or spirits could possibly be valid. Sadducees did not accept individual communications with God, and they rejected angels and disembodied spirits as well as the idea of a resurrection and an afterlife. Paul, who was himself a Pharisee and had actually dealt with angels and spirits, was able to divide his accusers on one occasion and defuse a dangerous situation by invoking the resurrection that the Pharisees, but not the Sadducees, accepted. The Pharisees sided with Paul to make a point that was important to them, saying, "We find nothing wrong with this man. What if a spirit or an angel has spoken to him?" (Acts 23:9).

Like the Sadducees, far too many believers, in their effort to honor the Bible, adopt an unbiblical teaching about God's relationship to his children.

Leaders: Turning People On, Not Off

Speaking pastorally, I believe one of the greatest harms church leaders can do to those in their care is to convince them that God isn't going to meet them personally or that he is meeting them only if *the leaders* approve of what's happening. If our gospel does not free the individual for a unique life of spiritual adventure in living with God daily, we simply have not entered fully into the good news that Jesus brought.

God does take care of his church, and all our efforts as leaders must be directed toward fostering each person's individual adventure with him. We can trust God and nothing else, not even the sterling soundness and sobriety of our own "faith and practice." If we trust anything else, we as leaders will cause those we care for to trust something else as well, and we may end up with very proper spiritual corpses filling our pews. We should shudder before these words of Jesus to the ministers of his day: "Woe to you, scribes and Pharisees, hypocrites! For you cross sea and land to make a single convert, and you make the new convert twice as much a child of hell as yourselves" (Mt 23:15).

There are dangers to encouraging people to hear from God. Of course there are. The adventure can get disastrously out of hand. We know that people do go off the deep end, and this problem must be addressed. Yet after gravely warning that death and disaster may also come from going off the *shallow* end, what must be done pastorally is to lead people into an understanding of the voice of God and how it works in their lives.

Most importantly, and right at the outset, they must be helped to see that recognizing God's voice is something they *must learn to do through their own personal experience and experimentation.* They must especially be encouraged to do so if they do not already expect God to speak to them. And we may even have to help identify the voice of God for them and instruct them in how to respond. Those who are older in the Way should be prepared to do this from their own experience.

How wonderful that Eli recognized what was happening to young Samuel and could tell him what to do to begin his lifelong conversational walk with God! Otherwise, it might have been years before Samuel would have found his way by himself. We must not mistakenly assume that if *God* speaks to someone, he or she automatically knows what is happening and who is talking. If Samuel did not know, surely many others also would not.

How wonderful that Abraham could assure his puzzled servant that God was guiding him back to the city of Nahor to find a wife for Isaac (Gen 24:1-7)! How wonderful that the servant could come to an utterly new understanding of God because he *did* experience guidance and was, indeed, guided into knowledge of guidance itself! If you turn to that great story now, you will enjoy reading and meditating on one person who certainly learned by experience to work with our God *who is available.*

The Priority of the Voice

Knowledge and experience of hearing God teach us many things that can keep us from harm and keep us from harming others in our spiritual adventure of life in God's kingdom. One of the most important things we can learn is *the superiority of the voice*— however the "voice" may come, even as the still, small voice within the silence of our own minds—over the other types of encounters. This superiority lies in two things: the clarity of its content and the advanced spiritual condition of those who can hear and receive it.

Earlier we looked at how Aaron and Miriam, brother and sister of Moses, criticized him because he had taken a woman from Ethiopia for a wife. In fact, they were jealous of the way God spoke to Moses, saying, "Has the LORD spoken only through Moses? Has he not spoken through us also?" (Num 12:2) The fact that God spoke through others certainly was no problem for Moses himself. He wanted everyone to prophesy (Num 11:29), and he was a very unassuming man. But God did not disregard what Miriam and Aaron were saying. He called the three of them into the meeting tent. He then came down in a cloud and called Aaron and Miriam forward and said,

Hear my words:
> When there are prophets among you,
>> I the LORD make myself known to them in visions;
>> I speak to them in dreams.
> Not so with my servant Moses;
>> he is entrusted with all my house.
> With him I speak face to face—clearly, not in riddles;
>> and he beholds the form of the LORD.
Why then were you not afraid to speak against my servant Moses? (Num 12:6-8)

"Not in riddles"—this phrase is important for our contemporary understanding of God's voice and guidance. Riddles are obscure, barely intelligible sayings. They lie on a par with the gibberish of "ghosts and the familiar spirits that chirp and mutter" from which people sought guidance in Isaiah's day as well as today (Is 8:19). We cannot know for sure what riddles mean, and they provide an all too fertile field for wild conjectures and manipulative interpretations.

Many who claim to speak for God refer to their visions, dreams and other unusual phenomena—or to their vague impressions or feelings—but they cannot articulate a clear, sane meaning of them. This does not mean that they have *not* truly been spoken to. Prophecy will often come in an indefinite form, requiring interpretation, but the still, small voice doesn't have to be interpreted. Usually, its meaning is clear as it was to Moses. He was spoken to directly face to face—"mouth to mouth" or *conversationally.* His meaning when he spoke for God was, therefore, always specific, precise and clear.

Notice that Jesus never had a vision, but Paul had visions. Why would this be true? God does not have to get certain people's attention, because they are already paying attention in that interchange that characterizes the conversational relationship. Perhaps they are not as in tune with what God wants done, as Miriam and Aaron were not. Instead, they were in tune with what they wanted done, so God got their attention. So the individual that is closer to God receives the clearer communication

If we do have a vision that turns out to be of God, we should not feel inferior however. We simply give God thanks. We thank him for the presence of the Bible in our lives because it allows us to grow closer to God and his ways of dealing with us. We should look forward to the time when our interaction with God is quiet and constant for our guidance and usefulness in ministry as we do the work God has placed before us. For example, we will be able to love our neighbor as ourselves only if we are in inward conversation with God. What our neighbor needs is often something we don't know, and so we need to be guided. When our neighbor has done something awful to us, we often have to be taught how to love that neighbor because we don't know how. Loving an enemy (who may be our neighbor) is to do what is in our power for their good, but sometimes love means opposing what they want. We learn how to do this as we hear from God about it.

As Bible history proceeds onward from Moses, we notice that in the process of divine communication the greater the maturity of the listener, the greater the clarity of the message and the lesser the role played by dreams, visions and other strange phenomena and altered states.

Of course, it is impossible to argue conclusively from silence. But in the lives of New Testament personalities—especially Jesus himself—there is a great preponderance of strictly spiritual—nonphysical—communications between God and his people. Visions, dreams and angels continue to play some part—as I think they may do today. It would not be too much to say, however, that where these phenomena are the main, as opposed to occasional, means of interaction, *it indicates a less developed spiritual life both in the individual and in the church group.* I am not trying to be judgmental here; I am merely trying to be helpful by pointing out the kind of with-God life into which we should expect to grow—a life in which one hears from God amid frequent times of conversational prayer.

I have found much help in the words of E. Stanley Jones, who firmly believed in and practiced interaction with God's voice throughout his life:

> God cannot guide you in any way that is not Christ-like. Jesus was supreme sanity. There was nothing psychopathic about Him. He went off into no visions, no dreams. He got His guidance through prayer as you and I do. That is, He got His guidance when in control of His faculties, and not when out of control as in dreams. I do not say that God may not guide through a vision or dream; but if He does, it will be very seldom, and it will be because He cannot get hold of our normal processes to guide them. For God is found most clearly and beneficially in the normal rather than in the abnormal. And Jesus is the Normal, for He is the Norm.[15]

The More Spectacular Is the Less Mature

I believe that the predominance of the spectacular encounter generally goes along with the *less mature* levels of the spiritual life. On the other hand, the absence of such spectacular events must not be taken as indicating great spiritual development; it is also consistent with utter deadness.

Spectacular encounters are obscure in their content and meaning, perhaps for our protection. In general, knowledge tends to be destructive when held by anything less than a mature character thoroughly permeated by love and humility. That is true even in the secular areas of life. Few things are more terrifying in the spiritual arena than those who *absolutely know* but who are also unloving, hostile, proud, superstitious and fearful. That Aaron and Miriam *could* be jealous of Moses is a sure indication that God could not trust them with the kind of knowledge he shared freely with Moses. That Moses was untroubled by their attack and glad to share the prophetic ministry just as surely indicates that he could be trusted with such knowledge.

When the spectacular is *sought*, it is because of childishness in the personality. Children love the spectacular and show them-selves as children by actively seeking it out, running heedlessly after it. It may sometimes be given by God—it may be necessary—because of our denseness or our hardheartedness. However, it is never to be taken as a mark of spiritual adulthood or superiority. If spectacular things do come to them, those who are more advanced in the Way of Christ never lightly discuss them or invoke them to prove that they are right or "with it" in some special way.

> *When the spectacular is* sought, *it is because of childishness in the personality.*

How Obscurity Can Serve Us

Having said that, it is important to understand that God in his mercy often speaks to us in obscure ways in order to allow us the room and time we need to respond. He lets us know that we are indeed being addressed but also that we need to stretch out in growth in order to receive the message. Perhaps we often think, *Well, God, why don't you just come out and say it? Tell me in detail how to live.* But we are usually full of mistaken ideas about what that would actually mean.

Our minds and values have to be restructured before God's glory, but at the same time our interests are truly appreciated and understood. We may be tempted to cry out, like Isaiah, for God to rend the heavens, come out of hiding and stand before us telling us what to do (Is 64:1), but we do not really understand what we are asking for when we ask that. Probably it would literally kill us or at least unbalance us if it actually happened, so God in his mercy continues to approach us obliquely, in one way or another. But this is increasingly less so as we mature—even until that time when we can safely know him as he knows us (1 Cor 13:12).

It is therefore natural and right that God's word comes to us in forms that we must struggle to understand. This is even true of the Bible, which is very explicit in many respects but still requires persistent and energetic work to understand. In the process of struggling we grow to the point where we can appropriate and assimilate the content of truth *as* it becomes clear. It is one of the oldest and most common stories of human life that in its most important moments we have little more than the foggiest idea of what it is we are doing and saying. And our ignorance is partly for our own good.

Did you *really* know what was happening when you entered the university or military training, got married or brought a child into the world? In some vague sense you did, perhaps, but you also had very little idea of what it meant in the long run. If you had appreciated all that it meant at the time, you probably would not have had the courage to proceed. Then you would have missed out on much good that has come to you through those events.

In faith also we come very slowly to appreciate what is happening to us. James and John came to Jesus and said, in effect, "Lord, when you become president we want to be your vice president and secretary of state." Jesus replied, "You do not know what you are asking. Can you drink the cup that I will drink of, be baptized with my baptism?" With great assurance they replied, "Oh yes, Lord, we are able to do that; bring it on" (Mk 10:37-39, paraphrase).

In fact, they had no idea what they were asking. In the end it turned out that by the Lord's mercy they *were* able to drink his cup and take his baptism. They were prepared when the time came. James was the first one of the apostles to be martyred. According to tradition, John lived longer than any of the apostles, but he was

tortured with hot oil, and we know that he was exiled on the barren island of Patmos, where he received a revelation of Jesus Christ
in a form utterly new to all previous experience, recorded in the
book of Revelation.

These things were not what James and John had in mind, by
any means, but they did very well with them when the suffering
came because God was with them. They grew to the vision and
the task as they stepped forward in faith. They lived and finally
died as the friends and colaborers of Jesus and of his Father.

The "Signs" Are Not the Reality

Bob Mumford, discussing the spectacular forms of communication
from God, remarks that

> signs are given to us, because God meets us on the level
> where we operate. . . . In guidance, when God shows us a
> sign, it doesn't mean we've received the final answer. A sign
> means we're on the way. On the highway we may pass a sign
> saying, "New York: 100 miles." The sign doesn't mean we've
> reached New York, but it tells us we're on the right road.[16]

But on the other hand, he continues,

> God wants to bring us beyond the point where we need signs
> to discern His guiding hand. Satan cannot counterfeit the
> peace of God or the love of God dwelling in us. When Christ's
> abiding presence becomes our guide, then guidance becomes
> an almost unconscious response to the gentle moving of His
> Holy Spirit within us.[17]

How glad I am that humankind was finally ready to be addressed by the still, small voice of Jesus! How good it is that God
left the spectacular forms that had been necessary—and perhaps
still are necessary for some purposes—and came to deal with us
by the very whispers of his Spirit. Who among us would really

know what to do if the great God came down in splendor and somehow stood before us? As Job said,

These are indeed but the outskirts of his ways;
　and how small a whisper do we hear of him!
　But the thunder of his power who can understand?
　(Job 26:14)

The incarnate Son comes without strife, so gentle that his voice is not to be heard above the chatter of the street (Mt 12:19). It is because of this approach that the Gentiles, or people generally, will finally come to have confidence in him.

I am so thankful for the quiet written Word, for the history and presence of the church of the Lamb, for the lives of the saints and for the tireless, still conquests of the Spirit of God. These approach me. These *I* can approach, and through them I can approach God while he safely draws ever closer to me.

The rivals of God's voice—still and small, still and within—continue to be necessary, then, and have their place. But as we are earnestly seeking God, we get beyond the need to have big things happening to reassure us that somehow we are all right, and possibly that others are not. Then we begin to understand and rejoice that (as Jesus so clearly lived and taught) the life of the kingdom is "righteousness and peace and joy in the Holy Spirit" (Rom 14:17).

Then we begin to understand that God's whole purpose is to bring us to the point where he can walk with us quietly, calmly and constantly, leaving us space to grow to be his (often fumbling) colaborers. We will still have some distance from him and yet be united with him because we are being conformed to the image of his Son, bearing the family resemblance.

Beyond Words
Even at the merely human level, one of the highest forms of communication is that kind of communion in which no overt word is

needed or wanted. What are we to make of a poet (Ben Jonson) who says,

> Drink to me only with thine eyes,
> And I will pledge with mine?

He has touched upon an element of what God would finally bring us to in communion with him: a union sometimes beyond communication, a life constantly before him in this world and the next.

There is, finally, a *silence that speaks*—which, paradoxically, "says" all:

> Love culminates in bliss when it doth reach
> A white, unflickering, fear-consuming glow;
> And, knowing it is known as it doth know,
> Needs no assuring word or soothing speech.
> It craves but silent nearness, so to rest,
> No sound, no movement, love not heard but felt,
> Longer and longer still, till time should melt,
> A snow-flake on the eternal ocean's breast.
> Have moments of this silence starred thy past,

> Made memory a glory-haunted place,
> Taught all the joy that mortal ken can trace?
> By greater light 'tis but a shadow cast:
> So shall the Lord thy God rejoice o'er thee,
> And in His love will rest, and silent be.[18]

Some Topics for Reflection

1. Do you see any reasons to be concerned about Virginia Lively's story? How might leaders guide people in their responses (possibly envious, possibly critical) to her story?

2. What do you think of Gustave Oehler's "principle that a clear consciousness when receiving revelation is placed higher than

ecstasy or other abnormal states of mind"? How would this relate to cases like Moses and the burning bush or Joshua and the "commander of the army of the LORD"?

3. The cases of an "audible voice alone" are today most likely to be associated with mental unbalance. Is this justified? Is there any well-based objection to God's simply producing the sound waves appropriate to audible language? Or might skepticism about such cases really rest on outright disbelief in God?

4. Have you experienced any cases that could be described as God's speaking to you *with the words of some other human being*? Biblical words? Those of a contemporary? What is it about those cases that leads you to describe them as such?

5. It is very common to hear church leaders speak of having a *personal relationship* with God through Jesus Christ. In your opinion, can such a personal relationship make sense *without* God's speaking directly to the individual?

6. Some reasons are given in this chapter for regarding the voice as the superior form of God's communication, given God's announced purposes in interacting with humanity. Do you find those reasons convincing?

7. Have you ever seen Bible deism in action (the idea that God gave us the Bible and then went away, leaving us to make what we could of it, with no individual communication either through the Bible or otherwise)? What makes it attractive?

6

The Word of God and the Rule of God

By the word of the LORD the heavens were made,
and all their host by the breath of his mouth.

Psalm 33:6

He sends out his command to the earth;
his word runs swiftly.
He gives snow like wool;
he scatters frost like ashes.

Psalm 147:15-16

Then they cried to the LORD in their trouble;
and he saved them from their distress;
he sent out his word and healed them,
and delivered them from destruction.

Psalm 107:19-20

Where the word of a king is, there is power.

Ecclesiastes 8:4 KJV

*T*he phrase "still, small voice" might seem to suggest something weak and marginal, but that is far from the truth. Hearing this divine but small voice is what lies at the heart of a relationship with God. One who hears God's voice is operating from the foundation and framework of all reality, not from the fringe. But what does this mean? *What place do words and God's Word have in reality?* This is a difficult question, but answering it will bring rich rewards. It is all about understanding the larger context in which we hear God. Let us explore further.

Astonishing Faith in the Power of Words

He is known to us only as "a certain centurion" (Lk 7:2 KJV). He was a Gentile, a Roman soldier of considerable rank: the top man, possibly, in the area of Capernaum. He was also a good governor who sacrificed his private wealth to help his subjects (Lk 7:5) and a good man who loved his servant, sick to the point of death. And he was humble. But all this was not what impressed Jesus when the man came to request healing for his servant. Jesus was particularly impressed by the quality and magnitude of the man's faith. The centurion seemed to understand, from his own experience of authority, how Jesus accomplished what he did. Therefore he had complete trust in Jesus' power. In an almost casual and offhand manner, he said to Jesus,

> Don't trouble yourself, sir! I'm not important enough for you to come into my house—I didn't think I was fit to come to you in person. Just give the order, please, and my servant will recover. I am used to working under orders, and I have soldiers under me. I can say to one, "Go," and he goes, or I can say to another, "Come here," and he comes; or I can say to my slave, "Do this job," and he does it. (Lk 7:6-8 Phillips)

Jesus looked at this man with astonishment. Then, turning to the group following along after him, he said, "I have never found faith like this anywhere, even in Israel!" (Lk 7:9 Phillips). What? Did John the Baptist not have greater faith? What about those who heralded and welcomed the child Jesus as the Messiah? Did his own family and disciples not have greater faith than this Gentile soldier? Apparently not.

Great faith, like great strength in general, is revealed by the ease of its workings. As "the quality of mercy is not strained"[1] (cannot be forced), faith also cannot be forced. Most of what we think we see as the struggle *of* faith is really the struggle to act *as if* we had faith when in fact we do not. We will look again at this centurion later. He has much to teach us about faith and about its dependence on a proper understanding of the word of God.

Words and the Word

God *created*, God *rules* and God *redeems* through his word. God's creating, God's ruling and God's redeeming is his word. This is the single basic truth about the overall relationship that he has to his creatures. And in this truth we see the all-encompassing mediation of Jesus his Son. If we wish to understand God's personal relationship to us, including how he speaks to us individually today, we must understand what the word of God is in general and how both the Son of God and the Bible are the Word of God.

What words are. If you find a word written on a wall or simply overhear one spoken in a crowd, you cannot tell who spoke it and so whose word it is. Its ownership does not reside within itself, but it is considered merely as a mark or a sound. In contrast, *my* word is not just *a* word. It is I who am speaking or writing. But even my name written ever so clearly on a check is not my word or my signature if *I* did not write it and thereby express my*self*—my thoughts and my intentions.

What is essential to a person's word is the meaning given to it by that person—the thought, feeling or action *that person* associates with it and hopes to convey to others. Through our words we literally give to others a piece of our mind. By hearing or reading others' words, we may know their thoughts and feelings and share in their lives.

Through words, soul impacts soul, sometimes with a great spiritual force. As marks or sounds alone, words are nothing. It is their mental side, their spiritual force, that hooks into the hidden levers of mind and reality and gives them their immense power. If we do not understand Spanish or Greek, we hear the sounds, but they have little or no effect because they are without meaning for us.

The power of the word lies finally in the personality that it conveys. Children learn to say, "Sticks and stones may break my bones, but words can never hurt me." Adults teach them to say this in order to ease the terrible pain that really is inflicted on them by the words of their playmates. How deeply children can be hurt by words! The school playground can become a chamber of horrors where young souls are left permanently crippled and scarred by malicious or mindless chatter.

Jesus saw this, no doubt, for *he* had eyes that saw. He also saw adults ravaging the lives of little children with their words. Surely it was largely his sense of the damage done in this way that made him say, "If any of you put a stumbling block before one of these little ones who believe in me, it would be better for you if a great millstone were fastened around your neck and you were drowned in the depth of the sea" (Mt 18:6).

The true view of the power of words is forcefully given in the book of Proverbs: "Death and life are in the power of the tongue" (Prov 18:21); "a soft tongue can break bones" (Prov 25:15); "a gentle tongue is a tree of life, but perverseness in it breaks the spirit" (Prov 15:4). This theme is carried into the New Testament. James remarks that the tongue is "a small member, yet it boasts of great exploits. How great a forest is set ablaze by a small fire!" (Jas 3:5). Jesus himself regarded words as a direct revelation of our inner being: "For by your words you will be justified, and by your words you will be condemned" (Mt 12:37).

Words as Spiritual Forces

In trying to understand the great power of words we cannot afford to overlook their *spiritual* nature. Spirit is unbodied, personal force. It is personal reality that can and often does work independently of physical or bodily forces. It can also work in conjunction with them. We can most clearly see spirit in our own selves as the force that belongs to thought, emotion and intention. In the biblical view, spirit reaches far beyond these—and beyond our limited understanding—and ultimately serves as the foundation of all reality. "God is spirit" (Jn 4:24).

The view of words as spiritual forces is common to both Scripture and pagan philosophers. Once, when his followers were struggling to understand him and were overemphasizing the material realm, Jesus said to them, "It is the spirit that gives life; the flesh is useless. The words that I have spoken to you are spirit and life" (Jn 6:63). This meant that through his words Jesus imparted *himself* and in some measure conferred on those who received his words the powers of God's sovereign rule. Through him they "have tasted the goodness of the word of God and the powers of the age to come" (Heb 6:5). This imparted power is referred to in Jesus' later explanation that "if you abide in me, and my words abide in you, ask for whatever you wish, and it will be done for you" (Jn 15:7).

Plato, the great philosopher of ancient Greece, also spiritualized words by treating our thinking as an inner "conversation" that the soul holds with itself.[2] In treating thought as a kind of language—as words, but as words hidden away in the nonphysical realm—he set a pattern that many thinkers have followed up to the present day.

St. Augustine carried that tradition on, joining it to Christian thought, in saying that "he who thinks speaks in his heart." He explicitly founded his view,[3] in part, on Gospel passages such as

Matthew 9:2-4, where "some of the scribes *said to themselves,* 'This man is blaspheming' " (italics added; see also Lk 12:17).

The word as *a person's speaking* is therefore to be understood as a spiritual power—whether of ourselves, of God or of some other personal agency and whether for evil or for good. It is the power of the one who is speaking. It is precisely in this realm that God seeks for those who would worship him "in spirit and truth" (Jn 4:23). He desires truth in the "inward being" and will "teach me wisdom in my secret heart" (Ps 51:6).

William Penn says, with a characteristically Quaker emphasis,

> For the more mental our worship, the more adequate to the nature of God; the more silent, the more suitable to the language of the spirit.
>
> Words are for others, not for ourselves: nor for God who hears not as bodies do; but as spirits should. If we would know this dialect we must learn of the divine principle in us. As we hear the dictates of that, so does God hear us.[4]

The *word of God,* when no further qualification is added, is his speaking, his communicating. When God speaks, he expresses his mind, his character and his purposes. Thus God is always present with his word.

All expressions of God's mind are "words" of God. This is true whether the specific means are *external* to the human mind (as in natural phenomena [Ps 19:1-4], other human beings, the incarnate Christ [the Logos] or the Bible) or *internal* to the human mind (in our own thoughts, intentions and feelings). God's rule over all things, including the affairs of humankind, is carried out through his word, understood in this way.

A Kingdom of Words

We are under constant temptation to think of the universe as a place in which the only relationships between things are certain physical or mechanical relationships. Our dominant idea systems lead us to think of blind forces pushing and pulling among physical objects as the way in which all things relate to one another. This is the naturalistic outlook discussed in chapter four. Such a view, however, can never bring understanding of the common deeds and affairs of human beings, let alone of higher culture or the religious life. After centuries of attempts at such understanding, it still falls pathetically short of that goal.

In contrast, the religious life and the religious outlook on the universe (especially the outlook identifiable with the mind of Christ and with life in his footsteps) is one that sees the universe as a *kingdom*. A kingdom does not work merely by pushes and pulls. Essentially it works by the *communication* of thoughts and intentions through words or other symbols, for a kingdom is a network of personal relationships.

> *A kingdom works by the communication of thoughts and intentions through words or other symbols, for a kingdom is a network of personal relationships.*

This is a point about the nature of social reality that we cannot afford to miss. Some of our greatest problems in understanding and entering into life in the kingdom of God come from an inadequate appreciation of how that kingdom—like all kingdoms—works: that is, by communication, the speaking or use of words for the expression of minds and intentions. The Scriptures are the best place to look for illustrations of how the speaking of a word works in the kingdom of God.

Creation by Words: God's and Ours

We begin, naturally enough, with the first chapter of the first book of the Bible, at creation. We are told that in the beginning God created the heavens and the earth. How did he do it? By speaking, by a sequence of directly creative words.

It should come as no surprise, given what we know of the physical universe, that God's first creative act was to create light, a form of physical energy (Gen 1:3). How did he create light? According to the record he *said,* "Let there be light." God's speaking—the word of God—is simply the expression of his mind. By the expression of his mind, then, he created light.

The coming into being of light and the result (light itself) are both to be viewed as a word of God. The writer of Hebrews observes that the things that are seen (light and so on) were not made of things that are visible (Heb 1:1-3). The word of God is *invisible*; it is the spiritual reality that produces all that is visible (cf. 2 Cor 4:18; 2 Pet 3:5-7).

Is it possible to clarify these passages from Genesis in some small measure by reflecting on how we ourselves create? I think so. You may express your own mind both through the creation of things and in what you create. But you will usually have to do more than just "speak" these into being. For example, if you are to create a bouquet of flowers or a cake, you cannot just think or say, "Let there be a bouquet!" or "Let there be a chocolate cake!"

In this way we can see the meaning of our finiteness. Finiteness means limitation or *restriction.* You and I are under some restrictions regarding how we can make a cake. We must work with and through the eggs, the flour, the sugar, the heat of the oven and the time. We must adapt ourselves and our actions to our ingredients. The structures within the substances with which we must work dictate the order and limitations of our actions. God, by contrast, dictates the structure and order in all things.

Eventually, however, the cake is finished, if we know what we are doing, and it is an expression of ourselves, our thoughts, feelings and intentions. Without them the cake would not exist. The husband or wife or child who eats the cake without comment has not grasped that point. He or she must find it good and say so. Better yet, he or she must say, in so many words, "How good of you to make this cake for me!" For *you*, the cook, are invested in that cake.

At a still more creative level of human life we have inventions. Normally a cake will be thought of just as something nice that you produced by following a recipe or knowing how to make it. But if a person conceives of a new type of engine, clothing or communicative device, that is an invention. It, too, is an expression, at a deeper level of individuality, of the mind of its creator. Hence we glorify inventors and authors as special kinds of people. Here also, thought—the internal word—governs events in the material world, yet here also it works under restrictions. We cannot create a jet engine just by saying or thinking, "Let there be a jet engine!"

There is, however, one arena where the human mind simply "speaks" and what it wishes is done. This is in the voluntary motions of the body—such as the hands, the feet and the face—and the voluntary wide-ranging journeys of our inward thoughts.

God is *always* able to speak and to create without going through channels, without working under restrictions (though he does not always choose the direct route). This constitutes his infinity. Within a certain range we too have been given a similarly unrestricted ability in our own natural powers, though it is very narrow, in contrast to God's. In the realm of our finiteness we must *learn how* to do things. We learn how to break the eggs and how to stir the batter, how to steer the car and how to apply the brakes. But we do not *consciously learn how* to move our fingers, our tongues or our feet. Here there are no channels we must go through under normal circumstances. The action is immediate, and in our conscious processes there is no "how" about it. Our thought and intention is there, and the body with all the physical intricacies moves in obedience.

Similarly, we know or can learn how to interpret a passage of Scripture, read music, solve a crossword puzzle or dissect an argument. There is, therefore, also a "how to" aspect across broad ranges of the mental life. But at a certain point you can only think *directly* of some things or decide on a course of action. If I ask you to think of a kitten, you do so immediately, without first thinking, "How shall I think of a kitten?" for that makes no more sense than asking, "How shall I move my little finger?"

This all goes to make the following point. Here, in this restricted range of direct action, God has given us a power that, so far as our conscious control is concerned, is as immediately creative as his own. *A realization of how our own thoughts (inner words) translate themselves into an act of creation is absolutely vital if we are to gain any concrete sense of God's rule through his word.* Only if we have some understanding of what it means for his word to *act* will we have any grounds for believing that God can have a personal, guiding relationship with us.

Returning to Genesis 1, we see God continuing to create by the direct action of his word on the results of his first creative word—the one that produced light and energy from itself alone, energy that we now know to be the substance of matter. Thus we read:

> And God said, "Let there be a dome in the midst of the waters, and let it separate the waters from the waters. . . . Let the waters under the sky be gathered together into one place." (Gen 1:6, 9)

He spoke and thereby formed these specific things into existence.

> And God said, "Let there be lights in the dome of the sky. . . . Let the waters bring forth swarms of living creatures. . . . Let the earth bring forth living creatures of every kind. . . . Let us make humankind in our image, according to our likeness." (Gen 1:14, 20, 24, 26)

In all these cases, as God spoke the object concerned came into existence (whether in an instant or over a more or less extended period of time does not matter) in the same way that your hand moves in response to your thought and intention. *That* is the creative power of the word of God. With all this in mind you may wish to interrupt your reading here to undertake a meditative and worshipful study of Psalm 104!

The word of God—the thought and mind of God—continues its presence in the created universe, *upholding* it. "Lasting to eternity, your word, Yahweh, unchanging in the heavens: your faithfulness lasts age after age; you founded the earth to endure. Creation is maintained by your rulings, since all things are your servants" (Ps 119:89-91 JB).

What we call natural laws, then, must be regarded as God's thoughts and intentions as to how the world should run. Because of this, as the Christian philosopher and Anglican bishop George Berkeley said long ago, echoing Psalm 19, "God himself speaks every day and in every place to the eyes of all men."[5] The events in the visible, material world—the unfolding of a rosebud, the germination of a seed, the conception and growth of a child, the evolution of galaxies—constitute a visible language manifesting not only a creative mind but, as Berkeley continues,

> a provident Governor, actually and intimately present, and attentive to all our interests and motions, who watches over our conduct and takes care of our minutest actions and designs throughout the whole course of our lives, informing, admonishing, and directing incessantly, in a most evident and sensible manner.[6]

Hearing God in Scripture
Psalm 19:1-6; 119:89-91

Before doing this *lectio divina* exercise, take a minute to review what was written in the previous seven paragraphs. The ideas in this chapter about the place that words and God's Word have in reality will help you settle into the passage in an informed, expectant way.

To prepare to read in order to receive from God—to hear God—please set the book or electronic reader down for a minute. Close your eyes and breathe out slowly. Ask God to give you an openness to hear whatever the Spirit wishes to bring to you today.

Read—*lectio*

Read the passage slowly, considering the invitation that reading Scripture is "encountering God himself or hearing his voice."

> *The heavens are telling the glory of God;*
> *and the firmament proclaims his handiwork.*
> *Day to day pours forth speech,*
> *and night to night declares knowledge.*
> *There is no speech, nor are there words;*
> *their voice is not heard;*
> *yet their voice goes out through all the earth,*
> *and their words to the end of the world.*
>
> *In the heavens he has set a tent for the sun,*
> *which comes out like a bridegroom from his wedding canopy,*
> *and like a strong man runs its course with joy.*
> *Its rising is from the end of the heavens,*
> *and its circuit to the end of them;*
> *and nothing is hid from its heat. (Ps 19:1-6)*
>
> *Lasting to eternity, your word, Yahweh, unchanging in the heavens:*
> *your faithfulness lasts age after age; you founded the earth*
> *to endure.*
> *Creation is maintained by your rulings,*
> *since all things are your servants. (Ps 119:89-91 JB)*

Now that the words are familiar to you, please read them again. This time, also listen with the ear of your heart for a word or phrase that shimmers or stands out to you. Do not choose this yourself. Let the Spirit bring it to you. Welcome it with meekness and see what happens (Jas 1:21).

Reflect—*meditatio*

Read the passage again slowly. As you do so and for a few minutes afterward, reflect on the word or phrase that stood out to you. Why do you think these words resonated with you? Give yourself a few minutes to do this.

Then ask God, How does this connect with my life today? What do I need to know or be or do?

Respond (Pray)—*oratio*

Read the passage one last time, preparing yourself for what you want to say to God about what you think the Spirit might have said to you or what came to you.

Pray however you are led pray. You might thank God for something or ask God for something. Or you might want to use the last four lines of the passage as your prayer.

Rest (Contemplation)—*contemplatio*

Do as you are led. You may wish to wait on God—to simply *be with* God. You may wish to pay attention to God, pondering especially how this passage adds to your wonder about God. What about him makes you want to worship him, or at least *be with* him? Sit in the companionship of God—the one who seeks you.

The Word of God as the Son of God

At a certain point in history this word—this visible language, the upholding order of the universe—came to us through the womb of

Mary: "He was in the world, and the world came into being through him; yet the world did not know him. He came to what was his own, and his people did not accept him" (Jn 1:10-11).

The *redemptive* entry of God on the human scene was no intrusion into foreign territory; it was a move into "his own"—a focusing of that divine thought, which is the order of all creation, into the finite form of one human personality. He, as the ancient prayer says, "did not abhor the Virgin's womb." Even there, as always, the "control panel" of the entire universe lay ready to hand. By voluntarily emptying himself (Phil 2:7) during his incarnation, he refrained from all but a very selective use of it.

The apparent paradox of the incarnation is that Christ's "infleshment" was really not an imposed restriction but rather the supreme exercise of the supreme power, as the end of human history will make abundantly clear:

> Here is my servant, whom I have chosen,
>> my beloved, with whom my soul is well pleased.
> I will put my Spirit upon him,
>> and he will proclaim justice to the Gentiles.
> He will not wrangle or cry aloud,
>> nor will anyone hear his voice in the streets.
> He will not break a bruised reed
>> or quench a smoldering wick
> until he brings justice to victory.
>> And in his name the Gentiles will hope. (Mt 12:18-21)

The story of the New Testament is the story of people's increasing understanding of who Jesus was. Those among whom he was reared said, "This is Mary and Joseph's boy. We know him." His own disciples thought he might be Elijah or one of the old prophets risen from the dead. In a flash of divine revelation Peter announced, as Jesus quizzed the disciples on his identity, "You are the Messiah, the Son of the living God" (Mt 16:16).

Only in the later parts of the New Testament does there emerge
the concept of Jesus as a *cosmic* Messiah: a ruler spanning all geographical and ethnic differences, providing the glue of the universe
(Col 1:17) and upholding all things by the word of his power (Heb
1:3), or, as the Jerusalem Bible beautifully translates it, "sustaining
the universe by his powerful command." Thus he is, as described in
the book of Revelation, the Alpha and Omega, the Faithful and
True, the Word of God, who leads the armies of heaven, the King of
kings and Lord of lords (Rev 1:8; 19:11, 13, 16).

In all its manifestations in nature and in the incarnate Christ,
the word of God is characterized by overwhelming power. It is the
awareness of this power that brings the prophet Isaiah to contrast
the thoughts of humankind with the thoughts of God, which in
their expression are the *words* of God. Mere human thoughts,
though effective within their appointed range, are as far below the
power of God's thoughts (and words) as the earth is below the
heavens (Is 55:8-9). For God says that, with a force comparable to
the forces of nature—the rain and seed bringing forth plants, seed
and bread to nourish the hungry (Is 55:10)—

> so shall my word be that goes out from my mouth;
> > it shall not return to me empty,
> but it shall accomplish that which I purpose,
> > and succeed in the thing for which I sent it. (Is 55:11)

The *unity* of the natural order with God's redemptive community under the word of God is seen in Psalm 29. Here the behavior
of the waters and the forests are attributed to the voice of the Lord:
"The voice of the LORD causes the oaks to whirl, and strips the forest bare" (Ps 29:9). But while "the LORD sits enthroned over the
flood," he will also "give strength to his people! May the LORD
bless his people with peace!" (Ps 29:10-11). This same unity is
exhibited in the life of Jesus. He could turn water into wine, calm
the billowing waves with his word and walk on them as on pave-

ment. But he could also place the word of God's kingdom rule into people's hearts, where it would bring forth fruit a hundredfold, or sixtyfold, or thirtyfold (Mt 13:23).

This, then, is the Word of God and the Son of God, united in the ordering of the cosmos. To understand how the Word of God is related to the *family* of God, however, we must consider more closely the *role of ordinary human words* in ordinary human life. This should then, later in the chapter, help us to see how the *power of the Word of God*, operating among human beings, differs from superstition, magic and voodoo. That is crucial if we are to make sense of hearing God and to keep Christian spirituality clearly distinct from other spiritualities.

The Power of a Word

In the book of Ecclesiastes a wise man reflects in depth on how human life and society work. Among other things he considers how kings or governments function. Psalm 29 told how the Lord sat as King at the flood, and we know that he is indeed King over all the earth and master of the most terrible of situations. But a king, contrary to what is often thought, does *not* rule simply by brute force.

The emperor Napoleon Bonaparte was about to use great force to subdue a certain population when a wise lieutenant, one of his aides, said to him, "Monsignor, one cannot *sit* upon bayonets." This man understood that the use of brute force could not lead to a *settled* political rule. All government exists to some degree by consent of the governed. No one can totally rule a people by force alone. Instead, the ruler rules by words, understandings, allegiances and alliances.

The writer of Ecclesiastes, himself a king, was amazed at what the word of a king could do. He observes that a king's word "is powerful, and who can say to him, 'What are you doing?'" (Eccles 8:4). Take his authority, his role, away from him, and a king is like any other person. But when he is indeed kingly, his smallest word has awesome effects: heads roll, nations prosper, cities burn, armies march, enemies are crushed. Seeing clearly the power of words at the merely human level may help us to understand the power of the creative word of God in *his* kingdom.

Words in the Kingdom of God

If we turn to the kingdom of God with an understanding that it *is* a kingdom and that it too works in large measure by words, numerous events from the life of Jesus on earth are easier to appreciate and enter into sympathetically.

At the opening of this chapter we met "a certain centurion." He had implicit faith in Jesus—not, it seems, on a religious basis but from his secular knowledge of the power of authoritative words. So far as one can tell from the story, he did not have any special degree of faith in God, though he was a good man and respected the Jewish religion. He simply knew how authority worked, and he recognized that Jesus was working with authority to heal.

When, as recorded in Matthew 8, Jesus entered the city of Capernaum one day, this centurion came to ask for help, saying, "Lord, my servant is lying at home paralyzed, in terrible distress" (v. 6). Without being asked, Jesus said, "I will come and cure him" (v. 7)—just like that! It seemed to be nothing extraordinary to him. For Jesus, his healing this servant would be like our saying, "Now I'll raise my hand."

The centurion was in a position to understand Jesus' response. He replied, "Lord, I am not worthy to have you come under my roof" (v. 8). The centurion was acting with both humility and courtesy, for he knew that he was speaking to a Jew and that proper Jews thought that entering into the house of a Gentile would defile them. So he said humbly to Jesus, "But only speak the word, and my servant will be healed" (v. 8).

"Only speak the word"? Yes, for where the word of a *king* is, there is *power!* The word is enough. The centurion understood this because he was like a king within his own small arena, who was authorized to speak for a higher king, Caesar.

In both Gospel accounts of his meeting with Jesus, the centurion is allowed to explain fully how he knows that Jesus need "only speak the word" to heal his servant: "For I also am a man under authority, with soldiers under me; and I say to one, 'Go,' and he goes, and to another, 'Come,' and he comes, and to my slave, 'Do this,' and the slave does it" (Mt 8:9; cf. Lk 7:8).

What we see here is *trust* based on *experiential knowledge of the power in the words spoken by authorized individuals.* In a personal universe (whether our own small arena or God's cosmos) the word directs actions and events. The centurion understood this, and Jesus marveled at his understanding: "When Jesus heard him, he was amazed and said to those who followed him, 'Truly I tell you, in no one in Israel have I found such faith'" (Mt 8:10).

> *In a personal universe (whether our own small arena or God's cosmos) the word directs actions and events.*

At this point our practical atheism or skepticism may abruptly emerge, and we may find ourselves saying (or thinking), "Things just aren't like that!" But what is it, exactly, that we find wrong here? What is amiss with a universe in which reality responds to a word? What is wrong with a universe in which reality responds to thoughts and intentions? Surely we live in precisely such a universe. But our faith does not normally rise to believing it—at least not to the extent to which it is true. In part, no doubt, our skepticism comes from the fact that we often speak words unaccompanied by faith and authority. Such words do not have the effect on reality that words laden with faith, spoken in the fulfillment of an authoritative role, do have. Thus *our* experience, unlike the centurion's, hinders rather than helps our faith.

For the centurion, by contrast, it was all perfectly easy, because he recognized that he was dealing with someone in high authority. He knew what authority was. He knew what it was to command an event. He knew that Jesus was doing the same kind of thing, so it was a simple matter for him to step into the situation by faith. Where *he* had no authority—and thus he could not say, "Be healed!"—he could recognize the one who did have such authority. In faith he could ask that one, Jesus, to use his authority to direct processes within the material universe, namely, the healing of his servant.

This Power of Words Given to Human Beings
To some who doubted in his day, Jesus said,

> "But so that you may know that the Son of Man has authority on earth to forgive sins"—he then said to the paralytic—"Stand up, take your bed and go to your home." And he stood up and went to his home. When the crowds saw it, they were filled with awe, and they glorified God, who had given such authority to human beings. (Mt 9:6-8)

C. H. Spurgeon appropriately comments that "miracles of grace must be the seals of our ministry; who can bestow them but the Spirit of God?"[7]

According to the biblical record, powerful words such as Jesus spoke *have* been given to other human beings to speak also. In Numbers 20:8-12 we find a fascinating case study on this point. The Israelites, on their wilderness wanderings, were dying for lack of water. Moses' leadership was under violent criticism from his people. This drove Moses to prayer, as was right. Then God appeared to him, telling him to command a rock that was close by to give forth water: "Thus you shall bring water out of the rock for them" (v. 8).

Instead of doing this, however, Moses took the rod that God had given him earlier as a sign and he and Aaron called the people together, saying, "'Listen, you rebels, shall we bring water for you out of this rock?' Then Moses lifted up his hand and struck the rock twice with his staff; water came out abundantly, and the congregation and their livestock drank" (Num 20:10-11). Pretty impressive. But, because Moses had struck the rock instead of speaking to it, God dealt sternly with him for his disobedience: he did not allow him to cross into the land of promise "because ye believed me not" (v. 12 KJV). Was Moses' action truly such a serious offense? Did it deserve such a strong reaction from God? And if so, why? Without understanding the matters we have already discussed, one might see little wrong in what Moses did.

Possibly by striking the rock Moses was attempting to answer those who criticized *his* power. Or possibly he did not believe that his merely *speaking* to a rock could bring water out of it. Possibly he misunderstood and thought he had to bring forth the water by his own physical strength—"Shall *we* bring water for you out of this rock?" he asked. But the rock he struck, as we learn in 1 Corinthians 10:4, was Christ. If what we have come to understand about the Logos, or Word, within creation and nature is true, rocks are things that might well respond to words spoken with the appropriate kingdom authority and vision of faith.

The transfer of the power of God's word to the words of ordinary humans was something that Jesus, during his days in human form, approached experimentally. *He* could exercise this power of God's government, but could it be transferred to his followers? That was the question they faced together. He commissioned his disciples to do what they had so often seen him do, and he sent them on their way: "As you go, proclaim the good news, 'The kingdom of heaven has come near.' Cure the sick, raise the dead, cleanse the lepers, cast out demons. You received without payment; give without payment" (Mt 10:7-8; cf. Lk 9:1-10).

This first trial run was conducted only with his twelve apostles. When they returned and reported good success in acting in the

power of God's word, the question was then whether this transfer
of God's power could be extended beyond the close followers and
on to more ordinary believers. And so, according to Luke 10:1,
Jesus sent out "seventy others." It seems to me to be a matter of
great significance that these "seventy others" were not his closest
associates; we might say they were not the best-trained troops in
the army of the Lord. Yet they too returned rejoicing in the knowledge that even demons were subject to them through the name of
their Master (Lk 10:17).

This seems to have had the effect of settling the Lord's mind on
what we might call "the extended incarnational plan" for deliver-
ing humanity. It was apparently only at this point that Jesus saw
Satan in defeat, through the transfer of the word of God and its
power to ordinary people who could then speak *for* God under his
government (Lk 10:18).

In this touching passage (Lk 10:21-24), Jesus seems positively
gleeful, as in no other scriptural passage. Luke says Jesus "rejoiced
in the Holy Spirit"; the Greek word used here (*agalliao,* v. 21) suggests the state of mind in which people may jump up and down
with joy. Then Jesus turned aside, perhaps, for a moment of thanks
to his Father: "I thank you, Father, Lord of heaven and earth, because you have hidden these things from the wise and the intelligent and have revealed them to infants; yes, Father, for such was
your gracious will" (v. 21).

Realizing vividly the meaning of these events, he then informed
his followers with assurance that his Father had turned everything over to him—"All things have been handed over to me by
my Father"—and that he, Jesus Christ, was to be totally in charge
of the revelation of the Father to humanity (v. 22). He congratulated those around him on their good fortune in being able to witness what had happened, in seeing just plain folks succeed in operating with the power of God's authoritative word. Prophets and
kings had longed to see this but had not been able (vv. 23-24).

In this way the governmental rule of God reaffirmed itself *through* the actions and words of human beings within the people of Israel just before it was removed from their exclusive control. Because Israel failed to fulfill its divine appointment of being the light of the world, of showing the world how to live under God, Jesus finally said to the Israelites of his day, "Therefore, I tell you, the kingdom of God will be taken away from you and given to a people that produces the fruits of the kingdom" (Mt 21:43). It was not as if the Jews were to be excluded as individuals from the exercise of the word of power in God's kingdom. Far from it. But this was no longer to be *exclusively* their role *as Jews*. The Jewish people would no longer be the exclusive people of God, God's official address on earth. The story of the transfer of the kingdom from the Jews to the church, which was indicated by Jesus in Matthew 21:43, is the story of the New Testament book of Acts, which begins in Jerusalem and ends in Rome. Today participation in the kingdom rule of God through union with Jesus is open worldwide.

Prayers, Actions and Words

A proper understanding of the ways of the word of God among humanity, within the kingdom rule of God, illuminates something that has troubled many thoughtful students of the New Testament. Rarely does Jesus ever *pray* for a need brought before him. Rather, he normally *addresses* it or performs some *action* in relation to it.

Such a case is described in Mark 9. While Jesus was on the Mount of Transfiguration a man brought his child to be healed. The child was possessed of a spirit that rendered him mute. The disciples tried to cast the spirit out, but they failed. After some conversation with the child's father about the child's condition and about the father's own faith, Jesus cast the demon out with a command. When the disciples asked why they had not been able to cast it out—apparently they had previously had some success in such matters—Jesus replied, "This kind can come out only through prayer" (Mk 9:29). Yet Jesus himself did not pray on this occasion. What is the explanation?

I believe this is an illustration of the principle that (as experience readily shows) there are *degrees of power* in speaking the word of God and that prayer is necessary to heighten that power. Prayer is more basic in the spiritual life than is speaking a word and, indeed, is the indispensable foundation for doing so. The role of speaking the word of God has become limited today because of a widespread lack of understanding of such "speaking," coupled with the generally low quality of the life of prayer.

Certainly in some situations we will encounter, and perhaps in most, a *direct* word or action from God himself rather than from ourselves is what is required. And for that we can only pray. Sometimes, on the other hand, *we* should be in a position to speak, to say on behalf of God and in the name of Christ how things are to be. To do this will be more or less difficult, as Jesus indicates in Mark 9, depending on the specifics of the case. This kind of situation will frequently differ from other kinds and will call for other abilities, which we may or may not have available at the time. But I believe we are called to *grow* into this capacity to speak with God, in the degree of power appointed by him for us individually.

In the works done by the apostles of Jesus, we see the apostles *speaking with* God—as in the book of Acts and less so in the Gospels. They did not *always* pray to God for help in the matter at hand, and they certainly dealt with different situations in different ways. When Peter and John were confronted with the lame beggar as they entered the temple in Acts 3, Peter commanded the man in the name of Jesus Christ—that is, he commanded him on Jesus' behalf—to rise up and walk (v. 6). Then Peter took the lame man by the hand and pulled him to his feet (v. 7). Peter did not kneel down and pray for him, nor did he pass by saying, "We'll be praying for you!" He put his whole bodily self on public display as an agent of Christ. Scary, isn't it?

When dealing with Dorcas, the deceased sister who "was devoted to good works and acts of charity" (Acts 9:36), Peter put everyone out of the room. Did he learn this from Jesus (compare Mt 9:25)? Kneeling down, he prayed. Then he faced the body and commanded Dorcas to arise, and she returned to life (Acts 9:40). Perhaps Peter also learned from Elisha's practice in a similar situation (2 Kings 4:32-35). Elisha was one of the greatest practitioners of kingdom rule with his God.

At Lystra, Paul spoke the redemptive word of God to a lame man whose faith had been raised by hearing Paul preach. Paul loudly commanded the man, "'Stand upright on your feet.' And the man sprang up and began to walk" (Acts 14:10).

Today, with the return of the *charismata*, the gifts of the Spirit, to prominence across all denominational boundaries, multitudes of disciples once again dare to *speak* in the name of Jesus to the needs and dangers that confront them. And the practice of so-called spiritual warfare has prepared countless others to "speak to the mountain," as Jesus said (Mk 11:23). Testimonies of remarkable results find their way into many fellowships and into an abundance of Christian literature. This is to be expected as we grow in our confidence that reality, including the material world, is ultimately a *kingdom* in which authority, personal relationship and communication (words) are basic to the way things run. We have, of course, much still to learn.

We Are Called into Question

There are many ways in which these matters might be misunderstood, however. They will be especially unsettling if we are already used to living our lives untouched by them and are convinced that they should have nothing to do with our faith or our service to God. The suggestion that we *should* possibly be healing the sick, casting out demons or raising the dead by our participation in the word and power of God may leave us baffled, angry, rebellious and guilt-ridden.

At a meeting where I had been speaking on accomplishing things through prayer, a woman confronted me in great agony and tears and with not a little anger. She had earlier believed that prayer could actually make a difference in the course of events around us, and she had tried very hard to make this work in her life. But, for whatever reason, she had failed in the attempt, and that failure had left her feeling guilty and deeply hurt. To protect herself she had readjusted her faith—at least on the surface—to consist of believing the creeds, helping out at church and being a good person generally (as that is commonly understood in our society). My words had reopened the old wounds and disturbed her hard-won peace. I have since come to understand that she was representative of many fine people who are convinced that the biblical mode of life in God's kingdom simply cannot be a reality for them.

On another occasion I met a very devout woman who had been raised in a fellowship where stress was laid on receiving a "second work of grace." She had been driven to distraction in her frantic efforts to obtain this "deeper life" and cease being a second-class citizen among her religious friends. She too had "failed." She had moved to a different denomination and had recoiled into a life of mere mental assent to the truth about Jesus and some degree of effort for her local church. That day I had only been teaching about the joyous possibilities of life opened up by Jesus' invitation to enter his kingdom and about how gladly that invitation was received by his hearers. But this woman was thrown into agony by the talk of a life of real interaction with God in the manner described in the Old and New Testaments.

I cannot deal effectively here with all the issues involved in such cases, but there is one thing I can and must make clear: In a life of participation in God's kingdom rule, *we* are not to make things happen, but only to be honestly willing and eager to be made able.

If we are to exercise the word and rule of God in ways regarded as spectacular by human beings, Jesus is our model, as always. And that means above all that there will be nothing forced or hys-

> *In a life of participation in God's kingdom rule, we are not to make things happen, but only to be honestly willing and eager to be made able.*

terical about it and that we can count on God himself to lead us into whatever we are to do. He will do this in a way that is suitable to our lives and his calling for us.

Beyond this we should always keep in mind the words of Jesus to his seventy friends on their return from their mission: "Nevertheless, do not rejoice at this, that the spirits submit to you, but rejoice that your names are written in heaven" (Lk 10:20).

Keeping all this firmly in mind, I want to turn now to two final questions for this chapter: How does a life in which one speaks the creative word of God differ from a life of voodoo, magic and superstition? and, What does the Bible have to do with the word of God as discussed so far?

Voodoo, Magic and Superstition

The word *magic* in this context refers not to sleight of hand or trickery but to the attempt to influence the *actual course* of events, not just how things *appear to be*, by manipulation of symbolisms or special substances such as effigies and incantations. Voodoo and witchcraft—sometimes lumped together under the term "black magic"—are the forms of magical practice most familiar to the Western mind.

Satanism and demonism, though they sometimes merge with magic in practice, operate on a quite different principle—service to or from a power that is personal but evil. Magic and witchcraft, by contrast, are forms of superstition. They work from belief that some action, substance or circumstance not logically or naturally (or even supernaturally) related to a certain course of events does nonetheless influence the outcome of those events if "correctly" approached. Prayer and speaking with God must be carefully distinguished from superstition in how they work.

The word *superstition* is derived from words that mean "to stand over," as one might stand in wonder or amazement over something incomprehensible. The famous Connecticut Yankee in King Arthur's court in Mark Twain's fictional portrayal was able—as the story goes—to get the ignorant and generally superstitious people of ancient England to attribute unusual powers to his own actions, while he himself understood the natural causes of the events he manipulated. Martin Buber rightly says that "magic desires to obtain its effects without entering into relation, and practices its tricks in the void,"[8] the void of ignorance and selfish obsession.

Superstition, then, is belief in magic, and magic relies on *alleged* causal influences that are not actually mediated through the natures of the things involved. Suppose, for example, someone says they can throw you into great pain or even kill you by mutilating a doll-like effigy of you, a practice common in voodoo and other forms of witchcraft. It is superstition or magic, for there is no real connection between someone's sticking a pin in a doll and your feeling pain.

I am sure that in some cases there is much more reality to the *results claimed* than we might wish to credit, from either a commonsense or a scientific point of view. For example, there seems to be good evidence that in some settings people do suffer or die when certain rituals are performed with reference to them. However, it is not the mutilation of the doll or the incantations over it that produce the effects. Rather, the effects—where effects occur—are produced from the realm of the mind or spirit, in a social context where a certain set of beliefs about voodoo or magical rituals is shared. Possibly in some cases spiritual beings are also involved.

This does not mean that the effects are illusory or unreal, but whatever actual causation is involved has nothing *magical* about it. No causation has. The voodoo process is, so far as any results are concerned, an entirely natural process achieved through the prevailing psychosocial order.[9] The power involved is not the power of the ritual itself. It is the power of personal force, often involving something like hypnotism, along with the social context and perhaps the satanic dimension of the spiritual realm.

The Christian's faith is not superstition. If we look at the ways in which Moses, Jesus, Peter and Paul did the work of God—exercising his rule by speaking and acting with his word—there is neither magic nor superstition to be found. The same can be said for the astonishing results of believers' speaking God's words, results that are once again becoming a part of ordinary Christian life today.

Many people have difficulty accepting the more spectacular episodes of God's word at work, such as we have seen from Scripture. The same people, however, still believe in the healing power of prayer and in the capacity of some individuals or some rituals practiced by the church to minister at the physical level in the healing of the body and so forth. Is *this* not just more superstition?

The answer is that, in our faith, *we do not believe that the power concerned resides in the words used or in the rituals taken by themselves.* If we did, we would indeed be engaged in superstitious practices. Instead, we regard the words and actions simply as ways ordained in the nature of things, as established by God, for accomplishing the matter in question. They work as part of life in the kingdom of God. They enlist the personal agencies of that kingdom to achieve the ends at their disposal and are not mere tools by which we engineer our desired result. We are under authority, not in control.

The combined condition of faith, love, hope and understanding that is present in those who work with the word of God is *in its very nature* connected with the effect to be brought about. As part of the kingdom this condition forms the appropriate channel from the supply to the need—relating the nature of the human body or mind (in the case of healing) to the creative and redemptive Spirit who is God. This forms a natural (though really supernatural) order of influence and causation.

This process might become more clear if we return briefly to the matters discussed at the beginning of this chapter. We saw there that the very nature of the material universe is to be subject generally to the word of an all-present, all-powerful, all-knowing divine mind. (Recall this discussion in chapter four.) This mind is what mediates between the word spoken by God's servant on his behalf and the physical structure of the waves or the rocks, or of the body or mind to be healed. That is why Moses, Jesus, Peter and Paul were not magicians and did not practice anything like voodoo.

Superstitious Attitudes Creep In

Sometimes I fear that we Christians do engage in truly superstitious uses of words and rituals. This occurs when our activities are not an expression of an understanding of the connection between the desired result and our faith and union with God. In other words, this arises because we do not really understand how the kingdom of God functions among us.

A few years ago, for example, many Christians in the United States were caught up in a fad involving the phrase "what you say is what you get" (or "name it and claim it"). Some still are. It was suggested that if you just affirmed what you wanted, you would get it. Furthermore, if you said what you *did not* want—for example, if you voiced something you were worried might happen—that also would happen to you. Now this *is* superstition, placing us in the category of those people, described by Jesus, who "heap up empty phrases as the Gentiles do" in prayer, thinking "that they will be heard because of their many words" (Mt 6:7). Possibly many professing Christians have little *except* superstition in their religious activities. They may have no understanding at all of the nature of God's kingdom and of how he rules in the affairs of humanity through his word, especially within the family of the faithful. We must each search our own heart on this matter. We do not have to be superstitious if we seek above all the kingdom of God.

Legalism is superstition. The legalistic tendencies found throughout our religious and cultural life also thrust us toward superstition. Legalism claims that overt *action* in conforming to rules for explicit behavior is what makes us right and pleasing to God and worthy of blessing. Jesus called legalism "the righteousness . . . of the scribes and Pharisees" (Mt 5:20).

Legalism, superstition and magic are closely joined by their emphasis on controlling people and events. Legalists are forced toward superstitious behavior because, in the interest of controlling life through their laws, they depart from the natural connections of life. They bypass the realities of the heart and soul from which life really flows. That is why Jesus tells us we must go *beyond* the righteousness of the scribes and Pharisees if we are truly to enter into life.

Life does not come by law (Gal 3:21), nor can law adequately depict or guide life. The law is the letter, and "the letter kills, but the Spirit gives life" (2 Cor 3:6). Legalists are evermore forced into merely symbolic behavior, which they superstitiously suppose to have the good effects they seek. Magic or superstition, as is well known, also place absolute emphasis on doing everything "just right," which is the essence of legalism.

"Speaking the word" confused with magic: Two biblical cases. Living and acting from the power of God, through reliance on Christ, has nothing to do with superstition, as it has nothing to do with legalism or salvation through the law. In two different cases in the book of Acts the word and work of God were *mistaken* for magic by those without understanding.

The first case is that of Simon the sorcerer in Acts 8. Seeing how Peter and John conferred the Holy Spirit on others with the attendant manifestations, Simon offered money to them if they would give him power to do the same (vv. 18-19). Peter saw from this that Simon, though apparently a believer (v. 13), did not have his heart right with God. He rebuked him severely for thinking that he "could obtain God's gift with money" (v. 20).

In Acts 19 there is a rather more humorous story. A traveling troupe of Jewish exorcists, the seven sons of Sceva, saw the miracles worked by God with Paul and Paul with God. They listened to the *words* Paul used, mistaking them for incantations rather than intelligent, rational discourse within a society or kingdom.

They then tried exorcism by pronouncing the name of Jesus over a person possessed of demons, saying, "I adjure you by the Jesus whom Paul proclaims" (Acts 19:13). The scriptural account of what happened then is so good that it must simply be quoted: "But the evil spirit said to them in reply, 'Jesus I know, and Paul I know; but who are you?' Then the man with the evil spirit leaped on them, mastered them all, and so overpowered them that they fled out of the house naked and wounded" (vv. 15-16).

This vastly impressed everyone in Ephesus, and the name "Lord Jesus" was held in great respect. Believers who had been using spells and practicing magic forsook such practices, realizing the great disparity between the realm of the magical and the kingdom of God. They burned magic books worth fifty thousand pieces of silver, while for its part "the word of the Lord grew mightily and prevailed" (v. 20).

As followers of Christ we are not to believe or act on things that make no sense and that we only hope to make work for our own ends, no matter how respected those things might be.

The Bible and the Word of God
Finally, how are we to understand the relationship of the Bible to this word of God that we have just seen growing mightily and prevailing around Ephesus and to the Word that is God and that upholds the world?

The Bible is *one* of the results of God's speaking. It is the *unique* written Word of God. It is inerrant in its original form and infallible in all of its forms for the purpose of guiding us into a life-saving relationship with God in his kingdom. It is infallible in this way precisely because God never leaves it alone.

The inerrancy of the original texts is rendered effective for the purposes of redemption only as that text, through its present-day derivatives, is constantly held within the eternal living Word. Inerrancy by itself is not a sufficient theory of biblical inspiration because, as everyone knows, the Bible in our hand is not the original text. Inerrancy of the originals also does not guarantee sane and sound, much less error-free, interpretations. Our dependence as we read the Bible today must be on God, who now speaks to us in conjunction with it and with our best efforts to understand it.

In light of our discussions so far it is clear that, *while the Bible is the written Word of God, the word of God is not simply the Bible.* The way we know that this is so is, above all, by *paying attention to what the Bible says.*

If you take just the passages studied so far and carefully examine what they say about the word of God, you will see that that word is much greater than the Bible, though inclusive of it. The Bible is the Word of God in its unique *written* form. But the Bible is not Jesus Christ, who is the *living* Word. The Bible was not born of a virgin, crucified, resurrected and elevated to the right hand of the Father.

Neither is the Bible the word of God that is settled eternally in the heavens, as the psalmist says (Ps 119:89), expressing itself in the order of nature (Ps 19:1-4). The Bible is not the word of God that, in the book of Acts, expanded and grew and multiplied (Acts 12:24). It is not the word that Jesus spoke of as being sown by the active speaking of the ministry (Mt 13). But *all* of these are God's *words*, as is also his speaking that we hear when we *individually hear God.*

So the Bible is the unique, infallible, written Word of God, but the word of God is not just the Bible. If we try to dignify the Bible by saying false things about it—by simply *equating* the word of God with it—we do not dignify it. Instead we betray its content by denying what it says itself about the nature of the word of God.

God reigns in his kingdom through his speaking. That speaking is reserved to himself, but it may in some small measure be communicated through those who work in union with him. The Bible is a finite, written record of the saving truth spoken by the infinite, living God, and it reliably fixes the boundaries of everything he will ever say to humankind. It fixes those boundaries *in principle*, though it does not provide the detailed communications that God may have with individual believers today.

> *God reigns in his kingdom through his speaking. That speaking is reserved to himself, but it may in some small measure be communicated through those who work in union with him.*

The Bible has its own special and irreplaceable role in the history of redemption. We can refer any person to it with the assurance that if he or she will approach it openly, honestly, intelligently and persistently, God will meet him or her through its pages and speak peace to his or her soul. This is assured to any person whose deepest self cries out,

> Beyond the sacred page I seek Thee, Lord;
> My spirit pants for Thee, O Living Word.[10]

Paul therefore instructed his protégé Timothy that "the sacred writings . . . are able to instruct you for salvation through faith in Christ Jesus. All scripture is inspired by God and is useful for teaching, for reproof, for correction, and for training in righteousness, so that everyone who belongs to God may be proficient, equipped for every good work" (2 Tim 3:15-17).

The word of God in the larger sense portrayed *in* the Bible is therefore available to every person *through* the Bible, the written Word of God. All may hear the living Word by coming to the Bible humbly and persistently, with burning desire to find God and live in peace with him.

As for others, the Bible may prove a deadly snare, as it did for those in Christ's earthly days who actually used Scripture to dismiss him and his claims on them (Jn 5:36-47). Because of this we are warned in the Bible that we can even destroy ourselves by Bible study: specifically, by the study of Paul's epistles, for "some things in them [are] hard to understand, which the ignorant and unstable twist to their own destruction, as they do the other scriptures" (2 Pet 3:16).

The Scriptures are an unbelievable treasure, but people can use the Bible to support their position. When they come to the Scripture with an open heart, they will see the Word light up. I encourage people to memorize passages so that it is in their bodies and things come out of that which they have never seen before. The test is: Is this serving what I want or what God wants? The conversation breaks down that tendency to try to control the word of God. When living in a conversational relationship with God, we have to let go of our efforts to manipulate him or others. We must be ourselves and receive the word that comes from him through the Scriptures.

Our only protection from our own pride, fear, ignorance and impatience as we study the Bible is fellowship with the living Word, the Lord himself, invoked in constant supplication from the midst of his people, as we see here:

> O send Thy Spirit, Lord, now unto me,
> That He may touch my eyes, and make me see;
> Show me the truth concealed within Thy word,
> And in Thy book revealed, I see thee Lord.[11]

We see it also here:

> Light up Thy word; the fettered page
> From killing bondage free:

Light up our way; lead forth this age
In Love's large liberty.
O Light of light! Within us dwell,
Through us Thy radiance pour,
That word and life Thy truths may tell,
And praise Thee evermore.[12]

Some Topics for Reflection

1. How is it that words can have such power to affect reality? Is it through their relationship to personality? What is that relationship? In what way are words a spiritual force?

2. How is the use of words involved in creation by God and creation by human?

3. How is a kingdom a verbal, not a merely physical, reality?

4. How are natural laws related to God's word? (Recall Psalms 19 and 104.)

5. Compare the Word as the Son and the Word as the Bible.

6. What exactly was it that the Roman centurion knew, and how did it relate to his faith in Jesus?

7. Explain the relationship between prayer and speaking *with* God.

8. The rock that Moses struck was Christ. What do you make of this statement (see 1 Cor 10:4)?

9. Do you feel threatened in any way by the contents of this chapter? Did anything in this chapter encourage you?

10. How can you distinguish Christian faith in the power of God's word from voodoo or the general belief that engaging in a certain action or saying certain words (if done "correctly") changes the course of events?

7

Redemption Through
the Word of God

He says, "It is too small a thing that You should be My Servant
To raise up the tribes of Jacob, and to restore the preserved of Israel;
I will also make You a light of the nations
So that My salvation may reach to the end of the earth."

Isaiah 49:6 NASB

You are the light of the world.

Matthew 5:14 NASB

*T*o understand how God speaks we must understand to some extent what the word of God is. In the Way of Christ, as I have said, discerning God's voice is essentially *just one dimension* of a certain kind of life, the *eternal kind of life*, a life lived in conversational relationship with God (Jn 17:3).

Studying the word of God helps us understand what this eternal life is, how we are to take part in it by the graciousness of God, and especially how hearing God is part of it. We will truly be at ease hearing God only if we are at home with the word of God, with his speaking throughout creation and redemption. Hearing God is not a freakish event.

God speaks not just for us and our purposes, nor does he speak primarily for our prosperity, safety or gratification. Those who receive the grace of God's saving companionship in his word are by that fact also fitted to show humankind how to live. They, and they alone, are at home in the universe as it actually is. In that sense they are the light of the world. Their transformed nature automatically suits them to this task. Therefore, this task is not an option or afterthought. The light that they radiate is not what they do but who they *are*.

World events as well as situations we're aware of demonstrate the great need for light on how to live. The popular media of newspaper, radio and television, as well as scholarly research and publications, constantly update us on our burgeoning social and personal problems. These problems remain unsolved because of the confusion, ignorance or perversity among both our leaders and among most of the world's population about the fundamental causes of human happiness and misery.

Solutions to humanity's problems—from incest to atomic warfare, from mental illness to poverty and pollution—are by no means easy or simple. But what we know of human nature seems to indicate that insight on how to live can be provided effectively only by those who are prepared to lead the way by example. Only by *showing* how to live can we teach how to live. It is by the *kind of life* that is in us and that makes us examples of God's indwelling that we reveal the foundation for communicating God's redeeming word and Spirit to an ever-larger circle of human beings. This is the pattern set forth in the New Testament book of Acts and later points of Christian history. In us, as in Jesus Christ himself, *the Life* is to be "*the light* of all people" (Jn 1:4).

Collectively, the church as the "called-out" people of God is empowered to stand up for wandering humanity to see, just as the cloudy pillar by day and the pillar of fire by night guided the Israelites through the desert (Ex 13:21-22). When faced with starvation, crime, economic disasters and difficulties, disease, loneliness, alienation and war, the church should be the certified authority the world looks to for answers on how to live. The resources of God's power are at the church's disposal. We sense this, however dimly, and announce it when we say, "Christ is the answer!" Although you might not have thought of these problems as "questions," they do present the precise difficulties of life that Jesus alone can resolve.

Individuals who are disciples and friends of Jesus who have learned to work shoulder to shoulder with their Lord stand in this world as a point of contact between heaven and earth, a kind of Jacob's ladder by which the angels of God may ascend from and descend into human life (Jn 1:51; Gen 28:12). Thus the disciple stands as an envoy or a receiver by which the kingdom of God is conveyed into every quarter of human affairs (Lk 10:1-11). This, as Hannah Hurnard has so beautifully described it, is the role of the intercessor:

> An intercessor means one who is in such vital contact with God and with his fellow men that he is like a live wire closing the gap between the saving power of God and the sinful men who have been cut off from that power. An intercessor is the contacting link between the source of power (the life of the Lord Jesus Christ) and the objects needing that power and life.[1]

But what is the *process* by which we can be fully transformed into children of light? Into "blameless and innocent . . . children of God without blemish in the midst of a crooked and perverse generation, in which you shine like stars in the world . . . holding fast to the word of life" (Phil 2:15-16)? How are we to understand the ongoing process (which involves hearing God's voice) by which our present life is to be redeemed, shaped and conformed to the likeness of the Son (Rom 8:29)? And what is the role of the word of God in this process? When these questions are answered, we shall be in a position to deal in a practical manner—in chapters eight and nine—with hearing God's voice.

An Additional Birth by the Word of God

How are we to fulfill the following words of Scripture?

> Let the same mind be in you that was in Christ Jesus. (Phil 2:5)

> For to this you have been called, because Christ also suffered for you, leaving you an example, so that you should follow in his steps. "He committed no sin, and no deceit was found in his mouth." When he was abused, he did not return abuse; when he suffered, he did not threaten; but he entrusted himself to the one who judges justly. (1 Pet 2:21-23)

In the light of the previous chapter on the word of God, we can now give a clear and thorough answer to the question about the process of redemption—one that goes beyond mere figures of speech and poetic language. *It is through the action of the word of God upon us, throughout us and with us that we come to have the mind of Christ and thus to live fully in the kingdom of God.*

As we have seen, the word of God is a creative and sustaining substance, an active power, not limited by space and time or physical constraints. It organizes and guides that which it is directed to by God and by people in union with God. It is what lies at the foundation of all the kinds of life and beings there are.

What is life? In all its various levels and types, *life is power to act and respond in specific kinds of relations*. For example, a cabbage has certain powers of action and response and a corresponding level of life. There is a big difference between a cabbage that is alive and one that is dead, though the dead one still exists. This can also be said of a snail or a kitten.

But a live cabbage can make no response to, say, a ball of string.

That is precisely because of the *kind* of life that is in it. Though alive as a cabbage, it is *dead* to the realm of play. Similarly, a kitten playing with the string can make no response to numbers or poetry, and in that sense the kitten is dead to the realms of arithmetic and literature. A live cabbage, though dead to one realm (that of play) is yet alive in another—that of the soil, the sun and the rain. The situation is similar with the kitten.

Human beings were once alive to God. They were created to be responsive to and interactive with him. Adam and Eve lived in a conversational relationship with their Creator, daily renewed. When they mistrusted God and disobeyed him, that cut them off from the realm of the Spirit. Thus they became dead in relation to the realm of the Spirit—much as a kitten is dead to arithmetic. God had said of the forbidden tree, "in the day you eat of it you shall die" (Gen 2:17). And they did.

Biologically they continued to live, of course. But they ceased to be responsive and interactive in relation to God's cosmic rule in his kingdom. It would be necessary for God to confer an additional level of life on humans through "being born from above" (Jn 3:3). This would enable them once again to be alive to God, to be able to respond toward him and to act within the realm of the Spirit.

Human beings "born of water" (Jn 3:5)—that is, through natural birth—are alive in the flesh, in the biological and psychological realm of nature. But in relation to God they remain "dead through the trespasses and sins" (Eph 2:1). Therefore they inhabit a world "without hope and without God" (Eph 2:12 NIV). They can, however, be born a second time, "born from above" (Jn 3:3). This is not merely to be born again in the sense of *repeating* something or to make a new start from the same place. Instead, it is a matter of an *additional* kind of birth, whereby we become aware of and enter into the spiritual kingdom of God. Imagine an otherwise normal kitten that suddenly begins to appreciate and compose poetry, and that image will give you an impression of the huge transition involved in this additional birth.

This additional birth is brought about by God's word and Spirit, and it is spiritual in its effects. "What is born of the flesh is flesh, and what is born of the Spirit is spirit" (Jn 3:6).

The Teacher Who Did Not Know

A respected spiritual leader of the Jews was very impressed with what he had seen of Jesus and approached him with the words, "Rabbi, we know that you are a teacher who has come from God; for no one can do these signs that you do apart from the presence of God" (Jn 3:2). Thus Nicodemus, this leader, complimented Jesus, yet at the same time he complimented himself on being an insider who had the good sense to recognize God at work.

Jesus' reply to him was a stinging rebuke, though it was delivered in such a gentle way as to be digestible and helpful. In effect Jesus said that Nicodemus had not the slightest idea what he was talking about. Nicodemus came claiming to be able to recognize, to see, God at work. Jesus said, "No one can see the kingdom of God without being born from above" (Jn 3:3). Without this birth we cannot recognize God's workings: we do not possess the appropriate faculties and equipment. We are like kittens trying to contemplate a sonnet.

Nicodemus was immediately tripped up by this simple observation, revealing the true limits of his understanding. He could only think of the usual sort of birth. So he gropingly inquired, "How can a grown man have *that* again?" Then Jesus explained that unless someone has had the usual birth (of water) and an additional birth (of Spirit), she or he cannot participate in God's governance, his kingdom.

Those born of the Spirit manifest a different kind of life. Remember that a life is *a definite range of activities and responses.* The spiritually born exhibit a life deriving from an invisible spiritual realm and its powers. In natural terms one cannot explain what is happening with them, where they come from or where they go (Jn 3:8). But just as with the invisible wind and its effects, we recognize the presence of God's kingdom in a person by its effects in and around them as they progressively become transformed into children of light.

> *The spiritually born exhibit a life deriving from an invisible spiritual realm and its powers.*

Birth Through the Spirit and the Word of God

We have already seen how the words of Jesus are Spirit and in what sense the Spirit is also Word. The additional birth that brings a person to life in the realm of God is attributed both to the Spirit (Jn 3:5-8) and to the Word. In 1 Peter 1:23 those who are alive to God are described as being "born anew, not of perishable but of imperishable seed, through the living and enduring word of God." And James 1:18 tells us that "in fulfillment of his own purpose he gave us birth by the word of truth."

This testimony of James and Peter was based on their observations of the effects that the word of God through Christ had on them and of the effects that God's word through them and the early church had on others. Paul expressed this as a sober matter of fact: "So faith comes from what is heard, and what is heard comes through the word of Christ" (Rom 10:17).

As the word of God in creation brought forth light and matter and life, so the gospel of Christ comes to us while we are biologically alive but dead to God. The gospel both empowers and calls forth a response by its own power, enabling us to see and enter the kingdom of God as participants. It opens the door of the mind and enters the heart. From there it is able to progressively transform the whole personality. Thus "the sower sows the word" of the kingdom (Mk 4:14). When this takes root in the heart and mind, a new life enters our personality and increasingly becomes *our* life as we learn to "be guided by the Spirit" (Gal 5:25) and "sow to the Spirit" (Gal 6:8).

Redemption in this respect is simply a further aspect of creation—a new creation. This new creation is the only thing that matters in our relation to God, as Paul says (Gal 6:15). Without it we have no relation to God, in the sense of something in which we *live*, and from it arise all further developments of God's rule in our individual souls.

This is what C. H. Spurgeon had to say on the matter:

> Even so we have felt the Spirit of God operating upon our hearts, we have known and perceived the power which he wields over human spirits, and we know him by frequent, conscious, personal contact. By the sensitiveness of our spirit we are as much made conscious of the presence of the Spirit of God as we are made cognizant of the existence of souls, or as we are certified of the existence of matter by its action upon our senses. We have been raised from the dull sphere of mere mind and matter into the heavenly radiance of the spirit-world; and now, as spiritual men, we discern spiritual things, we feel the forces which are paramount in the spirit-realm, and we know that there is a Holy Ghost, for we feel him operating upon our spirits.[2]

The Word of God Planted in Our Hearts

James, the brother of Jesus, uses the image of planting to portray the relationship of the additional life in the Spirit to our natural, fleshly life. He encourages us to "welcome with meekness the implanted word that has the power to save your souls" (Jas 1:21).

After the "additional" life has been planted in us, our natural powers are not left to run their own way under or alongside the new life; they are to be channeled through and subordinated to that life from above. All are redirected to spiritual ends, appointed to higher purposes, though they remain in themselves normal human powers.

The uniqueness of each individual personality remains in the beauty and goodness of its natural life. But a holy radiance rests upon it and shines through it because it is now the temple of God, the area over which the larger and higher power of God plays. An additional, spiritual life comes through the word of God as that word possesses and redirects the energies of the natural life to promote the ends of God's kingdom.

Washed in the Word of God

A different description of the function of the word of God in our redemption is seen in Ephesians 5:25-27. Here, speaking of the church, the apostle says that Christ "gave himself up for her, in order to make her holy by cleansing her with the washing of water by the word, so as to present the church to himself in splendor, without a spot or wrinkle or anything of the kind—yes, so that she may be holy and without blemish."

Here Christ, the Word of God, is pictured as *washing away* the impurities and clutter that have permeated our human personalities during our life away from God. These impurities and distractions, which in fact do not automatically disappear at the additional birth, limit and attack both individual spiritual growth and the role intended for Christ's followers as the light of the world.

By his sacrificial death and triumphant resurrection, Jesus Christ finished welding his immediate followers into a totally new kind of social unit—the redemptive community, the living temple of the living God (Eph 2:21-22). This community in turn provided an environment within which God's word would be present with such richness and power that the church *could* stand forth on the world scene as beyond all reasonable reproach. This is how it is to fulfill its calling to be the light of the world—the haven and guide of all humanity on the earth.

Just think for a moment about what happens when you wash a dirty shirt: the water and laundry soap move through the fibers of the shirt material and carry out the dirt lodged within those fibers. When we come to God, our minds and hearts are like that dirty shirt, cluttered with false beliefs and attitudes, deadly feelings, past deeds and misguided plans, hopes and fears.

The word of God—primarily the gospel of his kingdom and of the life and death of Jesus on our behalf—enters our mind and brings new life through faith. As we open our entire life to this new power and as those sent by God minister the word to us, the word moves into every part of our personality, just like the water and soap move through the shirt's fibers. God's word pushes out and replaces all that is false and opposed to God's purposes in creating us and putting us in our unique place on earth.

We are transformed by the renewing of our minds and thus are able to "discern what is the will of God—what is good and acceptable and perfect" (Rom 12:2). *Hearing God becomes a reliably clear and practical matter for the mind that is transformed by this washing of the word.*

The Amazing Extent of the Dirt

What a multitude of things must first be washed from the mind, and what an obstacle they pose to our hearing God! Only the powerful and living word of God is capable of removing them. For example, we usually think that if we are mean enough to people, they will be good. We hope to control people by threatening them and punishing them. Yet this was not the way of Jesus. He let others punish him and said, "And I, when I am lifted up from the earth [on the cross], will draw all people to myself" (Jn 12:32).

We are also apt to believe that we must serve ourselves or no one else will. But Jesus knew that those who would save their life must lose it (Lk 9:24-25). We are pretty well convinced that we gain by grabbing and holding. But Jesus taught us, "Give, and it will be given to you" (Lk 6:38). An untold number of other false ideas and attitudes corrupt our minds and lives and must be washed out by the entry of God's word. "The unfolding of your words gives light" (Ps 119:130).

Even for many of us who already profess to follow Christ, much inward change will still be needed before we will be able to hear God correctly. When trouble comes—for example, when we have car problems or get into a dispute with someone in our family or at work—how long does it take us to get around to bringing it to God in prayer? When we see an accident or some violent behavior or we hear an ambulance down the street, do we even think to hold those concerned up to God in prayer? When we go to meet with a person for any reason, do we go in a spirit of prayer so that we would be prepared to minister to them, or they to us, in all ways possible and necessary? When we are alone, do we constantly recognize that God is present with us? Does our mind spontaneously return to God when not intensely occupied, as the needle of the compass turns to the North Pole when removed from nearer magnetic sources? Our answers to these questions make us sadly aware of how our mind is solidly trained in false ways.

Today, with all our knowledge, all our technology and all our sophisticated research, we find our world in the same basic situation as that described by Isaiah many centuries before Christ:

> We wait for light, and lo! there is darkness;
>> and for brightness, but we walk in gloom.
> We grope like the blind along a wall,
>> groping like those who have no eyes;
> we stumble at noon as in the twilight,
>> among the vigorous as though we were dead. (Is 59:9-10)

This is all because our minds—perhaps our very brains—need to have the false thoughts and habits washed out of them. They so badly need to be washed that we rarely understand what life would be like if they *were* cleaned, and many of us do not even sense the need for cleaning.

A recent report from a mental health clinic told how the removal of coffee from the waiting rooms transformed the patients' behavior. Before, while the coffee was available, there was constant bickering and even violence between patients as well as between the patients and the staff. After the coffee was removed and the stimulation of caffeine was withdrawn, there were only two or three unpleasant scenes per week. Like the caffeine, the poisonous thoughts, beliefs, fears, lusts and attitudes inhabiting our minds compel us to destructive behavior that we ourselves do not understand and whose source we do not recognize.

Earlier I explained that a word is fundamentally an expressed thought or feeling. The *literal* truth is that Christ through his word removes the old routines in the heart and mind—the old routines of thought, feeling, action, imagination, conceptualization, belief, inference—and in their place he puts something else: *his* thoughts, *his* attitudes, *his* beliefs, *his* ways of seeing and interpreting things, *his words*. He washes out our minds, and in the place of confusion and falsehood—or hatred, suspicion and fear, to speak of emotions—he brings clarity, truth, love, confidence and hopefulness.

So where there was fear, there is now hope; where there was suspicion, there is now confidence; where there was hate, there is now love; and all are based on a new understanding of God conveyed into us by his word. Vessels of wrath become vessels of patience and kindness. Where there was covetousness and lust, there is now generosity and courteous consideration. Where there was manipulation and possessiveness, there is now trust toward God and encouragement of others toward liberty and individuality. We now have the *character* to which listening for God's voice is natural.

Union with Christ

Until now we have been dealing with the word of God as it comes to, on and through us. But in the progress of God's redemptive work, communication advances into communion, and communion into union. When the progression is complete we can truly say, "It is no longer I who live, but it is Christ who lives in me" (Gal 2:20) and "For to me, living is Christ" (Phil 1:21).

> *In the progress of God's redemptive work* communication *advances into* communion, *and* communion *into* union.

Communication often occurs over a certain distance, even amid possible opposition. We can still communicate with those with whom we are at war. God communicates with us even while we are his enemies, dead in our sins. When communication between two people rises to the level of communion, there is a distinctness but also a profound sharing of the thoughts, feelings and objectives that make up our lives. Each recognizes the thought or feeling as his or hers, while knowing with joy that the other is feeling or thinking in the same way.

When communion advances into union, however, the sense of "mine" and "thine" may often be absent. There is only "ours" and, while "mine" does mean mine, it no longer thereby also means "not thine." This condition of union is realized in a marriage where the two partners have indeed become one. For this reason marriage can serve as a picture of the relation between Christ and his church, and between the soul and God.

It is this union beyond communion that Paul speaks of when he says the redeemed have the mind of Christ (1 Cor 2:16) as well as when he exhorts us to have the mind of Christ (Phil 2:5). Jesus prays the faithful might have this same union: "that they may be one, as we are one, I in them and you in me, that they may become completely one, so that the world may know that you have sent me and have loved them even as you have loved me" (Jn 17:22-23).

For the good that Christ offers us in the redeemed life to become real in ourselves, we must at some point begin to appreciate
the *literal* character of the Scriptures that speak of Christ's being
in us. Jesus Christ imparts himself to his church. In what may
have been his first attempt to make this plain, he told his followers, "Very truly, I tell you, unless you eat the flesh of the Son of
Man and drink his blood, you have no life in you. Those who eat
my flesh and drink my blood have eternal life, and I will raise
them up on the last day; for my flesh is true food and my blood is
true drink" (Jn 6:53-55).

Those who heard these words were deeply offended, for they did
not understand that when he spoke of his flesh and blood he was
speaking in the most concrete terms of himself. As he immediately
explained, his actual flesh, when taken apart from his *spiritual, personal reality*, would do them absolutely no good at all (Jn 6:63). In
this same verse he goes on to describe his *words* as "spirit and life."

It was through his words that he literally, not figuratively, imparted
himself while he lived and taught among the people of his day. On the
foundation of his words to his followers, the powerful events of Cal-
vary, the resurrection and Pentecost brought forth a communion and
then a union later described by the apostle Paul as the great mystery
of the ages, "Christ in you, the hope of glory" (Col 1:27).

Christ's Faith as My Faith

The faith by which Jesus Christ lived, his faith in God and his kingdom, is expressed in the gospel that he preached. That gospel is the
good news that the kingdom rule of God is available to humankind
here and now. His followers did not have this faith within themselves, and they long regarded it only as *his* faith, not theirs. Even
after they came to have faith *in him*, they did not share his faith.

Once, in the middle of the Sea of Galilee, the disciples' boat was
almost beaten under by the waves while Jesus slept calmly. His
disciples woke him crying, "Lord, save us! We are perishing!" (Mt

8:25). Jesus reproachfully replied, "Why are you afraid, you of little faith?" (Mt 8:26). Now the disciples obviously had great faith in Jesus. They called upon him, counting on him to save them. They had great faith in him, but *they did not have his great faith in God.* It was because they did not have *his* faith that he spoke of how little faith they had.

Some Christians too commonly demonstrate that the notions of "faith *in* Christ" and "love *for* Christ" leave Christ *outside* the personality of the believer. One wonders whether the modern translations of the Bible are not being governed by the need to turn our weakened practice into the norm of faith. These exterior notions of Christ's faith and love will never be strong enough to yield the confident statement, "It is no longer I who live, but it is Christ who lives in me" (Gal 2:20). They can never provide the unity of the branches with the vine, where the life that is in the branch is literally that which flows to it through the vine and is the very life of the vine to which it is attached (Jn 15:1-4).

Such exterior notions cannot provide the mutual abiding (Jn 15:5) that causes us branches to bring forth much fruit and without which we can do nothing. It is as such abiding branches that we "were reconciled to God through the death of his Son, [so] much more surely, having been reconciled, will we be saved by his life" (Rom 5:10).

> *Our additional life is also God's life in us: his thoughts, his faith, his love, all* literally *imparted to us, shared with us, by his word and Spirit.*

Our additional life, though it is still our life, is also God's life in us: his thoughts, his faith, his love, all *literally* imparted to us, shared with us, by his word and Spirit.

Paul on Salvation

The substance of Paul's teachings about salvation is drained off when we fail to take literally his words about our union and iden-

tification with Christ. Without this his writings can be handily
subjected to elaborate plans of salvation or made into a "Roman
road" of doctrinal assents, by which we supposedly gain God's approval *merely* for believing what every demon believes to be true
about Jesus and his work. James S. Stewart's profound book *A Man
in Christ* deals with this tendency in interpreting Paul and forcefully corrects it:

> Beyond the reproduction in the believer's spiritual life of his
> Lord's death and burial lies the glorious fact of union with
> Christ in His resurrection. "Like as Christ was raised up
> from the dead by the glory of the Father, even so we also
> should walk in newness of life" (Romans 6:4). Everything
> that Paul associates with salvation—joy, and peace, and
> power, and progress, and moral victory—is gathered up in
> the one word he uses so constantly, "life." Only those who
> through Christ have entered into a vital relationship to God
> are really "alive." . . . But what Paul now saw with piercing
> clearness was that this life into possession of which souls
> entered by conversion was nothing else than the life of
> Christ Himself. He shared His very being with them.[3]

Stewart points out how Paul speaks of "Christ who is your life"
(Col 3:4) and of "the life of Jesus" being "made visible in our bodies" (2 Cor 4:10). He points to Paul's contrast of the law of sin and
death with "the law of the Spirit of life in Christ Jesus" (Rom 8:2).
And he emphasizes that "this life which flows from Christ into
man is something totally different from anything experienced on
the merely natural plane. It is different, not only in degree, but
also in kind. It is *kainotēs zōēs* (Romans 6:4), a new quality of life,
a supernatural quality."[4] This is what Paul means when he says
that if one is *in* Christ, one is a new creation (2 Cor 5:17).

It is this identity between the additional life of the regenerate,
or restarted, individual and the person and life of Christ himself

that turns believers into "a colony of heaven" (as Moffatt translates Phil 3:20) and enables them to fulfill their call to be the light
of the world, showing the world what it is really like to be alive.

Focusing on Our Aliveness to God

The person who has been brought into the additional life by the
creative action of the word of God now lives between two distinct
realms of life and power: that of the natural or fleshly and that of
the supernatural or spiritual. Even while dead in our sins and unable to interact constructively with God, we are still capable of
sensing the vacuum in the natural life apart from God and of following up on the many earthly rumors about God and where he is
to be found. Once the new life begins to enter our soul, however,
we have the responsibility and opportunity of ever more fully focusing our whole being on it and wholly orienting ourselves toward it. This is *our* part, and God will not do it for us.

We can see how this happens by looking in Romans 7. Here Paul
speaks of a time when he found that the impulses of his personality,
solidified through lifelong training in the ways of sin, continued to
move in their old patterns and not in conformity with the new life
that had entered his soul when he encountered Christ. In this condition, he said, "I fail to carry out the things I want to do, and I find
myself doing the very things I hate" (Rom 7:15 JB).

This condition is rather like that of a boat traveling through the
water. The boat does not immediately shift to the direction the
pilot wants at the very moment he moves the rudder. And it may
even continue moving forward for some time while the engine is
in full reverse. The pilot must learn how to direct the boat partly
in terms of powers that move independently of his will and do not
as such represent *his* intentions.

Paul chooses to identify with his new life. He *acknowledges*,
reckons and *affirms* his union with what in himself cleaves to
the good:

When I act against my own will, that means I have a self
that acknowledges that the Law is good, and so the thing
behaving in that way is not my self but sin living in me. The
fact is, I know of nothing good living in me—living, that is,
in my unspiritual self—for though the will to do what is
good is in me, the performance is not, with the result that
instead of doing the good things I want to do, I carry out the
sinful things I do not want. When I act against my will,
then, it is not my true self doing it, but sin which lives in
me. (Rom 7:16-20 JB)

Or, as the King James Version simply says, "It is no more I that
do it, but sin that dwelleth in me" (Rom 7:20).

The "not I, but sin" of Romans 7 must be taken in conjunction
with the "not I, but Christ" of Galatians 2:20. Of course some
people might say such things and only be seeking to excuse themselves from responsibility for their inner sinfulness, as referred to
in Romans 7, or from responsibility for their sinful actions, as referred to in Galatians 2. But not Paul. Speaking for hosts of men
and women who have come to life in Christ throughout the ages,
Paul is beyond the point of excusing or accusing. He has accepted
the full measure of his guilt. He is now concerned with how to
enter into the new life to its fullest.

This requires that *we* take a stand as to *who we are* in this new
life, that we identify *with* the Christ-life in us and *against* the sin
still present in ourselves, and that we settle in our will the question
of who we intend to be. This is what it means to "consider" ourselves "dead to sin and alive to God in Christ Jesus" (Rom 6:11).

As men and women of the additional birth, we stand at the
intersection of the merely natural (fleshly) and the spiritual. St.
Thomas Aquinas coined a word to express just this state: *aevum*,
as distinct from *tempus* and *aeternitas. Aevum* is the mean between eternity and time, sharing in them both. It is two lives, two

streams of awareness and power, mingling together in the individual who must choose which one he or she will truly be.

Our identification with the one life or the other is not a fact to
be discovered by subtle examinations of theological treatises or of
our soul-life and state of mind. It is a *set of the will*. Is it my will to
be in the old, dead life of sin? Or is it my will to be in the resurrection life of Christ, which has entered into me through the impact
of God's word?

If you choose the latter, you still "work out your own salvation
with fear and trembling; for it is God who is at work in you, enabling you both to will and to work for his good pleasure" (Phil
2:12-13). It *is* I. Yet it is *not I* but Christ. We move beyond mere
communication and communion toward union with him, and we
have the opportunity of progressively unifying all aspects of our
personalities with him so that, literally, "to me, living is Christ
and dying is gain" (Phil 1:21).

◇◇◇

Hearing God in Scripture
Romans 5:10-11; 6:4, 8-11

Before doing this *lectio divina* exercise, take a minute to review
the ideas in the last three sections:

- "Christ's Faith as My Faith": His thoughts, his faith, his love, all
  literally imparted to us, shared with us, by his word and Spirit.

- "Paul on Salvation": The new life is a new supernatural quality
  of life. It is a different *kind* of life.

- "Focusing on Our Aliveness to God": As we take a stand as to
  who we are in this new life, identifying *with* the Christ-life in us
  and *against* the sin, the "boat" of our life begins to turn around.

These ideas about our aliveness in Christ will help you settle
into the Scripture passage in an informed way.

To prepare to read in order to receive from God—to hear God—

please set the book or electronic reader down for a minute. Close your eyes and breathe out slowly. Ask God to give you an openness to hear whatever the Spirit wishes to bring to you today.

Read—*lectio*

Read the passage slowly.

> *For if while we were enemies, we were reconciled to God through the death of his Son, much more surely, having been reconciled, will we be saved by his life. But more than that, we even boast in God through our Lord Jesus Christ, through whom we have now received reconciliation. . . .*
>
> *We have been buried with him by baptism into death, so that, just as Christ was raised from the dead by the glory of the Father, so we too might walk in newness of life. . . .*
>
> *If we have died with Christ, we believe that we will also live with him. We know that Christ, being raised from the dead, will never die again; death no longer has dominion over him. The death he died, he died to sin, once for all; but the life he lives, he lives to God. So you also must consider yourselves dead to sin and alive to God in Christ Jesus.*

Now that the words are familiar to you, please read it again. This time, also listen with the ear of your heart for a word or phrase, a detail of the story that shimmers or stands out to you. Do not choose this yourself. Let the Spirit bring it to you. Even if you don't like it, try to welcome it with meekness and see what happens (Jas 1:21).

Reflect—*meditatio*

Read the passage again slowly. As you do so and for a few minutes afterward, reflect on the word or phrase that stood out to you. Why do you think these words resonated with you?

Then ask God, How does this connect with my life today?

What do I need to know or be or do? Give yourself a few minutes to do this.

Respond (Pray)—*oratio*
Read the passage one last time, preparing yourself for what you want to say to God about what you think the Spirit might have said to you or what came to you.

Pray however you are led to pray. You might thank God for something or ask God for something.

Rest (Contemplation)—*contemplatio*
Do as you are led. You may wish to wait on God—to simply *be with* God. You may wish to ponder, How did God *seem* in the passage? How did Christ seem in this passage? Is there anything about Christ that makes you want his life in you, or at least want to *be with* him? Sit in the beauty and hope of that.

◇◇◇

The Written Word in the Progress of Redemption
Once the life of Christ has entered into us there are many things that we may do to increase the extent and depth of our identification and union with him. But the proper use of the *written* Word is most central to our cooperative efforts with God toward full conformity with Christ.

The written Word may come to us in many ways. It may come through sermons, through art, through casual conversation, through dramatic performances, literature or song. All of these are important. For many centuries the contents of the Bible were present to the people of Europe through the architecture and artistry of their great cathedrals and churches. Indeed, even today, Christians who have read the Bible and know its contents

well are often powerfully impacted on first seeing the content of
the Bible communicated in magnificent stone and rich, sweeping
stained-glass windows, such as are found in the cathedral at
Chartres, France.

Although all these means are good and helpful, however, the person who wishes to grow in grace is by far best advised to make a
close and constant companion of *the book*—the Bible. I do not mean
that it should be worshiped. Its uniquely sacred character is something that does not need to be exaggerated or even insisted on, because it is self-authenticating to any earnest and open-minded user.
For just as openness to and hunger for God leads naturally to the
Bible, if it is available, so the eager use of the Bible leads naturally
and tangibly to the mind of God and the person of Christ.

The written Word of God is an expression of God's mind just as
surely, though in a different manner, as are creation and Jesus, the
living Word. As we read and study it intelligently, humbly and
openly, we come increasingly to share God's mind.

This use of the Bible is not superstitious or magical, because a
natural connection exists between a proper use of the Bible and its
ideal result—union with Christ. The Bible expresses the mind of
God, since God himself speaks to us through its pages. Thus we,
in understanding the Bible, come to share his thoughts and attitudes and even come to share his life through his Word. Scripture
is a *communication* that establishes *communion* and opens the way
to *union*, all in a way that is perfectly understandable once we
begin to have experience of it.

We will be spiritually safe in our use of the Bible if we follow a
simple rule: *Read with a submissive attitude.* Read with a readiness
to surrender all you are—all your plans, opinions, possessions,
positions. Study as intelligently as possible, with all available
means, but never study merely to find the truth and especially not
just to prove something. Subordinate your desire to *find* the truth
to your desire to *do* it, to act it out!

Those who wish to hear the word and know the truth are often not prompted by their desire to *do* it. The light that such people find frequently proves to be their own snare and condemnation.

"Praying" the Scriptures

William Law comments, "Therefore the Scriptures should only be read in an attitude of prayer, trusting to the inward working of the Holy Spirit to make their truths a living reality within us."[5]

There is a simple technique that every believer, no matter how trained or untrained, can follow with assurance that the very bread of life will be spread out for them on the pages of the Scriptures. It is a practice very similar to one encouraged by Madame Guyon in her little book *Short and Very Easy Way of Prayer*, first published in 1688 in Lyons, France. This book is still available today, republished with some modifications under the title *Experiencing the Depths of Jesus Christ*. The first four chapters of it could usefully be read as a supplement to what I am about to say here.

When we come to the Scriptures as a part of our conscious strategy to cooperate with God for the full redemption of our life, *we must desire that his revealed will should be true for us.* Next, we should *begin with those parts of Scripture with which we have some familiarity,* such as Psalm 23, the Lord's Prayer, the Sermon on the Mount, 1 Corinthians 13 or Romans 8.

You may think that this is not a big beginning. But keep in mind that your aim is not to become a scholar or to impress others with your knowledge of the Bible—a dreadful trap for so many fellowships aiming to be biblical. That aim will only cultivate pride and lay a foundation for the petty, quarrelsome spirit so regrettably, yet so commonly, observed in those outwardly identified as the most serious students of the Scriptures.

It may help to remember these words of Thomas à Kempis:

Of what use is it to discourse learnedly on the Trinity, if you lack humility and therefore displease the Trinity? Lofty words do not make a man just or holy; but a good life makes him dear to God. I would far rather feel contrition than be able to define it. If you knew the whole Bible by heart, and all the teachings of the philosophers, how would this help you without the grace and love of God?[6]

Your aim must be only to nourish your soul on God's word to you. Go first to those parts of the Bible you already know, therefore, and count on your later growth and study to lead you to other parts that will be useful.

Do not try to read a great deal at once. As Madame Guyon wisely counsels, "If you read quickly, it will benefit you little. You will be like a bee that merely skims the surface of a flower. Instead, in this new way of reading with prayer, you must become as the bee who penetrates into the depths of the flower. You plunge deeply within to remove its deepest nectar."[7]

You may have been told that it is good to read the Bible through every year and that you can ensure this will happen by reading so many verses per day from the Old and New Testaments. If you do this you may enjoy the reputation of one who reads the Bible through each year, and you may congratulate yourself on it. But will you become more like Christ and more filled with the life of God? It is a proven fact that many who read the Bible in this way, as if they were taking medicine or exercising on a schedule, do not advance spiritually. It is better in one year to have ten good verses transferred *into the substance of our lives* than to have every word of the Bible flash before our eyes. Remember that "the letter kills, but the Spirit gives life" (2 Cor 3:6). We read to open ourselves to the Spirit.

Come to your chosen passage as to a place where you will have a holy meeting with God. Read a small part of the passage and dwell on it, praying for the assistance of God's Spirit in bringing *fully* before your mind and into your life the realities expressed. Always ask, What is my life like since this is true, and how shall I speak and act because of this? You may wish to turn the passage into a prayer of praise or request.

> *Read a small part of the passage and dwell on it, praying for the assistance of God's Spirit in bringing* fully *before your mind and into your life the realities expressed.*

Perhaps you are reading the great "God is love" passage from 1 John 4. You find written here, "There is no fear in love, but perfect love casts out fear; for fear has to do with punishment, and whoever fears has not reached perfection in love" (v. 18). You may prayerfully dwell on the ways in which love—God's love for us, our love for him and love among people on earth—pushes fear out of all relationships. You may think of the fearless child surrounded by loving parents, of how loving neighbors give us confidence and relieve our anxieties. You may dwell on how the assurance of God's love given to us in the death of his Son suggests that we will never be beyond his care. You may seek God's help in comprehending this and in seeing what your fear-free life might be like. Then you may lift your heart in joyful praise as you realize how things are for you, living in God's kingdom. God's word now speaking in you, not just *at* you, creates the faith that appropriates the fact *for you.*

Or you may read, "The LORD is my shepherd, I shall not want" (Ps 23:1). First, you will find *information,* which you may not automatically transfer to yourself. You may say, "This was true just for David, the psalmist." But, as you dwell prayerfully on the plain information, a *yearning* that it might be so for *you* may arise. You may express this, saying, "I wish the Lord were my shepherd; that the great God would have for me the care and attention that the shepherd has for his sheep!" And as you meditate on the psalm, *affirmation* may arise, as it has for so many people ("It must be so! I will have it be so!") followed then perhaps by *invocation* ("Lord, make it so for me") and *appropriation* (the settled conviction that it *is* so, that it is a statement of fact about you).

Do not hurry. Do not *dabble* in spiritual things. Give time for each stage to play itself out fully in your heart. Remember, this is not something you are doing by yourself. *Watch* and pray.

Now practice again with those great passages from Romans 8, beginning with verse 28, "We know that all things work together for good for those who love God, who are called according to his purpose," and ending with the declaration of triumph that no matter what befalls us "we are more than conquerors through him who loved us" (v. 37). Again, the general train of development is as follows:

1. *information*
2. *longing* for it to be so
3. *affirmation* that it *must* be so
4. *invocation* to God to make it so
5. *appropriation* by God's grace that it *is* so

This last stage must not be forced or, especially, faked. The ability for it will be given as you watch for God to move in your life.

When there is an inner agreement between our minds and the truth expressed in the passages we read, we know that we have part of the mind of Christ *in us as our own*. For these great truths conveyed by Scripture were the very things that Jesus believed. They constituted the faith, hope and love in which he lived. As they become our beliefs, his mind becomes our mind. We are fitted out then to function as true colaborers with God, as brothers, sisters and friends of Jesus in the present and coming kingdom of God. And we are in a position to know and understand fully how God speaks now to his children.

The practice of *lectio divina* introduced in this book will draw you deeper into this kind of devotional use of the written Word. In order for the written Word of God to have its best effect, it should be made part of an overall plan of disciplines for the spiritual life.[8]

Some Topics for Reflection

1. Redemption is understood in this chapter to cover transformation of whole persons and their lives into Christlikeness. It is not merely a matter of the forgiveness of sins, to guarantee our entrance into heaven when we die. Do you regard this view of redemption as biblical? Does it make sense in your theological background?

2. In what way is a *redeemed life* automatically the light of the world?

3. What is life, say, in a cabbage or in a kitten? Can you characterize the "life from above" in terms of its presence in day-to-day human existence?

4. Planting and washing are two metaphors relating to the additional life of the Christian. Can you explain the meaning of each metaphor and illustrate each in a practical context?

5. Did the discussion of communication, communion and union make sense to you in terms of experiences you have had or know about on a purely human level? What about in terms of your experience of Jesus?

6. What is the distinction between the faith *of* Christ and faith *in* Christ? What difference does the distinction make? How do both of them help us?

7. What does it mean to "*consider* yourselves dead to sin" (Rom 6:11)? What will be the results of not doing this?

8. Our identification with the sin-life or with the Christ-life in us "is not a fact to be discovered by subtle examinations of theological treatises or of our soul-life and state of mind. *It*

is a set of the will." What is this about? Do you agree?

9. Experiment several times with praying the Scriptures, and summarize the results of the exercise. Share them with a friend.

8

Recognizing the Voice of God

*The shepherd of the sheep . . . calls his own sheep by name and
leads them out. . . . He goes ahead of them, and the sheep follow him
because they know his voice. . . . I am the good shepherd.
I know my own and my own know me. . . . My sheep hear my voice.
I know them, and they follow me.*

John 10:2-4, 14, 27

*The doctrine of the inner light is not sufficiently taught.
To the individual believer, who is, by the very fact of relationship
to Christ, indwelt by the Holy Spirit of God, there is granted
the direct impression of the Spirit of God on the Spirit of man,
imparting the knowledge of his will in matters of the smallest and
greatest importance. This has to be sought and waited for.*

G. Campbell Morgan, *God's Perfect Will*

*W*hen a word or thought comes to us—through others, the inner
voice, some special experience, the Bible or circumstances—*how*
do we know whether it is a word from God to us? What is it about
it that indicates it has a divine source? We can, of course, know

that the word is from God if it corresponds with the plain statement or meaning of the Bible, construed in such a way that it is
consistent with soundly interpreted biblical teaching. We can all
know at all times, for example, that God directs us not to worship
an idol or be covetous.

Beyond this, however, the only answer to the question, How do
we know whether this is from God? is *By experience.* Even a word-
for-word quotation from the Bible can be put to a use that makes
it only a message from the Dear Self or from Satan. The dangers of
so-called proof texting—of taking biblical passages out of context
to serve some preconceived purpose—are well-known. A single
statement taken directly from the Bible, even statements that are
often invoked for personal application, may be used in ways *contrary* to the purposes of God, contrary to any meaning that he may
have in mind for us. That is why *only the Bible as a whole* can be
treated as the written Word of God.

In any case, we must certainly go beyond, though never *around,*
the words of the Bible to find out what God is speaking to us. As
we have already seen, the teachings of the Bible, no matter how
thoroughly studied and firmly believed, can never by themselves
constitute our personal walk with God. They have to be *applied* to
us as individuals and to our individualized circumstances, or they
remain no part of our lives.

Voice Recognition in Nature

It is a remarkable fact that sheep and other domesticated animals
and pets unerringly recognize the voice of their master or mistress.
When they first hear that voice, they do not recognize who is
speaking, but they learn to do so very quickly. They do not need a
voice meter or other device to analyze it scientifically; they simply
recognize it immediately.

I once saw on television a story about a man named Charlie
Frank and his elephant Neeta. Frank raised Neeta from birth and

trained her as a circus performer. On retirement he gave her to the San Diego Zoo. They had not seen each other for fifteen years at the point when the program filmed their reunion. Frank called to Neeta across a distance of about a hundred yards. She came to him immediately and performed her old routines on command. Her past experience gave her the power to recognize his voice. In a similar way, we human beings learn from experience alone how to recognize the color red, with its various shades and characteristics, and to distinguish it from blue or yellow. A musician learns by experience to distinguish a minor key from a major one simply by hearing a melody.

Comparing humans with animals on this point echoes a prophetic theme. Isaiah marvels that

> the ox knows its owner,
>   and the donkey its master's crib;
> but Israel does not know,
>   my people do not understand. (Is 1:3)

Jeremiah makes a similar complaint with reference to non-domesticated creatures:

> Even the stork in the heavens
>   knows its times;
> and the turtledove, swallow, and crane
>   observe the time of their coming;
> but my people do not know
>   the ordinance of the LORD. (Jer 8:7)

By contrast, the light that shines on every human being who comes into the world, according to John 1:9, vainly strikes the blinded eyes of fallen humanity. The word that has gone out to the very ends of the earth, according to Psalm 19:4, falls on deaf ears. But those who have been given the additional birth—the new birth through the redemptive message of Christ that has entered their lives—can learn by experience to hear God as he speaks, to recognize his word and confidently interact with it.

Knowing by Experience

The simple statements from the Gospel of John, chapter 10, quoted at the beginning of this chapter are not merely a record of words that Jesus spoke. They are also an expression of John's own experience with Christ, his Lord and friend. The emphasis given in the opening of John's first epistle to seeing, hearing and touching the Word of life is quite startling (1 Jn 1:1, 3). But it was in the presence of the visible, touchable Jesus that John learned to recognize when God was speaking.

In the course of later experience John became so confident of the inner teacher that he could tell his children in the faith—even as he was warning them about those trying to deceive them—that they had no need of anyone other than the inner teacher, the Holy Spirit: "The anointing that you received from him abides in you, and so you do not need anyone to teach you. But as his anointing teaches you about all things, and is true and is not a lie, and just as it has taught you, abide in him" (1 Jn 2:27).[1]

John therefore speaks to us from the authority of his experience, just as Abraham spoke to his eldest servant when sending him into an unknown land to find a wife for Isaac (Gen 24) and just as Eli did to little Samuel (1 Sam 3). We may mistakenly think that if *God* spoke to us we would automatically know who is speaking, without having to learn, but that is simply a mistake— and one of the most harmful mistakes for those trying to hear God's voice. It leaves us totally at the mercy of any stray ideas we have picked up about what God's speaking is like.

Perhaps our inability to recognize his voice right off is a result of our fallen and distorted condition. Or perhaps it lies in the very nature of all personal relations—certainly you and I did not recognize the voice of whoever is now most dear and intimate to us the first time we heard it. Or perhaps it is because of the very gentleness with which our heavenly Father speaks to us. Whatever the reason, it seems that at first we must be *told* that God is speaking to us and possibly even be helped to detect his voice. Only later do we come, without assistance, confidently to distinguish and recognize his voice as *his* voice. That ability comes only with experience.

> *To confidently distinguish and recognize his voice as* his *voice— that ability comes only with experience.*

With assistance from those who understand the divine voice from their own experience and with an openness and will to learn on our part, we can come to recognize the voice of God without great difficulty. On the other hand, we should understand that it is in Satan's best interest to make an inherent mystery of God's word coming directly to the individual. In this way the power of God's specific word for our lives can be hindered or even totally lost. Without qualified help (which works alongside our own desire to learn and readiness to cooperate), God's direct word will most likely remain a riddle or at best a game of theological charades. This is generally the condition of the church today, I suspect. This would explain why such great confusion and difficulty exists about what it means really to walk with God (Mic 6:8). Such confusion allows evil impulses to move into the vacuum and sweep us away.

The Three Lights

God's impressions *within* and his word *without* are always corroborated by his providence *around*, and we should quietly wait until those three focus into one point. . . . If you do not know what you ought to do, stand still until you do. And when the time comes for action, circumstances, like glowworms, will sparkle along your path; and you will become so sure that you are right, when God's three witnesses concur, that you could not be surer though an angel beckoned you on.[2]

Many discussions about hearing God's voice speak of three points of reference, also called "three lights," that we can consult in determining what God wants us to do.[3] These are

- circumstances
- impressions of the Spirit
- passages from the Bible

When these three things point in the same direction, it is suggested, we may be sure the direction in which they point is the one God intends for us.

If I could keep only one bit of writing on hearing God outside the Bible itself, it would be hard to pass over a few pages from Frederick B. Meyer's book *The Secret of Guidance*. Many other authors have very fine and helpful things to say on the subject, but Meyer draws the issues together in a complete and yet simple fashion; and the spirit of his remarks—as is usual with him—is so sane and so spiritual that I would choose him over most others who have written on this subject. According to Meyer,

> The circumstances of our daily life are to us an infallible indication of God's will, when they concur with the inward promptings of the spirit and with the Word of God. So long as they are stationary, wait. When you must act, they will open, and a way will be made through oceans and rivers, wastes and rocks.[4]

It is possible to understand this precious advice in such a way that it completely resolves any problem about hearing God's voice. I believe that this will normally be the case for those who have *already* learned to recognize the inner voice of God. Probably none knew it more clearly than Meyer himself.

For those who do not yet have a confident, working familiarity with this voice, however, trying to discern the three lights may speedily result in a swirl of confusion, leaving them hopelessly adrift or wrecked on the shoals of spiritual misadventures. These lights can be especially dangerous and disappointing for those without a deep experience and commitment in the Way of Christ. Such people will almost certainly try to use them as a spiritual gimmick or quick fix. They will then fall prey to the desire to get their own way and to secure their own prosperity and security. Let us look more closely at the problem with using the three lights.

The Problem of Their Interdependence
A large part of the *practical* problem in working with the three lights comes from the simple fact that they are *interdependent*. It is difficult or impossible to tell what the one is saying without already knowing what the others are saying.

First of all, it is commonly understood that the Holy Spirit works through the Scriptures to make them effective for guidance as well as redemption. A conference of biblical scholars has affirmed "that the Holy Spirit who inspired Scripture acts through it today to work faith in its message" and also that "the Holy Spirit enables believers to appropriate and apply Scripture to their lives." Furthermore, the members of this conference denied "that the natural man is able to discern spiritually the biblical message apart from the Holy Spirit."[5]

Many people commonly regarded as evangelicals seem prepared to make even stronger statements on the role of the Holy Spirit in Bible study. Consider these comments made by William Law:

> Without the present illumination of the Holy Spirit, the Word of God must remain a dead letter to every man, no matter how intelligent or well-educated he may be. . . . It is just as essential for the Holy Spirit to reveal the truth of

Scripture to the reader today as it was necessary for Him to inspire the writers thereof in their day. . . . Therefore to say that, because we now have all the writings of Scripture complete, we no longer need the miraculous inspiration of the Spirit among men as in former days, is a degree of blindness as great as any that can be charged upon the scribes and Pharisees. Nor can we possibly escape their same errors; for in denying the present inspiration of the Holy Spirit, we have made Scripture the province of the letter-learned scribe.[6]

But how are we to recognize or authenticate a thought or message as an intervention of the Holy Spirit—even in our studies of the Bible—*except* from the teachings of the Scriptures?

The biblical test of a spiritual impulse weighs the impulse by whether or not it confesses Jesus as Lord (1 Cor 12:3) or as Son of God (1 Jn 4:2-3); yet this test is not very helpful in practice when we are, for example, trying to decide whom to marry or which job to take. And testing of spiritual or mental impulses or messages cannot in general be done by invoking the teachings of Scripture, if Scripture itself cannot be understood without spiritual assistance from those very impulses and messages.

Finally, the mere open or closed doors of circumstances cannot function independently of the other two lights or of *some* additional factor; for one does not know merely by looking at these doors who is opening or closing them—God, Satan or another human being. Indeed, one often cannot tell whether they are open or closed until after one has acted. It is not, therefore, practically possible to use the criteria of openness or closedness by themselves to determine what to do. Scripture and inner promptings must be brought into consideration to determine whether doors are open or closed.

No doubt those who think they can make the three lights formula work will be very impatient with me for raising these difficulties. My experience suggests that people who, for whatever reason, do not really need help in the practical context of hearing God may think that this formula can be made to work *as* a formula—which is how it is normally presented. Those who do need help, on the other hand, frequently drive themselves to distraction trying to use it. Also the formula is often thought to have worked *in retrospect*—after one has taken a certain alternative at the suggestion of the lights and all has turned out well. But by that stage, such confidence is no longer needed.

It is, therefore, simply not true that we can get a reading of what circumstances say, a separate reading of what the Bible says and yet another separate reading of what the Spirit says. Consequently, we cannot strengthen our reading of God's will from one of these sources just by mechanically checking it against the other sources, as we might get a safer reading of the time of day by consulting three clocks running independently of each other. Also the three lights tend to be limited to guidance, not to helping us understand the conversation.

The Conditions of Responsible Judgment

All who have much experience in the Way of Christ, however, will know that it *is* somehow right, when trying to hear what God is saying to an individual, to look to circumstances, the Bible and inner impulses of the Spirit. And all will know that these three do *somehow* serve to correct each other. That is why Frederick B. Meyer's words are so valuable. While they provide no formula, no mechanism, for making decisions, they must not simply be abandoned. How are we to understand the role they play in hearing God's voice? The answer to this question comes in two parts.

First, a life lived by listening to God speaking is not one that excludes our own judgment. Listening to God does not make our own decision-making process unnecessary. We ourselves, as well as others who come under the influence of God's voice, are still the ones who make the decisions. This is something we have already discussed, and we shall consider a new and very important aspect of it in chapter nine. *The three lights are simply the factors that we must consider in the process of making a responsible judgment and decision about what we are to do.* To be responsible in judgment and action is to humbly and fully consider these factors.

Second, while neither one light taken individually nor all of them taken together simply *give* us God's word, each or all together may be and usually are the *occasion* of God's directive word coming to us. This is the way it usually works in practice.

The voice of God is not itself any one of the three lights nor is it all of them together. But the inner teaching of which John speaks in his first epistle—the voice or word of God coming to individuals, as repeatedly displayed in biblical events—*usually* comes to us in conjunction with

- responsible study and meditation on the Bible
- experience of the various kinds of movements of the Spirit in our heart
- intelligent alertness to the circumstances that befall us

Although there are exceptions to the rule, God's directive voice does not usually come to us out of the blue. This point is important to us practically. *It enables us to do specific, concrete things that will help us as we seek to know the will of God.* These things we do—reflecting on the three lights—turn out to be the very things that go into exercising responsible judgment. As we reflect on our circumstances, our impressions of the Spirit and passages we read in the Bible, we also listen for the divine voice. But when God speaks and we recognize the voice as *his* voice, we do so because our *familiarity* with that voice enables us to recognize it. We do *not* recognize it because we are good at playing a guessing game about how the occasions through which his direction comes do or do not match up with each other.

Three Factors in the Voice

The voice of my beloved!
  Look, he comes
leaping upon the mountains,
    bounding over the hills. (Song 2:8)

I slept, but my heart was awake.
Listen! my beloved is knocking. (Song 5:2)

To say that we learn to recognize the voice of God by experience is not, however, all that we can or must say. Certain factors distinguish the voice of God, just as any human voice can be distinguished from another.

The most immediate factor in the human voice, which by itself is usually enough to tell those familiar with it whose voice it is, is a certain *quality* of sound. This is mainly a matter of which *tones* are produced and the manner in which they are modulated. Quality, at the human level, also includes the *style* of speech. For example, is it slow or fast, smooth or halting in its flow, indirect or to the point?

Besides quality, a certain *spirit* attaches to the human voice. A voice may be passionate or cold, whining or demanding, timid or confident, coaxing or commanding. This is, of course, not merely a matter of sounds but also a matter of attitudes or personal characteristics that become tangibly present in the voice.

Finally, there is the matter of *content* or of information conveyed. Although this is rarely the most immediate sign of who is speaking, it is in the end the most conclusive mark, for it reveals the history and conscious experience of the speaker. No matter if quality and spirit were totally different, a specific bit of information could conclusively identify a speaker in certain cases. For example, we might identify someone's words even when those words are spoken by another (as we do when one person reads another's writings aloud) or when we read those words in written form, without the author there to read them to us.

The three factors of *quality*, *spirit* and *content* by no means exhaust the complexity of the voice. Modern-day science and linguistics find in the voice vast fields for theoretical and practical study. From the philosophical point of view, much more could be said.[7] But enough has been said here to allow us to turn next to an examination of the voice of God in our hearts.

The Weight of Authority

The question then is, What are the factors of God's voice that enable us to recognize it as his? In this case, too, there is a distinctive quality with which we can become familiar—but it is not strictly the quality of sound, as it would be with a human voice. In chapter five I explained how the voice of God will usually (though not always) take the form of certain *thoughts* or *perceptions* that enter our minds. These obviously are not sounds.

The quality of God's voice is more a matter of the *weight* or impact an impression makes on our consciousness. A certain steady and calm force with which communications from God impact our soul incline us toward assent and even toward active compliance. Our innermost being seems to say *Yes, this is true and right*. The assent or compliance is frequently given before the content of the communication is fully grasped. At least I find it so, and others do as well.

We also sense inwardly the immediate *power* of God's voice. And once we have experienced it, we no longer marvel at how nature and spirits responded to this divine word in scriptural accounts. The unquestionable authority with which Jesus spoke to nature, humans and demons clearly manifested this quality of the word of God.

Addressing the question of how we can distinguish the voice of God from the voice of our own subconscious, E. Stanley Jones says,

Perhaps the rough distinction is this: The voice of the subconscious argues with you, tries to convince you; but the
inner voice of God does not argue, does not try to convince
you. It just speaks, and it is self-authenticating. It has the feel
of the voice of God within it.[8]

When Jesus spoke, his words had a weight of authority that
opened up the understanding of his hearers and created faith in
them: "for he taught them as one having authority, and not as their
scribes" (Mt 7:29).

The authority of the scribe or the
scholar comes only from his foot-
notes or his references to and associations with someone other than
himself, someone who is really supposed to know. The word of God, on
the other hand, comes with a serene

> *When Jesus spoke,*
> *his words had a weight*
> *of authority that opened*
> *up the understanding*
> *of his hearers.*

weight of authority in the word itself. People left the presence of
Jesus with heads and hearts full of thoughts and convictions that
he had authored in them through the power of God's voice and
word with which he spoke.

The immediate *qualitative* distinction of the voice of God is
emphasized in John Wesley's first sermon on "The Witness of
the Spirit." Here he poses the question, "But how may one who
has the real witness in himself distinguish it from presumption?" He answers:

How, I pray, do you distinguish day from night? How do you
distinguish light from darkness; or the light of a star, or a
glimmering taper, from the light of the noonday sun? Is
there not an *inherent, obvious, essential* difference between
the one and the other? And do you not immediately and directly perceive that difference, provided your senses are
rightly disposed? In like manner, there is an inherent, es-

sential difference between spiritual light and spiritual darkness; and between the light wherewith the Sun of righteousness shines upon our heart, and that glimmering light which arises only from "sparks of our own kindling": and this difference also is immediately and directly perceived, if our spiritual senses are rightly disposed.

To require a more minute and philosophical account of the manner whereby we distinguish these, and of the criteria, or intrinsic marks, whereby we know the voice of God, is to make a demand which can never be answered: no, not by one who has the deepest knowledge of God.[9]

In my own experience, I first became aware that it was God's word that was coming to me by the effects it had on myself and others around me. My main work for God is that of a teacher. I have occasionally received insights that, while perhaps of little significance in themselves, were experienced by me as literally staggering. Then, as I became aware and began to trust that these insights were God's word, I immediately began to observe the qualitative difference that Wesley emphasizes. And I began to find that certain others also understood, from their experience, exactly what this difference was.

Adela Rogers St. John remarks (perhaps somewhat overconfidently but yet to the point), "The first time you receive guidance you will know the difference. You can mistake rhinestones for diamonds, but you can never mistake a diamond for a rhinestone."[10]

The Spirit of God's Voice

The voice of God speaking in our souls also bears within itself a characteristic *spirit*. It is a spirit of exalted peacefulness and confidence, of joy, of sweet reasonableness and of goodwill. His voice is not the voice of a bully. It will not run over you and your will. It is, in short, the spirit of Jesus, and by that phrase I refer to the overall tone and internal dynamics of his personal life as a whole.

Those who had seen Jesus had truly seen the Father, who shared the same Spirit. It is this Spirit that marks the voice of God in our hearts. Any word that bears an opposite spirit most surely is not the voice of God. And because his voice bears authority within itself, it does not need to be loud or hysterical.

Bob Mumford has a vivid illustration of this point. One day the voice of God spoke to him when he was in Colombia, South America, and very distinctly said, "I want you to go back to school." His description of this experience brings out the quality and spirit of the voice:

> It couldn't have been any clearer if my wife had spoken the words right next to me. It was spoken straight and strong and right into my spirit. It wasn't a demanding, urgent voice. If it had been, I would immediately have suspected the source to be someone or something other than the Lord. The vocal impression was warm, but firm. I knew it was the Lord.[11]

The sweet, calm spirit of God's voice carries over to the lives of those who speak with his voice: "But the wisdom from above is first pure, then peaceable, gentle, willing to yield, full of mercy and good fruits, without a trace of partiality or hypocrisy" (Jas 3:17). If we would only heed this statement, we would never lack for sure knowledge of who speaks for God and who does not.

Content

Finally, there is a *content* that marks the voice of God. This is a matter of what information the voice conveys to us. Perhaps we had better speak of a *dimension* of the content, since the specific content of an individualized word from God may not of itself be easily identifiable as having come from God. But this much we can say: The content of a word that is truly from God will always conform to and be consistent with the truths about God's nature and kingdom that are made clear in the Bible. Any content or claim that does *not* conform to biblical content is not a word from God. Period! As Charles Stanley comments, "God's Voice will never tell us to engage in any activity or relationship that is inconsistent with the Holy Scriptures."[12]

Evan Roberts, when he was in college studying for the ministry, was deeply moved by the sermons of Seth Joshua, who visited his school.

> Roberts could not concentrate on his studies after that and went to the principal of his college, and said, "I hear a voice that tells me I must go home and speak to the young people in my home church. Mr. Phillips, is that the voice of the devil or the voice of the Spirit?" Phillips answered, very wisely, "The devil never gives orders like that. You can have a week off."[13]

While this response may seem a little glib, it was basically right. Subsequent events in which he was involved strongly confirmed that Roberts was indeed directed by the Lord on this occasion.

The Principles Are What Count

In order to qualify as the voice of God, a thought, perception or other experience must conform to the principles—the fundamental truths—of Scripture. It is the *principles*, not the incidentals, of Scripture that count here. Study of the Scriptures makes clear that certain things are fundamental, absolute, without exception. If the Bible says something once, notice it but don't count it as a fundamental principle. If it says it twice, think about it twice. If it is repeated many times, then dwell on it and seek to understand it. What you want to believe from the Bible is its message on the whole and use it as a standard for interpreting the peripheral passages. The principles show up with stunning clarity as we become familiar with the overall content of Scripture.

You must distinguish between the peripheral messages of

Scripture and the essential messages. Keep to the principles in interpreting the voice of God. For example, in 1 Corinthians 11, we find women being advised not to have short hair and men being informed that on them long hair is shameful. Such things are clearly *incidental.*

On more serious matters, in Mark 10, Jesus tells the truly fine young man who had come to him that he must sell all he has and give the proceeds to the poor. This too, contrary to what many have thought, is *incidental to people generally* (for Jesus did not ask this of everyone he met). In the particular case of this young man, of course, Jesus' directive went right to the heart of his special problem with wealth. But it is not a principle to which all must conform. Why? Because it is not a teaching emerging from the whole of Scripture; and it should not, without further consideration and guidance, be taken as God's word to you or anyone else.

When you read the writings of John the apostle, however, and learn from him "that God is light and in him there is no darkness at all" (1 Jn 1:5), you are on to a *principle*—something that wells up from the whole Bible and the totality of the experience of God's people through history.

We are also discovering principles when we hear Jesus saying that the most basic of all the commandments is "you shall love the Lord your God with all your heart, and with all your soul, and with all your mind, and with all your strength" and that the second is "you shall love your neighbor as yourself" (Mk 12:30-31). And his declaration that "those who want to save their life will lose it, and those who lose their life for my sake, and for the sake of the gospel, will save it" (Mk 8:35) is also conveying a principle, as is his statement that we are to "strive for his kingdom, and these things will be given to you as well" (Lk 12:31). *No specific word that is from God will ever contradict such principles.* Such principles place an ironclad restriction on what content can come with God's voice.

Principles of Scripture are to be identified most of all from the actions, spirit and explicit statements of Jesus himself. When we take him in his wholeness as the model to follow (which is what it means to *trust* him), we will safely identify the content of the inner voice of God, for "whoever follows me will never walk in darkness but will have the light of life" (Jn 8:12). In the awareness of this we are set free to be open to the new and special things that God wants to do in us and through us. We will be free to develop the power and authority that come from the experience of dealing directly with God—free *and* safe within the pattern of Christ's life and teachings.

Beware the Spiritual Panacea

Something should also be said on the negative side about the content of voices. Any voice that promises total exemption from suffering and failure is most certainly not God's voice. In recent years innumerable spokespeople for God have offered ways we can use God and his Bible as guarantees of health, success and wealth. The Bible is treated as a how-to book, a manual for the successful life in the way of the Western world, which, if followed, will ensure that you will prosper financially, that you will not get cancer or even a cold and that your church will never split or lack a successful minister and program. To the question from the old hymn

> Shall I be carried to the skies,
> On flowery beds of ease;
> While others fought to win the prize,
> And sailed through bloody seas?[14]

these people shout, "Yes, most certainly!"

But if we consider those who stand throughout history as the best practitioners of the Way, we will find that they went through great difficulties, often living their entire lives and dying amid these trials. The word of God does not come just to lead us out of trouble—though it sometimes does this—or to make sure that we have it easy and that everything goes our way. When we hear a suggestion that his word does in fact come to free us from all difficulties, we will need to recall this interchange between Jesus and Peter: "I'm going to go up to Jerusalem, and they are going to kill me," said Jesus. Peter—because he just *knew* it—replied, "Far be it from you, Lord. Such a thing shall not happen to you." Peter did not have such events in mind for himself, and hence they were not for his Messiah, the star to which he had hitched his wagon. But Jesus said to him, "Out of my sight, Satan; you are a stumbling block to me. You think as men think, not as God thinks" (Mt 16:23, paraphrase).

We must not be misled by wishful thinking. We are going to go through the mill of life like everyone else. We who are disciples are different because we *also* have a higher or additional life—a different quality of life, a spiritual life, an eternal life—*not* because we are spared the ordinary troubles that befall ordinary human beings. "Many are the afflictions of the righteous, but the LORD rescues them from them all" (Ps 34:19).

In summary, then, what we discern when we learn to recognize God's voice in our heart is a certain *weight or force*, a certain *spirit* and a certain *content* in the thoughts that come in God's communications to us. These three things in combination mark the voice of God. To those well experienced in the Way of Christ, these give great confidence and great accuracy in living day-to-day as the friends of Christ and as colaborers with God in his kingdom.

The Voice of Satan

There are other "spiritual voices" too. It is in *contrast* with the kind of voice I have just described that the voice of our adversary, Satan, is made known to us, for he too will speak in our heart once he sees he no longer holds us in his hand. Only if we learn to recognize this voice as well can we avoid many silly attributions of events to

Satan ("The devil made me do it!"). And only then can we correctly
identify and firmly resist him and make him flee from us (Eph
6:11; 1 Pet 5:9).

Satan will not come to us in the form of an oversized bat with
bony wings, hissing like a snake. Very seldom will he assume any
external manifestation at all. Instead, he will usually, like God,
come to us through our thoughts and our perceptions. We must be
alert to any voice that is in contrast with the weight, spirit and
content of God's voice, for that may signify that we are under subtle attack.

The temptations of Jesus in Matthew 4 illustrate this well. It
does not take much imagination to realize that, if some bat-like
creature suggested to Jesus that he turn the stones into bread, this
would certainly have tended to curb his appetite. How, then, did
the tempter come to him (v. 3)? Actually, the Gospel passages give
no indication as to how he came.

Perhaps—and this is just a suggestion—as Jesus suffered extreme hunger, the stones about him reminded him of—perhaps
began to *look* like—the loaves from his mother's oven. Perhaps he
began to *smell* them and then to think how easily he could turn
those stones into such loaves—with butter. But then he also realized the *conflict* between this vision and the great truth that the
word of God is a substance, a meat (Jn 4:32). He refused to allow
himself to be turned away from learning that God's word is sufficient for his every need. Human beings live by every word that
issues from God's mouth (Deut 8:3). The voice of temptation was
clearly opposed in spirit and content to God's word, and Jesus
recognized Satan and successfully resisted him in this and in the
other temptations which followed.

Likewise, followers of Christ must be encouraged to believe
that they can come to understand and distinguish the voice of
God. They need only to look within their thoughts and perceptions for the same kinds of distinctions as they would find in spo-

ken or written communications received from other human beings: a distinctive quality, spirit and content.

All of the words that we are going to receive from God, no matter what may accompany them externally or internally, will *ultimately pass through the form of our own thoughts and perceptions.* We must learn to find in them the voice of the God in whom we live and move and have our being.

Infallibility

But, someone may ask, When I am sure that God is speaking to me and sure about what he says, *couldn't I still be mistaken,* even though I've had apparently successful experiences of hearing and understanding his voice? Yes, of course you *could* still be wrong. God does not intend to make us infallible by his conversational walk with us. You could also be wrong about most of the beliefs on which you very successfully base your life. But you are usually correct. You could also be wrong in believing that your gas gauge is working, that your bank is reliable, that your food is not poisoned. Such is human life. Our walk with the Lord does not exempt us from the possibility of error, even in our experienced discernment of what his voice is saying.

We don't become infallible because of what we have heard from God. We should be cautious in sharing what we have heard. Sometimes it is appropriate, but it is not a fix-all and is not meant to be. Infallibility, and especially infallibility in discerning the mind of God, simply does not fit the human condition. It should not be desired, much less expected, from our relationship with God.

The Centrality of the Bible (Once Again)

Personally, I find great comfort and encouragement in the face of my fallibility by maintaining a close relationship with the Bible. In this book I have repeatedly emphasized the centrality of the written Word in hearing God's voice. It cannot be stressed too much that the permanent address at which the word of God may be found is the Bible. More of God's speaking to me has come in conjunction with study and teaching of the Bible than with anything else. As Frederick B. Meyer says, "The [written] Word is the wire along which the voice of God will certainly come to you if the heart is hushed and the attention fixed."[15]

> *More of God's speaking to me has come in conjunction with study and teaching of the Bible than with anything else.*

Reading in the lives of the saints seems to confirm this. From the many available illustrations, I have selected a few words from John Bunyan:

> One day, as I was traveling into the country and musing on the wickedness and blasphemy of my heart, and considering the enmity that was in me to God, that scripture came into my mind: "Having made peace through the blood of His cross" (Colossians 1:20). By which I was made to see, both again and again, that God and my soul were friends by his blood; yea, I saw that the justice of God and my sinful soul could embrace and kiss each other, through his blood. This was a good day to me; I hope I shall never forget it.
>
> At another time, as I sat by the fire in my house and was musing on my wretchedness, the Lord made that also a precious word unto me: "Forasmuch then as the children are partakers of flesh and blood, he also himself likewise took part of the same; that through death he might destroy him that had the power of death, that is, the devil; and deliver them who through fear of death were all their lifetime subject to bondage" (Hebrews 2:14-15). I thought that the glory of these words was then so weighty on me, that I was both once and twice ready to swoon as I sat, yet not with grief and trouble, but with solid joy and peace.[16]

It is *by experience* that many have come to know that there is a huge difference between an experience of the Scriptures in which a word of God seizes me and an experience in which I am simply seizing the words on the page (however interesting this may be in the process of biblical scholarship). In the former case I find myself addressed, caught up in all the individuality of my concrete existence by something beyond me. God acts toward me in a distinctively personal manner. This is the common testimony across wide ranges of Christian fellowship and history. I think it is this sense of being seized in the presence of the Scripture, in a manner so widely shared, that gives the Bible its power to assure us in the face of our continuing fallibility. We stand within a community of the spoken to.

In experiences with Scripture and other things—circumstances, our own inner thoughts and impulses, reading history or biography—God's word frequently comes in a way that at least approximates the experience of an *audible* voice. When examined closely, the data of Christian experience reveals that this is much more common than is generally thought. But the audibility of the voice is not anything essential to it, nor does it have any effect on the reliability of our experience of the voice. The essentials remain, once again, the distinctive quality, spirit and content that we have learned through experience to associate with the personal presence of God.

Scholarship too, both biblical and otherwise, is certainly important to the individual and to the church as a whole. It is a part of *our* part in responsible living before God. But it can never stand in the place of experience of the living voice of God, and it cannot remedy or remove our fallibility.

In general, no person is totally dependent on the expertise of biblical or other scholars for a saving and living knowledge of God. Humble openness before the recorded Word of God is sufficient for receiving his saving and guiding word to us. Those who *know all about* the word of God may yet never have *heard* it and recognized it. And those who have heard it and who recognize it readily may have little to say *about* it. But we need many who both know it and know about it, in order that it might come to have freer course and more competent reception in the community of believers and in the world. Only in this way will his people learn how to follow God's voice more successfully.

Practical Results in Life

Knowing the voice of God and having a *practical understanding* of that voice in our minds and hearts is not a luxury for the people of God. It is not to be allocated only to those who enjoy special spiritual high points. Let us consider four aspects of the importance of this understanding to a vibrant life in God's kingdom.[17]

Direct, daily access to God and his kingdom for all believers. First of all, without this direct communication with Christ, who is the head of the church, the rule of God will not be promoted through our lives as it should and could be. The understanding of the voice of God gives substance to the relationship between Christ and his church. *He talks to it.* That is a major part of what it means for his word to live in the church.

When we align ourselves with the kingdom of Christ and come into the family of God, we become an outpost of that kingdom. You might say, though these are crude metaphors, that we have the telephone installed so we can take the heavenly orders and participate in decisions as we do kingdom business; we have the computer terminal put in place, from which we can communicate, act and interact with God in his work. It is important that we have God's instructions and directions for what we do. And, to repeat a crucial point, it is just not true that the Bible *alone*, or our subjective experiences *alone* or the interpretation of circumstances *alone* is going to give us the kind of direction we need. It was never so intended. We must be spoken to by God, specifically and concretely guided in thought and action, to the extent and through the channels he chooses. In this book I have tried to make sense of what that might amount to.

Confidence, comfort and peace. We as individuals must have the confidence and peace that comes from knowing we are indeed in communication with God himself.

Think of the benediction that contains the blessing of Moses upon God's people in Numbers 6:24-25: "The LORD bless you and keep you." What does this mean? "The Lord make his face to shine upon you." What does that mean? We might rephrase this: "The Lord look right at you." That is what God has made us for—his presence. God seeks us. The basic nature of God is one of loving community. What is our response to God? When God says to us, "Seek my face," our response is: "Thy face, O LORD, will I seek" (Ps 27:8, paraphrase).

Have you ever watched a little child who loves her father when the father's face is *not* directed toward that child and shining upon her? Have you perhaps been in that place yourself? Do you remember what it was like to experience your father's or mother's turning away from you in anger and *withdrawal*—when their faces did not shine but instead scowled at you or ignored you? Communication was cut off. You were agonized by it until you learned to harden your heart against it. In a similar way a certain communication is absolutely necessary to our having the kind of confidence and peace appropriate to a child of God.

A little child's mother died. He could not be adequately consoled and continued to be troubled, especially at night. He would come into the room where his father was and ask to sleep with him. He would never rest until he knew not only that he was with his father but that his father's face was turned toward him. He would ask in the dark, "Dad, is your face turned toward me now?" And when he was at last assured of this, he was at peace and was able to go to sleep.

How lonely life is! Oh, we can get by in life with a God who does not speak. Many at least think they do. But it is not much of a life, and it is certainly not the life God intends for us or the *abundance* of life that Jesus Christ came to make available. Without real communication from God, our view of the world is very im-

> *We can get by in life with a God who does not speak. Many at least think they do. But it is not much of a life, and it is certainly not the life God intends for us.*

personal, however glorious we may find God's creation. But there is all the difference in the world between believing that this is our Father's world (or that God has arranged for our eternal redemption) and having *confidence* based in *experience* that the Father's face is turned toward us and shining on us, whether in the dark of the night or the brightness of the day, and that he speaks to us individually.

Protection from mad religionists and legalism. It is also important for us to know on a practiced, experiential basis how God speaks, so that we might protect ourselves and others about whom we are concerned.

We all know what foolishness sometimes follows on the heels of the words "God told me." Indeed, we all know not only what foolishness but even what tragedies can come when people say these words. We need to know what the voice of God is like, how it comes and what kinds of things God might say if we are to protect ourselves and those around us in the fellowship of the faithful. Otherwise, we are at the mercy of ideas from others who are malicious or who are being carried away with voices contrary to God, which they themselves may not understand.

It is of vital importance that we are able to recognize when people in positions of power do not know what they are talking about (even with all their authority) or when they are being guided by evil. We need to understand how God's voice works for our own protection as well as for the protection of those we love and for the prosperity of the church as a whole. Hearing God's voice must therefore be taken out of the realm of superstition or mere guesswork and put in terms that everyone who wants to understand it can understand it.

We can clearly identify cultic leaders, without exception, if we understand what has been said above about the spirit and content of God's voice, and if we understand the proper character of God's leaders. The 1978 tragedy of Jim Jones and Jonestown could have been stopped if even a few of the people he gathered around him had been in a position to see through his claims to speak for God. We now know this tragedy began long before the actual mass suicide in Guyana among the decent citizens of various cities across the United States. But these people had no competence in dealing with the voice of God as a practical, experiential matter. Through mystification of that voice and by "spiritual" bullying, they were literally led to the slaughter.

Every few years a new version of this same tragedy is played out. Right this minute, some less overtly destructive version of the Jonestown deception is being played out in hundreds or thousands of Christian settings throughout the earth. If those leaders who try to bring others under their supposed "guidance" knew that they would be examined by compassionate but strong individuals who understand God's true guidance, things would go much better for individuals, for our churches and for communities at large.

Danger comes not only from the wild side of religion, however; it can also come from the respectable side. In John 9, Jesus healed a blind man on the sabbath. The leaders of the people, proud of being Moses' disciples (v. 28), "knew" that Jesus could not possibly be of God because he did not observe their restrictions on working during the sabbath (v. 16). They just "knew" that this man Jesus was a sinner because they "knew" the Bible.

And they "knew" that the Bible said you were not supposed to do the kinds of things Jesus was doing on the sabbath. Therefore, since this man Jesus did these kinds of things on the sabbath, he was a sinner.

These leaders had good, reliable general knowledge of how things were supposed to be. For his part, the man healed could only report, "I do not know whether he [Jesus] is a sinner. One thing I do know, that though I was blind, now I see" (Jn 9:25). But *that* was not in the Bible, in the law. The leaders had their own guidance, and they thought it was sufficient. But it was not sufficient, though it was very *respectable* and generally accepted. For it allowed them to condemn the power and works of love in Jesus himself: "We know that God has spoken to Moses, but as for this man, we do not know where he comes from" (v. 29).

"We don't know!" That is perhaps the most self-damning statement they could possibly have made. They looked at what Jesus did and said, "We don't know what this person is doing. We don't know where he is coming from. We don't know that he is of God." Why didn't they know?

What they were really confessing was that they did not know who God is or what his works are. In their own way they shared Nicodemus's problem of not being able to see the kingdom of God—though they were sure that in fact they did. Many stand in that same place today. They could look at the greatest works of love and righteousness and if those works did not conform either to their legalistic ideas of what the Bible or their church teaches, or to what their own subjective experiences confirm, they could condemn those works without batting an eyelid, saying, "We *know* that this is wrong!" We all need to be delivered from such knowledge!

When facing the mad religionist or blind legalist, we have no recourse, no place to stand, if we do not have *firsthand* experience of hearing God's voice, held safely within a community of brothers and sisters in Christ who also have such knowledge of God's personal dealings with their own souls.[18]

A quality of life like those in Scripture. Finally, experience and understanding of God's voice can alone make the events of the Bible real to us and allow our faith in its truth to rise beyond mere abstract conviction that it *must* be true. This is a theme that we have already touched on a number of times, but it is so important that it is worth returning to it once again.

Consider, for example, the events recorded in 1 Samuel 16:1-13. This is the story of the selection of David as king over Israel. As with so much of the Bible, the passage is filled with "the LORD said to . . ." In this case, the Lord is speaking to Samuel.

> The LORD said to Samuel, "How long will you grieve over Saul? I have rejected him from being king over Israel. Fill your horn with oil and set out; I will send you to Jesse the Bethlehemite, for I have provided for myself a king among his sons." Samuel said, "How can I go? If Saul hears of it, he will kill me." And the LORD said, "Take a heifer with you, and say, 'I have come to sacrifice to the LORD.' Invite Jesse to the sacrifice, and I will show you what you shall do; and you shall anoint for me the one whom I name to you." (1 Sam 16:1-3)

The sons of Jesse came before Samuel; the first was Eliab. Apparently Eliab was a fine-looking person, for Samuel said, "Surely the LORD's anointed is now before the LORD" (v. 6). But the Lord said to Samuel, in words we should never forget, "Do not look on his appearance or on the height of his stature, because I have rejected him; for the LORD does not see as mortals see; they look on the outward appearance, but the LORD looks on the heart" (v. 7).

Abinadab, Shammah and all of Jesse's other sons (besides David, who was not present) then passed before Samuel with the same result. Finally, David was called out of the fields, where he was keeping the sheep. When he came before Samuel, "The LORD said, 'Rise and anoint him; for this is the one.' Then Samuel took the horn of oil, and anointed him in the presence of his brothers; and the spirit of the LORD came mightily upon David from that day forward" (vv. 12-13).

It is essential to the strength of our faith that we are in some measure capable of inwardly identifying with Samuel's experience as he *conversed with the Lord* in the midst of Jesse's family. Hopefully the earlier discussion of the nature of the inner voice will help in this.

Not Mere Impressions

King David's own conversational interactions with God are documented at many points in the Bible, nowhere more graphically than in 1 Chronicles 14. After he had taken the throne of Israel, the Philistines came to war against him. David "inquired of God" (v. 10) what he should do. This was probably done by standing before the ark of God. The ark had been used earlier in the history of Israel for such inquiry, and it had been recently relocated by David in an effort to place it in Jerusalem, which he had chosen as his capital city (see 1 Chron 13). "David inquired of God, 'Shall I go up against the Philistines? Will you deliver them into my hand?' The LORD said to him, 'Go up, and I will give them into your hand'" (v. 10).

And so it happened. The Philistines then regrouped and later set themselves in array once more in the same valley. "When David again inquired of God, God said to him, 'You shall not go up after them; go around and come on them opposite the balsam trees. When you hear the sound of marching in the tops of the balsam trees, then go out to battle; for God has gone out before you to strike down the army of the Philistines'" (vv. 14-15). It occurred just as God said.

One of the most interesting things about these cases and many other similar biblical passages is the specific information, the clear and detailed cognitive content, given in the movement of God on the minds of Samuel and David. What we have here are not mere impressions, impulses or feelings, which are so commonly thought to be what God uses to communicate with us. Rather, we have a specific and full cognitive or propositional content concerning what is the case, what is to be done and what will happen.

David and Samuel were not left to wonder about the meaning of their impulses to do this or that or their feelings about this or that. Nor did they have to test them against the Scriptures or circumstances. They were simply told. David did not have to speculate about the meaning of "the sound of marching in the tops of the balsam trees" (v. 14); he was *told* its meaning.

Hearing God in Scripture
1 Chronicles 14:8-17

Before doing this *lectio divina* exercise, take a minute to review what was written about this passage in the section above, "Not Mere Impressions." This will help you move into the passage in an informed, picturesque way.

To prepare to read in order to receive from God, please set the book or electronic reader down for a minute. Close your eyes and breathe out slowly. Ask God to give you an openness to hear whatever the Spirit wishes to bring to you today.

Read—*lectio*

Read the passage slowly, considering the invitation that reading Scripture is "encountering God himself or hearing his voice."

When the Philistines heard that David had been anointed king over all Israel, all the Philistines went up in search of David; and David heard of it and went out against them. Now the Philistines had come and made a raid in the valley of Rephaim. David inquired of God, "Shall I go up against the Philistines? Will you give them into my hand?" The LORD said to him, "Go up, and I will give them into your hand." So he went up to Baal-perazim, and David defeated them there. David said, "God has burst out against my enemies by my hand, like a bursting flood." Therefore that place is called Baal-perazim. They abandoned their gods there, and at David's command they were burned.

Once again the Philistines made a raid in the valley. When David again inquired of God, God said to him, "You shall not go up after them; go around and come on them opposite the balsam trees. When you hear the sound of marching in the tops of the balsam trees, then go out to battle; for God has gone out before you to strike down the army of the Philistines." David did as God had commanded him, and they struck down the Philistine army from Gibeon to Gezer. The fame of David went out into all lands, and the LORD brought the fear of him on all nations.

Now that the words are familiar to you, please read it again, remembering that "those who lived through those experiences felt very much as we would have if we had been in their place."

Also listen with the ear of your heart for

- a word or phrase, a detail of the story that shimmers or stands out to you

- where you find yourself in the passage: David standing before the ark of the Lord (in all probability), the Israelite soldiers waiting and listening for the sound of God marching in the tops of the balsam trees, an Israelite soldier's family listening later to the soldier tell the story, an Israelite commander wondering if David heard correctly, a Philistine soldier baffled at the sound and wondering what it might be. Or you might find yourself in the role of an object such as the trees themselves. That's not silly or unusual. Just go with it.

In either case, do not choose this yourself. Let the Spirit bring it to you. Even if you don't like it, try to welcome it with meekness and see what happens (Jas 1:21).

Reflect—*meditatio*

Read the passage again slowly. As you do so and for a few minutes afterward, reflect on

- the word or phrase that stood out to you. Why do you think these words resonated with you?

- who you found yourself to be in the passage. How does it feel to be this person or object? What are you thinking about the situation? What are you thinking about God, or maybe how God interacts with people?

- what it would mean to be a person who is not left to wonder about the meaning of their impulses to do this or that or their feelings about this or that.

Give yourself a few minutes to do this.

Then ask God, How does this connect with my life today? What do I need to know or be or do?

Respond (Pray)—*oratio*

Read the passage one last time, preparing yourself for what you want to say to God about what you think the Spirit might have said to you or what came to you.

Pray however you are led to pray. You might thank God for something or ask God for something, perhaps for help in believing that our life can have the same quality of life as those in Scripture.

Rest (Contemplation)—*contemplatio*

Do as you are led. You may wish to wait on God—to simply *be with* God. You may wish to pay attention to God, pondering especially, What sort of God is interested in communicating with humans so clearly? What about him makes you want to worship him, or at least *be with* him? Sit in the companionship of God—the one who seeks you.

<><><><><><><><><><><><><><><><><><><><><><><><><><><><><><><><><><><><><><><><><>

Plain Communication

It is possible to talk about hearing God in terms of mysterious feelings, curious circumstances and special scriptural nuances of meaning to the point where God's character is called into question. We must reply to this tendency by stating emphatically that *God is not a mumbling trickster.*

On the contrary, we can expect (given the revelation of God in Christ) that if God wants us to know something, he will be both able and willing to communicate it to us *plainly*, as long as we are open and prepared by our experience to hear and obey. This is exactly what takes place in the lives of such biblical characters as those we have just seen.

We may be sure that "no prophecy ever came by human will, but men and women moved by the Holy Spirit spoke from God" (2 Pet 1:21). With very little exception, the form such inspiration took was nothing more than thoughts and perceptions of the distinctive character that these people had learned by experience to recognize as the voice of God in their own souls. The thoughts and perceptions were still *their* thoughts and perceptions. It could not be otherwise. But the thoughts and perceptions bore within themselves the *unmistakable stamp* of divine quality, spirit, intent and origination.

Thus we find that Paul distinguishes clearly between what the Lord said through him and what he was saying on his own (for example, 1 Cor 7:12). Yet, when he composed his letters under divine inspiration, he did not stop thinking or set aside his own perceptions and feelings to become an unconscious writer or mindless voice box. His thoughts and perceptions were his, *but they were God's also.* Paul recognized them as such by virtue of the distinctive character that he knew so well and worked with in utter confidence.

When we have learned through experience to recognize the voice of God as it enters into the texture of our souls, the lives of biblical characters become real to us, and the life of God in them becomes something with which we can identify. Our faith is strengthened by this, and we are able to claim our part in the unified reign of God in his people throughout history on earth and in heaven.

Some Topics for Reflection

1. It is a fact of nature that sheep recognize and respond to the voice of the one who takes care of them (Jn 10:3-4). What do you make of how Jesus uses this metaphor to explain the interaction between his voice and his people (Jn 10:14-27)?

2. What are the "three lights" referred to in this chapter, and what problems arise because of their interdependence?

3. Explain in your own words the "three factors in the voice" treated in this chapter: quality, spirit and content. Do you regard any of them as more important than the others? If so, why?

4. God's voice or word does not usually come to us via sound waves, unless he is speaking to us through and *with* a human being, as explained earlier. Does the lack of an audible quality diminish the reliability of our experience of his voice?

5. "Any voice that promises total exemption from suffering and failure is most certainly *not* God's voice." What do you think of

this claim? Why do you think people so readily reduce the Bible to a how-to book, a manual for the successful life?

6. What would be some indications that a communication that comes to you is from Satan? From yourself? (Remember this is very individualized and might appear to be good or biblical.)

7. Our ability to recognize the voice of God serves as protection against leaders on both the wild side and the respectable side of religion. Discuss or reflect on any examples of this you have experienced or know about.

8. Which of these practical, life-related results of hearing God have you longed for most recently?

- direct, daily access to (and often interaction with) God and his kingdom for all believers
- confidence, comfort and peace
- protection from mad religionists and legalism
- a quality of life like those in Scripture

9

A Life More Than Guidance

*To deliver the soul from the sin which is its ruin and bestow on it
the holiness which is its health and peace, is the end of all God's dealings
with His children; and precisely because He cannot merely impose, but must
enable us to attain it ourselves, if we are really to have the liberty of His
children, the way He must take is long and arduous.*

John Wood Oman, *Grace and Personality*

*If you indeed cry out for insight,
and raise your voice for understanding,
if you seek it like silver,
and search for it as for hidden treasures—
then you will understand the fear of the LORD
and find the knowledge of God.*

Proverbs 2:3-5

◆◆◆

*I*n the previous chapters we have dealt with many aspects of how
God speaks individually to his children. This discussion may
sometimes have seemed remote, scholarly or merely philosophical. It is an unavoidable fact, however, that *what we do or do not*

understand, in any area of our lives, determines what we can or can-
not believe and therefore governs with an iron hand our practice and
action. You cannot believe a blur or a blank, and the blanks in our
understanding can only be filled in by careful instruction and
hard thinking. It will not be done on our behalf.

Contrary to what many in our culture will tell you, this does
not cease to be true when we enter the realm of the religious life.
Perhaps you've seen the book called *The Lazy Man's Guide to
Riches*. Misunderstandings about faith and grace lead people to
think that the Christian gospel is *The Lazy Person's Guide to Getting into Heaven When You Die* or perhaps *The Passive Person's Path
to Paradise.* But it is not.

Faith is not opposed to knowledge; faith is opposed to sight.
And grace is not opposed to effort; it is opposed to earning. Commitment is not sustained by confusion but by insight. The person
who is uninformed or confused will inevitably be unstable and
vulnerable in action, thought and feeling.

Misunderstandings, mental confusions and mistaken beliefs
about God and communications between him and his creatures
make a strong walk with him impossible, even if we don't think
about how we hear God or not. I have seen repeatedly confirmed
in often tragic cases the dire consequences of refusing to give
deep, thoughtful consideration to the ways God chooses to deal
with us. Instead people often rely on whatever whimsical ideas
and preconceptions about his ways happen to be flying around.
That is very dangerous to our health and well-being.

Indeed, when we do not make the effort to understand God's
dealings with humanity or to study the Bible and whatever else
may help us to understand it, we are in rebellion against the express will of God. For he commands us to love him with *all our
mind* as well as with all our heart, soul and strength (Mk 12:30; cf.
Prov 1–8). We can therefore say on scriptural grounds that it is the
direct and inclusive will of God that we *study* his ways of commu-

nicating with us. The conscious rejection of thoughtful and careful study is not faith, and it does not spring from faith. It is the rejection of the God-appointed means to God-appointed ends.

But now you have made that study. You have done the hard work of thinking carefully and in depth about hearing God's voice in general and about the presentation of it given within the Scriptures. It is time to bring our results to bear on the life that any serious disciple of Christ consciously undertakes from day to day. If the previous chapters have communicated successfully and if you are concerned about hearing God and knowing his will for you, you can come to a place of rest and assurance, confident that the Lord's face does indeed shine upon you.

The question that we will deal with in this final chapter is, therefore, essentially a how-to question:

- How may we come to live confidently and sensibly with God as a conversational presence in our lives?

This leads on to subordinate questions such as

- How much can we count on hearing God?

- What does it mean when we don't hear his voice?

- What are we to do then?

The Framework for Our Answers

Let us set out toward the answers to such questions from a brief summary of the fundamental points presented in the course of this book. Repetition counteracts our powerful habits and misconceptions about hearing God that are buried deeply in customary religious behavior and thought patterns.

While God's communications come through experiences of many kinds, their detailed content or meaning always takes the form of the inner voice, a characteristic type of thought or perception. Without this the accompanying events (circumstances), appearances or biblical passages remain puzzling, mystifying and open to conjecture.

God may, of course, direct us mechanically, *without* speaking to us and guiding us through our own understandings and choices. He *can* guide us just as we guide our car, without speaking. But whenever he guides us in our conscious cooperation with him as friends and collaborators, he does so by speaking to us, by giving to us thoughts and perceptions that bear within themselves the marks of their divine origination.

His speaking most commonly occurs in conjunction with study of and reflection on the Bible, the written Word of God, wherever the Bible is available. Less commonly, though still often, it comes in conjunction with a human being who is speaking to us. But it may come in any of the other ways God chooses.

Our ability to recognize God's voice in our souls and to distinguish it with practical certainty from other competing voices is acquired by effort and experimentation—both on God's part and ours. It does not come automatically by divine imposition and command.

Those who want to live under God's guidance and who by proper teaching or God's other special provision become convinced that he will speak and perhaps *is* speaking to them can learn through experience the particular quality, spirit and content of God's voice. They will then distinguish and understand the voice of God; their discernment will not be infallible, but they will discern his voice as clearly and with as much accuracy as they discern the voice of any other person with whom they are on intimate terms.

I emphasize once again that this does not mean that they will always correctly understand what God says to them or even that it will be easy for them to get his message straight. One great cause of confusion is that people make infallibility a condition of hearing God. It helps, I believe and hope, to understand that God's word is *communication* and that communication occurs constantly in contexts where infallibility is completely out of the question.

The infallibility of the *speaker*—as is the case when God is the speaker—does not and need not guarantee infallibility of the *hearer*. But fortunately, as we all know, speakers who are not even close to being perfect still communicate reliably and regularly. I know my children's voices well and would recognize them under a very wide range of circumstances. Generally I understand what they say. But I would know it was one of them speaking even if I could not understand what was said. (This has actually happened on numerous occasions!)

Indeed, careful study of personal relationships shows that recognition of a certain voice is often the cue for someone to *stop* listening or even to distort the message in particular ways that are relevant to the specific nature of the relationship between the people involved. I am convinced that this often happens in the divine-human conversation, and it almost always happens when God speaks to those who are in covert rebellion against him.

Paying Attention to How We Hear

One of Jesus' deepest teachings concerned the *manner* in which we hear. This is so important that it cannot be emphasized enough. Specifically, Jesus alerted his hearers to the fact that they might not be using their ears simply for hearing but for other purposes as well—such as to filter and manage the message so it fits better their own lives and purposes: "'Let anyone with ears to hear listen!' And he said to them, 'Pay attention to what you hear; the measure you give will be the measure you get, and still more will be given you. For to those who have, more will be given; and from those who have nothing, even what they have will be taken away'" (Mk 4:23-25). Listening is an *active* process that may select or omit from, as well as reshape, the message intended by the speaker. Both listening and our other ways of perceiving turn out to be fundamental displays of our character, our freedom and our bondages.

Those who really do *not* want to hear what God has to say—no matter what they may say to the contrary—will position themselves before God in this way:

> they may indeed look, but not perceive,
>   and may indeed listen, but not understand;
> so that they may not turn again and be forgiven. (Mk 4:12)

If we do not want to be converted from our chosen and habitual ways, if we really want to run our own lives without any interference from God, our very perceptual mechanisms will filter out his voice or twist it to our own purposes.

God on Demand

The doleful reality is that very few human beings really *do* concretely desire to hear what God has to say to them. This is shown by how rarely we listen for his voice when we are not in trouble or when we are not being faced with a decision that we do not know how to handle. People who understand and warmly desire to hear God's voice will, by contrast, want to hear it when life is uneventful just as much as when they are facing trouble or big decisions. This is a test that we should all apply to ourselves as we go in search of God's word: do we seek it only under uncomfortable circumstances? Our answer may reveal that our failure to hear his voice when we want to is due to the fact that we do not *in general* want to hear it, that we want it only when we think we need it.

> *People who understand and warmly desire to hear God's voice will want to hear it when life is uneventful just as much as when they are facing trouble or big decisions.*

Usually, those who want a word from God when they are in trouble cannot find it. Or at least they have no assurance that they have found it. This is, I think, because they do not first and foremost simply want to hear God speaking in their lives in general. At heart they only want to get out of trouble or to make the decisions that will be best for them. I have spoken with many who think of divine communication *only* as something to help them avoid trouble.

Besides engaging God mostly when we're in trouble, people also often seem to lack desire to receive God's word merely for what it is, just because we believe it is the best way to live. This is shown by a disregard of the plain directives in the Scriptures. Sanctification from sexual uncleanness (1 Thess 4:3) and a continuously thankful heart (1 Thess 5:18) are among the many specific things clearly set forth in God's general instructions to all people. It is not wise to disregard these plain directives and *then* expect to hear a special message from God when we want it.

I do not mean to say that God absolutely will not, in his mercy, communicate and instruct those who have departed from the general guidance, the Word, he has given. Contrary to the well-meaning words of the blind man whom Jesus healed (Jn 9:31), God does, on occasion, "listen to sinners," and he speaks to them as well. But this cannot be counted on as part of a *regular and intelligible plan for living in a conversational relationship with God.* Anyone who rejects the general counsels of Scripture is in fact planning not to be guided by God and cannot then rely on being able to be delivered from their difficulties by obtaining God's input on particular occasions.

Many people, however, honestly desire God's word both in its own right and because God knows it is best for us. As a part of their plan for living in harmony with God, these believers adopt the general counsels of Scripture as the framework within which they are to know his daily graces. These people will most assuredly receive God's specific, conscious words through the inner voice, to the extent that it is appropriate in helping them become more like Christ. There *is* a limit to which such guidance is appropriate, and we will return to this point later. But it is true in general, as G. Campbell Morgan has written, that "wherever there are hearts waiting for the Voice of God, that Voice is to be heard."[1]

With this summary of what we have learned so far before us, we turn now to deal with some final practical questions.

Listening for God

James Dobson has given some of the best practical advice I have heard on how someone who really wants the will of God and who has a basically correct understanding of it should proceed. Describing how he does it himself, he says, "I get down on my knees and say, 'Lord, I need to know what you want me to do, and I am listening. Please speak to me through my friends, books, magazines I pick up and read, and through circumstances.'"[2]

The simplicity of this should not mislead us. When we are in a proper, well-functioning relationship with God, this is exactly what we are to do. And then we are, as Dobson says, to *listen*. This means that we should pay a special kind of attention both to what is going on within us and to our surrounding circumstances.

We are talking about practicalities now, so it might be a good thing, until it becomes a habit, to write down Dobson's simple prayer for guidance and put it somewhere—on the bathroom mirror, for example—where you can see and use it often. In conjunction with doing that it is important to observe *regular times for listening* with respect to the matters that especially concern you.

Frederick B. Meyer is once again helpful at this practical level:

> Be still each day for a short time, sitting before God in meditation, and ask the Holy Spirit to reveal to you the truth of Christ's indwelling. Ask God to be pleased to make known to you what is the riches of the glory of this mystery (Colossians 1:27).[3]

If we maintain this general habit, then, when we are aware of a need for a particular word from God, we will be able to listen for it with greater patience, confidence and acuteness.

When I want to hear from God, I ask him to speak to me, and then as I go through my days, I listen for that voice or the thought that comes from him to help me understand things. It is amazing how often we don't ask for what we need. But when we do ask, we expect it and watch for it. I'm often in the midst of something else when the answer comes.

After I ask for God to speak to me in this way, I find it works best if I devote the next hour or so to some kind of activity that neither engrosses my attention with other things nor allows me to be intensely focused on the matter in question. Housework, gardening, driving about on errands or paying bills will generally do. I have learned not to worry about whether or not this is going to work. I know that it does not *have* to work, but I am sure that it *will* work if God has something he really wants me to know or do. This is, ultimately, because *I am sure of how great and good he is.*

Often by the end of an hour or so there has stood forth within my consciousness an idea or thought with that peculiar quality, spirit and content that I have come to associate with God's voice. If so, I may write it down for further study. I may also decide to discuss the matter with others, usually without informing them that "God has told me . . ." Or I may decide to reconsider the matter by repeating the same process after a short period of time. If you are uncertain if this is from you or from God, ask for further confirmation as Gideon did (Judg 6:11-40). You might say, "Please speak to me again" or "Lord, would you make that more clear?" That is the natural way we would relate to another person. We ask for clarity. I usually put a limit of two to three days on it.

Being uncertain doesn't mean you haven't heard. Remember too that scientists check their results by rerunning experiments. We should be so humble.

If, on the other hand, nothing emerges by the end of an hour or so, I am not alarmed. I set myself to hold the matter before God as I go about my business and confidently get on with my life. Of course I make it a point to *keep* listening. Very often, within a day something happens through which God's voice, recognizably distinct, is heard.

If I am given nothing, my next step is to say, "Is there anything in me that is preventing you from speaking clearly about this matter? If there is something in my attitude, please tell me." That answer may come in various ways. I don't believe God messes with our minds. He is not mean, and if he has something to say to me, he will say it.

If this does not happen, I generally cease to seek God's word specifically on the matter in question. I do not cease my *general* attitude of listening. But I am neither disappointed nor alarmed, nor even concerned, and I shall explain why as we proceed further. (I am not speaking here of prayer generally, where a different approach of greater persistence and tenacity is often called for.)

I have followed this simple method of listening for God's voice in many situations—in university teaching, research and administration; in family and business affairs; in writing and conducting sessions in conferences and seminars. It is the furthest thing from a legalism or formality for me, and God also takes ample occasion to slip up on me by speaking to me words that I am not seeking in this way. Generally, it is much more important to cultivate the *quiet, inward space of a constant listening* than to always be approaching God for specific direction.

> *It is much more important to cultivate the quiet, inward space of a constant listening than to always be approaching God for specific direction.*

From my own experience, then, and from what I have been able to learn from the Scriptures and from others who live in a working relationship with God's voice, I am led to the following conclusion: Direction will always be made available to the mature disciple if without it serious harm would befall people concerned in the matter or the cause of Christ.

If I am right, the obedient, listening heart, mature in the things of God, will in such a case find the voice plain and the message clear, as with the experiences of the friends of God recorded in the Bible. This is a claim that must be tested by experience, and anyone willing to meet the conditions and learn from failures as well as successes can put it to the test. In every congregation we need a group of people who, in front of everyone, are explicitly learning and teaching about life in dialogue with God.

This Is Not a Gimmick

God often speaks *without* our initiating any such procedure of seeking his individualized word as I have just described. We must also not be misled into thinking that there is some surefire *technique* for squeezing what we want to know out of God. A life surrendered to God, a humble openness to his direction even when it is contrary to our wants and assumptions, experience with the way his word comes to us, and fervent but patient requests for guidance—these do not constitute a *method* for getting an answer from him.

For hearing from God is not a gimmick. Strictly speaking, talk of method is out of place here, although it is possible and helpful to lay down general, practical guidelines. After all, God is not someone we "work on" for a result, even though certain behaviors before him are more or less appropriate. Above all, we must beware of trying to *force* God to speak. This is especially true just when we are most likely to attempt it—that is, when we are not in peaceful union with him.

A scene from the life of Saul, the first king of Israel, poignantly illustrates the folly of such attempts. Saul's highest priority certainly was not waiting on God to see his will done. To keep control over his armies in the face of the Philistines, he sacrificed without waiting as he should have for Samuel, the priest, to arrive. He blundered ahead on his own, even though it was not his place, and made peace offerings and burnt offerings (1 Sam 13:5-10).

When Samuel arrived at last, he asked Saul why he had sacrificed without him. Saul's reply goes to the very heart of his character:

> When I saw that the people were slipping away from me, and that you did not come within the days appointed, and that the Philistines were mustering at Michmash, I said, "Now the Philistines will come down upon me at Gilgal, and I have not entreated the favor of the LORD"; so I forced myself, and offered the burnt offering. (1 Sam 13:11-12)

Samuel immediately announced that Saul would lose his kingdom (1 Sam 13:13-14), for he clearly saw that Saul was a man who would take things into his own hands to get his way and that he would also find a "good reason" for doing so. Samuel knew that God would not stand by such a man.

A little later Saul disobeyed again when he did not utterly destroy Amalek and once more he found a "good reason" (1 Sam 15). He even pretended to Samuel that he had obeyed (v. 13), and when his deceit was uncovered he again blamed his disobedience on the people (v. 24). And again Samuel announced that the kingdom would be taken from him (v. 26).

Finally, Saul came to his extremity, facing death (1 Sam 28). Samuel himself was dead by that time, and when Saul inquired of the Lord, "the LORD did not answer him, not by dreams, or by Urim, or by prophets" (v. 6). Now, as was his way, Saul tried to *force* the knowledge he sought. Even though he himself had banned witches from Israel, he sought out a witch and compelled her to call up the spirit of Samuel (vv. 7-11) to tell him what to do. Samuel arose "up out of the ground" (v. 13) and said to Saul, "Why have you disturbed me by bringing me up?" (v. 15).

Saul poured out his tale of woe: "I am in great distress, for the Philistines are warring against me, and God has turned away from me and answers me no more, either by prophets or by dreams; so I have summoned you *to tell me what I should do*" (v. 15, italics added). How sadly typical this is of the human view of God and his guidance! We treat him like a celestial aspirin that will cure headaches brought on by the steady, willful tendency of our lives away from and even against him. We treat him as a cosmic butler who is to clean up our messes. To compel him to serve us, we seek gimmicks and tricks suited only to idols.

Samuel then read Saul's sentence to him: "Why then do you ask me, since the LORD has turned from you and become your enemy? . . . Tomorrow you and your sons shall be with me; the LORD will also give the army of Israel into the hands of the Philistines" (vv. 16, 19). At these words Saul fell flat on the ground, weakened by hunger and terror—a tragic picture. God refused to be used by him any longer.

Deciding On Your Own

We now turn to what surely is one of the greatest problems in the devout person's attempt to receive God's word. Even if we are not in disobedience to God, even if our hearts are attuned to his will, there will be many times in which God does not send a particularized word. What, then, *are* we to do?

We must not automatically assume that, if God does not communicate with us on a particular matter, we are displeasing to him. *If* that is the cause—which of course remains possible and should always be considered—there are ways of finding this out. It will be something that can be discovered and clearly known if we seek it out through honest examination of our lives, through counsel with Christian friends and leaders, and through asking the Lord to reveal it to us.

It is crucial to remember that God will not play little games of hide-and-seek with us. As I emphasized earlier, it is very important that we believe God is the kind of person Jesus revealed him to be. Such a person will show us what the problem is, if there is a problem, provided that we sincerely and with an open mind pray and seek to be shown. He is not frivolous or coy; he will not tease or torture us. In our relationship with him there is no mysterious catch to receiving his word for us, no riddle to solve, no incantation to get just right—not with the God and Father of our Lord Jesus Christ! We must make a point of not thinking of him in terms of human beings (relatives, supervisors, authorities and others) who may have enjoyed tricking us by not explaining what we were supposed to do.

There are reasons other than his displeasure why a specific word may not be forthcoming to us in a particular case. One of the major other reasons is that, *in general, it is God's will that we ourselves should have a great part in determining our path through life.* This does not mean that he is not with us. Far from it. God both *develops* and, for our good, *tests* our character by leaving us to decide. He calls us to responsible citizenship in his kingdom by saying—in effect or in reality—as often as possible, *"My will for you in this case is that you to decide on your own."* God is preparing us for a life of initiative, so I know that God will be with me even when he does not tell me what to do. His presence is known in ways different from his specifying what he wants done.

In his profound chapter titled "The Will of God," John Wood Oman gives us an excellent statement on this point:

> We can only be absolutely dependent upon God as we are absolutely independent in our own souls, and only absolutely independent in our own souls as we are absolutely dependent on God. A saved soul, in other words, is a soul true to itself because, with its mind on God's will of love and not on itself, it stands in God's world unbribable and undismayed, having freedom as it has piety and piety as it is free.[4]

From the apostle Paul and the saints through the ages rings out the full meaning of that robust and powerful saying, "I live! Yet not I, but Christ liveth in me!" (see Gal 2:20 KJV). In this way individual human personality is not obliterated, but rather it is given its fullest expression.

We are dealing here with the essence of human personality as God has ordained it. A child cannot develop into a responsible, competent human being if he or she is always told what to do. Personality and character are in their very essence inner directedness. This inner directedness is perfected in redemption. That is Oman's point. Moreover, a child's character cannot be known—even to herself—until she is turned loose to do what she wants. It is precisely what she wants and how she handles those wants that both reveal and make her the person she is.

What we want, what we think, what we decide to do when the word of God does not come or when we have so immersed ourselves in him that his voice within us is not held in distinction from our own thoughts and perceptions—these show *who we are*: either we are God's mature children, friends and coworkers, or we are something less.

Spiritual hypochondria. There is also a neurotic, faithless and irresponsible seeking of God's will, which is always taking its own spiritual temperature. In this state, people are far more concerned with being righteous than with loving God and others, and doing and enjoying what is good. One can be over-righteous (Eccles 7:16). We may insist on having God tell us what to do because we live in fear or are obsessed with *being right* as a strategy for *being safe.* But we may also do it because we do not really have a hearty faith in his gracious goodwill toward us. If so, we need to grow up to Christlikeness, and nothing short of that will solve our problem. Certainly more words from God will not!

We may in our heart of hearts suspect that God is mean and tyrannical, and therefore we may be afraid to make a move without dictation from him. We may even have the idea that if we can get God to tell us what to do, we will no longer be responsible for our decisions. Far from honoring God, such an attitude is blasphemous, idolatrous and certain to prevent us from ever entering into that conversational relationship with God in which sensible words, clearly revealed and reliably understood, are given as appropriate. How much would you have to do with a person who harbored such low opinions about you?

Often we just do not think through the things we say about God. A well-known American minister of some decades ago, Bud Robinson, was called by a parishioner whose husband had recently died. The lady informed the minister that God had told her to give the husband's suits to him. Would he please come over, she asked, to see if the suits would fit? Pastor Robinson very sensibly replied, "If God told you to give them to me, they'll fit." How refreshing it is to hear from someone who actually believes in a competent God!

The Perfect Will of God

We cannot be groveling robots or obsequious, cringing sycophants and *also* be the *children of God!* Such creatures could never bear the family resemblance. A son or daughter is not their father's flatterer, and groveling does not come from either humility or worship before the God and Father of Jesus Christ. To suppose so is to live within a morbid and anti-Christian view of who God is. "The humility that cringes in order that reproof may be escaped or favor obtained is as unchristian as it is profoundly immoral."[5]

In this context I must say something about being in the *perfect* will of God. If our lives conform to the general counsels of God for his people, as given to us in the written Word as a whole, then we are perfectly within God's general as well as moral will. If, in addition, we have received and obeyed a specific word of God to us concerning a particular matter, then we are *perfectly* in God's *specific* will for us, relevant to that matter.

But suppose that no such specific word has come to us on some matter of great importance to our lives. (For example, Should we enter this school or that? Should we live here or there? Should we change employment?) Does this mean that in the matter at hand we *cannot* be in God's perfect will or that we can be so only by chance, following some anxiety-ridden guessing game about what God wants us to do?

Most assuredly it does not! We must resolutely resist the tendency to blame the absence of a word from God automatically on our own wrongness. And we must equally resist the idea that it means we must be somewhat off the track and living in something less than God's perfect will. If we are living in sincere devotion to the fulfillment of God's purposes in us, we can be sure that the God who came to us in Jesus Christ will not mumble and tease and trick us regarding any specific matter he wants done. I cannot emphasize this point too much, since the tendency to think otherwise is obviously so strong and ever present.

Think of it this way: no decent parents would obscure their intentions for their children. A general principle for interpreting God's behavior toward us is provided in Jesus' words, "If you then, who are evil, know how to give good gifts to your children, how much more will the heavenly Father give the Holy Spirit to those who ask him!" (Lk 11:13). How much more will our heavenly Father give clear instructions to those who sincerely ask him—in those cases where he has any to give? Where he has none to give, we may be sure that is because it is best that he does not. Then whatever lies within his moral will and whatever is undertaken in faith *is his perfect will*. It is no less perfect because it was not specifically dictated by him.

> *Where God has no instructions to give, we may be sure that is because it is best that he does not. Then whatever lies within his moral will and whatever is undertaken in faith is his perfect will.*

Indeed, it is perhaps more perfect precisely because he saw no need for precise dictation. He expects and trusts us to choose, and he goes with us in our choice.

Several different courses of action may each be God's perfect will in a given circumstance. We should *assume* that this is so in all cases where we are walking in his general will, are experienced in hearing his voice and find no specific direction given when we seek it. In these cases there are usually various things that would equally please God, though he directs none of them in particular to be done. All are perfectly in his will because none is better than the others, so far as he is concerned, and all are good. He would not have you do other than you are doing. (Of course, being in his perfect will does not mean you are quite flawless yet! You can be in his perfect will without being a perfect human being.)

In his book *Decision Making and the Will of God*, Garry Friesen has done a masterful job of critiquing the view that God always has one particular thing for you to do in a given case, that correct decision-making depends on your finding out what that thing is and that if you miss it, you will only be in God's permissive will at best—and a second-class citizen in the kingdom of God. Arguing against this extremely harmful view, Friesen remarks,

> The *major point* is this: God does not have an ideal, detailed life-plan uniquely designed for each believer that must be discovered in order to make correct decisions. The concept of an "individual will of God" [in *that* sense] cannot be established by reason, experience, biblical example or biblical teaching.[6]

So the *perfect* will of God may allow, for a particular person, a number of different alternatives. For most people, for example, a number of different choices in selecting a partner (or none at all), various vocations, educational institutions or places of residence may all equally be God's perfect will. None of them may be in themselves better or preferred by God in relation to the ultimate outcome desired by him.

The sincere seeker should assume that this is so and should move forward with faith in God if no specific word comes on the matter concerned after a reasonable period of time. All of this is consistent with there *sometimes* being only one choice that would perfectly fit God's will for us. Our choices must be approached on a case-by-case basis, just as life is lived one day at a time, trusting God.

Just as character is revealed only when we are permitted or required to do as we want, so also the degree and maturity of our faith are manifested only in cases where no specific command is given. It is not a great and mature faith that merely does what it is told. Rather—in the words of William Carey, as he went out to India as a pioneer missionary—such a faith is one that "attempts great things for God and expects great things from God." It actively gets on with the work to be done, the life to be lived, confident in the good-hearted companionship of the Father, Son and Holy Spirit. Human initiative is not canceled by God redeeming us; it is heightened by immersion in the flow of God's life. People with a mature vision of God and extensive experience in his ways have no need to be obsessively anxious about doing the right thing. For the most part they will simply *know* what is right. But their confidence is, finally, not in a word from the Lord but in the Lord who is with us.

Caught in Cosmic Conflict

Sometimes we find ourselves without God's specific communication not because our Father wishes us to decide something. There are also times when we are face to face with the powers of darkness that inhabit our universe along with us. Many people have fallen under some affliction and have cast about desperately to find out what *they* did wrong, but often it was nothing, or whatever wrong they may have done was not what was responsible for their problem.

A battle is going on in the universe. As we live in this universe and share in God's activity both of creation and redemption, there are moments when we stand alone. Jesus knew what that was like. You will remember how he speaks in Luke 22:53 of the time when *his* hour would come—the hour of darkness, the hour of the powers of evil. In that hour he cried out, "My God, my God, why have you forsaken me?" (Mt 27:46).

You and I are going to face these hours too; though, I believe, we will never be *actually* forsaken and alone. As that magnificent little giant John Wesley said at his death, "Best of all, God is with us!" But words from God, no matter how well we know his voice, will not spare us the times of grief and pain, as Jesus was not spared. Our confidence remains that these times also "work together for good" for those who love God and are called according to his purposes (Rom 8:28). In that we can rest and refuse to harass ourselves with doubt and blame.

It is a similar situation when we are given a word from God and are sure of it, but the events indicated do not come to pass. Others may be involved, and *they* may not know or may not do the will of God. And God may not override them. Our world is the crucible of soul making, in which we can still remain always certain of inevitable triumph, "more than conquerors." The will of God made plain to *us* is sometimes not fulfilled because of the choices of *other* people. We must not, because of that, lose confidence in God's guiding words.

Greater Than a Word from God

There is something even greater than always knowing what is the right thing to do and always being directed by the present hand of God. Paul brought this out very clearly in 1 Corinthians 13. In this passage he writes of knowledge, prophecy and many other great things that we might find desirable. But he says that all of these are only partial and incomplete goods. The three greatest things—

truly inseparable from each other when properly understood—are faith, hope and love.

Even in the hour of darkness, these three—faith, hope and love—remained with Christ. They will remain with us. The great height of our development as disciples of Christ is not that we always hear God's voice but that we are trained under the hand of God (which includes hearing God as he speaks and guides) in such a way that we are able to stand at our appointed times and places in faith, hope and love *even without a word from God:* "and having done everything, to stand firm" (Eph 6:13).

At a certain point in my progression toward spiritual maturity, I can be assured simply that "the one who sent me is with me; he has not left me alone" (Jn 8:29). It should be the hope and *plan* of every disciple of Christ to come by gracious assistance to this place of rest in God's companionship and service. Then we will, as Brother Lawrence advises, "not always scrupulously confine ourselves to certain rules, or particular forms of devotion, but act with a general confidence in God, with love and humility."[7] We will simply "stand fast . . . in the liberty wherewith Christ hath made us free" (Gal 5:1 KJV). The liberty is not an opportunity to indulge the flesh but the arena within which we "serve one another in love" (Gal 5:13 NIV), precisely because "the one who sent me is with me." The branch thus abides in the vine. The branch and the vine share a common life and together produce abundant fruit for God (Jn 15:1-8).

But Never Beyond Risk

It is absolutely essential to the nature of our personal development toward maturity that we venture and be placed at risk, for *only risk produces character.* This truth is intensified when it comes to our walk with God. In this matter I find myself disagreeing with certain very wise people, such as A. T. Pierson, who regard God's guidance as *precluding* risk:

One great law for all who would be truly led by God's pillar
of cloud and fire, is to take no step at the bidding of self-will
or without the clear moving of the heavenly guide. Though
the direction be new and the way seem beset with difficulty,
there is never any risk provided we are only led of God. Each
new advance needs separate and special authority from Him,
and yesterday's guidance is not sufficient for today.[8]

This is a beautiful and helpful statement, *except* for what it
seems to be saying about risk. In this respect it is not a completely
accurate account of what it means to live with God's words in our
lives. The immaturity of many Christians today is due to their
adopting the attitude toward risk expressed in this statement as
the *whole* truth about hearing from God.

Having adopted this attitude, we then mistakenly try to *use* our
ability to hear God as a device for securing a life without risk.
When it does not work—as it certainly will not—we begin attacking ourselves, someone else or even God for being a failure. Such
a response partly explains why God remains humanity's greatest
disappointment. Who doesn't have a grievance against him? In
truth, we don't need to seek risk but we will never be without it, at
least in this world. Nor should we try to be.

Living Well with God in All of Life

The key concept underlying all the themes I have raised in this
book is this: *Hearing God's word will never make sense except when it
is set within a larger life of a certain kind.*

To try to locate divine communication within human existence
alienated from God is to return to idolatry, where God is there for
our *use*. To try to solve all our life's problems by getting a word
from the Lord is to hide from life and from the dignity of the role
God intended us to have in creation. As John Boykin remarks,
"God does not exist to solve our problems."[9] We exist to stand up
with God and count for something in his world.

We must ultimately move *beyond* the question of hearing God and into a life greater than our own—that of the kingdom of God. Our concern for discerning God's voice must be overwhelmed by and lost in our worship and adoration of him and in

> *God does not exist to solve our problems.* We *exist to stand up with God and count for something in his world.*

our delight with his creation and his provision for our whole life. Our aim in such a life is to identify all that we are and all that we do with God's purposes in creating us and our world. Thus, we learn how to do all things to the glory of God (1 Cor 10:31; Col 3:17). That is, we come in all things to think and act so that his goodness, greatness and beauty will be as obvious as possible— not just to ourselves, but to all those around us.

God's speaking will always be an essential part of this, to the extent and in the manner God deems suitable. It will come without threat to the full participation of the redeemed self, as a unique individual, in the work of God. For those who come to this point, their life will be *theirs*—irreducibly, preciously so—and yet also God's, and through them will flow God's life, which is also theirs. This is the life *beyond*, and yet *inclusive of*, his guiding word. It is the life that has its beginning in the additional birth and its culmination in the everlasting, glorious society of heaven.

With this life in view, John Wesley answered an intelligent and serious man who said to him, "I hear that you preach to a great number of people every night and morning. Pray what would you do with them? Whither would you lead them? What religion do you preach? What is it good for?" Honest and searching questions, which no minister should allow out of his mind. Wesley replied,

> I do preach to as many as desire to hear, every night and morning. You ask, what I would do with them: I would make them virtuous and happy, easy in themselves and useful to

others. Whither would I lead them? To heaven; to God the Judge, the lover of all, and to Jesus the mediator of the New Covenant. What religion do I preach? The religion of love; the law of kindness brought to light by the gospel. What is this good for? To make all who receive it enjoy God and themselves: to make them all like God; lovers of all; contented in their lives; and crying out at their death, in calm assurance, "O grave, where is thy victory! Thanks be unto God, who giveth me the victory, through my Lord Jesus Christ."[10]

While I was teaching at a pastors' conference, one pastor asked me what was the *human* issue, irrespective of church life or religion, that Jesus came to address. This is the question facing the Christian church today. My answer was this: Jesus came to respond to the universal human need to know *how to live well.* He came to show us how, through reliance on him, we can best live in the universe as it really is. That is why he said, "I came that they may have life, and have it abundantly" (Jn 10:10). His supremacy lies in the greatness of the life he gives to us. Putting Jesus Christ into a worldwide competition with all known alternatives is the only way we can give our faith a chance to prove his power over the whole of life.

A Formula for Living with God's Voice

Within such a life as Wesley described to his inquisitor, God's word is to be reliably and safely sought and found—free of mystification, gimmickry, hysteria, self-righteousness, self-exaltation, self-obsession and dogmatism. Presupposing such a life, we can lay down something close to a formula for *living with* God's guiding voice.

Note, however, that it is *not* a formula for *getting God to speak to us* on matters that may concern us. Any such "formula" is ruled out by the very nature of God and of our relationship with him. This much should be clear by now. It is, instead, a formula for *living with* God's voice, for hearing his word in a life surrendered and brought to maturity by him.

The first two steps in the formula may be described as foundational, since they provide the basis for hearing God's individual word to us but do not exclusively and specifically concern it as the rest do.

Foundational steps. We intend, plan and make provision to do what we know to be morally right and what we know to be explicitly commanded by God—so far as it lies within our understanding and conscious will. Such strategy is possible because we have entered into the additional life by the additional birth. This commitment includes the intention to find out what may be morally right or commanded by God and hence to grow in our knowledge.

At the impulse of the Spirit of God, we do service to the good wherever it may appear. In so doing, we venture into the fullness of the new life in Christ beyond our merely natural powers and rely on God's upholding power. Thus we move from faith to more faith (Rom 1:17), as we find him faithful. Above all, we venture in the proclamation of the gospel of Jesus Christ and his kingdom, as presented in the New Testament Gospels.

Steps to hearing God. We meditate constantly on God's principles for life as set forth in the Scriptures, always striving to penetrate more deeply into their meaning and into their application for our own lives.

> Happy are those
>> who do not follow the advice of the wicked,
> or take the path that sinners tread,
>> or sit in the seat of scoffers;
> but their delight is in the law of the LORD,
>> and on his law they meditate day and night.
> They are like trees
>> planted by streams of water,
> which yield their fruit in its season,
>> and their leaves do not wither.
> In all that they do, they prosper. (Ps 1:1-3)

We pay close attention to what is happening in our life for God's communications in our mind and in our heart. For here is where God's communications come and identify themselves, whatever the external occasion may be. It was said of the prodigal son that he came *to himself* (Lk 15:17) and then he found the truth and repentance that saved him from his plight.

When God came to Adam after he had sinned, he did not ask, "Adam, where is God?" but "Adam, where are you?" (Gen 3:9). We must purposefully, humbly and intelligently cultivate the ability to listen and see what is happening in our own souls and to recognize therein the movements of God.

We pray and speak to God constantly and specifically about all matters that concern us. This is essential to our part of the conversation with God. You would not continue to speak to someone who did not talk to you; and you could not carry on a coherent conversation with someone who spoke to you only rarely and on odd occasions. In general, the same is true of God.

Nothing is too insignificant or too hopeless to bring before with God. We share all things with God by lifting them to him in prayer, and ask for his guidance, even—or perhaps especially—in those things that we think we already understand.

We listen, carefully and deliberately for God, paying close attention to what we hear. We may perhaps use a regular plan such as the one described in chapter eight.

When God does speak to us, we pay attention and receive it with thanks. It is a good habit to write such things down until we become so adept at the conversational relationship that we no longer need to. If he gives us an insight into truth, we meditate on it until we have thoroughly assimilated it. If the word he has given concerns action, we carry it out in a suitable manner. God does not speak to us to amuse or entertain us but to make some real difference in our lives.

In those cases where God does not speak to you on the matter concerned, take the following steps:

1. Ask God if some hindrance is within you, informing you in whatever way he chooses. Be quiet and listen in the inner forum of your mind for any indication that you are blocking his word. But do not endlessly pursue this. In prayer, set a specific length of time for the inquiry about hindrances: normally no more than three days. Believe that if a problem exists, God will make it clear to you. Share the robust confidence of Abraham Lincoln, who said, "I am satisfied that, when the Almighty wants me to do, or not to do, a particular thing, he finds a way of letting me know it."

2. Take counsel from at least two people whose relationship with God you respect, preferably those who are *not* your buddies. This may be done in a group setting if it does not concern an inherently private matter.

3. Correct any causes for why God's word could not come. Do this mercilessly. Whatever it is. Just do it.

4. Act on what seems best to you if you cannot find such a cause. Do this after considering the itemized details of each alternative. If certain alternatives seem equally desirable, then select one as you wish. This will rarely be necessary, but your confidence, remember, is in the Lord who goes with you, who is with his trusting children even if they blunder and flounder. In this instance you may not know God in his specific word to you, but you *will* know him in his faithfulness. "His mercies never come to an end; they are new every morning; great is your faithfulness" (Lam 3:22-23). These words were written by the prophet Jeremiah in a time of utter failure, when the guiding hand of God was totally hidden from Israel and his punishing hand was raised against them.

If we proceed in this way, we will come to know God's voice as a familiar personal fact, which we can both comfortably live with and effectively introduce others to. We will know what to do when

God speaks, but we will also know what to do when he does not speak. We will know how to find and remove any hindrance if there is one and how to move firmly but restfully onward, in loving peacefulness, when there is none. We will know that God is inviting us to move forward to greater maturity, relying on his faithfulness alone. We will know, in short, how to live in our world within a conversational relationship with our Father who is always there for us.

Some Topics for Reflection

1. What is your honest response to the idea that hard study and thinking about basic issues of faith is *commanded* by God, as the way of loving him with our mind? Surprise? Gladness? Discouragement?

2. What do you think are the three most important points to understand about hearing God? *Patience, Understanding - humbulness*

3. What would be some signs that you really do not want to hear God (although you don't say this or even realize you think this) and give his word a place in your life?

4. What is the difference in results and in motives, if any, between

   • *not planning* to hear God's voice (an act of omission; you don't make any provision to enable yourself to do it)

   • *planning not* to hear God's voice (an act of commission such as avoiding thoughts that come to you that have the tone, spirit and quality of God)

   Do you notice any similarities or differences between the two?

5. What do you think it is like to listen for God to communicate with us, and what are some practical tips that will help us to do it successfully?

6. What is the effect of too much guidance on a personality? How

are receiving directions from God and deciding on your own interrelated?

7. How can we be in God's perfect will with respect to matters where he has given us no specific word?

8. Is it right to expect that a person who hears God word will be beyond risk in life? Is it desirable to live without risk? What is the *ultimate* safety that we have in God?

9. What more is there to life in Christ than hearing God's voice?

Epilogue

The Way of the Burning Heart

Blessed are those who have not seen and yet have come to believe.

John 20:29

*Were not our hearts burning within us while he was
talking to us on the road, while he was opening the scriptures to us?*

Luke 24:32

I have tried to clarify what hearing God amounts to and to make
a life in which one hears God's voice in the Way of Jesus accessible
to anyone who would enter it. I have aimed to give a biblical and
experiential understanding of the theory and practice of that life.
Now as we come to the end of the book, I am still painfully aware
of *the one great barrier* that might hinder some people's efforts to
make such a life their own. That barrier is what Henry Churchill
King many years ago called "the seeming unreality of the spiritual
life."[1] We could equally speak of it as "the overwhelming presence
of the visible world."

The visible world daily bludgeons us with its things and events.
They pinch and pull and hammer away at our bodies. Few people
arise in the morning as hungry for God as they are for cornflakes
or toast and eggs. But instead of shouting and shoving, the *spiritual* world whispers at us ever so gently. And it appears both at the

edges and in the middle of events and things in the so-called real world of the visible.

The Gentleness of God's Approach

God's spiritual invasions into human life seem, by their very gentleness, to invite us to explain them away. These moments soberly remind us that to be obsessed and ruled by the visible is death, but that to give one's self over to the spiritual is life and peace (Rom 8:6).

We are hindered in our progress toward becoming spiritually competent people by how easily we can explain away the movements of God toward us. They go meekly, without much protest. Of course God's day will come, but for now he cooperates with the desires and inclinations that make up our character, as we gradually become the kind of people we will forever be. That should send a chill down our spine.

God wants to be wanted, to be wanted enough that we are *ready*, predisposed, to find him present with us. And if, by contrast, we are ready and set to find ways of explaining away his gentle overtures, he will rarely respond with fire from heaven. More likely, he will simply leave us alone; and we shall have the satisfaction of thinking ourselves not to be gullible.

The test of character posed by the gentleness of God's approach to us is especially dangerous for those formed by the ideas that dominate our modern world. For centuries now our culture has cultivated the idea that the *skeptical* person is always smarter than one who believes. You can be almost as stupid as a cabbage, as long as you *doubt*. The fashion of the age has identified mental sharpness with a posture, not with genuine intellectual method and character. Therefore only a very hardy individualist or social rebel—or one desperate for another life—stands a chance of discovering the substantiality of the spiritual life today. Today it is the skeptics who are the social conformists, though because of powerful intellectual propaganda they continue to enjoy thinking of themselves as wildly individualistic and unbearably bright. This social force toward skepticism remains very powerful even in Christian congregations and colleges for ministers.

Partly as a result of such skepticism, very few people develop competence in their prayer life. Their respectable uncertainty *prepares* them to explain away as coincidences the answers that come to the prayers that they do make. Often they see this as a sign of how intelligent they are ("Ha! *I* am not so easily fooled as all that!"). And in their pride they close off a possible entrance into a life of increasingly confident and powerful prayer. They grow no further, for they have proven to their own satisfaction that prayer is not answered.

Nearly all areas of life in which we could become spiritually competent (hearing God and receiving divine guidance among them) confront us with the same type of challenge. They all require of us *a choice to be a spiritual person, to live a spiritual life.* We are required to "bet our life" that the visible world, while real, is not reality itself.

> *We are required to "bet our life" that the visible world, while real, is not reality itself.*

We cannot make spirituality "work" without having a significant degree of confidence in and commitment to the truth that the visible world is always under the hand of the unseen God. Our own spiritual substance and competence grows as we put what faith we have into practice, and as we thereby learn to distinguish and count on the characteristic differences that emerge as evidence of God's presence in our life. This is how, through the gospel of Christ, God's righteousness—what it is about him that makes him absolutely good, "really okay"—is revealed from faith to faith (Rom 1:17).

Life from "Beyond"

The greatest divide between human beings and human cultures is between those who regard the visible world as being of primary importance and those who do not, between those who view what is visible as all that's real or at least the touchstone of reality, and those who do not. Today we live in a culture that overwhelmingly gives primary, if not exclusive, importance to the visible. This stance is incorporated in the power structures that permeate our world and is disseminated by the education system and government.[2]

But neither God nor the human mind and heart are visible. It is so with *all truly personal reality*. "No one has ever seen the Father," Jesus reminds us. And while you know more about your own mind and heart than you could ever say, little to none of it was learned though sensory perception. God and the self accordingly meet in the *invisible* world because they *are* invisible *by nature*. They are not parts of the visible world, though both are related to it.

The second of the Ten Commandments tries to help us find God by forbidding us to think of him in visual terms (Ex 20:4). It forbids the use of *images* as representations of the divine being. The entire weight of the history of Israel—and its extension through Jesus and his people—presses toward the understanding of God as personal, invisible reality. This God invades history to call human beings individually to *choose* whether they will live in covenant relation with him or whether they will put something else—something visible—in the place of ultimate importance.

This is the challenge that I face every day when I wake. It walks with me through the events of each day. Will I, like Moses, "endure as seeing him who is invisible"? Will I listen for God and then obey? For me this tension is what it means to live as one who is learning from Christ how to live in the kingdom of God. Right where I am, moment to moment, I sweat it out with my brother Paul: "My visible self may be perishing, but inwardly I am renewed day to day, . . . producing something far greater than my troubles, and eternal in its glory, while we disregard the seen and focus on the unseen" (2 Cor 4:16-18, paraphrase).

God is not insensitive to our problem of overcoming the power
of the visible world. He invades the visible. The elaborate *visible*
provisions dictated to Moses by God—the rituals and equipment
of sacrifice, the tabernacle, and so forth—provided a point of constant interaction *in* the visible world between the invisible God
and the people he had selected to reconcile the world to himself.
Continual sacrifices, morning and evening, took place at the door
of the tent for meeting between God and the Israelites, "where I
will meet with you, to speak to you there" (Ex 29:42). This is the
form in which God chose to "dwell among the Israelites, and I will
be their God" (Ex 29:45).

This speaking was not metaphorical, as the biblical records
clearly indicate. There was an audible voice, usually with no visible presence. Although physical in nature because of its sound,
the voice of God was a step away from the visible toward the unseen and spiritual world (Deut 4:10-14). As for Moses himself,
when he "went into the tent of meeting to speak with the LORD, he
would hear the voice speaking to him from above the mercy seat
that was on the ark of the covenant from between the two cheru-
bim; thus it spoke to him" (Num 7:89).

We have seen that the audible voice unaccompanied by visible
presence continued well into the events of the New Testament. No
doubt it can occur today as well, since God is still alive and well
on planet Earth. But the tendency of life in Christ is progressively
toward the inward word to the receptive heart. The aim is to move
entirely into the hidden realm of spiritual reality, where God desires to be worshiped (Jn 4:24).

God's audible voice that comes from heaven also came in the
presence of Jesus. But, as he himself explained on one occasion
where an audible voice came from heaven, "This voice has come
for your sake, not for mine" (Jn 12:30). Jesus constantly presses us
toward a life with our "Father who is in secret" (Mt 6:6), toward an
eternal kind of life in the invisible and incorruptible realm of God.

The Invisible Companion

After his resurrection, Jesus appeared to his disciples in visible form only on a very few occasions over a period of forty days. His main task as their teacher during these days was to accustom them to hearing him without seeing him. Thus it was "through the Holy Spirit" that he gave instructions to his apostles during this period (Acts 1:2). He made himself visible to them just enough to give them confidence that it *was* he who was speaking in their hearts. This prepared them to continue their conversation with him after he no longer appeared to them visibly.

An instructive scene from these important postresurrection days of teaching is preserved in the last chapter of Luke's Gospel. Two of Jesus' heartbroken students were walking to Emmaus, a village about seven miles northwest of Jerusalem. He caught up with them in a visible form that they did not recognize, and he heard their sad story about what had happened to Jesus of Nazareth and about how, it seemed, all hope was now lost.

He responded by taking them through the Scriptures and showing them that what had happened to their Jesus was exactly what was to befall the Messiah that Israel hoped for. Then, as they sat at supper with him, suddenly "their eyes were opened, and they recognized him; and he vanished from their sight" (Lk 24:31). But their recognition was much more than a visual recognition, and *that* was the whole point. They asked one another, "Were not our hearts burning within us while he was talking to us on the road, while he was opening the scriptures to us?" (Lk 24:32).

What were they saying to one another? They were recalling that his words had always affected their heart, their inward life, in a peculiar way. That had been going on for about three years, and no one else had that effect on them. So they were asking themselves, "Why did we not recognize him from the way his words were impacting us?" The familiar "Jesus heartburn" had, no doubt, been a subject of discussion among the disciples on many occasions.

Soon he would meet with them one final time as a visible presence. There, in the beauty and silence of the Galilean mountains, he would explain to them that he had been given authority over everything in heaven and on the earth. Because of that, they were now to go to every kind of people on earth and make them his students, to surround them with the reality of the Father, Son and Holy Spirit and to teach them how to do all the things he had commanded.

You can imagine the small degree of enthusiasm with which these poor fellows rose to greet the assignment. But his final words to them were simply, "Look, I am with you every minute, until the job is done" (Mt 28:20, paraphrase). He is with us now, and he speaks with us and we with him. He speaks with us in our heart, which burns from the characteristic impact of his word. His presence with us is, of course, much greater than his words to us. But it is turned into *companionship* only by the actual *communications* we have between us and him, communications that are frequently confirmed by external events as life moves along.

Christian spirituality as practiced through the ages takes the form of this companionship with Jesus. Spiritual people are not those who engage in certain spiritual practices; they are those who *draw their life from a conversational relationship with God.* They do not live their lives merely in terms of the human order in the visible world; they have "a life beyond."

> Spiritual people are not those who engage in certain spiritual practices; they are those who draw their life from a conversational relationship with God.

Today, as God's trusting apprentices in the kingdom of the heavens, we live on the Emmaus road, so to speak, with an intermittently burning heart. His word pours into our heart, energizing and directing our life in a way that cannot be accounted for in natural terms. The presence of the physical world no longer has to be a *barrier* between me and God. My visible surroundings become, instead, God's gift to me, where I am privileged to see the rule of heaven realized through my friendship with Jesus. He makes it so in response to my expectation. There, in some joyous measure, creation is seen moving toward "the glorious liberty of the children of God"—all because my life counts for eternity as *I* live and walk with God.

> Now is the shining fabric of our day
> Torn open, flung apart, rent wide by love.
> Never again the tight, enclosing sky,
> The blue bowl or the star-illumined tent.
> We are laid open to infinity,
> For Easter love has burst His tomb and ours.
> Now *nothing* shelters us from *God's desire*—
> Not flesh, not sky, not stars, not even sin.
> Now glory waits so He can enter in.
> Now does the dance begin.[3]

APPENDIX

Key Questions and Answers

This appendix will help you quickly find answers to some of the most frequently asked questions about how people hear God. You might want to use it as a review after reading the book or as a preview before you begin. It can also help you when you start thinking, *I know I read that somewhere in this book, but where?* or when you're preparing to teach on this topic.

A Preview
Here are the questions listed below.
1. How can I know God is speaking to me?
2. What about when we don't hear from God? When God doesn't seem to answer us?
3. How do I know I'm not hearing the voice of Satan?
4. Why do some people seem not to hear God's voice? What are they to do?
5. What am I to think when someone tells me that God told them something about me? Can I count on that?
6. What do leaders need to think about in terms of hearing God?
7. What sort of Bible reading helps us become the kind of people who are better able to hear God?
8. What sort of use of the Bible does *not* help us hear God?
9. How does our view of God affect if and how we hear God speak?
10. Is it true to say that hearing God isn't very scientific?

1. How can I know God is speaking to me?

- Chapter eight, all sections, pp. 217-52

2. What about when we don't hear from God? When God doesn't seem to answer us?

- Chapter five, "Silence Is *Not* an 'Answer,'" pp. 138-39

- Chapter nine, tenth paragraph of "Listening for God":

If, on the other hand, nothing emerges by the end of an hour or so, I am not alarmed. I set myself to hold the matter before God as I go about my business and confidently get on with my life. Of course I make it a point to *keep* listening. Very often, within a day something happens through which God's voice, recognizably distinct, is heard. (pp. 261-62)

- Chapter nine, "Deciding On Your Own," pp. 265-68

- Chapter nine, the seventh point in "A Formula for Living with God's Voice," which begins: "In those cases where God does not speak to you on the matter concerned, take the following steps," pp. 278-80

3. How do I know I'm not hearing the voice of Satan?

- Chapter eight, second paragraph:

Beyond this, however, the only answer to the question, How do we know whether this is from God? is *By experience.* Even a word-for-word quotation from the Bible can be put to a use that makes it only a message from the Dear Self or from Satan. (p. 218)

- Chapter eight, "The Voice of Satan," pp. 235-37

4. Why do some people seem not to hear God's voice? What are they to do?

- Chapter four, "Truth 2: God Does," pp. 90-94

- Chapter nine, first six paragraphs, pp. 253-55

5. What am I to think when someone tells me that God told them something about me? Can I count on that?

- Preface, seventh and eighth paragraphs from the end:

Furthermore, if we are firmly gripped by a true picture of life with Jesus and are moving by experience deeper and deeper into its reality, we will be able to resist strongly but calmly the mistakes and abuses of religious authority. From the local congregation up to the highest levels of national and international influence, we hear people and groups claiming that they have been divinely guided as to what *we* are to do. This is sometimes benign and correct, both in intention and outcome. But this is not always the case.

Those who understand how individualized divine guidance, on the one hand, and individual or corporate authority, on the other, meld together in Jesus' community of transforming love will know how to respond appropriately to misuse of religious authority. Today there is a desperate need for large numbers of people throughout various arenas of life to be competent and confident in their practice of life in Christ and in hearing his voice. Such people would have the effect of concretely redefining Christian spirituality for our times. They would show us an individual and corporate human existence lived freely and intelligently from a hand-in-hand, conversational walk with God. That is the biblical ideal for human life. (p. 15)

- Chapter eight, "Protection from mad religionists and legalism" (third subhead under "Practical Results in Life"), pp. 242-45

6. What do leaders need to think about in terms of hearing God?

- Chapter one, "Our Leaders Hear from God," pp. 22-25

- Chapter two, "How to Believe the Bible Stories," pp. 44-46

- Chapter four, "Sheepdogs or shepherds?" to the end of the chapter, pp. 106-8

- Chapter five, "Leaders: Turning People On, Not Off," pp. 142-44

- Chapter eight, "Protection from mad religionists and legalism" (third subhead under "Practical Results in Life"), pp. 242-45

7. What sort of Bible reading helps us become the kind of people who are better able to hear God?

- Chapter two, "How to Believe the Bible Stories," pp. 44-46

- Chapter five, "Reaffirming Our Participation in Biblical Experience," pp. 119-20

- Chapter six, near the end of "The Bible and the Word of God":

The word of God in the larger sense portrayed *in* the Bible is therefore available to every person *through* the Bible, the written Word of God. All may hear the living Word by coming to the Bible humbly and persistently, with burning desire to find God and live in peace with him.

As for others, the Bible may prove a deadly snare, as it did for those in Christ's earthly days who actually used Scripture to dismiss him and his claims on them (Jn 5:36-47). Because of this we are warned in the Bible that we can even destroy ourselves by Bible study: specifically, by the study of Paul's epistles, for "some things in them [are] hard to understand, which the ignorant and unstable twist to their own destruction, as they do the other scriptures" (2 Pet 3:16). (pp. 186-87)

- Chapter seven, "The Written Word in the Progress of Redemption" and "'Praying' the Scriptures," pp. 209-15
- Chapter eight, "The Problem of Their Interdependence," pp. 223-25

8. What sort of use of the Bible does *not* help us hear God?

- Chapter five, "Bible Deism," p. 142
- Chapter eight, second and third paragraphs:

Even a word-for-word quotation from the Bible can be put to a use that makes it only a message from the Dear Self or from Satan. The dangers of so-called proof texting—of taking biblical passages out of context to serve some preconceived purpose—are well-known. A single statement taken directly from the Bible, even statements that are often invoked for personal application, may be used in ways *contrary* to the purposes of God, contrary to any meaning that he may have in mind for us. That is why *only the Bible as a whole* can be treated as the written Word of God.

In any case, we must certainly go beyond, though never *around*, the words of the Bible to find out what God is speaking to us. As we have already seen, the teachings of the Bible, no matter how thoroughly studied and firmly believed, can never by themselves constitute our personal walk with God. They have to be *applied* to us as individuals and to our individualized circumstances, or they remain no part of our lives. (p. 218)

- Chapter eight, "The Principles Are What Count" and "Beware the Spiritual Panacea," pp. 232-35

9. How does our view of God affect if and how we hear God speak?

- Chapter two, "God as Taskmaster," pp. 40-42

- Chapter four, "Truth 1: God Would," pp. 89-90

- Chapter eight, "The Spirit of God's Voice," first two paragraphs, pp. 230-31

10. Is it true to say that hearing God isn't very scientific?

- Chapter four, "Truth 3: God Certainly Can" (to the *lectio divina* exercise), pp. 94-103

Notes

Chapter 1: A Paradox About Hearing God

[1]John Calvin, *Institutes of the Christian Religion* 1.7; and chapter five of William Law, *The Power of the Spirit*, ed. Dave Hunt (Fort Washington, Penn.: Christian Literature Crusade, 1971).

[2]George Fox, *The Journal of George Fox* (London: J. M. Dent, 1948), pp. 8-9.

[3]Wilhelm Hermann, *The Communion of the Christian with God*, 3rd ed. (London: Williams & Norgate, 1909), p. 14.

[4]John Baillie, *Our Knowledge of God* (New York: Charles Scribner's, 1959), p. 132.

[5]C. Austin Miles, "In the Garden" (1912).

[6]J. A. Sargent, "Astrology's Rising Star," *Christianity Today*, February 4, 1983, pp. 37-39.

[7]Russ Johnston, *How to Know the Will of God* (Colorado Springs: NavPress, 1971), p. 5.

[8]Frederick B. Meyer, *The Secret of Guidance* (Chicago: Moody Press, 1997), p. 12.

[9]E. Stanley Jones, "For Sunday of Week 41," in *Victorious Living* (Nashville: Abingdon, 1938), p. 281.

Chapter 2: Guidelines for Hearing from God

[1]The first edition of this book refers to the 1975 film version. This edition refers to the 2004 version in which events are slightly different.

[2]The Council of Chalcedon (A.D. 451) makes this use of the idea of virgin birth: "That Christ was really divine and really human; in his divinity co-eternal, and in all points similar to the Father; in his humanity, son of the Virgin Mary, *born like all others*, and like unto us men in all things except sin" ("Monophysites," in *Cyclopaedia of Biblical, Theological and Ecclesiastical Literature*, ed. John McClintock and James Strong [New York: Harper & Row, 1894], p. 509, emphasis added).

[3]A. W. Tozer, *The Root of the Righteous* (Harrisburg, Penn.: Christian Publications, 1955), p. 34, emphasis added.

[4]A. T. Pierson, *George Mueller of Bristol and His Witness to a Prayer—Hearing God* (New York: Baker & Taylor, 1899), pp. 185-86.

Chapter 3: Never Alone

[1]Anonymous, "Never Alone" (19th cent.).

[2]Anonymous, "Where'er Have Trod Thy Sacred Feet" (1889).

[3]Thomas à Kempis, *The Imitation of Christ* (Chicago: Moody Press, 1958), pp. 106-7. A. W. Tozer sharply states the contemporary need in this connection: "What we need very badly these days is a company of Christians who are prepared to trust God as completely now as they know they must do at the last day. For each of us the time is coming when we shall have nothing but God. Health and wealth and friends and hiding places will be swept away and we shall have only God. To the man of pseudo faith that is a terrifying thought, but to real faith it is one of the most comforting thoughts the heart can entertain" (A. W. Tozer, *The Root of the Righteous* [Harrisburg, Penn.: Christian Publications, 1955], p. 54).

[4]Augustine, *The City of God*, 22.30.

[5]Westminster Shorter Catechism, first paragraph.

[6]The Beatles, "Eleanor Rigby," *Revolver* (1996).

[7]D. L. Moody, quoted in A. P. Fitt, *The Shorter Life of D. L. Moody* (Chicago: Moody Press, 1900), p. 67.

[8]Ibid., p. 76.

[9]Brother Lawrence, *The Practice of the Presence of God* (Old Tappan, N.J.: Revell, 1958), pp. 37-38.

[10]Leslie Weatherhead, *The Transforming Friendship* (London: Epworth, 1962), pp. 155ff.

[11]An excellent supplementary discussion to this is found in Jeremy Taylor, "General Manners of the Divine Presence," in *The Rule and Exercise of Holy Living* (n.p., 1650), sec. 3, chap. 1.

[12]E. Stanley Jones, *A Song of Ascents* (Nashville: Abingdon, 1979), p. 191.

Chapter 4: Our Communicating Cosmos

[1]Catherine Marshall, *A Man Called Peter* (New York: Fawcett, 1962), p. 24.

[2]David Pytches, *Does God Speak Today?* (Minneapolis: Bethany House, 1989).

[3]Agnes Sanford, *Sealed Orders* (Plainfield, N.J.: Logos International, 1972), p. 98.

[4]E. Stanley Jones, *A Song of Ascents* (Nashville: Abingdon, 1979), p. 188.

[5]G. Campbell Morgan, *How to Live* (Chicago: Moody Press, n.d.), p. 78.

[6]Frank Laubach, *Letters by a Modern Mystic* (Syracuse, N.Y.: New Reader's Press, 1955), p. 14.

[7]Alfred, Lord Tennyson, "In Memoriam A. H. H.," 1850.

[8]Blaise Pascal, *Pensées* (Baltimore: Penguin, 1966), p. 88.

[9]A. H. Strong, *Christ in Creation* (Philadelphia: Griffith & Rowland, 1899), p. 3.

[10]James Jean, *The Mysterious Universe* (New York: E. P. Dutton, 1932), p. 27.

[11]Jack Sarfatti, quoted in Michael Talbot, *Mysticism and the New Physics* (New York: Bantam, 1981), from the introduction and chap. 1.

[12]William Temple, "The Divinity of Christ," in *Foundations*, ed. B. H. Streeter (London: Macmillan, 1920), pp. 258-59.

[13]Stevie Wonder, *Superstition*, Motown Records (1972).

[14]For elaboration of this point please see chapter three of Dallas Willard, *The Divine Conspiracy* (San Francisco: HarperSanFrancisco, 1998).

[15]Francis Thompson, "The Kingdom of Heaven, God" (1913).

[16]Henri Nouwen, *Creative Ministry* (Garden City, N.Y.: Doubleday, 1978), pp. 12-13.

[17]C. H. Spurgeon, *Spurgeon's Lectures to His Students*, ed. David Otis Fuller (Grand Rapids: Zondervan, 1945), p. 187.

[18]St. Francis de Sales, *Introduction to the Devout Life*, trans. John K. Ryan (Garden City, N.Y.: Doubleday, 1957), p. 106.

[19]Ibid.

[20]Joyce Huggett, *Listening to God* (London: Hodder & Stoughton, 1986), p. 141.

[21]George Wade Robinson, "Loved with Everlasting Love" (1876).

Chapter 5: The Still, Small Voice and Its Rivals

[1]Letter 117-2 in *Guideposts*, December 1982.

[2]Ibid.

[3]See the preface of Mortimer J. Adler, *The Angels and Us* (New York: Macmillan, 1982). See also Billy Graham, *Angels: God's Secret Agents*, rev. ed. (Waco, Tex.: Word, 1986); and A. C. Gaebelein, *What the Bible Says About Angels* (Grand Rapids: Baker, 1987).

[4]Gustave Oehler, *Theology of the Old Testament* (Grand Rapids: Zondervan, n.d.), p. 143.

[5]Ibid.

[6]Today we unfortunately do not have on hand an adequate, common vocabulary to discuss the movements of God within and upon the soul. We are now without a psychology of the spiritual life. Distinctions in the indi-

vidual's experience of God that were once widely understood and used are now either unknown or wholly the object of scholarly curiosity. On vital distinctions to be drawn in experiences of voices and visions, Teresa of Ávila, for example, has this to say: "Some of them [voices] seem to come from without; others from the innermost depths of the soul; others from its higher part; while others, again, are so completely outside the soul that they can be heard with the ears, and seem to be uttered by a human voice" (from chapter three of the Sixth Mansion in Teresa of Ávila, *The Interior Castle* [many editions]). See also the remarkably analytical and sane discussion in Evelyn Underhill, "Voices and Visions," in *Mysticism*, 12th ed. (New York: New American Library, 1974).

[7]Samuel Shoemaker, *With the Holy Spirit and with Fire* (New York: Harper & Row, 1960), p. 27.

[8]Russ Johnston, *How to Know the Will of God* (Colorado Springs: NavPress, 1971), p. 13.

[9]Thomas Goodwin, *The Vanity of Thoughts and Let Patience Have Its Perfect Way* (Wilmington, Del.: Classic-a-Month, 1964), p. 4.

[10]Rosalind Rinker, *Prayer: Conversing with God* (Grand Rapids: Zondervan, 1959), p. 17, italics added.

[11]Ibid., p. 19.

[12]Leona Choy, *Andrew Murray: Apostle of Abiding Love* (Fort Washington, Penn.: Christian Literature Crusade, 1978), pp. 152ff.

[13]Ibid.

[14]Charles H. Spurgeon, *Morning by Morning* (London: Passmore & Alabaster, 1865), p. 191.

[15]E. Stanley Jones, *The Way* (Nashville: Abingdon/Cokesbury, 1946), p. 283.

[16]Bob Mumford, *Take Another Look at Guidance: A Study of How God Guides* (Plainfield, N.J.: Logos International, 1971), pp. 140-41.

[17]Ibid.

[18]Frances Ridley Havergal, "Silent in Love."

Chapter 6: The Word of God and the Rule of God

[1]William Shakespeare, *The Merchant of Venice*, act 4, scene 1, line 183, Portia speaking.

[2]Plato, *Theaetetus*, p. 190 (Stephanus edition).

[3]Augustine, *On the Trinity*, 4.10.

[4]William Penn, *The Peace of Europe, Etc.* (London: J. M. Dent, n.d.), p. 65.

[5]Mary W. Calkins, ed., *Berkeley: Essay, Principles and Dialogues with Selections from Other Writings* (New York: Charles Scribner's, 1929), p. 370.

[6]Ibid., p. 373.

[7]David Otis Fuller, ed., *Spurgeon's Lectures to His Students* (Grand Rapids: Zondervan, 1945), p. 182.

[8]Martin Buber, *I and Thou*, trans. Ronald G. Smith (New York: Collier, 1958), p. 83.

[9]Consider on this point the studies of physiologist Walter Cannon, referred to in *Psychology Today*, June 1983, pp. 71-72.

[10]Mary Ann Lathbury, "Break Thou the Bread of Life" (1877).

[11]Ibid.

[12]Washington Gladden, "Behold a Sower! From Afar" (1897).

Chapter 7: Redemption Through the Word of God

[1]Hannah Hurnard, *God's Transmitters* (Wheaton, Ill.: Tyndale House, 1981), p. 12.

[2]David Otis Fuller, ed., *Spurgeon's Lectures to His Students* (Grand Rapids: Zondervan, 1945), p. 172.

[3]James S. Stewart, *A Man in Christ* (London: Hodder & Stoughton, 1935), pp. 192ff.

[4]Ibid., p. 193.

[5]William Law, *The Power of the Spirit*, ed. Dave Hunt (Fort Washington, Penn.: Christian Literature Crusade, 1971), p. 62.

[6]Thomas à Kempis, *The Imitation of Christ*, trans. Leo Shirley-Price (London: Penguin, 1952), p. 27.

[7]Madame Guyon, *Experiencing the Depth of Jesus Christ* (Goleta, Calif.: Christian Books, 1975), p. 16.

[8]For an introduction to disciplines for the spiritual life, see especially Richard Foster, *Celebration of Discipline: The Path to Spiritual Growth* (San Francisco: HarperCollins, 1998).

Chapter 8: Recognizing the Voice of God

[1]It is possible to understand the teaching of the sufficiency of the anointing in various ways, but no biblical Christian can deny it. Since the flood tide of European mysticism in the thirteenth and fourteenth centuries (for a good introduction see Jeanne Ancelet-Hustache, *Master Eckhart and the Rhineland Mystics* [New York: Harper/Torchbooks, n.d.]), this teaching has been nowhere more strongly defended than by the Quakers or Friends; their best presentation is in propositions 1, 2 and 3 of Robert Barclay, *An Apology for the True Christian Divinity* (many editions).

    I believe that on the whole a more correct view of the relationship between the Bible and the anointing is given by William Law, John Wesley and Andrew Murray. See William Law, *The Power of the Spirit*, ed. Dave

Hunt (Fort Washington, Penn.: Christian Literature Crusade, 1971); William Law, *Serious Call to a Devout and Holy Life* (many editions); Andrew Murray, *The Spirit of Christ* (London: James Nisbet, 1899); John Wesley, "The Witness of the Spirit," in *Sermons on Several Occasions* (New York: Waugh & Mason, 1836), 1:91-92; and Wesley's various discourses on the Spirit.

[2]Frederick B. Meyer, *The Secret of Guidance* (Chicago: Moody Press, 1997), italics added.

[3]In addition to Meyer's book, see also chapter seven of Bob Mumford, *Take Another Look at Guidance: A Study of How God Guides* (Plainfield, N.J.: Logos International, 1971); and G. Campbell Morgan, *God's Perfect Will* (Grand Rapids: Baker, 1978), pp. 155ff.

[4]Meyer, *Secret of Guidance*, p. 18.

[5]Beth Spring, "What the Bible Means," *Christianity Today*, December 17, 1982, pp. 45-48.

[6]Law, *Power of the Spirit*, p. 61.

[7]Professor Don Ihde of the State University of New York has published a very helpful guide to a deeper examination of the phenomenon of voice in Don Ihde, *Listening and Voice* (Athens: Ohio University Press, 1976).

[8]E. Stanley Jones, *A Song of Ascents* (Nashville: Abingdon, 1979), p. 190.

[9]Wesley, "Witness of the Spirit," pp. 91-92, italics added.

[10]Adele Rogers St. John, *Guideposts*, December 1968, p. 8.

[11]Mumford, *Take Another Look*, pp. 85-86.

[12]Charles Stanley, *How to Listen to God* (Nashville: Thomas Nelson, 1985), p. 51.

[13]J. Edwin Orr, "What Made the Welsh Revival 'Extraordinary,'" *The Forerunner* 2, no. 8 (n.d.): 11.

[14]Isaac Watts, "Am I a Soldier of the Cross?" (1721-1724).

[15]Meyer, *Secret of Guidance*, p. 31.

[16]John Bunyan, *Grace Abounding to the Chief of Sinners* (Grand Rapids: Baker, 1981), pp. 46-47.

[17]I recommend reading Stanley, *How to Listen,* chaps. 1 and 2, with this section.

[18]The communal side of discerning God's voice is not studied in this book. See Richard Foster, *Celebration of Discipline: The Path to Spiritual Growth* (San Francisco: HarperCollins, 1998), pp. 150-62; see also section two of Danny E. Morris, *Yearning to Know God's Will* (Grand Rapids: Zondervan, 1991). In general the same features that characterize the individual's process of hearing God apply also to the process individuals use in groups, but there is a greater certainty of the message when a spiritually

qualified group is involved. Group guidance is deadly, however, when the group is dominated by legalism, ignorance or superstition.

Chapter 9: A Life More Than Guidance

[1]G. Campbell Morgan, *How to Live* (Chicago: Moody Press, n.d.), p. 76.

[2]James Dobson, "The Will of God," radio broadcast, December 3, 1982. See also the excellent chapter "Interpretations of Impressions" in James Dobson, *Emotions: Can You Trust Them?* (Ventura, Calif.: Regal, 1981).

[3]Frederick B. Meyer, *The Secret of Guidance* (Chicago: Moody Press, 1997), p. 43.

[4]John Wood Oman, *Grace and Personality* (Cambridge: Cambridge University Press, 1931).

[5]W. R. Sorley, *The Moral Life* (Cambridge: Cambridge University Press, 1911), p. 138.

[6]Garry Friesen, *Decision Making and the Will of God* (Portland, Ore.: Multnomah Press, 1980), p. 145.

[7]Brother Lawrence, *The Practice of the Presence of God* (Old Tappan, N.J.: Revell, 1958), p. 51.

[8]A. T. Pierson, *George Mueller of Bristol and His Witness to a Prayer—Hearing God* (New York: Baker & Taylor, 1899), p. 196.

[9]John Boykin, "Rethinking the Will of God," *The Door*, May-June 1992, p. 13.

[10]John Wesley, *Selections from the Writings of Reverend John Wesley*, ed. Herbert Welch (New York: Eaton & Mains, 1901), p. 138.

Epilogue

[1]Henry Churchill King, *The Seeming Unreality of the Spiritual Life* (New York: Macmillan, 1908).

[2]You will be tremendously strengthened in your understanding of this situation by a study of P. A. Sorokin, *The Crisis of Our Age* (New York: E. P. Dutton, 1941). See also my book *The Divine Conspiracy* (San Francisco: HarperSanFrancisco, 1998).

[3]Elizabeth Rooney, "The Opening." I have been unable to find a bibliographic reference for this poem or locate the author.

Scripture Index